THE CORMANY DIARIES

The Cormany Diaries

A Northern Family in the Civil War

James C. Mohr

Editor

Richard E. Winslow III

Associate Editor

UNIVERSITY OF PITTSBURGH PRESS

The preparation of this work was made possible in part by a grant from the Program for Editions of the National Endowment for the Humanities, an independent federal agency.

Published by the University of Pittsburgh Press, Pittsburgh, Pa. 15260
Copyright © 1982, University of Pittsburgh Press
Feffer and Simons, Inc., London
Manufactured in the United States of America

Library of Congress Cataloging in Publication Data

Main entry under title:

The Cormany diaries.

Includes index.
1. Corman family. 2. United States—History—Civil War, 1861–1865—Personal narratives. 3. United States—Social life and customs—1783–1865. I. Mohr, James C. II. Winslow, Richard Elliott, 1934–
E464.C66   973.7'81   81-16345
ISBN 0-8229-3447-7   AACR2

Contents

Contents

Illustrations

Introduction

What follows is a unique pair of diaries. One was kept by Rachel Bowman from the autumn of 1858 through the summer of 1865. The other was written by Samuel Cormany from the spring of 1859 through the summer of 1865. Both diaries begin before either diarist knew the other and continue through their meeting as fellow students at Otterbein University, their separate attempts to find a place in American society as young adults, their eventual courtship and marriage, and their honeymoon trip on the eve of the Civil War from Ohio to the Grand River Valley in Canada, where Rachel had been born. After almost two years of uneasy exile among Rachel's Canadian relatives, and the birth of their first child, Rachel and Samuel decide they must return to the United States, even though they realize they will be casting their fates into the greatest upheaval American society had ever experienced.

The Cormanys return in the summer of 1862 to the Cumberland Valley of Pennsylvania, Samuel's birthplace. After a brief reunion with his kinfolk in the area, Samuel enlists in a volunteer regiment of Union cavalry, and from that point onward his diary evolves into a firsthand account of what it was like to fight as an ordinary horse soldier in the eastern theater of the Civil War. Because Samuel participated in most of the major eastern campaigns from Chancellorsville through the final chase to Appomattox, his account is rich in significant detail. In the meantime, Rachel, who has been left with her baby in a rented room in Chambersburg, Pennsylvania, records the ordeal of life on the home front in a town that is twice occupied by the Confederate army and intentionally burned by the Southerners in 1864. The diaries end in the summer of 1865 as the Cormanys are reunited.

Both diaries are rich sources of historical insight. Samuel's, for example, is the only diary known to exist from his regiment, the 16th Pennsylvania Volunteer Cavalry, and it would be important to military historians for that reason alone. Yet it also contains fresh evidence on such diverse subjects as farmmaking, childbirth, infant care, troop morale, and promotion in the federal army. Samuel practices hydropathic medicine, and his comments help explain why an educated young person of the 1860s might find the so-called water cure therapies, with their stress on natural forces, self help, and good diet, more attractive than the therapies advocated at the time by professional physicians. Samuel came from a large family, and he alludes several times to his own desire for children, especially a son. Yet he defers to Rachel's desire to limit the size of their family. This is an important piece of evidence in the historical debate over the relative roles of men and women in the dramatic reduction of fertility among white Protestant Americans during the nineteenth century. Samuel's sections on the occupation of Virginia and the demobilization of the Union army are also valuable. Most Civil War soldiers' diaries stop with the cessation of actual combat and therefore miss the anticlimactic tensions and personal frustrations that provided the Cormanys some of their most trying months of separation.

Rachel's diary by itself is an even more fascinating document than Samuel's. Rachel was one of only a few hundred women in the United States to graduate from a coeducational college prior to the Civil War, and her impressions of undergraduate life are valuable. So also are her firsthand accounts of how difficult it was for a single woman of the common classes to establish a secure place for herself in antebellum America, even with a college education. Her diary contains several deft descriptions of rural family life in Ohio and Pennsylvania that help peel away old generalizations and expose the variety and complexity that actually existed: good marriages and bad, intergenerational squabbling and bucolic harmony, public spirit and narrow selfishness, religious commitment and debilitating alcoholism. Rachel's many references to the behavior of children, including her own, indicate that most of the hypotheses offered thus far by the historians of childhood and childrearing may be too unidimensional. Finally, historians know a great deal about what life was like for the hundreds of thousands of young men who went off to fight against the slaveholders but surprisingly little about the women who were left behind, often with small children and little money. How did they survive? Where did they live? To whom did they turn? How did the experience affect their marriages and their sense of themselves? What emotions did their situations evoke? These are crucial questions for social history, the history of the family, and the history of women; Rachel's diary provides an important new source of direct answers.

The two diaries share certain characteristics that add further to their merit as historical sources. The most significant of these is that they are both the diaries of common folk. The personal observations, impressions, reactions, and assumptions of ordinary people are not readily available either in published or manuscript form. Both Samuel and Rachel were from middling farm families and rural areas rather than from commercial, entrepreneurial, or industrial backgrounds or from urban areas. In this respect they resembled the majority of their fellow citizens on the eve of the Civil War, but were quite different from most of the Americans whose diaries have survived. The latter tended to be individuals in the upper echelons of society, and they were usually located near major metropolitan areas. They were the people who had the most leisure time, the best sources of information about aspects of life that seemed noteworthy, and the best education with which to express themselves. Subsequent generations saved their comments.

The vast majority of common folk, on the other hand, either did not or could not record their thoughts (there is a large literature on who keeps diaries and why they do it), or they wrote journals that tended to be excessively routine, poorly expressed, and irregularly kept. While those qualities are important to an understanding of the lives they led, their descendants tended not to save such seemingly mundane materials. Thus, one of the important aspects of the Cormany diaries is that they record individual experiences from a social stratum that American historians are often forced to treat in extremely generalized, impersonal, or statistical terms.

Notwithstanding the value of the Cormany diaries separately, however, it is the relationship between the two that ultimately makes them so intriguing. The editors are unaware of any comparable pair of diaries for the Civil War era. Together they constitute, in effect, the autobiography of the early years of a marriage—a marriage begun within weeks of Lincoln's election and tested, like the nation itself, in the intense crucible of the Civil War.

The Diarists

Rachel Bowman had been born April 12, 1836, on her father's farm near the tiny agricultural hamlet of Carlisle Hill in what was then called Canada West (now the Province of Ontario). She had lived her early life there before coming to the United States to seek an education. She had studied in the preparatory department at Oberlin College in Oberlin, Ohio, during the 1854–1855 school year and in Oberlin's literary course during the 1855–1856 school year, before persuading her family to let her continue toward a collegiate degree at Otterbein University, a United Brethren school in Westerville, Ohio, just north of Columbus.

In October 1858, as the surviving sections of her diary begin, Rachel Bowman was in the fall semester of her senior year at Otterbein. She was twenty-two years old and quite stout. She had dark hair, dark eyes, and plain features. She lived directly across the street from the college in a large house owned by her father, Benjamin B. Bowman. The location of the house and the name of its owner are clearly marked on an 1858 map of Westerville. Benjamin Bowman himself was in Canada, tending to postharvest business and preparing to move his family back there, but Rachel's mother, Mary Clemens Bowman, and five younger sisters were in Westerville. The younger sisters, in descending order of age, were Mary, Leah, Susie, Lizzie, and Carrie.

To finance their residence in Westerville the Bowman women opened their large house to student boarders. Boarding was a common practice in nineteenth-century America, particularly in college towns. Westerville had a permanent population of 275 people at this time; Otterbein registered 267 students for the spring term of 1859. Since the college provided only a few dormitory rooms and no food services whatsoever, boarding was an important element of the local economy. The Bowmans had temporarily become hotel keepers in order to allow Rachel to attend Otterbein. Notwithstanding Rachel's frequent annoyance with many of the details of this arrangement (she complains often about the division of labor among the six sisters), it shows a remarkable commitment to education in the Bowman family at a time when few women were sent to college and few colleges accepted them.

In addition to her five younger sisters, Rachel also had two brothers and an older sister. Abraham Clemens Bowman, whom the family called "Clem," had studied hydropathic medicine at the New York Hygienic Institute and was trying to establish a practice of his own near Blair, Canada West. Rachel's other brother, Amos Bowman, was a reporter for the New York *Tribune.* Lydia Bowman, Rachel's older sister, had married a dry-goods merchant, Samuel S. Weaver, and was raising a family in Elmira, Canada West, not far from where she and Rachel had grown up.

Samuel Eckerman Cormany was the son of Jacob Cormany, a Pennsylvania farmer, and Mary Eckerman Cormany, Jacob's third wife. Samuel had grown up where he had been born May 24, 1838: on his father's farm eight miles north of Chambersburg in the Cumberland Valley. Samuel had four older half-sisters (Mary Jane, Wilamina, Hannah and Lydia), two older half-brothers (John and Bernard) and two younger sisters (Sarah and Eleanora). Samuel had also seen his parents lose three children in infancy.

When Samuel's father died in 1855, the farm passed jointly to his mother and his oldest half-brother, John. The other siblings received modest cash settlements, and Samuel decided to use part of his inheritance to pursue a college education. He enrolled at tiny Mount Pleasant College, a United Brethren school in Pennsylvania, but the college closed during the economic slump that followed the panic of 1857. By 1859 Samuel's mother had decided to remarry and was in the process of selling her share of the original Cormany farm to John, who would then become sole owner. Since John's family was already living on the property, and since his mother was moving to a nearby farm to become Mrs. Daniel Byers, Samuel decided it was time for him to leave home and seek his fortune farther west. Consequently, in the spring of 1859, he accompanied several other Pennsylvanians who left Mount Pleasant to enroll at the nation's only remaining United Brethren college: Otterbein University. He was twenty-one when he began the diary published here, slightly under five feet six inches tall, and he weighed a little over 130 pounds. He had hazel eyes, a light complexion, and dark hair.

It is significant that these two young adults encountered one another at a church-related school, for both Rachel and Samuel were steeped in the traditions of evangelical Protestantism. Samuel had been raised in the United Brethren faith. His father had served the United Brethren as a lay minister. That denomination had its origin in a wave of revivals among German Reformed and Mennonite congregations in the valleys of Pennsylvania and Maryland near the end of the eighteenth century. The United Brethren in Christ (not to be confused with the Unitas Fratrum or Moravians) organized formally in the early nineteenth century and expanded their geographical base out into Ohio. Theologically the United Brethren might be characterized as Germanic Methodists; indeed, the United Brethren and the Methodists began to cooperate closely after the Civil War and eventually merged into the present United Methodist church. Their personal spirituality was intense, their commitment to ethical behavior was unwavering (some of the most dramatic incidents in Samuel's diary deal with his personal agonies over the sale and use of alcohol), but their doctrinal positions and their forms of worship were remarkably flexible and tolerant (the Cormanys frequently attend the services of other evangelical denominations). Otterbein University, founded by the United Brethren in 1847, was in no uncertain terms a denominational college.

Rachel's religious roots were less denominationally specific than Samuel's, but just as spiritually intense. She had grown up among the Mennonites and German Reformed groups who farmed the Grand River Valley. Her father's family had been among a group of "Pennsylvania Dutch" Mennonites who emigrated from eastern Pennsylvania to the Canadian frontier after the American Revolu-

originals remained legible, but finally discarded the last of those disintegrating booklets in the 1970s. The published edition of Samuel's diary was prepared entirely from the 1916–1917 transcript.

Both Rachel and Samuel had apparently kept diaries prior to 1858, but their earlier journals have not survived. The transcripts that follow begin with the first extant entry in both cases and continue through August 1865: there are no omissions of any sort from either record during that period. The decision to stop September 1, 1865, resulted partly from the changing circumstances of the Cormanys' lives and partly from the nature of the later material. That date may fairly be said to mark the close of a distinct period in the lives of Rachel and Samuel; their later entries reveal an effort to put the war behind them. After a round of visiting family and friends, the Cormanys strike out for Missouri, where they try to resume their pre-war lives. But that new phase of their lives is not so well documented as the one they just concluded. Rachel wrote only sixteen entries in the nine months following September 1, 1865, and their substance has been incorporated into the Epilogue. After May 26, 1866, Rachel either ceased diarykeeping altogether or, more likely, what she wrote was lost. Samuel maintained his diary on an almost daily basis after September 1, 1865, but the extant record ends abruptly on November 15, 1865. The rest has been lost. What survives has also been incorporated into the Epilogue.

Editorial Format

This project presented few technical problems. The editors standardized the datelines (including the day of the week only when the diarist did so) and the physical layout of the entries. We also eliminated all underlinings in Samuel's diary, primarily because many of the underlinings appear to have been added later, possibly generations later, than the entry itself. In Rachel's diary, where the underlinings appear to be original, they have been retained. Otherwise, the diaries are given here just as they were written. This may cause some inconvenience to readers. There are many misspellings, some repetitions, and a few missing words. Samuel often used dashes in lieu of commas and periods, and Rachel's punctuation was irregular. Both diarists occasionally capitalized words that would normally be printed in lower case, and both diarists frequently failed to capitalize the first word of a sentence. But neither used excessively idiosyncratic forms, codes, or notations. The editors feel confident that any difficulties for the reader will be more than offset by the authenticity of encountering Rachel and Samuel in the prose they actually wrote.

If the technical problems of transcription were easily resolved, however, the larger question of overall presentation posed a difficult series of choices. The two diaries could be printed, for example, in separate volumes. Yet that would involve a great deal of cumbersome cross-referencing and still fail to exploit fully the unique interrelationship between the two documents. At the other end of the spectrum of possible arrangements were several types of day-by-day or double-column presentations. Yet those seemed equally unattractive because they would chop the diaries up to such an extent that readers would find it nearly impossible to follow either one of them in a coherent, cumulative fashion. These formats would also be inappropriate for the substantial portions of Rachel's diary that deal with her struggles to find a place for herself as a single woman and for the lengthy sections of Samuel's diary that were written either in behalf of his wife and himself or primarily as military narratives.

To resolve this dilemma, the diaries have been divided into reasonably self-contained sections and arranged in an alternating sequence. This allows the reader to hear one voice at a time without losing the continuity of the narrative. At some points the appropriate breaks were obvious; at others they were judgmental. It is hoped that the essential integrity of each diary has been preserved within a format that emphasizes the relationship between the two.

Acknowledgments

Much of the credit for this project belongs to the Editorial Division of the National Endowment for the Humanities. The NEH recognized both the paucity of published material on the lives of common citizens (particularly women) during the Civil War and the unique merits of the Cormany diaries as documents of social and family history. Consequently, they helped underwrite this project with an editorial grant. I wish to thank the Endowment for its support, and to acknowledge specifically the assistance of Kathy Fuller, who represented the NEH on this project.

Support from the NEH allowed the editor to obtain the services of Richard E. Winslow III as associate editor. Dr. Winslow proved a tireless, skillful, and congenial colleague, whose deft abilities as an historical sleuth have greatly enriched this volume. Dr. Winslow, who subsequently joined the Papers of Henry Clay project at the University of Kentucky, wishes in turn to acknowledge the help of Dr. Frank G. Burke, executive director of the National Historical Publications and Records Commission, for the experiences he gained as an intern in the National Archives and the Library of

Congress, and for the skills he acquired in a Historical Editing Seminar and Conference at the University of Wisconsin.

The selfless efforts of the Ray E. Kiefer family have already been mentioned, but they bear reemphasizing here. Without their efforts there would be no project. Other descendants of the diarists also gave generously of their time, information, and family records. These included E. Irving Wines of Chambersburg, Pennsylvania, a great-grandson of Samuel's oldest half-brother, John Hampsher Cormany. Mr. Wines shared years of independent genealogical research with the editors and helped doublecheck the many kinship references in the diaries. Robert B. Cormany of Boiling Springs, Pennsylvania, and J. Roy Cormany of Chambersburg, Pennsylvania, also offered useful genealogical assistance and family records. Henry B. Bowman of the Waterloo Historical Society identified important materials on the Canadian branches of the Bowman family.

Many excellent reference librarians and archivists helped the editors over the past two years. Several deserve special mention. Mary-Jean Whittaker, Binnie Syril Braunstein, and the rest of the staff of the library at the University of Maryland Baltimore County cheerfully and patiently answered a lengthy series of obscure questions. Dale Floyd of the National Archives expedited our efforts to use the Old Military records at Washington. Richard Sommers, archivist-historian at the United States Army Military History Institute in Carlisle, Pennsylvania, shared his interests in Civil War cavalry records.

Terry Tilden of the Pennsylvania State Library at Harrisburg handled several long distance inquiries with great skill and patience. The reference staff at Otterbein University in Westerville, Ohio, was especially courteous and helpful each time we asked them for assistance. W. E. Bigglestone, archivist of Oberlin College, kindly searched some of his college's records for us. Mary E. Dickerson, head of Information and Reference Services, Legislative Library, Toronto, Ontario, went out of her way to be helpful, as did Jim Montieth and James L. Murphy of the Ohio Historical Society. Richard Stephenson and Jim Flatness made working at the Geography and Maps Division of the Library of Congress in Alexandria, Virginia, a professional pleasure.

Frederick A. Hetzel, director of the University of Pittsburgh Press, has been consistently encouraging from the outset of this project and offered valuable technical and editorial advice on several occasions. Catherine Marshall, managing editor at the Press, did a superb job copyediting this manuscript and overseeing its production to book form. Elizabeth A. Mohr revealed, once again, both her acute editorial skills and her great reserve of patience during the difficult proofreading stages of this undertaking.

Competent secretarial help is critical to the success of a project like this. B. Joan Watson and Mary A. Dietrich provided just that in fulfilling some very difficult typing and transcribing assignments.

For help in securing illustrations, and for permission to print them, I wish to acknowledge Tim Boles of the Anacortes Museum, Anacortes, Washington; Janet Mae Book Boydon, author of *Northern Rendezvous: Harrisburg During the Civil War* (Harrisburg, 1951); the Ray E. Kiefer family; the Louisiana State University Press; the Maps Division of the Library of Congress; and the Division of Prints and Photographs of the Library of Congress.

Finally, I wish to thank my family for the understanding they have shown throughout the course of this project.

James C. Mohr

Kinship Glossary

*H*undreds of individuals are mentioned by name in the Cormany diaries. Because few of them were previously known to historians, their appearance in the diaries posed major problems of identification and presentation. The editors decided to discuss selectively in footnotes only some of the persons named, while allowing most of the others to continue to enjoy their historical privacy. Whenever we singled out a particular person for identification or discussion, it was either because that person was (or became) an important historical figure or because we believed that some details of that person's life were important to a full appreciation of the diaries.

There was one category of named persons, however, for whom the preceeding general decision proved inappropriate: the diarists' closest relatives. Rachel and Samuel are part of large kinship networks that function for them as subsystems within the larger society. Rachel, for example, does not go to New York City per se, but to her *brother* there. She does not go to Quakerstown because there was a teaching job available, but because her mother had relatives there who would help her find a position. Samuel's diary ironically begins with his effort to break away from the kinship network in which he was raised, but later reveals his decision, when the chips were down, to entrust his wife and infant daughter to that network when he goes off to fight, even though that meant they would spend the war in one of the most vulnerable towns in the North.

The importance of those family networks and a full appreciation of the way they worked make the identity of close relatives essential to an intelligent reading of the diaries. We therefore prepared kinship glossaries for the Bowman and Cormany families. The glossaries include only the most frequently mentioned close relatives (generally siblings and their spouses) of the two diarists; aunts and uncles, for example, are not included, even though many of them appear in the diaries. Each relative is identified by a letter or letters that will appear as a superscript whenever that person is mentioned.

Cormany Kin

a. *Jacob Cormany (1797–1855).* Samuel's father. He had lived on a farm some eight miles north of Chambersburg and served as a United Brethren minister. Died before the diaries open.

b. *Mary Eckerman Cormany Byers (1811–1879).* Third wife of Jacob Cormany and mother of Samuel. Married Daniel Byers in 1859 and resided throughout the period of the diaries on the Byers farm about five miles north of Chambersburg.

ba. *Daniel Byers.* Married Samuel's mother, Mary Eckerman Cormany, in 1859. Farmed some five miles north of Chambersburg.

c. *Mary Jane Cormany Wenger (1821–1848).* Eldest child of Jacob Cormany and his first wife, Margaret Hampsher; half sister to Samuel. Married Samuel Wenger, 1841. Died before the diaries open.

d. *John Hampsher Cormany (1822/23–1892).* Second child of Jacob Cormany and his first wife, Margaret Hampsher; half brother to Samuel. Lived with his family on the old Jacob Cormany farm throughout the period of the diaries.

e. *Catherine Ann Myers Cormany.* Married Samuel's older half brother John Hampsher Cormany, 1848. Lived with her husband on the old Jacob Cormany farm throughout the period of the diaries.

f. *William Cormany.* Son of John Hampsher and Catherine Myers Cormany, lived with his parents on the old Jacob Cormany farm throughout the period of the diaries.

g. *Fred Cormany.* Son of John Hampsher and Catherine Myers Cormany, lived with his parents on the old Jacob Cormany farm throughout the period of the diaries.

h. *Maggie Cormany.* Daughter of John Hampsher and Catherine Myers Cormany, lived on the old Jacob Cormany farm throughout the period of the diaries.

i. *Wilamina (variant spellings) Cormany Karper (b. 1825).* Third child of Jacob Cormany and his first wife, Margaret Hampsher; half sister to Samuel. Resided with her husband, Philip Karper, on a farm outside Chambersburg during the period of the diaries.

j. *Philip Karper.* Married Samuel's older half-sister Wilamina, 1843, and farmed outside Chambersburg during the period covered in the diaries.

ja. *Maggie Karper.* Daughter of Philip and Wilamina Cormany Karper.

k. *Hannah Cormany Karper (b. 1827?).* Fourth child of Jacob Cormany and his first wife, Margaret Hampsher; half sister to Samuel. Resided throughout the period of the diaries on the farm of her husband, John Karper, outside Chambersburg.

l. *John Karper.* Married Samuel's older half sister Hannah, 1844, and farmed outside Chambersburg.

m. *William Karper (1844/45–1863).* Eldest child of John and Hannah Cormany Karper.

n. *Rose Karper.* Daughter of John and Hannah Cormany Karper.

o. *Richard Karper.* Son of John and Hannah Cormany Karper.

p. *Lydia E. Cormany Rebok (1829–1891).* Fifth child of Jacob Cormany and his first wife, Margaret Hampsher; half sister to Samuel. Lived during the period of the diaries with her husband, the Reverend Henry W. Rebok, first in Chambersburg, then on a farm some ten miles north-northeast of Chambersburg not far from the village of Orrstown, on the road from Orrstown to Shippensburg.

pa. *Henry W. Rebok.* Married Samuel's older half sister Lydia, 1849.

pb. *Naoma Rebok.* Daughter of Henry and Lydia Rebok.

q. *Bernard Anthony Cormany (b. 1834).* Only child of Jacob Cormany and his second wife, Lydia Hampsher; half brother to Samuel. Farmed outside the village of St. Thomas, some five miles west of Chambersburg.

r. *Elizabeth Strock Cormany.* Married Samuel's older half-brother Bernard A. Cormany, 1857.

t. *Daniel Cormany (b. 1840).* Second child of Jacob Cormany and his third wife, Mary Eckerman Cormany Byers. Died in infancy.

u. *Sarah A. Cormany Thompson (b. 1840).* Third child of Jacob Cormany and his third wife, Mary Eckerman Cormany Byers; a twin to Daniel, and sister to Samuel. Married Isaac Thompson, 1861, and lived on his farm near the village of Strasburg during most of the period covered by the diaries. Emigrated from the Cumberland Valley to Iowa, 1865.

v. *Issac Thompson.* Married Samuel's sister Sarah, 1861.

w. *Jacob Cormany (1841).* Fourth child of Jacob Cormany and his third wife, Mary Eckerman Cormany Byers; a brother to Samuel. Died in infancy.

x. *Lacinda Cormany (1843).* Fifth child of Jacob Cormany and his third wife, Mary Eckerman Cormany Byers; a sister to Samuel. Died in infancy.

y. *Eleanora Jane Cormany Slichter (b. 1845).* Sixth child of Jacob Cormany and his third wife, Mary Eckerman Cormany Byers; sister to Samuel. Lived with her mother on the old Jacob Cormany farm at the outset of the diary, then married Benjamin Slichter in 1863 and moved to his farm outside Chambersburg. Emigrated to Iowa, 1865.

z. *Benjamin Slichter.* Married Samuel's younger sister Eleanora Jane Cormany, 1863.

aa. *Benjamin B. Bowman (1811–1872).* Rachel's father. Thirteenth child of Joseph and Mary Baer Bauman. Emigrated with his parents from Berks County, Pennsylvania, to Blair, Canada West, 1816. Moved to Michigan, 1865.

bb. *Mary Clemens Bowman (b. 1815).* Rachel's mother. One of eight children born to Abraham and Rachel Dierstein Clemens. Grew up in the Waterloo area of Canada West, but had many relatives on both the Clemens and Dierstein sides in Bucks and Montgomery Counties, Pennsylvania.

cc. *Abraham Clemens "Clem" Bowman (d. 1905).* Eldest child of Benjamin and Mary Clemens Bowman; Rachel's brother.

dd. *Lydia Bowman Weaver (d. 1866).* Second child of Benjamin and Mary Clemens Bowman; Rachel's sister. Married Samuel Weaver and lived in Elmira, Canada West, throughout the period covered by the diaries.

ee. *Samuel S. Weaver (b. 1828).* Married Lydia Bowman. Partner in a dry-goods firm in Elmira, Canada West, where he and his family resided throughout the period covered by the diaries.

ff. *Astor Weaver.* Son of Samuel and Lydia Bowman Weaver; nephew to Rachel. He is a baby during the diary period.

gg. *Angus Weaver.* Son of Samuel and Lydia Bowman Weaver; nephew to Rachel. He is a child during the diary period.

hh. *Amos Bowman (1838–1894).* Fourth child of Benjamin and Mary Clemens Bowman; Rachel's brother. Living in New York City, where he was a reporter for the New York *Tribune* during most of the period covered by the diary.

ii. *Mary "Mollie" Bowman.* Fifth child of Benjamin and Mary Clemens Bowman; Rachel's sister. Married Joseph Peterson and lived with him on a farm in Kansas.

jj. *Leah Bowman Adams.* Sixth child of Benjamin and Mary Clemens Bowman; Rachel's sister. Married James W. Adams, 1859, and moved from Westerville to the Waterloo area of Canada West.

kk. *James W. Adams.* Canadian merchant who married Rachel's sister Leah Bowman, 1859.

ll. *Joel Bowman.* Seventh child of Benjamin and Mary Clemens Bowman; Rachel's brother. Died in Ohio at the age of fourteen, prior to the period covered by the diaries.

mm. *Oscar Bowman.* Eighth child of Benjamin and Mary Clemens Bowman; Rachel's brother. Died at the age of one year.

nn. *Susannah "Susie" Bowman.* Ninth child of Benjamin and Mary Clemens Bowman; Rachel's sister.

oo. *Lizzie Bowman.* Tenth child of Benjamin and Mary Clemens Bowman; Rachel's sister.

pp. *Carrie Bowman.* Eleventh and last child of Benjamin and Mary Clemens Bowman; Rachel's sister.

Abbreviations Used in Footnotes

AFCP D. G. Beers, *Atlas of Franklin County Pennsylvania* (Philadelphia, 1868; rpt. Knightstown, Ind., 1974).

BHWT Ezra E. Eby, *A Biographical History of Waterloo Township and Other Townships of the County, Being a History of the Early Settlers and Their Descendants, Mostly All of Pennsylvania Dutch Origin As Also Much Other Unpublished Historical Information Chiefly of a Local Character* (Berlin, Ont., 1896), 2 vols., supplement 1931 by Joseph B. Snyder, index, notes, and revisions by Eldon D. Weber (rpt. Kitchener, Ont., 1971).

CWH *Civil War History.*

CWTI *Civil War Times Illustrated.*

DAB *Dictionary of American Biography.*

H16PC Charles H. Miller, comp., *History of the 16th Regiment Pennsylvania Cavalry, for the Year Ending October 31st, 1863* (Philadelphia, 1864).

LC Library of Congress, Washington, D.C.

NA National Archives, Washington, D.C.

NCAB *National Cyclopedia of American Biography.*

NUC *National Union Catalogue.*

OMACW George B. Davis et al., *The Official Military Atlas of the Civil War* (Washington, D.C., 1891–95; rpt. New York, 1978).

OR *War of the Rebellion: A Compilation of the Official Records of the Union and Confederate Armies* (Washington, 1880–1901).

PV Samuel P. Bates, *History of Pennsylvania Volunteers, 1861–5* (Harrisburg, 1870).

TQRGO *Twelfth Quadrennial Register of the Graduates of Otterbein University, 1857–1905* (Westerville, O., 1905).

THE CORMANY DIARIES

I

Rachel at Otterbein

October 30, 1858–June 26, 1859

*R*achel's *diary opens when she is a senior at Otterbein University and continues through her graduation with the antebellum equivalent of a B.S. degree. Although the first entry records an excursion into Columbus, most of this section is set in the small college town of Westerville, some twelve miles northeast of the Ohio capital. Most of the characters are Rachel's classmates or members of her household.*

This section offers a rare glimpse of undergraduate life at a small church-related college on the eve of the Civil War. The glimpse is especially valuable because the college was one of only three or four coeducational colleges in the United States and because it is written from a woman's point of view at a time when few women in the country had been through the experience of completing a bona fide college education. Otterbein was founded in 1847 by the Ohio Conference of the United Brethren church, but did not award its first two baccalaureate degrees until 1857. In 1858 it conferred seven more. Rachel's class of nine seniors was the third to complete one of the three college courses prescribed by the Otterbein board of trustees. Rachel was taking the science course, which included modern subjects and was taught in English. Her classmates who studied the classics received a Bachelor of Arts degree, and some of the women at Otterbein were taking a Mistress of Arts degree.

Several of Rachel's entries deal with the social pressures of her senior year. Her classmates were beginning to pair off, but Rachel's own relationships—with Wilberforce Boggs and Jacob Burgner—turn sour. In the frustration of those relationships, however, and in her acid comments on the widower Hellane (February 12, 1859) Rachel reveals that she has both strong views and high expectations regarding marriage.

October 30, 1858 This morning we got up at 8 O clock to get ready to go to Columbus to market for the purpose of seeing how it goes there. Mr. Pennell, Mother,[bb] Mary Miller and I were the ones that went.[1] We got to Columbus at about 9 A.M.. Just as we entered town

1. Hezekiah C. Pennell (1829–1904) and Mary Lucretia Miller (1839–1898) were fellow students at Otterbein. For biographical sketches of both, see *TQRGO*, pp. 26, 29.

we met six nuns walking two and two. I felt as though I would like very much to talk with them and convince them of their error. Poor things I pitied them. We next came on Market street, and such a crowd of wagons and people I scarcely ever saw before in one place. On passing some turnips Mother[bb] and I got dreadful hungry for some. We wished to buy a few to eat, and asked the man to sell us two or three to eat. He laughed at us and told us we might have as many as we wished to eat for nothing and would not accept of our money. After we got tired of market we went shopping had quite a time at the auction store. Got through shopping till dinner. After dinner we with Mr. Wiebling went to the Assylums.[2] The hack went and left Mr. Wiebling. they then came home with us.[3] We had six for one horse. Almost a respectable Methodist load. Within about a mile from home we met young Mr. Wiebling on his way to Columbus to fetch his parents. We got home safe but were very tired.

October, 5, 1858 [actually November]   This has been a very unpleasant rainy day. Mother[bb] is sick this evening, I did not go to society[4] on that account, wrote a composition for tomorrow morn-

2. Rachel probably refers here to the Central Lunatic Asylum, the State Asylum for the Blind, and the Hospital for the Deaf and Dumb, all located in Columbus. They attracted sightseers in part because of their size and impressive architecture. Moreover, many nineteenth-century Americans viewed such institutions as reassuring symbols that their form of government worked well to protect the unfortunate and to solidify community spirit. While historians have questioned the accuracy of such perceptions (e.g., David J. Rothman, *The Discovery of the Asylum: Social Order and Disorder in the New Republic* [Boston, 1971]), ordinary citizens seem to have clung to them tenaciously. Daryl E. Jones and James W. Pickering, in "A Young Woman in the Midwest: The Journal of Mary Sears, 1859–1860," *Ohio History* 82 (1973), 223–24, document a similar example of asylum visiting in Columbus. For more on the asylums themselves, including illustrations, consult Jacob H. Struder, *Columbus, Ohio: Its History, Resources, and Progress* (Columbus, 1873). The Wieblings were friends from Westerville who had also come into Columbus for the day.

3. A hack was a small stagecoach. Westerville lay on the so-called State Road between Cleveland and Columbus, so townsfolk could use the regularly scheduled stage for transportation to and from Columbus. Mr. and Mrs. Wiebling had missed the departure of the public coach so Rachel's group offered them a lift in their one-horse buggy. See Henry Garst, *Otterbein University, 1847–1907* (Dayton, Ohio, 1907), pp. 289–93, and Ohio Writers' Program, *Westerville in the American Tradition* (Works Projects Administration, 1940), pp. 38–39. Both Rachel and Samuel often refer to families and to couples simply by the name of the male head of the house. Thus, "visited John Smith" often means the writer went to see the John Smith family at their home; John himself was not necessarily there.

4. The Philalethean Society, a literary society for undergraduate women. Two similar societies competed for the loyalty of male students at Otterbein at this time. Garst, *Otterbein*, pp. 166–71. Literary societies, which were common on American campuses,

ing, received a letter from Ella Chambers, she is going to come here to school. I see that I have some little influence. I got acquainted with her while teaching in their district. Answered her letter, and now am going to sow at the little girls bonnets. Yesterday evening instead of lecture, Dr. McFadden tried chemical experiments, exploded some powder on land, and some under water, had quite a time in getting the rope across the stream.[5]

November 18, 1858 I see it is quite a while since I last wrote in my journal. Miss Chambers is here now, we three room together, that is Mary,[ii] Miss C, and I, hope we will get along well. Cousin Isaac[6] is with us now, he thinks of giving one lecture before he leaves, he wants me to go home with him, wish I could. Last Friday I was elected secretary in literary society. I am afraid I won't fill the chair well, well I guess I can do as well as I can, Saturdy night M. Miller and I sat up with a sick girl, sowed nearly all night. I have to read in "public" in a week from Saturday, those public exercises do take me down dreadfully, wish it was over.[7]

November 27, 1858 This was the day for our Monthly rhetorical exercises. It commenced snowing in the morning and snowed all day. I had hard work to get my essay finised. got through just in time, the snow was so deep that we could scarcely get down to the chapple. After the exercises, all those that read went to Proffessor

---

functioned as joint-stock library associations, providers of entertainment, debating and composing teams, and proto-fraternities and sororities. Much of the extracurricular college life available to students like Rachel was organized by and around these societies. Thomas S. Harding, *College Literary Societies: Their Contribution to Higher Education in the United States, 1815–1876* (New York, 1971).

5. Thomas McFadden, M.D., educated at Dickinson College in Carlisle, Pennsylvania, had been appointed professor of natural sciences and scientific agriculture and horticulture in 1858. He resigned from the faculty during the Civil War to become an army surgeon with the 46th Ohio, then returned to Otterbein as professor of natural sciences in 1866. He occupied that chair until his death in 1883. Garst, *Otterbein*, pp. 113–26, 184–86. Otterbein was not only teaching natural sciences, but offering its students rudimentary laboratory work and geology field trips (see May 18, 1859). On the important role of small schools like Otterbein in the dissemination of modern knowledge see Colin B. Burke, "The Quiet Influence: The American Liberal Arts Colleges and Their Students, 1800–1860," forthcoming, New York University Press.

6. Probably Isaac L. Bowman (1830–1893), youngest son of Rachel's father's brother John B. Bauman and his wife Nancy Bechtel Bauman. Isaac was a prominent educator in the public school system of Waterloo Township, Canada West. *BHWI,* II, 25.

7. The public recitation of original essays was a standard pedagogical technique in nineteenth-century colleges.

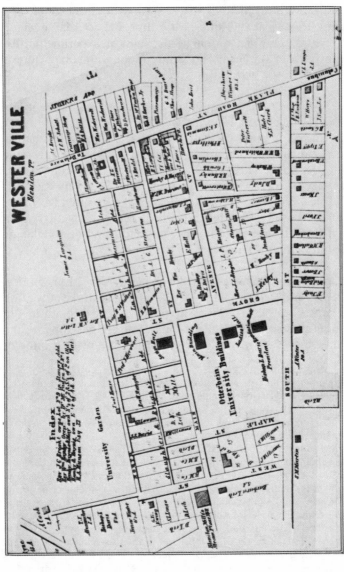

Westerville, Ohio, in the late 1850s. Rachel (B. B. Bowman) lived directly across Grove Street from Saum Hall. The homes of many of the people Rachel mentions can be located on this map. Detail from John Graham, *Map of Franklin County, Ohio, from Actual Survey and Records* (Philadelphia, 1856). Maps Division, LC.

Walkers[8] to a supper, we had been invited for some time, we had a very nice time. Amanda Hanby, Miss McKinney and Miss Gilbert[9] were the extra ones, they did not read, we had a very nice time, it rained when we came home. W. Hiskey took Miss Gilbert, W. Haynie Miss McKinney, W. Boggs, M. Miller, J. Clark, A. Hanby, A Zehring, me.[10] such a time we had getting home.

November 29, 1858 It is raining yet. the snow is not gone yet, it is very sloppy and almost impossible to get along. it is raining so fast, and so bad to get along that I do not know whether I can get to church today or not.

December 5, 1858 Sabath afternoon. Was to church this morning Bishop L. Davis preached,[11] it is very windy. I have been contemplating on my bad heart, read some in Mrs. Sigourney's letters to her pupils,[12] was reading of their amiable dispositions how I have to deplore my unamiable one, by my horid temper I loose friends, but never gain any. I feel as though our family could and would gladly spare me. I have been accustomed to look on their treatment as though they thought me not smart and tried to impose on me, and that is what made me act as I did. I see now that it is my own doing, would to God that I could overcome, I wish from my heart to be a true christian, to fit myself to do good, but without that true love and pure religion in my heart I cannot expect to do much, I have made a resolution to act so that my folks here can love me, I am very easily discouraged naturally, and am often only taunted when I

8. Ralph Manning Walker, who came to Otterbein from Grand River Institute in Austinburg, Ohio, had been appointed professor of ancient languages in 1853. In 1858 he was serving as professor of latin languages and literature. He remained on the faculty until 1862. Garst, *Otterbein*, pp. 73–74, 306. The Walkers lived next door to the Bowmans.

9. Mary L. Gilbert was principal of the Ladies' Department (dean of women) from 1856 to 1862. Garst, *Otterbein*, p. 307. The other two were fellow students.

10. Biographical sketches of William O. Hiskey (1838–1871), John Wesley Haynie (1836–1897), and Wilberforce K. Boggs (1839–1872) are in *TQRGO*, pp. 29, 30. Note that the group was clearly paired off into couples.

11. The Reverend Lewis Davis, a bishop in the United Brethren church, had led the drive to establish Otterbein in the 1840s. He served as the school's president from 1850 through 1857 and again from 1860 through 1871. Garst, *Otterbein*, pp. 9–78, et passim.

12. Although her work is excessively sentimental and moralistic by modern standards, Lydia Howard Sigourney was one of the most popular versifiers and authors of the nineteenth century. Among her sixty-seven published books was *Letters to My Pupils: With Narrative and Biographical Sketches* (New York, 1851), to which Rachel refers here.

express it, but I expect if I would act right all would be better, I generally do the dressfitting and cutting and bonnet making. This year I had to make two by fixing old foundations into new ones, which of course did not look as well as new. The girls (sisters) acted so about them that I felt that I could almost pray to be delivered from bonnet making. I think their actions make the owners of the bonnets dislike them, as they do, when the bonnets are plenty good enough.[13] I am going to write my resolutions on a paper and carry them in my pocket, and mark it every time I don't come up to the mark, and also when I do right at the close of each. It seems to me that victory is sure. Sabath evening, Had Missionary meeting this evening.[14] Prof. Walker addressed the society, advanced the idea of colonies emigrating to evangelize the world. An essay was also read by Mr. Gharst.[15]

December 15, 1858 Just finished a large washing. Mary[ii] and I washed. last Sunday we had quarterly meeting. I long before wished to take sacrament and prayed for it. I took sacrament, and ever since I feel almost as though I had committed a sin by it. I meant well. O! that I knew in my heart that I was the Lords, I want to be a good christian. I desire to be prepared to do some good, but how can I if my heart is not ful of the true kind of religion.

December 20, 1858 We have had a protracted meeting in operation here two weeks now, two have experienced religion, I think we are going to have a great revival.[16] I hope so at least, I that would get my

13. The Bowman women supplemented their income by dressmaking and bonnet-making. Sewing was an extremely common source of extra money in low-income households, especially where daughters were still at home. Sons could earn money outside the home; daughters, at least in preindustrial towns like Westerville, generally could not. Rachel will return to needlework, first as a struggling newlywed with an unemployed husband and then as a soldier's wife during the war.

14. This missionary society was founded in 1852. The fact that the United Brethren's missionary secretary, John C. Bright, resided in Westerville and sat on the Otterbein board of trustees no doubt helped sustain interest in foreign missions among the faculty and students. Otterbein functioned as the unofficial headquarters for the United Brethren missionary effort around the world. Garst, *Otterbein*, pp. 234–36.

15. Henry Garst (Rachel misspelled his name) was a fellow student who returned to Otterbein in 1869 as professor of Latin, served as president of the university, 1886–1889, and published the first definitive history of the school in 1907. Willard W. Bartlett, *Education for Humanity: The Story of Otterbein College* (Westerville, Ohio, 1934), p. 43.

16. Revival meetings were held frequently throughout the United States during the nineteenth century; in 1860, a meeting in Westerville conducted by the Reverend William Hanby lasted six weeks. Harold Hancock, *The History of Westerville, Ohio*, rev. ed. (printed privately, 1974), p. 51.

heart full of God, so that when I leave that I may go to do good. I desire very much to be truly pious, that my influence may be felt wherever I go, that I may be fitted for whatever position it will become my duty to fill. I want Ella C. to be a christian. I hope she will become truly good and a blessing to her unchristianized family. Saturday evening I received a good letter from I.B.K.[17] blessed man, may God bless him.

December 21, 1858 Have just returned from our christmas ride we started from here at ten Oclock Fryday evening and went to Columbus, we had intended to go to catholic church but we came too late for the midnight church we staid at a little market tavern till four in the morning when we went, the church was very prettyily fixed off, they had about three hundred and twenty two wax candles on the rostrum. of all flowers and strange things that catholic church had the most I ever saw and the priest has most curious actions I ever heard of After church we went to market, which very full. after we got tired of that we went back to our little hotel to warm and then went up on high street to do some shopping, got a bible Philopena for Meno,[18] we went to the printing office saw them setting tipe, we run round a great deal, we even went to the china store, we had a great deal of fun. We then went out to Mr. Chamberses,[19] had a splendid dinner, and in the evening we went to a singing class about three miles off, had to sit on the carriage about an hour before the key came never saw Mr. Pennell so full of mischief. from there back to Mr. Chambers' again and after we got warmed a little we had our supper, had a great time, it was eleven Oclock until we got through, we were very sleepy the boys knew it although they were sleepy too, having done without sleep as long as we but would not leave and go to bed on the plea that it was unhealthy to retire so soon after supper, that we ought to wait three hours It rained all day sunday so that we could not go to church but went to Mr. Detwilers for dinner, and in the evening to Mr. C. had to get up real early to get home for school the boys got up at eleven one but went to bed again. upon the whole we had a very nice time and got home in time too.

17. I. B. Kilbourne, Rachel's first serious boyfriend, still lived in Canada near the Bowman's home farm.
18. A cousin, Menno S. Bowman, the youngest son of Rachel's father's brother Jonathan and his wife Polly Schneider Bowman. Menno, who was the same age as Rachel, had just come from Canada to seek his fortune in Ohio. *BHWT*, II, 24–25.
19. Ella's home.

1859

January 1, 1859 Was at home all day till afternoon. had quite a time baking cakes, especially little curiosities for the little girls, they were almost wild about it. In the afternoon Ella Chambers and I went to call on Rev. Mr. Halls, but they were not at home, we called also at Mr. Haynies to see Melissa[20] but she had gone to her school already. We then went home to enjoy home.

January 3, 1859 Have been attending my classes as usual. Misses Smith and McClure paid us a little visit. E. Walker called too.[21] She told me some of the party at Mr. Hanby's.[22] I felt very much slighted and insulted by their actions, whenever they have any sickness they can be here in a short time to have us come and help them, but at partys they never think of us but dont feel quite right about it and try to smooth it over, presuming that we are so green and will take it all. If they dont want us there just let them hush up and not try to plaster it up afterwards.

January 9, 1859. Today and yesterday it has been real cold, was to church this morning Mr. W. Hanby preached, this afternoon there will be preaching to the children but I must go to my class.

January 11, 1859 Yesterday was to Columbus, to a musical concert by the continentals, four gentelmen dressed in continental style, or in the continental style of 1776, they looked real pretty, and sung real well, one of them had the prettiest hands for a gentleman I ever saw. I cannot begin to enumerate the pieces sung, but they were very good. We went down in the new umnibus[23] (Mr. Lawson &

20. Melissa Ann Haynie, a classmate of Rachel's, served as principal of the Ladies' Department during the 1863–1864 school year. Garst, *Otterbein*, p. 307.

21. Ellen Louise Walker (1840–1870), a classmate and next door neighbor, was the daughter of Rachel's literature professor. *TQRGO*, p. 28; Garst, *Otterbein*, pp. 73–74.

22. The Hanbys were among Westerville's most illustrious families. Amanda Hanby has already appeared in the diary (see Nov. 27, 1858). Benjamin Russel Hanby (1833–1866), who graduated a year ahead of Rachel, became a minister and a song-writer. He wrote his best-known composition, the antislavery ballad "Darling Nellie Gray," while he was a sophomore. Garst, *Otterbein*, pp. 141–44. Cyrus M. Hanby (1837–1868) was also a student at Otterbein during 1858–1859. *TQRGO*, pp. 25–26. The Reverend William Hanby, who appears in the next extry, had played a key role in founding Otterbein and later rendered an even more critical service in helping the college through the financially troubled 1850s. Garst, *Otterbein*, pp. 58–62, 111–12, and opposite 80. Hanby's house, which also faced the college from Grove Street, was just across Main Street from the Bowmans' house.

23. An omnibus was a large coach. The one introduced on the Westerville-to-Columbus route in 1859 was drawn by four horses and held thirty-two passengers. Hancock, *Westerville*, p. 49.

Shanck) we started at four in the afternoon, got down a little after six, the gentlemen had sent word to have a special supper prepared for us, after the concert, but thinking that we might be hungry got some of the very best plum pie for us before concert, the plum pie was a real treat being that fruit is so scarce this year, after concert we had a good supper and then a pleasant little time in the parlor and then started home at nearly twelve Oclock, got home till two in the morning. Those that went were, Mr. Ebersol & R. Winter, Mr. Ambrose & L. Winter, Mr. J. Clark & L. Bright, Mr. M. Shank & P. Watson, Mr. Boggs and I.[24] I was quite astonished at Mr. B. asking for my company. I thought that he was mad at me because Father[aa] had done as he did, he said that he was not angry at me at any time yet. I did not or would not talk about those old affairs because I thought that there was not the place to talk about them. he seemed very friendly. Mr. Pennell was along too, he was to take a lady but on account of some misunderstanding did not, so he done the singing for us. we had quite a jolly time coming home. I did not act quite as prudent as I might have done, hope to do better next time.

January 20, 1859 School has closed now, passed through all my examinations pretty well, better than I expected. Last Saturday evening was to a party at Proff. Walkers had quite a nice time. Tuesday evening had a surprised party here, quite a number were here, had considerable sport with Mr. Nickless as some one spelt his name. Today while I was writing here Jenny Streeter[25] came to tell me that her mother wished to see me, I went down, she wished me to help her to get up a party for the Miss Nortons, that is to get up a list of people who were to be invited, hope we will a nice time. I had quite a talk with Mr. Boggs the other evening those old things were talked of some, but not quite to my satisfaction. Returned from the party, it was very rainy and dark, but quite a number were there after all, when we started home, Mr. P. asked for my company. I told him that I had other. Mr. B brought me home. had quite a talk after we came home, he asked for my company regularly next session, in the parlor, I granted it. I think he has sufficient excuse for

24. TQRGO, pp. 31 and 33, contains biographical sketches of James Clark and Rachel Winter. Rachel Bowman's date was Wilberforce K. Boggs (1839–1872), who graduated in 1861 and became a Presbyterian minister and schoolteacher. TQRGO, p. 30.

25. A daughter of the Reverend Sereno W. Streeter, who had come to Otterbein in 1857 and was teaching rhetoric and belles lettres in the spring term of 1859. Garst, *Otterbein*, pp. 78, 306.

his actions last session and all other things according to my notion. I shall allow him visits, if not why I can anytime tell him.

January 22, 1859 This morning Mary,[ii] Leah,[ii] Miss Smith and Miss McClure went to visit for a few days at Miss Chambers home, Mr. B went away also to spend the vacation with his uncles at Mt. Vernon.

January 23, 1859 Am at home, am not going to church today it was very cold this morning

January 26, 1859 This evening the girls came home, last evening Mr. E. Light came. I just got to speak to him before I had to leave to go and sit up with Elizabeth Leib[26] who has been very sick, Mollie Mille[r] and I sat up together, had some sport while eating our midnight luncheon. Was to a party at Mr. Barbees, went with Mr. Sowers,[27] he is quite a nice fellow, but think he has not been out in company of ladies very much. we had quite a nice time.

January 27, 1859 Sewed all day, am very tired, my shoulders ache very much, was to hear Mr. E. Light preach, he preaches well. Mr. Dorcas closed meeting and preached about as long as Mr. Light yet.

January 28, 1859 Had a dinner for some of the old folks. I have worked all day as fast as I could, had intended to go to Mr. Pennells school, the girls both declared that they would not go, Mr Light spoke of going. as soon as they heard that the both said they would go, but changed their minds and Mr. Light and they went to J. Adams school.[28]

January 31, 1859 The students are just pouring in this evening   last Saturday Mary[ii] and I cleaned nearly the whole house, had an awful time, were both nearly sick by the time we got through. Monday,

26. The Leibs lived just down Main Street from the Bowmans. They had two daughters attending Otterbein, the older of whom, Sarah (1840–1888), was in Rachel's class. *TQRGO*, p. 28.

27. Erastus W. Sowers (1830–1871), Otterbein class of 1860, served briefly as a newspaper reporter during the Civil War before establishing a real estate firm in 1864. *TQRGO*, p. 29.

28. Several of Rachel's classmates were teaching in the public schools around the Westerville area (see also Nov. 15, Dec. 21, 1858, Jan. 1, 1859). This was a common practice during the antebellum period wherever colleges and universities were found. Nearby villages were guaranteed a ready supply of reasonably well qualified teachers (by the standards of the day), and the college students could earn some money and gain teaching experience while pursuing their degrees. Burke, "Quiet Influence," chs. 2 and 5.

Mary[ii] and I did a very large washing. Today made me a headdress, had quite a time, worked some at my picture, got so tired that I put it by before I finished it. Nan McClure and Mollie Smith called this afternoon, Ella Chambers came again, tomorrow school will commence again, Now hard times will commence again   we will have a lot of boarders and I will have a number of studies. I would wish to begin this session right, but of myself, I will be incompetent. God help me to do right in all things.

February 2, 1859   School has commenced today, quite a number of students are here, but not all the old ones yet. I have my studies made out, this session finishes my school life for some time perhaps forever. Mr. B——gs has not called on me yet, I am not going to give him a chance to speak to me in public if I can help it. I am going to test his sincerity, and if he does as he did last session, he is awful mean. it is worth considerable to get to know a man, I judge him to be a true hearted man, and above mean deceit, or coquetry, and just about *the* fellow, but this session will tell, and I bet too, if he dont fulfil all his promises he will learn what I think, I am not going to take such things from any fellow, by the last interview I have accomplished what I desired to, this long time. I know now that he knows the cause of Fathers[aa] actions and he knows now how much to blame him and how much to blame me, I am going to assert more independence and act more dignified now and I am going to let Mr. B——gs understand that I can live without *his* attentions. It has been raining all day, it has made a fair start for school too I guess. I am the only girl in the Chemistry class. I want to do my best and let the world know that I can do as well as the boys.[29] I want to do well in all my classes, there, the hack is just coming. Evening. Already I have broken over my above resolutions. E. Chambers were going to Mrs. Leibs on an errant but found it too muddy to get along so we turned back, & Mr. B——gs caught up to us, and commenced talking to us so pleasant, and laughing at our being out such a rainy evening.

February 3, 1859   Attended recitations today, was to call on Mallissa Haynie, it was very muddy. Sarah Leib went with me   we also

29. Oberlin, where Rachel had gone to preparatory school, is generally considered the first college in the United States to admit men and women on an equal basis. Otterbein claims to be the second, and unlike Oberlin, Otterbein never placed any restrictions on the courses women were allowed to take. Garst, *Otterbein*, pp. 79–93; Ronald W. Hogeland, "Coeducation of the Sexes at Oberlin College: A Study of Social Ideas in Mid-Nineteenth-Century America," *Journal of Social History* 6 (Winter 1972–73), 160–76; and Lori Ginzberg, "Women in an Evangelical Community: Oberlin 1835–1850," *Ohio History* 89 (Winter 1980), 78–88.

went to the ambrotype room,[30] was also to see Miss Gilbert. Kate Kumler was here to see us.

February 8, 1859 Nothing of any importance happened through last week, until Saturdy afternoon. I with some more of my lady classmates were to B. Davises to help Mollie Miller quilt, had an excellent supper came home expecting Mr. B——gs. when he did not come I just sat down and wrote him *such a note*, but did not get to put it in the office until Monday, on Monday afternoon he came to ask me to go to concert, I had fully made up my mind not to go, but he looked as though he was troubled about something, I supposed it to be that note, and I like a fool went, I have wished often since that I had not gone, he never said a word about the note until on the way home, he came in and such a time of explaining as we had, I fear that I hurt his feelings, feel sorry, there was a misunderstanding between us, etc, but still I think he is not the fellow for me, he dont care enough for me, I like to have fellows almost break their necks for me, and dont like such that think that you have to do just so. Mr. B however went away apparently good, God do to us as seems good to him, and help me to act better. Mr. B. says that he saw as soon as he caught a glimpse of my face that something was wrong. It seemed so rediculous to me last evening to sit down there having a fuss with a fellow and making up again that I could not keep my face straight.

February 12, 1859 Am not well, am troubled with headache, have been all this week. I get along pretty well with my lessons, Mr. B. looked rather troubled a few days after that great note was sent looks right pleasant now again, guess he got over it. Never does any thing take me down worse that to feel that I have hurt any ones feelings, but thinking as I did I think I was right in writing as I did, I think we will understand each other after this. Leah[j] and M. E. Spade went last night to sit up with Mrs. Hellane who was sick with consumption,[31] they were there but a short time when she died. The old man (her husband) even while she was in the agony of death was

---

30. A photography studio; ambrotyping and tintyping were two of the earliest photographic processes used commercially.

31. Consumption referred specifically to pulmonary tuberculosis, but was often used more generally to denote any debilitating condition centered in the respiratory system, such as pneumonia and flu. Dr. S. S. Fitch, *Family Physician* (New York, 1868), p. 12, noted that at least twenty-four different diseases were commonly and indiscriminately called consumption by his contemporaries.

ammusing himself with the pictures in an agricultural book, and as soon as she was dead went and got his smoke pipe, saying that he guessed that he might smoke now again, that Mommy did not allow him to, she could not stand it. The old brute said too that he thought he would wait one whole year before he would get another wife. I hope in my heart that he may never get another, he is not fit to have one, but if he does get one, I hope he may get his match, one that will pay him up in a measure at least.

February 15, 1859 Just returned from the store with a pair of new shoes, have them, they fit pretty well. Yesterday was valentines day. I got a comic one, it made me feel bad, but what is the use of feeling bad for such a thing, Last evening Mr. Boggs called, I fear that I hurt his feelings more than I thought, well I cant help it. I thought just as I wrote and I think after explaining as I did and knowing too that his brother wrote one about as sharp to M. L. Miller and knowing that he knows it. I just think if he wants to pout about it he may, he need not think that I have no eyes. At times I feel real bad over it but other times I feel as independent as you please I hope all will at last come right. God can make it so.

February 19, 1859 Saturday. Was out to tea a Mr. Sanders this evening, we had a very nice super, a few more beside me were asked in, had quite a nice time, it rained nearly all day, had to read a composition this morning, the roads are very muddy but we have sawdust walk so that [with] it we can get along pretty well after all but I must get ready for Sunday now. I dont like to miss my bible class. Mr. Allen[32] is such an interesting teacher, he is my class leader too, Of late, I have thought much about missionary life, I think sometime that I am yet to be one. I sometimes think of talking to Miss Gilbert or say something at class meeting, but then again it seems to me that I am not good enough to have so much money spent for me, and were I good enough, am perhaps not talented enough. I pray God daily to direct me and make me truly good and fit me for the place he would have me occupy.

February 20, 1859 Sunday. Was to church this forenoon and afternoon, went to sacrament this afternoon. I felt as though I was not good enough, but desired so much to go, so I went, I know that it is

---

32. Though more than six years older than Rachel, Samuel B. Allen (1830–1886) also graduated in 1859. *TQRGO*, p. 26.

my desire to be good and to do good. I wish to live a life devoted to God and his service. today I felt as though I had almost done wrong in thinking about not be tallented enough to be a missionary, for if God directs us to do something, *he* considers us talented enough to do it. It seems almost like blaming God for not bestowing more. God help me ever to live right.

February 24, 1859 Wednesday. I attended my classes as ususal, Proff. Streeter is sick so that he cannot hear his classes recite and has been sick since last Friday. Prof. Haywood[33] teaches some of his classes. This is a very pleasant and warm day it seems like spring. I have been thinking very much about the missionary work, but the more I think of it the more I feel that I must get better. I would do some good. I cannot bear the idea of being a mere blank in this world but if Christ help me not I shall not be able to accomplish any thing. I feel that if I live as I ought, all, all, will be right. I took a walk down the plank with some of the girls this evening, enjoyed very much.[34]

February 25, 1859 Today was appointed for prayer in behalf colleges in our land, we had no recitations, I sewed nearly all day. Quite a number of our boys are down to Columbus to hear Mr. Pennells trial for whipping a school boy. This evening, we went out with the little girls into the yard to help them play. It does a body good to have such runs when studying.

February 26, 1859 Was to society this eving. after society S. Leib Mr. Norton, F. Galagher and I sat up with K. Perdue. S. Leib and I were to sit up the first part of the night and sat there with the sick girl quite a little bit when the girl took some kind of a spasm with an unearthly laugh which quite unnerved us. we called up the other girls and all sat up the whole night. Why is it that we are so affected by any thing that seems like death. O, that I had more courage in my heart, O! More of all good qualities.

33. John Haywood was professor of mathematics. He graduated from Oberlin in 1850 and joined the Otterbein faculty in 1851; he was professor emeritus when he died in 1906 after more than half a century of service to Otterbein. Haywood had helped organize the first formal United Brethren church in Westerville and in 1859 was also serving as the town's first elected mayor. Garst, *Otterbein*, pp. 72–73, 306; Hancock, *Westerville*, p. 50.

34. The main road to Columbus had been "planked"—covered with wooden boards—in 1853 by a private road company, which then charged a toll for its use. Hancock, *Westerville*, p. 49.

ffaculty of 1859

Miss M. L. Gilbert	John Haywood	Thomas McFadden
R. M. Walker	L. H. Hammond	S. W. Streeter

From a photograph reproduced in Henry Garst, *Otterbein University, 1847–1907* (Dayton, Ohio, 1907).

February 27, 1859 Today Prof. Haywood's little girl got cut very bad, her cheek was quite cut through. it had to be sewed up, the poor child suffered much, was also to the monthly rhetorical exercises, had pretty good performances. In the evening Mother[bb] and I called at Mrs. Leibs a little bit, while we were gone Mr. B——gs called to see me, wonder what he wanted, surely no quarterage this time.

February 28, 1859 Received a note from Miss Gilbert this morning requesting me to take her place at sabath school, she was not able to attend. I did so, found that the little children were harder to teach and keep straight than a body would think, was to church too, Mr. Weaver[35] preached and real good too, I find when sitting listing to a sermon that my thoughts have to be watched continually or they will be roving. O! that I were real good, my stack of patience is so very small that it seems as though I had none at all. God help me to do right.

35. The Reverend Jonathan Weaver was Otterbein's financial agent. Garst, *Otterbein*, pp. 101–03.

March 1, 1859 Cousin M. T. Bowman came this evening, it seems quite good to see him again after these few months absence, his term of school is out. Mr. J. Weaver addressed the people here on the subject of temperance,[36] did pretty well, at one time Mr. Dorcas screamed out Amen when it was altogether out of place, it created quite a laugh.

March 3, 1859 Was almost sick today, did quite a large washing yesterday afternoon, and somehow it made me sick, was sick all night, and today have attended only two recitations, did not go to lecture. Moral Science is quite interesting. I have learned that I must guard my thoughts more.

March 7, 1859 Yesterday Bishop H. Humler preached both german and english.[37] I finished reading Shady Side,[38] it is a very good book, to see how the minister and his good wife did, urges one on to take a higher stand gives one new ideas of life, new motives to live for. I felt as though I should desire just such labor, however hard. I have been trying to show more of a christian spirit at home. I feel that Mother[bb] is wearing herself out, while we are going to school, I know that I have not done as much as I might have done to make her labors fewer and lighter. I have resolved to live more effectionate toward my parents and the rest of the family. I feel so often as though they dont care for me, but I must overcome that. O! I must get a better heart. I desire very much to be real good and to do good. I feel that I am prone to think too much of my own happiness. I scarcely know how to express what I wish to say, But it seems as though there were a dark spot in my heart that must come out, but how to get it out is the question. I think I dont see my utter helplessness as I ought. I should like to send Shady Side to several gentleman at the hall[39] to read, but fear that they would think that I was trying make love to them I must forbear.

36. After the Civil War, Westerville gained national fame as a prohibitionist center; one of Otterbein's later presidents, Henry A. Thompson, ran for vice-president of the United States on the Prohibitionist party ticket in 1880. Garst, *Otterbein*, pp. 145–65; W.P.A., *Westerville*, 59–66.

37. Henry Humler was one of the most prominent members of the United Brethren hierarchy in Ohio. His father had also been a bishop in the church. Garst, *Otterbein*, p. 16.

38. Martha Stone Hubbell, *The Shady Side; or, Life in a Country Parsonage. By a Pastor's Wife* (Boston, 1853; rpt. 1854, 1858).

39. Saum Hall, the men's dormitory, was built in 1855. It stood directly across the street from Rachel's house. Garst, *Otterbein*, p. 105.

March 9, 1859 Have such a headache. Ellen Chambers has come back again. M. Miller and I were up street shopping.

March 11, 1859 This is a very windy day, had quite a thunderstorm the clouds looked very pretty, from nature we should look to natures God, just finished an essay to read in the morning. I received another letter yesterday from the district where I taught my first school, requesting me to come and teach there. I dont know whether I shall go.

March 12, 1859 Ellen Chambers and I went to Mr. Brights, or duch [Dutch] Brights as they are more generally called, with the little girls. They treated us with maple sugar and a very good supper, we had a right pleasant time. On the way home as we came into town we were met by Mr. Baker and Miss Hanson, who said that I was just the person they were in search for, and told me then that they desired me to go with them to little gathering, at Mr. Sanders, there were but few there but we had a nice time, had a very good all round supper. After I came home I wrote a long letter to Father.[aa]

March 19, 1859 Was to Mrs. Leibs this afternoon and for tea had quite a nice time. on our way home we called at Mr. Allens M. Smith is sick. Mr. J. Fisher came in. I had quite a talk with him, when we came home there was a letter here fr Father,[aa] telling us that we were not going to move to Canada this year, and that Mary[ii] and I are both to keep studying right along this session. I would stay at any rate until I graduate, then we will go to C. W. to teach.[40]

March 21, 1859 This evening I took another lesson in gunmanship, I fear that I give way to my wild nature too much do not restrain myself enough. I have been trying to live better. I feel that I need to be very much better to do any good I desire to be of some use, I have not thought so much of missionary life of late. At classmeeting my feelings overcome me and I can never tell my mind half as I would wish. I have been greatly tempted not to go again, but that must be wrong, I do wish to be truly good.

April 5, 1859 It is quite a while since I wrote in my journal, and consequently have considerable to write A few weeks ago I was

---

40. C. W. was the standard abbreviation for Canada West, now the Province of Ontario. See Walter S. Avis et al., eds., *A Dictionary of Canadianisms on Historical Principles* (Toronto, 1967), p. 113.

induced to take a class in the infant Sabbath school, at first I thought I could not do it but at last consented and I am right glad that I did. I like my little class, there is one little colored girl in the class, a smart little girl. Last Thursday evening Mr. Pennell had his school exibition, the chapple was very much crowded not near all could get in, Mr. B——gs escorted me home came in and stayed quite a while, he is to me like some intricate mathematical problem. I dont know what to make of him, his health is very bad, he has gone to spend a few weeks with his Uncles to recruit Yesterday evening My good Papa[aa] came home again, we were all so glad to see him that we scarcely knew how to do, he brought us ever so many nice things, he brought me a lot of nice Canada pine and cedar trees, or perhaps I had better say he brought them for himself, but I wrote to him and was the cause of them being brought he brought us a lot of nice maple sugar and a few apples too, we have not had such a nice treat since we live here.

April 6, 1859 Was just out getting rosebushes and flowers got them and planted them on the graves of our dear brothers and little sister,[41] the Live forever[42] that Mary[ii] and I planted there last spring grows the prettiest kind. the Mr. Lights, Mr. Much and Father[aa] are down there now planting the cedar and pine, I am afraid that the trees will die. I do hope they will live. I think those trees are more appropriate than any others that could be planted there.

April 13, 1859 Have just finished writing in an Album. Since I last wrote Leah[jj] and Mary[ii] have made up their minds to go to Canada, I do not know how we will get along with the work, having such a number of boarders. I will have more to do this last half than any time yet. I guess we will get along some way.

April 20, 1859 The girls Mary[ii] and Leah[jj] started yesterday morning I have scarcely a minute to run round or think, my studies and work take up all my time, I tremble when I think of my graduating essay and clothes, I cant see where or when I can get

41. See the Bowman kinship glossary, entries ll and mm for the brothers. The Bowman family Bibles and genealogical sources account for eleven siblings, but Rachel's obituary (*Johnstown Tribune*, Feb. 20, 1899) claimed she was one of twelve. This unnamed sister must be the twelfth.

42. Live Forever is a variety of Orpine, specifically *Sedum telephium*. Because it remains alive for months after picking, it was a favorite garden flower in the nineteenth century. Robert Shosteck, *Flowers and Plants: An International Lexicon with Biographical Notes* (N. Y., 1974), 167–68.

time to write or sew, I ought to have some time to read, but that is out of the question, how I will get along is more than I can tell I did not like for the girls to go on account of the work but I only got snapped up when I said any thing. I sometimes doubt whether I have a true friend in the world, those everchanging ones I do not like. Religiously, I get along as usual, I feel as though I could desire nothing more than be permitted to do some good, would that my heart were better. I desire to live right. We have two more boarders. Pensylvanians, right good fellows I guess.[43] We had two pretty heavy hail storms this evening.

May 9, 1859 My poor journal has been almost neglected, but I am kept so very busy that I do not get time to write. I have not had the blues much since the girls are gone, I do not get time to write on my graduating essay. I fear that I will be pushed with that and my clothes, cant see now how I can do all, have to work pretty hard. Our boarders are so good and kind to me. Was to Columbus last Saturday, had a nice time, got my grad. clothes etc, am pretty well pleased with them

[Undated] Do not recieve letters from Mr B——gs, dont care either, he is not the man for me, I guess it is best that it went as it did but still I cannot understand something. A group of us girls had our minitures taken for Mr Burgner[44] I guess they will be real good, but I must study now and leave writing.

May 18, 1859 Yesterday the this year geology class and the ladies of last year went out on a geological excursion, there were twenty of us beside the teacher, we all took our dinners along, had the two umnibusses to take us, started at five in the morning, we went to the Whetstone first, which is just beyond Worthington, did not find any thing of importance so we went on farther, to the Sciota at Doublin we all got out of the hacks and in one lot started up the river, we walked along the waters edge, climed the rocky mountainous banks, in some places it was almost impasible to get along, but the gentlemen were such good gallants and helped us along the

---

43. Facing financial hardship after the panic of 1857, the United Brethren decided in 1858 to close a small college they had been trying to maintain in Mt. Pleasant, Pa., since 1851, and to concentrate all their remaining educational resources on their original college at Westerville. Garst, *Otterbein*, pp. 110, 128. This decision not only saved Otterbein but brought to Westerville a substantial influx of undergraduates from Pennsylvania, including Samuel E. Cormany, one of the new boarders.

44. Jacob Burgner was a member of the graduating class. *TQRGO*, p. 27.

best kind, and helped us get our specimens. Mr. C. helped me, I got quite a number, some real nice ones too, we walked until we were all nearly tired to death, Miss Hanson took sick and had to go to the buss long before the rest. At nearly dinner time we all went to the 'buss and got our baskets and again took up our line of march up the river until we got to some shady trees. There we spread our cloths and laid our dinners on and all sat round there in a circle and the ground and eat. After dinner we went up the river, had to go over the worst rockyest road I ever saw, at some places we had to leap from one rock on the other, got to one ravine—went through one ravine, then went on further to another, walked nearly quarter of a mile till we got to the uper end, there was a very pretty clear sprink of clear cold water at the way far end. The walls on either side of the ravine are nearly pirpendicular, two caves were partly explored by some of our company. we were very tired till we got back to the 'busses, E. Walker lost her duster. I forgot to speak about the panorama, J. B——r[45] took me down.

May 25, 1859 I am very irregular in writing in my journal   last Saturday evening had quite a talk with Mr B——s, I dont like him much, I think he could improve considerable yet, but he seems rather selfconceited, thinking that he is about right. I often feel ashamed of myself that I cannot keep up a more interesting conversation. I sometimes think that perhaps let my love of fun carry me too far. Religiously I am still not any better, I often feel that I desire very much to be entirely given up to God. I want to do some good, I have written some of my graduating essay but know it not near finished yet. Dont know what I shall do, I fear I wont get my things ready.

June 2, 1859 Have been feeling bad for some time and scarcely know about what, one thing is that I expect I will have to stay here this summer, and teach some where not far off. I expect it will all be right. I pray God daily to guide me and lead me into just such places as he would have me go. I feel so much as though there was not a soul in the universe that cared for me, I have the blues most awful bad in general and about every thing. It is very hard to give up the idea of going to Canada. Parents dont know it, and I am not going to tell them if they say I should stay, I will stay. Old matters too will come up sometimes. I think of Mr. Kilbourne very often. I still cant get quite over that, but guess it was for the best.

45. Jacob Burgner; Rachel later wrote the full name in the margin.

June 5, 1859   Was to church this morning. Prof. Streeter preached.
real good,   Last evening, had a call from J. B——r. I dislike the man
so that I can hardly bear to talk with him, he is certainly a verdant
youth, and as selfconceited as he can be and withal horibly jealous
and sensitive, he tried to rake up a fuss out of nothing. I let him
understand a little what I thought of it. It makes me feel quite indignant when I think of it. Yesterday some of our boarders were to
Columbus   Mr. C——[46] brought me the nicest bunch of cherries   he
is such a good fellow, he tells me that he is going to be my good
brother since my sisters and brothers have all left.

June 8, 1859   I expect all is finished up with Mr. B——r he said
some things in notes that were a little more than I could bear so I
just closed all up and wont have a thing to do with him, sent all old
notes and stuff of his back that I did not destroy, he looks rather
down today, but he need not think that I can take all his impudence.

June 26, 1859   The commencement is all over now. I left many
things that I ought to have written. Mr. B——r and I are friends but
would have nothing to do with him as a beau. I had to work pretty
hard to get my things ready, had to work till after midnight some
nights. I liked my dress, but was not so well satisfied with my essay.
I thought I was not scared one bit, but I must have been for all, for
Sis tells me that I was cheered and I never heard it   I got along very
well, I have the satisfaction of knowing that my essay was liked by
some, by the Honorable J. R. Giddings for one,[47] although it was not
so entertaining to the crowd. Nearly all the students have left. It is
beginning to get lonely

46. Samuel Cormany.

47. Joshua R. Giddings, the first avowed abolitionist to serve in Congress, was
elected to the House of Representatives by his northern Ohio district in 1838 and
continuously reelected until he decided to retire rather than run again in 1858. As a
warhorse of the antislavery cause, his willingness to deliver the principal address
made Rachel's graduation a notable event. Rachel's speech, her own copy of which
has survived, was a rather typical graduation piece: full of generalized truisms, references to past human achievements, and exhortations to strive onward in the future.
Rachel urged her classmates to emulate Amos Lawrence, for his philanthropy, and
Florence Nightingale, for her selfless service to others during the recent Crimean
War.

II
Samuel Comes to Ohio
April–September, 1859

Samuel's diary opens with retrospective summaries covering the period from his arrival at Otterbein in the spring of 1859 through the end of his summer vacation. His affection for Rachel, in whose home he boards, is apparent from the outset.

———————◆•●•◆———————

April, 1859 I left my old Home in Franklin County Pennsylvania for "Otterbein University" at Westerville Ohio in April 1859 in company with Tiras Enterline. We entered the Spring term of O. U.

I recited to Miss Gilbert—in "Bullims Grammar[1]—To Proffessor Haywood in H. Arith. & Algebra: To Proff Degmeyer—in German and Proff Hammond in Music—Played 2nd violin in Orchestra—Father Saml. Hively showed me great kindness——

I roomed and boarded at B. B. Bowmans[aa] across from Saum Hall. We were a Jolly Crowd Tiras Enterline and I, and Israil, Stephen, and Job Light—John Mutch—Jerry Nicklas and Mills——

The Bowman Family are a wholesome lot. Clem[cc] & Amos[hh] away—Rachel—Mary[ii]—Lea[jj]—Susie[nn] Lizzie[oo] and Carrie.[pp] The last two half grown, bouncing day school girls and Susie about full grown—— An evening Party—our first Sat night—in the home dining room—Students, and family—brought us all together, and made us better acquainted.

We enjoyed the new play "Consequences." It occasioned fun, better freedom in each others company all around. How strange that Miss Rachel and I should be several times mixed up in Consequences!

At once—Miss Rachel strikes me as an exceptionally fine specimen of young Christian womanhood——

In fact all the girls are decidedly Sisterly to me—Rachel seems somehow just a little more so than the others. I wonder why!

---

1. Almost certainly Bullions; Peter Bullions (1791–1864), a clergyman and college professor, wrote several textbooks on English grammar that were widely used in schools throughout the United States. *Appletons' Cyclopedia of American Biography* (New York, 1888), I, 446.

Original Main Building   Original Ladies' Dormitory   Main Building   Saum Science Hall
Removed   Torn Down 1871   Destroyed by Fire Jan. 26, 1870   Built in 1855

View of Otterbein University as it would have appeared from the Bowmans' front window. From a lithograph in Henry Garst, *Otterbein University, 1847–1907* (Dayton, Ohio, 1907).

(A whisper! Miss Lydia Strock[2] has for years seemed to me the best and most lovable girl in the world——But the last night I was in her company—she said she would never go West—would never go so far away from her parents—and I responded, "Then I'd as well quit coming to see you. Since I'm pretty certain to go West to Educate, and most likely would settle there) Well! Rachel seemed to me like one who would go to the ends of the Earth with the man who won her love——But I can scarcely hope to win her. I only a Prep.[3] and She graduates in June——The Lord knows best about such things—and I've been committing all my ways to Him—

May, 1859 I enjoy Student life and association, and my Studies—— I find close application to study is not agreeing well with me——I lack in the out-door-hustling I have been accustomed to——

My old throat troubles are showing up at times again——I do hope I do not have "cankered sore throat" again—and away from home——Lord help me!

May 24, 1859 This is my 21st Birth Day anniversary. Yes! and I have been having a fearful time with my throat.

I had thought I was forever cured of that plague, but here the siege has been on again.

The Bowman Family—The Sisters all have been so interested in me in my illness——

Especially Rachel, who seems to be ever ready to do little things to help me out, or when she is crowded with her preparations for graduation sets the others to doing——

Being away from home—& underpar & suffering and weak is not so bad after all with such surroundings as this home affords, and especially with Miss Rachels attentions and interest——I am able withal to keep up all my studies—had to miss some recitations, but on xamination passed after all——

May 30, 1859 I have so many such good talks with Miss Rachel these days in social and religious topics—She says I help her so

2. A young woman whom Samuel had courted before leaving Pennsylvania. The Strocks lived in St. Thomas township, just west of Chambersburg. Bernard Anthony Cormany, one of Samuel's older half brothers, had married into the Strock family in October 1857. Keister family Bible; E. Irving Wines, personal communication.

3. Prior to the Civil War many American institutions of higher education, even those designated universities, had preparatory departments or divisions. Hence, many "university" students were actually seeking a level of education later provided by separate high schools.

26

much in her religious life——On matters of common life as social beings we agree so fully too—someway we happen to get together quite frequently, and have talks on the most important problems of life Social, intellectual and spiritual.

May 31, 1859 I have written Miss Lydia Strock that I wish her to hand to my Sister Sarah^u my Picture Locket in her possession and that my future home and work is to be chiefly in the West, and that I surely wish for her a happy and most useful life in the East——

June, 1859 Commencement over and past! Miss Rachel Bowman read a good address——Original—fresh Sound, just what one would expect of a lady of her make up——

Her pasing-appearance and manner throughout were *winning*— Strikingly modest and unassuring tho impressing one with decided force of Character——

How nice does seem this vacation freedom. Free from constant hard study and also more free to associate with the family of girls, and it happens someway that Miss Rachel and I quite often meet— so unexpectedly & on the Hall Stairway, and have time to sit on the wide steps and talk over our past studies and future prospects——

Most of the Students have gone home——I decide to spend the long vacation in Ohio.

George Beam, Jacob F. Wilt and I decide to do up Southern Ohio— and Canvass to pay our xpenses, and add to our treasury——

We buy Commercial Note paper by the ream—Envelopes by the thousand—Steel pens and holders & lead pencils by the Gross— and large Envelopes by the thousand——Then together we place into a large Envelope

> 24 sheets of paper—different kinds
> 24 Envelopes   "   "
> 2 steel pens—a pen holder & Lead pencil
> with eraser, and sell the pkge for
> 25 Cents—Costing us 12¢——

We rushed business, and sight seeing as well—Operating in Springfield, Xenia, Lebanon, Dayton, Urbana, Cin'ti—Covington & Newport Ky. and whenever special sights scenes, doings &c came up anywhere we were free to take a day or days & nights off from business and enjoy them——At the close of vacation we were ready again to take up College work—I had $90 nett profits, besides the instruction, pleasures and experiences incident to such an employ-ment of time——

September, 1859 So September found us glad to resume at O.U.—
—SURE! I am glad to return to the Bowman Home. And—I whisper
it—delighted to come into closer communication with Miss
Rachel—for whom——I actually admit I entertain what I suppose is
called love, but being so far away, my superior in College Education, I dare scarcely hope for actual return, were I to declare my
feelings, and desires, and actual longings——

The Lord knows all, and if He wills it, the way will be made open
and clear, and I may win the heart and hand of this Charming
woman——

I have a good many drawbacks to my studies—My throat, and
nerves give me much trouble—So that I almost dispair of being able
to go through with my intended College Course——

My old desire to "go West and grow up with the Country" comes
bobbing up—and increaces, whenever sedentary life takes a tight
grip on my physical structure, and makes my studies a kind of bore.

Now I am hearing incidentally of openings in Missouri for young
fellows——

Mr. Bowman[aa] has some land interests in Macon Co. Mo.——and
by the way Mr. and Mrs. Bowman seem to me to be favorable to my
attentions to their daughter Rachel, and, honest John! I begin to
hope I may become acceptable to her ladyship—Miss Rachel herself
in course of time—She certainly gives me indications that she cares a
good deal for me.

III
Rachel Seeks a Job
July 10, 1859–January 11, 1860

*H*oping to become a teacher, Rachel travels by train to New York City and lodges with her brother Amos while she seeks a job. Her search proves unsuccessful, and she falls back on the support of relatives, friends, and co-religionists in eastern Pennsylvania. She finally obtains a position as the sole teacher in the Quakertown public school and becomes embroiled in a bitter debate over the place of prayer in the classroom.

———————◆•◆•◆———————

July 10, 1859 My long neglected journal. I ought to have written in here long since, but was to busy preparing for commencement. Now I suppose I am a graduate from Oterbein University. But I feel too that my responsibilities to my God have increased with my knowledge and I desire very much to be made useful. We had one boarder Mr. Cormany from Pa. a very fine young man. I had some good talks with him, which did me so much good, he seemed like a brother to me, and he calls me his good sister, I often think of Mr. Kilbourne yet, but think that must have been for the best It seems hard to have none to love me. I had cherished the hope of visiting my native country as soon as I finished my education, but after Mary[ii] and Leah[ij] went I thought it almost cruel to go and leave my parents here alone. When I told Mr. Cormany that I was going to stay he exclaimed "Good, I am glad of it." Some thing makes me half think that he loves me. But I am older than he, if it were the other way something might grow out of our regard for each other.[1]

July 21, 1859 Have just finished two letters. I receive a great many letters and all good ones, it does me so much good to receive letters. If one week passes without I receiving two or three letters it seems awful, I cannot be thankful enough for the friends the Lord has given me. I often wickedly repine and murmur but I ought not. Still

---

1. Rachel's impression that mid-century American grooms were usually older than their brides has since been confirmed. See Michael Drake, "Age at Marriage in the Pre-Industrial West," in F. Bechhofer, ed., *Population Growth and the Brain Drain* (Edinburgh, Scotland, 1969), p. 206.

I do not possess that evidence of my acceptance with God. O! that I had it. but I must lay this by for our folks have just come home and I must go down.

I had such a siege at housecleaning, I was nearly worn out till I got through.

July 30, 1859   I was to church this forenoon, did not go this afternoon, read and wrote letters etc, we had a little sprinkle of rain but not enough to wet the dust, every thing is drying up.

July 31, 1859   Have just hung out a pretty large washing I wash all alone since the girls are gone, have to work pretty hard. I am making shoes, it is very hard on my hand to put on the soles, finished one pair, they look right well, wore them and in the country visiting on Saturday, they are so light, my feet feel go good in them. Every week one except one and some weeks two letters come from S. E. C.   they are so ful of life and cheer that I just love to get them, he is such a good fellow too.

August 21, 1859   I neglect my poor journal too much, many things take place that would be of interest in after life if recorded so that they could be remembered. Those good little letters from S.E.C. are still coming as regularly as ever. Mr. J. K. Bilhimer, missionary from Africa is back to America to recruit his health and was to our quiet W.[2] in search of a better half, he is not certain of one yet, he is intending to be back this month again, then I suppose his doom in that respect in W. will be sealed, he is a right smart looking man. I had a letter last evening from an old school mate in C.W., he speaks almost plain enough. Religiously I think sometimes I get along a little better and others worse. I wish to become very good and be prepared for any thing the Lord would have me do

September 17, 1859   Writing in here seems almost a task. I feel very badly this evening. I feel as though I had no friend in the world. Why am I such an unlikable creature. Perhaps I am punished in this way on account of my sins. O, that I were better. I feel like sitting down and taking a good cry, I believe it would do me good. I scarcely know what I wish, but surely I wish, I was out of Westerville. Next Tuesday, sister Lea[ii] will be married, we have been having quite a time to get her ready, she is not the best natured these few

---

2. Westerville.

days. I have a very bad cold, it seems to me more than just cold, I have to cough so much. I have often wished that I had never been born, and were it not so wicked, I would wish that I could lay me down and die, But must leave off writing now for the tears blind my eyes. Why did fate blast my early budding hopes. God only knows. He can make all right

September 29, 1859 Thursday. This time I will have a long epistle to write. The great hustle of Lea[jj] wedding is over, we had quite a nice little party for her. Brother Clem[cc] had R. Winter, Rev. E. Light and H. Hively Mr. Clase and Tilla Baker, Mr. Cormany and myself composed the young people. Mr. Hanby married them. T. Baker and I were the brides maids, Mr. Clase and Mr. Cormany grooms men, we had a nice supper, the company staid till about nine, in the evening, the ceremony was performed at about five. The next morning, Lea[jj] and Mr. Adams[kk] started for their Northern home, Mr. Cormany and I went along to Columbus, put up at the Buckey house.[3] Lea[jj] and Mr. Adams[kk] did not wish to go out, so Mr. C. and I went alone, we went to the state house, state library, etc. had a very nice time. Went back to the hotel for dinner, after dinner, we went up street to do some shopping, helped Mr. C. pick a winter shawl, went back, took a city hack to take us to the depot to see L[jj] and her worser half[kk] on the cars,[4] left word for the Westerville buss to call for us, we saw them off, took comfortable seats in the depot and were enjoying a nice chat, but thinking it about time for the buss to come Mr. C. stepped out and inquired, when he was told that it had left. We both agreed as to the meanness of the affair but could not better it, so we just laughed over it and concluded to stay, being that we could enjoy ourselves better than by going on an express in the night. Rooms were then spoken for and we settled down easily in the little Parlor, After supper we took a walk through the principle part of town, went into the museum then returned to the hotel pretty well tired, and soon found ourselves easily fixed on the sofa and engaged in a tete a tete, where 10 oclock found us before we were aware of it, then drawing out his watch, and seeing the time it surprised him and in his surprise one arm found its way round my waist and drawing me gently to him and imprinting a ―― on my lips, he said, Darling hadn't you better retire.   long long have I wished some one would say darling to me, now it was spoken, and I had something new to

3. The Buckeye House was a prominent Columbus hotel.
4. Railroad cars; in modern usage, "the train."

muse on not dreamed of before. The next day was spent as pleasur-
ily as the previous one, and at 3 in the afternoon we were seated
enroute for Westerville, where we arrived in due time. We had
scarcely set foot inside of the door when the congratulations came
like a torrent, and questions were asked about the Pa. mountains,
all knew how much I desired to see mountains, and they said they
supposed that we had eloped. I was told too on my return that I
had received a letter from brother Amos[hh] and that Clem[cc] had
answered it and told him[hh] that I would start the following Monday
for N.Y. City. As a matter of course preparations had to be made
now, and at last it was agreed upon that Tuesday night should be
the time for starting. Many were the regretts expressed by Mr. C.
on account of my leaving, all was passed off in a joke until Monday evening when the final adieu came then in spite of all my
stoical resolutions the tears came. I am ashamed of it ever since but
it cant be helped. I started with many good wishes and many
blessings and I doubt not with many prayers. The traveling was
very pleasant. I had the company of Mr. J. L. Hewit till to Whel-
ing, the conductor was quite a pleasant man and very kind. I saw
mountains for the first time. O! I just feasted on the scenery. When
we neared the Cheat river the conductor came and asked me
whether I had ever seen it I answered in the negative, he then
led me to another seat, staid there, and called my attention to the
particular interesting parts, he then took me out on the platform to
show me the tressel work over which we passed, led me back to
my seat then told me that he would turn two seats together so that
I could rest better and would bring my things there. Somehow it
seemed to me he was getting a little too good, so I would not do
it. thanked him though and told him that I preferred the seat I
had, night was just coming on, and I fixed myself to take a sleep
and did sleep too, did not see any more of the conductor until
about four the next morning, when I was arroused from sleep by
somebody pulling at my head, which by the way was completely
envelloped in my large shawl. I hopped up so quick that he and
the man with the light just laughed. he thought I had curled up
into the seat rather comfortably, and asked whether I had slept,
told him I had. I then brushed my hair and donned my bonnet,
and got ready for any bidding, soon the good conductor came
round, and told me to keep my seat after we came to Baltimore
until he would come for me, that he would take me to a buss
which would take me to the other depot. According to his word he
took me over then, made those old hack drivers stand round, and
every body else that came in the way, bid me good morning and

off I was.[5] I shall always love to remember him. From Baltimore to N.Y. the conductors acted as though all womankind were nothing but bothersome baggage. Let them go on in their glory. I guess the time will come when they will pray for some of that kind of baggage to come round their way. In Baltimore a man got very much interested in my welfare, and was going to get my breakfast I thanked him and told him that I was able to pay my own way, but he insisted on me taking breakfast. I then thanked him, not in the most affectionate way and told him to mind his own business that I knew what was best for me, he disappeared and left me alone in my glory. I happened to fall in with an honest hearted old lady from Baltimore who had once lived in N.Y. she helped me along very much, arrived safe at my brothers boarding place without any trouble and am now in the midst of N.Y. City, and am acquanted with none but my good brother,[hh] who looks well, and who is doing his best to get me a good class to teach and helps me along. I like the appearance of Mrs. Underhill very much, and also of her Mother and sister.[6] It is cloudy today, there is a never ceasing rattle and clatter in the streets but I scarcely mind it Now I am ready to commence my labors, and I know if I trust in the Lord that I shall succeed and may be able to do a great deal of good. I find that I am rather to timid to succeed well in this great city. brother is to busy to help much.

October 1, 1859 N.Y. City. Still I have not the evening class. am rather encouraged to think that not only an evening class but also a day school may be had. Yesterday my brother[hh] took me to the public school, was presented to Mr. Howe, brothers good friend, who presented me to the principle, who formed quite a favorable opinion of me, had quite a chat with him. I must brush up on some of my studies now so as to stand an examination. My desire to do good. I often long for someone with whom I am acquainted to be

5. Baltimore was the terminus of two of the most important rail systems in the eastern United States: the Baltimore and Ohio, which ran both south from Baltimore toward Washington and west from Baltimore toward the Ohio Valley; and the Philadelphia, Wilmington, and Baltimore, which ran north from Baltimore to Philadelphia with connections to New York and New England. Rachel had arrived on the former and wished to continue her journey on the latter. But the two systems had separate depots in Baltimore; passengers had to cross the downtown section of the city when changing trains (Rachel uses the local omnibus service). This peculiarity led to a serious riot at the outset of the Civil War, when pro-Southern mobs attacked Massachusetts troops as they marched from depot to depot en route to Washington.
6. Rachel had taken a room in the Underhills' boardinghouse where her brother lived.

engaged in the same business and then go with me to visit some of the poor and do them good. I just finished a long letter for the home folks. My religious state is not what I want it to be, I dont feel near enough to my Savior I desire to be in close sympathy with him. I know if I trust in him that he will keep me from all harm and bring me safe to the heaven of rest.

October 2, 1859 Sabath. This is my first in New York City. Brother[hh] and I were to H. W. Beechers church,[7] was very tired till I got there, had to stand a good part of the time, like Mr. Beechers mode of speaking very much, the whole congregation joins in singing I like that very much. If it were not out so far to go over there I should go every Sunday. he say so many new and grand things there is something said or rather old things are said in a new way, he said that when we did the wickedest deeds, the Saviour was nearest us and pities us, that He looks at us then like a parent at the missteps of an erring child, etc. I came home very tired, we intended to go church in the afternoon again but Amos[hh] was called away to report about two men being killed in a fight. I then spent the rest of the day in reading and writing letters.

October 3, 1859 Monday. This evening we, Amos[hh] and I, were down Broadway to some picture galleries. in the first gallery were mostly engravings and oil paintings very pretty, some very *very* pretty landscape pictures. It made me want to be an artist O! that I had my evening class started so that I could persue my pet study, drawing and painting.

October 4, 1859 Tuesday. This afternoon we were to the Cooper Institute, did not have much time, consequently did not see many of the paintings, was introduced to Mr. Wise the principle, got a catalogue and was told to come and recieve instruction.[8] Want to very

7. Henry Ward Beecher, reform-minded, pro-Republican Congregationalist minister, regularly attracted 2,500 listeners to the sermons he delivered with tremendous skill and presence in Brooklyn's Plymouth Church from 1847 to 1887. *DAB*, I, 132, notes that "visitors to New York from all over the country and from abroad made it a point to hear him." See also Lyman Abbott, *Henry Ward Beecher: A Sketch of His Career: With Analysis of his Power as a Preacher, Lecturer, Orator and Journalist, and Incidents and Reminiscences of his Life* (Hartford, 1887).

8. The Cooper Institute, which still operates as part of the Cooper Union, was a gift to the City of New York from Peter Cooper, a millionaire who decided to devote his fortune to enriching the lives of the working classes. It housed a free public library, art galleries, a large public lecture hall (four months after Rachel's visit, Abraham Lincoln gave one of the most important speeches of his career there), and

Rachel's brother Amos Bowman. Anacortes Museum, Anacortes, Washington.

much, shall as soon as my evening class is established. Was to the evening school, news rather unfavorable, made the acquaintance of Mr. Slack and Mr. Mason.

October 5, 1859 Wednesday. Wrote a long letter to Mr. C——y before breakfast, waited on Amos[hh] so long that I came nearly losing my breakfast. the servants were like bears, I ordered Amoses[hh] breakfast too and carried it to my room. I then fixed for washing, wend down to that old Ireland of a laundry got along well, promised A[hh] to be at the Tribune office till two but did not get there in time so he was off. I sat there a long time then was informed that he went way off to report something. So I started home again met him at the door, he[hh] was very busy. I walked home came upon broadway, which was crowded very much, got a pack of envellopes, and some paper, found my envellopes lined with green, dont like it. but it cant be helped. Rested in the parlor as I came up a middle aged man tried to make up acquantance, took particular pains to inform me that he was a widower. The old sheep. Feel a little lonely this eveing, I want somebody to talk to. I wish Mr. C. was here, or sister Mary.[ii] Yesterday I was to the America Bible Society,[9] went through without A[hh] being along, thought myself almost a hero for it, but to, after I got out I had to change my mind for I got on the wrong way and almost lost. got right again by going back and starting in a different direction. That is just what we ought to do morrally, when we see that we are in the wrong way we ought to turn immediately and go in an opposite direction, but we seem to be so ignorant with regard to our spiritual welfare.

October 6, 1859 Thursday. Was down Broadway to see the suprintendent about the eveing school, did not find him at home. Amos[hh] had to go to his office then and I came home alone, went into three or four picture galeries, saw some very pretty crayoning   also went

---

classrooms for tuition-free instruction in such subjects as art, literature, foreign languages, and design. See James D. McCabe, Jr., *Lights and Shadows of New York Life; Or, The Sights and Sensations of the Great City* (1872; facs. rpt. New York, 1970), pp. 673–74; and Allan Nevins, *Abram S. Hewitt, with Some Account of Peter Cooper* (New York, 1935). Mr. Wise was probably a temporary principal in the School of Design for Women, but no record of his service has survived in the Cooper Union's own archives; John K. McAskill, Assistant Librarian, Cooper Union, to Richard Winslow, May 30, 1979.

9. Bible House, national headquarters of the American Bible Society, was in Astor Place.

into a carpet and a music store to inqure the prices, to tell Mother,[bb] did my ironing was quite tired till I got through. After supper I had quite a talk with an old man the same I talked with yesterday. The old baggage wanted me to go out walking with him, but I guess he wont catch this child quite so easy, he wants to take me to the theater or opera, but I guess he will *know* when I go with him, I am not quite that big a fool, he wants a wife mighty bad. I had quite a long talk with Bridget this evening, she cleaned my room and casses. I find that she is getting rather too free. Today I gave an old beggar woman an old basque[10] of mine the poor thing could hardly thank me enough, said she would pray for me, that I would be rewarded, passing along the street an old man asked alms. O! a body ought to be made of gold to live here, it pains me to have to pass them without giving them something. Those Irish servant girls are a very course set   the yell and talk and laugh the awfulest. The days seem to go so fast that I scarcely know where they get to, we are gliding down the stream of time so swiftly and will come to the end before we think of it, we should therefore be always prepared to exchange worlds.

October 7, 1859   Fryday. Staid in my room all day, got some sewing from Mrs. Underhill, am getting a little lonely, and feel anxious about the evening class, it takes so long to get it straightened out. felt like taking a good cry this afternoon. This evening I got some more letters from home and also one from Mr. J. K.   letters do me so much good. I am so thankful for them, was down to the parlor for the first time, they wanted me to dance, but I refused.   enjoyed it pretty well. Two of the servant girls went to a ball, so Miss Post and I went to help them get ready, or rather to see them, such a time as they had, and of all the brass jewelry that was piled on, it was enough to make any body laugh, have a bad headache.

October 8, 1859   Saturday. Sewed nearly all day, had a headache in the evening, thought I would not go down to the parlor but Miss Post sent up for me, so I went down. I dont like to go into company much because I have not the means of dressing like they do which makes me feel so odd, did not stay very long, called on Mrs Shott. a Danish lady.   she speaks german too, like her, she is so friendly, retired with the blues

---

10. A fitted jacket.

October 9, 1859 Sunday. Was to Dr. Alexanders church, Presbyterian.[11] Dr. Alexander died not long since and today his funeral sermon was preached, brother Amos[hh] had to report it so I went with him.[12] At dinner we had a quite a talk with Mr. Carpenter, like him better than any gentleman I have seen yet in this city. he seems like a good hearted man. Some of the ladies here paint, one in particular it looks so senseless to do that. Was to D. Chapmans church this evening. Universalists, he preached pretty well,[13] his belief and mine dont quite coincide, had quite a discussion with Amos[hh] after we came home, he has some strange notions about Christianity. O! that I were better that my influence over him might be real good.

October 10, 1859 Monday. Spent the morning at that much disliked business of mending torn dresses, then went to brothers[hh] room and by permission hauled a large trunk out and commenced examining its contents, but could not do it ample justice but did enough to satisfy my curiosity. At 1 oclock I started for the Tribune Office. Stopped in at a shoemakers and had a shoe mended the shopkeeper was quite talkative, got some apples from a little round-faced duch girl, brother[hh] was out when I got to the tribune office but returned in a little while, he then went with me to the city superintendants.[14] Was examined and recieved a diploma, came up in Broadway which is alway crowded. I went down on Third Avenue saw some of the worst looking people, some were the living pictures of poverty and distress, passed one woman that looked so fierce it made me quake to pass her Amos[hh] is scarcely ever here for dinner, so I have to sit at my table all alone, it dont seem at like home here. I shall try to get into a private family as soon as I get my school started. I was very tired when I got to my room again this afternoon, rested a little and then went to Amoses[hh] room again and hauled out another dusty trunk which was filled with books scraps, catalogues, &c. I seated myself before it on the floor and had quite a feast in reading select scraps, and this evening after supper looked over a Phrenalogical Journal, found some good pieces, marked some and

11. James Waddel Alexander, minister at the Duane Street Presbyterian Church, died July 31, 1859. *NCAB*, VI, 490.
12. Amos's story appeared in the New York *Tribune*, Oct. 10, 1859, p. 7, col. 2.
13. Rachel probably refers to Dr. Edwin H. Chapin. Like Henry Ward Beecher, Chapin invariably spoke to overflow audiences that included many visitors. One of the regular members of the Fourth Universalist Church of New York City, where Chapin presided from 1848 to 1880, was Amos's boss, Horace Greeley. *NCAB*, VI, 89; Ernest Cassara, *Universalism in America* (Boston, 1971), p. 205.
14. The Superintendent of Public Instruction, whose office issued the antebellum equivalent of teachers' certificates.

would sent it to my friend S.E.C. but fear that he would think me rather too fast.[15] My daily prayer is that I may be real good and do good, nor do I ever in my prayers forget the folks at home. I know that they are interested in my welfare, they are alarmed about my cough, which seems to be some better, but it sometimes comes back with all its disagreeableness, there is such a never ceasing clatter here that I long to be out again, but still I do not wish to go yet. I have not accomplished what I came here for viz become expert if not profissient in drawing and painting.

October 11, 1859 It is nearly ten oclock already. I have just got through reading letters from home. One from Mother,[bb] the dear good woman tells me how hard she has to work. O! how I do wish that I could make enough money to send home so that they would not need to keep boarders, I also received one from Sis which is full of good cheer and jokes, just like herself, also one from Clem,[cc] full of the same. Bless their dear hearts, they are all too good to me, I also received one from Mr. S.E.C——y such a long one too, and so good, the dear man, wish I could kiss him, his letter was so good that I could not help to kiss it. It seems too that he is rather smearing the paint. Sis tells me that Mr Bilhimer[16] thought that I was

15. Phrenology reached the height of its popularity in the United States during the 1850s. It assumed, first, that human behavior could be divided into forty-six abstract qualities, each controlled by a particular section of the brain, and second, that the skull bone accurately reflected irregularities in the brain beneath it. Hence, a trained phrenologist could analyze a person's innate tendencies by examining his or her skull. As anatomists at the time protested, neither of phrenology's two basic assumptions was correct, yet such prominent public figures as Horace Mann and Henry Ward Beecher took phrenology seriously. Moreover, the commercial success of the *American Phrenological Journal* testifies to substantial popular support.

Part of phrenology's appeal lay in its entertainment value; it was often treated as a sort of parlor game, similar to fortune telling. Much more significantly, however, phrenology was linked both commercially and in the popular mind with other reformist ideas then current in the United States. The interest shown by Rachel and Samuel in such subjects suggests a willingness to explore the various social, medical, and dietary reforms of their era. On phrenology and its chief backers, see John D. Davies, *Phrenology, Fad and Science: A Nineteenth-Century American Crusade* (New Haven, 1955); Madaleine B. Stern, *Heads and Headlines: The Phrenological Fowlers* (Norman, Okla., 1971); and J. C. Furnas, *The Americans: A Social History of the United States, 1587–1914* (New York, 1969), pp. 438–49. In her long standard *Freedom's Ferment: Phases of American Social History to 1860* (Minneapolis, 1944) Alice Felt Tyler also made the significant point that phrenology and the many fads and reforms associated with it became "extremely popular with *intelligent women*" (emphasis added), who were themselves grappling with profound changes in their potential social roles.

16. The American missionary, back from Africa, who had been in Westerville seeking a wife.

married, I must not insert his remarks it would look too vain, he told her to tell me that he is going to call on me. I shall be glad to see him. I do get such good letters from Westerville. God bless them all. I spent the day in sewing, I made my old buff calico into a morning dress, am fixing over my old dresses so that I wont have to get new ones, I am going to shift with as little as I can, so that I can send things home, wish I could make up a trunk full for them.

October 13, 1859 Do not feel in very good trim for writing this evening, but must relate some of my todays adventures. This morning early A.[hh] and I went to see Mr. Byrn.   not find him at home, so we went to his store. he was not there. I waited there a long time but did not get to see him. Amos[hh] is gone to see him again this evening.   but felt discouraged, thinking that he would not get to see him   Amos[hh] is getting a little out of humor about it   he has to run round so much.

October 14, 1859 This morning the first thing I did was going to see Mr Byrn.   found him in his office this time. I presented my letter of introduction. he looked over it then said that he could not do much for me. I told him then that I only asked his concurrence, &c, he talked like a bear but smiled over it every little but that I guess it is his way of talking but indeed it made my heart sink within me. I felt like going home and spending the rest of the day in weeping, but that would not do, he told me he would appoint me if I got a class[17] and gave me a letter of introduction to the principle of the evening schools. Last evening I was to go and see them. But Amos[hh] did not come to go with me.   although I had gone all the way down to the Tribune Office to tell him to come, it made me feel a little out of humor, how can I expect a class if it goes this way all the time like it has been so far, I cant bear it. I am going now this evening if I have to walk all night. I am going to have it done, surely I realize now that the old bird in the wheatfield told the truth, when she told the little one, that they need not fear that they would be disturbed so long as the farmer and his son did not say that they were going to take hold and reap it themselves   I know Amos[hh] wishes I had not come, but he had no business to write for me. I am going to do the best I can and make him glad yet. Bridget was in to tell me her sorrows, was weeping, I tried to comfort her, I pity the

---

17. I.e., if Rachel could find a class (either by recruitment or by inheriting one abandoned by a previous teacher), the official in charge, Mr. Byrn, would offer her a formal appointment.

poor girl, wish I could teach her, she expressed a desire to be taught.

October 14, 1859 Had to breakfast alone again, but brought some up to my room for Amos,[hh] which I often do. I mended and cleaned his coat today and this evening I was to the evening schools. Am much encouraged, think I shall have a class soon, Monday evening I am to go again to receive the names, came home alone, got lost but found myself again like Mr Hill says, received a good letter from my friend Hattie, was much pleased with it. But I am so tired

October 15, 1859 I staid at home all day, sewed read studied, but did not do as much of either as I might. my mind is filled with blisful dreams. O! how I fear that all, *all* will be blasted, It is so sweet to love and be loved, but in this fast age a single breath may blow all away. Often I forget myself and catch myself sitting listlessly looking into the future and see myself in a neat little home and surrounded with nothing but love, and a strong arm to protect, and a manly kind heart to love and guide. O! he is so good. I fear to mention his name for fear of disappointment. It is natural for me to fear, having had such bright visions destroyed so suddenly once before, but this one seems much dearer. I did not know that I cared much for him until we had to part, and his letters seem so good that I cannot refrain from pressing them to my lips and heart. Today I let an old besetting sin overcome me again. O! when shall I conquer, only those that conquer shall be served. I fear for myself. O! that I were real good I long so much to feel that I am that Lords indeed. this evening there is a party in the parlor, I dont know whether to go down or not.

October 16, 1859 Was to Dr Cheevers, or the Puritan church.[18] liked it very well. In the evening to hear Prof. Shaff from Chambersburg, Pa. german preacher, he would speak in german a while and then glide off into english, he went from one to the other so often that at the end his sermon was about as much english as german. To both meetings we were late. Amos[hh] dont like to go early, and gets quite out of patience when I say any thing.

18. George Barrell Cheever was pastor of the Church of the Puritans on Union Square from 1846 to 1867. An inveterate and controversial reformer, Cheever was another of the nation's leading voices of evangelical abolitionism. *NCAB*, VII, 82; *DAB*, II, 48–49.

October 17, 1859   Today was the great Trienial parrade of the fire companies, they gathered in from different cities and made quite a fantastic appearance. I went up to Broadway to see them but there was such a great crowd that I could not see much. They had their carts fixed very pretty, there were so many that it took them two hours or more to pass, they had about sixty bands of music.[19] In the evening I went to my school, found two schollars and the promise of about eight more. I went home thinking Amos[hh] might be here yet but he had gone, so I will have to wait till morning.

October 18, 1859   Got up early, took a bath, read my usual bible lesson and had my devotions.   Then wakened A.,[hh] took breakfast and then suggested to him the idea of going to see the german teacher to inquire the encouragement about a class. A.[hh] spoke rather indignant at the idea of having him go along, he has a novel that he likes to read a little better than do any thing for me. I felt quite out of heart to think that even a brother should think it too much trouble to help a sister a little, and thought too if men were all so, I should never want to get married. I can bear almost anything better than neglect. I told A.[hh] that I thought I might as well start right off for some unknown part not knowing whither. If women could travel with the safety of men, this night would not see me again in N.Y. city.   but to me it seems as though the commencement of such a wandering life would be but a prelude to the commencement of wretchedness and abandonment, how could I bear the thought if such should be my lot, friends should never hear of me again. Nay I can be servant and be still pure. I will not consent much longer to tax his patience, attendance or purse.   I cannot consent to it. But I must away now to see what I can do for a class.   if that fails, then measures for the other can be taken. Am back, no signs of a class. I went to some of the houses, but could not do anything. It makes me lose my compassion for their ignorance when laziness keeps them from an education   perhaps I ought not to feel so but I cant help it.

October 19, 1859   This morning Amos[hh] and I concluded that it would be best for me to go to Pa and visit a while, perhaps I can get

19. New York City still depended on volunteer firemen. Their companies also functioned as political and social clubs and competed for influence, prestige, and members. Some six thousand men took part in the parade that Rachel refers to here. New York *Times*, Oct. 18, 1859. For details see Augustine E. Costello, *Our Firemen: A History of the New York Fire Departments, Volunteer and Paid* (New York, 1887), pp. 379–84; and George W. Sheldon, *The Story of the Volunteer Fire Department of the City of New York* (New York, 1882), pp. 275, 509–41.

a school there, and perhaps he can get me a class here by New Year   I can hardly consent to give up the idea of taking lessons in drawing. My cough is worse too, and have quite a head ache and often a pain in the side, and considering all, it may be the very best thing I can do. I desire very much to become real good and to do good. Today I walked out again into some of the worst parts of town. The poor sallow looking women were engaged in almost all kinds of drugery work, shoveling coal, carrying wood on their shoulders &c &c while the men look like walking rumbarrels, loafing round.[20] I just read an account of that dreadful insurrection at Parkers Ferry, it was dreadful.[21]

October 20, 1859   I was out this afternoon first I went down to the tribune office waited about an hour for Amos[hh] but he did not come so I started off alone down to the battery, where all the imigrants land, walked along the shore stood awhile to see the vessels move along, but it was so cold that I could not stay long and I felt unsafe to stay long there were so many ugly looking men round all the time, was very tired till I got home, after dinner this evening I went down to see about my class but it is all of no avail to try to get one, there were only three girls there. So I concluded to give up the idea of teaching here for the present and am making preparations to go to Pa.   What the design of all this is I dont know, I thought I came here trusting in the Lord, surely it must be to teach me some good lesson.   I have no money. Amos[hh] is going to give me enough to take me to Pa.   how it will go then I dont know, God help me. After I came back from my school I went to the parlor, Mr Carpenter stepped up and asked me to go with him to a music society. I went   they were rehearsing the Oratoria of Elijah.[22] Mr. Carpenter is so very tall that I had to reach way up to take his arm, my shoulder would nearly go under his elbow. I like him pretty well

October 21, 1859   This day I staid in nearly all the time to sew, write, etc. I was to Mrs. Underhills room a little while. It is very cold. I am most freesing.

---

20. While Rachel appreciated the potential advantages of the city, she was shocked by much that she saw there. For more on the ambivalence of nineteenth-century Americans toward the city, see Lucia White and Morton White, *The Intellectual Versus the City: From Thomas Jefferson to Frank Lloyd Wright* (New York, 1964), and Paul Boyer, *Urban Masses and Moral Order in America, 1820–1920* (Cambridge, Mass., 1978).

21. The reference is to John Brown's raid at Harpers (not Parker's) Ferry, Va., two nights earlier.

22. Felix Mendelssohn's *Elijah.*

October 22, 1859 It is quite cold today, I staid in all day and read Tenysons poems, like them very much. I have read Longfellows poems too. I not only like but love his. wrote letters home. Was down in the parlor this evening, had quite a long talk with Mr Carpenter, I think him a very fine young man. Mr Niely declare that Mr Carpenter is in love with me, what an idea, getting in love before getting really acquainted. Mr. Niely is a rich old southern widower and is a little more interested than need be himself.

October 23, 1859 Sunday morning. Am a little provoked this morning. I wanted to go to church this morning   wakened Amos[hh] but he would not get up so I took my breakfast alone, brought him some to my room and waited till about about 10. then told him again and still he would not get up. Now it is past 12, and he is just eating his breakfast, now who would not be provoked.

November 5, 1859 Aaron Moyers school house, Pa. Bucks Co.   I had my journal in my trunk so that I did not get to write till now, but will now write an account of my travels. I had intended to start on Monday Oct-24th, but the porter made such a mistake and took Amoses[hh] empty trunks to the boat instead of mine. I bid them all goodbye and started for the Tribune office to tell Amos[hh] and to get him to help me to fix all right. When I got there he had been apprised of it, and told me too that the boat would not leave till the next day. So I left my basket in the office, but took a book along which I had just received by mail. A Cottage Testament from Mr. C——y, a Phila. I did not expect it or any thing else. I like it very much, shall prise it very much. I strolled up Broadway and at dark reached Mr Underhills again. Mr Carpenter was standing in the parlor by the fire when I entered, he looked so funny, scarcely knowing what to say. I went to room but it was already taken up by somebody else so I went to the parlor again, Mr Carpenter soon came in again, we then took, or went to dinner together and then to the parlor again, where we sat till ten oclock when I got Bridget to get me another room

November 23, 1859 I started from N.Y. city on Oct. 25 on board the boat Boston, Amos[hh] went with me to the boat, got my state room and spoke to the clerk to have me in his care and see me safe on the cars in Philadelaphia. All went right on boat till night the first day when the engine gave out, the captain got the mate at it and fixed it and run a little while when it got out of order again, the sails were then put up and we run within sight of Cape May by sail,

44

there the wind and tide came against us. We anchored then and got help and material and had our ship or boat repaired. In the afternoon of the 27 of Oct, we started again, rounded the cape and went along right smart for a while, but it got so dark that we anchored again and laid by for that night   Although I was quite strange to every body and every body to me, yet by this time I have got acquanted with some. Our crew[23] consists of about twenty four.   all rather respectable looking ones except one, who looked rather suspicious. I got pretty well acquanted with a Mrs Crump from Reading Pa. This afternoon we (the crew) were sitting round the stove in the Cabin, for it quite cold, the men were plaguing a little boy when the suspicious looking man fell off his chair and had a very hard spasm, it frightened me, and I started for my room but turned round and went back, thinking to teach myself to be able take hold and help in any case of emergency, of such or any other kind, but could not force myself to go near and felt quite sick and faint. My friend Mrs Crump and her husband went right up to the man and did for him what they could and told every body just what to do. I staid in the cabin until all was over, i.e., the man came to. I then went to my room, I felt quite faint and sea sick but could not vomit, was very sick for a while. In the course of the evening Mrs Crump came to my room to see whether I was sick, she came in and we sat there together talking for a long time, learned that she belonged to the same church as myself and also that she was acquainted with persons that I was acquainted, this interview made us good friends, we went round together to see the boat. The captain showed us the machinery &c   All the crew got pretty well acquainted, we sit round the stove and talk.

October 28, 1859   This morning early Mrs Crump was to my room to inquire about my welfare, which— The boat started again at daybreak, we went on a little while when down our engine broke again, the wind was contrary so we just go where the wind drove us to. We were almost discouraged, thinking that we would have to stay on there another night.   but fortunately a boat came from Philadelphia and us on board and took us on to Philadelphia and sent a tugboat to fetch our poor disabled boat. We (the crew) got so well acquainted that we hated to bid each other adieu. A Mr. Lentz went with me to the depot, saw that my trunks were brought there and found out that I had to wait about four hours, he asked me then to go with him to see some of the city.   I walked with him quite a

23. I.e., the passengers.

distance when we came to a nice house when he said "There lives my uncle, wont you call with me a few minutes." I went in with him, before we knew it dinner was ready and we took a good dinner, had some fine catawby grapes, the lady took me out into the garden showed me her things her grape vines &c., and when I went away she had some nice grapes put up in paper for me to eat on the cars. McClarrens is their name, Mr L. went along to the cars, saw me all safe, gave me his card and after making me promise to let him know of it when I came to the city he took his leave, and I was soon lande safe in Quakertown. On the cars I heard a man, a Mr. Clemner say that he was going to get off at Quakertown so I asked him whether he knew the man (mentioned his name) where I wished to go to. he said he did, but he lived a good piece from the station. The old lady, the mans wife then spoke up and said that I should go home withe them and that they would take me to where I wished to go the next day. I took them by their offer, went home with them, found them very clever people, helped the girls to dress a doll for the little girl.

October 29, 1859 This morning I cut and fit a dress for one of Mr Clemners little girls. In the afternoon Mr C. took me over to Milford Square to Mrs Crotz found her a very pleasant and Motherlike lady. I went with her to some of her neighbors till sunday when we went to church, for dinner to widdow Clemners, for supper and all night to Rev. J. Oberholzers, found them all clever people, they think me one of the seven wonders, having *come all alone from Ohio,* why their men would be afraid to do that. No wonder they chew and smoke so much tobacco that their nerves are weakened, and look as black as a common chimney and their mouths, who can describe.

October 30, 1859 This morning I walked from Mr. Cs. to Mrs Crotzs again, was going to do some washing but cut a dress instead and she washed for me, we always talk late every evening and still can never get through.

October 31, 1859 This morning Anna Oberholzer came early with the horse and buggy to take Mrs C and myself to Quakertown from where we walked on the track down the country about two miles to Mr Rosenbergers, who are cousins to my mother there are also other cousins over there. At dinner they were talking about their teacher and accidentally told where he was from and his name and lo, here it is. Aaron Moyer to whom I had written that he should fetch me. Right after dinner I went to his school house but he was not in then but came in a short time. He was so surprised to see me that he scarcely knew what to say. We spoke but a few words for his school had to commence. In the evening he came to where I was. after supper he and Mr. Rosenberger, my cousin, and I went to a husking frolick, such cutting up as they had there, they acted almost like wild cattle, we did not stay verry long. Mr Rosenberger girls also cousins went along, and when we got back the old folks were up yet but soon went to bed   Aaron went home, but the three girls, Christian and I sat round the stove talking till after three in the morning.

November 1, 1859   Were to J. Fellmans for dinner and just before dinner, Maria F and Mr. R. and I were to A. Moyers school. Dont like Mr Fellmans very much, they dont seem the best hearted people in the world. In the afternoon I went with C. Rosenberger to Mill in the large market wagon, he took Mrs Crotz home and fetched my trunk from the M. Square, got some little stones at the mill, we did not get back to Mr R's till after night.   after supper the girls C and I went to a Mr Martins to hear him play on the melodean and pianno, his instruments are not good, we run race on the way home.

November 2, 1859   Went out with the girls to husk corn, did not do much at that however, Mary Ella and I then went to pick up some hickery nuts. In the evening I went with A Moyer to Mr Chiles, liked them pretty well.

November 3, 1859   This morning I went out among the rocks at Mr Chiles, tore my shoe among the rocks. Miss Kity C. and I went to another Cousins of my mother. Mr P Segenfouses. were there for dinner, in the afternoon we went back to A. M.s school, he then went with us to Quakertown to see one of Kritzs cousins who is staying with a quaker family Mr Mathers, took supper there   liked the people very much, we accidentally learned there that the village school was not taken up, so we went to one of the directors, but he could not give me an answer until after a meeting of the board. We then went back to Mr Chiles and was there all night.

November 4, 1859   Went back to Rosenbergers again. In the evening Mr. Derstein[24] and Mr Hunsberger and their ladies from Hilltown township. We all sat there and talked till after twelve, then went to bed.

24. Rachel's maternal grandmother was a Dierstein.

November 5, 1859 Sunday. This day the great flatland church was dedicated. C. Rosenberger took me in his nice new buggy, he had asked another girl but last evening he told her that he could not take her. I did not like it very much, he and I went alone to a strange place for dinner, went home to Mr. R's for supper and then went with Mr. Derstein home to Hilltown he and his mother and two sisters live together. They were in bed already but the one would get up and got some pie for us, these people would nearly kill a body with kindness if they would be allowed.

November 6, 1859 Was to J. Hunspergers for dinner. Isaac their son cracked hickory nuts for and nearly filled my pocket. for supper I was to Mr Springers all night to A. Hunsbergers, quite a number of young folks came there in the evening to see me.

November 7, 1859 Was to J. Hunspergers for dinner, all night at Isaac Hunspergers.

November 8, 1859 for breakfast to I wismers, went to see the sawmill. he showed and explained all the machinery to me. for dinner I was to A. Wismers went to the barn with the old man to see his stock on the farm to see other things. J. Hunspergers went with me all this while, we went back to their house and then started right off to Mr J. Crouts. I got acquainted with the young folks when they were on a visit in Canada, we got

November 9, 1859 Those that took me to Mr Crouts took me to Mr A. Dersteins where I was for dinner. after dinner Mrs D. and I walked round over the farm, they have a pretty view of the country. Were I a good painter I would paint some of the scenery there. Young Mr D. took me to J. Hunspergers again. I had been there only a short time when two official looking men drove up and inquired for me. they were told that I was there and were brought in to where I was. They then told me that they were the *directors* of the *Quakertown public school*, and wished to employ me as their teacher. I made a bargain with them to teach for $26 a month, and commence on the 20th of Nov. In the evening Mr and Mrs J. Hunsperger went with me to Mr J. Moyers, quite a number came there to see me. I went back with Mr. H's to stay there all night—

November 10, 1859 Today I staid at Mr H's all day and looked over the branches a little in which I was to be examined, but they talked

48

to me so much that I could not study much. In the evening I went to Mr. J. Dersteins but went back again to stay all night at Mr H's

November 11, 1859   Today I went with Mr H. to Centreville where he had business with a doctor then down another way to Buckingham township to Mr W. Johnson's the school suprintendant, and was examined and received what would be called a good certificate. from there we went to Charles Moyers for dinner. In the afternoon we went to S. Moyers, from there one of their sons and one daughter went along to Mr Landise's, Mr. H did not go along in but went home. Quite a number of the young folks from Hilltown township came there to take me along up there again. I did not like Mrs. Landises extra well but still they were as kind as they could be and I liked them as well as the folks in general, but they are not like our folks but yet kind in their own ways. Benjamin their son took sick, so that he could not be up, going home I went in Mr Shrougers carriage. I went to J. Hunspergers again, when we got there lo and behold Mr. Shrouger stepped up and asked me for my company that night, it being midnight already. I knew their customs, but still I was surprised, being a comparative stranger at the place and he to me and I to him. Yet I thought best to allow him come in, he took his seat in a corner of the room and the most he said was yes and no, I talked all that I could think of, tried to entertain him but could not get him to say much more than yeas and no. At two I told him in as sly and polite a way as I could that I thought it time for him to go home, he had sense enough to take a hint and went. I could not refrain from laughing at my strange adventures.

November 11, 1859   Sunday.[25] Went to J. Dersteins early to get my clothes to go to church (I had my trunk there) and was going with J. Hunspergers if Mr D. was not going. he did not go, so I told a little boy to tell Mr H's that I would go with them, but the little fellow misunderstood me and told them that I was going with Mr D. so they started right off and of course when I got over there they were off, so I went back to Mr D's. At about eleven it commenced to rain very fast, and rained very fast when the people went home from church so that many of them got wet. As soon as Mr H's came home, Isaac their son came over to explain for they had learned how it went from the little boy they had there. We

25. Rachel is still catching up on her diary entries (see the entry above for Nov. 23, 1859), and she has now lost track of exact dates. This is the second entry for Nov. 11, which was actually a Friday.

had promised Shrougers young folks that we would be there for dinner but as we missed that through the above circumstance we went in the afternoon and were there for supper When we got there it was raining hard. I. H was allowed to help all the girls down except me. Young Mr I. who was standing there all the time just stepped in before him. During the afternoon we were treated with nice apples and some kind of drink and in due time had a supper that would do credit to a kings house. shortly after partaking of that rich repast we started off to Mr H's again, Mr I. was ready to help me on the carriage, but allowed some other one perform that duty to the other girls. I was amused with the undue defference shown to me by other members of the family as well as by him.

November 12, 1859   This afternoon Mr. J. D. took myself and Mrs H who went with me to Hatfield Montgomery Co. Whitehall station where we took the cars to Hatfield to visit the Clemence[26] relations. Mr. G. Clemence is the proprietor of H. hotel   old Mr Cassels live in the same house, we staid there that night. I did not like it there, everything goes helter skelter.

November 13, 1859   John Clemence another cousin of my mothers happened to come to Hatfield today for coal, so I went home with him in his coal wagon   we passed through Harleysville and there I received three letters, one from home, one from brother Amos[hh] and the other from J. B. Slichter from Canada. It does me good to receive letters especially from home. I read them after I got to my room which was not very early.   Those who have been on such visiting tours well know how it goes.

November 14, 1859   Mrs. J. C. went with me to Henry Clemences a brother of Johns, she left her two little girls at home with their Pappa of whom they are very fond and took only the babe along. We took dinner there, like the people pretty well, but it seemed to me that they were not very accomodating, were to worldly or too stingy. In the afternoon the widow Clemence whose husband died so suddenly in Canada and who lives in the same house came in. She and I had quite a talk. I like her very much. I went with her to her room and there got acquainted with her daughter a girl of seventeen who as well as her mother seemed subdued by their late grief.

26. A variant spelling of Rachel's mother's maiden name.

This is the old house in which my Grandpoppa Clemence was born, but it has been fixed over so that it does not look so very ancient. Grandpoppas brothers old farm was near and the old house was standing yet. One of the widow Clemences daughters went with me over there to see the old stand. The house is not now used for a dwelling house, but as a storehouse to store old trash in. We went to the new dwelling house and asked permission to go through the old house, stating our reason for visiting such an old revolutionary habitation. It was truly ancient looking. Our first entrance was into the kitchen which was a long narrow room with a large fire place in the middle, we passed to the far end of the room to enter into the parlor which was a fine square looking room. I imagined how the furniture was arranged which no doubt would be a curiosity if preserved. By the way I did see some among my friends which was still preserved, we passed through the room to the family sleeping room, which was not quite square, but still a very nice room for that purpose. We then had to pass through the parlor again to the kitchen, and pass the old fireplace to the outside entrance near which were the stairs to take us to the upper story, which consisted of two small attick room, no part of the house was ceiled, and to me it seemed as rather an uncomfortable and unhandy house, we then decended the winding stairs again and went out to get an outer view of the old farm, from there we went to the Brange as it is called, a pretty strong stream of water. I picked up stones from the bank, and not satisfied with those as relics, I walked on rocks to the middle of the stream and picked two out of the bed of the stream. We then went back to H. C's house took supper, and after supper, H. C's sorrowed daughter and the widdows daughter went to see Susannah the other of the widdows daughters, we had a pretty long walk through the woods, had a nice visit. like Susannah very much, returned to Mr C's was very tired and glad to retire.

November 15, 1859 Susannah C. and I went to Mr J. Crotzs. Mrs C is a cousin to Mother.[bb] Mrs H. C. took us part way, she went to the shoemakers and we rode with her, we walked the rest part of the way. I was received with the warmth of an old friend. In the afternoon Mr Crotz took us to Mr J. Landises. Mrs L. is a cousin to Mother[bb] too. Susannah is still with me, we staid all night at Mr L. they are right clever people too, two of their daughters are married but are at home yet. The one and her husband live there and follow cigar making as their business Horrid. I think we need tobacco reforms as well as liquer reforms.[27]

November 16, 1859 This morning S. and I went to her grand mothers, she is quite an inteligent woman we had a nice visit. when we were going to return to Mr L. it rained very hard but we started in the rain. Mr L. then took us back to Mr Crotzs again where we staid all night, in the evening Mr and Mrs C showed us their dishes, dresses, harness etc &c, are very talkative.

November 18, 1859 It is raining fast yet this morning. Mr C. took me to Francony station (from there I was going to Quakertown on cars) through all the rain, he thought the train went up at eight but we learned that it would not leave till near eleven, so I had to wait there, it rained very hard for a while but ceased before I left and the rest of the day we had fair weather. I got to Quakertown between eleven and twelve. I took an umnibus to take me to Dr Meridiths who is one of the school directors, took dinner with them. In the afternoon Issabella M. one of Mr Dr M. daughters went with me to get a boarding place. I got a place with Mr Grants. I am to have a *room to myself* with a *melodean in it* for $1.75 per week. I went home with Miss M. again took supper there, in the evening I went with her to the reading circle, did not feel well, went home with Amanda Grant—daughter of Mr. G.

November 19, 1859 Did not have my clothes so I could not go to church, so I staid at home and read and wrote letters. In the afternoon C. Rosenberger brought my trunk as soon as he was gone I went and dressed and in the evening I went to church. I felt almost homesick.

December 1, 1859 This is my second week at teaching. I have a very large school, over sixty schollars some very bad ones, I have been getting along pretty well till today, some have acted very bad and I have to record the humbling fact of having had to close school in a flood of tears, truly it is humbling but I could not help it.

---

27. Among the many organized reform efforts of the antebellum period was an antitobacco movement led by Orin Fowler, Joel Shew, and George Trask. According to the *NUC*, an antitobacco journal was published from 1859 to 1864. Increased use of tobacco by soldiers during the war, however, effectively blunted this nascent reform. Samuel himself will experiment with tobacco while in the Union army. See *About Tobacco* (Lehman Brothers, 1955), pp. 22–23, and Joseph C. Robert, *The Story of Tobacco in America* (New York, 1952), pp. 105–12.

Received a letter from Sml. E. C. did not expect one. The man is truly in love I really believe, and I must confess that I am not ill pleased with it for my heart longs for something true and noble to cling to. But what is near my heart now is grace to teach and govern my school right. God help me and help the children.

December 2, 1859 All went right well today, even those that acted so bad yesterday are unusually kind and good. I feel as though the good Lord was helping me. I felt my dependence and flew to Him for help, and He has been good to me. In the evening, I went to hear Mr Wm. C. Hunter from N.C. to lecture on Sunday schools. Before the lecture the Demosthenian Lyceum had a meeting which was rather interesting.[28] The two meeting together made it rather late till we got home, it was half past ten.

December 3, 1859 The county suprintendant and two of the school directors were to my school this fore noon, the Suprintendent and one of the directors staid all the forenoon. I learned quite a number of new things from their visit. Mr Jamison, a director promised to be a strong support in my teaching. This afternoon Mr Jackson and Mr W. Jacoby were into my school. I think I have had visitors enough to do for awhile.

December 4, 1859 Sat up in my room reading till afternoon when I got ready and went to Sunday school, after S. School I staid to Bible class, liked it pretty well, promised to call for Miss Jacoby to go to evening preaching, she being gone her brother went with us to church, it was rainy and icy so that it was hard to get along. Mr J. escorted us home from church again, he seems like a sensible man.

December 5, 1859 All went pretty well in school today. It is still very icy and hard to get along, received two letters, or rather two envelopes full of letters. I opened one and looked from whom it was, I just glanced at it and thought it was signed Saml and addressed me as dear Sister. I thought he had already repented of his late declarations, in anger and grief I flung it from me. I began to feel quite faint and sick. I did not know that I had allowed him so much power over me already. I looked again and saw my

28. The Lyceum movement, launched in the 1820s, provided intellectual stimulation for the general adult population, usually in the form of lectures. By the time Rachel wrote this, tens of thousands of local chapters existed in America's towns and cities, and hundreds of paid lecturers toured among them. See Carl Bode, *The American Lyceum: Town Meeting of the Mind* (Carbondale and Edwardsville, Ill., 1968).

mistake   it was signed Susie[nn] instead of Sml.   but still I did not get over the first effects the whole day.

December 6, 1859   This was a pretty hard day again, some of the boys are so bold, the larger ones make the most trouble. The two from where I board seem to think themselves priveledged characters and the boy is so bold too. I am almost at a loss to know what measures to take   Was to prayermeeting at Mr Jacobys, there were but very few there, after the meeting I had quite a discussion with W. J. about secret societies.[29] I have to laugh at myself.   he got quite in earnest about the temperance association, which they wish me to join   I think I shall too, for I think it a good society and is not strictly speaking a secret society

December 7, 1859   All went pretty well today the large girls have taken a streak to cut up. I need wisdom from on high to guide me. How any person can teach school without the aid of prayer is more than I can see. My leaving home, and being brought here to teach this school seems to me truly providential and it seems to me that there must be some design in it all, I desire to be a true whole hearted christian. I come so far short of what I want to be. I feel too that the Lord is very good to me and feel a degree of trust, but do not trust Him as I should, I know that *all* is in His power and that every thing that I enjoy comes from Him. I desire to walk in the way that leads to life everlasting and do good while I live. It is very rainy and muddy today and my old schoolhouse is in as bad a place as there is round, but still I can get along.

December 12, 1859   Nothing of any consequence happened since I last wrote.   only that I was to Quaker meeting yesterday, which was certainly the strangest meeting I ever was at. All sat there perfectly still, the men kept their hats on. One man, The preacher as they call him, kept moving and twisting round, making the ugliest faces possible, then all at once he got up and spoke a little while about how strange it may seem to to those who are not accustomed

---

29. Passionate concern over secret societies was more than a quaint notion among nineteenth-century Americans, particularly those who shared Rachel's evangelical ethos. Indeed, American citizens frequently expressed in political terms their almost paranoid opposition to anything that smacked of conspiracy. See David B. Davis, comp., *The Fear of Conspiracy: Images of Un-American Subversion from the Revolution to the Present* (Ithaca, N.Y., 1971). Otterbein students founded literary societies rather than fraternities largely because the opposition to organized secrecy was so strong within the United Brethren that fraternal rites were suspect. Garst, *Otterbein*, p. 271.

to such a mode to come there and worship with them in their silent way, and tried to prove that their mode of worship is the only right one. I felt very much depressed this morning. It seemed to me as though something was going to happen to me. I had quite a time to get the fire burning this morning. All thing else are going pretty well. I have been writing a letter home again.

December 13, 1859   Two boys acted pretty bad today. I had to whip a little colored girl too.   she is so mischievous. I had the blues all day, and they get worse this evening. If I were alone I believe I would take a good cry, But I must go to prayer meeting now perhaps that will do me more good. There were but very few at prayermeeting   the men only pray here, so there was but one that prayed. I had quite a talk with Mr Jacobys family again, but still the blues did not all go away. I fear something is wrong at home.

December 15, 1859   This evening I united with the Temperance Society—like it pretty well.

December 16, 1859   This forenoon Mr. Green one of the school directors was in my school, and told me that the directors have concluded that henceforth I must not open my school with prayer. I told him I did not know whether I could consciencously do so, but I would think over it. I feel bad over it, feel like taking a good cry. Either I must leave the school or leave that. God direct me how to do. This evening on the way to the lycium, Amanda G and some other girls went in for T. Jacoby. I with some others waited at the gate. Sarah came out for us telling me Washy wished to see me. I went in and had quite a talk about this school affair. They advised me not to give it up. And since I have thought over it, I have concluded that let the consequences be what they may that I would at least *open* the school with prayer let the consequences be what they may. I asked the all the pupils to raise their hands who were in favor of having it opened as heretofore. All but two raised their hands, some of the larger ones expressed themselves very indignantly about the manner.

December 17, 1859   This morning, I went to the schoolhouse rather early, but not before I had a season of prayer. At the schoolhouse, I had another as generally have every morning. Some boys were here bright and early all full of what happened yesterday, each one asking what harm it could do, sure enough, what harm can it do. Those who fear that it will contaminate their children, must just keep them

55

out.   Mr Green thought that if only one family were opposed that it should be dropped   I told him I did not believe that. We spoke much of the great riots in Boston and Philadelphia.[30] I know nothing of those but his arguments made no impression on my mind. Mr H. Ball, Mr. Jackson, Mr Coxe and Mr Walter, were in my school this forenoon. This affair causes great excitement among the people. Mr B and Mr J adviced me too as Mr Jacoby's did. The approved highly of the course I had persued, and Mr B. said I will see that you are paid. I have not decided how to do yet.   but think I shall send a note to Mr Green to inform him of my conclusion. I know that the Lord *will* sustain me, and He too will provide for me. I know that I need very much the little that I would earn but he can provide a way for me. He has provided for me in the past, and He will provide for me in the future too. This will make me more fixed and decided, I never knew how appropriate that little hymn "A charge to keep I have" but now I feel it.   All, *all* will be right.

December 18, 1859   Read my bible and wrote letters this forenoon. this afternoon I was to Sunday School, they gave me a class to teach. I staid for Bible class after S. School. In the evening I went to church again. Mr Horn preach a sermon on public opinion. The whole sermon seemed to point to my case, all the way through. After church W. Jacoby saw me home, and told me that my affair was the base of the sermon, he told me too how much the people sympathized with me and how warm they were on the subject.   One old man wanted him to write a piece about it for the paper, he told me too not to fear, that there were many to plead my cause.

December 19, 1859   I had school today as usual. Nothing of any consequence happened, till evening. Mr Jamison one of the directors called to see me, and to find out whether I had decided as to what I should do. I told him that for the present I was decided, and did not think that any deliberation would change my mind, that we must obey God first.   Yes he said, it was all so, and he did not object to

---

30. Both Boston and Philadelphia experienced serious battles between Protestants and Catholics, which had been partly sparked by (though hardly limited to) issues involving religion in the public schools. The 1844 riots in nearby Philadelphia, the bloodiest in that city's history, had broken out following a dispute over which version of the Bible would be authorized for use in school exercises. See Michael Feldberg, *The Philadelphia Riots of 1844: A Study of Ethnic Conflict* (Westport, Conn., 1975); Elizabeth M. Geffen, "Violence in Philadelphia in the 1840s and 1850s," in *Riot, Rout, and Tumult: Readings in American Social and Political Violence*, ed. Roger Lane and John J. Turner, Jr. (Westport, Conn., 1978), pp. 112–32.

my way at all, but he said that the opinion of many of the citizens differed so much on that subject and that they must try to please the people, and that he was sory I had decided as I did, that he was desirous that I should continue the school, and that the people generally were pleased with every thing about it except the praying part. he said too that they would call another meeting and then they would decide the matter. I forgot to say that Mr Green also told me that those under six years, were to be excluded from school. I told the children, but one little boy will come, the next morning he came to bid me goodbye, and gave me a large apple, he pretty near cried, and since he has been here every day, and his folks say they cant keep him at home.

December 20, 1859   I was to prayermeeting last evening, was called on to pray, it was somewhat of a cross, but still I think it is good for me, I did not get a talk with W. J. but I think he had intended to see me home, had not Mrs Grant been with me. Mrs G. said that she never was to prayermeeting before. The other day the little ones were frightened thinking a crazy man would take them   I assured them that I would not let him.

December 22, 1859   Nothing of any consequence happened today in school. I have a few large schollars that try my patience rather badly. I have been expecting a letter from S.E.C. this whole week but did not get one yet.   I have not heard the descision of the directors yet as to whether prayer will be allowed or not. I feel a little blue this evening. I do not know how it will go yet. Above all things I desire to be a good christian. From school I went to Dr. Merediths, recieved an order for my school money, from there I went to Dr Greens but he was not at home, so I went home. After supper I Amanda Grant went to Dr Greens again he was not at home but we waited till he came.   he then signed my order.   he was crusty and seemed cross, perhaps I just thought so. We went from there to Mr Jamisons to draw my money but there was none in the treasury, but have the promise to receive it as soon as posible. On the way home we passed Mr Jacobys and were going to stop to see whether they had gone, they had but Mr Horn was there on the same errant, so I just went with him to the Division.[31] After the exercises, Mr Jacoby saw me home   we talked a long time on the porch. I like him, think he is an excellent young man. I

31. The local branch of the Temperance Society that Rachel had joined.

scarcely know how to do. I hope he will think of nothing beyond friendship. I promised to go with him to the teachers institute.[32]

December 23, 1859   This school affair makes me feel a little unpleasant. I wish the directors would decide so that I would know what to do. Just now one of my school boys Sml. Johnson came and give me some nice candies, which I am going to send home to the little girls. I like my schollars, yes love them. O! that I might be an instrument in the hand of God to do good to these little ones. A few evenings ago two little girls swept.   after they got through, they came up to me and said, "Miss Bowman let us have a little prayer-meeting again." I was in a great hurry to get home to wash, but I could not disappoint them. I feel that I am not near good enough. I would that my heart might be filled to overflowing with love to God and love to man. That I might do much good, A talk with S.E.C. on that subject would do me so much good.

December 30, 1859   This is the last time I suppose I will be able to write in my Journal for this year. I have neglected to write this week. The directors I learned from Mr Horn, Prin. of the bording school, Sent a man to Philadelphia to see what could be done with me according to law for not minding their directions with respect to praying in my school. They only learned that they could not do much. The directors have met now, but I have not heard their descision yet.   more than this, viz. Mr Grant asked L. Jacoby how they had decided with respect to praying, he said "He guessed they would let her pray." I do not care how they talk about it just so they let me go on. I know that the noblest and the best are on my side. Religiously I scarcely know how I do get along. I think however, that this opposition is doing me good, but I am not satisfied with myself. I do not have that bright assurance which I desire. We have snow today. I heard some sleighbells go. Yesterday evening I had a tooth extracted, the night before I had toothache all the night.   I also went to temperance division. W. and E. Jacoby called for me. W. saw me home, it snowed fast going home. I felt quite sick from loss of sleep and toothach. I got me quite a lot of new wearables, that I must make up now. I got me a cloth circular, and a velvet

---

32. By the 1850s, the Lyceum movement had become one of the strongest advocates of improved public schooling in America. Local lyceums pressed state and local authorities to upgrade education and, according to Carl Bode, "acted at times as a training school (usually called a county institute) for teachers before the days of the normal school." *American Lyceum*, p. 115.

basque. I have also commenced me a nubia.[33] I do not get much time to practice on the melodean. This week I also sent off a box of things home, I guess it will surprise them, I had some thing for each of them, I think Papa[aa] will be pleased with his. The Bible in three volumes with notes and explanations.

December 31, 1859 Did not have any school today. I cut and made my cloth circular. During the forenoon T. Jacoby came to invite me to their house to tea, I went, but took my sewing along. Washy had school, but came in the evening, I had quite a pleasant time, had quite a discussion with W. on the womans rights question. It being the night before New Year, so there was to be watchmeeting. I staid at Mr J's till time to go.   Miss L. Nagel came to spend the evening and to go allong to church which was to commence at eleven oclock. All seemed to get sleepy so I suggested the usefulness of a game at snow balling. No sooner said than some of us were out but it being to cold to make snowballs and not satisfied with that we began to wash each others faces. Sml. Ball came there too, so Miss E. J——y marched right up to him and began to rub his face with snow. When I saw that he was getting the upperhand of her I went to her assistance from that it went helter skelter, and next I knew Washy was at me rubbing my face as though he meant to purify it from every shame. Once in a while, I got a little snow in his face.   he had me cornered for about one hour. I was a pitiful looking object by the time he let me go, My hair was all down. My nice clean underleeves all black, my combs and hair pins lost &c &c.   Neither could all be found. next we all had to take a regular washing and brushing up time by the time we got through we had to start for church.

January 1, 1860 Was to church this morning. after preaching Mr Horn got at me to take dinner with them. I did so, they had a turkey and excellent dinner, Was to church in the evening again.

January 2, 1860 The large schollars turned out today again. I would rather have small ones for the large ones cut up so. I scarcely know what to do.

January 16, 1860 Nothing of any great importance happened since I last wrote, except that I was elected Vice President Secretary and Editress of the Gem,[34] in the Lyceum and in the T. division I was

33. A soft fleecy wrap for the head and neck, worn by women.
34. Evidently the local lyceum newsletter.

also elected Editress. I read the Star last time we met.[35]   The directors after having aplied to a Philadelphia lawyer and State Suprintendant for information concluded to let me go on. I still receive such good letters from S.E.C. I am so happy. It is sweet to be loved and to love, I believe that our attachment is from God, for why was not my heart inclined to love others who sued for my hand before he did.

35. The *Star and Covenant* was a religious journal published in Chicago from 1848 to 1883.

IV

Samuel's Winter of Decision

November, 1859–April 10, 1860

This section begins with Samuel's resolve not to reenter Otterbein following his summer stint as a traveling stationery salesman. After a desultory autumn of visiting friends and relatives in Ohio, he makes two significant decisions: he will use his inheritance to try to establish his own farm in Missouri and he will go east to ask Rachel to marry him and share that new life. As Samuel's future comes more sharply into focus, so does his diary, which now becomes a disciplined day-by-day record of his experiences.

———————◆–◆·◆·◆———————

November, 1859 Time has worn away, and I have decided to quit O.U. this fall—I will do some reading and study alone, and continue—what I long have been at—the study of Hydropathy and Phrenology—under direction of Dr. A. C. Bowman[cc]—I go on a visit of Uncle Pipers in Summit Co. O. and other friends in Richland Co. and will likely go to Missouri in the Spring and see what there may be there for me to do—I hope to find something more condusive to my health than College life—and in line with what the good Lord has in his plans for me——

I shall soon be receiving my share of Fathers Estate $1300.00 Thirteen-Hundred dollars, and it seems to me I can do better with that out West, than East[1]——So I'll visit friends—Read—study—and await further guidance——

Miss Bowman—Rachel—goes East to N.Y. City—or possibly to Quakertown to Teach—We often talk over the idea of her going east to seek her Fortune, and I west to seek mine——She is assured that her "Brother Amos"[hh] will help her in N.Y. City, And should she go to Quakertown, Friends are there calling for her.

If I go to Mo—Kimmils are there, they and Bowmans are Friends—

---

1. Thirteen hundred dollars was a substantial amount of money in 1859, and Samuel was right about its enhanced purchasing power in the recently opened districts of the upper Mississippi and Missouri basins. In most midwestern states it was more than enough to purchase a farm capable of supporting a family and to get in a first crop. See Clarence H. Danhof, "Farm-making Costs and the 'Safety Valve': 1850–60," *Journal of Political Economy* 49 (1941), 317–59.

and my coming from O.U. and from the Bowman home will be ample recommendation for me out there——

Say little Journal! This is a trying time for a young fellow without any Father or Mother, and pretty deeply in love with a good girl who is about starting East, and he doesn't know whether She'll ever come back, whether she really loves him more'n just like a whole-souled—tender-hearted—Sister loves a good brother like I've been to her without trying a bit—It just does itself—

You see I'm just whispering it like—I'm in a big bunch of perplex-ity—maybe before She goes east I'll know, and maybe not——

Later! O Jolly! We—Miss Rachel and I had a good sociable all to ourselves before she started for N.Y. and she is going to write me, and I say "Letters is pretty apt to tell"——I am pretty sure—since this last talk before leaving—that I'll be O.K. by and by——I'm next to certain Miss Rachel Bowman loves me, and loves me good, and I can afford to wait a while yet, to find out. I'd like to get down to something real before I in any way press my suit——

December 22, 1859 I am at Mansfield O—visited Jacob Lehmans (Mrs Lehman is sister to Stephen Huber—and was girl chum to my Mother) Had a fine visit there, and amongst other folk orignally from Franklin Co. Pa——

December 26, 1859 I have been having a great time over Christmas at Criders, Hoovers & Kauffmans—I fell in with a Charming young Lady—Miss Kauffman—through Hoovers—She is 19 or 20—Still in School, Black wavy hair, piercing dark blue eyes, almost black—very fair—rosy cheeks—a perfect female figure—smart—springy in move-ment—specially intelligent for a Country girl who has grown up on a Farm—

I am in her company frequently, through the week—while I am visiting at Hoovers and Criders—Sat with her several evenings til near 11 OCK—She is a charming girl surely, and will make some man a wife to be proud of and happy with a life time if he is the right kind of a man.

I have been getting letters weekly from Miss Bowman. Her experi-ences in N.Y. City not quite satisfactory, so she came to Quaker-town where her school proves to be a hard proposition—Between my visiting about so much, and falling in with this Miss Kauffman, maybe my letters to Miss Rachel showed a little warning, while hers to me were more confiding, and full of expressions of confidence in me, and were not lacking in expressions of desire to be enabled to sit with me, and talk over the ins and outs of life as we used to do at the old Bowman home not so long ago.

January, 1860 My Westward outlook seems opening up—I am about decided to go to Mo. Early in the Spring—Our having fine times with my old Franklin Co. friends here and near Akron at Uncle Pipers etc—Lots of revival meetings going on—Have fine oppertunities to grow in grace—I certainly feel need of a deeper work of grace—a more complete consecration to The Saviour—My Lord and Master—

January 15, 1860 Miss Bowmans letters draw on me decidedly—I want to see her, and that soon, I cannot allow Miss Kauffman to in any way draw me away from Miss Bowman—or even get a little corner in my affections—Oh! No! She is too near to me—and I whisper it too dear to me to allow any one to come in and in any way crowd her back—even if she is far away, and even though I am not yet certain that I can win her heart and hand——

In our letters we have been calling each other pet names, and using some rather endearing terms of expression but nothing has transpired that could make me certain that I am acceptable to her in the deep deep sense, nor have I ever given her any assurance that she is the best in the world to me and in my heart——

January 28, 1860 Saturday. Still at Uncle Pipers—Revival Meetings—Visiting, writing letters and receiving—The routine. Recd a strong letter from my Honey, decides me to go east to see her and talk face to face. So as to remove all this suspense. I shall start East Monday—In the meantime, I have just written her a real good letter, quite strongly pointing in the direction of our approaching decussion, though not at all clear or binding. Nor do I intimate that I am coming to see her—But her mind will be made up, and the answer prompt I am quite sure——

January 29, 1860 Sunday. I am too full of love affairs to get much good out of Church today. Uncles may think me queer—No matter! I'm going to see Her, Rachel Bowman, and know my fate is to Our future——

January 30, 1860 Monday. Left for Pittsburg—Struck a wreck on Ft Wayne Road. Lay over on our train til Tues 31" 9:30 we climbed past wreck and boarded a train that came from Pittsbg for us—3:30 P.M. Took Sleeper for Harrisbg and slept most of way—

February 1, 1860 Wednesday. Breakfast at Baumgardner House—Left for Phil'd'a 7: A.M.—Arrived 4 P.M.—SNOW! Put up at Union Hotel——

February 2, 1860 Thursday. 12° below zero——Left Philad'a 9:30 for Quakertown arrived 11½ A.M. Dined at Depot House P.M. Strolled up town—Put up at "Corner House" across street from where "Miss Bowman—a Cousin from O.U. Ohio—the School Ma'm—lodges & Boards—Home of Mr. Grants——

Near 4 OCK I went to the School House—several blocks away. Surprised Miss Bowman? SURELY! A pleasant meeting indeed. I closed school for her with prayers—Accompanied "The Teacher" to Mr. Grants—Then we took a walk til supper time——

The Grant family is real pleasant, and our breaking bread together and chatting, was a delightful occasion——

Early the family retired leaving us in possession of the Parlor—Such a face to face talk we had never had before, and such a blending of hearts we had not before experienced—Spontaneously we flowed together, and I felt as I never did before in degree—That we must become one someday, and that it should be settled soon—yes now——

About 11 OCK I ventured to propose that she give me her name. What would I do with it? Have it changed into mine——After a brief silence, I ventured to say "Will you be mine?" Our hands clasped—as never before—and She said "YES!" and rested her head upon my bosom as never before—Thus the Rubicon was crossed.

We sat together til 1 OCK lovingly talking of our future, and planning with refference to it.

I went across to my Hotel with altogether a new sett of thoughts and feelings, and aspirations——

February 3, 1860 Friday. Very cold—I am a new Man! Henceforth I live for another—P.M.—I took "The Teacher" Sleighriding to Milford Corners—to Charleston—and back to Q——We had a very pleasant time indeed—Evening a Mr. Moyer and two ladies called, and we enjoyed a nice Sociable hour—I remained with Honey til two oclock—What a change a few words produce in our lives—slept at Hotel—

February 4, 1860 Saturday. Very cold——

Some 3 or 4 men were "Shooting Mark" near by—I nebbed in a little—The best shot bantered me—I took it up—and beat the kit at

100 yds. First shot I cut the edge of the "Bulls eye"—No one had done better. Second I made a center shot—They wanted me to shoot again, I declined "til some one else does as well"—No one did— P.M. Honey and I took a two hours walk——

Evening we attended a "Reading Circle"—It lasted from 10 til 2 OCK—was rather more of a "detention circle"—on our walk to Grants we xpressed our feelings to each other which were by no means insignificant.

February 5, 1860 Sunday. at Hotel I slept til 10 A.M.   P.M. I was at S.S. and evening at Church—a good sermon—Took Honey home, and we had a happy time together til "wee hours." Surely these few days, and evenings spent together are welding us into oneness— demonstrating that we belong to each other.

February 6, 1860 Monday. Got up to Breakfast at 8 OCK—went over to give the dear one the parting hand—It seems hard to part. But I have now a new life to live, in which a new one occupies first place of all on earth, and I tarry at Allentown to sit for a Dauguer- reotype and send back to Honey.

February 7, 1860 Tuesday. Slept in Reading last night——Reach Harrisburg 12:30—Met Will Peacock—Enjoyed fine stroll and visit reviewing old times—Left Hb'g 4:30 P.M. reach Pittsbg 1:30 A.M.

February 8, 1860 Wednesday. Left Pittsb'g 2:A.M.   Breakfast at Al- liance. Weight 134½ lbs.   Reach Columbus 1:40 P.M.   Put up at Buckey House—meet some acquaintances——

February 9, 1860 Thursday. I visit Menno Bowmans School Today—we discuss Missouri and plan to start out 10th or 12th of March

February 10, 1860 Friday. I leave Menno—walk to Columbus— Dine at Buckeye House and P.M. Hack to WESTERVILLE. Meet with very pleasant reception all around—Spend the evening, very pleas- antly, in the Dining room with the Bowman Family—Sleep with John Mutch[2]——

---

2. It was common for people of the same sex to share a bed, particularly under temporary circumstances. Mutch had been one of Samuel's fellow boarders at the Bowman's during the previous spring semester.

February 11, 1860 Saturday. I went to Prayers—Lots of pleasant greeting—Wrote letters, and spent several hours with Mr. Bowman[aa] xamining charts of lands he owns in Mo & Iowa—Eve attended revival meeting—Rev J. M. Spangler in Ch'ge.

February 12, 1860 Sunday. Mr Deaner call'd on me also H. M. Crider—We went to church—Good sermon by Spangler. Eve Prof Haywood addressed the Missionary Society—W. O. Hiskey read a paper—I joined. Fee $1.00——

February 13, 1860 Monday. Looked over Draft of B.B.Bs[aa] Farm in Canada—and discust real Estate problems—&c——

February 15, 1860 Wednesday. Recd letter from Darling. O it rejoices my heart to get such good letters—I responded at once——

February 16, 1860 Hunted Rabits awhile—re-read Darlings letter. O what a delight—Recd letter from Geo W. Bean—and called on J. M. Strasburg——

February 17, 1860 Eve attended Literary—Clark and D. A. Tawny present—Spicy speeches.

February 20, 1860 Monday. I attended numerous religious services over Sab. Am feeling quite well physically & spiritually.

February 27, 1860 I am devoting much time to reading. Study and writing——

February 29, 1860 I recd a business letter from Brother John[d] on Estate matters I sign and forward receipt necessary Have concluded to remain in Westerville until April.   Then go to Missouri—

March 2, 1860 "Clem" Dr. A. C. Bowman[cc] and I took a long walk and had an extended talk—I am still making Hydropathy & Phrenology Special studies, and Clem helps me very much indeed——

March 3, 1860 I confided my "engagement"—to Menno—Miss Rachel is his favorite cousin of the Bowman Girls—I hoped for a letter from her—None today!

March 4, 1860 Sunday. Attend M. E. Church——

March 5, 1860 Monday. Menno and I go to Shrocks Sugar Camp—
Fine time— P.M. visit Weiblings—The mail bro't me Darlings Ambrotype—My! but it is precious, but the original is many times more
so——

I have been making a very agreeable acquaintance—Mr. Wm
Eadie—a Canadian Scottsman—Fine fellow——

March 7, 1860 Wednesday. Eve at a good German pr'm'tg

March 9, 1860 visited H. C. Pennels School—Letter from Kimmels—
in Missouri—full of news of interest to me—Missouri—Darling and
Me—Home! by and by——

March 11, 1860 Sunday. A.M. M.E. Ch—— P.M. Sunday School
I made a little speech to Primary Department—Evening wrote to
Darling—Monday routine—Tuesday took Mollie McKinny to The
Sam Galloway Lecture.

March 14, 1860 Wednesday. Clem.[cc] Wilt & I went to Columbus on
business—Put up at Buckey House—Eve I came home alone—A
letter from Darling, Full of good for me—a Feast!

March 16, 1860 Friday. I am suffering from a severe cold acquired
from my Columbus trip Wed.

March 17, 1860 Saturday. Israil H. Light and I tossed ball a long
time—Eve Pa[aa] and Ma[bb] Bowman and I talked over future prospects
til 11 OCK—They are very open, candid. Alls O.K.——

March 18, 1860 Sunday. Bad cold. remain in doors—and lie on
bed—drop asleep—my Darling came to me—so full of love and
tenderness—that I seemed to be in a little Heaven of love—Evening
I am not feeling at all well——

March 19, 1860 Monday. I moved to other end of House—Spent
P.M. writing to Darling etc. Evening Mr. & Mrs. Pennell, Amanda
Hanby—Emma Crout—Susie[nn]—Lizzie[oo] Carrie[pp]—John Mutch & I
spent hours together in Our dining room. A jolly season sure——

March 20, 1860 Tuesday. Sold my Ten-years Scholarship to Z. Z.
Graves, went with him to see President Owen and Doctor McFad-

67

den about the transfer[3]—all O.K.—Evening went to young mens prayer meeting—H. M. Crider led—

March 21, 1860 Wednesday. Wrote letters—and in Eve Clem^{cc} and I called on Miss Hively and Pennels——

March 22, 1860 Not any new thing

March 23, 1860 Friday. Read and wrote some—I accompanied Prof Streeter & Mr. Bonner to the woods to get hoop poles to bind Prof's Boxes when he moves——The Professor almost put me in the notion to go to see Mich. before going to Missouri——
Evening a letter from my Darling Rachel, chuck full of devotion and Love—I am reading my Bible more, and desiring, praying, and striving to be a better man in every way——

March 24, 1860 Saturday. Had quite a talk with Susie^{nn} on personal religion—I hope I helped her——

March 25, 1860 Had a good sabbath.

March 26, 1860 I am reading extensively on Matrimony—Brother Clem^{cc} supplies me with the Books—as also on Hydropathy & Phrenology

April 3, 1860 Tuesday. James^{kk} and Lea^{jj} came today for a visit— Delightful companionship. I confided in him my secrets

April 4, 1860 J.W.^{kk} & Lea^{jj} occupy my room in part today, so I get little reading, study or writing done——
Eve a letter from Darling—I am informed that my money is in Columbus for me——A week of home doings in a social way—I do

3. One of the many fund-raising schemes tried by educational institutions was the sale of tuition vouchers at reduced rates. Families could buy perpetual scholarships or, as in this case, tuition waivers for a student of their choice for a specified number of years depending upon the price. The colleges hoped to build up enough endowment to cover the prepaid tuition through investment income. But the experiment failed, and most schools, including Otterbein, abandoned it after the Civil War. Garst, *Otterbein*, pp. 107–09. Samuel had probably purchased his scholarship in Pennsylvania, where this form of fund raising was widespread. Saul Sack, "A Nineteenth Century Scheme for Financing Higher Education in Pennsylvania," *History of Education Quarterly* 1, no. 3 (Sept. 1961), 50–54. Owen was the Reverend Alexander Owen, president of Otterbein, 1858–1860.

some study, but we are full of discussions of Bowmans Missouri land and of my going out soon——

April 10, 1860 Eve Pennels—Miss McKinney—Clem,[cc] Adamses[kk]— with all the rest of us make up quite a company—and time flies cheerily all the evening.

V
Rachel's Return to Westerville
January 30–April 13, 1860

In this section Rachel concludes her stormy teaching career in Quakertown and returns to Ohio to be with her family, make her wedding plans, and prepare for her future as a Missouri farmwife.

‌ ——————————◆·●·◆———————————

January 30, 1860 I have not written in here for so long. Since I last wrote I have been really affianced to Mr S. E. Cormany, who is going to start to Misouri in the spring to seek a home for us in the western wilds. I think likely I shall go home in the spring, or I may not get to be at home much before I leave for the west. but I am not off yet. something may happen to blast all again. The people here are quite troubled about this western maiden. Some really believe that Mr Jackson goes to see her. Others that Mr Cope who took her to an institute once does, and worse than all that Mr Shaw want to go and see her, he has tried several times to see me home but did not succeed, he tries to find out from Mr Grann[t] or Amy and Henry G. whether I would allow him to come. He will find out if he comes. My school goes pretty well, I have to switch some like every thing and am getting tired of teaching I like some of my scholars very much, but others I cant like so well I try to like them too but they act so ugly. Yesterday Sacrament was administered. I partook. O, how I desire to live good now. Anew I tried to consecrate myself to the Lord. O! for assisting grace to live right and to set a right example before these children. I feel that my position as teacher is a very responsible one, and truly I need help from above to perform my duties rightly.

February 1, 1860 It is very cold today. Last night it snowed considerable and till this morning it was rather hard for me to get along on my way to the schoolhouse. It is very cold in here, the house is so old and airy. Two of the directors were in to visit the school. Yesterday evening I had to send one of the boys home for misbehavior.

February 3, 1860 This will be the last day we will spend in this old schoolhouse. Yesterday afternoon, we had an awful time I had to

70

punish a few little boys and one of them turned round and fought me, but I conquered him. I whipped him till he gave up. Just as I had called the rool, and was about to sing and have the evening devotions some one stepped in and to my surprise when I looked right, there stood Mr Cormany. I was rather beat. he prayed with us. he went home with me then. I changed my old garb and went out walking with him. I got him to stay for supper, but he would not put up then, but went to the tavern. he was at my boarding place till after twelve.

February 7, 1860 I did not have time to write for the last few days. Mr C——y staid till yesterday morning he was to Mr Grants every evening till after twelve, and during the day we slept or walked out. I love him so, to me he seems the dearest object on earth. It is so sweet to love and be loved. Many many things are said while together and arrangements will be made to have me go to the far West with him till Fall or Winter. he called over in the morning to bid me good bye and staid till schooltime. I started for the new schoolhouse, for this was to be our first morning there. I got there ten minutes too late, all were waiting for me. All the directors except Dr Meredith were present. I commenced right away to organise the schools, viz to divide it into two schools. It took nearly all the forenoon to do that. A few classes recited yet till noon. I like it much better already, but find that I have plenty to do as it is. I think I shall like it much here now. I almost had the blues on Sunday evening. Mr Jamison was to my boarding place and spoke in rather a scolding way. Mr C was present while he spoke. he told me afterwards that he could hardly take it, and that he almost felt like saying, she shall stay no longer, but shall pack up and shall go right home with me. Yesterday Mr Jamison almost made up with kindness for the talk of Sunday evening. All saw right away that it would not do to have the two schools in the same room, so they sent carpenters right down to fix the upper room and are going to move the other school room. I did not mention that Miss Reeder has charge of the primary department. I open and close school with prayer as before, the directors told me that I was helmsman, and must guide the ship. I do not wish to have any control over the other department. Some are coaxing me to let them come back to my school. I scarly know how to do, I pity them, but I must let judgment and reason and not pity guide me. O! how I wish that I could induce these children to become christians.

February 9, 1860 On tuesday evening I went to the P.O. and was handed a neat little package, on opening it I found it to be S.E.C.s miniature[1] with a few lines telling me where he was &c. &c. and charging me not to allow any one to impose on *him*, refering to me. The dear soul. I does me good to look at his miniature only, and infinitely more to look on himself in reality. That miniature is the dearest little thing I ever saw, it is in such a pretty case too, and in my estimation not another man in the world could grace it to better advantage than he. He is good, pretty and smart. Yesterday the primary school was moved up stairs, and I had to change the seats of mine, both boys and girls wanted the same. I felt as though the girls ought to have their choice and acted accordingly, the boys got very angry about it. One, and by the way one that I am not sorry for, has not been here since. I hope he wont come again. The girls say he is a disgrace to the school. L. Grear the one that left spoke in an unbecoming manner to me, but I think he did it when angry, and I guess it is best not to be too touchy. Till evening all were good again, and the boys told the girls that they might have that side, and both sides joined together and cleaned the house and this morning I found quite another atmosphere in here.

February 12, 1860 On last Saturday we (our schools) had the rhetorical exercises public, quite a number of visitors came in, the house was crowded and the children did right well for the short time they had to prepare, After the exercises I went to have my miniature taken, but the chemichals were not in good order consequently the picture would not take well. I was quite tired and did not feel well, and consequently did not go to the division, was to the P.O. and received a letter from S.E.C.. a good and long one. Yesterday was to church and Sunday school. Mr. Horn preached a good sermon. This morning I went to school.   L. Grear is back to school, I was surprised to see him, he looks rather sheepish, as though he hated it that he acted as he did and I think he ought to feel ashamed. Mr Harry Ball is very sick. I hope he will be sorry for his bad deeds and never do so again

February 14, 1860 I went to the store on my way to the school this morning. Mr. Kaul was in, and as full of talk as ever, he told me about one of his nephews who was such a noble man, he said "John (his nephew) is a little fellow just about like that little man of yours," and then laughed rather knowingly, the mischief. Nobody believes him to be cousin, and I would not for all the world that he

---

1. The daguerreotype that Samuel mentions in his entry of Feb. 6, 1860.

were cousin. I also met R. Green one of the directors, who thought I ought to open my school a little earlier, But I just wont do it. I will leave first. These old directors need not think that I am going to be knocked round by them, just as they please. I am not going to be imposed on, by them, nor any one else.

February 20, 1860 Last thursday evening I was to hear Mr Philips from Easton Pa. lecture on the subject of marriage, It was right good. He gave us some good hints on the subject. He first spoke of the obstacles which should prevent a union, 1st Extreme poverty. 2nd Near relationship. 3rd Great difference in age. 4th Ignorance of Domestic Economy 5th,   . He also spoke of the opposition of Parents. He said if none of the above obstacles were in the way, and true genuine love existed between the parties, they should run off and get married, and if the ministers up here would not marry them, they should come to Easton, he would tie the knot so tight that no man could open it. He said many more things that I cant remember now, but he made out that if christians really love each other and are married, that they would have a little heaven on earth already. If it is not so, it ought to be. On Fryday evening my school went out sleighing, (some of them I mean) for when it came to the starting point some that were to give horses and sleighs backed out, so the boys had to say at home. It was too bad. I pitied them but could not help it. On Saturdy the Institute met in Shaws schoolhouse, I was to take a class there, but it snowed and stormed so that I could not go. Mr Moyer called in the afternoon to see me, we had quite a chat and made out that I would go along with him to Philadelphia and to Hilltown next week when he goes home. This morning Rich. Green one of the directors, and Mr Faulk were in to see my school. I almost hate those old directors. They as much as tell me that the children dont learn much. How do they know, how can they know, just coming in a few minutes in a month. Not for all Pa. would I teach here another term. If I will ever rejoice it will be when I get out of this place. But I am going to try to do my duty to the children and advance them as much as possible

March 2, 1860 Since I last wrote I have had quite a trip. Mr Moyer asked me to accompany him to the city when he went home. Last Saturday was his last day   in the evening he had told me he would be over for me in a carriage, he thought of course Rosenbergers folks would fetch me, but no indeed the roads were a little muddy, so they would not take their horses out.   he told them that I would stop my school, expecting to go along, but they would not do it.   I shall disown them as friends and would as relatives if it were posible. I could do only two ways, stay at home or walk, so I walked, the roads were so bad that it was almost imposible to navigate. but we got over it safely, but O! my feet were so sore that I could scarcely walk afterward, and are sore yet. On Sunday we went to Hilltown and in the evening to a wedding where two sisters were married the same day to distant cousins of mine. they made me think of heathen countries, for surely they did not act like civilized people. On Monday we went to Philadelphia on the market wagon. I caught a very bad cold, and was tired most to death. Took supper at a Hotel but staid overnight at a Mrs Alabach's   Tuesday, got me a blue silk dress, and a traveling dress for a particular occasion some time not very far hence, for dinner went to Mr Dersteins a cousin of my mother. I did not like it there. In the afternoon had my miniature taken for_____. Mrs D. talked about nothing but parties and how people praise her cooking &c.   I dont like such. In the evening I was to Methodist meeting but did not enjoy it much, went to Mrs. A's for the night   Wednesday Kate A. went with me to the public institutions. In the afternoon I started to Quakertown again, instead of going in a market waggon, I went on the cars. When I handed the conductor the money for my fair he tooked a little gold dollar that I handed him, and then handed it back saying, That is not good, I was beat for I had only money enough to take me home, but he told me to hand it to him some other time, and just laughed over it.   I was glad to get back. In the evening I mailed my miniature, also got such good letters from S.E.C.   If ever man loved, he does. I believe all he says is meant too. Today I had a very small school, only ten. I wish instead of six weeks I had only six days but these six weeks will not be without end. This is a delightful day.

March 21, 1860   This is a rough windy Morning. My school is going on like ever   two of the boys have been acting pretty bad.   one new one has come, and it seems he has come just to be troublesome. I am a little troubled to know just how to do. I fear I will have to have a regular row with him yet. How I hate such things, that is what makes schoolteaching such a horible business. My schollars are preparing for an exibition, they are in a great [s]tew about it. In three weeks from today we will have our last day, they are preparing to sing some too. I guess we will have quite a nice time.

March 24, 1860   This morning Dr Meredith and Mr Jamison were in my school. Jamison is finding fault nearly every time he comes. I feel just now as though I had rather leave the school than stay, but I fear it

74

would please them too well so I wont do it and I wont take much from them either. I would not teach school another summer on no considerations. I do not like this ruling of directors, nor faultfinding.

April 2, 1860   I am anxiously waiting for my school to close. In nine more days my term will close. I can hardly wait for the time to come. I count the days and almost the hours. Some days my school seems very pleasant—others again I get almost sick at the thought of staying yet another day. I have written my last letter for this town, I am going to wait to answer those I have till after I get home.

April 3, 1860   After school I was over to Mr Brunners to see that sick man, he is very sick, his disease is at the heart.   his head is also affected so that he is delirious all the time. I never saw anyone in greater distress than he seems to be. Today I had only ten scholars   this is the great moving week and so many have to stay at home to help, which affects my school very much. Quite a number of my schollars have moved away.[2] Yet seven days, O! ho but I am glad. After supper Mrs Grant and I went to Mr Kauls on a visit, but before going to Mr K's I went to the P.O. and got such a good letter from brother Amos[hh] from New York. Mr Smoo[k]er, assistant teacher at the Normal school had just returned. I had quite a talk with him. I tried my skill in playing on the Pianno forte, but it would not go very well having forgotten most of my pieces. I returned to my boarding place very much pleased with my visit. I love to look on that dear little miniature of Mr C's, he is my beau ideal of a true man.

April 4, 1860   It is rainy this evening but for all that, Mrs Grant and I went to Mrs Erdmans to see her flowers and got some very nice ones. After I got home I fixed my bonnet over a little so as to look fit to travel.

---

2. The common people, particularly those who rented in towns and cities, frequently changed their places of residence. Since virtually all leases in a given area expired on the same date, a "great moving week" took place once a year in most American towns and cities. Some of Rachel's students (the children of those moving within the Quakertown area) had to take a week off to help relocate their families, and others (the children of those seeking new opportunities or driven out by rising rents) disappeared from the school forever. For a delightful commentary on moving day in New York City in 1855, see William S. Walsh, *Curiosities of Popular Customs and of Rites, Ceremonies, Observances, and Miscellaneous Antiquities* (Philadelphia, 1897), p. 728. Marshall B. Davidson, *Life in America* (Boston, 1974), II, 365, reprints a contemporary painting of that same annual event.

April 5, 1860   This evening I was to Mrs Reeders for tea with Albina. I enjoyed my visit right well, she came over with me after tea. I got my viganette[3]   we then went to the P.O.   I got such a good letter again from S.E.C.   It is sweet to be loved. My school went a little better than common. I had a few more schollars. I brought the matter before the board frequently and this morning I felt as though my prayers were heard.

April 6, 1860   Today school was a little larger than usual, I mean than it has been this week. This has seemed the longest I ever spent, but I must fix my things to pack. Evening was to church. Mr Horn preached. Balinda Brunner her brother Charley and Mary Snyder were confirmed as the lutherans say, or as we would say joined church.

April 7, 1860   This forenoon I had but very few schollars, this afternoon a few more.   the girls attend pretty regular but the boys dont half come. O! but I wish that the last day were here. I can hardly wait till I can start for home. The hours seem to have grown three times their usual length. If my summer school is to be such a one like this I shall hope that I wont get it. After school, I with the whole school went to Taylors hill. Balinda Brunner went along. We had a pretty nice time. I do like my children that is, some of them, but Henry Grant I can not like, he is such a conceited little brat, and real ugly in the bargain. I mean ugly in actions. I am pretty tired this evening. I had quite a bunch of flowers to bring home, the children run up and down hills spying into every nook for flowers for me. Indeed I cannot help loving some of them. I do not know why the attendance is so slim. If it is my fault, God grant to help me remove the cause.

April 8, 1860   I have been to Sabbath school I suppose for the last time here. I got little testaments for my little Sabbath school class, the books of course are cheap as my means are too small to get nice ones, the parents of these children would be doubly able to get them but do not care enough about having their children learn them. Tomorrow evening those little ones are going to come to my room where I will have another opportunity to speak to them. O! that I could say but a few words that would induce some to become christians and be useful while they live. This forenoon I did not attend church it being so very rainy, but wrote a long letter to Mr. J. B. S. [?] in Canada. And

3. A head-and-shoulders photographic portrait characteristic of the 1860s; probably a replacement for the one mentioned on Feb. 12, 1860.

since I came back from Sunday school I read awhile in my pretty testament, which was presented to me by my intend liege lord, and then in my Ladies Reposatory,[4] and after that I indulged in a good cry on the thought of leaving the children. Although there may be some here who do not like me, still I know there are many who are my friends, the children nearly all, if not quite.

April 9, 1860 Still some who are to perform absent themselves I scarcely know what to think of them, but now today will tell whether we can have an exibition In the evening I was to Mrs Jacobys and from there to Sunday School teachers meeting, after S.S. meeting to Missionary meeting, had quite a chat with Mr. Smooker on the way home.

April 10, 1860 This morning I was up early and packing my trunks. I can hardly wait till the starting day comes. It is raining very hard this morning. I scarcely know how I shall get to the schoolhouse

[May 9], 1860 On the 11th of April My school had an exibition and a picnic after the exercises, the day was so rainy that we had to have it all in the house, quite a number of parents were out but not one director, both children and old folks seemed to enjoy it. the children spoke their pieces very well. Mr. J. Hunsperger from Hilltown and another man came up to see me yet before I left. I had quite a time in the evening to bid the little ones goodbye. Miss Reeder went with me to hand in my report and get my money which was all ready.

April 12, 1860 I started for home. My schollars went down to the depot to bid me farewell again, when I saw their tearful eyes I could not but weep too, strange feelings reigned. I was almost overjoyed at the thought of going home and still I was sad on account of leaving the children. I was not well the morning I started. I had to wait a long time at Allentown from there I went to Reading, changed cars, then to Lebanon. At Lebanon when the cars stopped and as soon as they had fairly stopped Job & Stephen Light were standing beside my seat trying to get me to go home with them.

4. *The Ladies' Repository: A Monthly Periodical Devoted to Literature and Religion* had been a popular journal since 1841. Published in Cincinnati and affiliated with the Methodist Episcopal church, it featured highly moralistic stories, usually by ministers. Mrs. Sigourney also wrote for this publication. In 1876 it was superseded by the *National Repository*. See Frank Luther Mott, *A History of American Magazines, 1741–1850*, vol. I (New York, 1930), p. 388.

being almost too sick to travel, it did not take much to persuade me to stay. I could eat no supper which seemed very hard to their good old mother. Quite a number called in to me.[5] Eleven Oclock came before I thought of it. the evening passed so pleasantly that I almost forgot that I was sick.

April 13, 1860 Fryday. Felt much better. eat a good breakfast, then went with Stephen to his store and then with Job to Isreal's Fathers and to J. Much's Fathers then in a round about way to Stephens store again, eat dinner, after which both of the boys went along to the depot—I was going to send a telegram to S. E. C. but it cost $1.50 I thought it would not pay, so I did not send one. The boys then took me on the roof of a large hotel to get a good view of town. at 11 Oclock I took my seat in the cars again, and was soon out of sight. I passed through the Lebanon valey, which is a delightful country. Arrived at Harisburg at one oclock, met Mr Will there had quite a talk with him, he gave me to understand that he was on his way to York to get a wife. he is a good fellow, if he did not tell me a story. if he did woe be to him. I talked with him bout two hours when the cars again wheeled me away. The scenery just west of Harisburg is delightful, nay grand, sublime, the mountains, the rivers and every thing in nature help to make it such. The bridge across the susquehanna is very pretty. Night overtook us before we got to the Aleghanies. between 1 and 2 at night we got into Pittsburg. I had taken a good nap already and did not feel any too well for being roused. I could not get water to quench my thirst, so I got me an orrange. could not eat it all at once, the conductor took me to the other cars where we had to wait nearly an hour at last we were off again and I again settled down for another nap. at day break we had just crossed the line and had got to the first station in Ohio. I raised my head to get a glimpse of the dear old state when lo! what a sight. it was snowing as fast as possible. the ground was white and every thing looked dismal, and the farther we went the more dismal it got, the low ground was covered with water leaving only the track out in many places. at some places scarcely that. the road was very much injured so that we had to go very slow. Stopped to take breakfast but it snowed so fast that none but the gentlemen could go out. On account of the bad roads we got behind time at Crest Line. I was much disappointed. I desired very much to get home that day. Another train was to leave at midnight

5. Some of the Light boys had boarded with the Bowmans while attending Otterbein.

which as we thought was the only one as we now thought to take us.[6] I bethought myself of the good dinner which was in preparation. My stomach too did not object to the idea for his wants had not been attended to for more than a day, but just as we were about to go to the table word came that a passenger car was to be annexed to the burden[7] train. Of course dinner went by the board. The traveling with the burden train was slow and tedious. arrived at Columbus at 8 P.M. I was so glad that I was so near home that my feet scarcely touched the pavement. I went to the Buckeye house, rung the bell, which brought the landlord. I enquired whether any one was there from Westerville waiting for a lady from the east "Yes Ma'm Mr. C——y is here, and has been here since Fryday, but he has retired so as to be ready to go to the depot by the time the night train arrives." Would you please tell him she is here. In a few minutes he came. More than a few questions were asked and answered, supper was ordered. After supper the carriage and horse were brought and we started enroute for home. That ride was the happiest I ever had. he is the dearest man. Surely none could fear to trust their keeping to him.

6. The travelers thought they would have to wait until midnight for the next passenger train.

7. I.e., freight.

VI
Frontier Farmmaking in Missouri
April 11–November 18, 1860

It was fairly standard procedure on the American agricultural frontier for a man to go west alone, select a farmsite, prepare the land, and build a house. Only then would he return to fetch his wife and family. This section of Samuel's diary recounts his efforts to follow that pattern. Like many of his fellow migrants, he goes to a specific place, a district where his prospective father-in-law had already bought land. And, again like many others, he gets a helping hand from those who went ahead, in this case the Bowmans' old friends the Kimmels.

April 11, 1860 Wednesday. A letter from Darling—My! but she's a Bird——Will soon be here now—will Dispatch me at Columbus—13th—Care Buckeye House.

April 13, 1860 Friday. Sim Whisler and I went to Columbus—Put up at Buckeye House—Did up Deaf and Dumb Asylum—But no telegram came[1]—at mid-night went to Depot. No honey came—and no news——

April 14, 1860 Saturday. Spend the day doing up the City—writing—and watching trains, for that "Miss Bowman" to arrive—Had seen the last likely train—and returned to my room to read and write til midnight train—when the words came to my room "A Lady calls for your name at the Office" "You will find her there now" and sure enough there was Miss Bowman—in a side parlor. Whom I for the first time greeted as "My Darling," and embraced with such a kiss of rapture.

We sat and talked a wee, and at 8 OCK took supper together. There at 9:30 P.M. we started for Westerville in The Bowman Family buggy—Arrived at 1 A.M. Sunday—After many Family greetings—Miss Rachel and I were left to ourselves, and a joyful time we had til 2 OCK—when we lovingly retired—each to our rooms——

---

1. See Rachel's entry for April 13, 1860.

April 15, 1860 Sunday. Of course I slept late, and at home all day— P.M. All in Parlor and dining room—a general good time. Evening Darling and I had The Parlor to ourselves—My inward and uppermost thought being "Oh! how sweet to love and to be loved"—11 OCK the time of "good nighting" came——

April 16, 1860 Monday. I present Darling with a watch—Do some packing preparatory to going—I spent much of the P.M. and evening with my Rachel in the Parlor—Every one seems to shape up so as to have us be alone much of the time—Right and Proper says I!

April 17, 1860 Tuesday. I finished packing—Enjoyed several hours more discussing future plans and appreciating each others love and affection——

P.M. Darling and I strolled down the plank road. We indulged in our old sport of target practice, She is becoming a real good shot with my pistol, much to my satisfaction, a Lady in the wild west needs to be——

We had an all around Family evening in the Parlor til 9 OCK when all withdrew, leaving Darling and me to interview on until 11 OCK—and we did most of our Good-bye-ing preparatory to my leaving in the morning for Missouri——

April 18, 1860 Wednesday. After a lot of tender adieus I left W. for Columbus—Then 1:55 P.M. left—For Lafayette Ind where I spent several days looking up some land interests for Father Bowman[aa]—I find his investments have been rather questionable as to outcome—I struck Jacksonville Ill Sat Eve—Put up at Dunlap House—

April 22, 1860 Sunday. Attended Prot. Epl. Church—not very inspiring

April 23, 1860 Monday. Hotel bill for 2 Beds & 3 meals $2.50—— Leave 5. A.M. reach Quincy 10:20 Cross Miss. River on Ferry— Change cars at Palmyra for Bavair at 3 OCK took Buss for Bloomington Macon Co. Mo—some 3 miles Put up at Bloomington House[2]—

April 24, 1860 Tuesday. Here I am in Missouri—A fine day—warm enough for Spring fever—and I really have the Blues awfully— Things here look so forbiding——

2. Bavair (Bevier) was on the recently completed Hannibal and St. Joseph Railroad. Bloomington, a thriving stage stop until the tracks bypassed it, was three miles to the north. *General History of Macon County, Missouri* (Chicago, 1910), pp. 55, 58.

I walk out to the Kimmel Home by 12 OCK—I am very kindly recd Had a nice dinner at 2 OCK— P.M. Mr. Kimmel and I walked over to Atlanta. I was introduced to John B and Sister Bell Kimmel and some others—The looks of the country pleases me pretty well—

I engaged a Surveyer to come tomorrow to Survey the Bowman[aa] land so as to be able to consider more certainly its locality and quality, and value——

April 25–26, 1860 Wednesday and Thursday. Father Kimmel John B and Doc helped, Each 1½ days—to Survey—for $1.50 each.

Evening—John—Sis—& I had a fine sing—and say! I wonder—in a whisper—what Darling is doing? God bless her and me too——

April 27, 1860 Friday. John and I went calf hunting and Fishing—I caught 6—John 8, made a fine mess—

P.M. wrote several hours giving B.B.B.[aa] an a/c of his lands and then to Darling a letter aglow with business, and love and hopes as to our future——

April 28, 1860 Saturday. Martin Atterberry showed me his 10 acre timber lot—and 40 acres of Prarie—I like the location and looks of both—Spent the evening with the Kimmels reading, singing and in general sociability, and withal religiously. So this week ends real satisfactorily.

April 29, 1860 Sunday A.M. Read, wrote meditated—prayed, and P.M. went along with The Kimmels to prayer meeting—I led it—It was a good spiritual service, a real waiting on the Lord—Evening! My first sunday evening in Missouri closes up quite satisfactorily all around——

April 30, 1860 Monday. I start in, landlooking, in good earnest, and am arranging to get down to business establishing a Home for Darling and me

May 3, 1860 I have settled down to be at home with the Kimmels for the summer—They board me and wash for me for six dollars per month—

May 4, 1860 I closed in with Martin Atterberry for his Forty acres of Prairie East of Atlanta, and ten acres of Timber west—for Five Hundred Dollars Cash—and now comes the fencing of the Prairie,

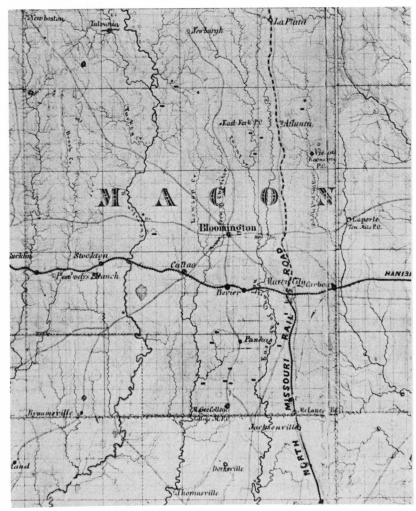

Map of Macon County, Mo., as it appeared when Samuel bought his farm-stead near Atlanta. Detail from John T. Fiala and Edward Haren, Jr., *A New Standard Map of the State of Missouri* (St. Louis, 1860). Maps Division, LC.

and the building of a House—A Cage—for my prospective Bird—My assured Darling Birdie——

May 6, 1860 Sunday. Slept til 7. Write letter to Darling in A.M.— P.M. went to Prayer meeting—I conducted it—Pap Kimmel seems to think I must do about all the leading—It proved to be an excellent service—Thus my second Sunday ends quite satisfactorily in Old Missouri.

May 7, 1860 Monday. John B. Kimmel agrees to work for me the summer for Eighteen dollars per month and board himself—at home——We started making rails to fence my 40—I made 50 ten foot rails—all but 7—and 10 ground chunks—which we called equal to 7 rails so my 1st days railmaking was 50 "from the stump"—while John made 95——100 is called a fair days work—we took it easy the first day.

May 9, 1860 Wednesday. My hands some stiff—but soon limbered up, So today I made 80 and John 100—Eve wrote letter to Darling—

May 10, 1860 Thursday. Surveying in A.M.— P.M. I made my 50 rails in ½ a day—So I am really already capable as a chopper and splitter in this Missouri White Oak timber——

May 13, 1860 Sunday. Organization At 10 A.M. Rev Burns preached in S.H.—I handed in my certificate of Membership— P.M. we organized a Union S.S.[3] They Elected me Superintendent so now I am in the harness Rev Burns all night with us—another good Sabbath in Mo—

May 16, 1860 Monday John and I made 213 rails Tuesday 15′ 240 and Wednesday 16′ 255—and spent the evening singing and chatting at the little Kimmel Home—

May 17, 1860 Thursday. I soon acquired the ability to do as much rail-making as John, and so we kept no separate count as we did at first—Soon will have enough for the fence.

May 20, 1860 Sabbath. Our S.S. opens up nicely today—and the Pr. meet'g was good——

---

3. Sunday School.

May 21, 1860   Monday. Rail hauling has been going on some days. Mr. Still, John K, and I "lay up" fence all day——This tires me more than splitting—or chopping—

May 23, 1860   I have decided on building an Octagonal house, using "Grout" for the walls[4]—

May 24, 1860   Thursday. This is my Birthday—22—worked all day industriously—Anti-snake day. Enroute to the woods I killed a rattlesnake with 9 rattles—and in P.M. a black snake 4½ feet long—

May 29, 1860   Started team at Prarie-breaking—Tiny Atteberry dropped corn for 30¢ a day—Will break up 20 acres.

June 3, 1860   Sunday. A.M. John and I walked to Hatters S. H.[5] to organize a Singing School—a poor go—Left appointment for next Sat. a week—4 P.M.— P.M. we had our S.S. and singing exercises—A good turnout, and interesting time—

June 5, 1860   Tuesday. John Harper helps me stake off my House or cellar, and start the diging.

June 6, 1860   Wednesday. My throat and mouth are ailing—Strong indications of sore throat again. Cankered sore throat. I assist in Cellar diging as I am able——
 My trunk arrives from Westerville—Besides my other things, it has ½ bushel of Potatoes, and a bunch of flowers from Darling—I studied their language—Oh! such love, such devotedness—I think so much of darling these days when so unwell—and starting The Home—I yearn for deeper religious life——

June 7, 1860   Thursday. Not well—So am not doing much—Wrote over an hour to Darling in A.M.—At noon got a letter from my precious one. Oh! such a good one, with more flowers and other xpressions of love and endearment——

4. Cormany is attracted by the ideas of the Fowler brothers and the other reformers whose notions the Fowlers popularized. In *A Home For All, or the Gravel Wall and Octagon Mode of Building* (Fowlers and Wells, 1853), Orson S. Fowler extolled the advantages of eight-sided houses (more direct sunlight, better ventilation, and efficient floor plans) and the virtues of grout (a cementlike mixture of sand, gravel, stones of varying sizes, and lime, which was poured wet between wooden forms and covered with plaster). See also Carl F. Schmidt, *The Octagon Fad* (Scottsville, N. Y., 1958).
5. School House.

June 9, 1860 Saturday. My mouth and throat ill—Confided in Sister Bell Kimmel. Showed her Darlings likeness—

June 10, 1860 Sabbath. A.M. wrote to Darling— P.M. our S.S. and Singing practice comes off nicely—My throat in bad condition—Places for singing opening up——

June 11, 1860 Monday. Throat improving—Letter from my Mother[b], and one from Darling—for whom I realize—my love grows stronger—as the time draws nearer when I shall be united with her forever—I feel it is so now.

June 17, 1860 Sunday. Experience meeting at S.H. at 9:30—People much moved—10:30 Rev Michael preached a pretty good sermon—I dined at McGiltens—at 3:30 P.M. Rev Beckwith preached well. Evening Rev Burns preached—Good attendance, People very attentive—I enjoy services well——

June 22, 1860 Friday. Quarrying Stone. Excavating for Cellar & foundation & cistern goes on—Cistern nearly done—I am needing more money from Bro John[d]—and more religion too, to enable me to wear this world and its cares as a loose garment, and to avoid all worry over what I cannot avoid——

July 1, 1860 Am kept from S.S. etc on a/c of a sore foot—Wrote most of day to Darling—Sister Ella[y]and in our S.S. Record——

July 2, 1860 Monday. Carpenter Brooks offers to work on my house for one at $1.00 per day and board himself——

July 4, 1860 Wednesday. Slight celebration—Harvesting for Pap Kimmel—Hauling lumber, stone, &c&c the order of the passing days— Eve. in meditation and prayer my soul obtained such a gracious uplift—I am so happy! and my Rachel is so precious to me and seems so near——

July 12, 1860. Brooks works on Frames & cellar, stone hauling goes on—and each employee is faithfully doing his part towards putting up our Home—

July 15, 1860 Sunday. Sunday School becomes more and more interesting—Our new Library is such a luxury—Have each reader of a Book relate some point or points obtained—Proves real interesting—Receive some good reports——

July 16, 1860 Monday. Work goes on nicely   a busy week on cellar wall—John and I help Pap K on haying one day—

July 24, 1860 Darlings letter fails to come, Saddens me a good deal—I wrote her one all the same—and one to Mr. Bowman[aa]——

July 29, 1860 Sunday. Fine S.S. and good singing after—Took long walk with Bell. She is an interesting girl—made me to long so for my Darling—

July 30, 1860 Monday. Brooks busy on Door and window frames—and John and I on grout wall are just fairly started on it—So much work finishing up Cellar for the beginning of wall——

August 4, 1860 Saturday. P.M. a pretty satisfactory weeks work— Eve. Singing School. Good—I escorted Bell to an from—called in at Semen Atteberrys—I met Sally Ann Atteberry. The Lady J.B.K is in love with, but Father is mad opposed, I find Bell a good confidant & Sister—

August 5, 1860 Sabbath. Interesting S.S. and fine Sing after—Eve I held the tin for Bell to milk the Cow—Later we had a family sing— Good time—After all The thought of my Darling Rachels loving me makes me happy as nothing else on earth——

August 7, 1860 Tuesday. My Cistern becomes a well—Seeing dampness in the cementing at the side next the house near the bottom, I drilled outward, and struck a weak vein last evening, and this morning found 5 or 6 barrels of water in my well for use in my building work and for our Home. Brooks busy on Joist, Rafters &c. John and I on beginnings of wall——Meditations—I have this day resolved to live a more happy life, and not allow things which I cannot avoid to trouble me so much—I resolve to be a better Christian—Oh! for a good heart! Temporally I am so well, and spiritually I should be, and I will be by the grace of God—

August 10, 1860 I have decided to build only one Story in height.

August 13, 1860 Completed the cellar wall—and now it must stand a few days to settle and dry—Then we continue the grout wall upward. The Grout consists of sand stone any size, sand & lime to fill all interstices—we use the sheeting lumber and 2 × 4 studding, and rafters for boxing—leaving one foot space between for thickness of wall—filling in 4 or 5 feet height at a time, then allow several days for hardening before putting more on top———

August 16, 1860 Saturday. I delivered a private message for John B. K—to Miss Sarah Ann A.—and told her I wished to speak to her in the evening—Evening I escorted Miss S. A. to an from writing class—Had a fine chat Made her my confident as to my arrangements for the future, and assured her that I was willing to be a helper in any way, between her and John B. K—

August 26, 1860 Sunday. Wrote all A.M. for Darling. She writes me such great good letters—am very happy— P.M. went to S.S. Good time—Gallanted S.A.A. to Mr. Stills for a "Melon-eating" Took supper with the Atteberrys—Eve escorted S.A.A. ("Sally") to and from pr. meet'g—Gave her a letter from John—and carried one from John to "Sallie."

August 29, 1860 Wednesday. Eve. Escorted Sallie to writing school—some suspicion leaks out that I escort Sallie for John—Mrs Kimmel so mad she wont let Bell go—Later she understands and is reconciled—

August 31, 1860 Friday. Work has gone on finely—and we now put on the Joists and fill in between them nicely—So the completion seems nearing—

September 15, 1860 Roof on and about finished—but the work drags some. Brooks seems to lie on his job somewhat———
    A trowel fell into the Cistern—I undress—wash, and dive to the bottom and bring it up—a Cool job———

September 22, 1860 I see I cannot be ready to go East as soon as I had intended—Receive O such a good letter from Darling. I feel awfully badly on A/C of having to disappoint my Rachel—
    Hi! Ho! Johns, Sallies & my affairs have been figured out by Zeph A (I hope he keeps cool) Work on my House goes slowly—a little draggy—

October 6, 1860 My money fails to come promptly—Two letters from Pet. O that I know how to answer her satisfactorily—
    Eve had a confidential consultation with John and Bell on my affairs———

October 8, 1860   Completing the Cage for my Bird goes on slowly—I resolve to try to borrow money so I can go for my Darling as soon as she gets ready for me to come.

October 9, 1860   Martin Atteberry is willing to go my bail, if I need to borrow money—Thank God for good friends—I am somewhat more happy—
Evening—Recd check for $100.

October 13, 1860   a good singing—I escorted Sallie—all night—for John—Letter from Darling & Sister Ellie[y] this Eve.

October 14, 1860   House now about done, and the surroundings graded up—

October 16, 1860   Brooks' child dies   They feel it sorely—I assisted about getting ready for burial—

October 21, 1860   Sabbath. I feel so badly because John B.K. has measurably lost confidence in me.   11 A.M. Rev. Burns preached a very good sermon for us—Evening preached again, real good, gave universalism Fits—Bell and I saw Sallie home. Then we had a long talk on Johns and my affairs.

October 23, 1860   Tuesday. Dug Potatoes—scrubbed the 2 back rooms. Then helped Sol Moore thresh Buckwheat—Evening two letters from Darling—The day of our nuptials is now set for Nov 27th—The letters are so good. How dearly I do love her—Soon now we will be happy in each others embrace and practically each the others—

October 25, 1860   Thursday. Sol & I cleaned up 40 Bushels of Buckwheat—I put into our cellar Potatoes
4 bu Peach Blows
1–¾ bu Neshannooks
5 Bu Semens Tubers[6]
Eve small Pr. meeting

October 26, 1860   Friday. Eve—John & I have acquired a better state of feelings for some reason—Spent the evening singing in the home—a happy little band.

6. Popular varieties of potatoes.

October 27, 1860 Saturday. Busy day—I am not well—and need more holiness of heart and life—Eve a good singing & pleasant time——

October 28, 1860 Sabbath. Wrote most of A.M. for Darling—Time shortens when we shall be together instead of writing and longing to be—Had a fine Sabbath School—and singing afterwards—went to McGiltons to tea—Had a fine talk on religion with the Old Gentlemen and George.

Evening had a good little Pr. M'tg—I led it—only Bell, John & I led in prayer—

October 29, 1980 I scrubbed my room and Kitchen—Laid a floor for Corn Crib—Cut poles for it—

Eve wrote letter for Pet—

October 30, 1860 Hauled stuff for crib—Snapped some corn—Letters from Bros John[d]and Bernard[q]—am pretty well and happy—In 4 weeks I will be a married man—How I do long to see my Rachel and be with her to stay.

October 31, 1860 Wednesday. Hauled in Corn—J.B.K. and John Storm had a fight—

Eve escorted Bell to Pr. Met—

November 1, 1860 Thursday. I worked for Kimmels—I am pretty well temporally and spiritually   I feel the importance of doing more towards saving the Souls of my fellowmen——

November 3, 1860 Saturday. A fine letter from Darling—She still has the idea in mind that we should spend our honeymoon in Canada. In fact spend the winter there, as she has so many kindred there whom she has not seen for a long wile, and then too going to Missouri to start our new life, it would likely be a long while when things would be as favorable for a visit as right after the wedding. So I approve, and she will be very happy to learn the fact.

November 4, 1860 Sunday A.M. Wrote Darling to plan affairs with the view of our visiting Canadian friends right after the Wedding. Wrote her a long letter—   P.M. Did not go to S.S.—Evening went to Pr meeting—We had a good service—Oh! that I might be enabled to do something to induce some of these dear young folks to become Christians and Oh! That my Darling were here now——

November 6, 1860 Tuesday. John Kimmel and John Storm start for Iowa—I gave Storm hail for revealing my secrets—John Kimmel and I kissed on parting—How sorry I am to lose the companionship of such a good friend—John and I have made peace—and he has written Sally—and recalled certain things—wherein he found that he was mistaken as pertained to his Sally and me. Poor fellow, it was hard, tho it was for him, and their interests that I was in Sallys company quite often.

November 7, 1860 Wednesday. Bell is at Sols—"Sis" has a baby girl—P.M. I went over—was so glad to see Sister Bell—Our Kimmel home seems real lonely with John in Iowa, and Bell at Sals—Eve quite a lot of young folk at Pr. mt'g—But so few to pray—

November 12, 1860 Am busy touching up things for my going— Martin Atteberry offered me the money I need to go to Ohio, provided mine dont come from Brother John[d] in Penna.

November 13, 1860 Have my Corn Cribbed— Received my box of goods, and leather from home. am glad for it—I meditate so much on my future—The Ministry is impressed on me a great deal—From nine years of age I have studied my Bible a great deal—and read many religious works—and spent much time reading and studying Matthew Henrys Commentary so as to be versed in Scripture[7]—

November 14, 1860 Pulled Turnips—have 10 bushels fine ones— Later burried them—Covered by Potatoes in the Cellar and the pumpkins & squashes, So they can't freeze even if I did not come back with My Darling til near Spring—

November 18, 1860 Sunday A.M. wrote Darling 3 sheets of a letter, as the last one, til I meet her face to face.
    Evening had a good prayer and class meeting—I had good liberty, and feel that some impressions were made on the people—

---

7. Matthew Henry's *Exposition of the Old and New Testaments* (1708–1710). Note the parallel to Rachel's ruminations about the possibility of becoming a missionary. The agonizing desire to serve society in some visible or overtly religious fashion was characteristic of the evangelical temperament.

VII
Rachel Waiting for Her Wedding
April 13–November 27, 1860

Rachel has just returned from Quakertown in the spring of 1860 as this section begins. Faced with the prospect of several months of lonely waiting while Samuel is in Missouri, she decides to teach another term of school to support herself and to pass the time until her wedding. She accepts a post in the rural district of Worthington, Ohio, only a few miles west of her parents' home in Westerville. Part of her compensation involves room and board in the homes of her students, and the result is an inside view of village life in the Old Northwest on the eve of the Civil War.

April 13, 1860 It was past midnight when we got home. As soon as my voice was heard Mother[bb] and Father[aa] were out. After having talked with them awhile I went from room to room to see the rest of the family. Lea[jj] and her husband[kk] were at home too, on a visit. Next day (Sabbath) I was not at all well. I had taken cold, could scarcely talk loud. I had quite a time greeting the acquaintances. Mr. J. Kumler called in the afternoon to see me. I had quite a talk with him, but it hurt me to talk so I had to be excused, went to the Parlor, was not there long till S.E.C. came. it did not hurt me to talk with him, the wee hours were not far off when we adjourned. If ever mortal loved I think, nay know that he loves me. during the day on Sabbath I kept my bed awhile. he feared I was ill, and looked like he was sick too. Monday morning I was not any better, they wanted me to take a cold water sweat. I took one and in the course of an hour I could speak loud again, but I did [not] sweat. consequently, my cold did not get much better.[1] S had intended to start for Mo. and tuesday morning, but he put it off another day. The evenings were very pleasantly spent in the parlor. On those eventful evenings the day on which I should no longer be R. Bowman but

---

1. A cold water sweat, one of the standard therapies of hydropathic medicine, involved wrapping the patient in a cool damp sheet which was in turn covered with several layers of blanket. The patient remained thus bundled for perhaps an hour. The technique was used primarily to reduce fevers. Russell T. Trall, *Hand-Book of Hygienic Practice: Intended as a Practical Guide for the Sick-Room* (New York, 1864), p. vii.

Mrs. S.E.C. also who was to perform the ceremony. Where we would go on the wedding tour, or in country style where the infore should be. conclusion. At Elmira C. W. and from there to Misouri, where our place of residence will be. On Wednesday morning he started away, when no one could see me I could not keep the tears back, but when with the rest I cut up worse than usual. Such is the teaching we get from the cold world. The straight jacket which custom compels us to wear is horible. Lea[jj] and Clem[cc] staid till the following Wednesday when they went away too. After they had all gone I commenced cutting and fitting dresses in earnest. Mother[bb] had so much sewing to do that I worked just as fast as I could. I should have written before this that most of my lady friends have called on me. Miss Gilbert was to see me too. On the first of may Pappa[aa] took me over to my school but the house was not ready for me so I went along home again and staid till the next monday when Mr. Gardner, one of the directors came for me and took me along. I should have written before that I was to Columbus on the 5th of May to be examined. I received a certificate for 18 months.[2]

May 12, 1860 I have now been teaching one week. My school is small. I have only fifteen on the list. I think I shall like the school very much there are a few who I think will need to be reproved pretty often. I have got along well so far. I like some of the children very much. I am getting along finely too with my sewing. I have a good bid to sew these few weeks that I shall stay. I had a good letter from Mo. It is settled now I suppose that if life be spared that Mo. will be my future home. I almost grew sick at heart at the thought of going so far, but still with[al] I shall feel better at home with Saml. there, than with any other man even if I should dwell in the richest pallace in the highest style. Even if poverty and hardships should be my lot, I would go with him rather than live anywhere else without him. He is indeed more than life to me. I should not wish to live were he taken away, unless I could do some good in the cause of religion

May 15, 1860 Yesterday evening I went to old Father Gardners where I expect to board this week.[3] The old lady is very corpulent, weighs about two hundred. the old gentleman is very slim both are very pleasant. The two daughters at home are rather odd look-

2. Although this entire entry was dated April 13, Rachel obviously wrote most of it in May.

3. It was a common practice at this time for those families with children in the school to take turns providing room and board for the teachers.

ing girls, the one is always trouble with sore eyes. After tea, the girls took me out into the grove along a very pretty stream, then up the hill to the cymetery, which is not very large nor pretty. In the evening all the family with myself were seated round the little stand sewing and telling stories. I learned in the course of the evening, by their conversation that I was to a regular underground depot.[4] They told me that many had passed through there, took refreshments and changed cars. The old gentleman is so consciencious in using any thing made by slave labor that he does not use any of the southern cotton material for clothing, but gets cotton at the quaker settlement, and for shirts wears course linnen.[5] They are religious, have prayers Mornings and evenings, which seems quite good. They are great folks to tell stories. I judge they are great readers. I thought surely this evening I should get a letter from Mo. but none came. Surely this evening one will come.

May 16, 1860 Was to Worthington this morning with Miss Gardner in her carriage. Stopped at the P.O. got a letter from Mo. that had been there some time, it was advertised already, which seems strange, for some one inquired every evening except last evening S.E.C. has bought a tract of land and is preparing to build a house. &c &c &c.   Evening, scrubbed the School house. I helped till all the desks and seats were washed off. I then thought surely they can now finish, but they got stubborn so I went back again, some had started to go home, but I brought them back and made them work. just as we were nearly through, two Lewis girls came to scold their little sisters for staying to help. I felt badly. I wanted to go home.

May 17, 1860 This is another fine morning, every thing went off very well so far, only that I am not very well. Evening Misses P & A Gardner and I went out on the R. R.   the brakesmen threw kisses at us which almost insulted us.

---

4. I.e., of the underground railroad, the quasi-covert network of antislavery sympathizers who helped escaped slaves make their way to safe areas of the North or to Canada. One of the "trunk lines" ran through the Worthington-Westerville area. Wilbur Henry Siebert, *The Mysteries of Ohio's Underground Railroads* (Columbus, 1951), pp. 170–71, mentions the Gardners specifically.

5. It was widely believed by antislavery reformers that if people would refuse to buy slave-produced goods, slavery itself could not survive. Only the Quakers acted upon the idea: they established the American Free Produce Association and operated stores that stocked only nontainted merchandise. See Ruth Ketring Nuermberger, *The Free Produce Movement: A Quaker Protest Against Slavery* (New York, 1942).

May 18, 1860 It is rather cool today and cloudy. it rained a little this morning, but so little that the dust was not laid. we need rain very much. it is so dry.

May 21, 1860 Monday morning, at school again. On Fryday evening as expected, our folks came for me. Israel, Job, Jacob Light & J Much with our horse and little waggon. we had quite a nice time. did not get home till dark. first I was told, was that they had the itch and I being tormented with the hives as I thought, was tormented with the itch instead.[6] Somebody brought it to town and set the whole borrough on fire with it. I felt provoked, but did for it all I could. am not rid of it yet though. I have brought some stuff along to cure it. It is awful. I fear some of the children will get it. I slept with two girls last week. they will get it I know and I cant bear to tell them of it. I knew nothing of it. I never dreamed of such a thing as itch or I should not have asked them to sleep with me. I trimmed the little girls bonnets on Saturday. Sunday I could not go to church on account of this old tormented stuff I wrote letters and read all day. I wrote to S.E.C. his trunk was sent off this morning. I put a lot of scraps, papers &c. with potatoes in.[7] I had a letter from S.E.C. when I got home he has been working very hard, his hands had got so sore that he could hardly hold the pen, poor fellow. I guess he nearly works himself to death to get ready to come back in the Fall. Evening. Went to a new boarding place. Mr. Carters. I saw before I dismissed school that it was going to rain I hurried them through with their lessons and dismissed them, but it began to sprinkle. I started as soon as I could get ready with Nettie Carter for her home. we got about half way when it began to hail. we went in to the nearest house and waited till it stopped hailing. we then started on in all the rain. it was very muddy but we finally got to Mr. Carters, it blew and rained so that I could scarcely get into the house. "Racher hard introduction said the old gentleman. "Why we did not expect you this week," chimed the old lady, I was wet, tired, muddy, and it was raining, but I just felt like packing up and being off, but I thought I would not please them enough to go. After making about five thousand apologies they became rather pleasant. I staid from Monday till Fryday May 28. On

6. The itch referred to any psora or contagious skin eruption, of which the two most common were mite-born scabies and the so-called straw mattress dermatitis. William A. N. Dorland, *Dorland's Illustrated Medical Dictionary*, 25th ed. (Philadelphia, 1974), pp. 805, 1381; Robley Dunglison, *A Dictionary of Medical Science* (Philadelphia, 1868), pp. 532, 807.

7. Its safe arrival in Missouri was noted in Samuel's diary, June 6, 1860.

Fryday evening after school Mr. Carters took me home. their little girl Nettie went home with me, they had their mule to take us home, the first ride I had after [i.e., behind] mules. I had a pleasant time at home, got ever so many letters, one from Ellen Norah Cormany[y] her letter was short but good for the first one.[8] I went to church Sabath afternoon. Pres. Owen preached.[9] My mind was not in a frame to listen good. I fear sometimes that it is too much taken up with Samuel. One thing I know if he were taken from me that I would never be of much account, for my whole heart seems bound up in him. I do not wish to make an idol of him to worship more than God. I should fear greatly that he would be taken from me if I should, but he is next to God. I love him as I never loved before, with a devotion that seemed to me to be impossible. J. A. Kumler called to see me on Sabath evening, he told me many things, he seems to put almost unbounded confidence in me, he told me of his engagement and disappointment. I pity the man. I think him to be a real good fellow we took a stroll to the cymetery. I like to talk to him. i told him of my engagement. Monday Morning Father[aa] brought us over to Worthington, we walked from there, it is about 2 miles. I got very tired. When I got to Mr. Gardners they handed me two letters. One from S. E. C. such a long good one. I love to get letters from him, better than from any one else. It seems too that his whole life seems to be centered in me. It is sweet to love and be loved, it seems to me we are less selfish when we really love some one, our aim then is not to live for ourselves, but for the one we love. I often wonder why I do not put that implicit confidence in my Redeemer like I do in S.E.C. It must be because the one I see, the other I cannot see, and I am too faithless to trust without seeing. I have a fine boarding place this week, the people are very pleasant. I know I shall like it there. I like my school too. I feel at home among the children. God help me to do my duty. I have been writing to Ellie Cormany.[y]. I am going to send her a big letter School did not go very well today, the children did not have their lessons good. I am going to make them get their lessons better.

June 1, 1860 It is quite cold this morning. I came over from home and got quite chilly. On Wednesday evening after I went to my boarding place (Mr Carpenters) there was a second cousin to Mr Carpenter there to ask the yoing folks to his sisters wedding. Ma-

8. Samuel's younger sister was fourteen years old.
9. The Reverend Alexander Owen, president of Otterbein, 1858–1860. Garst, *Otterbein*, p. 306.

rinda was to be bridesmaid, and if she would not, Joab was to bring some lady to be bridesmaid, they got at me to go. I thought I could not go on account of my school, and I had nothing to wear that suited me for a wedding. I bethought myself. I made out to have plenty to wear, if I took my graduating dress, I told him then that the children would go to the school house and would not know what the matter could be, he would see to that he said if that was all, and started off for a horse, and to send word to the schollars, it was about six Oclock till we got off, we (Joab and I, Marinda and Geo. Comstock) started almost by telegraph speed.   got to Westerville in a short time. I changed my clothes and packed up some to take along, and then we were off again   stopped at the store to get a belt for M.   got to Mr Comstocks after ten Oclock, a distance of sixteen miles or more. It was not long till we found ourselves in bed, the rest of the family had all retired before we arrived. First we knew in the morning was the entrance of the bride expectant to tell to walk out to breakfast.   but before we could do that we had walk out of bed and don our garments. When we got out to &, behold if it was not raining real hard. M & I had a little fixing to do (pressing our dresses &c &c) Joab got out the pony and took me to Sunbery to see the place. I enjoyed my rides very much.   M. & J. sat in our room telling stories and talking till time for dinner, when they brought us a piece,   we were in another room then talking with all till the man came. we went and dressed then. Just as I got through, Mr. Carpenter came and told me that he and I were to be gromsman & bridesmaid   What arrangements thought I to myself, but I dared not refuse.   we marched up stairs where the groom and bride were to make some better arrangements. They did not seem to know anything how to do. What a time thout I to myself, but got arranged prety soon and then marched on down. A Justice of the peace performed the ceremony. All sat round the room as we entered, we took the seats reserved for us and sat there awhile when the justice asked whether the party were waiting on him, the gromsman answered, he then stepped forward and told us to rise to our feet.   we did so, he next asked whether there were any objections to these being joined in the holy bonds of matrimony.   none. "Jine your right hands." (done) Will you have this woman to be thy wedded wife if so,——, (The man made a low bow) Will you have this man to be thy wedded husband, if so——(the lady bowed) Inasmuch: he then looked on the floor and got a little red and then said, "I am not used to say this ceremony. I have forgotten it.   but I have it wrote it down on a bit of paper in my pocket." and so saying he pulled out the paper and read off the rest of the ceremony. After the usual congratulations were over we all started to take a ride so as to give room to the cooks. I had to laugh as soon as we got out for it seemed so comical, we went about a mile and back, but supper was not ready yet so we took another, supper was till we got back, the supper was very nice, but all seemed to be bashful. I told the groomsman that he would have to carve the chicken, he did so, every one pitched and commenced eating as fast as they could. I waited till the chicken was carved, they did not have spoons in any thing so we could not get many of the nice things, the cake and pie were cut in the illest way I ever heard of. Supper over, we changed our dresses, and started on home, the whole company went along a piece. It was a cold dreary day, and every little bit it would rain a little. We got to Westerville just at dusk, in a pretty smart rain, Mr C. had his horse put up and he and Miss C. staid there till next morning. In the morning bright and early we started for my school. All the schollars did not come, they feared there would be no school

June 4, 1860 Nothing of any consequence happened since then. Yesterday I took my second ride after mules. I went with Mr Carpenter to Sunday school up country, in Hardscrable. Rainy. Dismissed school at the usual time, but it rained so that the children could scarcely get away. I had them fixed out, and had them sent, and was just going out myself when Mr. C jr came along with his teem to take us home, he was at the door in a minute to gallant me to the wagon. I gave my umbarella to some of the little girls so I went in the rain, the mules scared and run off which made the mud fly in every direction. I was so muddy and wet that I had to wash out my dress. Every one had to strip. Joab not excepted. I think he is one of those true hearted gentleman, but notwithstanding his good qualities he is not My Samuel, nor could he ever fill his place.

June 5, 1860 It is rainy yet. I am going to stay at Mr Gardners the rest of the week, so as to have my Sunday house at Mr Carpenters.

June 6, 1860 It is cold and cloudy this morning again. I if we would not get to make our expected visit. I do not care so much for the visit as for the strawberries. This morning Mr J. Carpenter sent me a nice boquette of roses and rose buds and a slipp of paper with the names of the roses, Hail Columbia. he is getting rather fresh, wonder if he aint going to fall in love. Evening. I let out school nearly an hour sooner. I saw that a storm was coming. The children had no more tha[n] got home if the[y] hurried, and some scarcely that till it began to rain hard. It rained very hard for some time, then began to hail.

The storm continued for several hours. Such a fearful raging of elements is not often seen, the ground was almost covered with hailstones, some of which were nearly as large as hickery nuts. The rain prevented me to fulfil my intended visit. After tea I wrote a letter for Susan Alston (a colored girl) to her friends who are still held in bondage in N. C. Also engaged her to help us a week at the time I am going to leave home.

June 7, 1860 Was up early, after taking a good bath and completing my plain toilette I seated myself by the half raised window and burried myself in some good pieces in the L[adies] Repository. I do love that magazine. The reading is so solid and yet quite spicy too. While sitting there a little bird came and sat in the open window but as soon as it espied me it flew away. After breakfast I started pretty soon to the school house so as to be there in time to make up the hour for yesterday, but it began to rain before I got there, and rained pretty hard for some time, which detained the children for some time but at last they came in all the rain. It was damp and cool, so we had a fire built. Thina Gardner is one of the most awkward and disagreeable of all human beings I ever saw. If any of the children get near her, she will be sure to knock them over. Inkstand and flowerpots, if within reach will be kocked over, and that is not all, she is always so dirty and slovenly looking that a look is enough set a bodys stomach in an uproar. Let me be never so hungry, only one look at her takes all appetite away.   and an other thing, she has no more manners than an insolent sneaky cat. For all this I do not blame her so much as her folks, who ought to have taught her better. She always has sore eyes which makes them let her go as she pleases more. Evening was to choir meeting at Worthington, with Mr Carpenters. I had promised them for more than a week to go with them some time. I was staying with Mr W. Gardners, on account of the rainy weather. Joab came over after me in a carriage. I went along to his home to wait until they got ready, he drove all round town for me to see it. The choir met at the ladies Seminary.[10] They sing pretty well, but I had heard better singing before. Marinda and I left before they got through, and went up into one of the young ladies room to visit. It was past eleven Oclock when we got back to Mr Carpenters. Joab tried his best to get orranges for us, but

---

10. This seminary, chartered in 1839, was the first Methodist school for women in the Midwest. The building Rachel visited had been dedicated in 1842. Frank Corbin, *A Walking Tour of Old Worthington: First Center of Culture in Central Ohio* (privately published, 1969), pp. 78–80.

The Worthington Seminary where Rachel heard the local choir. Detail from John Graham, *Map of Franklin County, Ohio, from Actual Survey and Records* (Philadelphia, 1856). Maps Division, LC.

there were none to be had in town so he got candies and fed us on those. Mrs. W. Gardner speaks of Mr C's folks in such a way that I scarcely know whether to go with them or not. I have been trying to find out of the children what they were thought of and concluded they were fully as well thought of and as respectable as Mr. Gardners, I rather think Mrs G is rather to fault finding

June 8, 1860   I have just closed school. As I had written the above, Sis and Mr Light came. I put by my writing. Sis came in.   Mr L. went to Mr Carpenters with the horse and had it put up.   then, he, Joab & Marinda came back to the schoolhouse, we all started to the creek to gather gooseberries. We wandered along down the stream a good piece but did not find many berries. We came to very high banks. Sis & J. Dickson had got tired and sat down under a tree to rest while the rest of us clambed the bank. It was very high. I got very tired, but after we got to top we were well paid. We stood under a large oak tree.   on the other side were the high banks.   a little to the south was a deep ravine.   way down was the silvery stream rippling along. Sis and Miss D were down by the stream and their merry laugh came up to us borne by the gentle breeze. We wandered along till evening when we all returned to Mr Carpenters, had supper, but I had got so tired that I was quite sick. At 9½ Oclock we started home, got there at midnight.

June 9, 1860   Was at home sewing and fitting dresses. Mrs Pennel came and invited us there to supper. We had a very nice supper. We staid till after 12 Oclock waiting for Mr P. but he did not come at all. Got a nice letter from Mo, and a number of others.

June 10, 1860   Wrote letters all forenoon, went to prayermeeting, and to church in the evening Mr Weaver preached. I was so sleepy that I did not get much good of the sermon. My state of my mind too is not as it should be. O! that I were better, I have got quite indifferent.   I have toothache and am about half sick.

June 11, 1860   Father[aa] brought me over to my school this morning, just got here in time, it was quite cold so we had fire   I am not very well, have toothache. Joab C. came to my school. I gave him my watch to get a key for it.   the one I had was too large. Evening, Was to church at Wor[thington].   heard a good old fashioned methodist sermon   broke the buggy going, Mr Carpenters were just on before us, he came and fixed it, got my watch all right.

June 12, 1860 It is not quite so cold this morning. It has been quite pleasant all day. School is going all right. My mouth is sore yet but it is better. After school, I sewed till after sundown when we saw M. C. coming down the lane on old Charley (horse), she rode up to the fence and I jumped on behind her, but he jolted so hard that I came near going off so we went back again. she then galloped off at a fast rate, returned soon with her brother along, they rode up to the fence, Marinda jumped off & Joanna D. on and gallopped off with Joab so they came back and I got on old Charley but did not gallop off for I was not a skilled equestrian. I learned though how to stick on without holding to the horn of the saddle.

June 13, 1860 It rained a little this morning but is quite pleasant now. quite warm My mouth is nearly well. The children bring me such nice flowers. Evening. Mr Carpenter Jo. Dickson & I were up to Mrs Gardner's we did not get honey as we expected, but had a very nice supper, but somehow or other my appetite always leaves me when I get there to eat. a look at Althina is enough to turn any bodies stomach. I was very tired when we got home.

June 14, 1860 I slept till six, but feel all right this morning. I had some ripe gooseberries brought for me to eat before breakfast this morning. When I got to school one little girl brought me cherries and another currants, and others flowers. Comstocks children said they had a baby at their house, that their Poppa traded strawberries for it. They think it the richest present they ever got Last night the mice got into my drawer and spoilt some of my nice white cloth which I had cut out for the great occasion. Eve. took a little horseback ride on a mans saddle came very near going off.

June 18, 1860 It rained a little this afternoon I feared we would not get our expected horseback ride but it cleared off till evening. At 5½ P.M. Joan D. and I were up to Mr Carpenters already to start for Westerville, they were not quite ready, it did not take them long however. Miss D expected Mr C to go with her but instead of that he rode up beside me and off we went. We had one glorious ride. We did not wish to get into Westerville till dark, For it had got quite muddy from the rain, & we were all spattered up with mud & worse than that, had no habits to wear, we got near town long before dark, so we went along the river to Lockwin, when we got within sight of town we got to the end of the road, so we had to turn round & go back. I got pretty tired till we got home & a little sick. Mother[bb] got supper for us, I changed my clothes & by 10 Oclock P.M. we started again on our way home. Of course I went with Joab again, Joanna went way on ahead. Marinda a good piece on behind her & we on behind her. I got very tired before we got back, when about 2 miles from our journeys end, I got so faint that I could scarcely keep on the saddle, but I kept on till we got home Joanna went right on home. I went along to Mr C's. & waited till the horses were put up, when Joab went down with me to Mrs Dicksons. he helped me off the horse, but by that time I was so sick that I could scarcely stand up. I got into the house, but was so sick that I rooled right on the floor. I was so sick that could not go to sleep. I slept some though, but had not got over it by morning. Saturday Morning or rather forenoon. Joab, Marinda & I went to town to a Sunday School picnic. we staid till after dinner when we went to Mr Genangs, where we were invited to go for tea, and from there we took a ramble to the high banks, we had a fine time, only it is a perfect bore to go with Joab all the time. He asked me again and in earnest too whether I was engaged to be married. I answered him as careless as possible in the affirmative and laughed over it. I told him all when it was going to come off, and asked him to the wedding, and laughed over it. Of course he does not believe a word of it. Mr C got a lot of candy & nuts, when we got into a pretty shady place we eat just as much as we could, we then went to Mr Genangs for tea, they had the nicest table set I ever saw for a private table. I liked their appearance very much, they all are so easy in their manners. I though to my self if I ever get to be mistress of a house I should to preside as gracefully as she & have a brother half as easy as Mr Genang. I believe that Samuel will preside even more graceful than he. We went to Worthington to the P.O. on our way home & got a letter from S.E.C. I was to awful tired to read it all. Sunday Morning. I wakened early and read my letter. I felt bad over some things, that to save my life I could not keep the tears back. I feared that *that* would be cause of unhappiness yet. The rest of the letter was just like himself. just as good as it could be. I went down to Mrs Dicksons this morning. Marinda went along, they acted awful crusty. I have felt bad all day, it seemed as though her children pertook of the surly nature. In the evening, Marinda came down, she told me many things, what they said. but I am not going to mind them, they are so mad because Joanna was not taken along to the high banks, we went on special invitation & I think her foolish to get mad about it especially to be mad at me about it. It looks very simple in my estimation, by what I can hear she is jealous because Joab goes with me, he used to go with her. Before we went to Westerville she told me she was going to run race with Joab. but she did not get the chance, for he kept with me as though he my gauardian and feared I would run off, if he were not by my side all the time. If she is going to get her pay for jealousy by acting ugly to me she will get poor pay. I do not mean to mind them.

June 19, 1860 It is quite warm this morning, and pleasant, the folks act a little awful yet, but not quite as bad as yesterday. The school goes better too. Evening. The school ended very pleasantly. Alan Beulen came in just before I dismissed and spoke a little to the children, he is going to lecture to the people here this evening. I fear it will be something of not much account. After lecture. The lecture was not of much account. Joe Dickson acted like a fool, as soon as Joab & Marinda came, she was off, & after lecture home again. It seemed to me she was trying to get rid of me, but she is not going to get rid of me so easy.

June 20, 1860 This is a pretty morning. I took my little trunk to Mr Gardners, to get ready to go home Fryday. If Thina comes I shall go home with her. It is not necessary to stay where they act so crusty. Noon. I have changed my mind I will go down there this evening again and offer to help Joanna to make her riding habit & show them if posible the meanness of their actions, perhaps they will stop acting so if I be real kind. I prayed God to help me & the above plan came into my mind.

June 21, 1860 I went to Mr Gardners after all. Thina came and said they expected me so I went but told Laura to tell Joanna that I would help her. I like old Mr Gardners folks they are such clever people. At dusk Mr Gardner got a note from Worthington telling him that a fugitive slave was there ready to be expressed on the underground road. He spoke to Miss Parintha and me about going, told us he thought it just something for us. It was made out then that we get up at 3 Oclock & go to Worthington and bring her to Mr Potters, from where she was to be taken to the next station. It was 4 Oclock this morning before we got started, but still got to Worthington and got the girl (who looks as though she was about 18 years old & quite smart) before many folks were astir & got back to Mr Potters before six Oclock. Our old horse went so much faster than he generally does that it seemed to me he must have been inspired with his mission. As soon as breakfast was over and the horse could be gotten out, he was taken to Mrs Potters & Mrs P. and little daughter with the fugitive got in the covered buggy. When they came to old uncle Ozems, as the neighbors call him, they stopped.[11] we all went out to see them, she had no gloves & it was a little dangerous of being detected without, so I gave her mine. Noon. I have no dinner this noon, Mrs Gardner would have sent my dinner but I thought Mrs D. would send it. Noon came & I had no dinner. I guess Mrs D. did not want her girls to lug my dinner up as she said one morning. Carpenters little girls brought me some such nice currants & Thina G. brought me a little cake which made my dinner. Well if this aint to bad, Just as I was going to call school Thina G came all in prespiration with my dinner. she went home and got it. Dicksons never made any apology for not bringing it

June 22, 1860 It is quite cool this morning. Still I think it will be warm. Last evening Dicksons acted much better. I helped Joe to sew on her riding habit. they seem quite different. Joe & I went up to Mr C's to see how Marinda is getting along with her suit. Joab came home with us & asked me to go out riding with him on the 4th of July. I do not know whether I will go. Noon Ellie Gardner brought me the nicest little cherry pie done up in a bit of paper, with my name on a slip of white paper pinned on. she said her mother sent it. Let others say what they will, Mrs G is truly a kind lady at least to me. Evening. I have closed school for a week. I expect to rest a week now, and attend commencement at Westerville. I expect our folks to come for me this evening. nearly two months of my school are gone, five more weeks will finish the term. I will have to bid my dear old journal adieu for one whole week, which seems rather hard.

July 2, 1860 I went home on Fryday evening. Poppa[aa] came for me in the buggy. I was glad to get home. Sat. we cleaned up a little. Sunday Pres. Owen preached a sermon to the graduates very good text."Be ye always sober minded. The new building was pretty well filled.[12] Monday. We washed, had a very large washing. Tuesday ironed. Mr Light & Mr Staub came in with the buss in the evening, to our house. had trustees for dinner. were very busy all day. Mr Evans and J. A. Kumler called to see me, also Maggie Moore & Lizzie Miller. went to the Society lecture in the evening delivered by Sam Galaway, subject Civilization. it was pretty good, but we got very tired, he also presented the diplomas. Mr & Miss Carpenter

11. Ozen Gardner was a leader of the area's underground railroad. Siebert, *Ohio's Underground Railroads*, pp. 170–71.
12. The new building refers to Otterbein's central chapel and meeting hall, which was still partially unfinished but in full use. Fire destroyed the building in 1870.

from near Worthington came too. Wednesday Morning all the students, faculty Alumni, trustees, met at the old chapple at 8 oclock A.M. & marched to the new in regular order as usual. Mid the wildest military music. the com. exercises were very good, they were short. Jacob Burgner was there & went home with us to dinner. I dislike him as much as ever & I cant like him We had a great deal of company all day. Mr. Evans & Mr Mattox called and asked Sis & I to go to concert in the evening. Sis had no excuse whatever so she said she had rather be excused from going with him. I told Evans I had company. Mr. Carpenter took me to concert. the music was good. The Choral Society. the Bethovan orchastra & the University Orchistra were the performers. I forgot to notice that sometime very early Wednesday Morning a new paper called the Westerville Nemesis was distributed, by being thrown into the front yards. The editors & contributors are all unknown. It comes pretty hard on some of the Mo. land speculating Ministers.[13] It may do some good. Quite a number of the students went away yet after concert. Thursday Morning the greater part left, till evening the town was almost desolate. I had quite a talk with Rev. E. Light. he tried to gather all the information about Ivery Norton. I told him all the good I knew. That very afternoon he called on her. In the evening he preached, & after preaching took her home. Such an odd match as that would make. Fryday I served as fast as I could N. & T Norton & a few others came to take dinner with us. A Zehring also called. I went with him to Mrs Winters to see the folks there. Mr Gharst was there to see Lydia. Saturday we cleaned house finished all up, but were nearly tired out till evening came. I could not eat super, had another good letter from Mo. The dear good soul is working like a hero. Sunday Morning I did not go to church, felt awful over it. Went in the evening. Mr Bright preached. Monday morning Poppa[aa] brought me over to school. It began to rain soon after we started and kept on raining faster & faster till past nine Oclock. I could not get to my school till ten. I had only nine pupils. In the evening I went to Mr Carpenters

13. No details of this incident could be found. The *Nemesis* was probably an anonymous broadside of protest rather than a true newspaper. It may have been produced by some departing students who resented the role of the local clergy in pushing certain real estate ventures. Rachel's father was one of those induced to invest in Missouri land. For the repercussions of this land speculation crisis on the local economy in Westerville, see entry for Nov. 9, 1860. The important link between real estate and clergymen in the nineteenth century is impossible to document, for it is buried in hundreds of local histories and church narratives; nor is there, at present, a major study on the other business activities of the nineteenth-century American clergy.

again. After supper I went with them to town. Marinda got a new swiss dress, & I am to help make it. I have hardly time to do so. It is quite warm & looks like rain. Evening. it did not rain more but was a little muddy. Joab came after us.

July 3, 1860   After dinner it begain to rain & kept on till dark. Joab came for us again. We worked till late at her dress, & finished it

July 5, 1860   Yesterday Morning it rained very fast so that we could not start for Columbus till noon. The roads were a little muddy, we were spattered a good deal. Got to C's till three.   spent the afternoon in shopping, got me a shaker,[14] had quite a time in getting it, went to nearly every store in town before I could get one large enough. We also visited the State house. Mr Merrell went with us there, the doors were closed & for some time we could not get any admittance.   we could get only into a few rooms, it being after the time.   we went up into the dome.   got very tired.[15] Mr C. is perfectly green when compared with Mr Cormany as a gallant, he does pretty well however. By the time we got out, it was supper time.   we went back to the Buckeye and eat a good supper, after which we called on A Mr Goos, then went back to the state house yard where the people were assembling fast to see the fireworks. as soon as dark enough the rockets began to fly as well as many other things which I can not describe.   soon after 10 P.M. we started home, tired enough, got there safe till 12. There are a few more pupils today. Evening. Went to a new boarding place this evening. Mr R. Comstocks. I have a very nice little room. I like the folks only I think the children are not very well trained.   they do not mind when told any thing, nor can they well be coaxed to do any thing they do not wish to do. Ada would sleep with me, & both George & Ada declare they are going home with me when I go. The children just feed me on berries & apples these days. O! that they may learn fast. Nothing troubles me more than not being a better christian, so as to be able to teach them better the way to the better world

July 7, 1860   I have great things to write this morning. Last evening after I had been to my boarding place a little while Joanna Dickson came there. They were talking and laughing about something.   at

14. A large bonnet.
15. After more than twenty years of political haggling and intermittent construction, the new Ohio state capitol building had nearly reached completion. This two-acre structure, with its Doric columns and central dome, was considered one of the most magnificent buildings in the Midwest. Studer, *Columbus*, pp. 331–47.

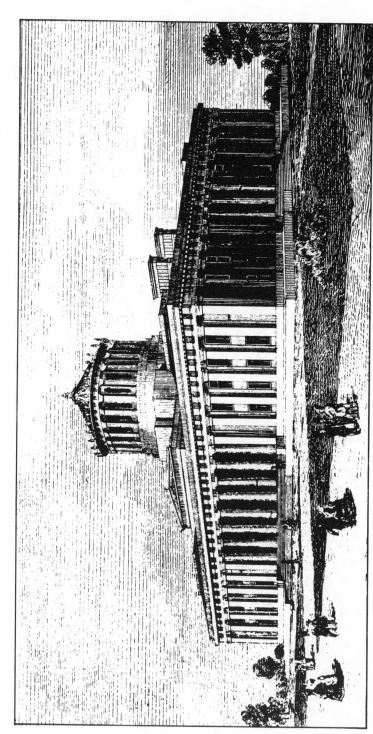

The new capitol at Columbus. Detail from John Graham, *Map of Franklin County, Ohio, from Actual Survey and Records* (Philadelphia, 1856). Maps Division, LC.

last Joanna said. "Miss B. you did not know that Joab C——had become daddy." I was perfectly dumb founded. I did not know what to say. I was to Mr Carpenters on Monday night & at about 12 oclock at night some men came there. Marinda & I had just gone to bed, it scared us, we thought they were robbers, we were silenced by being told that they must be drunk. I have found out since that it was the Constable & that he came & took Joab off that night up to Orrange station, where the girl lives. Early in the morning Mr C—r went up, to help to settle it. I was at their house helping Marinda make her dress. On the 4th M. Joab & I went to Columbus & never found a word of it out till last evening. I fear it will injure me some, being a stranger here. Although I never once went with him alone, still I was in his company. I can hardly bear to stay over here now, it makes me feel awful to think I had any thing to say to such a man. It is a little cool this morning, we have had so much rain   I feel like taking a good cry.

July 9, 1860 Saturday evening Parintha Gardner came down to have me go home with her, we went together to Mr Carpenters to get my dress.   They all feel very bad about this affair of Joabs, he feels very bad himself. I pity him. Joanna Dickson is dreadfully pleased about it & the whole family are as good as they can be now. I spent the Sunday at Mr Gardners, went with them to church & Sunday school. It rained very much in the forenoon, but cleared off nicely in the afternoon. Joab was to meeting   he looks bad. It is very pleasant this morning   it will be warm through the day. I received a note from Joab, he seems to feel awfully. Marinda came to see the babe, looks very bad.

July 10, 1860 Marinda staid with me all night   she does not believe Joab to be guilty.   received another note from Joab. I answered his of yesterday pretty sharp which seems to have cut pretty deep. I find that he is not blamed by many, and that quite a number do not believe that he is the father to the child. I must answer him again. Since this is a good opportunity to get rid of him now I am going to improve it.   It is quite warm, no rain.

July 11, 1860 Had an awful time last night. Ada Comstock the little codger took a notion to sleep with me, well last night she got sick, vomited all over the bed and on me. I lighted the candle and fixed up the bed as well as I could but got almost sick too, it raised such a stench. Got another note from Joab. I am not going to answer this.   it is warm again this morning. I did not get a letter from S.E.C. last week   I dream of him nearly every night. I fear something is the matter of him. I had quite a time with my schollars today, the whole school turned against O & F Carpenter. I scarcely knew how to do with them. First I asked them one after another to give the golden rule, then asked them questions about the rightfulness or wrongfulness of some actions, then came plain out that I meant them. At noon all acted as bad as ever. I called them all in at the regular time as soon as all were seated and still I told them I wanted to have this great quarrel settled (O&FC were crying) I commenced by asking each for their complaint.   none had any except Maggie Dickson & one or two more.   that was that. Olive called them a fool one day. O. confessed that she was sorry & wished the pardon of girls   All granted her pardon if she would pardon them, except M Dickson & H. Carter. I then read them from Mathew 6–14 & 15.[16] I read it over several times, explained it to them and told them all to think of it. At recess all were as good as they could be.

July 12, 1860   It is quite cool this morning. The night are quite cool. I am taking lessons in rocking the cradle this week. Mrs C's girl is not of much account & the babe is sick.   so I sit by the cradle with my sewing & rock.

July 13, 1860   It is quite pleasant this morning. I am looking forward with bright anticipation to this evening when I shall get home. I hope to get some news from Mo then. Last evening I began to pick gooseberries, did pretty well, but got my hands all scratched up and full of briers, they are quite sore this morning. I do not feel very well this morning.

July 16, 1860   I picked all the berries in the evening I had spoken for. Our folks came for me, the little girls came along, and with a few of my schollars, went berrying   got but a few. It was ten oclock when we got home. There were two letters there from S.E.C. great long and real good ones. Sunday went to church. Rev. Walker from some distance preached a real good sermon. Was not well, consequently did not go to church in the evening. Wrote to S.E.C.   called on Elizabeth Leib who is quite sick again. She is much better. Ellen Walker is quite poorly too, her folks think she has the quick consumtion.   they took her to Grannville to the Watercure.   they

16. A passage on forgiveness.

doubt her recovery.[17] Early this morning Susie[nn] & I got ready and Poppa[aa] took us over to my school. Susie[nn] will stay with me this week. was not very well all day, had to reprove more today than any day before. Received a note from Mr Lewis that they could not take me to board. I am going to board with Mr Gardners their time & they will pay it.

July 17, 1860 Sis[nn] went to Mr Carpenters this morning & I this evening. Mrs C. looks almost like a shaddow. this trouble of theirs is almost killing her. We went out to the R.R. and were tired most to death.

July 18, 1860 Was at Mr Carpenters all night. got up early and smoked glass to look at the eclipse of the sun.[18] had quite a talk with Marinda last evening. I believe she is under conviction of her own sinfulness, we were in the barn door where we talked a long time and before we went to the house, we went into the barn & kneeled down together and prayed. I had quite a talk with Marinda & Mrs C this morning, they feel so bad Evening. School went very well today, after school went to Dicksons. When I entered Mrs D. said Good evening Mrs Carpenter & tried to plague me with Joab. I wish the folks would quit plaguing me so with him. Dicksons girls & Carpenters & Sis[nn] & I went down to the narrows. Mrs D. & Joana pitched into Marinda and tried & did rake up a fuss about some of the childrens quarrels that took place three or four years ago which seems so childish & foolish.

July 19, 1860 School went very well today, nothing of any consequence took place. It has been quite warm. Sis[nn] & I went to Grand Pa Gardners after school, I like to visit there, they are so kind. We feasted on berry pie & berries & cream.

July 20, 1860 Sis[nn] Staid up at Mr Gardners while I came down to school early to write letters I wrote to Marinda with regard to the quarrel, as she requested. I also answered a note from Joab. Yester-

17. Dr. William W. Bancroft established a water-cure sanitarium in Granville in 1852. By 1860 it had acquired a strong reputation and was drawing patients not only from other Northern states, but also from the South. William T. Utter, *Granville: The Story of an Ohio Village* (Granville, 1956), pp. 224–25. Quick consumption, also called galloping consumption, would probably be labeled acute pneumonia today.

18. The eclipse of July 18, 1860, was the first to be photographed successfully, and as a result, it allowed scientists to make great strides in their understanding of the sun's surface. Samuel A. Mitchell, *Eclipses of the Sun* (New York, 1924), pp. 134–35.

day Mr Gardner spoke to me about teaching another month. I do not know whether I shall. I do not know what time S.E.C. will be back. perhaps he will tell me in this weeks letter.

July 21, 1860 It has been quite rainy today. Sis[nn]is still with me, we expect Mama[bb] & Poppa[aa] today. I thought they would come this morning, but it is too rainy. Evening. They came this afternoon. My good Ma[bb] brought me a lot of nice clean clothes. They are so kind to me. It seems to me they are thinking all the time perhaps we will never again have another opportunity of doing anything for her. I went with them to Mr Carpenters where we took supper. Ma[bb] brought me some letters, one from Samuel. He writes such good letters, he tells me of the death of G. B. Millers intended bride, poor George, his heart seems almost broken. I shudder, fearing such may be our lot. I spoke of him getting a dog to guard me in his absence, in sport only. in this letter he tells me that my little dog is doing finely. The dear Pet, he seems to forget self altogether & lives & labors only for me.

July 22, 1860 Afternoon. Mrs Gardner & I went to church up the country in their buggy. The little log schoolhouse was quite full. It seems quite odd to go to such a place to meeting. It rained quite hard this morning so that it was quite muddy. I love to go to meeting. I like to write too. I long so much for a true hearted person to talk with. I can talk with none, that live round here with ease. I like so well to get home to talk, but when I have none to talk with I take my pen & talk with my dear trusty Journal & to Samuel, those are true & tried friends, & it seems almost a hardship to have to write to any one but our own family beside those, although I have other correspondents that I esteem very highly. I fear sometimes that this sweet dream will never become a sweet reality. I have learned to look at death as a dreadful monster, since my acquaintance with Samuel E. C. I fear something may happen to Samuel that death will take him from me. My *Savior knows* what is best & *He* will *do all things well*. The people where I board are not religious. Their children are not brought up to know God, rather like little heathen, perhaps that expression is rather hard for they are brought up very moral.

July 23, 1860 School went pretty well. Dicksons children were not here this forenoon. Maggie was here this afternoon, bringing a special message from Joanna to have me come to stay with her tonight. I will go this evening but not to stay all night. I want to go to meeting & I can go with them, the little girls bring me apples, There were two very nice ones brought & hid under a paper on my desk the little pets. How they try to please. I feel a little sad this evening. I have this dear little miniature of Samuels with me. he is so noble. though small in statue he is noble & great in spirit.

July 24, 1860 I have not felt very well today, school went very well. I guess I took cold last night. my teeth feel a little inclined to ache I received & answered another note from J. R. Carpenter today. I told him just what I thought. I do not know how it will take neither can I help it. This evening some of the girls quarreled about their merits. those Dickson children seem such ill disposed children toward all who get along a little better than they. I do not think them too truthful either. Marinda C. came down to see me this evening. I started to go a piece with her & went all the way, to please the little girls who wanted Frankie C to come & stay with them. On the way home they told me how much they loved me, they were talking together, one declared that Miss Bowman was her lover, & that she loved Miss B best, while the other declared that she did not. Somehow I do not feel at ease with Mrs G. I do not know why. My candle is gone.

July 26, 1860 I am quite tired & sleepy today. I went to Mr Pitkins for tea last evening, & from there Cora P. & P. Gardner & I walked to hardscrable to meeting. After meeting back. Cora came home with me & staid all night, we talked till after midnight. Joab Carpenter asked the prayers of christians at meeting. Hope he is sincere.

July 30, 1860 My dear good trusty Journal, it is some time since I had a good talk with thee. I have just finished three letters I have been writing every spare minute I had all day. The meeting are still continued I do not get to go every evening.[19] last evening a man got religion & shouted so that it scared a horse so that he broke the waggon & came near running away. Joab Carpenter also experienced religion, when the penitent ones were invited to the alter he came over to the carriage where his sister & I were sitting & asked her with tears in his eyes to go with him, but she would not. he went alone. I tried to persuade her to go but she refused positively. two of my schollars were at the alter. I went to speak with them, & staid till the congregation were dismissed. J. C. refused to

19. There was a prolonged revival, or camp meeting, underway near Worthington.

rise from his knees, but kept on praying. I went back to the carriage. was not there long till he came with face all bright & alive, shook hands with his old comrade, Gen. G. H. [?] telling him how happy he was & asking him to become religious, he then took my hand, saying as he did so, "I am all well now, (he had been nearly killed on Sat. and was scarcely able to be up at all on Sunday) he shook as with the ague, alternately laughing & weeping, scarcely knowing what he was doing. He held my hand I should judge nearly ½ hour, when some one told him his wagon was broke. "Is it, well I guess I will have to go & fix it then," this was spoken in such a changed & cheerful way that I could not but feel happy, but before he left he had one request to make, nay two. 1st that I would pray for him. 2nd that I would stay & teach another month. I promised him the first but the last I could not. I could not stay. the bare thought of staying makes me almost sick I like all the school except Dicksons children. I would like them, & I think if they had better bringing up at home I should like it better. but the old folks, Joanna & her mother, are so crusty & hateful & the rest seem to catch it too. The reason of their actions is jealousy of Mr. J. C. I cannot help allowing his attentions when *they* can see it, just to taunt them, for it seems so simple for them to act so. there may be something else but what I cannot tell. Saturday afternoon M. C. & I went to Westerville on horseback, she borrowed a hat & habit for me so we were fixed in style. It was very warm, & we were tired nearly to death. After resting awhile we came back. I have been very lame & bruised up every since. My left arm was almost useless. I forgot to mention that the meetings are held in the grove since Sat. evening. In a very pretty place. I never saw the woods look so grand as last evening the moon from above & the lights from below gave it an appearance of grandeur the like of which can never be seen in the most finished architecture. There seemed to be a sacredness round the place It is getting quite late. I must retire now too.

July 31, 1860 I spoke with Mr Gardner this morning about staying another month. I told him I could not stay if I was to board round. I would rather help My Father[aa] plow than board round he told me I need not bother on that account. I could board with them. he knew all would be willing to pay for my board. I told him I would stay then. O! that I could inspire those little children with energy now to commence with renewed zeal in their studies. Some how some stay out so much. I sometimes feel like saying, Dicksons are a perfect nuisance to the whole neighborhood. I would too that they would all become christians. God help me to do my duty to the children.

August 2, 1860 We have had quite interesting meetings since I last wrote. Sunday eve two experienced religion. A Mr Sulivant & Joab Carp. J. C. seemed to be very much engaged in prayer all evening, when the rest rose he still kept on his knees & staid in that position till after meeting was dismissed. Miss C & I were sitting in the buggy close by (Miss C is not a christian & would not yield to either my entreaties or her brothers, although the strong man begged her to go with tears in his eyes). Soon after the congregation had been dismissed, before many got away he received a blessing & first he did was to come to the buggy to shake hands with us. he trembled like a man with the ague. He held my hand a long time. it seemed to me almost an hour. he seems quite happy ever since Mr Slaughter preached one evening I was sorry that such men as he are allowed to preach, his practice does not agree with his preaching & the people have no confidence in him. Last evening, Mrs G & I went up in their buggy. During meeting time the Boid families near the place where the meetings are held got into a fight & one shot at the other, but did not hurt him much. but still it caused great excitement the congregation scattered off in a short time. Mrs. G. was pretty badly scared. My school is going on finely now. I have been desiring a full salvation for a long time. Today it seemed to me I had found what I had so long desired. I could but go & write it to S.E.C. before I got through I felt that after all I did not have it. I have been reading in the "Beauty of Holiness,"[20] and found things which seemed to suit my case. The great trouble seems to be that I cannot claim the promises as mine. I have been. The entrance of a little girl has made me forget what I was going to write. It is quite cloudy I fear it is going to rain. If it does it will break up the meetings, but God knows what is best.

August 3, 1860 The children are all alive this morning. They brought me pretty little stones for my curiosity box, & flowers & apples. all are very good. All expect a great time in the woods this afternoon where I propose taking them to speak their pieces.

August 5, 1860 After I came back from the woods Mother & Mrs L. Hammond were at my boarding place ready to take me home with them. But I must tell the my good journal of last Saturdays exploits. At 2 oclock we started for the grove, all in high spirits, we climbed

---

20. The Ohio and Pittsburgh Conferences of the Methodist Episcopal church published a religious journal under this title twice a year from 1853 to 1855 and then annually through 1864.

up a high hill, there I had them all seated & then conducted the exercises as usual, after the exercises I told them all to go & play just as hard as they could. I went with the little ones & such a time. they all seemed like birds let out of their cages, we roamed up & down the river more than on hour, & while along the river one little girl fell in & rolled right over in the water, another one got her eye hurt by a twig snapping into it. I got dead sick of children & of teaching, we all got tired, but the children seemed to have enjoyed it well. At home all goes like usual. Father[aa] brought me over to the woods meeting yesterday. I came here with Mr Carpenter. I do wonder sometimes whether there ever was any one with a religious like mine. I feel miserable. last week I felt much encouraged but all is dark again. Joanna Dickson & Mrs. Comstock were to the alter to be prayed for. Last evening Joanna would not go. M. C. is stouborn, I fear she is hardening her heart.

Well if that dont beat all [nature?]. Joab C. sent me a paper full of the nicest kind of mandrakes.[21]   the little girls have been telling me that he had gathered some & laid them in bran to ripen. He is another simpleton. If I liked him I could not but dislike him after acting, well it seems to me green. I never could bear this thing of being fed on candy & such stuff by a gentleman. Evening. Dicksons stopped for me & took me along to church. I was surprised to have them stop for me. A stranger preached. Marinda, Joanna & I were sitting together.   as soon as he was through M told me that she & J were going to the alter to be prayed for & wanted a lady that was sitting right before us to go with them, but she refused.   they went alone. It seemed to me that deep selemnity & determination was written on M's brow. Three of my schollars say they have found peace in christ.   O! that more would seek.

August 7, 1860 Before daylight this morning breakfast was announced. I scrabled out & got ready as soon as posible. After I got back to my room the clock struck five, so I just went to bed again. Near school time Olive C. brought me another note from J. C.   such an odd one. I could not but laugh at it. He gets powerful near popping the question

August 9, 1860 I have good news to tell thee my dear trusty Journal this morning, but since it is in school hours I may not get time to

21. The root of the American mandrake, closely related to the Asian ginseng, was believed to have medicinal powers and in many folk traditions was considered an aphrodisiac. Joab's gift, in light of the trouble he was in, is more than a little ironic. See C. J. S. Thompson, *The Mystic Mandrake* (New Hyde Park, N.Y., 1968).

say all, but since the most of the children have nearly all gone to the S.S. celebration I do not have so much to do only five are here. Well Wednesday evening I went to meeting & home with Minnie C. she was seeking religion, but had not found. Thursday evening I went with them to church again. J. Dickson got religion, sister Corrie went out to the alter & soon got to shouting. Minnie still kept on her knees, at 10 oclock the meeting was dismissed, but Minie refused even to get off her knees, we staid there till after 12 oclock, still she had not found peace. I went home with her by request of her parents but felt that instead of instructing her & praying for her I needed to be prayed for. I read to her from the Bible & tried to encourage her but all seemed of no avail. I then pulled the pillow to the foot of the bed & laid my head on it intending to pray, but soon fell asleep. I had slept about an hour when I was awakened by a strange noise. I raised up, the candle was still where I had set it, the Bible was open before her & she was down before the bed on her knees, her mother, on hearing the noise, came in & asked her whether she could not trust now. "O! Yes." she said in a clear tone, we got her up on the bed, she was laughing & crying together, her father soon came in, & such a time of rejoicing is not often witnessed or heard of. We at last got to bed but it was near four oclock till we got to sleep. In the morning she was as happy as ever. She said she felt so very happy that she thought she could not live & that she had felt very bad just before & had got down & prayed, then read in the Bible & while reading she got so happy that she thought she could live no longer.[22] O! that I could too have such a bright evidence. Yesterday after school I took Mrs. Gs hired girl home, she lives about a mile beyond Westerville & had time to stop but a few minutes at Home. I do have such a good Mother.[bb] I did not see Father,[aa] he is good too. It was dark coming home I felt a little fearful coming through the woods, the little girl that was with me fell asleep so I had none but My God to commune with. O! for a full salvation. A bright evidence of my acceptance with God. Lord lead me into the right way. I expect to go home again tonight Joab C wants to take me home after the meeting. I fear it will be quite late & at 3 in the morning our folks want to start to Columbus. I fear it will be rather a hard day for me. I must go to Worthington today sometime to get my money. I do not know yet how I shall get there.

22. Minnie has experienced a classic nineteenth-century conversion: an unusually heightened realization of sinful unworthiness followed by an ecstatic state of acceptance and joy.

August 13, 1860 It is quite cool   we have a fire in the schoolroom. I have but five schollars today. I do not know why the children do not come more regular. It plagues me very much to have them stay out. I do not know why the people are so indifferent about their children coming to school. If I ever rejoice it will be when this month is out. I do wish to do right with the children. I was to Columbus on Saturday & got most of the things (I mean wearable things) I shall at the nuptial festival. It seems so strange that I should love Samuel, who was an entire stranger less than two years ago, as I do, & that I am going to be married to him. Yet I would not have it otherwise for the whole world.

August 18, 1860 Saturday. I have not talked with you my good old Journal for sometime. My school is quite small today, only six pupils.   but for this place it is not so small for a Saturday school. I am much pleased with the school this week. I like it as well as I did at first. Nothing of importance took place this week. I have been drawing some, finished one piece. I find that reading a good piece to the children is a good plan. Even if my school is little I find many things to perplex. I am reading "Sweet Home" and find it real good, instructive & refining.[23] I like to read such books.

August 19, 1860 Sabbath afternoon. I have not been out today. In this quiet country every thing is so very still, they do not have preaching here very often & when they do have it is in the afternoon. I have been reading & writing all morning until I am getting quite tired. I have been writing to Samuel. When writing to him I cannot help thinking of my future western home. I have it all blocked out in immagineation and see myself duly installed.   every thing is in perfect order & looks cosy. My dog which Samuel has gotten for me is lying in the shade beside the door sleeping & yet ever wachful to keep all danger away. Now I should like to say I am very corageous, but have to say the contrary. Smls dressing gown & slippers are out airing & waiting for his return. Supper is all ready (Land! wonder whether I can ever get supper that I wont be ashamed of.) All will seem so strange. It seems to me I have much more to live for since my acquaintance with him. Much more to induce me to be good. Ah, yes to be a better christian. Sunday Evening. I sent home today again for a letter, but none has come for me, what can the matter be that I do not get one. I think he must have written, for he writes every week.

23. George Canning Hill, *Sweet Home; Or, Life in the Country. Showing the Joys and Sorrows of Every-day Home-life in New England. By the Editor of a Boston Daily Paper* (Boston, 1854; rpt. 1858, 1859, 1860).

August 20, 1860 Am not well at all. I let school out ten minutes sooner at noon on that account. Thought I had rather make up some other time when I felt all right. The children have been quarreling again. It troubles me when they quarrel. It makes me hate teaching. Wonder why I did not get a letter. A letter would make me feel all right I know. It is very warm today, the sun seems almost scorching.

August 26, 1860 I have been up several hours & have been reading my Bible. Just now the rest of the family are beginning to stir. Mrs G. wants to go to Westerville today. I was hoping we would get started in time so as to get to church there. Pres't Owen is going to preach & I should like to hear him, but it is too late now, we ought to be starting soon. It will be almost meeting time before we will get breakfast. I have not talked with my journal since Monday & still I do not have a great deal to say, the last week was not a very eventful one. I suppose Joab has concluded since I have not answered his last note with the "big wish" that it is of no use to say more to me. So I judge he has turned to Gettie Goss. I have been staying closely at home this week. I think it more profitable than to be gadding round so much. I have regular hours to read & find it very profitable. I believe in several hours of good solid reading every day & the light newspaper reading can be caught up while waiting for dinner or any other odd minutes. If I had thought that I would not need my things till winter I should have devoted more time to reading since I have one place to board at. while boarding round it was imposible to read much, or even to sew much. I do not think boarding round a good plan, it has some advantages, but the disadvantages more than counterballance them. I have not had a letter from Samuel for more than two weeks, which makes me feel a little anxious. I hope to get at least one from him today. I can hardly wait till we get started. Some of the people over here beat all in sleeping I ever heard of. & Minie Carpenter beats all the rest. I can hardly wait till we get started for home. I would be off by this time if I had myself only to start.

August 28, 1860 I was home Sunday & got two long letters from Samuel, such good ones too, he is working so hard to get ready to come east. I have been writing rather too indifferent I must not do so he is so very sensitive & feels it so keenly. I felt as though he was indifferent about how soon he came back. I was wicked to judge him so wrongfully. I do not feel sad to think I am going away so far I do not know why it is, for I know that it is not on account of affection for them for I believe no one can love their parents better. but still I love Samuel better than them. I do not fear in the least to go with him even if it were double or trible the distance I know he loves me as his own life. This morning it rained very hard I feared I would not have my scholars, but nearly the usual number were there after all. Dicksons make me more trouble that all the rest put together. To get along well with them it is necessary to almost kneel to them, but I wont do that so of course they dont like me. But I dont care, their friendship is worse than none. I do not crave it.

September 1, 1860 Well I am once more at home to stay. My School closed yesterday. I am not at all sorry, but still I could scarcely keep the tears back when I bade them goodbye. I had quite a nice little time with the children in the woods. Now I suppose I shall be as busy as a bee till I take my departure from home forever. I cannot but feel a little sad when I think of it in that light.

September 3, 1860 It seems quite good to be at home again. I helped to do a large washing today & to fix up the rooms. Quite a number of students came this evening. Six came here for supper Now I suppose school life will commence again in earnest for those who go to school and for those who take boarders. I expect to pitch in and help to cook for a short time at least. I would need all this time to sew, but will do my sewing after I get to my western home. I long for the next letter from Sml.

September 16, 1860 I have been so busy since I am home that I have almost neglected my journal. I have had general hauling, over washing and mending time since I am home. I have scarcely touched my own sewing. I shall be very busy till I leave, which will be on the 20th or 27th of November. Tomorrow Mother[bb] is going to Columbus to see whether she cannot get her hearing bettered by a Buffalo Doctor.[24] Wednesday Morning Father[aa] is going to start to C. W. on business about the farm. I scarcely know how to account for the fluctuation of my feelings with respect to Sml. I do not realize that I am really going to be married to him & going with him to Mo. It will seem so strange. I should like if he were better educated, but it is not necessary that he stay so, he will undoubtedly in a few years be as far in an education as I. How gladly I would teach

---

24. Itinerant healers were common in antebellum America. They would come to a city, advertise their specialities in the local newspapers, stay awhile, then move on to another city.

or do almost any thing to have him go to school longer. I never loved any one as I do him. It is so different from the love I had for Kilbourne.

September 25, 1860 I have just returned from a long walk down the plank to Mr McQuirks & Mr Brights. Polly Spayd was with me, we got very tired, got such a pretty boquet of flowers. Went to the P.O. got some papers one from C. W. in which was recorded the marriage of J. B. S. & Hannah Bristow which surprised me a little, promised H. H. to call to see her this evening yet.

September 29, 1860 I received a letter from Mr. S. E. C. on Thursday which tells me that he has been disappointed in getting his money in Pa. & consequently our nuptials must be put off till spring. I do not like it much for the reason that postponements often result in final separations. I believe him to be sincere at present, but I cannot help thinking of a letter I received in Pa. & I feel a little shaken I am troubled beyond expression. My head just thumps & aches whenever I think of it. Mother[bb] shakes her head at the postponement, & thinks the would not be put off so. This is the second, already. I must confess it looks a little a ruse to pave the way for worse things. Pride says reject him before he will have the chance to tell you he does not love you. My heart whispers, be not too hasty. I have written him a little how I felt about it & too that I do not like the idea of another postponement. To be fooled in marriage by any man is a little more than I am willing to bear, especially by one whom to marry according to the estimation of many I am coming down a little. I have just let them understand in pretty plain language that *that* is my business. I know what I am about & can be my own adviser, but now the idea of being fooled by such an one is more humiliating than I can well bear. I do not think Friends or acquaintances should be trouble with me long. however I should not choose to die for any man, but I would go to where never mortal man had seen me.

October 1, 1860 I have just put out a large washing I thought it would not rain any more so I hung them out, but now it is raining already. I have washed all alone the several last times. I have been thinking of Samuel very much. I cannot portray my thoughts and feelings with pen & ink. When I think of him as altogether unable to help these postponements I love him all the more, but when I think of him as a little indifferent I get mad, & feel myself wronged, & as if I wanted revenge if it killed me, & like refusing him, no difference

121

what pleas he may bring. It seems to me if he was very anxious for my company he might make all other things bend to this. Above all things this setting the day & putting it off is something I cannot endure. I can take almost anything before the idea of being imposed upon it makes me feel like a bear robbed of its whelps and I have not the goodness to keep me from resenting.

October 21, 1860 Father[aa] has returned from C.W. has arranged his affairs there that we need not go at least not till spring. brought is a lot of maple sugar. we had quite a feast. he also brought us a number of letters from the friends. Mr. S. E. C. will be here in five weeks. I judge I will not get to C. W. as I had expected, it is quite hard for me to give up, indeed it almost seems like an imposibility. My will says give up but my heart refuses. I have told him I would give up, & I am going to, but it is hard to think I shall never in this world see some of the friends again.[25] Two cousins ill with consumption will scarcely see another spring, they say "Rachel come & see us, ere we die. O! I would love to, but what could I help them if I did. If Mr C. knew how hard it is for me to give up he would go if it were in his power, but I must not tell him, for I know it is almost imposible for him to go. I have wronged in thinking as I did & writing as I did. I trust all will be for the best let it go as it will.

November 9, 1860 My trusty journal I have quite neglected thee in this bustle of getting ready to be married. I have not all done yet, but cannot forebear unburdening my heart: 1st This is one of those chilly drizzly Nov. days which always make me feel a little sad, but what makes me more sad is that Westerville is in such a bad condition financially. The leading men are breaking. their property goes to pay debts or is signed away to secure it. & the creditors have to loose. Father[aa] has bailed some who we thought good financial men, & now those sums come on him to pay. He & Mother[bb] are greatly troubled about it. they do not feel willing to let their property go to strangers after having worked for it their lifetime. Father[aa] trusted those ministers who were in high standing too much, for they have turned out to be the veriest knaves and wear the ministerial cloak only to deceive the honest the more easily.

November 11, 1860 Was to church, had preaching in the new chapple & will have it there henceforth. L. Davis preached. I do not

25. Because the wedding was delayed, Rachel agreed to skip their honeymoon trip to Canada and go directly to Missouri. But as Samuel's diary already revealed, the Canadian honeymoon was reinstated.

like him as a minister. I cannot but think of his swindling Father[aa] in a land sale, he seems so self righteous. I have just finished my last loveletter. I judge the last one for my life I cannot but feel sad when I think of leaving home forever. O! that I may do just right in all things & live Godly so that we may all meet in Heven at last.

November 24, 1860 My Husband elect is here arrived on the 21st he looks well. The dear man I love him as my own life. It is quite late. I have been very busy today, but all is done now. I fell very solemn as though something dreadful was about happening me. Although it is midnight I am not sleepy. I am happy deep down in my heart.

November 25, 1860 The dye is cast. The Rubicon is crossed. I am now R. B. Cormany. We were married in church by the Rev. J. M. Spangler, after evening preaching. Rachel H. Winter & Mollie L. Miller were my attendants. J. A. Kumler & S. E. Ebersole were Mr Cormanys. I was attired quite plain. My dress consisted of plane bule silk, white collar & undersleeves & a long bridal veil. My attendans were dressed in white. I felt quite composed. Every body seemed to be well pleased with the sight. I should have prefered a private marriage, but having graduated in this place, & my parents not feeling able to make a large party it was thought best to have it in public. I am happy & yet my heart is almost full to bursting O! that I could get somewhere alone to weep off this load. Day & evening beautiful

November 26, 1860 Rainy & disagreable. Mr C. & I are packing my things. I love my husband very much & know that he loves me Evening. Received quite a number of calls, notwithstanding the inclemency of the weather. It seems so odd to be called Mrs. Cormany.

November 27, 1860 Finished packing our things and received quite a number of calls through the day. Tomorrow we leave for my native country. Canada. The thought of leaving home seems hard. how will the reality be. Sisters & Parents are very kind to me.

VIII
The Decision to Remain in Canada
November 19, 1860–January 13, 1861

While the Cormanys are in Canada on their honeymoon, conditions in the United States grow increasingly unsettled. Samuel reluctantly decides to postpone any return to the farm in Missouri, pending some resolution of the secession crisis.

———————◆•◆•◆———————

November 19, 1860   Monday. I start East for my "helpmeet"—My Darling! Dine with friend Barnes in Macon City—Leave at 2:15 for Saint Louis—Fare $5.90, Arrive 9 P.M.   Put up at Everett House— Well and Happy—Bathe Evening and Morning—Left St. Louis 20″ 7. A.M. Tuesday.   Fare to Columbus Ohio $13.50—Read most of the day—Reach Cinti 9:40 P.M.   Leave for Columbus at 11 P.M.   Arrive 3:40 A.M.   Put up at Buckeye House—Good Sleep——

November 21, 1860   Wednesday. Met Mrs Haney—a little chat— P.M. Took Buss to Westerville—Put up at my old Boarding house. Met Darling at Dining-room O So Joyfully——Very very few know any-thing of our Engagement—I am only calling as a former boarder— Our correspondence was veiled all the while I was in Mo.   My old Friend Israel Light addressed and mailed all letters to me—and all my letters to Darling were addressed to him with a secret private mark which only he understood—and so he handed them to Rachel. Un-less indeed herself or some other member of Home carried all the mail to the House, when of course each recognized his or her own— Evening, of course We visited in the Parlor—and talked til 11 OCK—

November 22, 1860   Thursday. A day of important talks with Father B. B. Bowman[aa]—and Rachel and Mother[bb] Bowman.
   Eve. my money has not yet arrived for our Canada trip—But we have our other arrangements settled—Ceremony Sab Eve in Church—Brides Maids Miss R. Winter, Miss May Miller, Grooms-men J. A. Kummler and E. C. Ebersole—I called on them and talked things over with them—Later spent an hour joyously with Darling.

November 23, 1860 Friday. A busy day arranging details. &c
Spent the evening very pleasantly in Parlor with Darling.

November 24, 1860 Saturday. Very cold—We went to Columbus
for our License. Dined at Buckey—Home at dusk. Supper at Pennels. Later Groomsmen and Brides Maids called on us—consum-
mated arrangements for the Ceremony—Darling and I had a fine
chat til 11 OCK

November 25, 1860 Sunday. I am happy—This is the last time the
sun shall arise on me in the single state.
    Had a fine chat with Darling during A.M.—Did not go to church.
    It was announced that there would be a marriage in the evening—
during service—by Rev. J. M. Spangler—Few know who were to be
married—
    J. L. Kephart acted as Page—Evening! We were all in the Bowman
Parlor—save the Pastor and Page—fully ready, and waiting notice
from the Page that the sermon was nearing the close—on notice The
procession walked across street to Chapel—as we entered the Vesti-
bule, the congregation was closing the singing of a verse of "On
Jordans Stormy Banks I stand"—at its close the doors opened and
we marched up the aisle—The house was full. E. C. Ebersole & Miss
Winter led—Darling and I followed, and J. A. Kumler and Miss
Miller brought up the rear. On reaching the alter—the group fell
easily into the proper curve, and ceremony was very brief—
    Then as Mrs and Mr Cormany we led the way out the other aisle,
the attendants following. While passing out the congregation struck
up singing the verse "Filled with delight, my raptured soul would
here no longer stay &c" Completing the song as we moved out,
and the dismissed audience soon filed out—We proceeded to the
Bowman Home—where a little group of Specials—Viz The Family—
The Pastor and Mrs Spangler—The Brides Maids and Grooms
men—and the Page, and several others Enjoyed an hour or so
socially—About 10:30 all withdrew, and we were left to ourselves,
and each other, our cup of happiness full to the brim, and we
kneeled together offering Praise to God, seeking His special blessing
on our life, and anew consecrating our selves, soul and body to
Him, for a life of service—Thus we began our new life upon our
knees—and closed the first evening in Family worship together—

November 26, 1860 Monday. We look out upon a new day in our
new life, with Joy and gladness in our hearts. Had some callers—We

packed up our things to start for Canada on our HoneyMoon just as soon as my money arrives—Eve it has not come—

November 27, 1860 Tuesday. Too bad to have my Darlings plans so disarranged—But we have delightful calls, and accept the situation quietly.

November 28, 1860 Wednesday. I've now got the needful—and we start. Reach Buffalo at 3:40 P.M.—Do some sightseeing—

November 29, 1860 Thursday. 9 A.M. we go to Niagara Falls—O! This is glorious scenery—we donned oil cloth suits—and posatively when we came face to face in the hallway we took each other for Esquamaux, just a flash, then laughed boisterously—

Crossing through under the falls—sheet—was a thrilling experience, which we enjoyed greatly—and in the Evening we went to Jordan Station to visit "Albrights"—old friends of Rachels—We were royally received—and entertained—and the height of my joy is in seeing how greatly my Darling enjoys it all—

November 30, 1860 Friday. We spent the day so cheerily visiting with these kind hearted people—

December 1, 1860 Saturday. at 9 we took train for Preston arriving at 11:15 and were met by Sister Mary[ii] Cous J. L. Bowman—who conveyed us to Hon J. E. Bowmans,[1] where kindly greetings and a sumptuous dinner awaited us—P.M. we went via Berlin,[2] and Waterloo to Elmira—to the home of S. S. Weaver[ee] and Sister Lydia[dd]— Darlings eldest sister—where we were received royally—and feasted and entertained in best of fashion—

December 2, 1860 Sunday. A quiet day in the Home—S. S. Weaver[ee] and Sister Lydia[dd] and their little sons Angus[ff] and Astor[gg]— make up such a happy home group——

1. This is almost certainly "I" (for Isaac) Erb Bowman, the only prominent officeholder among the many branches of Rachel's father's family. At this time he was treasurer for the Township of Woolwich, which included Elmira, and was later elected to the provincial and national parliaments. J. O. Coté, *Political Appointments and Elections in the Province of Canada from 1841 to 1865* (Ottawa, 1918), p. 117, however, gives the initials as Samuel does, so there may be some confusion over the rendering of the first name. J. K. Johnson, ed., *Canadian Directory of Parliament, 1867–1967*, 2nd ed. (Ottawa, 1968), p. 65; Waterloo Historical Society, *Annual Report* (1932), p. 334 and (1933), p. 21.
2. Now Kitchener, Ontario.

Evening I do feel very happy in my new state—
I am only beginning to know what it really is to love and be
loved—Darling is ideal.

December 3, 1860 Monday. I spent much of the day in the store,
counting room and noting . the business of the Firm "Wenger,
Weaver and Company" wholesale and retail dealers in Dry Goods,
Groceries &c and Manufacturers of Woolen Goods—all kinds of
Farm products taken in exchange—Had a good social day dotted
with business—and I practiced considerably on the violin to fill in
time—

December 4, 1860 Tuesday. Darling helps Mary[ii] to wash. J. L.
Bowman and I discuss Slavery freely—and possibility of war over
it[3]—Evening I am a little unwell—Quite happy—but feel I need to
be better, a more perfect Christian man—

December 5–7, 1860 We visit at Uncle Noah Bowmans—They
took us to Elora Falls—see wild romantic scenery in abundance.
Darling and I fairly enraptured with The Falls, rock walls, & cliffs—
a delightful christian family—a son George—daughter Rachel—
another son Clemens, pretty well grown, and growing is the
group—active in U.B. Church work—and practical family and
neighborhood religion[4]—

December 8, 1860 Returned to Elmyra, to S. S. Weavers[ee]—we take
tea at Peter Wengers, and go to a "singing"—proves a bore—

December 9, 1860 We visit "Burkholders"—Aunty Burkholders—
and then Grand Father Clemens[5]—I am much pleased with my Darlings Kin-folks and Friends. We remain at the Clemenses over 10th

---

3. Although South Carolina was already trying to withdraw from the Union, no
one yet knew either what the other slaveholding states would do or how the Buchan-
an administration would respond to the crisis. Lincoln's election in November had
provided the pretext for South Carolina's dramatic move, but he would not assume
office until March 1861.

4. Rachel's mother's sister, Lydia Ann Clemens, had married Noah S. Bowman,
the eldest son of one of Rachel's father's older brothers. Though technically Rachel's
cousin, Noah was sixteen years older than she. The family later had a fourth child
(see Samuel's entry for July 28, 1862). They were farming near West Montrose.
BHWT, II, 23–24, 105–06.

5. Rachel's maternal grandfather, Abraham Clemens. *Ibid.*

& 11—Take in the Uncle George Clemens[6] family under the same roof—and then "Uncle Amos Clemenses"[7] and The great Flax Factory—These people delight in entertaining us in their homes—and showing us points of interest. We were weighed at the Factory— Rachel 165 and I 135 lbs—

December 11, 1860   Eve. We arrive at "Uncle Sam Bowmans" near Blair[8]—I do love this place and these folks very much.

Darling not very well—Too much excitement, and too many changes. It is very cold too—hovering along zero every night, and even below some mornings.

December 12, 1860   Cousin "Nancy" took us to Uncle Wendel Bowmans[9] for the day, had a nice time. Eve took Tea at J. B. Slichters—and enjoyed a good little pr. meeting—Met Rev Price— Returned to Uncle Sams for the night——

December 13, 1860   10° below zero—We visited Uncle Dave Snyders til P.M.—Then Cous Danl Snyders for Tea[10]—returning to Uncles for the night—we are very happy in each other these days, and also in Our Saviours love—God is so good to me, and mine—O! for more love to Him—

December 14, 1860   We visit Cous Amos Weavers—Fine time—Evening they took us to Uncle Amos Clemenses to enjoy a Turkey roast. We remained all night—

December 15, 1860   Sunday. At Freeport—Toll Bridge Church— Cous Rev J. B. Bowman preached.   was a good service—We dined at Mose Eshelmans   P.M. attended S.S.—I taught a class, and closed

---

6. George Clemens (b. 1831) was Rachel's mother's youngest brother. He had married Salome Bowman and they had five children at this time; more to follow later. *Ibid.*

7. Amos Clemens (1821–1875) was Rachel's mother's oldest brother. He lived with his wife, Mary Wismer, and their seven children near the village of Chickopee in Waterloo Township. *Ibid.*

8. Samuel Bowman (1802–1883) was one of Rachel's father's older brothers. He lived with his wife, Elizabeth Bauman Bowman, and their seven children on the original Bauman farmstead at Blair. *Ibid.*, pp. 25–26.

9. Wendel Bowman (1806–1876) was another of Benjamin B. Bowman's older brothers. Nancy was Wendel's oldest daughter, who was married to Joseph Stauffer and also lived at Blair. *Ibid.*, p. 26.

10. Leah Bowman (1804–1876), one of Benjamin B. Bowman's older sisters, married David Snyder. Daniel was one of their sons. *Ibid.*, p. 16.

with prayer—We took Tea at Uncle Sams—Later went to Uncle Amoses—We had Experience Meeting in the evening—were all happy—

December 17, 1860   23 Vis—47 its etc[11]—

December 18–19, 1860   Cold. We are letting up a little in our visitings—Darling has cold—and so we tarry about Old Carlisle—Blair—Gault—Preston—McNallys—and take in the Sights & scenes of Rachels early days—and meet many of her early associates—and enjoy many many jolly sleighrides.

December 20, 1860   Do up Gault—

December 21, 1860   McNallys—Shoutzs—Kolbs—

December 22, 1860   at Jacob Kolbs—The day and night, Sleighing—Singing—and good times generally—
   It is very cold—but sleighing is good, and 15 to 25 packed into a sleigh, make merry as they glide along, and every place they stop—soon partakes of hilariousness—Darling and I are well and happy—and overflow with jollity—
   I feel that I am too great a fool—Oh! for grace to be a better Christian, and show a more holy example—O! That our lives were more hidden with Christ in God

December 23, 1860   Sunday. Today Mr Kolbs took us to Elmira—we were very happy to get back after our long visiting tour of weeks and Weavers[ee] received us most cordially—Evening we went to prayer meeting—It seemed good—I feel that I want to be doing more posative good—I seem to be doing so little—O! That I were better——

December 24, 1860   Monday. A letter from Brother John[d]—He has sent my money to Missouri. A letter from Bell Kimmel from Missouri. Well my money matters will straighten out by and by—Evening S. S. Ws[ee]—gave us a party—some 9–10 pairs present—Singing—Playing games—and a little make-believe waltzing, with good eating was chief in the program—we had rather a wild time of it, and every one seemd to enjoy every bit of it–Retired about 1:30 OCK Darling and I are well and so happy in each other.

11. Apparently a tally: twenty-three visits and forty-seven items, presumably wedding gifts.

December 25, 1860 Christmas We had a great Dinner at Mrs Johnsons and a fine time for certain—Eve went to Uncle Noah Bowmans. Had a big Supper and a splendid time as a Christmas affair. After Supper had an "Animal Show"—creating lots of fun. A large Mirror resting on a Small table against the wall, and draped by a large curtain which parted at the center of the mirror—Lights so arranged as to strike the face, and also the glass when the curtain was parted and the person looked in to see their desired animal—

Now of all the company who desired to see some special animal were in a special room awaiting the Show, while the Operators—Rachel and Myself—and the older people—were in the Show-room to take in the fun—Two operators—stood ready to part the curtains carefully at the right moment—Another—This was myself—inquired of each desirer what animal they most desired to see—and insisted they must be explicit, have the supposed appearance of the animal or object on their mind, and expect to see it when the curtain was drawn aside, and they looked into the Cage—Take J. L. Bowman who was a bearded man with bushy hair and large eyes—and nose & lips—especially the lower lip—and he wished to see a Buffalo.

I took him alone into the show room—told him he must stoop a little, before the curtain would open—and pretty close to it—instantly the operators drew it aside, and—the scene was stunning—Mr. B. was startled for sure and declared he had never known that he could, by lights, and shades and position be made to look so much like a Buffalo—

Now Mr. J. L. B remained and another was brought in to see—An Ape—Baboon—an Angel—anything—The operator usually suggesting, &c. &c.

The ½ hour was hilarious—About 10 OCK Four sleigh loads of us started out for a ride and sing, and good time—and we had all of it, and reached S. S. Weavers[ee] at 11 OCK.

December 26, 1860 SURE! These exciting occasions leave us a little enfeebled spiritually—In fact we are a little trifling—tho I hope not wicked—I want to be really good—My wife is so good, and so dear to me—and is such a favorite in all our gatherings and doings—Another day of sleighing—we dined at Mr. Moyers.[12] Then went to Snyders ½ hour—Then to Uncle Burkholders a while—and to Uncle Weavers for Tea—Cousin Ira, Noah, Nancy and Eliza Bowman went

12. Canadian relatives of Aaron Moyer, who had helped Rachel get her teaching job in Quakertown the year before.

along to tea and for an evening—We returned about 10 OCK—Our visits and calls were pleasant indeed all around—

December 27, 1860 Thursday. I had such a glorious season of secret prayer this morning—I have so much to be thankful for—Our good health and happiness. I wrote to Mother,[b] and in my diary. Helped Rachel and Mary[ii] about the washing—hangout clothes &c., I read a good deal—Practiced long on violin—A home day—

December 28, 1860 Friday. Rachel, Mary[ii] and I in Cutter—with Charliyhorse—took a ride to Peel—we called on Rev. Brown—a colored brother—who is laid up with a broken leg—but he thinks it is "beginning to ignite," as it is "kind o sumwhat—jaggy, curus" we did have a funny time hearing his quaint talking—Called also on Major Hardin—also colored—and is interesting as the Rev. Brown[13]—

December 29, 1860 Saturday. Wife and I had a long talk on Child bearing—we differ on some points, but sweetly agree to disagree, and avoid any risks by continued abstinence &c, &c.[14]

December 30–31, 1860 Visiting with the Clemenses, we close the old year with many thanksgivings for each other and our numerous Kindred and friends—I am so happy to have a darling wife. Such a dear good one—Our daily aspiration and prayer is to both become better Christians. Thus we end the Old Year 1860.

January 1, 1861 We spent the day and evening at Carneys and Kilburns, and Hollidays til 11 OCK P.M. a very social time throughout—On way home Darling & I—all enwrapped in Robes—had such delightsome times all the way—Oh! I do thank God that He has made us for each other, and that our union is such a continual cup of happiness—we got home about 12 OCK.

13. Blacks had been in the upper Grand River Valley in small numbers since the early 1830s. Despite a substantial influx from 1850 to 1860, however, they still constituted only a tiny percentage of the population. The welcome extended to black members by the Canadian Brethren testified to their liberal position on the issue of race, for the norm in most Canadian churches was de facto segregation. See Robin W. Winks, *The Blacks in Canada: A History* (New Haven, 1971), pp. 146, 337–61, et passim.

14. This short entry indicates that the Cormanys discussed family planning openly and that Rachel was a cautious young bride, unwilling to risk an unwanted pregnancy. It becomes evident later in Samuel's diary that he is more anxious to have children than Rachel, yet he defers to his wife's views. For a full exposition of the importance of this evidence that some women asserted control over their own destinies within the nineteenth-century marriage bond, see Carl Degler, *At Odds: Women and the Family in America from the Revolution to the Present* (New York, 1980), pp. 207–08.

131

January 7, 1861 Monday. Well we have been sleighing and visiting, then visiting and sleighing and withal 3, 4, or 5 times the day and night feasting, with amusements sandwiched in, and then more amusements—so this is great honeymooning indeed—

There is much excitement and discussion of possible WAR IN THE UNITED STATES—

Matters surely are in lamentably unsettled condition.

The hotheadness of the South, and the invinsibleness of the North, on the Slavery question, i.e., That slavery shall not be extended into the Teritories—nor into the North,[15] and that the Union can not be dissolved, but must stand: and stand one and inseparable as a Body of States. This is the Slogan of all really sober-minded Statesmen of the great majority of the States.

Poor Missouri! A house divided against itself—

A sorry looking prospect, for a young man to take his young wife to, to start the making of a new home—But the Octagon Cottage is builded—

Nearly all Darlings Friends advise us not to think of going out there in the Spring.

WAIT! They say, until things become more Settled—

Surely there is no telling what we would be going into as matters now stand—and are likely to stand in the Spring.[16] S. S. Weaver[ee]—My Brother-in-law, proposes to give me work in the Firm of Wenger Weaver and Company, and The firm suggests that Rachel and Lydia[dd] set up a Millinery Department in connection with the Store, and so be busy until developments suggest more favorable conditions for our "going west to grow up with the Country"— Monday P.M. Uncles took us to visit Cousin Sipes near Blair—

January 8, 1861 Tuesday. We do up Gault, and have our Family group taken—7 for $4.75—To send to Friends—

15. Following the Dred Scott decision, Lincoln and the Republicans had raised the possibility that slaveholders were conspiring not only to extend slavery into federal territories, but also to re-legalize it in the Northern states. David M. Potter, *The Impending Crisis, 1848–1861* (New York, 1976), pp. 288–89. The charge was taken seriously. See, in this context, Michael F. Holt's discussion of the widespread loss of faith in the political process in *The Political Crisis of the 1850s* (New York, 1978).

16. It was already evident that the citizens of Missouri were badly divided during the secession crisis. A large number, especially those of German descent in the St. Louis area, were fiercely loyal to the Union. Yet Missouri was a slave state, and there were paramilitary organizations pledged to defend both that institution and the right of the separate states to decide their own destinies. When the Civil War began, both sides claimed the state, rival governors struggled for control, and residents endured long periods of anarchy and guerrilla warfare.

January 9, 1861 Wednesday. We visit GrandPa Clemens—Evening—return to Elmira and enter agreement with Wenger Weaver and Co to start in next Monday Collecting & Settling accounts for the Firm—

January 10, 1861 Thursday. We are both well and happy, and are pretty well through with our protracted visiting, and are becoming restless to be doing something aside from spending time, money and energy almost entirely for entertainment and amusement—
But ah! me! We have all this while sought to be a blessing to those we have met, and associated with, and have been entertained by—Thank God for grace to be unashamed of our religion, willing to be known as Christians, and as aspirents to greater attainments—

January 13, 1861 Sunday. Now that we have concluded to remain in Canada til Spring or until War Matters take a different form, we are taking more special interest in the S. S. work, and other Church work.

January 14–16, 1861 Monday &c &c We are moving our things into The vacant Gross rooms—and leisurely getting into shape for having a home of our own possibly soon—I have entered upon my duties with The Firm as an Accountant.
The Firm does a credit business, but requires settlement of all a/cs about the end of the year—
My work is to go over the Books make out Bills of all unsettled a/cs at 1st of the year—Then call on such for settlement, taking cash for ballance, or notes bearing 6% interest—
Sleighing is fine—"Charlie" The Horse is a very fleet-footed little fellow, and my Cutter (sleigh) is very light about 100 lbs, and with Buffalo Robe under me, and another over me, and fur Gloves—Zero weather is not to be dreaded at all—So I go out on "concession" ½ the day and back another settling with residents as I stop here and there—
A pretty nice employment this—Darling and her Sister Lydia[dd]—Mrs Weaver—are busy working up the Milinery business each day. And in the evening we compare notes of our days work—And later we go to our room and it is most delightful to love and be loved.

IX
Rachel's Life in Rural Canada
December 2, 1860–May 1, 1862

What *began as a honeymoon visit was becoming an ever-lengthening period of exile. Rachel is frustrated with the lack of direction in her life and complains about the behavior of some of her kin. Her situation is further aggravated when Samuel quits his job and the Cormanys are forced to relocate and face the prospect of becoming little more than dependents of Rachel's parents. To make matters worse, Samuel nearly dies of diphtheria. Rachel's record of the Cormanys' long waiting period in Canada ends as she is preparing for the birth of her first child.*

December 2, 1860 (In sister Lydias[dd] parlor. At Elmira[1] C. W.) It went very hard to bid adieu to my old home with its many pleasant associations. It seemed like an imposibility to leave but the tie— love—that bound me to my husband was still stronger. Yea much stronger than that which bound me to my childhood home. We had a very pleasant journey. Spent some time at Niagra Falls. Went under the sheet.[2] the view is *grand*, superlatively so. The scenery round is beautiful beyond description It is vain to try to describe or say more. I had quite a chat with a Sister of charity at Niagra depot. We took the evening train for Jordan to visit an early very intimate lady friend. It was dusk when we got there. We had not seen each other for such a length of time that we did not recognize each other at first It was a joyful meeting. The dear woman I do love her. We stayed two nights & a day with her, then started enroute for the old home. Sister Mary[ii] & Cous J. L. B.[3] awaited us at the depot, & conveyed us to Elmira 20 miles (where we now are), where quite a party was waiting to welcome us. O! how glad I was to see them.

January 14, 1861 Elmira. We have now been visiting a month & a half. We enjoyed it very much. I could not begin to tell all the particulars, & deem it not necessary since Mr C. has them in his

1. The village of Elmira was located in the upper Grand River Valley, some twelve miles north of the larger town of Waterloo.
2. I.e., under the falls.
3. Probably John B. Bowman, the son of Rachel's father's brother.

134

diary. Today he commenced collecting & clerking for the firm of Wenger & Weaver. Sister[dd] & I are going to commence the bonnet & dressmaking.

February 20, 1861 Our papers Telescope & Valey Spirit came this evening[4] In the Telescope I noticed the death of Sml. Evers. One of my schoolmates. It made me feel quite sad. One by one of those dear ones are going to their last quiet resting place. Schoolmates, & in particular, Classmates become very dear to each other. Almost like members of the same family.

February 22, 1861 Sister[dd] & I laid in more stock for our trade. We read a great deal, are reading Livingstons travel.[5]

February 23, 1861 Bought some muslin for a counterpane sheets &c &c. I have not yet been initiated into housekeeping but am preparing for it. All seems so odd. More like a dream than reality. I read a great deal we do not have much sewing to do so I read.

February 24, 1861 It is quite cold this morning. the sun however shines very brightly which gives an animated appearance to nature. I am happy & well this morning I do not regret that I have given myself to such a noble man. I love him more every day. Washed this forenoon, did not feel well. Attended Gabrait's lecture. The lectures are good, but his delivery *very poor*. Made some very unbecoming expressions.

February 27, 1861 Went along with my dear good husband on a collecting tour, spent a few minutes at Mr Kilbornes. Thence to the 8th line of Peel.[6] We called in at many places. The buildings are

---

4. The *Religious Telescope* was the leading journal and the chief source of denominational news for the United Brethren church. It was published, usually biweekly, from 1831 to 1963 (under various titles), when denominational mergers ended its separate existence. The *Valley Spirit* was the dominant newspaper in the county where Samuel grew up. Published in Chambersburg, Pa., the *Spirit* was also the voice of the Democratic party in the Cumberland Valley. I. H. M'Cauley et al., *Historical Sketch of Franklin County, Pennsylvania* (Chambersburg, 1978), appendix, pp. 294–96; Richard H. McDonnell, "The Chambersburg *Valley Spirit,* 1850–1861," *The Pennsylvania Magazine of History and Biography* 104 (April 1980), 200–20.

5. David Livingstone, *Travels and Researches in South Africa* . . . (Philadelphia, J. W. Bradley, 1860). It is easy to imagine how an educated woman isolated on the Canadian frontier, who not only knew several African missionaries but had also considered such a life for herself, would find volumes like this absorbing.

6. I.e., the eighth range of surveyed farmsteads in the township of Peel. This section of Canada was still quite sparsely settled.

mostly small & of log, the roofs also of log. The people were friendly nearly every where. There are some real jolly old fellow in these new countries. Dined at Mr. Cards. The old gentleman was once a sailor, they are real fine folks, had a good plain dinner. Towards evening we got into still newer & rougher country & met some rough people, went through some dreadful bad wood roads. I wonder how people could ever imagine such crocked roads. got O! so tired. Still I enjoyed the ride, the weather was delightful.

February 28, 1861 O! What a lovely day this is. It will not be long until gentle Spring will depose grim old Winter & banish him to the north pole. In the afternoon Mr[ee] & Mrs[dd] Weaver & I went to A. Cavanaws on a visit. His Bachelorsanctum looks finely. he got us a grand supper Returned in time for lecture by Golb.

March 1, 1861 The first day of spring with weather to suit. Got a chart of my head. Husband did of his also.[7] Dear Land! What a sight I was when acting out Bridget from the Emerald Isle, to scare off some bad boys. It was well that I had a mask on or I should have betrayed myself by laughing, so they could not see me laugh.

March 2, 1861 Mr.[ee] & Mrs W[dd] & children[ffgg] went to Berlin. Cous. Lydia & I were left alone, finished our work then read. Evening attended lecture again, had my head examined in public.

April 1, 1861 Have been at Fathers[aa] a week to help them clean house & fix up. took a severe cold so that I was sick several days. Unger was so unreasonable about the house that they moved in H. Bechtels granddady house. All things came safe except one of my teacups & glass preserve dish. My dear good Samuel came for me I was so very glad to seem him it seemed so long since I had last seen him. We brought my summer wear & pictures along up.

April 10, 1861 Mr[ee] & Mrs[dd] Weaver have been away since the 7th. It seems a little odd. Yet O! so good for my Sml. & I to be alone. I sometimes make horible mistakes in cooking. The greatest trouble is that I am so fearful when alone evenings. There is a drunken man in the store. I hear the cutting up all evening. he swears so dreadfully.

April 11, 1861 Mr Weaver[ee] & Angus[gg] came home this evening. Lydia[dd] staid down to help them (Fathers)[aa] move, they have bought the house from Unger.

7. Phrenological charts.

April 12, 1861 This is my 25th birthday. Dear & I had such a nice talk this morning before getting up. I do love him very much, he is so very good. He gave me such a splendid birthday gift. Such a pretty book. he does not know how much I thank him for it way deep down in my heart. I witnessed such an awful deed of depravity. A man commiting masturbation. A feeling of horror came over me. My face burned with shame for the brute. Sister[dd] has not come yet. It is raining so fast, has been raining more or less all day & last night. My precious dear is sitting beside me covering my neck with K——, I do love him more than is possible for me to express.

April 13, 1861 Sister L.[dd] is home again. She had quite a time helping fathers clean the house. Unger made some money out of father but lost all their regard for him through it. We baked & served. Had an old flame for dinner. Visited at J. Bowmans in the afternoon.

April 14, 1861 Dear & I were to church this morning Mr Swan preached. Text "And their hearts were fully set in them to do evil." Afternoon. Read our Bridal Gift through & some of my old essays, retired early.

April 15, 1861 L[dd] & I did a large washing I was not well, several times I came near giving out.   still I tugged through with it. Some Pa. visiters came yet for dinner. I was glad to see them, felt very tired in the evening & had to suffer considerable. Dear sympathizes with me very much. I appreciate his sympathy. I do love him very much

April 16, 1861 Feel some better than I did yesterday. Cut a sack by measure. Ironed the clothes, & straightened up my room. My precious has toothache would that I could relieve him. I fear he will have to get it extracted. Am somewhat tired. It is already quite late. My thoughts are quite serious. I desire to live according to the "Golden rule."

April 17, 1861 Sister Lydia,[dd] My Samuel & I were to Uncle Noahs to eat sugar. They had not been boiling sugar for several days & had not intended to do so until we came.   he boils in large pans has it arranged well. Dear & I strolled away down to the river which is pretty high. We had a grand time sugaring off.[8] It was quite cold to be out.

8. "Sugaring off" refers to the process of tapping and boiling maple sap to produce syrup and sugar.

April 20, 1861 A. Cavanah was with us last night & this morning while doing up our work he read for us among the rest of the pieces he read was a ghost story. Dear & I are truly very happy in each other.

April 21, 1861 Were to preaching. S. Fear preached. Afternoon wrote letter to R. H. Winter then we read in my pretty birthday gift, & in the Bible together & prayed. Took a stroll to the river, on the way home called on Christian Lieks spent a short time in prayer before retiring Dear got so happy. O! he is so good. If tears could wash my sins away, I could weep myself away. I do want to become a better christian.

April 22, 1861 L^{dd} & I did a pretty large washing, got through till ten. Got ready to go to Josep Fears. Had such a droll time to get off. Sister L.^{dd} wished the baby wagon fixed to haul her heavy boy. One of the clerks said he had a new one which she might have. I took the boy down. Sister took pillows for the wagon. In the Hurry I sold a bonnet & took the order for another. Knowing that it had taken me quite a while I thought the rest must have gone. Still I thought best to see whether Mrs W.^{dd} had gone. When I got there she was waiting for a call to tell her we were ready. when we got out Sister^{dd} was piling the children into a big wagon. I asked what all this meant, "Why says she instead of a baby wagon John brought a light spring wagon. We took a hearty laugh & I with the children was piled into a big wagon & rode a short distance We were very much fatigued when we reached Mr Fears. Had quite a jolly time there eating sugar. Walked home in the evening. My feet suffered much. I fully realized the evils of a bad foundation. A. Cavanah was here when we returned had quite a jolly time after our return. I brought some taffy along for Dear

April 23, 1861 Ironed the clothes this morning, am quite tired. Trimmed strawbonnets this afternoon, & gave L.^{dd} a lesson in drawing. She does pretty well. Angus^{gg} has been very ugly & hateful all day. It does agravate me so much at him that I can scarcely help chastising him. Am very tired & sleepy. It is raining hard.

April 27, 1861 Have been very busy all week making & trimming bonnets. Am very tired this evening. Trimmed a hat for Ls baby^{ff} after 9 oclock, it was past 12 oclock when I retired L.^{dd} had gone to bed only a short time before I went

April 28, 1861   L. A,[dd] & S. S. Weaver[ee] & children went to Blair today. Dear & I went to church. Mr Brown preached, a prety good sermon. We were too late. It is a shame that we did not get up earlier. Were to S School in the afternoon. My shaker was quite a curiosity to the rising generation there. Am not very well.

April 29, 1861   Finished a letter to Dears Mother.[b] Am not well at all, could not eat any breakfast. Got a breakfast which would not be equaled in any circle.   forgot to salt the hash. Do [i.e., ditto] the potatoes. Coffee not strong.   doughnuts hard as rocks. Well to redeem my name I must exert myself & show my skill at getting dinner. A very pleasant delightful morning. Adieu My dear Journal, or dinner will be late too.

May 6, 1861   I had to neglect my journal for a whole week on account of sister Lydias[dd] illness   She needed a great deal of my time to supply her wants. Very frequently I did not get the breakfast dishes washed until nearly dinner & the dinner dishes until near supper time. I had to work quite late to get through in the evening. Not being used to such hard work I felt it very much. My limbs pained me so of evenings that I could scarcely sleep   Lydia[dd] was quite badly ill, she had something like spasms on fryday. I was very much frightened. The babe[ff] is being weaned too. Mr C & I take care of him nights. The first two nights he cried himself nearly hoarse, since then he has slept pretty well until last night. I think the teeth trouble him. Yesterday Mr C & I were over to Uncle Noahs, took Angus[gg] along. Was not well. Mr. C. is not well today, he has a pain in his shoulder. The Dear Good Pet, he is so very kind to me. Yea more than *kind,* so *tender, affectionate, true,* & *loving.* How could I be otherwise than happy with such a husband. Today they got a little girl to take care of the children which is indeed quite a relief to me. I am getting quite expert in the cooking line. I make a good deal of music with the pots & kettles. What if they did laugh at my first attempt at bread making & said that it would take a week for the yeast to rise, it being so stiff. I am sure it was not burnt when done anyhow. It is good. My pies were scorched rather too much. It is raining. O! these onions give a horibly delicious scent to our room. Mr Weaver[ee] has gone to visit a sick brotherinlaw. O! it does seem so nice to have a few minutes to sit down to rest.   last week, day after day I could rest only while eating

May 11, 1861   Another week has passed. Sister[dd] is getting better. Ma[bb] & Pa[aa] were up to see us. too[k] Angus[gg] along down, which is quite a relief for he is so contrary & hateful.   we still have the babe[ff] up with us. Made a good many bonnets this week. This was an eventful day. 1stly we slept too long & did not get breakfast quite in time, 2ndly, waited on Lydia[dd] 3rdly stired in the bread, 4thly, bathed & dressed the babe,[ff] 5thly sent the girl for the diaper pin who came down stairs like a whirlwind & knocked bread tray bread & all over, & spilled bread, flower & all on the floor, 6thly, She instead of putting the dipper into the water bucket stuck it into the yeast 7thly, I went to milk the cow   8th Helped the girl to wash dishes for I surely thot she would not get through this day 9thly Had to hurry her all day to keep her at work. Lastly, Had quite a time, tore my dress only 4 times today. I could scarcely help saying "Confound the nail kegs. Yet many more wonderful things happened during the week, for instance I had several pretty warm discussions with Dr Pattison on the mode of treating patients. He could not establish his assertions with sound reason. Made a boiler full of blood purifying stuff for L.[dd] to take   Such foolishness. It is quite late.   O! I did not say that we have made arrangements to go to housekeeping.

May 12, 1861   Washed today. Had quite a large washing. It was pretty late until I got the morning work done to commence. I washed with all the strength I had to get through. Am not well. Am full of pain.

May 13, 1861   Am scarcely able to be up. O! It seems as if I would be pulled to pieces with pain.

May 14, 1861   Some better, but not near well. Ironed all the clothes. Lydia[dd] is still sick but is gaining a little daily

May 18, 1861   All the bonnets are finished. We have taken in quite a little pile of money for bonnets   I baked bread & pies, finished a bonnet, planted some beets. Prepared some things to take along home. I am very tired. Dear worked very hard today fixing up the yard to the little home we have rented. We want to bring our things up on Monday & go right to housekeeping. It is quite late.

May 19, 1861   Went to S. School. There were more there than expected, even those who were so bitterly opposed to having it in the morning were at their posts in good time. We started home right after Sunday school. Had quite a pleasant ride. We met Father[aa] on his way to S School & Mother[bb] was on her way to Uncle Sams with Aunt Lea. We insisted on their going to the places intended, so they went & we went to the old burying ground. Many narrow beds have been made there since I last visited there. Relatives & acquaintances rest there.

May 20, 1861   Were out quite early. After we had breakfasted Mr C. & Pa[aa] went to Preston & got a cooking stove.   Lizzy[oo] & I took a strool in the Nursery.   got a few flowers. Mother[bb] gave me a jug of Applebutter & a jug of Elderberries, a basket of apples, a small roll of butter & a piece of cheese. We started right after dinner. Angus[gg] went home with us. Just above Avon, Mr C. got out & gathered a lot of pine cones for me. All went safely until we got into Waterloo when the axle of the wagon broke. Fortunate I Mussleman came along & too[k] the goods, & Mr C got a pole & fastened it so as to keep the weight off the wheel. The Applebutter jug lost the cork out & split nearly all the butter. I was so sorry for the good applebutter.

May 21, 1861   Did up the mornings work for Lydia[dd] & then went to clean our house. O! but it was dirty. Mrs Gross whitewashed up-stairs. I did not get through until after dark. Mr C. came over & helped me. Am very tired, so much so that I ache all over

May 22, 1861   Got breakfast & did up the work, then carried my things over, which was no small job. Made up the bed. In the evening got supper for the first time in our own home. Although it was but simple, it tasted well. Am quite tired this evening too. Have such a bad taste in my mouth & sore throat. Had some of it all week.

May 23, 1861   Am still fixing up. Did a large ironing for Lydia.[dd] I milk the cow for her and am to have a pint of milk a day for it. Mr C. is working over here today, making fence, table, lounge &c. planting &c &c.   Slept in our own house for the first time last night. It seems so nice to have a home of our own, it seems more like living.

May 24, 1861   This is Mr C's 23 birthday. Also the queens birthday. S.S. W's[ee] & we were up to A. Cavanaws on a fishing excursion. S. S. W.[ee] acted rather small & mighty selfish so that we got insulted which spoilt the enjoyment of the day. I have sometimes wished for Mr Cs sake that we had gone right to Mo. instead of coming up here. Nothing puts me out quicker than to be lorded over & nothing excites my ire sooner than to see some one trying to lord over My Samuel. However it is always better to suffer than to do wrong.

May 25, 1861   Baked for Lydia,[dd] Scrubbed & baked for us This is a delightful day, took a good footbath after I got through with my work. I do not feel near so tired since.

May 26, 1861   Six Months ago today we were married & are happier today than ever. We are truly very happy in each other. We were to S. School   I do like my class. The school seems like another set of children since My Samuel is at the head.

May 27, 1861   Cloudy & rainy. Had to attend a lawsuit as witness in a dirty duch [i.e., German] mess. My S. took me over in the buggy. Aunt Lydia was here, brought us about 2 bus. of potatoes. I cut out two dusters for her   Evening attended S. School meeting. Mrs Johnson acts like a heathen in those meetings.

May 28, 1861   It is raining hard this evening. I covered a centre table. Sewed all day as fast as I could. O! The roof leaks & letts the water into the kitchen.

June 9, 1861   Were to S. School this morning. Prizes were distributed   all seemed to be well pleased. Dear Husband spoke so good to the children. Mrs Moore & H. Weaver were here for dinner. Afternoon Dear & Angus[gg] & I went to Benners to meeting.   buggy broke on the way. Was not well.

June 10, 1861   Monday. Made a bonnet & 2 borders & read considerable. Walked about ½ mile this morn & eve to milk the cow, felt very tired when I got back. Was much troubled with vomiting yesterday & today   Dear was out collecting   brought me such a beautiful boquet of wild flowers. He made such a good little speech when presenting it. I wish I could remember it. I would insert it. Here he comes. Hear him. "This boquet my beloved wife, though simple, composed but of wild flowers, comes to thee laden with love as strong the restless tide, and free as the breath thou breathest."

June 11, 1861   Sister Lydia[dd] & I were to Uncle Noahs on a visit. We had a fine time. It was quite warm, still quite pleasant. We did not return until it was cool this evening. Aunt Lydia gave each of us a little chickie for pets. I also took a dress & bonnet to make. I am glad I have a good deal of work. I am so happy in my Samuel. He is so good.   we are very happy together.

June 19, 1861   Did my washing. Had quite a lot of clothes   I almost gave out before I got through. Afternoon scrubbed my kitchen & sewed. My pet chick got so troublesome that I had to give him to Lydia.[dd] Mrs Thomas called in, we are just getting acquainted.   I think I shall like her. Mr. J. Fear took supper with us. Had orranges for supper.

June 21, 1861   I have been so very busy this week that I could get no time to write.   Last night we had a powerful rain, & today was a general planting day. I planted beets & cabbage plants & am very tired   These are delightful moonlight evenings. My S'ml & I are very happy together

July 7, 1861   This is Sunday again. We were to preaching & S. School. The S. School is quite interesting. There is quite a competition between my class and Mrs Johnsons, each is trying to exceed the other in the No. verses they recite. It is quite warm & cloudy. Mr. Foreman preached a good sermon. Last week My Samuel & I were to my Fathers.[aa] We spent the greater part of the week there.   we had intended to visit my uncles but could not get through at home. We canned Rubarb, currants & strawberries for winter use & put down carpets for Mother.[bb] We had a fine time. Brother Clem.[cc] is back. I think he will stay & practice in C. W. now. My Samuel sprained his wrist last Wednesday a week, it was very painful, & is yet.   I fear it will be more serious than we thought. Mr. Weavers[ee] are away today. We have little Amos over here, he is such a pretty little pet.

July 9, 1861   I helped Lydia[dd] can fruit in the A.M.   the rest of the day I sewed at a coat for My Samuel. Evening read war news quite a while. It looks dreary enough on the other side of the great lakes. It fairly makes my heart to read the horrible accounts of war. We have had several fine showers today, also such a beautiful rainbow. My Samuel & I are still very happy in each other. I do love him so much.

July 12, 1861   Just now a funeral procession passed through the village. I knew nothing of it until I saw the procession. A gloom passed over my spirits on beholding the coffin. I wondered whether the departed spirit had gone to that world of light or that deep abyss of woe. Oh! how important to live holy, for our last day will surely come also. I could not but think of my brothers[llmm] who have exchanged worlds, & it seems as though

Over the river they becon me.
Loved ones who have gone to the farther side

July 30, 1861 Can it be that I have neglected my Journal so long. I did not even note the fine time My Samuel & I had visiting & canning strawberries at Fathers.[aa] We put up a quantity of fruit for winter use while there. Another great event that transpired was the campmeeting. We staid from Tuesday morning until Wednesday evening. I did not enjoy one part of the exercises of the camp, viz being gazed at. I wore my shaker, it being the most suitable bonnet for the occasion I had. If I had gone to a heathen country I should have thought nothing of it, but it seemed passing strange that civilized people should be guilty of such heathenish actions. Otherwise I enjoyed the meeting. We visited Grand fathers, Uncle Moses Bowmans, &c. &c. they gave us lots of good things. Last Sabbath was quarterly meeting over at Benners. Sister Lydia[dd] was baptized. She seems quite happy since. My Samuel has felt some scruples of concience since he has been clerking in selling liquor, but ever tried to think it not wrong, since he did only what his employers asked of him. lately however he has been fully convinced in his own mind that in order to retain to favor of God he must quit the sale of liquor. He told Mr W.[ee] that his concience forbade him selling the stuff any longer. It is plain that it will not go to have a clerk who refuses to sell a part of the articles to be sold. Mr. Weaver[ee] informed My Samuel of the fact, so as a consequence of following the dictates of conscience we will have to look for another situation.[9] I know the Lord will provide, for he has promised to do so to those who trust in Him.

August 1, 1861 This is the great emancipation day which the colored people celebrate.[10] Elmira is quite of of people this morning, quite a display of colors. The white people turn out well. Eve. A. Hunspergers took supper with us, also Aunt Lydia

August 2, 1861 Washed this A.M. & made a bonnet this P.M. & heated my dried fruit over in the oven to keep insects out Cous I & J. Bowman visited us. I dined & supped here.

August 3, 1861 Was very busy making a bonnet & got through just in time. was extremely busy all week

---

9. This episode is covered in greater detail in the next section of Samuel's diary.
10. In 1833, the English Parliament passed a law that ended slavery throughout the British Empire effective Aug. 1, 1834.

August 4, 1861 Went to S. School, felt a little depressed in spirit. Could scarcely keep the tears back. The school seemed to be very sorry that Mr Cormany could not stay on.[11] The house was full. The parents take an interest in the school too & come out. It is encouraging to see the great change for the better. After S. School we went down to the tolebridge to a basket meeting, it was very warm. Angus[gg] went with us. Eve. went to Pa's[aa] for supper then to Uncle Amoses. Had a fine shower.

August 5, 1861 Uncle Amos & My Samuel went to Galt to look for a situation. did not get one. Sml, Cous Henry C, & J. Master went spearing fish. got a large bucket full.

August 6, 1861 Started home early, got home at noon Afternoon I went to visit Mary Bristow & sister. Their Mother is dead, they keep their things very nice & seem to have excellent management. Eve. had a teachers meeting & elected A. Cavanah superintendant of the S. School whose term of office will commence as soon as we leave. Mrs Richer brought be a bowl of white gooseberries.

August 7, 1861 We had intended to go for berries this morning, but it having rained I did not go. My Sml however went & now it is raining pretty hard. I fear it will make him sick. We are writing to the girls today. Sml. returned at noon dripping wet with scarcely a teacup full of berries. It is raining hard & has been all day.

August 8, 1861 It is still raining this evening. It has been drizling all day & is just such a day as we look for in November. W. Cavanaws paid us a visit & took tea. A Cavanaw is married today. What a day for a wedding, rain, rain, rain all day. O well! So it frequently happens. They will live just as happily as though they had a pretty day. Lydia[dd] & I have been taking stock.[12]

August 9, 1861 Finished taking stock & settled. L.[dd] took all the stock. It is still raining. Three days rainy weather seems a very long time without the sun. If we would only take to heart the importance of the Son of righteousnes reigning in our hearts like we do to see the sun we would not have so many dark seasons. O Horrid! Now the cats howl. it fairly makes the chills run up my back.

---

11. After Samuel and his brother-in-law parted ways over the sale of alcohol at Wenger and Weaver, the Cormanys decided to relocate.

12. I.e., toward a dissolution and settlement of their millinery partnership.

August 12, 1861 L. A. W.[dd] & children, Sml, & I were to Mrs. Johnsons & Mr Seatons visiting. It is very rainy & cold & muddy.

August 18, 1861 We were to S. School, had quite an interesting school. Read my Bible after I returned then came to the parlor to write. just as I opened the window a man ran by followed by a woman who was weping aloud, then another woman who said that the report came that her brother was killed   My Samuel has gone to see what has happened. S. is back, the boy is not killed, only stunned, he climbed a tree & fell down.

September 7, 1861 Since I last wrote we made quite a visit at Fathers[aa] & neighborhood. We went to Berlin on the stage, walked from there to J. B. Bowmans. Were caught in the rain. Samuel has all the details of the visit in his diary so I will not repeat. I have not been well for several weeks, feel better today than I did for some time. take hydropathic treatment.[13] The weather is rather cool, rained last night.

September 13, 1861 This is a beautiful morning. I took quite a long walk before breakfast. Samuel is very good to me, yea more tender than ever since my p——y. he cooks nearly as many meals as I do. I am not well at all, the greater part of the time. My walk this morning seems to have done me a great deal of good. On the 11th Aunt Lizzy Burkholder was burried, her death surely was gain to her. A large concourse of people attended her burrial, her old husband seemed quite lost after she was gone. My pen is so poor that I make dreadful scribling

November 11, 1861 It is quite a while my good old journal since I last communicated with you. Well now for a long chat. The first event worthy of notice was our removal to Carlisle Hill on the 1st of Sept. We came down on the large team wagon of W. & W.[14] O! such a ride. We were jogged nearly to pieces. Samuel had not yet fully recovered from his sore mouth & fever (O yes! I did not say how very sick he was. I was much alarmed about him)   We took dinner at Berlin & arrived at C. H. at 5 oclock P.M.   The house we were to live in was quite out of fix, so we stored our goods into an outside shanty until we had the house in trim, & we took board & logings at Fathers.[aa] Sisters Sue[nn] & Mary[ii] have returned from col-

---

13. As becomes evident, she has morning sickness.
14. Wenger and Weaver's commercial delivery wagon.

lege & Lee[jj] & her husband[kk] & baby daughter are all back from Ohio, so we are having a fine time. They all got back just a week before we moved from Elmira & they with Fathers[aa] dined & supped with us several times yet before moving. & since we are down here Lee[jj] & staff have visited us several times. We have fine times on the Hill since all are at home again. Several times Fathers[aa] have had feasts—big dinners—for their children Several times some of the girls, Mother,[bb] S & I have gone to Galt shopping. On one of those occasions I laid in quite a stock of flannels &c &c for future use. on another Mary,[ii] Sue,[nn] & I got dress for our selves. My helth is much better. I am not troubled now with that deathly sickness with which I was so much troubled several months ago. On the whole my health is much better. I cannot endure much fatigue, but still much more than I could endure a few months ago. I have to be very careful with my diet. This is a clear but very windy blustry day.

November 12, 1861 A very beautiful day. Brother Clem[cc] took breakfast with us, we had cracked wheat & canned currants. O! but they were good I am not at all well today. Mrs J. B. Slichter & sister spent the afternoon with me. Mrs. S's babe is just 5 weeks old. she makes a great fuss over it. fed it molasses at the table which seemed outrageous to my way of thinking. We got a stove today for our parlor, borrowed it & pipe from the school section. It seems so much more like living to have a parlor to sit in. I feel quite badly this evening.

November 13, 1861 It is cloudy this morning & wet. it rained in the night. I walked nearly to the back end of the farm before breakfast & feel refreshed on it. Ate a light breakfast then performed my household duties. If I carry out this way of living, I will be a living monument for the water cure system during the pregnant state. Evening. Went to Moses Eshlemans to prayermeeting, had a very good meeting. A beautiful moonlight evening, had quite a little chat with aunt Mary.

November 14, 1861 Was crochetting mittens for Aunt Lydias children, was over to Fathers.[aa] Mrs. J. B. S. came there, she was over here a little while. I carried her babe home for her & had quite a talk with her.

November 17, 1861 Sister Mary,[ii] Pet & I went to Blenheim to church, were rather late. Father was nearly through with his sermon. Mr Plowman spoke quite a while yet, after which the sacrament was administered. I vowed again to live a better christian the Lord helping me. After meeting we went to Mr C. Rosenburgers for dinner. In the evening to meeting   Mr P. preached a good sermon, the house was crowded.

November 18, 1861   It is clear & pleasant out. Mary[ii] was over the greater part of the day. I am not at all well, have such a bad cold. Pet is very good to me. When I am not well, he is so attentive

November 21, 1861   Samuel & I were to Uncle Amoses for tea. After tea, Sml & Henry C went to Strawsburg to start a singing class. They succeded, & got back until 10 oclock. It being so late we staid at Uncles until morning. Took breakfast. Bo't a turkey for 50¢ from them. Aunt gave me a large dish full of sausage & pudding. At 7 oclock we started home well laden.

November 24, 1861   Attended Sunday School, had a pleasant time & meeting in the evening. L. L. Downey preached.

November 25, 1861   This is our first marriage aniversary & we have had quite a pleasant day of it. In the forenoon I baked & scrubbed, prepared the turkey &c &c for our aniversary dinner. At 2 oclock the guests began to assemble. The guests were all cousins, viz 4 of Uncle S. B's oldest children, 4 of Uncles Amoses, do. do., 2 of Uncle Wendels, J. L. B., 4 unmarried sisters, Clem,[cc] Lee[ji] & husband,[kk] Father[aa] & Mother.[bb] Had dinner at 5 P.M.   We had turkey roast, mashed potatoes, boiled cabbage, graham buiscuits, do. dropcakes, baked apples, canned strawberries, butter in pineaple shape. After dinner, Ma.[bb] & Pa.[aa] went home.   all the rest staid to have a play. Just when the clock struck 8, three cheers were given by the company for the memorable hour in which we were made one. From 8 to 9 oclock was spent by different ones relating the events of the past year. At 9, all dispersed again & Sml & I were left to ourselves to recount the pleasures of the past year. After comparing this with other years, we have truly never spent a year so happily in all our former life. We then kneeled down together & thanked our heavenly Father for having brought us together, & allowing us so much happiness, both spiritually & temporally. We were happy one year ago, but much more perfectly so today & we hope that we shall ever be able to say that as years multiply, our love increases.

November 26, 1861 Am quite sick tired & lame this evening. Sml. helped me wash our yesterdays dishes, after which I washed our dirty clothes & by it caught cold.

November 27, 1861 Am quite unwell this morning. Took a pack in the morning. fasted until 4 P.M. feel better.

November 28, 1861 Pa's,[aa] Jamses[kk] & we went to Cos. J. Bowmans for tea. Sml went to Strawsburg to teach a class in singing.

December 2, 1861 It is very cold this day. At 10 A.M. Mrs. J. B. Slichter took her first lesson in drawing. I also went to Uncle Sams to see whether their girls would not take lessons. Nancy & Eliza said they would take lessons. I felt a little dubious about going there to solicit pupils, but felt so elated at my success that I think I shall start out soon again to get some more I can teach a dozen as well as one, which would make quite a difference in the purse at the end.[15] While writing here Mr. Cormany is taking his first lesson. My health is pretty good now. Aunt Polly Bowman made us a short visit this evening.

December 3, 1861 This is certainly a strange world, or rather some of the people in it are passing strange. After all my large drawing class will be only one pupil. Uncle Sams girls have sent word that they think they wont take lessons. They changed rather suddenly.

December 6, 1861 Was to Uncle Sams to learn the cause of the sudden change of mind. Nancy told me that her father declared that he would not pay for it & their mother would not either & was quite unwilling that they should go. I do not like those people who are right in for any thing to your face but change as soon as your back is turned. Uncle Sams were quite willing that the girls should take lessons to me. How can I respect them as much as before. J. W. A's[kk] & we visited our rich cous. J. Erbs today. I am sure that elegant houses with elegant furniture are not always occupied by elegant people. J's[kk] & we felt better at home than they did. We also visited at B. Burkholders, had a very pleasant & instructive visit.

December 11, 1861 Sml. has gone to Preston to start a singing class. We took dinner at Pa's.[aa] sisters Lydia[dd] & Lea[jj] in passing through

---

15. Rachel hopes to earn some extra money by giving art lessons. Samuel is still out of work, earning meager amounts as an itinerant singing master.

large gate this morning were caught under the gate & were pretty badly hurt. Lydia[dd] had her sholdere slightly fractured. I must start to prayermeeting   Lydia[dd] & the children took breakfast with us.

December 25, 1861   Christmas day. We were to a dinner party at Uncle Amos Clemences, had quite a nice time. In the evening we went with them to meeting at the tolebridge Cous J. B. B. preached, had such a good talk with Aunt Mary.

December 30, 1861   James'[kk] & we went to Uncle Abram Clemences   had quite a sing in the evening. Drank tea this evening which makes me feel figetty. Am not well at all.

December 31, 1861   Dined at A. Hunspergers   Called at J. Clemences. Their little boy is getting better. Returned home in the afternoon. Went to watchmeeting in the evening,[16] quite a number were out, had a good meeting. S. Downey preached a good sermon but I felt too dull and sleepy to be benefitted, felt quite unwell. I am scarcely fit to go out evenings being subject to sick spells on short notice.

January 1, 1862   Were at home all day, am not very well. Lambs youngest daughter was married today, also 4, 5 or 6, or more couples not far off. It is cold & blustry.

January 6, 1862   Having been quite unwell for several days I allowed myself to be persuaded to try the curative effect visiting. We went to J. Hallmans.   In the evening Mr. H. & Sml. went to Dundee to start a singing class. A class of 33 was raised I had quite a pleasant visit with Cous' Mary & Rachel.

January 7, 1862   Returned home, not much better than I left. Pa's[aa] killed their pigs today.   S. helped.

January 10, 1862   Have been quite unwell all day. I think this illness is caused by eating apples that were stewed in a brass kettle.   the kettle had not been used for some time. Ate no supper.

January 11, 1862   The girls (Susie[nn] & Lizzie[oo]) breakfasted with us. We had quite a jolly time eating rivel soup.[17]   baked pies for

16. I.e., New Year's Eve service.
17. Rivel, or rivvel, was a basic milk and flour soup. Ruth Hutchison, *The New Pennsylvania Dutch Cook Book* (New York, 1958), p. 1.

them. Ma.[bb] being away to Elmira I also baked appllejourney cakes, which are real good. We can have a great variety in cooking Hydropathically, fully as much so as in the old way, with less expense & more healthful. In the evening Pet & I had such a good talk, he then mended my shoe & I finished the second pair of mittens for Mrs Downeys children. Father[aa] came home from Elmira, he was very cold. It has been snowing & blowing nearly all day. Pet had no singing.

January 12, 1862 It is not cold at all this morning, has been raining some. The snow is going fast again. Father[aa] has gone to the Tolebridge to preach, he went in the cutter.[18] Evening. It is quite cold this evening & is snowing a little. Saml was called to Uncle Georges to prescribe for their sick babe. Sally is rather oldfoggish & does not want to do all that the prescription calls for. They have nearly fed the child to death and got its little stomach quite out of order.[19]

January 13, 1862 Sml. helped GrandPa kill a calf. We took dinner with them (GrandPa's) On starting home they had half a quarter of veal done up in paper for us to take along. I enjoy a visit to Grand Pa's very much, nearly every time we go there GrandMa has something for us to take home.

January 14, 1862 This was the coldest morning we have had this winter. The Thermometre stood 16 below zero. I have not felt very well today. I get a little out of humor such days, but My Sam'l like a good man does not seem to mind it. I always feel so sorry afterwards. I desire to be a good christian, & this evening I feel quite cheered on my way. Although I am all alone I feel safe in the hands of my Savior. I know my Sm'l is praying for me. I feel it.

January 20, 1862 Got up at 4 oclock this morning so as to get ready to start early for Woolwich to meeting. We got away at six. Susie,[nn] Lizzy,[oo] My Sml & I went to Eshlemans large sled & Fathers[aa] horses. We were in good time for meeting, Rev. Plowman preached a good sermon, after sermon the sacrament was administered. Quite a number partook. Jacob Benner experienced religion a few days ago & is quite happy now. After meeting J. S. A's[kk] Mary[ii] & Mr Moyer & our

18. A fairly small one-horse sleigh.
19. Samuel has become the local expert on hydropathy. He will shortly take advantage of this reputation by merchandizing hydropathic literature in the small towns and villages of rural Canada. The sick baby was Milo B. Clemens (b. 1860), fifth child of George and Salome "Sally" Bowman Clemens. *BHWT*, II, 24, 105–06.

load went to Uncle Noahs. In the evening all went to meeting again, and all except Mary[ii] and Mr. Moyer went to Uncle Noahs again.

January 21, 1862 Uncle Noahs, J. W. A.'s[kk] & we went to S. S. W's[ee] to a birthday dinner & spent the day very pleasantly In the evening all went to Benners to meeting, got there rather late. Mrs Moore was at S. S. W's[ee] with her two children, she feels lonely & lost since her husband is dead.

January 22, 1862 Dined at J. E. Bowmans at St. Jacobs. Had a nice little visit there. Returned home in the afternoon, it got dark before we got home. My Sml. staid in Preston to teach singing.

January 23, 1862 Gave Mrs J. B. S. 2½ drawing lessons. After she got through she & I took a sleighride to New Aberdeen. We also stopped in a little at Uncle Amoses to see whether Mr Cormany could not go with them to his singing Feel right well for some time now. I think my general health is improving.

January 24, 1862 Did not feel well this morning, but since I have stirred round some I feel better. Gave Mrs. S. 2 lessons again today. Mother[bb] told me this morning that she did not think it would pay for Mary[ii] to go to J.B.S's every day to take drawing. It would take up too much time, & that she might take lessons from Susie.[nn] I offered to teach her if she would then take care of me while I would be sick, but it seems that was not cheap enough yet. I think it is hard to do any thing cheap enough for relatives. even if instruction were given gratis they would begrudge the time they would have to spend. I paid for instructions in the fine arts with my share of the money—I had earned myself—I was allowed to keep, & while at home instructed my sisters free. Since Married I thought that almost too cheap. I find too that they do not value those instructions as they would if they had to pay for them. It is not very cold today. Sleighing is good. My Sml is hauling wood.

January 25, 1862 Gave Mrs S one ¼ lessons, then sewed until two oclock when the children came to sing. Uncle Amoses came to hear them sing, they sing right well too. Uncles & their two little girls & Father[aa] took supper with us. Aunt & I had quite a pleasant visit. Evening. Cous. R. C & Carrie[pp] staid with me until 9 oclock. Sml. has gone to singing, feel pretty well, finished a shirt for Sml & read in Pioneer.[20]

20. *NUC*, 459, p. 288, lists a Philadelphia weekly under this title.

January 26, 1862 It is very cold & blustry this morning. Did not rest well last night & do not feel well all day. Sml & I learned several new pieces in the Oriental Glee Book. I wish I could take more interest in singing, I get tired of it so soon.

January 27, 1862 Gave Mrs Slichter 2 lessons this morning. Afternoon. Cut out three nightdresses etc. then sewed until evening. Evening. Visited at Fathers[aa] & had a long sing.

January 28, 1862 Mrs S took 1½ lessons. right after she got through Sister Mary,[ii] Mrs S & I went to Gau[l]t with Mr S's horse & sleigh. It was very cold & stormy. I got pretty cold. My hands were exposed driving. The horse acted rather ugly at the start, but we soon tamed him. I bought quite a lot of things but nothing special. My Sml. had supper ready when I got home I feel chilly and rather unwell this evening. My Sml is staying at home on account of the storm I am always so glad when he can be at home. I tried to get lithographs & crayon board but could not get the right kind.

January 29, 1862 Washed this morning, got very tired, until I got them ready to boil, so I just put them into the boiler without putting fire under it & rested several hours. had quite a little sleep. Pa's[aa] had company from the Twenty Penna.[21] & Uncle George. All came over to see us before I got through with my washing & of course had on my old wash dress.

January 30, 1862 Rinsed my clothes & cleaned house. Got very tired. My Sml told me of Sister Lydias[dd] improprieties with their teamster & of her husbands[ee] distress about it. Clem[cc] was over this morning & told us of Pa's[aa] scolding. After I got through with my work I did [not] feel well enough to go to give a drawing lesson. So I spent the rest of the day in making little things Had quite a crying spell when thinking of the above mentioned troubles. Sml. staid over home so long too that I felt a little hurt at that. I felt badly until he came home & told me why he staid so long. He & they have been having a long talk about all those things that have caused hard feelings. Evening. The girls, Sams Y folks, & we went to Strasburg singing.

January 31, 1862 It being so late when we got home last eve, we slept late this morning. Gave Mrs. S. her usual lessons, sewed the rest of the evening Mollie[ii] was here until 11 oclock.

21. The Twenty was the traditional name of an early Mennonite settlement in the Niagara district of Canada West. *BHWT*, I, 3.

February 1, 1862 Baked, ironed, sewed etc. all day, went to singing in the evening, enjoyed it pretty well.

February 2, 1862 Sml has been reading the Telescope to me. Now he has gone to Baptist church. Evening. Was to S. School this afternoon. My Sml spoke to the children with good effect. I enjoyed the school well.

February 8, 1862 Baked & cooked a number of things for next week I baked coarse & fine flour cup cakes & really believe the coarse cakes are the best. however there is not much difference. Evening. Mr. Mrs. & Miss Bowman from Elmira are at fathers.[aa] I am quite tired & shall not go to see them until morning. All have gone to Tolebridge to singing school & Sml too so I am all alone. Sewed some at dolls clothes. Lee[ji] was with me a short time.

February 9, 1862 As soon as I could get my work away & dressed I went over to see the folks. we had quite a sing together. I felt that my unusual frontal development was noticed. J.E.B. a widdow bridegroom, took several good looks at me. I felt a little awkward among so many young folks. All took supper with us, also Sisters & Brother,[cc] & J. Johnson making in all 12 with ourselves. J.L.B. & Clem[cc] spent the evening here, they discussed some of their own good & bad traits.

February 10, 1862 Visited at Mr Eshlemans. Mrs E. is quite poorly. still she felt pretty well while we were there. She & I had quite a talk on health. I am of the opinion if she would leave of[f] drugging & treat herself hydropathically she might be restored to health. In the eve. I went with Sml & a load of girls & boys to Preston to singing. We sing quite a number of pieces for them. The subscription was then passed round & more names added. the full number however to form the class was not obtained but some of the leading members took the responsibility of raising the amount regardless of the number of names, so that he has a class there too. I took sick in time of recess & almost had to be carried out. Slept pretty well all night.

February 11, 1862 We did not eat any breakfast. neither felt well. Sml. hauled wood part of the day. I sewed, made a sack. It has been snowing nearly all day, felt quite unwell after supper, so much so that Sml hardly knew whether to go to his singing or not. I told him I would feel better soon & encouraged him to go, so I am again alone. I feel better but not well yet.

February 14, 1862   It has snowed some last night again & is cold and cloudy. I feel pretty well this morning. Visited this afternoon at J. B. Slichters. Mary[ii] & Mrs took their 4th crayon lessons, have felt pretty well. Wrote letters all evening. Carrie[PP] got a valentine & feels quite elated about. Finished the 12th pair of mittens for this winter. Commenced the second dolls blanket or shawl. Dressed a chicken for our dinner tomorrow. The war news are glorious these few days.[22] 20 minutes past 10 already, so I am going to bed.

February 17, 1862   Gave Mary[ii] & Mrs S. 2 lessons. Mary[ii] told me that Uncle Sams folks feel quite hard toward us for expressing our minds so freely on Canadian issues that we did not like. I considered this a country where free speech was tolerated, & I am in the habit of thinking for myself & if my opinion is asked on any subject I give it with perfect freedom. If it is not the opinion of others they need not receive it & I am always open to conviction if I am in the wrong. It seems they think that we have no right to have opinions of our own especially if they do not coincide with theirs, but instead of reasoning the matter with us & trying to convince us that we are in the wrong, they assent to what we say while with them, but when gone they talk the matter over by themselves & make us out dreadful mean for not *thinking like they do* & especially for *saying* it yet. *Such a pack of fools.*   to our faces they are the best of friends, but soon as our backs are turned they act in that way. J.L.B. boarded there a year & heard these things & thought it no more than kindness to tell us that those hard feelings that existed between us might be prevented if we were a little careful what we said. We were surprised that there were hard feelings existing & inquired the cause & were told that we expressed our dislike to Canada & some of her customs rather too freely. How could we help laughing at the idea. Such a silly thing. Susie[nn] & I being the greatest talkers are the worst ones of course because we are quite free to tell any one who asks that we prefer living in America, & that we like the customs of her people better than those of Canada.   also we like the country best in almost every thing. Joseph thinks we have no right to have that prefference *"because* Canada is our Native Country." Bah on such narrow contracted little mindedness. I am ashame that I have such boobys for relatives. Perhaps this is not the most christian way

22. Troops under Major Gen. Ulysses S. Grant captured Fort Henry on the Tennessee River eight days before Rachel wrote this entry. One of the first Union victories of genuine importance, it was well publiciæed. This publicity, in turn, helped boost the reputation of the previously obscure Grant.

to look at such things, but such really are the thoughts that will naturally come. My Sml. has an attack of dyptheria.

February 18, 1862   It is not cold at all today, taught my class, came home at 12 oclock, commenced washing right away   Washed out the clothes & put them over to boil. While boiling gave My Sml. a wet sheet pack, which opperated well.   finished washing & put the clothes in rinsing water. Sml ate supper, both ate right hearty. We ate later than our usual time. The consequence was we did not feel well.

February 19, 1862   Quite out of fix in the somach. Sml's throat worse &c &c. the effects of our late supper. Gave Sml a dry pack. Had him in the pack four hours before he prespired, it opperated well.   the disease seems to be broken but he is weak. I wrote letters, read, made dolls clothes &c.   The war news are glorious all this week. Forts Henry & Donaldson were taken, also a number of prisoners.[23]

February 21, 1862   Fryday. Nothing of importance happened during the day. Amos Hunsperger visited us in the afternoon. Cous. Hery Clemens took dinner with us. We had boiled beef & soup for dinner. Evening. J. C. Buckannan delivered a lecture on Slavery. He has traveled considerably in the south, & has seen much of the peculiar institution. His whole discourse was mostly on what he really saw. Mr Cormanys class sung & did well. Others beside Mr B——n made short speeches. Clem[cc] was one of them.   he referred to the Trent affair in such a way as to create the ire of some of the loyal Brittians.[24] Uncle Georges were down. Grand Ma sent me a little bucket full of real nice applebutter with them.

February 22, 1862   Baked & ironed am very tired & almost sick. Did not do any thing after dark. Sml. is still sick.

23. Following his victory at Fort Henry, Grant advanced against Fort Donelson on the Cumberland River. The Confederates surrendered Donelson on Feb. 16, 1862.

24. The Trent affair had dominated the Canadian press two months earlier. During the second week of November 1861, an American naval officer, Captain Charles Wilkes, removed two would-be Confederate ambassadors from the British steamer *Trent*. Protests from London provoked bellicose replies in the American press, which had portrayed Wilkes as a hero. When the English government indicated a willingness to fight for its interpretation of international law, armed conflict seemed possible. Though believing itself correct in principle, the Lincoln administration backed down late in December 1861 rather than force the British into hostilities that the hard-pressed Union government could ill afford.

February 23, 1862   Did not go to meeting, had quite a long talk with Susie.[nn] Packed Sml in the afternoon. & read the biographys of Three Mrs. Judsons.[25] Were to prayermeeting in the eve. at Fathers.[aa] felt quite unwell. did not stay till meeting was out. felt very badly after I came home. feared that labor had really begun.

February 24, 1862   Mollie[ii] & I went to J.B.S's the snow is much drifted. at some places we had to wade in above our knees. it is very cold & stormy. Mended all the torn clothes. N. Raynolds dinned with us. had fowl & potatoes &c. Sml is not so well this evening. I am not well either, have a constant pain in my back which at times extends over my right side & upper part of my abdomen. Sewing goes hard with me. I do not know when I will get my dolls clothes made.

February 27, 1862   This is the day appointed to start a benevolent Society for the ladies of Waterloo. It is very cold & stormy. At 9 oclock I got ready & went over to get Mary.[ii]   when I found her not ready, I enquired the cause, she said she could not go.   Mother[bb] had work for her, & that she could not go to Elmira if she went today. I offered to help her do her work if would go, whereupon Mother[bb] replied that she (Mother) had her plan made out for Mary[ii] & she did not like to have any one interfere with that plan. She said it in a displeased tone. I told her then that I did not wish to interfere at all but thought it would be all the same whether Mary[ii] or I did the work, just so it would be done.   by that time Mary[ii] had shawl & hood on to go to take her drawing lesson, so we started without saying more. I felt very badly on receiving such a rebuff when no provocation was given that I can see. I cannot understand Mother[bb] at all. She does not seem like she used to at all. It at times seems to me she has lost all affection for her children, especially those that belong to the Brethren church, she seems to watch us as though suspicious of us. I could scarcely keep the tears back while teaching my drawing class. I felt almost as though I could not go the ladies meeting until I had seen my Sml & told him how badly I felt. I could

---

25. Probably Arabella W. Stuart, *The Lives of Mrs. Ann H. Judson and Mrs. Sarah B. Judson, with a Biog. Sketch of Mrs. Emily C. Judson.* First published in 1851, this book recounted the lives of the successive wives of the Reverend Adonian Judson, who was involved in missionary work in Burma. New editions of this popular volume appeared annually throughout the 1850s, and by the end of the decade the title had been shortened to the one Rachel uses. Joan Jacobs Brumberg, *Mission for Life* (New York, 1980), evaluates the Judson family and the impact of their story on American evangelicals.

not go home before going since I was to go with Mrs Slichter & the lessons lasted until nearly time to start. After eating a luncheon we started, & got there safely but not without getting very cold. We stopped in Preston to get a little alum, & when near Mr E. Snyders (Where the meeting was to be held) the bells dropped off the horse. I jumped out for them & suppose by so doing the sample constution for a ladies Society which I had borrowed from Mother[bb] was lost out of the sleigh. I felt sorry, but can get a coppy of the same by writing to Westerville. There were only six ladies present beside ourselves still we organized. Elected officers &c &c Scarcely one present knew anything about such societies. So I explained to them. Told them how other Societies of the kind were conducted &c &c As soon as they knew what it was to be like & what for all were ready to form a society provided they have leaders to help them into the way. I told them then what officers they needed & how to elect them. I acted as Chair Woman & put the business right through. I also had to act as secretary & was put in as secretary of society. Mrs. A. Weaver modestly told me they would like me as their Pres. but feared I could not be with them perhaps for some time After partaking of refreshments we adjourned to meet again in 2 weeks at J. Bergys. M.H.B. Mrs S & I are to draw up a constitution.[26]

February 28, 1862 It is very cold & stormy. I feel pretty well today. Sml is some better again. I gave him a wet pack this morning. Mary,[ii] Susie,[nn] Clem,[cc] Mr & Mrs Slichter, Cous. J. B. are going to Elmira. O! My! but they have a cold day. I am glad I am not going now. I judge I will have to stay at home pretty much now until our ———— comes. It pays to stay at home for such a cause.

March 1, 1862 Saturday. It was quite cold this morning, but turned out quite springlike & pleasant. I have been quite unwell today thinking want of exercise was the cause I ground a little tin bucket full of cracked wheat. We had quite a time fixing our bed over. After I had the straw tick ready to be filled, Uncle Abram Clemences came. Sml. had not returned from his singing. I entertained them as well as I could, but felt too sick to be very entertaining. Mother[bb] & Father[aa] (who came with them) did it for me. I got supper for them. Pa's[aa] staid too. Mother[bb] helped me get supp. After

---

26. This type of grass-roots organization may have been crucial in the development and spread of women's consciousness and in the emergence of women as active participants in the shaping of society. For an insightful discussion of this phenomenon, see Nancy F. Cott, *The Bonds of Womanhood: "Woman's Sphere" in New England, 1780–1835* (New Haven, 1977), pp. 154–59.

they had gone, Sml & Pa.[aa] filled the tick with straw. we changed the furniture in our bedroom &c &c. I felt quite tired & sick. I rolled together a full suit of doll clothes so as to be ready at a moments warning.

March 2, 1862 It is quite cold this morning. Do not feel at all well. Perhaps this is a prelude to an increase of family.

March 4, 1862 Was quite unwell yesterday. especially in the evening & through the night. I went through the sleet & rain out to Mrs S's to give her a drawing lesson in the morning & felt better for the walk. Today I am still more unwell. I am becoming weak & pale. It has been quite cold & stormy all day. This eve. Sml went to Dundee I do pity him when he has to go out when it is so cold. he is just over an attack of dyptheria & I fear he may get it again. He will not consent to stay away over night if he can help it. consequently he is often out until near midnight. Why there he comes again! I wonder what has happened. The roads were drifted so that he could not get through. I am so glad that he is going be at home this evening

March 5, 1862 This is another spring like morning

March 9, 1862 Pa,[aa] Sml, Carrie[pp] & I were to Tolebridge to meeting. Mary[ii] & Susie[nn] started with us but when we got to the front gate a number of young Moyers came along to visit them so they staid at home. The weather was real fine & springlike. Pa.[aa] preached, he is not a great sermonizer, but a practical speaker. The house was so very warm & the air so impure that I got sick before the first hymn was sung. I went out awhile & then took my seat by the door which I left ajar. After that I felt pretty well. It is raining this afternoon. Sml has gone to S. School. I feel cold spiritually. I find that by attending meetings so little I get indifferent. for a while I felt more earnestly engaged. I want to be a true christian

March 10, 1862 Had company early this morning (Mr & Miss High & Mr Albright from the Twenty & Telby High). Clem[cc] & I. L. B. Acted the fool awfully. Ironed. blackened the kitchen stove &c. Do not feel as well as I might.

March 11, 1862 Gave the usual drawing lessons. The weather is very springlike. Mary[ii] & I went to Galt this P.M. for drawing material but did not succeed in getting any. The roads are pretty bad. John Hallmans took supper with us.

March 12, 1862 Nothing special happened. The men are sawing wood & the machine does not seem to work well. Clem^{cc} left home in his usual way. Ma^{bb} & Pa^{aa} feel badly about it. It is colder again.

March 13, 1862 Spent the whole forenoon in framing & writing out a constitution for our missionary Society. Mrs. H. B. Slichter took Maryⁱⁱ & me over to Mrs. I. Bergys where the Society met today. There were but very few out. The meeting was opened by singing & prayer. The minutes of the previous meeting were then read & adopted. The constitution was also read & adopted. I was ordered to get a Secretarys book for the Society. Mrs. Bergy had a nice plain supper. The roads are getting quite bad. Sml & Sis & Maryⁱⁱ have gone to Strawsburg. I do not feel lonely. I do wish to become a better christian & to live just right every day

March 15, 1862 This is a very stormy rainy day. the rain freezes as it comes down, which makes it very slippery. To keep my neck from being broken I though[t] best to stay indoors. I ventured as far as Fathers^{aa} only once. I read the two last Globes[27] to Sml. while he was making spouts for sugar boiling. The war news are very interesting lately. Am pretty well today. Mrs Eshleman is very low, & as she & all who know her think, near heaven. I strange sensation comes over me when I think of death. A fear that all may not be right. It is then that I sigh for more religion. I ever sigh for more   My Rel. experience seems a strange & dark one. O! for more light.

March 16, 1862 I awakened happy as usual, happy in my Sml. he is so precious to me. O! that I could always feel as happy in my Jesus. I frequently think over this. Just now it seems as though something whispered in my ear. "You do not think in the right way." I am ever looking within at my own imperfections. I am rather doubting and fearful. & yet just now I feel happy & often when my mind runs in this channel I get happy. I know my greatest desire is to be good & to do good. I feel very much interested in the African mission. & am ever eager beyond expression for news from there. This has been so for some years. When reading the call

---

27. The *Globe* was a Toronto newspaper controlled by George Brown, a leader in Canada's Reform party and a man resolutely opposed to slavery. He continued to favor the union cause even after the Trent affair had driven most of the Canadian press into open hostility. J. M. S. Careless, *Brown of the Globe*, vol. I, *The Voice of Upper Canada, 1818–1859* (Toronto, 1959), pp. 40–45 and vol. II, *Statesman of Confederation, 1860–1880* (Toronto, 1963), pp. 36–37, 52–58.

for missionaries to go there, I almost felt like saying let us go. when I took a glance at self, I shrunk from it. I felt that I was not good enough a christian, had too many imperfections to be sent to a heathen country. I can do much at home. Ah, when I look at the home field & think what I have done I feel like hiding my face & saying no more about the much loved African Mission. The Lord alone knows who are the right persons for Africa & he will call. Mrs Eshleman is still getting weaker & as she says herself will not be with us much longer but is going to her home in heaven. Father[aa] said while praying with her she got so happy she clapped her hands & praised God.

March 17, 1862 Have felt happy all day, wrote a piece for an album, read some & thought a great deal. I think of our Mo. home a great deal, but much more still of our little hope. I often wonder whether another pair could be found who are so well adopted to each as I my Sml. & I. Religiously I feel about like yesterday O! that I may be still more revived.

March 19, 1862 Father[aa] & I were to Galt. I went expressly for drawing material which Mr Craig so faithfully promised to get for us, but lo! when I got there he had never sent for it, his excuse was that he thought it would not pay him to send for so little. It is real provoking. The class has been waiting over two weeks. Mary[ii] & I went down on purpose for it when his wife told us she thought it must be at the depot. I also got a package of books at the depot. Had quite a time with Capt. Monroe who did not want to deal with ladies. & was about sending me away without them, but I would not go. I stuck to it until I got them, but told me it was the last package he could give me. I should tell Mr C. to come for his own things. This is another specimen of Canadian gallantry & politeness. What an idea that a woman cannot even get a pack of books from a station because they "are not used to deal with ladies." I scorn such dependance & stupidity. I suppose Capt. M. does not dare to swear in the presence of ladies like of men, but I am sure he dares to get just as angry, he gave me a demonstration of that fact. Evening, I have been feasting in the new books. Now I shall have plenty of new matter to pry into. New & grand thoughts & theories to store up in my mind for present & future use.

March 20, 1862 Washed clothes etc. feel rather tired. Sml. & the girls have gone to meeting to Tolebridge. I am all alone, yet how could I get lonely with so many books & my journal, I do sometimes feel a little fearful but have been trying all winter to conquer that disposition. The sure cure is to think of my heavenly protector. It has been very blustery & windy today. I could not but think of the ships & sea.

March 21, 1862 Such a spring morning as this is. why the snow was drifted up our door at least two feet & you have to go up three steps before you get to the door. Sml. & Susie[nn] & Carry[pp] when coming home from Tolebridge meeting upset, & were nearly snowed in. Smls beard, hair & eyebrows were all matted with snow so that he had to thaw it out. one of his eyes froze shut on the way home. It was midnight when they got home. I could not get out this morning to take my exercise so I shoveled snow away from the door awhile. 2ndly (As the New Eng. preacher would say) I took a round at dancing, "Myself all alone" making my own music as I went 3rdly I hummed Bonepartes march across the Alps & marched to it on the double quick. Now I must get breakfast. Eve. There goes Father[aa] in the sleigh. How odd it looks to see a man so cosily nestled in a queer shaped box sliding after a horse. It makes me think of my early schooldays when the boys & girls would sit on planks & slide down the "big hill" Well those were joyous days. It is joyinspiring too to get on a sleigh slide along after noble spirited horse.

March 24, 1862 I just finished the reading of one of Horrace Mans Lectures delivered to the Boston Merchantile Library Association.[28] I was extremely pleased with it. To say it is grand is quite too tame an expression. I heard him lecture several times while at college, & was much interested, instructed & delighted. The recollections of the venerable manly form give a life to those valuable lectures which otherwise they would not contain, however full of life they are. I read, study & write a great deal lately. I also take exercise enough to keep the body well, & bathe frequently. I feel that I am responsible not alone for myself but for another also, I am alone the greater part of the day, & have no important sewing nor household duties to perform so I spend the greater part of my time in improving my mind & sould. My Sml. has not much time just now for mental improvement However his mind is so very active that without the aid my dull mind needs, it is ever expanding & his good heart is

---

28. Horace Mann, *Lectures on Education* (Boston, 1855; rpt. New York, 1969). Mann was one of the most famous champions of public education in nineteenth-century America.

ever growing better. I see a bright crown waiting for him beyond this vale & already he wears one which is a semblance of that brighter one.

March 25, 1862   Tuesday. This is a beautiful day. Mollie[ii] & I took a walk back the lane over the top of the snow which is nearly as high as the fence all the way back. The crust on the snow is hard enough to bear which makes it real good walking. Do not feel well to-day.   was quite sick last night.   heaved up some of the doughnuts I ate for supper.

March 26, 1862   Wrote to J.A.K.   am sending to him for drawing material   Cannot get it in Canada. Am so glad that Sml can be at home this evening. I am so lonely when he is away. This was a beautiful spring day.   the snow is thawing fast.

March 29, 1862   It is cold and raw all day.   feel pretty well. Walked out to the sugar bush & back. I went out for the express purpose of seeing how my "toth half looks when among the sweep maples   by the time I got there I felt more like resting than any thing else, still I romped round quite awhile. I poured the first bucket of sap into the pan &c &c.   by the time I got home again I felt rather loose about the joints, so I dived into the poetry of making apple dumpling, pealing potatoes etc etc which did not seem to relieve them much until we got down to the table & commenced making way with those nice mashed potatoes steamed buiscuts &c   Well by this time (8 P.M.) I feel a little like going to dreamland but I must read a while yet.

March 30, 1862   Sunday. When I wakened the sleet was pelting against the window at a furious rate, & continued raining until about 10 A.M.   I presume March is giving us his last pelting & blustering for this year. How swiftly time passes. A Month begins & is gone before we think of it. Years pass by & we grow old. Our end draws nearer & nearer still we do not realize it.   we live as though we would always stay in this world. O! that I could think of this propperly & take it to heart.

March 31, 1862   Commenced pasting my scraps into an old magazing to make a book of them. Sml. is helping me.   it being to cold to do any thing at the sugar boiling. Such a litterary looking room as we do have, scarcely a spot of carpet can be seen for the refuse papers strewn over it. I wonder what I. L. B. though of it.   I judge he put the whole mess to my ignorance of housekeeping. "O! just what I expected from a college girl. I suppose he thought the same of my paste bedaubed dress &c &c. Have felt quite unwell all day.

April 1, 1862 A beautiful day. Was quite unwell this morning. started with Sml to the sugar bush for a walk but felt unable to go & turned back before I got through the gates. Worked at my scrapbook, read awhile took a dance in the kitchen &c &c. by noon I felt pretty well. do not feel so well this evening. Sml. has gone to Dundee, Susie[nn] is staying with me awhile. We rec'd a letter from J.K. Mo.

April 3, 1862 Sugared off for the first time got ten lbs of real nice fine sugar. Worked at my scrapbook. finished one. & am so well pleased with it that I have commenced another. Recieved letters from Quakertown, rather bad news. One of my pupils died. poor girl. I hope she was a christian. Several others with whom I was slightly acquainted have also died. Sugared off again this eve.

April 4, 1862 Pa.[aa] & Ma.[bb] have gone to a sale near Uncle Elias B's. Also went to see Lee,[jj] who had the ague, but is well again. It is cold & stormy. Sml. has been to the woods nearly all day. had several narrow escapes. Once a tree nearly fell on him. another time the horse nearly run over him. It made me feel very strangely when he told me. He was wet through when he got home. last eve. he was caught in a thunderstorm while out boiling sap down. did not get home until late. felt very uneasy about him. It is raining & snowing. Pa[aa] & Ma[bb] will neary freeze.

April 5, 1862 Cold & rainy. Mrs Moses Eshleman was burried today. I could not go. so I sat by the window and watched them. It looked pitiful to see her husband & children following her to the lonely grave. I looked at my Sml. & thought how I would feel if he were taken from me. I could not but pray that even the tho't might be removed from me, I could not bear it. I thought too that before another month has passed it might be my lot to be carried there. Ah! would I be prepared. I fear. but look to God. Eve. Sml. has gone to Tolebridge to give his last singing lesson. I feel a little lonely & fearful. Read a long time after in bed. dropped asleep with the lamp burning & slept until S. came home.

April 10, 1862 Thursday. A beautiful day, so warm & summerlike so unlike the two preceeding ones which were very cold & stormy.

Mary[ii] washed for me. I cleaned house & blackened stoves. Clem[cc] is back again. Mary[ii] & he took dinner with us. had veal & soup. Mrs. J. B. S. called had quite a chatt with her. I do like our new books so well. I have plenty of reading matter now I grieve that I cannot sing. have to be able to do so again soon.

April 11, 1862 Fryday. Very pleasant, warm day, Mollie[ii] & I walked out to the sugar bush this morning. the ground was getting soft & muddy. Sml. was hard at work boiling sap & chopping wood & I got very tired going out & coming in, laid on the lounge ½ hour after I got back & rested. then got dinner. Sml. was displeased with the molasses. I feel badly ever since. The folks in the other house do not do quite as they would wish to be done by in fetching the mail. He felt hurt about that & it is no wonder for it is mean that after he pays for the paper they will not as much as fetch it from the office when they get the benefit of it just as much as we. Rec'd a letter from J.A. Kumler, with a bill of goods which he purchased for us.

April 12, 1862 Saturday. Well this is my 26th birthday it does not seem posible that so many years have passed over my head already. Year after year is added & soon is I live I shall be among the old while it seems but as yesterday when I was a little girl. Soon too it will be said, Rachel is no more. Ah! Will it be said too that she left a bright evidence of having gone to that better world where Jesus is? God help me to live richeously & uprightly all my days to do my duty at all times & in all things. I was looking at Mother[bb] & Father[aa] today & that soon, soon, they will be taken from us, but they will only go home to those who have already gone to that bright world & waid for us there. To the christian death is not so terible. Still I look at it with dread. I am fearful. yet I know my Savior sufficient for all trials & he has promised to help all who trust in him. When I look at my sinfulness I almost sink yet all my trying to make myself better makes me only worse. O! for more faith & childlike trust.

This is a very pretty spring day. Sml is in the sugar bush all day The sap runs so well that he does not take sufficient time to rest himself at night. I do pity him so much & wish I could help him. he is so good & I do love him so much. he does not seem one bit less lovable now than when a wooing lover as some predicted. because such was their experience, but the contrary is the case. each day he seems more dear. Neither does his love even seem to decrease for me the channel wherein it runs seems to grow deeper & wider as our days multiply. How can I thank God enough

165

for having granted me such a good husband. This & my 25th birthday have been the pleasantest I ever spent   My Sml. makes me so happy. All the world seems happy when his approving & loving smile rests on me. We sugared off this A.M.   I made some pies. had a regular fixing up time. Had quite an adventure in weighing the sugar, having only a small pair of scales with a little board & string to set things on.   well I set a jar full of thick molasses sugar on.   Sml was weighing & Ma^bb and I steadying it when lo! the string broke & down went jar & all making a general splash. O! what a plight I was in. My dress all in sweet stripes down before.   the sleeves sticking to my arms, my hands sticking together & feeling rather more than comfortably warm, for the sugar was not cold yet. Mothers^bb hands were in the same plight. There we stood licking our hands while Sml was gathering the stray drops from jar, box, dishes &c. &c. sending down the red lane. In short we had a sweet time without spilling much. We will sugar another time this evening.

April 14, 1862   Monday. Clem^cc examined or phrenologized our heads this morning, & will send us charts as soon as he get them written.   he started to Penna. to lecture on Phrenology   Did not feel well all morning, so I started to the sugar bush where my Sml was boiling sugar. I got quite tired   picked up a lot of cedar cones both on the way out and in. I was very tired when I got home. took a towel bath & then took a short nap.   did not waken until Sml. got home for his dinner. P.M. felt much better.   read considerable. Eve. Sugared off.   took until nearly midnight

April 15, 1862   Tuesday. Read in Combs treatise on digestion[29] & H Manns lectures.   felt pretty well all day. Uncle A.M.C. made us a short visit, & got my Sml. to write a letter for him.

April 16, 1862   Wednesday. This has been a beautiful warm day. The snow is nearly all gone, the fields are getting dry enough to allow us to walk out. The melting of the snow has swollen the rivers greatly. The grand river has spread all over the bottom land. I to a ramble to the sugar bush this P.M.   got very tired going out, rested

29. Andrew Combe's *Physiology of Digestion: Considered with Relation to the Principles of Dietetics* appeared in at least nine English and Scottish editions from 1836 to 1849 and in several American editions during the 1840s and 1850s. Though he held an M.D. degree, Combe had been one of the pioneers of the phrenological movement in the United Kingdom; he was a president of the Phrenological Society and a frequent contributor to the *Phrenological Journal* prior to his death in 1847. His various works on popular medicine sold well on both sides of the Atlantic.

there a long time. did not get so tired coming home. The frogs are singing this evening

April 20, 1862 Sunday. Easter. Rather cool this morning. Sml went to Menonite meeting in the schoolhouse I could not go so I read H. Manns lectures. Sml is pleased with the increased interest in Sunday school everybody seems to be more interested since he is superintendent Old Henry Bechtel had a stroke of the palsey last evening at about six O clock, he is speechless (neary) senseless & helpless, it is thought that he cannot live long. Uncle Amoses were here for supper. All went to prayermeeting at Fathers.[aa] I was all alone. felt a little fearful & sick. vomited nearly all my supper.

April 21, 1862 Monday. Am not well at all. took quite a walk before breakfast It is cold & rainy this morning. feel better since breakfast, but am so lame in both limbs.

April 26, 1862 Saturday. This has been rather a sad day to me. My Sml. is has another attack of dyptheria. Yesterday morn. when he wakened his throat was sore. still he went out to the sugar bush & worked hard all day & did not take time to attend to himself. he ate no breakfast, but ate dinner & supper. I was out in the bush with him the greater part of the afternoon. This morning his throat was much worse, even his tongue was stiff, & the throat seemed nearly swollen shut. I remembered reading a piece on dyptheria in one of our papers. hunted it up & found it to be Hydropathic & treated him according to that prescription he seemed much benefitted, took him through the same course this but he did not feel so well on it & worse than all he got thoroughly chilled before he got to bed. his mouth feels worse. He has been sleeping some since. Still, I feared this morning that he would be taken from me. I could not think of it. The tears came in spite of me. My feelings were indescribable. He is not out of danger yet O! he does suffer so much. That I could only help him bear it. I cleaned house & ironed some beside tending to my Precious. felt pretty tired. so much so that I got quite sick, but after a short nap I was all right again. I wish I were in better condition to wait on him, but all will be right.

April 27, 1862 Sunday. My Sml. seemed some better this morning, but not so well this evening.

April 28, 1862 Monday. Sml did not sleep much last night suffered a great deal. has been quite bad all day, still he was up & round.

April 29, 1862 Tuesday. Last evening after six oclock Sml had a dreadful spell for nearly two hours he was delirious. I packed him in a wet sheet to take the fever down but it seemed to have little affect. took him out & packed him a second time which soon took down the fever & delirium. I got Mollie[ii] to sleep over here, fearing that the fever & delirium might return. he did not have much fever during the night but still could not sleep well. Today he has kept his bed, being up long enough only to take baths & have the bed made. Uncle Sam visited him.

April 30, 1862 Wednesday. A very pleasant day. Sml seems some better but is very weak, walked out a little. Had no fever of any account Appetite pretty good but mouth & throat still dreadful sore

May 1, 1862 Rather cool this morning. Pet feels some better throat a little better also

X

The Birth of Mary Cora

May 15, 1861–August 4, 1862

Like his wife, Samuel finds the dependency and uncertainty of waiting out the American Civil War in Canada difficult to endure. He has a job as a clerk in his brother-in-law's store, but his Christian conscience prompts him to quit rather than dispense liquor to the customers. His real interest at this time is in hydropathic medicine, which becomes apparent in his description of the birth and care of the Cormanys' first child, Mary Cora Brittannia.

May 15, 1861 Darling has been rather unwell most of the week— Our hopes have been blighted again—so you see we are of one mind, and desire increace[1]—

May 18, 1861 My collecting business is now about done, and I spend a good deal of time in the Store as Salesman, besides doing most of the Book-Keeping, and in Evening and morning I am fixing up the little yard & garden where we intend to move soon—
Darling speaks well of and seems so pleased with the way I am fixing up things at our new prospective Home—Our First Home—

May 19, 1861 Sunday. Our S.S. met at 8:30 A.M. for the first time— The croakers are quiet—The school was decidedly larger and more interesting than before in the P.M.   After S.S. Darling and I drive to Blair to Pa Bowmans[aa]—My! how they did welcome us—and how happy Darling was to embrace her Father[aa] & Mother[bb] and how delightfully the evening was employed—

May 20, 1861 Monday. O how pleased I am this morning—to see my Darling so happy at Home with her Father[aa] & Mother[bb]—Father Bowman[aa] and I went to Preston and bought a Cook-Stove for US— me and mine $22.00—on returning we packed all Darlings things and at 1 P.M. started for Elmyra—At Waterloo we broke an axle— and were in a bad predicament. Isaac Musselman came along and took our load on his wagon and we fixed a slide-pole under the axle

---

1. After waiting six months, the Cormanys had decided to try to have a child.

and slid home, and it wasn't back sliding either even if I did loose my temper a little and speak unkindly to some one who was helping us adjust things. For I at once confessed and asked pardon, and was forgiven, and moved along nicely. Thank the Lord—

May 21, 1861 Set up and fired new stove and Darling & Mrs Gross cleaned up the rooms during the day—

May 22, 1861 Wednesday. I packed eggs yesterday & til 2 P.M. today. Then I got to work in our rooms—Put up a table to eat off and did other fixing—Darling got up our First Supper, on our new Stove, and we sat to our New Table—which I had made—in our new Home—O it seemed so nice to sit thus all alone, and Thank God for our meal, and then eat undisturbed by anyone. So happy in each other. The evening was passed so joyously—Before retiring we had Family worship our own family worship for the First time—O! That seemed so nice to read in The Book, and then bow together and pray, both to pray, and close the prayer with a Kiss——

May 23, 1861 Thursday. We used the whole day fixing up shelves—making a center table—planting flower seeds Beans and other garden stuff. However humbly, we start we are as happy in each other as can be imagined—I do think we have the nearest a little heaven this side of Heaven.

Darlings greatest object seems to be to make me happy and I am sure my greatest joy is make and see her so—

May 24, 1861 Friday. This is my 23rd Birth Day and The Queens Birth Day likewise. We hoist the Stars & Stripes on the Store, I fire a 4 shot salute—We have a fishing party at Abrm Cavenaughs not a perfect success—in P.M.—Evening happy time in our Home.

May 25, 1861 Very busy in Store—Happy restful evening at Home.

May 26, 1861 Sabbath. S.S. Excellent—I am proud of the way my Darling conducts her class—P.M. Rachel and I had such a delightful chat. She shows in so many ways that she loves me dearly, and is entirely happy in me. I surely am in her.

May 28, 1861 Tuesday. Very busy in Store—Darling covers & drapes our lounge and Table—and sets up such dainty meals for us. Thrice happy is our little unassuming Home.

May 30, 1861   Thursday. We are happy as the day is long.

It seems more and more pleasant to live alone—my wife! My darling wife and I. No one to disturb or hinder us. When I come in to meals I am met with a kiss, which I know comes right from the bottom of Darlings heart, when we sit to our table we pour out our hearts in Thanksgiving to the Giver of food, and all good, and before we retire, and in the morning we can hold worship and commune with God as we see fit, and rejoice in Him—

Thank God for a Free country, and in that country a Home and a jewel to beautify it. A true devoted wife——

June 1, 1861   Saturday. S. S. Ws^ee away—we keep house for them— Store affairs move along nicely—Evening had a singing practice— comes off pretty well—

June 2, 1861   Sunday. Good S.S. & preaching—

June 3, 1861   Monday. I work on the Road—
Office and Store dull——

June 5, 1861   Wednesday. S.S. Tea Meeting all day   Tea in school house. Speeches in Church. After Tea was on tables for noon, I went over to Ch. and got the pupils classified—Each Teacher took his or her class, and with Uncle Noah Bowman as my partner, we led the procession to the School House tables having Wm Linda as Flag Bearer. Mr. James Simms spoke to the people in church while noon T was being prepared—

The partaking was sociable, jovial—After noon T—The Church was full—

Mr. Saml Fear was chosen Chairman Mr. J. B. Slichter, J. L. Bowman, Hon J. E. Bowman and Rev. J. B. Bowman each addressed the Crowd quite interestingly.

I read my Report of the S.S. from its organization to the present time, and being called out, made several short speeches, at different times or points—

Had Tea again in the evening—at ½ price—and after that an auction Sale of surplus eatables &c.

Then followed short speeches by Hon J. E. Bowman M. P. J. L. Bowman, and myself—My Choir got along finely all the day and Eve singing at intervals—Adjourned about 11 OCK P.M.

June 6, 1861   Thursday. I am well, and happy since the T Meeting seeing my actions and labors in the building up of the S.S. are so generally satisfactory, and I am convinced that our God will be glorified as a result.

My happiness is greatly increased to find that my true devoted darling Wife is such a great helpmate in deed and truth—

June 9, 1861 Sunday. A Full S.S. I delivered Prizes to the Children—made a short address to them showing that Prizes were given to lead or induce greater faithfulness and continuous effort, and assured them that some who rec'd small prizes today may receive larger next time—

Things came off very nicely indeed, I was strongly complimented as having brought the school up to a decidedly improved state.

P.M. we went to Benners to Class and preaching—By request I led the Class—and there being a few Germans—I spoke some in the german language—

Rev J. B. Bowman preached in English—Good but too long—Evening Darling and I took a stroll to the River Woods—"Bush" Oh-h-h the Mosquitos!! We are so happy in each other. I would not be single again for all the world.

Our talks on all subjects are so full of interst, and we agree so nicely and when we do differ we agree to disagree and love each other all the same—Then too we are so well temporally and spiritually and find it so delightful to kneel together, evening and and morning, and pour out our hearts in prayer to God.

June 11, 1861 Tuesday. Very warm—a load of new goods came in—Busy day. Sales good. Rachel and Lydia[dd] spent P.M. over at "Uncle Noah's"—Evening Darling is so happy from having an a/c the visit—

I never had an idea that I could loved so intensely by any mortal as I have evidence I am loved by my darling We were very happy when first married but we are so very much more so now. Even as noonday exceeds the daydawn—I always meet with such happy reception and greetings when I go to the house. Just like I used to imagine I would like to have a wife to meet me.

June 14, 1861 Friday. Business brisk—I enjoy my work—Darling not real well—One bright hope blighted again[2]—

June 27, 1861 Thursday. Rachel, Lydia[dd] & I went to a S.S. Tea Meeting at Spring Hill. The Killburn and Allenville schools. We had

---

2. I.e., Rachel was still not pregnant.

some good speaking—Revs Fear, Adams & others—and good singing and Tea & Eatables and sociability—We spent the Evening at Wm Cavanaughs—Got home at mid-night—Darling and I have taken a good many drives, but never was I happier while out riding with her—She is such a good true woman, in fact all of a helpmeet. O! for grace to love my God above all other things for blessing me with such a good wife, one to love and cherish, as I easily can my Rachel.

June 28, 1861   Friday. Well & happy. Funny! Last night Darling, in crossing our "Stile," between yards, caught on picket on the fence—fell, and hung by her hoops. I was within hearing, and helped her off. Poor Dear. I feared she was much hurt, but thank the Lord she was not, so we laughed heartily.

June 29, 1861   Saturday. Routine busy day—Dr. A. C. Bowman[cc] and Aaron Moyer made us a visit—Very glad to have them with us—

June 30, 1861   Sunday. Fine Sunday School.
  P.M. Drove down to Pa Bowmans[aa]

July 1, 1861   Monday. Darling and I picked Strawberries and Currants for canning. Dr. A. C. Bowman[cc] wants me to go in with him and start up a "Water-cure Home"—Cant see it—No!—

July 2, 1861   Tuesday. We put up Berries, Rhubarb, &C
  Father Bowman[aa] talk with me about "The W.C. Home biz—S.S. Weaver[ee] to buy the Home Farm. I to be Overseer of the farm and Home, and A.C. Bowman[cc] to be the Physician——I replied finally I want to have it to say as soon as possible that I am free of any debt, and then I expect to keep out. I want to live in such a way that no one can say I was a miser, nor a spendthrift, but that I made a good honest living: made my family very happy and did much to make all around me so—I consider great amounts of money not the best legacy for offspring, but a well trained mind in a healthy body is beyond all computation——and thus, here the interview ended—We remained several days at B.B.Bs[aa]—I am happy to have such good Pa[aa] & Ma-in-Laws[bb]—such a loving and lovable wife, but above all that we have a Saviour who wills that we shall be happy in all our time, and to all Eternity—Oh to be more like Him.

173

July 4, 1861   Great excitement that Foley be elected to Parliament—We put out a Foley Flag[3]—

July 14, 1861   Sunday. After our S. School, Darling and I and a lot of other young folk went to the Holland-Camp-Meeting—I heard the Famous California Taylor[4]—a great man indeed! He simply carries Everybody with him—Got home about 9 ock P.M.—

July 16, 1861   Tuesday. Rachel, Lydia[dd] and I went again to Camp. Dr. Taylor lectured on California—It was truly masterly—Rev Wadsworth preached on Sanctification. Not very clear. At an after meeting I obtained a great blessing. O how sweet to feast at the Mercy Seat upon The Bread that comes down from Heaven—We slept in Mr Coofords tent. Cool! A light frost—Attended camp services all day—We made the acquaintance of many good people—Darling was the subject of many sly glances and whispered remarks on a/c of her "Shaker"—a new thing—in the bonnet line—just coming in—Mrs Weaver[dd] and Rachel handle them—and this is a good Ad as well as comfortable head wear—We arrived home at dark—

After camp, Darling and I had a long talk on evidences of acceptance with God and she seems considerably happier since—

July 19, 1861   The War goes on, and still on—Nothing seems to point to a time coming near when we can go to our Missouri Home—

July 20, 1861   My collecting and settling accounts is about cleared up, and all the office work is posted up in good shape—and this opens the way for me to give more time to Salesmanship which is a branch of the business I enjoy as a change from working over Books and accounts which I also delight in—The Firm also sells Liquors by the Jug and Quart, as well as Dry Goods and Groceries—and it is custom to treat customers to a glass of whiskey, brandy, or wine when they conclude their purchace—or pay a Bill—To do this be-

---

3. The Honorable M. H. Foley represented Waterloo Township in the provincial legislature until April 1864, when he resigned to become postmaster general. Rachel's cousin J. E. Bowman was then elected to his seat. J. O. Coté, *Political Appointments and Elections in the Province of Canada from 1841 to 1865* (Ottawa, 1918), p. 117.

4. Bayard Taylor (1825–1878) was a well-known world traveler, lecturer, poet, and author of a popular account of life in the California gold fields, as well as volumes on various places in Europe, Africa, and Asia. He was lecturing at a camp meeting that combined—quite typically—a religious purpose with cultural events, entertainment, and general sociability.

comes more and more a shock to my conscience—I dislike to sell drink, and still more to treat a customer to to strong drink, although it rarely becomes my duty—For some time I referred my customers—who wanted drink—to John Rupple an old Clerk who drank some himself, and he did the treating in my stead—

Some good customers however became rather insulted at this process, desiring the Clerk who sold them the bill to also treat them, and even sometimes insisted on his drinking with them.

While I had little compunction of conscience to taking a glass of wine myself, for my "stomachs" sake, yet to be down in the cellar drinking with a man struck me sorely—I must find a way out of this way of doing business—

True I am not selling for myself, I recieve no profit from the business. I am not in the business but I feel I cannot possibly enjoy the life and power of religion and continue selling, or serving strong drink.

July 21, 1861 Sabbath. Had a pleasant—nay—glorious time in S.S.—I spoke 15 minutes about the Heathen and our duty towards them.

Rev Wadsworth & Mr Maligan visited the school and each spoke briefly—

Later in Church Rev. W. preached a powerful sermon on The hardening of conscience, so he will be given over to hardness of Heart.

I feel that unless I give up doing that sin against my conscience I shall be damned after all I have professed, and really enjoyed.

On our way home I vowed to Darling that I would sell no more except for sacramental and medicinal purposes.[5] P.M. we went to Benners to Meeting—Then to Uncle Moses Bowmans for a visit—

July 22, 1861 Monday. We visited Grand Pa Clemenses—and then to Berlin on business and home by 6 ock P.M.—Evening we talked to Sister Lydia[dd] about my intention to sell no more Liquors and she gives me right. Then later had a long talk with S.S. Weaver[ee] I told him how I have felt for a long time, and still feel—He tried to persuade me there was no harm in my selling and handling it since I got no profits out of it. I am only hired on salary by the day or week

---

5. Many nineteenth-century Americans believed that alcohol had therapeutic value. Cormany is not a hypocrite; his attitude resembles that of a twentieth-century American who might abhor the indiscriminate use of hard drugs, but permit physicians to administer small amounts of morphine to relax a convalescing patient after a difficult operation.

to work   True! but I have no right to hire myself to do wrong, and he could not show me otherwise—

I assured him that I would posatively sell no more, that I would rather lose my situation, and if needs be go-a-begging.

So after continuing our parleying some time we parted in good humor—Darling and I talked the matter over further when got over to our little Home, and we were so happy to kneel together at our altar of prayer, with this old load off my heart. We had such a sweet time at our family worship—Darling is so good and dear, oh! that I could love her as she deserves, but it is not in to do so. Her true womanliness deserves more love and affectionate devotion than can be found in a coarse sinful heart like mine—I must have more of Gods own enobling grace.

July 23, 1861   Tuesday. Business brisk—Mr. Weaver[ee] asked me how I felt concerning our last nights talk—I replied "Just the same," and that I was willing to do as before save the whiskey   So I continued—but cut out the Rum.   and doing more on the Books, some that S.S.W.[ee] used to do—

July 25, 1861   Our man Crump leaves for Hamilton to work there. I shall miss him—

Oh! that awful war! That horrible Battle of Bull Run of which the papers are full today.[6]

My God save our country from the oppression of the South and from the Crime of Slavery.

July 26, 1861   Pete and I alone—Business dull—I work on the Journal and Ledger most of the day—My not selling Liquor don't work well—It don't suit some customers when they are in a hurry for a jug of whiskey and Pete is out, or busy, or at his meal—Row (Hotel Man) came in for a jug full—was about 99% mad about it—The thing has spread like wild fire, folks seem to know it pretty generally—and discuss my position pro and con—I am happy all day towards what I used to be—I have a clear conscience now void of offence towards God and man—My Darling! The pride of my heart, and more than life to me rejoices with me that That Thing is settled, and whatever may come as a result. We can trust Our God, and all will

---

6. The Battle of Bull Run, fought on July 21, was the first major encounter of the Civil War. It dealt a heavy physical, and even heavier psychological, blow to the Union side.

be well—A letter from Brother John[d] says the ballance of my Share of Fathers Estate may not be available for six months. I am sorry sure—

July 27–28, 1861 Quarterly Meeting at Bernims—Rev Plowman P.E. Quarterly Conference

J.B. Bowman p in C

J. Ariss C. Leader

S.E. Cormany Asst. Leader, the

german part, and Steward—

Communion Service small—but good. P.M. Mr. Shrader & Sister Lydia Weaver[dd] were baptized by emersion—

The whole service was enriching.

July 29, 1861 Monday. Rev & Mrs J. B. Bowman, Mr W and S.S.W.[ee]—Sister Lydia[dd] dined with us today. It was quite a house-full. But Darling was equal to it easily, and we had a nice social and religious time.

This P.M. I heard my doom. I am now thrown out of employment. Just because I dare to do right. But other employment awaits me Sure! O I am so sorry to leave my Sunday School—The little Benner class—and a host of good social friends—

But the business is not clean. I do not like working above so much Liquor as is in the cellar but would not have decided to quit had the Firm excused me from handling it and selling it—I see! of course, for me to refuse to sell & handle the stuff occasioned waitings discussions, and next thing to hard feelings at times when business was brisk and the Firm could not afford this kind of thing to grow.

Evening—I'm tired—I feel a little "out of heart," but Darling is so good and so true. So much of a comforter and happifyer that I can easily say after all "Alls Well"!

Oh! were it not for her I would be so unhappy just now but I dare not be. God lives! and Darling is here too——

Another thought stirs me up, and not a little—Mr. Weaver[ee] being so near to me—My Brother-in-law and such a good and kind man in all(?) respects and to every one. Just the bare thought that he may be forever lost, and have his doom magnified by some drunkards in the world of the lost—who have been led thither by the liquor he gave, sold, or induced to be sold to them—O! God save him from such an end.

August 1–3, 1861 Nothing special, only I handle no liquors, and am given time to find a new location or business—Darlings milinery business is good.

August 4, 1861   Sunday. A good S.S.—I gave a 15 min. talk—was well received—P.M. Darling and I went to Basket Meeting—Rev S. L. Downy preach a good sermon—We made his acquaintance—and later we went to Uncle Amos Clemens—Talked 'til after 11 OCK—

August 5, 1861   Monday. We walked up to Pa Bowmans[aa]—Then Uncle A. Clemens and I looked Gault over for a job for me—Business too dull. Most merchants would rather reduce than increase the number of clerks   P.M.—I helped haul in wheat—Evening. Henry Clemens, John Masters, and I go spearing fish in the Grand River—Got 140 by mid-night.

Oh! It did seem so good to get into a warm bed with my Darling so glad to have me come nestling up to her—We are so happy in each other—Our Love and enjoyment increacing daily.

August 6, 1861   Tuesday. This is Fish day—My! how good. Pa Bowman[aa] offered me a job on the farm—But They with us think I can do better by looking around—Returned to Elmira—P.M. I fixed up the Milinery Books for the Firm—

My! It seems kind of awful to be out of employment, but I have a little cash laid by, and I'll find something or make something to do.

August 8–9, 1861   We took stock, and settled up the Milinery Business. Darling has cleared some $40. with her needle and scissors since January—

August 10, 1861   These days put in chiefly looking for employment and visiting relatives dear to my Rachel   Although I am out of employment far from my kindred and know of nothing yet to do and the war is raging in my own Country Still I am happy for my Darling cheers me up so much—Never complains—and is so willing to do anything she can to help me, and daily encourages me. She is even willing to risk going with me to Missouri to our New Home, if I think best to make the venture which I may if I cannot soon secure employment here, and can obtain my money from the Pennsylvania Home; But that would seem hazardous owing to the unsettled state of affairs out there, and all over the United States—

August 13, 1861   Tuesday. Darling washed. I wrote and helped by spells. I am "Chief Cook and bottle washer"—I actually got the dinner—Beef, Carrots, Darling says it is x.x.t.y (double x.t.y) Sas I am a model husband on washday at anyrate, let me be never so bad at other times, and my worst is not very bad.

August 14–15, 1861 We are being entertained by the Cavenaughs, fishing, boating, strolling, and a good time generally, save the failure—as yet—to find any business to get down to regularly—

August 17, 1861 Saturday. With all my suspense—no work—the war ranging—and we cant safely go to our New Home, yet all our needs are well supplied. Temporally—socially—spiritually—and some of our desires as well—We have good reason to hope and believe that one of our desires is to be realized. Months have we wished and now we hope it is being fulfilled, or is on the way of fulfillment—Darling seems so happy. Oh! so happy, not only for herself but because she knows it will make me so very happy—

August 18, 1861 Sunday. A good S.S. I gave a short address—Mr. Seaton also spoke—By acclamation Hon J.E. Bowman was elected to succeed me on my leaving—

P.M. We went to Benners—Had a good meeting—I conducted the German Class—

August 25, 1861 Oh! That horrid war! Missouri is all in a ferment and is no place for a young couple to go to start a Home—

We are solicited so much, and so kindly, by so many of Darlings Kindred to "Come, and stay a while"—So we do a good deal of visiting and staying here and there, all the while looking for paying employment. But times are dull, awfully so. The war seems to have its effect adversely on this Country also—

August 28, 1861 We came here to Pa. Bowmans[aa]—To "Carlisle Hill"—We have been busying helping to fix up the old Carlisle Hill farm and Home—They want us to move our things from Elmira down here—

Propose that I help some about the farm and farming and Darling do sewing for the family—

That we fix up "Pig Stable Cottage" and plan to winter here on Carlisle Hill—where we can live cheaply and likely I will turn up some profitable employment.

September 1, 1861 Carlisle Hill—Well! We moved our things down here today—and while I shall do some work for Pa Bowman,[aa] Our leisure is employed in fixing up Our little House, close to the large one—about 50 feet south—wherein we now intend to winter—I am quite certain I can turn up something to make more than my living expenses—

September 7, 1861 We have taken up board and lodging at Father Bowmans[aa] until we can get settled down—Mary[ii] and Susie[nn] came home from Otterbein University and Lea[jj] and James[kk] have come also. So we are having a great time at the old Home.

Some big dinners! Yes! Sure! We had set up several big dinners to Pa[aa] & Ma[bb] Bowman and others just before leaving Elmira and now they go us several better—Ma[bb] Bowman is a wonderful cook and Mother as well.

September 8, 1861 In a whisper!—It is now settled that we are to have a little pledge of our love and affection—a Baby! by & by.

My! How happy my Darling is over the idea and I am more so—I prescribe for her "Hydropathically"—Sitz-bath contribute much to her comfort—

Dieting, and towel baths, and early morning walks are decidedly helpful. So altogether she is looking fine and keeps decidedly cheerful—

September 20, 1861 I am generally neglecting you—Miss Diary. Well I have been getting breakfasts generally, and help variously in routine affairs—Darling does a good deal of reading, some studying. Exercises her talent in art, and maybe will do some teaching in Art—

September 25, 1861 Hydropathic treatment is working firmly with Darling—I am finding time now the farm work is well out of the way, to do some Canvassing—Selling Tralls Hygienic Literature— Dr. Hollicks works[7] and am talking Vocal Music classes   I find interested people and some even enthusiastic—

October 1, 1861 I have been omitting a whole lot here on a/c of my pushing business, and also a little extra time required at home for my Darling. What a happy man I am to be rid of the accursed Liquor-Traffic, and to have my Darling so cozily fixed up in our pretty little Home—so close to her Mother and homefolks so when I am away on business, she has congenial companionship so near at hand—

November 1, 1861 My book business proves prosperous—Everything moves along smoothely and sweetly. Darling seems as "happy as the day is long," and I am quite certain she is all that—Singing

---

7. Cormany decided to try to sell, presumably on a commission basis, the kinds of home medical and self-help books that he found so fascinating himself. Russell T. Trall and Frederick Hollick each wrote numerous books on various applications of hydropathy and related subjects.

School classes and prospects are opening up brightly at various points.

November 12, 1861 "Clem"^{cc} came over for breakfast—cracked wheat and currants—Enjoyed it O.K.
I was on the business tramp today—Mrs. J. B. Slichter and Sister Mary^{ii} with Rachel the P.M.—To teach drawing is up Mrs may take lessons—I wish she would for her own sake and I'd like for Darling to have some such employment about this time for our sakes, i.e. the sake of us three—specially the 3rd

November 21, 1861 I commenced my class in vocal music at Strasburg this evening—Rachel went along to visit her Uncle Hiram Clemenses near by—We were there all night—nice visit—I bought a Turkey—a fine one—50¢—For our 1st Wedding Anniversary Dinner on the coming 25th N-o-v

November 25, 1861 ANNIVERSARY. Married 1 year Today about 2 OCK guests began to come in—Father,^{aa} Mother,^{bb} Sisters and Brother, Uncles Aunts and Cousins to the number of 20 and it was a jolly company that gathered around our table—laden with Turkey and good things plenty to partake of the 5 OCK Anniversary Dinner, occupying about an hour—The evening was very enjoyable—At 8 OCK the company let off three cheers for the memorable hour in which—one year ago—we were pronounced one—
An hour was enjoyed in listening to the rehearsal of events of the past year, and in general an[d] special sociability—
After all had gone, and we were all alone, we agreed that the year just past has been a long ways the happiest one of our lives—Later we kneeled together, encircled in each others arms, and the Good Lord for having brought us together and allowing so much happiness to be our lot this first year of our married life—both spiritually and temporally—and prayed that as years roll on our happiness and oneness may continually increace, and that a special blessing might continually rest upon the one, being entrusted to our care and keeping——

November 26, 1861 I helped helped Darling wash and polish all the dishes, and do the necessary cleaning up of affairs.

January 1, 1862 I find losing my position in the store proves a benefit. My Darling has it easier than when milinerying and housekeeping too—and she is so near her good Mother[bb] and homefolk—and I am making as much or more money and enjoy my work better and—best of all—I can give my Darling better attention and care, and furthermore I am not compelled to observe certain hours of business daily, and besides I enjoy this coming into contact with so much young life—and having a hand in giving them an uplift—all of which helps me to make and keep up a good cheery atmosphere in our blessed little Home—Last Night we closed the old year 1861 and commenced the New Year 1862 at a watch night service—at Freeport U.B. Church (old name Toll Bridge)

Pet—Mollie—Lizzie[oo] and I went over in the Spring-wagon—Rev S. L. Downey preached a good sermon on "So teach us to number our days as to apply our hearts to wisdom." After Sermon had a "Class Meeting" until 12 OCK—midnight—There on my suggestion we all joined in singing "Come let us anew our Journey pursue etc" All the members gathered about the Altar singing. Then all kneeled and Revs Downey and J.B. Bowman led in prayer the former English, the latter German—We surely had a glorious meeting, all seemed revived and prepared to start out in the New Year with genuine vigor—

Pet and I had such a sweet time at our Family worship this morning—

We spent New Years day at home—James[kk] and Lea Adams[jj] came over and ate supper with us—Evening I see anew that past defects cannot be recalled and undone. Therefore I vow to try by the grace of God to live more perfectly in future keeping my perspective home in view and living this life with reference to it as a goal—

January 4, 1862 Saturday. The Blair P.M. Singing class met at our house—The evening class failed to turn out sufficiently so I let it go—It is very cold and disagreeable—

January 5, 1862 Sunday. It seems as though the cold would bite the vitality out of a body—I read and write most of A.M.—and P.M. attend S.S. We had a good session and a good sing after—I feel myself such a poor Christian, am so often thoughtless and make so little advancement—

I vow and pray from day to day But still go on the same old way.

January 6, 1862 Monday P.M. Pet and I visit Cous John Haulmans—and in the Evening I organize a Singing Class at New Dundee—33 signed up—I gave an address to ¾ house on vocal music—good interest. Quite an interesting time all around—Rachel had taught school near here in her teens—gave me some interesting xperiences.

January 9, 1862 Thursday. Today Sister Sarah[u] is to be married to Isaac Thompson[v]—I fear she makes a mistake as Isaac[v] is not an active Christian—tho a presbyterian—and Sarah[u] is active and a U. B—God make them both to be devoted Christians—

January 10, 1862 Friday. Spent most of day reading. Pa Bowman[aa] and I had long talk on their financial losses—No use to allow them to sour life for him and Ma B.[bb] and so act on the family too, was what I tried to impress—

Darling is a wonderful wife to me. Constantly seeking my happiness before her own, and I am sure I ever seek hers first in point of importance and so we cannot be otherwise than very very happy in each other—O that I could take upon myself every pang she has to feel and could suffer for her, I should be ready to thank God that I was counted worthy to suffer it for her in her stead, and I love and cherish her still more because—in a sense—I am the cause or occasion of much of her pain and miseries.

But a few more months and we will be repaid for all. Yes doubly paid by becoming "Mother" and "Father"——

January 11, 1862 Saturday. Snowing fast. No class gathers for singing worthwhile, So I spend the evening with Darling reading and talking—Reflections: and now "another week of life is gone and doubtful few remain." O God for grace to spend my days so I eternal life may gain is my devout prayer tonight——

January 12, 1862 Sunday. Uncle George Clemens sent for Brother A.C[cc] to come and prescribe for their sick child. The Doctor being away, Pet and I went—The child is sick from excessive kindness—Nothing remains upon its stomache, and it is feverish—Gave it a rousing bath—had it drink much hot water—and no food til tomorrow—

We had a friendly visit in the evening with Grand Pa's also—They live in the same house—and are quite old—

January 13, 1862 Monday. Morning Gave the child a copious injection—warm—I had to insist on this—They feared it &c, &c. But the effect was fine—and later it took a little porridge—and it enjoyed and retained it—Gave strict orders against eating oftener than three times in a day, and then only lightly of cracked wheat—apple—

baked potato—very little milk but as much water as it wants and bathe in evening—and rub down in morning——Evening. Preston Singing Class numbers 35 now—

January 14, 1862 Tuesday. The child is better Eve—seems quite well—

January 15, 1862 Wednesday. O.K.—Eve go to my Dundee singing class good—Stormy night—Get home 11 OCK—Find Darling sweetly sleeping—

January 16, 1862 Thursday. Good day at home reading, and chatting. Pet and I —— Evening. Teach Strausburg singing class—Good time—

January 17, 1862 More snow and storm Eve Toll Bridge Class met in new church—Fine! This gives it new life—and now I feel the need of more spiritual life—

January 18, 1862 Saturday P.M. The Blair childrens sing class good Sure! Evening—adult class large but this class is certainly a one-horse-affair—There is no get-up about the young fellows. I hope to inspire them all later—News from Benner Revival brought by Rev S. L. Downy and uncle Amos. Old man Benner coverted from Universalist to Jesus Christ and United Brethrenism—Praise the Lord——

January 19, 1862 Sabbath. at 6 A.M.—midst all the snowing—— Rachel, Susie,[nn] Lizzie[oo] & I drove up to Montrose—near Benners to the Big Meeting—and it was big, and a good service. Rev Plowman preached earnestly, a glorious state of feeling prevailed—After service we—our load—also J. W. Adams[kk]—Mollie B[ii] and some more went to Uncle Noah Bowmans over dinner—Then had a fine sing—Eve—All went to meeting in 2 sleds—The House so crowded many had to stand—but the services were good—Old Mr. Benner is truly a changed man—seems so very happy—

January 20, 1862 Monday. We all went over from Uncle Noahs—to Elmira to celebrate S.S. Weavers[ee] 34th Birth Day—Great time—Eve I took eleven over to the meeting at Montrose—It was great—

January 21, 1862 Tuesday. Good sleighing After calling at various places we (four) & Clem,[cc] dined at Hon I.E. Bowmans M.P. at Saint

Jacobs—Had a very pleasant visit—about 2 P.M. we struck for Home—was real cold—we stopped at Potters Hotel to warm. Clem[cc] treated the Girls to wine—I felt hurt, and more especially because my Pet drank too—O! that Hell contained all alcoholic liquors—Pet asked my pardon later and I freely forgave her—

January 22–23, 1862 Wednesday and Thursday. I sleded wood for Pa's[aa] by day and taught my classes in evening

January 24–25, 1862 Routine generally

January 26, 1862 Sunday. At home for the most part save to S.S.— Eve such pleasant review. We are both so well and as happy as mortals can be—I believe I have the best, truest, most loving dearest wife on earth. She is continually doing little things to make me happy: Studies to please me in everything: Showing such constant attachment: meets me so pleasantly and lovingly when I come into the house, and never seeks her own happiness and pleasure as much as mine, and I do the same in return. So we must be happy. An then to cap the climax, we are so happy in religion too. Oh! I do. Yes! We do—thank God for each other, and for a full and free Salvation, and for the peace and joy it affords to know that salvation is ours—

January 29, 1862 Wednesday. My classes in music are progressing finely. I called at Uncle Amoses after pr meeting—Had a good sing—When I came home, Pet was still up   O that to one the grace were given to see my way more clear to heaven. Before retiring, I unbosomed my soul to my Rachel on the subject of my frequent impressions that I am not in my proper sphere, and that I am frequently troubled on that account—I told her how on former occasions I had felt about the subject—It seems no surprise to her—she loves me none the less, but proposes to do all she can to help me along—

Sometime, some way, the way will open more plainly. In the mean time I shall read, Study, Teach, and seek and strive to help make this world better in every way opening to me.

This cruel war has broken up our plans, But our God reigns and we may well look to Him for guidance and the path.

January 31, 1862 Friday. I am miserable—cant find a good reason— but am tempted to wish I could be annihilated.

Were it not for my dear good wife—my loving darling Rachel, and our little hope—a prospective Son—I would almost have dispaired entirely. I felt almost as though my mind would be thrown clean off its ballance—What an awful state! But the caresses, smiles, assurances and influences of my Darling drove all the gloom away, and I was restored—and spent the day in study mostly. Recd letters from Missouri—From J. B. Kimmel and M. Atteberry—makes me want to go out to Missouri—But No! That were foolish as things are out there on the war question—I must wait til affairs are more settled. I cannot take my Rachel away from all her Kindred into a strange country. When and where I cannot tell Friend from Foe, and where blood shedding is so common.

February 5, 1862 I feel that Mollie[ii] is true to us. She confides so in us and is so helpful—She certainly is second to no one in the Bowman Family except my Darling.

Oh! how dear to me is my Rachel. Time makes her only dearer Dearer DEARER!

Sore throat seems to be coming on in spite of all. Yet I can attend my classes.

February 16, 1862 My throat is bad—I was awake often and made appliances of cold compresses during the night and it seems broken up again this morning P.M. worse again I am so completely unnerved—unmanned that I have no control of my feelings scarcely consequently I cannot will this disease off me—

My religious feelings are not as I desire them to be. I do so desire to be a real good active living Christian man. One who can make a mark in the world, that will tell to the glory of God.

February 18, 1862 Ate rather much supper. Slept the worse for it— Read most of A.M.—Took a wet sheet pack—Helped me lots—My ravenous appetite is the hardest thing I have to contend with now. That operates against Diptheria or Cankered sore throat—Evening. I am unable to go to Dundee to meet my class Am feverish, slightly deranged in mind & feelings—I am well cared for by my merciful Heavenly Father and my unequalled in goodness Rachel. Helpmate—Wife

February 19, 1862 Wednesday. I took a "Dry Pack" this morning— was four hours in getting up a sweat but finally obtained some relief. This is surely a hard fight my throat is having day after day and night after night.

February 24, 1862 Monday. My mouth and throat seem to stubbornly resist getting well—
Evening had to miss my Preston Class.
I feel some discouraged about my mouth and throat. Most of today all seemed well except my lips which were sore and swollen— but since supper I feel so weak and my throat is worse—But I can lie down—

February 27, 1862 Thursday. I have been keeping pretty well on the go, but with my mouth and throat so bad much of the time I cannot do justice to my classes and work, and it is difficult to keep from becoming discouraged—But I dare not.

March 1, 1862 Saturday. Throat seems better. Pet quite unwell— Give her treatment. Eve attend my class—

March 2, 1862 Sunday A.M. Read for and chatted with Darling— Gave her cool Enemas—did her good—
My mouth and throat seem well now—I am so thankful. Surely I ought to serve God more faithfully—

March 5, 1862 Wednesday. Clem & I cut old Pine Tree—Snow deep and crust hard—Horrid job—Recd good letter from Mother[b] and Elly.[y] I am well again, and we are Oh! so happy—we become more happy in our marriage-relation every day it seems. Our Prospect is a source and subject of much conversation, and many prayers, and is long since dedicated to The Lord—

March 8, 1862 Saturday. Carrie[pp] and I went to Toll-bridge meeting in Evening—Some 14 "Mourners out" a good meeting. Pet was lonesome—I must not go away and leave her alone again in her present state.
She seemed so happy to have me come home, and made me so very happy too by her lavishing of love.
I feel a new strong desire to be and do good in the world—
Can I be saved if I do not better do my duty & O that heaven would open a way for me to do right—Oh! for Light! to see The Path.

March 12, 1862 Wednesday. I am preparing for Maple Sugar Making—Sawing wood &c——Eve—I am O so tired I can scarcely get along—But took a bath—ate supper—Then read the War News— Rebs Evacuate Manasses—

187

March 13, 1862 Thursday. Strasburg singing class closes this eve—
By unanimous vote they declare that they are pleased & satisfied
with my instructions, and feel that they have received the worth of
their money—

March 16, 1862 Sunday. Good Sunday School J. B. Slichter resigned Superintendency. Nominations were made to fill the
vacancy—Votes run—for Bechtal 1—Bowman 11—Cormany 25. So
here is additional work and new responsibility which I accept cheerfully—
Mrs Moses Eshelman is about to close out and is ready and happy
in the prospect.

March 19, 1862 Wednesday. The American War wears a brighter
aspect—Victory is crowning the U.S. movements on every hand—
Oh! I hope the Rebellion may soon be crushed[8]—

March 23, 1862 Sunday. I superintended the Sunday School—
Good attendance and fine interest—

March 26, 1862 Wednesday. Didn't get home from my class til
midnight. Pet was so glad to welcome me to her arms—and I—if
possible more so to be so tenderly and lovingly welcomed.

March 30, 1862 Had a good S.S.—
I gave them a talk on Joseph, which was well received—Spent the
day with my Rachel. O! so happily—and had a good rest up for the
coming weeks work—

April 1, 1862 Monday. My health is good, my singings are about
done—and life, for several weeks, has had in it much drudgery and
uphill work, and some unpleasantness.
Father Bowman[aa] is so strange a man that I can but wish I had
never become so well acquainted with him.

April 10, 1862 Sugar Making the order of the days and into
nights—Syruped off today—Left the bush at sundown.
I enjoy life better this week than for some time previously. Darling
comes out frequently and looks on and says a lot of pleasant things,
so making herself useful and more and more lovable—

8. This was written after the victories at Forts Henry and Donelson.

April 23, 1862 This has been a busy Period of toil and pleasure—
Everyday gathering sap, and nearly every day boiling more or less—
  Darling keeps up her walking out ¼ mile about daily. Often gathering chips, punching the fire, etc.
  She enjoys greatly being with me in the Bush, doing little things that are helpful, and Oh! how she does shower love and caresses upon me—
  We are daily so happy in our Prospect. The climax of which draws so steadily nearer—It astonishes me how strong Darling has become. Walking out and back almost daily. Exercising about in the "bush" much of the day, and doing her house work seems only to invigorate, instead of tiring or exhausting her—
  I am so delighted that we are so well, and above all so constantly happy in each other day in and day out——

April 24, 1862 Carrie[PP] and Lizzie[oo] out today helping to carry sap, and enjoying a good time. Carrie[PP] is most enthusiastic but wearies soon physically, but socially and poetically kept up a lively time indeed all day, or all the time out.

April 25, 1862 92 pails of sap today—Pet & Carry[PP] out helping—I syruped off 64 pails into 3½ pails of syrup and then at home the 3½ pails of syrup into 3 gallons of splendid molases—

April 26, 1862 My throat is swolen almost shut, and my tongue so stiff I can scarcely talk and I feel very badly—Rachel helped me take a sweat and a tub bath—later a wet sheet pack & bath—I wear wet compresses on my throat, and Fast for the fasting I have a pretty good reason—Evening I took another sweat Pack & bath, felt very badly on retiring—
  William and The Girls boiled sap, making 2¼ gallons molasses.
  My Darling is so good and helpful to me—Words cannot express how good a wife she really is—

April 27, 1862 Sunday. I feel that the disease is now broken, but my throat is very raw and painful—After 37 hours fasting I ate bit of Graham Gruel,[9] and some of the same with parsnip and milk for

9. Graham gruel was made by boiling a small amount of wholewheat meal in water. The hygienic and hydropathic medical books and cookbooks that the Cormanys used all referred to wheat meal as "Graham flour" in honor of Sylvester Graham, its chief advocate. Russell T. Trall recommended Graham gruel for convalescing patients in several of his books and included recipes for its preparation. See *The New Hydropathic Cook-Book: with Recipes for Cooking on Hygienic Principles* (New York, 1854), and *Hand-Book of Hygienic Practice: Intended as a Practical Guide for the Sick-Room* (New York, 1864), pp. xii–xxiii.

supper at 3 OCK—Took baths often, and wore compresses all the time—

I am having many serious thoughts as to what this spell might result in. Gods will be done not mine—

April 28, 1862 Monday. Pleasant Sugar Weather. My throat very bad yet—I keep up the same treatment—

William finished up the Sugar Making—Made 2 gallons molasses. Totals—192 pails of Sap, 7½ gallons No. 1 quality molasses—

Pet and I were over with The Girls most of the day—I ate two small meals—Had a high fever towards evening—was quite delirious for 1½ hours but my Dear was so good, and by her skilful treatment reduced the fever, and by 9 OCK P.M., I was quite natural again.

Pa Bowman[aa]—Ma[bb]—Mollie[ii] & Susie[nn] were over with us awhile—

I slept on the lounge——

April 29, 1862 Tuesday. I slept poorly—soon as I fell into a doze such flighty frightful dreams would startle me awake in a half choking state, my throat being filled with matter.   saliva etc—During the night Pet waited on me often, changing my chest wrapper, bathing my head, face and neck, and one time—God bless her goodness, She bathed my hands and feet too, and then I took a pretty good little sleep. The best of the night—

Today I kept my bed mostly being weak, and believing that quiet would be most conducive to restoration—

Pet waits on me with more than a mothers care—a care known only to herself. How sweet to be blest with such a wife——P.M. We had some callers, and I prespire instead of being feverish—a good omen!

I use burnt alum in my throat a little, but concluded not to use anything of the kind this time, but depend entirely on *Hygienic* treatment[10]—Evening I feel some better and am hopeful now of a speedy recovery for which I do thank God and my Darlings faithful attention—

April 30, 1862 Wednesday. Slept better last night, but am still not nearly well. I got up at 7 OCK—Took a bath—and ate some breakfast at 8 OCK—By diet—chiefly wheat meal gruel—apples—parsnips

---

10. Judging from the treatments that Samuel has described, he and Rachel were following Russell T. Trall's *Diptheria [sic]: Its Nature, Causes, Prevention, and Treatment on Hygienic Principles* (New York, 1862).

& the like I kept my bowels in shape—adding an occasional enema—

I walked out some with Darling for exercise—and then she read the war news for me, which is distressing sure.[11] Took a bath at 2 P.M. and a nap—8½ P.M. another bath to keep down tendency to fever—and then rested—but there came up a jaggy sensation in my throat and feverishness—

Pet warmed my feet and cooled my head and throat and soon I slept for a while, but was awakened by a sense of strangulation, and heat in my mouth and throat Bathed my mouth, neck, and face well, and then slept pretty well to remainder of the night—

May 1, 1862 Thursday. I am much better this morning—Took my baths and ate a nice little breakfast at 8 OCK. Took some outdoor exercise with Rachel and the girls, cleaning up the yard, etc.—

Then wrote up my Diary and the while, attending to my throat, which is getting better rapidly—I made out to enjoy my dinner quite well tho my throat is still delicate. Evening Darling and I had a nice talk over our late siege of affliction, and how kindly the good Lord sustained us and enabled her to do so admirably well for me—

Surely our afflictions work for good—and I resolve to be more devoted to my God, and a more faithful and devoted and loving and loveable husband to my Rachel.

May 2, 1862 Friday. I feel decidedly better this morning—William, Ma Bowman[bb] and The Girls brought the Sugar-boiling apparatus in from the "Bush"—

Susie[nn] and I went to Toll Bridge to U.B. Conference—Bishop Markwood presiding. The ride and associations greatly revived my spirits.

We dined at J. B. Bowmans. P.M. Conference session was intersting—warm speeches were made pro- and con on various subjects—

After an enjoyable day, a very pleasant ride and a lot of good cheer we arrived Home at 5 O clock. I found Pet in what seemed labor pains—She had been in bed most of P.M.—Had taken her sitz bath just before I came and the pain came on while in the bath—After I had my supper and had my little chores done I helped her take another sitz bath—Pains kept increacing gradually, at intervals.

11. Following his successes at Forts Henry and Donelson, Grant received a bloody setback at Shiloh, Tenn., April 6 and 7. Lt. Gen. Thomas J. "Stonewall" Jackson's wing of Lee's army was in the midst of its enormously successful campaign in the Shenandoah Valley, and the Union's Army of the Potomac under Gen. George B. McClellan was making slow headway on the Yorktown Peninsula southeast of Richmond.

The Intervals became shorter and the pains lasted longer. At 9 OCK I laid down to take a short nap—We had previously concluded to call no one in until necessity required—I slept very little—say 1½ hours. Pet napped some too, but 15–20–30 minutes a darting pain affected her back, various parts, and awaken her—at midnight pains were pretty severe every 5–10 minutes, and we concluded—as I was not very well—to call in Ma Bowman,[bb] and have Pa Bowman[aa] call in Mrs. Cress[12] from Preston—all this time Pet would be from lounge to the floor, then across the bed—and again on her knees to the lounge—with occasional easing intervals   about 2 A.M. Lady Cress came.

May 3, 1862   About 2 A.M.

Lady Cress came—after examination pronounced all things going on satisfactorily—The pains became more and more powerful—Too vigorous an effort was made by the Lady to have Pet—"Press"—"Pull on the towels fast to the bed-posts" "Beardown"—&c   I remonstrated that there was too much hurrying of nature—take time—I urged—give nature a chance—so I prevailed—6 Ock in the morning—all went to breakfast   I comforted Darling—she was so glad I stayed by her—

I encouraged her, and assured her all was going on perfectly—according to "The Books"—authority—But she needs to press the effort of expulsion as much as possible whenever the natural impulse arises——8Ock Pet seemed overcome—a little morose—discouraged—and needed much encouragement to impel her to believe that it would soon be over—She said several time "Oh! I cannot stand it"—"It will kill me"   I responded Oh no Darling, soon you will have relief—Do your utmost at expulsion—and our rejoicing will start in——9Ock! The little pet came—A Daughter! She cried lustily when the first Air entered her lungs—She seemed very much alive indeed——"Now Darling you are a Mother indeed and I am really a Father—and we are happy sure! Was my expression—as I placed a kiss on her forehead, which induced such a heavenly smile. In less than half an hour Darling was comparatively comfortable—Mrs Cress did her work nicely—but would not consent to our wish that she might have a spongebath—said it would kill her—she would do what was best—as she knew—and her own notions were carried out as to Darling. And Sister Mary[ii] took the child in hand—and dressed it—then presented it to me—I took it in my arms & kissed it.   and then I held it to its Mother—who smiled upon it, and named it Mary Brittannia.

12. A local midwife.

A sudden thrill flew through us all when Darling spoke out "There it is"—the Moment—I knew it was here I felt like pressing my Dear precious Rachel to my bosom and covering her with kisses—I did give her quite a number—and so now we have our desire—a Baby!—a dear—innocent—Angel Angelic—precious Baby The pain it cost was great but, ah! how dear, how precious it is—Worlds could not purchase it. The little household pet—and it a little girl, a dear pretty little girl—and all our own—with such a sweet, round face, and such sparkling eyes, and hair like its Pa...Pa...Pa...how funny that sounds. Me a Pa!—"Well Sammy you are now a Papa" my mother[b] would say—yes! and now my Ma[b] is Baby's Grand Ma—For the first time she is really fully Grand Ma in her life—though long called so—Good dear little Mary Britannia—God gave us her—She is even now dedicated to him. Oh! may she live to be a good, noble, useful, child, girl, virgin, woman. Oh! May God direct her that she may become a good woman True to herself, true to everybody, true to her country (U.S.A.) but above all true to her—our God—

At a little before 9 ock this A.M. a litle daughter was born unto us. and is named Mary Brittannia with room for another name to be given hereafter in between—Granny Cress left at about 10 ock. Soon after she had gone I gave Pet a general bath—and a little Soup at noon. Seemed to invigorate her a little—and rest her at once[13]—P.M. Pet gathers up nicely—so at 4 Ock—after a sponge bath she ate a little again and then rested nicely—Eve. All went to Tollbridge meeting Save Pet—Mary B. and myself—We three kept-house alone— Baby vomits occasionally during day & evening—a whitish-greenish-&darkish slime. Gave it a very little milk & water at bedtime—It cried very much before midnight—I dozed some—so did Darling— Folks came home midnight—Mother put Baby on the Lounge after warming it good, and covered it to almost the smothering point— and it slept til morning and so did Pet and I——

May 4, 1862 Sunday. I took a bath at 6 AM. Then gave Pet a bath—Ate my brekfast. Then gave Pet hers—wheat mush and

13. Samuel, a champion of the new hypdropathic and hygienic philosophies of medicine, has been impatient with Mrs. Cress, the embodiment of traditional midwifery. The midwife had wanted Rachel to try to help her natural contractions, while Samuel felt that a slower pace was more natural, hence safer and more desirable. After the delivery, Mrs. Cress, not unreasonably, refused to bathe Rachel; she had probably seen women die of puerperal fever and she probably believed from experience (though not yet from science) that all contact with potential sources of irritation and infection, including water, should be avoided. Samuel, on the other hand, could hardly wait for Mrs. Cress to leave so he could administer the kinds of baths recommended by his favorite medical counsellors.

strawberries—I wanted Baby bathed, but no one would do it—O what old fogies can do. I fed baby a wee bit of watered milk—a teaspoonful. at 9 Ock—and again at 12—Gave Pet Sitz bath of 10 min. and a full bath—She felt so well on it. I also renewed the Bed—all against law of Grannies—after an hours rest gave her some dinner—cracked wheat & Applesauce & m syrup—Fed Baby again between 2 & 3 Ock—I dined over at Pas[aa] at 3 Ock—I gave Pet an enema at 12½ Ock—It did not operate—another at 3½ PM. did not operate—Took one myself at 4—good Gave Pet another at 5—only the water passed off. & a very little sediment. Her bowels were entirely emptied before and during labor pains—and having eaten so little since the bowels contain but little—Pet is quite smart and feels well. Evening 6 ock she ate some toast-soup. (large clots of blood passed off this morning) Carrie[pp] came over at 7 P.M. to take care of Baby til Mollie[ii] comes—Baby has slept—all except 5 minutes. Since 2½ ock. Now 8¼ ock. Then til 10 cried some—Gave Pet a bath at 9 ock—went to bed about 10 Mollie returned about midnight—Baby slept well—fed it about 10—Mollie fed it near morning with all my doings. My throat and mouth have been getting well. and this eve. I am surely decidedly doing finely—

We have kept up our family worship at the bedside—my religious feelings are good. I feel so thankful for the dear little Baby and that all is so well with us—

May 5, 1862 Monday. Mother[bb] came over and gave Baby a bath—I took a bath—and then Pet was ready for her bath too. So we all were so clean. and now gave Darling her cracked-wheat brekfast. Baby cried wonderfully this morning. Catnip tea was urged by Ma B.[bb] but I said No. Let it cry—rather let it cry itself to death than commence drugging it—gave it a few sips of milky water at times— 10 ock. Pet begins to feel feverish. Milk is coming. Baby got a little this time—we feed Baby nothing, so it will suck lustily—11 ock. Gave Pet a good Sitz bath, and vaginal enema of cool water. Some clots passed off. Feels so good over it all. So much better. 12 ock cracked wheat and strawberry dinner, and a little soup. P.M. feels much better in every way. Baby slept well since 10 A.M. and it it is now 4 P.M. and I give Pet and her good bath. She feels so strengthened by it. 5 P.M. Baby got its fill of its proper nourishment, being the first time, and it is 55 hours old—6 ock. Pet ate ½ Graham biscuit and 2 inches square of Currant Pie. and 41 cherries for supper—7 ock. using a pipe—I drew the secretions out of Pets one breast which is defective—Darling sat up today several times—at bed time

I bathed her—we retired at 9 ½ ock   All slept till 12—Baby waked, and nursed—Then all slept well til morning—

May 6, 1862   Tuesday. Got up at 6 ock Baby nursed nicely—I gave Pet a sponge bath—and at 7 ock ate light brekfast.   rested nicely til 11 ock—suffers some feverishness and uneasiness. Gave her a sitz bath at 11 ½ ock.   decidedly strengthened by it—Ate toast biscuit—Potato parsnip, applesauce & milk—moderately—Baby nursed at 12 then went off to sleep—Rachel also rested til 2 ock.—Gave her an enema. Had a wonderful passage of the bowels—a long restful period followed—we had company—"Aunt Mary Clements—seemed to be restful to 5 ock   Baby nursed again. Then I gave Rachel a sponge bath. 65 to 70°—so refreshing to her.   slept sweetly til 9 ock. baby til 11, when it nursed again

My Pet made my heart so glad today. I expressed regrets that she had to suffer so many things when she responded "I gladly suffer it all and would even more just to have such a dear little angel given us"—and just so I feel meseems—I'd suffer all in her (Pets) stead, and ten times more rather than do without the little household angel—God direct us so we may direct its little steps aright, so as to bring the greatest honor to Our Heavenly Father.

May 7, 1862   Wednesday. Cool and windy—I got up at 6 ock—good bath—then gave pet a bath—in "checked water" Feels so much better. Sat up til 7—nursed baby while sitting up—Baby lay awake an hour—but Pet laid down and went right asleep—and so as not to disturb her, babys bath was deferred til 10–11   12 ock Pet awakened—Gave her a Sitz bath—65°—

Dinner, bean soup and baked potato. Lea[ii] dined with us—Mrs Bergy visited us—Pet is much stronger and livelier. Baby slept til 6 ock—then "nursed"—emptied the other breast too. P.M. Pet sat up several hours and ate her supper at 6:30—Grand ma insisted baby must "eat" some—quite a discussion—almost quarrelled—I finally yielded, and a wee bit of Grand-ma soup was given Baby—GrandMa—GrandPa and Hunsbergers Visited til past 10 ock—nevertheless I bathed Pet about 10—and we Pet, Baby & I went to sleep soon and slept til 3. A.M. when Baby waked—and nursed—my what a good Baby this is—

May 8, 1862   Thursday. We slept til 6 ock   Usual baths—Pet feels so much better on hers this morning   6:30 Baby waked and nursed and Pet sat up an hour—ate ¾ Graham Gem and milk for breakfast. 9:30 get Pet up and out on the big chair—sat up 1 ½ hours   Got rather tired—Gave her Sitz bath, and warm foot bath, and cold to her head, and soon—15 min.—equalized circulation and she felt much better. Then spongebath occasioned restfulness—Enjoyed dinner—Baby slept til 3 ock P.M. an 8 hours sleep and fast—nursed nicely—Pet feels much improved. Baby goes to sleep again and slept til 7 ¼ P.M. We had Cider soup for supper Mr. Brower called—pleasant man—nice little chat—Closing up the day Pet and I such a pleasant talk—we both are so happy—Happy in each other—happy in the Lord. Happy in our new charge. and all happy—9 ock gave Pet a bath, and then retired—all slept well til 3 ock A.M. when baby waked and nursed—and soon all were asleep again—

May 9, 1862 Friday. Warmer and stormy—usual baths—and nourishings—Pet a little feverish—and a little low spirited—Read some for her, and prayed with her—Noon feels better. Sitz bath did well—much revived—ate Some dinner—sat out in "the room" ½ hour then napped 2 hours—about 2 baby waked. nursed. is so greedy. gets too much, then vomits excess—but does not throw up at other times—

I am now chopping wood daily for xercise—killed Calf for Pa B.^{aa}—Jas W^{kk}—Lea^{jj}—Mollieⁱⁱ and I had a fine Sing after our supper—of cracked wheat. Apples &c The Sing seemed to do Pet so much good—Bedtime gave Pet bath—feels better—I am so happy this eve because Pet seems so much better—and because she is in so much better condition than most women are the 6th day after child-birth——Baby nursed again about 7 ock PM Then we all slept til 1 AM when baby nursed and we all slept till 4 A.M.

May 10, 1862 Saturday. Baby nursed—We bathed—Pet gave Baby an enema—did well—we ate full breakfasts—Pet feels much better and stronger—Helped Pa B^{aa}—Kill-dress and cut up Beef—Gave me 7 lbs   11 ½ gave Pet a Sitz bath—60°—Felt much better—was able to stand for a towel bath—

Pet ate Veal-rice-soup for dinner.—P.M. had a small family singing—good time   Today Baby slept till 9 A.M.—nursed   slept til 4 P.M. nursed again, but then about all up—Gave it some cold water—settled it 6 ock gave it short nurse—acted O.K.

6 P.M. Pet sat up an hour or so—ate supper with us—had her hair combed after—got a little tired. So to lie down seemed sweet—Baby cried excessively—gave it cold water—seemed better—gave it nurse again at 8 ½ then it went asleep—Pet Bath, & Enema—by 9 ½ all asleep   all slept till 4 A.M. when Baby wanted nursing—

This is the 1st day—without fire in room.

May 11, 1862   Sunday. Mollie[ii] up at 4—to get ready to go to Henry Weavers funeral   We slept 'til 6—Ma B[bb] came and bathed Baby & dressed it—I bathed and then helped Pet bathe—Pet feels much better this morning. Folks started for Funeral at 6 ½—I got breakfast—Pet and I ate together Veal-Rice-soup-biscut-fruit—Pet sat up to eat. Sat ½ hour—when Babe was 1 week old—Pet can now get out of bed pretty Easily alone—can stand and walk about with very little support.   rests comfortably.   might be up more but—we think—better too slow, than too fast—McNallys visited us—pleasantly—we both enjoyed it—11 ½ gave Pet Sitz bath. Baby nursed at 9 and then at 3—we dined at 1   Cousin Nancy stayed with Pet while I conducted Sunday School   Had a good S.S.   Then I was nurse. Had a big time doing for Baby—But baby slept most of time til 6 P.M.—nursed—Cous Jacob Bowmans visited us—surprised To find with a Daughter—I got supper   7 ½ ock S.S. Weavers[ee] called on us—Rather much xcitement for Pet. Last callers left at 10 ock Bathed Pet—then all went asleep—Baby waked at 2 ock—nursed—slept til 5 ock

May 12, 1862   Monday. up at 5. Baths—6 Baby waked—nursed. Slept til 9 ock   Mary bathed it—nursed again—Slept til 1 PM nursed—Pet ate brekfast—seems so much stronger—can handle herself freely—sat up an hour at noon   nursed baby while up—then took good nap rather than eat. 4 P.M. ate heartily—
     Baby cries considerably.   hiccoughs. Throws up some. Gave her cold water—settled it nicely   7 P.M. Pet Sitz bath, enjoyed it well, and soon after nursed baby   9:30 we all went asleep and slept well til 3 ock A.M.—
     I am well, and very happy, in most respects, only that I so long to be a holier man, and am making so little progress—

May 13, 1862   Tuesday. all slept til 7 ock—rainy—Baths self and Pet—8 ock baby nursed—8:30 ate our brekfast—after it Pet took good sleep—Baby slept til 2 P.M. Pet ate with us in Kitchen at 3 ½ ock, and was up most of the time til 8 ock. Feels much better—was quite unwilling to go to bed until quite tired out—Too tired for her bath, so retired without—seems too bad. I feel very sad over it—Had to yield to a weep—and can hardly tell why—my thoughts ran thus. 'My Rachel won't do what is best for her.   disregards my advice—will suffer for it.   and I must attend to her and help her thru—and I am going to have some throat again—Perhaps die with it—what will my Pet do? and my dear—little daughter!—Prayed long for Pet. and our little Mary Cora Brittania.   more   Perhaps Pet will overdo herself & die   and what would I do? How could I live without my precious Darling—all alone. and a little pet to care for—&c. &c.—. Having thrown up the 2 ock P.M. nursing, we nursed her again at 4 P.M. and again 7 ½ which stood, so at 9 ock all went asleep and slept til 4 ock in the morning.

May 14, 1862 Wednesday. Baby nursed at 4 A.M.—and then with Pet slept til 6 ock   Pet feels strong—stood for bath. Walked out into the room, and ate brekfast with us in Kitchen—Felt like walking out doors, but I objected—she was up most of A.M.   Took little nap on lounge—Baby nursed again at 10 ½—and is good all AM.—

Pet remained up most of day, Feels pretty strong—Baby nursed at 2 ock PM—a little painful for Pet on a/c sore nipple—Nursed at 7.PM   Then slept til 2 ock AM—nursed again slept til 6 A.M. Musings: Time flies! and bears us onward daily nearer home, It seems but a few months since I left Missouri and was married. a few weeks since I came to Canada. a few days ago when we first hoped that we would be blest in 9 months with a little Pet. And now we are Pa and Ma—have a dear little daughter. Eleven days old. Darling is able to be up all day, except, she takes little lounge naps several times a day. and she has been out in the Kitchen, and at the outer door a number of times—

I do thank God that things are as well with us as they are—O for grace to love and serve Him, as I should—in return.

May 15, 1862 Thursday. Baths—Their brekfast at 8—. I work out several hours, making a Shovel Plow for the Farm. I put in a good deal of time attending to Pet and baby—Baby nurses about every 3 hours, or 4 in daytime—and once in the night—at 2–3 ock AM

May 16, 1862 Friday. Pack and Bath for Pet—Baby normal—Today Pet came out to "Wood house" where I was working. Seemed so strong and cheerful. P.M. Baby Colicky—cries very much—gave it plunge bath, and injection[14]—In ½ hour quieted. Nursed naturally at 8 PM.   Then soon fell asleep. Slept til 5 ½ A.M.—and we did good sleeping too—

May 17, 1862 Saturday. Pet took her bath almost alone—Feels fine. Baby real good all AM—P.M. I had a Singing—Good but small turnout—Pet, and Mary Cora Brittanica were over at Grand Mas this

---

14. A plunge bath involved immersion in tepid water; an injection was an enema. Both were standard hydropathic treatments for colic. See Trall, *Hand-Book of Hygienic Practice*, pp. ix, xiii–xiv, xvii.

P.M.—Evening Pet so brisk, and Baby so good all day. we cannot but be happy—

May 18, 1862 Sunday. Baby slept from 8 last eve til 3 AM.—we did well too—Pet bathed herself—and we breakfasted, and at 8 ½ ock Baby nursed—and Baby and Pet took nice nap. We dined over at Grand Mas—Later took a stroll—called on Slichters—about ¼ mile s. east Pet enjoyed the walk and calling so much—Evening "The Girls" Mollie[ii] & Susie[nn] were over and we had a real jolly time—

May 19, 1862 Monday. War news exciting Pet and Baby getting on finely—Susie[nn] with us instead of Mary[ii]—Pet eats 2 to 3 times daily—and Baby 3 to 8 hours apart wakes only once in the night—and is real good during the day. Excepting occasional spells of colic—which always yields to warm enema and tepid bath—

May 20, 1862 Tuesday. Usual routine with Pet and Baby—9 ock I go to Galt. Canvass—Books—Hydopathic Phrendological & Hollicks works. Sell some $6.oo worth—circulate prospectuses—Home 5 ½ ock—Dined at Hotel—Supper at home—Eve killed & dressed Calf for Slichters—Rachel and Baby doing finely—

May 21, 1862 Wednesday. Same routine—Go at 9 ock—Take orders for $20.oo worth—Home 4 PM—Pet takes morning bath—and gives Baby one or two—nurses it every 3 to 4 hours by day and then from 2 to 4 ock at night—It seems so strange I cannot or do not become a better Christian. I have strong desires and yet they don't amount to much—

May 22, 1862 Thursday. renew ½—Me—Canvass $8.oo worth—came home 5 ock—Pet seems so glad when I come home, and Oh! I am so happy to meet her and the precious little Angel Baby—It truly is sweet to have a dear good wife and an angel of a Babe to live and labor for—This would seem no world to me without these blessed ones

May 23, 1862 Friday. All well and happy—went to Gault—canvass about 3 hrs. Five or Six $s worth. Ride home with Bro J. B. Bowman—Had a fine talk and religious visit Baby is bothered some with colic—Hiccough—&c—but soon yelds to sane treatment. The world and things generally move off pretty smoothly, and, but for hypocracy, folks in general, and I and mine in particular would be much happier. O! for grace to be true to God and all mankind—

May 24, 1862   Saturday. Queens birthday and mine. Lots of coming and going—Pet, Baby, and I intended to go to Gault to see the doings—But the Girls went so we couldn't—P.M. J. B. Slichter & wife—J. B. Bowman, J. Renshaw, Mollie,[ii] Lizzie,[oo] Nancy, Moriah & Eliza Bowman, Rose Syler met at our House to form a "Health Association"—J. B. Slichter Pres.,—S. E. Cormany Secy—Evening— Fine view of Fire works at Preston. It is great how—well and bright Pet and Baby are—

May 25, 1862   Sunday. Susie[nn] slept til I had breakfast most done— then went over home. So now we will do without a girl helper—Pet is so well and so happy. Took them out riding—Doon—Via Detwilers—called a wee at "Josephs"—

May 26, 1862   Monday. I got up early—cooked breakfast—leaving Darlings sleep—Pet enjoys sleep so much, and always is so refreshed that it does me good to work for her and let her sleep—

May 27, 1862   Tuesday. Got breakfast—and helped do things up— Canvassed in Preston—Dined at Burgys—Baby did not wake to nurse last night. Is good & well today—

May 28, 1862   Wednesday. All up betimes. Pet, Baby, Sue[nn] and I went up to Grand Pa Clemenses, 5 mile drive. John and Amos Hunsberger—Amos & Abram Clemens, Noah & Lydia Bowman and old uncle Jake Clemens were there—a great day visiting &c &c   Old women seem to think because Pet does not nurse baby— everytime it cries a little—like they used to do, Therefore she needs to be taught—but Darling knows what is best both for Baby & herself, and I stand by her.   Got home 8ock—Baby slept most of way—and Pet enjoyed the whole way—On retiring—Pet and I had a long openhearted talk concerning private matters—and we agree perfectly as to what were *best,* but I find myself lacking at times in self control and I must wonder how she can love me as she does—

May 29, 1862   Thursday. Pet & Baby put up at "Uncle Amos Clemenses" 2 loads of us—21 & 15 respectively went to Berlin S.S. celebration good grounds—we led the march—I conducted the singing and sang a solo on request—Addresses—songs—Sociability—Big crowd—Great time—Our loads sang, Much of the way, both ways Home by 8 ock—calling for Rachel and Babe on way and taking them along. They too had a good day—

May 30, 1862 Friday. Spent A.M. at home—chopped wood in bush—Darling keeps house herself—Evening Mr Jas W. Adamses[kk] came Lea[jj] remained with Pet and Babe, and J. W.[kk] accompanied me to my Strausburg Singing School—Had a good time instructing—Drilling—Testing &c &c and a fine social time going and coming home—and Lea[jj] Pet and Baby report lots of fun at home while we were off—

Looking back—and at myself I become so depressed and discouraged with myself, that I do not—seems cannot—better control my lower—my animal self—that I almost fall into despair of every reaching my ideal of a man—a Husband—a Father. Sometimes I feel as though I can never again become a really happy man—Lost lost lost rings in my ears so often and so long. I approach near to despair—But, Darlings love and devotion never fail—and she expresses both so tenderly—and here's our Babe and Jesus reveals Himself anew and joy arrives, and hope gladdens

May 31, 1862 Saturday. Usual routine—Today Adamses[kk] and me took inventory of our goods—at which they will take them if we decide to go to U.S. Had a real pleasant time—P.M. met my Blair childrens Singing Class at S. H. good Evening. our Health Association met Chairman & Secy—in place—adopted Constitution—and under it elected J.B. Slichter Pres. Mollie H. Bowman[ii] vice pres. S.E. Cormany secy.

June 1, 1862 Sunday. This morning Pet and I had a long talk about my feelings and evil forebodings &c—as with a magic wand, her goodness and womanliness dispelled the blues—and left happiness instead—P.M. after Sunday School—the Blair, Strasburg, and Toll bridge Singing Classes met for practice—Had fine time—are thinking of a coming concert—I am so much happier today—Life seems a pleasure when one is contributing to the sum of the happiness of so many young people, as my numerous singing clases embrace—and it is so sweet to live, when, at the close of day one has such a dear true, good wife—and precious Babe to retire to in the little home, and with plenty of the comforts of life—and encompassing all and permeating all. The one and only real Savior and experimental Knowledge of Him.

June 2, 1862 Monday. Canvass in Preston

June 3, 1862 Tuesday. I worked on Public Road as a Farmer—Mose Bechtal acted the wet cat all P.M.

June 4, 1862 Wednesday. Worked on Road—Home to dinner—Evening Joe Barlow & Sue Bechtol Menno Haymaker, Mollie[ii] Lizzie[oo] Sue,[nn] Darling and I had a regular Singing practice—good time till 11 Ock—

June 5, 1862 Thursday. Canvass Preston—Sell $3.25 worth books—Evening Toll Bridge Singing practice   Elias Snyder is acting the Wet Cat about the chapel key. O the delightful moonlight walk I had going & coming—and how happy I am.   but I am not as holy as I desire to be—

June 6, 1862 Friday. Slept late—Pet and Baby doing finely—Helped fix up house &c—
Saw Eshelman & Clemens. Can have Toll Bridge for Concert—Even James[kk] & Lea[ji] came—
met the Blair class and had a good sing—I am confident this class will do well at Concert—

June 7, 1862 Saturday. Busy day—James[kk] & Sue[nn] to Gault—I and The Girls—kill & dress Chickens for Pic Nic Monday at Puslinch Lake. P.M. I met jr Singing class—and then James,[kk] Lea[ji]—the Girls & I had a season of practice for concert   at 6 ock we started for Toll Bridge. Concert commenced at 8 P.M. Classes represented—Strasburg—Toll Bridge—Blair Sr & Jr—Preston—

Program

1st	All Classes	Omicron	page 220
2nd	Strasburg Class	Alleppo	" 164
	" "	Majesty	" 133
3rd	Blair Class	Forever With the Lord	" 183
	" "	Trumpet	" 237

4	"I am not young"	M.H.Bowman[ii] ⎫
	"Under the violet"	Lizzie Bowman[oo] ⎬ Sopranos
		Sue Bechtal ⎭
		Sue Bowman[nn] ⎫ Altos
		B.Bechtal ⎭
		J.W.Adams[kk] ⎫
		Jas Bechtal ⎬ Bass
		Menno Haymaker ⎭
		S.E.Cormany Tenor

5th	Strasburg & Classes Toll Bridge	Lifes Harvest 222
		Temperance Call 238
		Lord Dismiss us &c 219

6th	All Classes	Old House at Home	17
		Lips I have kissed	358
		Christmas Eve	202
7th	same singers as 4th	Anthem Be joyful	272
	adding Noah Stauffer on Tenor		
8th	Blair Class	The heavens declare &c	269
		Light and Gay (jolly)	20
9th	Rock Me To Sleep	M.H.Bowman[ii]—Sop	
		Sue Bowman[nn]—Alt	
		J.W.Adams[kk]—Bass	
		S.E.Cormany—Tenor	
10th	Same singers as 4th	Under the Birch	
		Rain on the Roof	
11th	I am not young—called for		
12th	Quartette—"Fallbrook" By	L.A.Adams[jj]	
		J.W.Adams[kk]	
		Sue Bowman[nn]	
		S.E.Cormany	
13th	Trio—"Farmers Girls"	Sue B[nn]—J.W.A[kk]—S.E.C	
14th	All Classes—German and		
	English.	"Good Night"	

(after 11—Speech By Rev. S. L. Downy—Collection $1.94¢—)

June 8, 1862 Sunday A.M. Mollie[ii]—Susie,[nn] Jameses[kk] and Pet—Baby and I went to Toll Bridge to meeting—Rev. S. L. Downy preached fine Sermon on Baptism—Some ½ doz were emersed—We dined at Pa Bowmans[aa] P.M. Had a good S.S.

J. W. Adams[kk] addressed the children nicely—Evening at˙Pa B's[aa]—It seems so cheery to be there all together, and sing the hours away as we have done this evening.

June 9, 1862 Monday. All in a bustle this morning for a Pic Nic at Puslinch Lake Started about 8 AM—James.[kk] Lea.[jj] Mollie.[ii] Susie.[nn] Lizzie[oo] Carrie[pp]—a pretty good day. But yes but there were a few butted in—only to mar. Had some good boating, and amusement—and a fine meal, and rather a pleasant partaking of the Pic Nic dinner—

I needed my Rachel and our Baby to help out and make my joy full—they were being companioned by Grand Ma—

June 10, 1862 Tuesday. at home all day with my precious ones—am well and happy still not satisfied with myself religiously—There are so many things yet to attain—and I make such slow progress—I need deeper earnestness and more faith

June 11, 1862 Wednesday. This P.M. Pet and I went to Gault Did some shopping—engaged a suit of clothes for me—Home dusk— Eve good prayer meeting over at Pa's[aa]—Saw Rev. S. L. Downy today—kindly invited me to attend a S.S. Celebration at Elmira, and "make a speech for them" Consented.

June 12, 1862 Thursday. a little blue on a/c of meager news from *Old* Home—"wish they would think ½ as often of me as I do of them."

June 13, 1862 Friday. I visited Ben Burkholders School to tender an invitation to Toll Bridge S.S. to our Blair celebration—I call at Dan Snyders—and Uncle Amoses. Supper there &c &c. Got home 9 ock Mollie[ii] and Susie[nn] were keeping Rachel company—I am well and as happy as the day is long—My darling is such a good dear that I could not be otherwise—

June 14, 1862 Saturday. Pa Bowman[aa] and I went to the Clemens fishing-bee—We caught about two bushels in about four hours— Had a great time indeed—P.M. met my jr singing class, pretty good time—

June 15, 1862 Sunday. Pet, Baby and I went to S.H. to hear Rev Hagey from Ill. preach—He is a shrewd Chap, sharp—scientific— uses strong, inductive reasoning in his preaching, is 50 to 75 years in advance of Menonites in Canada and Pennsylvania—He addressed our S.S. in P.M. very agreeably—Eve all at Pr. Mtg at McNallys— Good

June 16, 1862 Monday P.M. Pet Mollie[ii] and Sue[nn] visited at Eshelmans, while we menfolk selected place &c for our S.S. Celebration— Took supper there, and then had long talk on Hydropathy—Mr E intensely interested. I may sell him several works on the subject— Pet Mollie,[ii] Sue[nn] and Baby went home before I did. We are so well, and as happy and more so, then anybody we know—Life is sweet indeed since linked with one so good, and true, and precious as is My Darling. Thank God for a Perfect Woman.

June 17, 1862 Tuesday. I went to Uncle Sam Bowmans Mill Raising—Let a chizel fall on my foot cut it severely Dined at Uncle Sams—Brother Eshelman came home with me—Gave me his order for $5.50 worth of Books—Had a long fine talk on commonsense— The War seems slow about ending. Yet it seems the North moves,

Surely, tho slowly—I long to see the Secessionists run into the "last ditch——

I do so long to see it made safe for us to go to Our New Home in distracted—divided—Missouri to establish our little Home—which began to build in 1860—

O I do so wish I could get a letter from old Home once again—

June 18, 1862 Wednesday. Went with Pa B.[aa] to Gault—My suit not quite done—Pa[aa] went Home—I put up at Gault House—Seemed a long day in town. Had a long talk with Gavin Hume on U.S. war business, Hygiene &c. Eve walked home—

June 19, 1862 Thursday. Rainy—Gave Pet Turkish Pack for Boils & eruptions—and Baby also—Worked admirably—Noon Cleared—Prepare to go up to West Woolwich—to attend a S.S. Celebration—Started 2 P.M. Mollie,[ii] Susie,[nn] Pet, Cora and I—Nice drive—Supper at Uncle Moses Bowmans—a great little visit—Later went up to Uncle Noah Bowmans—at West Montrose—Met with a very warm reception and spent the evening very pleasantly—Discussed Religion—Health and Music—and had a fine Sing—

June 20, 1862 Friday. Frosty—Cold for June—
Uncle Noah ordered a lot of Books on Hygiene and treatment of ailments hygienically—

10 OCK a lot of us went over to Elmira—Met with very warm reception—more so than we expected   The Wengers and Weavers[ee] were sometime sore on a/c of my refusing to remain in their employ, since I could not handle whiskey—Brandy—Wine &c as a part of their business—

(But I make—and have made right along—more money teaching Music—and introducing Books on Hygiene Phrenology etc)—Dined at S.S. Weavers[ee] (sister Lydias[dd]) at 1 P.M. The S.S. assembled in the Bush for a Festival—Meeting was called to order by Hon J. E. Bowman M. P. cousin of Rachels—Song by Choir, Prayer. Speech by Rev Foreman and it rained, so we adjourned to the Chapel—Music—Then speech by myself—and a song—Address by Rev S. L. Downy—

Eating and Drinking & fun—Speech by J. L. Bowman—more songs and the Festival closed—Upon the whole it came off well Spent the evening pleasantly at S. S. W's[ee]—Rather cool all day.

June 21, 1862 Saturday. Sister Lydia[dd] (Mrs S.S.W) and Rachel settled up in part—old Partnership—Milinery affairs. Recd $1.13.

Had some very pleasant conversation with S.S. W^{ee} and Lydia^{dd} Baby Cora is a great center of attraction to very many—Started Home 10 OCK—Watered team and got Lemon aid at Waterloo. Got Home 2½ P.M.—I went to Quarterly Conference—at The Blair S. H—The most awful Quar. Conf. I ever witnessed—Plowman—The P.E.[15] showed a tremendous amount of scotchism and Downy too much Irish.

There certainly is power behind the Throne and it will manifest itself ere long unless matters change for the better.

Evening, we three Cormany's are all tired—Retire early and sleep sweetly—

June 22, 1862 Sunday. Woods Meeting in Uncle Amoses Bush—or rather "A Basket Meeting"—

We and Pa Bowmans^{aa} loaded up our Baskets and all went—

Good sermon by Rev Plowman—Followed by Sacrement, sweet but not ecstatic—Dinner was a pleasant season. Each group seated around or about a lot of Bread, Butter, Cakes Pies etc made things disappear, and the while made everything lively and mostly lovely as well—P.M. Rev J. B. Bowman preached in german and Rev S. L. Downey in English—both good, interesting—Large crowd of people in attendance.

For the evening—after coming home, Pet, Baby and I walked over to Slichters—Had a real pleasant visit—Conversation principally on religious matters—Bro Slichter is an honest true man wanting chiefly in sensativeness and energy to sharpen him up as a teacher and instructor—

June 23, 1862 Monday. Father Bowman^{aa} and I had a settlement. Our accounts agree nicely—He falls over $20. into my debt—Seemed to surprise him a little.

I am having considerable symptoms of "sore throat" again—

June 24, 1862 Tuesday. Make "store box" for packing.

In a whisper, Pa Bowman^{aa} seems decided to make an exception of me—Bro Clem^{cc} is bad on making debts, poor on paying. Pa^{aa} has been paying a good many but maybe won't pay me—In fact he has paid all I know of but me, and I had good reason to expect pay too— I am quite sure any of Clems^{cc} creditors could better afford to lose than I—

I hope he may see—what seems to me—his error before long—

15. Presiding Elder.

Joy! Got a letter from Mother.[b] O such a good one—She is expecting us to come to Pennsylvania soon. Offers me $18 as a favor and Motherly help—Guess we'll go—It seem to me I ought to go—Rachel and I have discust it frequently this summer—Tho going to Pa to visit my people, and old Home might mean my enlisting to defend my Home, Fireside and Country. What would be more reasonable were we to find on visiting there that our country needed me— as a loyal son—to step out in her defence, and for her perpetuation—and so the protection of what is nearest and dearest to Every Man.

Rachel—as a student at Oberlin caught the "underground R.R." idea—and later—at Otterbein University or near there, was connected with that R.R. line practically, and our reading together all the War news available, since the war began places her in a good position to make sacrifices—if needs be—in a different form to carry out her patriotic ideas——So we agree perfectly. We go over—not for the purpose of my enlisting but to visit my dear ones, Mother,[b] Sisters, Brothers &c—and then, to decide what we believe the good Lord would have me do, or rather have us do—

Some have come away from Pa to escape the war—We have decided to go and see for ourselves—and if needs be go into the War—Here we stand   We can see no way to honorably do otherwise—

June 25, 1862 Wednesday. Recd order for $3.00 worth of Books— Hollick—P.M. helped Pet some towards washing—Amused Baby— did what I could in general towards shaping thinks for packing up—Dont feel very well—wish so much to go to Pa to see my Mother,[b] Sisters &c, &c, and it seems I can hardly afford it.

I have never before felt so strong desire to go home—We will likely go

My health and Pets is so good, and we are so very happy in each other and The Lord.

June 26, 1862 Thursday P.M.   Mollie,[ii] Sue,[nn] Pet, Baby and I took a tour "Elmira-ward" again for a celebration—Called at various places en route—Eve. Turn in at Uncle Noah Bowmans—

June 27, 1862 Friday. about 10 A.M. all hands over to S. S. Weavers[ee]—Rev S. L. Downey—Levi Weavers—Uncle Noah's and J. L. Bowmans and we 3 dined at Sister Lydias[dd] (S.S.W's[ee])—

P.M. Struck for the woods—Speeches—singing—Raining a little &c.   Lemon-aid and cake gave spice to the gathering

Eve put up at S. S. Ws[ee]—Call on Isaac Wengers—Had a good sing—Good time generally

June 28, 1862 Saturday. Rachel and Lydia[dd] (Mrs S.S.W) Finished up their settlement of old millinery business—Homed by 3 OCK P.M.

—Nothing new—

June 29, 1862 Sunday. Routine—

June 30, 1862 Monday. Looking backward and Forward and upward—I am having some strong feelings as tho perhaps the Lord wants me to take upon myself the duties of a Minister—I seem hard to persuade—Mr Bridecker called on me and we planned some for a "singing school celebration" next Friday The Fourth of July—P.M. I went to Uncle Sam Bowmans to get out lumber for seating &c, &c, for S. S. Celebration—This to be a Sunday School and singing school affair—

Evening had a meeting to prepare singing program—

Had a fine time. All seem so interested—need more Bass.

July 1, 1862 Tuesday. We worked on seats, stand, etc—I feel somewhat disconcerted—So few take interest in the getting up of the necessary to a good celebration—

Would God, I could impress all parents with the responsibility resting upon them—i.e. Their whole duty towards their children—Young people—

July 2, 1862 Wednesday. I spent the AM going around giving directions concerning the preparations as to Cold Meats—Baking &c. &c.

Was treated respectfully in general. Excepting Old Uncle Wendel Bowman showed some of his Monarchical propensities—

Gossip has it that We—i.e. The B. B. Bowman Family[aa]—with J. W. Adams[kk] and myself as sons in Law—are planning to have a yankee 4th of July Celebration—

With the stars and stripes waving &c, &c, which the old Tories declare in advance—Can not be.

None of us have tried to disabuse their minds, but some have said, "Surely we must go with the Flag at the head of The column " (Not saying what Flag) but, never-ever-naming or denying what they assert—so leaving them in hot water.

P.M.—Pet, Baby & I went to Uncle Amos Clemenses—a delightful visit—

Evening a good prayer meeting. Came home right after—

July 3, 1862 Thursday. The famos "Celebration" comes off tomorrow—Gossip makes a good deal about the Flag Bugaboo, and Toryism says it just Shall not be—"All else is admissable, but no stars
and stripes—No Sirree" At 5 P.M. I, Pet and the Girls out to the
Bush to finish the Spot for the Celebration—near Sundown the Children and youngsters came for practice and a sing—

Had a fine time til dark—all seemed interested save "Uncle Sams"
and a few who were anticipating trouble—on a/c The Flag—

I am to speechify, and have not yet fully formulated my say—Put
in the evening preparing—

July 4, 1862 Friday. Early—busy—Day beautiful—S. S. Weavers[ee]
from Elmira arrived about 8 A.M.

People commenced gathering at The Carlisle Hill Chapel—The
place of rendesvoux at 8:30—About 9—Our B.B. Bowman Group—
Father[aa] & Mother[bb] Bowman—S. S. Weavers[ee]—J. L. Bowman—
James[kk] & Lea Adams[ji]—Rachel—Cora and Me—Mollie,[ii] Susie,[nn]
Lizzie[oo] & Carrie[pp] and a few others marched towards The Chapel
with the Flag—in a Sheath—

We were advised to keep it down—

The story was that an American Flag was to be raised—

A number of Old Tories and a few younger ones were on the
ground—in sight—and had said The Flag Shall not go up, nor lead
the procession From Chapel to Bush—

When the attempt was made to remove the sheath preparatory to
raising—Keep it down, Keep it down! was expressed—But amidst
the confusion, the sheath was jerked off, and the bearer quickly
unfurled The Flag—It was The "Union Jack" "The British Flag" and
The Tories looked crest fallen and walked aside—and We all of us
smiled complacently—[16]

Soon the Braslan—Berlin—Toll Bridge—and parts of other Schools
& classes were in the formation and Brother Eshleman and I met
them, and with the Flag marched into the prepared grounds—and
opening exercises were on—Songs—Prayers and Praise Speakers—

Hon J. L. Bowman

Benj Burkholder

S. E. Cormany—

16. Few Canadians were friendly toward the Union government at this time. They
feared annexation whenever the United States mobilized troops, and most Canadian
leaders would probably have welcomed a permanent division of the behemoth republic on their southern border. Moreover, memories of the *Trent* affair were still vivid.
Robin W. Winks, *Canada and the United States: The Civil War Years* (Baltimore, 1960).

Music—between speeches By the Berlin, Toll Bridge—Blair and other schools & singers   Dinner 12 til 2 P.M. Great   —Sociability—
P.M. Rev S. L. Downy
Rev. J. B. Bowman
and Hon J. L. Bowman
made short spicy addresses—The day was well spent and most interestingly—and Thank God Old Toryism was knocked out—put to shame—

Eve. we 3 & S.S. W's[ee] took tea at Amos Clemenses—nice time—and everybody one meets seems real happy—

July 5, 1862   Saturday A.M.   cleaning up the Grounds—P.M. Put up a big Swing for the Girls—Evening Health Assn meet on the Hill—I made an address of ½ hour on Diptheria—Its sane treatment—The Assn much interested. But we have some week kneed members and Mother B[bb] is one of them, sure!

July 6, 1862   Sunday. Cous Jacob Clemenses visit us—We do not approve of Sunday visiting.   P.M.—Sunday School—Fine—I gave my Farewell Address to the School, with good effect—The school deeply moved on a/c of our intending to leave for U.S. so soon—I am so glad for the love of these children and youths.

Eve. We—Jacob and Amos Clemenses—all took tea at Pa B's[aa]—Had a nice sing—

July 7, 1862   Monday. Pet—Baby & I start on a visiting tour—and good-byeing. To Geo Clemens—Dinner, Grand Pa Clemens for Supper—Spent day real pleasantly—Evening went to Uncle Elias Bowmans—Found James[kk] and Lea[jj] there—Good jolly evening all around—Pet & I bathed and gave Baby one too—Had delightful sleep——

July 8, 1862   Tuesday. The Women Quilt—I visit J. W.s[kk] school—we go to Eliases noon—We are all having some eruptions—Eczemic—Baby has a Gum rash, several days, and we are quite miserable at times. It don't yield readily to our treatment—

July 9, 1862   Wednesday. Still amongst the Bowman Uncles and Cousins—Delightful times xcept

July 10, 1862   Thursday. Baby is quite unwell—and we can't treat her as we would at home—so we will hie home soon, unless her rash &c lets up—

On our way to S. S. Weavers[ee] we drove to a secluded place along the Grand River, and each had a good bath—olive oiling after—

Dined at S.S. Ws[ee]—Supper at Wm Erbs—Had a pretty good time—Mr E is a first class man—and we had interesting interview on Politics—Hygienics—Morals and religion—Home at 10 P.M.—all abed—our bed occupied—Baby not well—Pet and I both have blues—What a time we do have—We slept over in our house on the floor, feeling almost sick of life—Quite grieved at the Home folks, and almost despairing for the life of Baby fixed it cosily. We lay in each others arms & soon sleep sweetly—

July 11, 1862 Friday. We all 3 slept late—Baby a little restless— Helped Pet give her treatment—we took baths and fasted—I mowed several hours for Pa B[aa]—before noon—

P.M.—Pet washed—Baby good—I mowed for Pa[aa] til Supper—

Evening helped bring in a load of hay—We put up at our own house again at bed time—

Poor dear Pet is so discouraged about Baby and also her own skin disease (contracted & cured (?) at Westerville—but shows up more or less occasionally) Pet always looks at the dark side of the picture. This has a tendency to make her "blue" and unhappy, and makes me much to do in the way of trying to make her happy. But Oh! she is still my own dear good true ideal of a wife, and Mother— Had she not these little weaknesses or failings, she might have greater ones, and harder for me to help her out of to overcome—

July 12, 1862 Saturday. Pleasant but warm—Helped Pet rinse and hang out the wash—

James W. A.[kk] and I settled O.K.—P.M. J.W's[kk] and we went to Gault to have Babys picture taken—Good

Recd Box of Books to fill orders Home at dusk—Baby seems quite sick—Gave it treatment—Seems helped—we retire early.

Maybe God will take baby from us—O! a kind Father forbid—But He knows, and we tremblingly say "They will be done"—we have her likeness now at any rate—

July 13, 1862 Sunday. Baby rested midling. Slept long and well in morning—Good bowel movement—Pores open nicely—Tepid bath—Cool on head—Gentle hand rubbing—soon seemed sleepy— Tucked it up and slept nicily til noon—and so shows she is decidedly improved by our treatment——P.M.—I went down—by request—and started up the S.S. then came home to our Company. J.

W. Adams[kk] and we enjoyed several hours singing & visiting preparatory to our going to U.S.—Eve James[kk] went home—
Baby is much better and Darling & I are so thankful—
Menonite P. Meet'g at Pas[aa] Fairly good—I feel somewhat cold and inactive in religion, still I love the cause of My Saviour—So often I quote Paul "The things I would do I not and the Things I would not I do" O for a deeper work of grace in my heart, and my rachel yearns for the same for herself—So we are of one mind and heart—

July 14, 1862 Monday. Rainy awhile—10 to 3 in Gault delivering Books At home then—Baby is still getting better—doing finely—Rachels skin trouble seems not to yield as it should—I have a little also, but not much—
I have so many things to distress me—I am so wicked and have so little control over myself—My Pet has not as much as she used to have, and I am to blame—I am not making her as happy as I wish to do and I sometimes fear it will cause her to love me less and O! What would become of me were I to lose her true love? Lost! Lost! Lost!

July 15, 1862 Tuesday. Great rain—Helped R and the Girls put out clothes to bleach—
P.M. Went to "Sep Bowmans" Fine Visit—Nice Tea—Saw a "Stump puller" in operation—Eve to Uncle "Abe Clemens—Visit til 11 OCK pleasantly—

July 16, 1862 Wednesday. Pleasant—Uncle showed me how to make "Buckskin"—10 OCK we went over to Amos Hunsbergers—Helped some on repairing Mill Machinery—as well as visiting—Nice time dining with the Family—and chatting—P.M. To Jacob Clemens Several hours there then started for home—stopped for supper at Amos Clemens—Has been to Mich—Full of praise of American Soldiers, and the war—Later, home. Our health and comfort good. Baby better too.

July 17, 1862 Thursday. Uncle Amos C—goes back on trip for to-day to Uncle Noahs—P.M. Mollie,[ii] Sue,[nn] Pet, Baby and I went to Mr Gowinloques—Splendid time—Showed us some fine art work—Oil & Crayon—and music—also Floral work—Home 10½ OCK—Delighted—

July 18, 1862 Friday. Pa Bowman[aa] a little contrary as to giving us—Ma B.[bb] Lizzie[oo]—Cora—pet & I the best team for us to go visiting—I am provoked—God forgive me—

About 11 A.M. we got off—Spent P.M. at Cous Sams and Uncle Jonathan Bowmans—Had a very pleasant time indeed. Tarried for Tea—Then went to Uncle Noah Bowmans—arriving at dusk— Pretty tired—but enjoyed the evening well—

We 3 are decidedly better physically—Pet used a little medecine. While I and Baby used none—But we seem about equally relieved—

July 19, 1862 Saturday. Aunt Lydia, Pet, Baby & I went over to Elmira—Dined at S.S. Weavers[ee]—Had a general good time all around. I was in the Store a while, and sold a bill of goods—as I used to do—

Supper at Isaac Wengers and a nice little visit—

Returned to Uncle Noahs Aunt L. and I had a long talk on her prospective—she is a believer in Hygienic treatment asked advice on many points—which I very gladly gave her—and encouraged her much—

I and mine well and happy.

July 20, 1862 Sunday. Rained all night and til 8 OCK—about 9 Uncles took us in carriage to Ch. dedication Service—I opened "Experience Meeting with singing & Prayer. Rev. S. L. Downy reading some scripture—This service lasted over ½ an hour—and was real spiritual—House nearly full—Rev S. L. Downy preached a good sermon—our Baby cried some—Darling was quite annoyed—Rev Downy said "Never mind sister Cormany—I can easily talk louder than your Baby will cry" and soon it quieted down, and the disturbance was not great—

P.M. J. B. Bowman preached a good sermon at the close there were 5 Baptisms—Mother[bb] and the girls went to Uncles—instead of to the baptizing—Evening Rev Cuthbertson preached—House crowded—Good singing—A day of spiritual services—Oh Yes! Religion is sweet—

July 21, 1862 Monday. Some pleasant chat with Uncle Noah and Aunt Lydia—wrote some—Then had a long talk with my precious— came more nearly resulting in hard feelings than I ever had in thought could ever come to exist between us—but all vanished, when we spoke over all candidly and openheartedly——Yes! I certainly do love my precious one more than ever. She is so good, true kind and loving and all of a real helpmate to me—Then too our little Babe—a precious little image of both binds us still stronger if possible together——Evening—early callers. Then—all to church—Rev S. L. D—preached well—a happy closing for Monday—

July 22, 1862 Tuesday. Pet is sick—Cholera Morbus[17]—Gave her treatment most of AM—P.M. we went to Elmira—to S. S. Ws[ee]—Pet being a little unwell—all retired early

July 23, 1862 Wednesday. S.S. W.[ee] is to be pitied!—Lord save me from every being brought to see that my wife loves another man more than me[18]—

Our Mary Cora Brittania Cormany is so much better, and is so interesting—she has learned to crow, and coo, and tries to jump when placed on her feet—

All the world, and the rest of mankind would be as nothing to me in exchange for my dear little daughter—

July 24, 1862 Thursday. I spent part of yesterday and this A.M. collecting old milinary bills for Pet & Lydia[dd]—P.M. visited Mr Jacob Bowmans—Hon J. E. Bowmans were home—Delightful visit, discussed his duties etc in Parliament—his Tannery business—Religion—and Sanctification as a doctrine

July 25, 1862 Friday. Pet, Baby & I went to visit "Croidly Snyders"—He is smart—Reads on Phrenology, Hygiene—Took his order for both Journals—Delightful time.

P.M. Called at Hon J. E. Bowmans for supper—Fine time—Home at dusk—Precious and I are truly happier than ever before in our love—constantly increacing instead of diminishing, as with all too many.

July 26, 1862 Saturday. Back to S. S. Ws[ee]—Work on Milinery a/c some——

P.M. Sister Lydia[dd] took us over to Uncle Noahs—I attend Quar. Conf—was sec'y—pretty good session—

We got to Noahs about 6 OCK—Aunt has slight labor pains—Bed time—more frequent & more severe—Pet gave her a sitzbath—Pains increase a little—I retire. Midnight I was called to give my opinion. Told them delivery might take place at almost any time—Sent for Mrs Wenger—and Dr Bowlby—The old family physician, on my preference—after some soothing treatment, stroking head—

---

17. Cholera morbus was the popular name for an acute gastroenteritis, often involving diarrhea, cramps, and vomiting. William A. N. Dorland, *Dorland's Illustrated Medical Dictionary*, 25th ed. (Philadelphia, 1974), p. 308; S. S. Fitch, *Family Physician* (New York, 1868), p. 66. It should not be confused with the far more serious disease called "Asiatic Cholera" in the nineteenth century.

18. See Rachel's entry for Jan. 30, 1862.

neck, hands—sponge bath &c She slept til morning—Some more pains creeping on stealthily but surely—

July 27, 1862 Sunday. Early. Dr Bowlby came—Pronounced her doing finely—No rushing desirable—Gave her a dose of Medecine. Dr and I had a little talk   He decided to go home—Mrs Wenger and Mrs Woodward retired for sleep—Aunt desired it, and we had a little prayer meeting—a most precious and glorious time. Evening a little delirious—I retired 10½ OCK—soon was called—pains more severe and oftener—11 OCK I went for Dr Bowlby—we were back by 2¼ OCK A.M.—Had a talk with him about Baby & Pet—Says "Its not itch" "It will yield to bathing & dieting"—said my treatment was rational[19]

July 28, 1862 Monday. Pains kept on increacing, and at shorter intervals—and at 12 min. til 8, after 3 very severe efforts, a 10½ lb boy was born[20]—Soon Dr B took placenta away without much pain and she felt remarkably well right off—talked and even laughed—10½ OCK I took Dr Bowlby home and went to Blair for Ma B[bb]—Aunt Lydias eldest Sister—Ma[bb] preferred Mollie[ii] should go—and so it was—Soon after Dr B & I left they gave Aunt a nice tepid bath as I had directed—on it she felt so refreshed and restful—and took a little sleep—and then after some soothing she fell asleep and slept til morning—Dr. Bowlby had told her after her last former delivery that she could never go through another. But thank God, and the despised system[21] I had counselled her in, had so invigorated her that instead of dying she says she had the easiest delivery and the best, and happiest feelings after, that she ever experienced.

July 29, 1862 Tuesday. Aunt received a good bath   Also Baby— and both rec'd clean clothes and beding and Aunt feels remarkably well and happy—

P.M. Pet and I went to S. S. Ws[ee]   Finished settlement—Bo't some goods   had good bye chat—returned to Auntys   The opinion of some of the Friends(?) prevented Aunt from her evening sponge bath—The consequence will show up later—Aunt sat up some yesterday, and again today—

Pet's health is decidedly better—Babies also. I am OK.

19. They are referring here to Rachel's recurrent skin problems.
20. Byron C. Bowman, Lydia's fourth and last child. *BHWT*, II, 24.
21. I.e., hydropathy.

July 30, 1862 Wednesday. Aunt slept almost none last night (for want of her regular bath) and feels a little tired still she rested midling—Baby was cross all night—Aunt received her bath and at once felt much better on it—Rev S. L. Downy came 10 OCK. At 10½ We bade all farewell and George[22] took us to Jas W. Adams[kk]—We dined at Sister Leas[jj]—

I wrote prescription for treatment lest they should forget—so Aunt might keep on as nicely as she has thus far—sent it back with George—

Jas[kk] came from his school about 5 P.M.—Chated awhile. Then over to Uncle Eliases for a good bye call—

James[kk] with their buggy took us to Grand Pa's and Uncle Georges—leaving us there—

Delightful evening visit at Uncle Georges—

July 31, 1862 Thursday. They took us home—Pet ails a little in her back—Baby is fine—I am well and happy indeed—Our lives as Man & Wife are very interesting. both are very openhearted—so not anything can mar our happiness much, since we always express our feelings freely and fully and as freely and fully forgive little mistakes. so true happiness is freely dispensed to us always.

August 1, 1862 Friday. About everything bends towards our preparations, packing &c for our going to my old Pennsylvania Home—

August 2, 1862 Saturday. Ma B[bb]—Rachel, Cora & I went to Gault—I made last of Book delivery—Got a satchel for 10/s = $1.25 Baby Bonnet 8/s = $1.00 Babys Likeness 13/s = $1.62 P.M. Grand Pa Clemenses came to see us and say Good bye—

I read and wrote some—Father[aa] is not yet done harvasting his fall wheat—Eve—Health Assn met—had an adjourned meeting—Gabrial Bowman and J. L. Bowman came down from W. Woolrich to say good bye—Delightful social evening on The Hill—

August 3, 1862 Sunday. Pet, Gabriel, Jas[kk] and I went to Toll Bridge to Church—Rev S. L. D. preached good—

I conducted the singing and made closing prayers—A general good-by hand shaking at close of service—P.M. Read—Talk—Sing at Home—Eve—Pet and I with Baby were going to Uncle Amoses and wished Adamses[kk] and Susie[nn] to go along—Susie[nn] said "too far"—

---

22. George was the oldest son of Noah and Lydia Bowman, i.e., the new baby's oldest brother. *BHWT*, II, 23.

but was only ½ mile, so we all went to Mose Eshelmans—½ as far—
Were having a nice visit—No 1—Jas[kk] Lea[ji] & Sue[nn] slipped off the
Dam—¼ mile—which showed that they didn't want to go with us to
Uncle Amoses   we felt hurt—But later went—Good time—

August 4, 1862   Monday. Doing up odds and ends—Preston and
Gault—Home about 10 AM—I cut Lea's,[ji] Carries[pp] and Pets hair—
P.M. Finished the packing—made settlement with Pa Bowman[aa]—He
don't reimburse me on the Clem[cc] affair—But I have $112.17¢ in my
purse yet—

Now I have finished my course in Canada, and am glad to leave,
even for a land of War.

XI

Home from Exile and Into the Army

August 5–November 25, 1862

This section opens with the Cormanys' trip from Canada, through New York City, and finally back to Franklin County, Pennsylvania, the area where Samuel grew up. Once home, and faced with the threat of a Southern invasion, Samuel takes the step he seemed fated for and enlists in the Union army. After some rudimentary basic training and a last brief visit with Rachel, he departs for the front.

━━━━━━━━━━━━ ◆•▬•◆ ━━━━━━━━━━━━

August 5, 1862 Tuesday. We good bye'd all around—Took train at Preston for Suspension Bridge—Fare $5.00—Time 8:20 Get to U.S. about 12 OCK M—

We hailed with joy the sight of the Star Spangled Banner—

Having to lay over til 5:20 P.M. we had a fine view of the Suspension Bridge[1]—Falls—Rapids, Whirlpool, &c.

Had some delights in the waiting—in touch with a newly married couple from Vermont—

Eve 5:20 Started for Albany on car all night—Pet did some good sleeping and I cared for Baby which slept considerably also—Reached Albany early.

August 6, 1862 Wednesday Morning. Took H.R.R.[2] after crossing river on Ferry—and made good time towards N. Y. City—How we did enjoy the sights and scenery cityward—Awfully hot day—Got to New York Hygienic Institute[3] at 10 A.M.—we met with very kind

---

1. The two-tiered suspension bridge over the Niagara River that so impressed the Cormanys was one of the engineering marvels of its day. Its chief engineer, John A. Roebling, later designed the Brooklyn Bridge. David B. Steinman, *The Builders of the Bridge: The Story of John Roebling and His Son* (New York, 1972), "Spanning Niagara," pp. 157–93.

2. I.e., the Hudson River Railroad.

3. Russell T. Trall's headquarters. The institute, at 15 Laight Street, functioned as an office, a clinic, a medical school, a museum, a hotel, and a sort of corporate headquarters for American hydropathy. Harry B. Weiss and Howard R. Kemble, *The Great American Water-Cure Craze* (Trenton, N.J., 1967). See advertisement following page 300 in Russell T. Trall, *Hand-Book of Hygienic Practice: Intended as a Practical Guide for the Sick-Room* (New York, 1864).

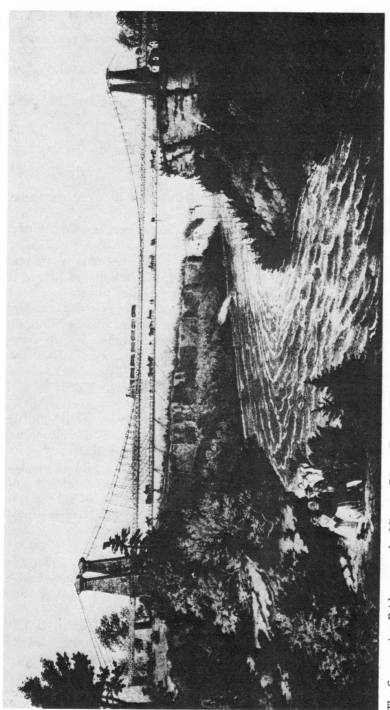

The Suspension Bridge over the Niagara River. From a lithograph by Currier and Ives.

reception by the Trall people (our Brother Clem[cc] was long a student here, and graduated, and had some practical relation later)

We found good accommodations. Splendid bath-rooms and everything in such good taste—

P.M. we walked out some—extremely hot—Baby good, but still a great care when it is so hot—

We like our rooms & board first rate—Made the acquaintance of Drs Miller and Jones—Interesting talk on Hygienics—Treatment of diseases &c—retired early—

August 7, 1862 Thursday. Baby went asleep at 4 P.M. yesterday and did not awaken til 6 this A.M.

We took general baths—Then breakfast   Then strolled the city, extremely hot—

P.M. obtained a Baby carriage to haul pussy in—Did shopping and sight seeing—Bo't Pet a Bonnet, me a silk hat—Babys little new Bonnet was stolen as we were doing up crowded places—

Saw some pleasant and some unpleasant sights and places and people—Visited some Picture Gallaries on Broadway—Paintings, Engravings, Statuary &c held us spellbound at times—were so entertained and detained, that we were belated and missed Theater to which we intended going—

Tired and heated—we took towel baths, and retired early—

August 8, 1862 Friday. Very Hot—Business call at and did up Fowler and Wells Establishment and attended to Book and Journal business in which I was engaged for several years in Canada[4]—

Pet & I hunted long and in many places for new baby bonnet but failed—Visited several Parks—See so many Soldiers and interesting sights—but not half so many as we would had we not Baby to care for and keep comfortable—Still Thank God for our Blessed Baby— and for each other to love and be loved by constantly

August 9, 1862 Saturday. We left N.Y. City at 4 P.M. Friday and arrived at Philadelphia at 8 P.M.—put up at Union House—Fine— retired early—and this morning finds us in good trim, and up early and out in the Park—

Took breakfast lunch there consisting of apples—pears & Trall crackers—9 A.M. called on Dr B. and Frank Palmers above 16th St on Chestnut—Assures us he can make Susie[nn] walk first rate without amputation in fact better than with—

---

4. This prolific publishing house was located at 308 Broadway.

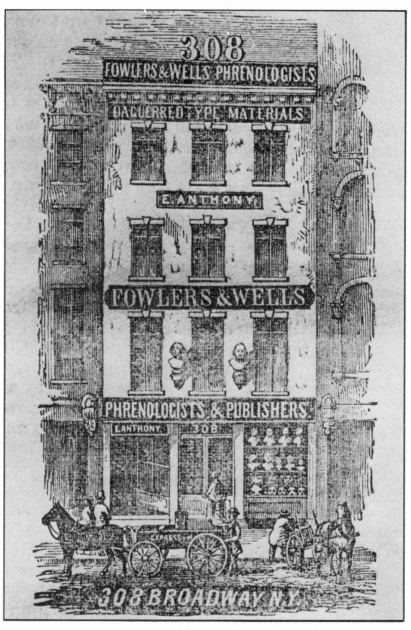

New York City headquarters of Fowlers and Wells. From *The American Phrenological Journal, 1854.*

Gave good encouragement in every respect, so we have good report to render to the Family[5]—Later called on Dirstines—at 436 2nd St—Very pleasant visit, and good dinner—P.M.—After several hours hunt we got a bonnet for Baby—tho not nearly as pretty as the other—Left at 4 P.M. for White Hall station. Hired team to take us out to Hunsbergers—Met with a warm reception—nice visit—Retired early—

August 10, 1862 Sunday. Met others of the Hunsbergers—
They took us to Menonite Church—Rather a dry service—P.M. visited Miss Reeder and her people—real pleasant time   war excitement pretty strong—many are in fear of a draft[6]—Eve at Jos Derstines for tea—Fine social time—The country fine and fertile—People very accommodating—

August 11, 1862 Monday. Spent day amongst Derstine Cousins &c—In P.M. we went to Jesse Springers—remained for tea—interesting discussion on Hygienic Medication—Gave prescription as to treatment of a Boys bad arm—a bad case—Evening—a lot of folks came to meet us at Abr. Hunsbergers—Jolly time—Baby is very troublesome—but oh! the dear precious one is worth ten thousand times the trouble—

August 12, 1862 Tuesday. Returned to Jacob H's. Our Head Quarters—They had done Pets Washing—she did some ironing—and we packed up for going—I never saw such universal willingness in persons to convey visitors from place to place to visit Friends and relatives—Took us to Rosenbergers near Quakertown.

August 13, 1862 Wednesday. A little cooler—Called at Zeagafooses a short time. Then took our Baggage to the depot at Quakertown—made several calls—at Kratzers for dinner—Pleasant time—P.M. returned to Quakertown—Called on Grants (where Rachel boarded when I came to see and we became engaged) and Smiths. Took Tea

5. Rachel's younger sister Susie was plagued by an injury or deformity of a leg.
6. The Militia Act of 1862, passed by Congress on July 17, authorized local or ad hoc drafts to fill state militia units for emergency service of up to nine months. Recourse to this in their sections of Pennsylvania was probably what the Cormanys' old friends and neighbors feared. On the other hand, the Confederate States of America had passed a national conscription act in April 1862, and many northerners feared that the Union government would soon be forced to follow suit. It did so in 1863. James G. Randall and David Donald, *The Civil War and Reconstruction*, 2nd ed. (Boston, 1961), pp. 251, 310–19.

at Jacobys. Called on Rev Mr Hornes—Mr. Balls, Shellys and a host of other places—In eve to Grants. Very pleasant time—remain all night—

We enjoy our visits and calls greatly and so do these dear good people, yet we are becoming rather tired even of a good thing, and dear Baby seems tired too.

August 14, 1862 Thursday. Slept rather long—Took 8:45 train to Bethlehem—Get Tickets and checks thro to Harrisburg, via Lebanon—at Lebanon we met the Light Boys[7]—Dined at Joseph Lights— Their carriage took us up—Very kind reception. Fine Dinner and pleasant time—P.M. were taken about calling on the Light Boys Friends, and Mutches—Spent delightful evening at Joseph Lights singing—talking, &c. &c—

August 15, 1862 Friday. A.M. visiting—12:10 train for Harrisburg— Good by visit with the Light Boys at station in H'b'g—Found Friends from Orrstown and St Tomas folks on C. V. cars[8] and some Chambersburgers—near Mechanicsburg my silk hat blew off—no chance to get it—We went to Reboks—Sister Lydia[P] didn't recognize me, nor did Henry[pa]—not knowing anything of our coming—and my being away since early in 1859—and I having grown quite a beard, and here was a woman and baby. But soon the case was clear and greetings were profuse—and time was well put in asking and answering questions—After supper Henry[pa] took us out to Mothers[b] place—

This was a sweet pleasant meeting and greeting—

We talked awhile—I am Oh so glad to meet Mother[b] and Sister Elly,[y] and pap Byers[ba] too and all who are about—

We being tired retired early—Oh yes! Sure! Mother[b] & Sister[y] greeted My Rachel & Baby most cordially and lovingly—

August 16, 1862 Saturday. A boil on my hip—a bad old fellow, rather interferes with my sitting comfortably—and sets me feverish.

Rachel does up our washing and ironing—and all hands are becoming acquainted—Baby Cora is the great center of attraction. P.M. went with Pa Byers[ba] to Cham'b'g—My lost hat failed to show up so I bought a new one—Saw many old friends in town—Chat with B. Y. Hamsher—Js Bollinger Sam Lehman, Andy Wenger, A. Holler

---

7. The same former Otterbein classmates whom Rachel had visited on her trip from Quakertown to Westerville two years before.
8. Cumberland Valley Railroad line.

and others.   very pleasant indeed after over 3 yrs absence—"Away out west."

Eve. My Boil made it more agreeable to walk home 4 Miles than to ride—

August 17, 1862   Sunday. Fine—Pet, Baby, Ella,[y] Mother[b] & I went to Old Salem Church—see Pa's[a] Grave—Go in to Sunday School– Brother John[d] met me with a Kiss—I took part—Closed with prayer—Rev Jerry P. Bishop preached a good sermon was a good service. at close, a great time shaking hands with old acquaintances and introducing My Rachel and our Baby—I was simply proud of my Wife and Baby—and rec'd many congratulations from very nice people——P.M., Pet, Elly[y] & I called at John Humbers a while—Fine sociable time—Oh such luscious pears and plums and Gages[9]—Back to Mothers[b] at Sunset—My Boils are retreating—

August 18, 1862   Monday. Pleasant all around—Darling and I strolled to the old orchard for 2 baskets Apples—a delightful time we surely had—we are so happy in each other. Rachel is so kind— Baby so sweet. Mother[b] and Elly[y] are so glad to have me home again and even old Daddy[ba] is real friendly. All of which goes to make our life and visit very pleasant—

August 19, 1862   Tuesday. Pa[ba] and Ma[b] took us down to Johns[d]— We met with a very warm reception. The children have grown very much   All things look Old Home like—The old well & Pump seem precious—

O Thou precious cooling refreshing invigorating fountain, how often thou hast given me nerve when week from toil and thirst—

Yes Tippy—the Dog knowes me—and seems so glad & frisky—I did up The Barn—Tannery[10]—Orchard— Meadow and Farm. My! how memories of boyhood days and pranks, their toils, and amusements come scampering along—P.M. John[d] and I had long conversation largely on Canada West and East—as regards Agriculture, Politics, Religion, Schools, Climate &c, &c, &c while The Women and Children were having a time of their own—and Ma[b] and Daddy[ba] returned home—

Evening: John[d], Catherine[e], Pet Baby and I—yes two Babies—went over to Sam Sollenbergers and old Johnies a little—Viewed the land-

9. Greengage plums.
10. The Cormanys operated a small tannery on the home (now John's) farm.

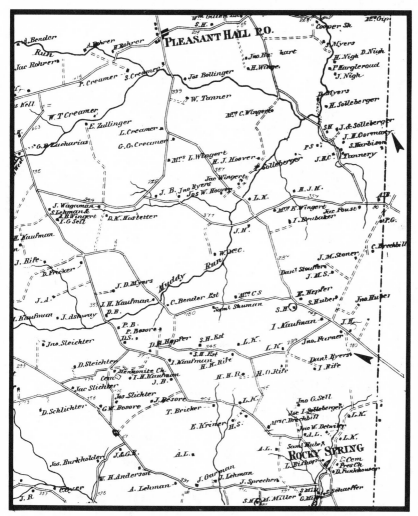

East-central section of Letterkenny Township. The arrows point to the home of Samuel's brother John H. Cormany (note also the tannery mentioned in Samuel's entry for Aug. 19, 1862) and to the farm of Samuel's stepfather, Daniel Byers. Salem Church was just down the road east of the Byers' farm. Chambersburg lay just south of Rocky Spring. The farms of many of the families mentioned in the diaries can be located on this map, which was first published in 1868.

scape over and called a bit at Stagers, and on returning, retired to sleep early

August 20, 1862 Wednesday. Bro John[d] gave me a/c of his difficulties as Executor of Fathers[a] Estate—I do look on Br John[d] as a pattern in almost anything and everything—most assuredly such as an Executor—John[d] & Cath[e] took us to visit Aunt Jane Shearers—nice visit   Then took us to Phillip Karpers[j]—Were welcomed most cheerfully—Enjoyed our visit pretty well—Johns[d] Wm[f] works at Phillips[j]—My! Wm[f], Fred[g], and Maggie[h] are nearly full grown—Bro Johns[d] went home—Pleasant evening all around with the Karpers[j]—

Pet is now troubled with boils—So we have our physical troubles and spiritually we are trying to grow better—

August 21, 1862 Thursday. We walked to Strasburg to Uncle Dan Gelwixes. Pleasant visit—Good dinner—Old Saml Lehman called to see me—Talked war—a little soaked—Cousin Sam Gelwix took us up to Thompsons.[v] Sister Sarah[u] not at home, Miss Martha and Mother very cordial—Sarah[u] came at dusk—Nice season of Family Worship—

August 22, 1862 Friday. Sarah[u]—Isaac[v]—Pet and I strolled up the mountain—above "White Rock"—Got a few huckleberries, and blackberries—and an awful sweating—Sights and scenery grand—O the refreshing springs we slaked our thirst at—

3 P.M. Sister Sarah[u] and Isaac[v] and Pet Babie and I walked to John Karpers.[l] Rained a little—nice visit—only J. K.[l] was a little too full of gossip to suit our tastes—

August 23, 1862 Saturday. Rose K——[n] washed and did up Rachels things for her and Babie—

Baby had tremendous Cholic last eve, caused—I think—by Rachels being so overheated yesterday on our mountain trip—Gave Baby a long warm bath—and injection which set her right very soon—P.M. Richard[o] took us home—to Mothers[b]—seemed so good to get Home. John Hollers came to see me—

August 24, 1862 Sunday. We attended Quarterly Meeting at old Salem—Communion day—Seemed O so good to meet so many dear ones—

War excitement is high—Everybody seems wound up—

Walked out home—Sarahs[u]—Bernards[q]—and Christ Snokes with us—Christ & I had a long tussel on the rightness of the war—

Eve—Mother[b] kept Baby, and Darling, Ella[y] and I walked to Church—Fine service—a new boil torments me—

August 25, 1862 Monday. Pet washed—I nursed Baby and boil—P.M. visited at Home—

August 26, 1862 Tuesday. Boil awful. Poulticed it opened at M—P.M. to Chamb'g—Supper at Reboks[pa]—Bro Barnys[q] come for us—took us to Saint Thomas their home.

August 27, 1862 Wednesday. Brother Bernards[q] are nicely fixed—Entertain us royally—My boils yielding—Visited at Home and Tannery & Town—

August 28, 1862 Thursday. Still at Brothers[q]—
We dine at Cous. Sol Hollers P.M. visit Cous Peter Hollers take supper there spent the evening pleasantly, and all night with them—

August 29, 1862 Friday. Cooler—8 A.M.—went to Brother Bernards[q]—Then to John Gillens—sr—Mr. Gillen and my Father[a] were warm Friends socially, Politically and Religiously—Pet Baby and the women folks generally got on finely. Mr. Gillen and I discussed politics some but Religion—U. B. ism—was his forte. Returned to Bro B. A's—Barnys[q]—

August 30, 1862 Saturday. Bernards[q] and we went to a S. S. Picnic—near St. Thomas—A fine time, met many dear ones.

August 31, 1862 Sunday. All to S.S. in A.M. Then went down to Daddy Strocks[11]—Spent the day quite pleasantly—It was a little embarassing for here was Lydia—whom I had courted so long in this home and gave up only because she had declared she never would go west nor far away from her parents for any man—so I responded "Well then my dear we had as well close up our courtship" and it was closed in a few months, very tenderly—and here I was visiting in the Family in the same rooms we so often sat together in 3 years ago and here was also My darling Wife and Our precious little daughter—while I could not avoid thinking of the past, and the great pleasure I often had enjoyed there in her company—Yet there came up not even a twinge of regret for I am O so satisfied and happy in my Precious wife and our child—

11. Bernard's father-in-law.

The day pleasantly, socially and religiously—and in the evening returned to Brothers[q]—

September 1, 1862 Monday. We went to Loudon in A.M.—Found Uncle Jerrys all "up down side" preparing to go to Westmoreland Co. to visit Aunts people—They had a quilting on go—saw Miss Lewis—also Kate Grafton—Jolly day—

Evening Wilson Owen and his intended—Miss Maggie Thompson—came to Uncle Jerrys—Taken all together this has been quite an eventful day socially—

September 2, 1862 Tuesday. Pet and I took a long ride to near top of Mountain[12]—

My O my! how Rachel did enjoy the scenery and outlook—Came back to Cousin John Hollers. We had a very pleasant visit all P.M. and evening—cool—

September 3, 1862 Wednesday. Quite a sharp little frost—Baby fell off her bed last night no harm—all well and happy—Go to Benj Hubers to Dinner Delightful visit—Mrs H. and My Mother[b] were girl chums—Eve to Bernards[q]

September 4, 1862 Thursday. Spent A.M. and part of P.M. at Bernards.[q] Eve. Went to Aunty Gelsingers—Were so warmly received and had such a fine time singing.

September 5, 1862 Friday. We—and Aunty went to Camp Meeting—There were 20 Tents—War feeling too high for Camp—Rev J. M. Bishop preached in A.M. and Tobias Crider in P.M.—Eve returned to Auntys—

September 6, 1862 Saturday. Early to Chambersburg for Fruit jars—P.M. Put up Pears—7 jars—

September 7, 1862 Sunday. We all went to Camp Meeting—War excitement great—A Battery went down the road en route for Baltimore.[13] Rebels reported near Hagerstown and coming this way—

---

12. Tuscarora Mountain, a long high ridge that overlooked the Cumberland Valley from the west.

13. General Lee had launched a major offensive three days earlier. Even as Cormany wrote, Southern troops were occupying Frederick, Md., and it was dawning on Cormany's old friends and neighbors that the Cumberland Valley was the point at which the enemy had decided to try to make a decisive breakthrough.

Meetings were not in good form—Too much War excitement—
Didn't remain for night meeting—Returned to Saint Thomas—Went
to hear J. W. Bird preach—a good sermon—

September 8, 1862 Monday. Boils have been harassing me for
some days—
We canned or sealed up 4 bottles Huckleberries—and 7 Bottles of
Tomatoes—and did over 2 cans of Pears—

September 9, 1862 Tuesday. Brother^q brought us to Chambersburg. I went to see about enlisting. There is great excitement about
Drafting men into The Army—The air is full of calls for men who are
patriotic to enlist[14]—I really inwardly feel that I want to go and do
my part—as a Man—as a Volunteer—leaving others to wait and be
drafted—and Darling is likeminded—That is, she is loyal and true—
and wants to see the South subdued—and however hard it would
be to be alone here amongst strangers—and to have me exposed—
and away. She calmly consents—That if I desire to go and make the
sacrifice for our Country—our Homes, our firesides, she calmly
says, though hard it is to say it—"Yes I am willing." "There will be a
way" and thus we wrestled with the problem. Spending a great deal
of time on our knees, before our God—and agreed that as a loyal,
patriotic Man I should Enlist—
The fear of being drafted, if I did not volunteer—had possibly
some weight in inducing decission—

September 10, 1862 Wednesday. NEWS! The Rebels are surely ad-
vancing on Hagerstown—Today—P.M. I enlisted in Capt. W. H.
Sollenbergers Cavalry Company[15]—I got Adam Yost to enlist also—
I was offered drink—I refused—Capt. approved my stand. Tho he

14. With the enemy literally at the state line, Pennsylvania authorities greatly
intensified their recruiting efforts.
15. William H. Sullenberger, a master carpenter from the Chambersburg area, had
served as a three-month volunteer from Aug. 5 to Nov. 9, 1861. He had been assigned to Battery A, 1st Pennsylvania Artillery, where he held the rank of lieutenant.
During the summer of 1862, Sullenberger was offered a captain's commission and
authorized to try to recruit enough local men to make up a cavalry company. Cormany agreed to become one of his recruits. Once full, Sullenberger's company would
be combined with other similarly recruited companies to form a full regiment, the
16th Pennsylvania Cavalry (Volunteers). Prior to the enactment of the Union draft in
the summer of 1863, the bulk of all Northern military units were organized through
enlistment processes like this one, usually under the supervision of well-known local
citizens. On Sullenberger, see NA, Civil War Pension Files, Application 511996, Certificate 318189.

drank himself—Brother John[d] was in town today. Said to me Sam, weight it well, I did so, and considered it a duty to serve my Country in her time of need.

September 11, 1862 Thursday. Spent all day recruiting Men—Rode out to Salem—Stauffers—&c—Sent word out to Pa Byers[ba] to come and fetch us out to bid them good bye—and arrange for my leaving—
This evening Martial Law was proclaimed—Many families are leaving Chamb'g[16]——
It is all Pet and I can do to keep Henrys (Reboks)[pa] cool enough to stay, and we stay with them——I went with a Company towards Marion—Lay out all night on our arms—No disturbance—

September 12, 1862 Friday. I am on the job—enlisting men—Have now met most of the men of our Company—
People are awfully scared—Many are leaving town—poor fools— When I came uptown to Henrys (Reboks)[pa] They had partly packed up to leave—I set to making fun of them. Then they unpacked again concluding to remain quietly in town and see!

September 13, 1862 Saturday. Still recruiting. Brave cool men are somewhat scarce—Reboks[pa] left Chambersburg today for the country. Will[m] came for them—and brought word that Daddy Byers[ba] is coming for us—needs a pass. I secured and sent him a Pass—amidst all the excitement we have no assurance that the Enemy is nearer than Hagerstown—and they may be detained—and defeated and caused to go back——Evening Daddy Byers[ba] came for us for over Sunday. He seemed very much afraid of town and hurried out— Mother[b] so glad we came—Had a long talk with Mother[b] seeking to get her reconciled to my going into the Army—She became pretty well convinced that I could even be saved if killed in battle defending my Mother[b] and Home and Country—I promised Mother[b] and Pet that I would keep evidence bright as to being right and at peace with God——

September 14, 1862 Sunday. Everybody seemed restful this morning—Mother[b] kept Baby—and Pet and I went to Salem—Took part in S.S.—Fine—I closed it.

16. A Confederate invasion seemed imminent, but Lee's plans went awry and he was forced to stand outside Sharpsburg, Md., then retreat. For a detailed study of this campaign see James V. Murfin, *The Gleam of Bayonets: The Battle of Antietam and the Maryland Campaign of 1862* (New York, 1965).

Rev J. M. Bishop preached and David Funkhouser and Landis exhorted.

Thompsons[v] were at Mothers[b], also Cous Jacob Slichters—He seems a little Secesh like[17]—Had a fine talk with Sister Sarah[u]—on my going into The Army—The bravery of my wife—and how all of them would be interested in her and Baby while I am away—

Darling and I are so well, and withal the outlook—separation exposure—danger &c. we are decidedly happy in each other, and can rest our future all in Our Heavenly Father's hands—

September 15, 1862 Monday. We all went to Daves for Peaches. I am still bothered with pesky boils. some pretty bad—P.M. I bade adieu to Mother[b] and Sister Elly[y] and Pa[ba] took us to town—

Seek for a place for Pet & Baby to call home—when I am away— Good rooms available at John Ploughs[18]—The best in sight—We'll see! It does seem very hard to be about to leave my dear loving Darling wife and our precious Baby Daughter—But so it must be, Oh! the horrors of War———

September 16, 1862 Tuesday A.M. helped Pet can some peaches— Sister Lydia Rebok[p] came back home from Johns[d]. The Enemy has been halted and battle is on beyond Hagerstown. So the tension is slightly relieved about Chambersburg—If our men win, the Enemy will surely need to fall back—south—if not gobbled up—

I and mine very busy getting ready to leave for Harrisburg. What a delight to know that Jesus Loves Me and Mine.

September 17, 1862 Wednesday. The noise of battle is in the air— occasionally[19]—

Brother Bernard[q] came from St. Thomas to see me once more before I am off—I enlisted Dan Croft today—Do some writing and loving at home between times. Evening We Boys met at the Bethel to Elect our officers—Elected W. H. Sullenberger Capt.

A. J. Snyder   1st Lieut
— Bohn   2nd Lieut.[20]

17. From "secession"; colloquial for pro-Confederate.

18. Jonathan Plough lived with his two daughters in a house that faced Chambersburg's main north-south artery, Front Street. His home was three blocks south of "the Diamond," the square at the center of town. See *AFCP*, p. 24.

19. Reverberations of field artillery at the Battle of Antietam could be heard in Chambersburg, some twenty-five miles north of the Union gun emplacements.

20. Union volunteer units elected their own officers as part of the organizing process. This practice, a carry-over from militia procedures, was formally acceded to

I had writing to keep me til 12 OCK. and some company—Struck bed at 1 OCK—

September 18, 1862 Thursday. Our Boys won out at Anteitem—and we'll hear later what next!

I got 3 or 4 more men—very busy til 8 A.M.—We failed to get off. So we Drilled till 1 P.M..—It was a solemn time saying good bye to Pet and Pussy this morning—But returned for Dinner, and had good byes over again, and then failed in getting a train all P.M. So I went home to my Darlings again for supper, and a little good bye visit—

I had prayers with Pet & Baby and was off again. It seemed harder this time than ever to leave—

September 19, 1862 Friday. Rained some—we stood, Sat and lay on the Depot Porch til 3 oclock in the morning. By and by we got started and reached Harrisburg at 8 A.M. I went with the Captain in a Cab to Camp Curtain[21] at 9:30 and the Company came out at 10—Got our breakfast at 3 oclock P.M. My first effort with tin plate, tin cup, tin spoon, Army knife and fork and Mess cookings—Spent my time writing up Diary—writing letter to Darling. Mostly alone in Captains Tent. Read my Bible—prayed and retired early—

September 20, 1862 Saturday. Up early—towel bath. Read & prayed Breakfasted on Fried Pork, Bread, Crackers & Coffee—My first coffe in a long time—

Wrote most of day for Capt. S—Made out Company mustering in roll—Alphabetically[22]—

---

by the Federal government during the early years of the war and affected all ranks below colonel. It was also customary for the organizer of the unit to become its commander. As the war progressed, the Lincoln administration began to take a firmer hand in the command structure of the Northern armed forces, but individual units continued to make the initial selection of those officers closest to the troops themselves. Randall and Donald, *Civil War and Reconstruction,* p. 326. Adam J. Snyder, the man elected first lieutenant, was a burly (5'10", 204 lbs.), hard-drinking tanner from Chambersburg. NA Invalid Application 731895; Invalid Certification 736580; Widow Application 492169; Widow Certification 325958. The second lieutenant was Valentine H. Bohn.

21. Camp Curtin, named for Pennsylvania's governor, Andrew G. Curtin, was located on the edge of Harrisburg. It became a major point of rendezvous and training for troops from Pennsylvania and other states. An estimated three hundred thousand men (a few of whom were Confederate prisoners) passed through Camp Curtin during the Civil War. Janet Mae Book, *Northern Rendezvous: Harrisburg During the Civil War* (Harrisburg, 1951), pp. 49–58, 130–31.

22. Samuel has established himself as a company clerk and special assistant to the captain. The record keeping required by the army created excellent opportunities for a

Fixed up tent some—Oh it seems so lonely here amidst all these men.

No dear Rachel, no precious pussy, and now night is here again and I must lie on the cold ground all alone and no cover except my blanket. It is a hard life and but for the defense of my country I should not make the sacrifice. Heaven bless Pet & Baby.

September 21, 1862 Sunday. Pleasant. Slept well—woke early— enjoyed a towel bath no one put on clean linen—Wrote 2 letters for Adam Frank   Poor fellow! Can't write[23]—

10 A.M. a Rev. came and preached for us a good sermon—

P.M. I read some, wrote some and was sick a good deal, awful diarhea[24]—Medical xaminer came—All had to strip stark naked, and submit to close scrutiny and examination. I passed O.K.   Tho a trifle Short of 5 ft 6 in.[25]

Eve.—I am "real bad off"—I cannot adhere strictly to hygienic principles here. O that I had my precious here to help me out.

Read & Pray & retire realizing a peace the world cannot give nor take away.

September 22, 1862 Monday. I feel as tho my whole insides were raw—Ate no breakfast—9 ock Examination in horsemanship, mounting, dis-mounting, riding &c—All passed save Adam Yost— Too stiff.

When mustering in time came nearly 1/2 seceded, or rather re-

---

man like Cormany with a smattering of higher education and experience as an account clerk and bookkeeper.

23. According to the 1860 census, 8.9 percent of the white population twenty years old and older was illiterate. *Historical Statistics of the United States* (Washington, D.C., 1975), pt. I, p. 365.

24. Chronic diarrhea was the bane of camp life. When simple diarrhea turned to dysentery, as it often did under the unsanitary conditions of the war, it became a mortal scourge. More men died of diarrhea and dysentery (57,265) during the Civil War than were killed in battle (44,238). Bell Irvin Wiley, *The Life of Billy Yank: The Common Soldier of the Union* (Garden City, N.Y., 1971), pp. 124, 136–37; Stewart Brooks, *Civil War Medicine* (Springfield, Ill., 1966), pp. 113–19, et passim; George W. Adams, *Doctors in Blue: The Medical History of the Union Army in the Civil War* (New York, 1952); Paul E. Steiner, *Disease in the Civil War, Natural Biological Warfare in 1861– 1865* (Springfield, Ill., 1968).

25. A medical examination for general fitness, however perfunctory, was required of every recruit. See *Soldier Life in the Union and Confederate Armies*, Philip Van Doren Stern, ed. (New York, 1961), p. 19; and Peter T. Harstad, "Billy Yank Through the Eyes of the Medical Examiner," *Rendezvous* 1 (Spring 1966), 37–51. The medical officer listed Cormany as 5'6". See NA, R. G. 94, Penn. Regimental Description Book, 16th Cavalry, R and P Office, Co. H.

fused, on a/c of some mis-understanding as to period. But it was adjusted and most all came in for 3 years unless sooner discharged. Several went home.[26]

My Diarhea is not much better. I ate very little dinner, and no supper but took some Brandy. Seemed to relieve me some—Read and prayed as usual before retiring.

God seemed my friend so very near—

September 23, 1862 Tuesday. Capt. Sullenburger slept with me. I showed some men how to make out Muster-in-rolls for their Co.

I wrote a letter home for John McKelvy and one for Jerry Leidig— We are busy and yet doing but little towards filling up our Co.

10 ock. Treatment. I took my syringe, went to the Canal. Took a bath and a most copious injection while in the water. Flushed myself good—Took drink of Ginger Brandy. Eve.—Feel much better.

September 24, 1862 Wednesday. Capt. and Lieut. Bohn went to Chamb'g to seek recruits to fill up Co.

Mondays heave up did us much harm—But we'll rally! I am improving generally but have sore throat and some symptoms of Diptheria—

Oh! What would I do were I to be sick and have no Rachel here to care for me. Tonight I sleep alone again. Would that I could lay my heavy head on my Rachels bosom and sleep.

September 25, 1862 Thursday. Early I awoke and read and prayed, but my prayers seem so dry and dull. Oh! for more holiness—

Wrote letter to Pet and a report for the Press of our late disaster— Drill 2 hours this A.M.

P.M.—My lips are quite thick & seem like when I have diptheria. Hope I can throw it off—Eve. Sam & Wm. McGowen in for a nice talk on religion. Lieut. Snyder fell in too & joined. I read and we had prayers. But how I missed Darlings closing kiss.

September 26, 1862 Friday. I feel much better this morning. Had another Drill. Then I went to the Canal again. Took good bath, and

26. Many volunteers got cold feet at the last minute or, as in this case, were legitimately upset to learn that the minimum term of service had been extended from three *months* to three *years* unless sooner discharged. In July 1861, Congress had authorized that volunteers be mustered in to serve "during the war"—i.e., to its finish. Not all potential recruits understood that they were making a commitment to see the war completed. Book, *Northern Rendezvous*, p. 56; Randall and Donald, *Civil War and Reconstruction*, p. 280.

Enema. Enjoyed it all and am much better. I ate and enjoyed a *big* dinner of Beef-Rice-Crackers-Stew. P.M. Did little save lie around and chat—Visited the Hospital tents—Poor Soldiers! Though wounded, they seem happy and cheerful—I was admited into Camp P.O. to get the mail for the Company.

Evening I fill much better. Injections. Baths—Dieting or rather fasting, and Ginger Brandy and will power won out—

September 27, 1862 Saturday. Capt. came back with some 5 new recruits. Seems good to have the Capt. here—

Time flies, one week follows another and one learns a little. One lives and what for. God only knows what lies out before. O that I were a better Christian Man—

I do have some pleasant talks with men on religion, and duty to our country.

September 28, 1862 Sunday. Read—Prayed and had breakfast. Took a walk to the Race, to the Hotel. Saw some Men who are about joining us.

Spent much time in Tent talking with Capt. S., Lieut. Snyder and orderly Sergeant largely on military affairs——Eve. I do so long for a letter from dear precious wife and for her presence and to press her to my bosom and to caress Our dear little pussy Cora my great joy.

September 29, 1862 Monday. Eight new men examined and tested in horsemanship Passed—

Wrote some letters for Boys—Recd a letter from my Dear precious Rachel—O such a good one. Poor dear, seems too hard she has to be so nearly alone—Mother[b] and Elly[y] are O.K. but old Daddy Byers[ba] is such a "sour" sample of Man—

P.M. I feel better and hardier than for a long time—Took long walk—Got fill of Melons—Good time generally—Eve—am happy, but am longing for Darling and Baby. They are constantly on my mind—

September 30, 1862 Tuesday. Moved our tent—I took bath—Enjoyed both hugely—Eve went to a preaching service—Musings—Darling and precious Baby are so near—wonder when I can see and caress them over again—Well! Well! I must be manly and never murmur—God make me a good soldier

October 1, 1862 Wednesday. Old routine—am well & happy. Do writing for Capt—make out Requisition for Mens Clothing—

Eve I still can keep up Reading and prayer—evening and morning—

October 2, 1862 Thursday. Rained powerfully. But I slept soundly—Tent O.K. Dry—

Capt Recd jug of old Rye——Eve. bunch of officers called— I "Phrenologised" them—Lots-o-fun Capt treated them—Chief twits were on candidacy for Regimental offices—are some aspirants—I have none other than to be a true noble soldier—learn efficiency—in my line as Private, and be efficient as such and Captains Clerk. Ever looking up and acquiring ability to occupy and fill higher positions should any vacancy come in sight—

October 3, 1862 Friday. Usual routine—Eating—Writing—Drilling—&c &c &c

Eve—Homesick? No. But I do think so much about my Rachel—and pussy (Cora) meseems I must see her soon, but I don't must—

I am a Man—a Soldier—a Christian—I am trying to become a more devoted Christian, a better Man—and the best Soldier I am capable of becoming, and to become and be either and all does not depend on seeing my wife and baby very often just now.

October 4, 1862 Saturday. Lieut Bohn brought five new men—Passed examination—Dress Parade 5 P.M. Our first—tiresome—

Two men—Kelly & Leidig skeedadled—

October 5, 1862 Sunday. Hot—slept late Read some in my little Bible—Prayed—and studied long—O that I could go to Church with Pet this Morning—

Capt., Lieutenants and I full of Co. business—Concluded to go and bring the skedadlers back—

5 P.M. Had Dress Parade—Our Camp rules are most awful strict.

Wm Karper^m is sick—I attend him—He has Cholera Morbus—Gave him some treatment—Got milk for him.

October 6, 1862 Monday. I made out W-Ks^m Descriptive list and we moved him to the Hospital—Were he not so awfully homesick he'd soon be O.K.—

Evening—went over to Hosp. Wm^m seems so glad to have me come—

I slept on the floor—near his cot all night—Both of us slept most of the night—

THE HOSPITAL AT CAMP CURTIN

From Janet Mae Book, *Northern Rendezvous: Harrisburg During the Civil War* (Harrisburg, 1951).

October 7, 1862 Tuesday. Billy^m some better. Capt S and Lieut Bohn went for the skedadlers.

We had Co Drill—Two men broke away—to Tavern—Serg't Peters, Hammond & I arrested them—brot them back—

P.M. I went to see Wm Karper^m again—is better, but lacks energy, snap, willpower—

October 8, 1862 Wednesday. Wm K——^m doing nicely—A.M.— Crowd bathed in Canal—I in Tent. P.M. To Hosp—Met Sam Risher—knew me at once—Little Chat—Wm^m improves—

Letter from Darling—O she is so glad in anticipation of my coming soon to see her and Pussy.

Hope she ain't disappointed   seems to me I just must see her and our little precious one soon—But there is no must to it, but it would be most gloriously fine & enjoyable—

October 9, 1862 Thursday. Ate lot of grapes last eve (have a fearful diarhea) was very sick in the night and this morning—A copious enema helped me I ate no breakfast—

Went to see Wm K.^m O the Boy! He is too homesick to get well— Noon I ate a little Beef broth—crackers—and an apple—P.M. am much better—was xcused from Dress Parade—

Ate no supper—Took a walk—went to Evening preaching—

I am still away behind my ideal of the Christian Man, but I press on.

I am greatly taken up with thoughts of and tenderest love for my Precious Wife and our sweet little center of double devotion—God bless them and keep them well and cheerful—

October 10, 1862 Friday. Glorious nights rest—am so happy this morning—and feel sure my Darling and Pussy are ditto.

Am having my Cavalry Jacket tailored some for a better fit.

Read a letter from John Karper^k—for his "son Will"^m—

The hardest most unreasonable thing I think I ever read. Seemingly blaming me for Wm^m having enlisted—and for all the ills he has been suffering. And Wills Sister Rose^n writes "Tell Sam I think he must not think much of his wife or he would not leave her as he did" &c.[27]

---

27. Among the most painful experiences endured by Civil War soldiers were recriminations from those back home and fears that their loved ones were suffering or uncared for. Desertion was relatively common on both sides during the war, but it probably resulted as often from letters like these as from ideology or cowardice. On desertion rates and their causes, see Randall and Donald, *Civil War and Reconstruction*, pp. 329–31.

All this must be imputed to their pitiable ignorance —

If others did not rally and protect their home and fireside, soon they would have neither but would be hunting for some place to hide their heads.

October 11, 1862   Saturday. All excitement today—Most of the Cavalry Boys have been marched to Harrisburg today to "draw their Arms" and to go on Guard duty—News has it "Rebels are in Chambersburg"[28]   We drew our Over-Coats and some other Clothing.

P.M. I went to see Billy Karper[m]   seems but little improved. Lieut Bohn is poorly too—was placed in Hospital[29]—

Eve. News is true that Chamb'g is taken—Capt S and Lieut Snyder have returned—They were in town when Rebels came, but escaped and came to their Company—Oh my dear wife and Baby! What will become of them. Heaven forbid that we should be separated. They amongst the Rebels, and I in the U.S. Army. But God! Yes He is our Keeper—News.   Rebels in Gettysburg and likely Carlisle—

October 12, 1862   Sunday. I had to make out Muster-in Rolls! A number have come to the Colors—

The excitement not quite so great as last Eve—I am well but can have no rest. Oh! My precious ones—wife and baby are enveloped in rebeldom—and my Mother[b] and Sisters and Brothers too—and I am helpless to do for them—

---

28. The previous morning, Gen. James E. B. "Jeb" Stuart had launched a cavalry raid that would take him in a giant loop around the Army of the Potomac, which was still based near Sharpsburg. Taking 1,500 (some reports indicate 1,800) specially picked Confederate horsemen, Stuart had dashed north from the Potomac River on October 10. The excitement in Harrisburg Saturday morning was justified, for the raiders had slept in the streets of Chambersburg on Friday night. The men at Camp Curtin did not yet know, however, that Stuart was already headed southeast on a route that would take him through Emmitsburg, New Market, and Hyattstown, Md., and back across the Potomac near its confluence with the Monocacy. This raid, which was completed by the night of Oct. 12, probably boosted Southern morale, but accomplished little of lasting military value. In Chambersburg, for example, Stuart's raiders captured several hundred horses and spoiled some supplies, but they failed to destroy the Cumberland Valley Railroad bridge, the primary objective of the raid. Matthew Forney Steele, *American Campaigns* (Washington, D.C., 1951), I, 139–40; Vincent J. Esposito, *The West Point Atlas of American Wars* (New York, 1967), I, text to map 70; OMACW, pl. XXV, no. 6.

29. Valentine H. Bohn, the second lieutenant in Company H, suffered from chronic rheumatism that kept him in and out of army hospitals and eventually occasioned his honorable discharge. See NA, Pension File, Adjutant General's Report (with copy of Dr. August Herrmann's certificate).

But Our God will save and protect them——

P.M. Listened to a sermon claiming Salvation for all mankind, and Evening one offering salvation for all who accept and believe in Jesus Christ as their Saviour—I led singing at both services. Only the last seemed at all acceptable to our Men—I long to be facing the enemy—and be doing all in my power to protect wife and baby—and our glorious old Flag—

October 13, 1862 Monday. Rumors still rife of great Rebel movements on Chamb'g—and in Perry Co—I believe much of it is wind—

P.M. We drilled awhile—Eve Capt. and I went down to the mens quarters—Captain made a speech to them assuring them that he was doing all in his power to secure for them their promised Bounty[30]—to get the Company filled up—That he was going down to the City this eve, and in the morning to Chamb'g in their interests—

I asked permission to go to see my precious wife and Baby—He consented and I am so happy I can hardly believe myself that such happiness awaits me on the morrow—Read, Prayed and Praised the Good Lord and retired calm and cool.

October 14, 1862 Tuesday. Slept well—Fixed for going home—ate no breakfast—Had quite a time to get Lieut Snyder's and Gen'l Tarbuttons[31] signatures to my Pass—Met Captain at station—Fare $1.65 Had a fine social chat on the way—Capt confided to me some of his "aircastles" to be builded after the war—Viz a pleasure boat to run on the Susquehanna and I am to be an officer on the boat—likely a swag of gin he took and I tasted was the chief inspiration of his talk—

30. The Federal government assigned each state a quota of men to be supplied to the armed forces. The states, in turn, parceled out their quotas to local subdivisions which began offering an enlistment bonus, or bounty, to volunteers. Since all the men who enlisted in a given unit were credited to the subdivision that organized the unit (regardless of where the men themselves were from), the bounty system had the added goal of inducing outsiders to help fill local quotas. This system was probably beneficial to individual volunteers and their families (Rachel, for example, certainly needed the money at this time), but rather irrational as a public policy (since some towns and counties approached bankruptcy competing with one another) and open to abuse (since "bounty jumpers" would enlist one place, collect a bounty, desert, enlist somewhere else under a different name, collect again, and desert again). Moreover, as was the case here, local governments could be frustratingly slow when it came time to pay.

31. W. C. Tarbutton, actually a captain rather than a general, was commanding officer of Camp Curtin at this time. Book, *Northern Rendezvous*, p. 55.

Got to Chamb'g 11½ ock—Met Elly[y] at Hokes[32]—Told me Rachel had just come in to town—

I took my Pet by SURPRISE. Met each other with warm kiss and caress—Dear one! She looks so well and so does pussy. Got my satchel up—ate dinner—and then we, Pet, Pussy & I spent most of P.M. in the parlor talking, loving and caressing each other. Oh! it seemed so sweet again to meet and pour out our very souls to each other.

Evening we read some letters from C. W. and talked about recent experiences til bed time—Then had worship and retired in exceedingly happy mood—

October 15, 1862 Wednesday. So nice to be at Home. We spent most of A.M. in parlor P.M. With livery rig (from 1 ock til 8 or 9 for $1.25) went to John Karpers[l] by 2½—Visit ½ hour—Then to Sister Sarah.[u] Has a fine little boy Baby—nice apples and cider and jolly chatting indulged in til 4 ock when we started for My Mothers[b]— Arrived at dusk—Took supper. Visited cheerily—Mother[b] gave us some dried Beef, applebutter, apples—and oceans of Love to take along—Awfully dark at 7 ock—Daddy Byers[ba] took his lantern and piloted us out ¼ mile to "The Big Road"—Then we sailed at 240 rate—reached Chamb'g at 8 plus OCK—

We had a pleasant P.M. all things considered. The greatest was the pleasant conversation pet & I had.

It is so sweet to have a true one to love and to live for—to find that we are of one mind & heart having for our object each the others happiness before his own—Pussy is so good—Surely we are a happy Family.

October 16, 1862 Thursday. Called to see Capt early—Has about enough men to fill up our Company—I got me ½ pint Brandy & ½ pt Gin to take along for medicinal purposes—

(During rebel raid last week The Fiends burned the Depot, Engine House, Machine Shop, Wunderlich and Neads Commission Warehouse) a terrible scare to the people as the threat was to burn the whole town. They made a horrible picture. But it proves a strong incentive to boys with the stuff in them to enlist and help clean out the Rebel Hoards—

Pet and Baby with me to Depot To see me off—We had ½ hour to talk, look at each other with emotions inexpressible, exchange kisses—say good bye and wave final adieus to the many onlookers—

32. A dry-goods store on Chambersburg's central Diamond.

Reached Camp at noon—Boys were at dinner—seemed glad to see me return.

I induced Levi M. Byers—a friend from boyhood—to come along—by paying his fare—hoping to secure his enlistment—

We discussed old times as boys and young men—and our doings since our marriage—

My return home—in the midst of the war—when I might easily have remained there, and enjoyed my family seemed to him and to many others a wonder—but we—i.e. Darling and I could not feel free to do otherwise, and however hard to be separated, and exposed, we do it cheerfully for Our Country and our God—

I tried hard to induce Levi to come and stand with me—But—God forgive him, he almost spurned me—I shall never esteem my chum as highly hereafter as I did in our earlier days—

October 17, 1862 Friday. Saw Levi safely off for Home—Called to see Will Karper[m] yesterday is much better—Lieut Bohn is almost gone—Wrote his uncle[33]—.

Evening had a drill, and later, some quiet meditations—Time bears me on, and still on, and everyday brings me nearer my Eternal Home—

October 18, 1862 Saturday. Had our Co drill early—It is not at all difficult for me to execute the movements—

John Karper[l] came to try to get his Billy[m] released and home—or at least—secure him a furlough—

Tarbutton would not consent at all. So I wrote a letter—asking a 10 days leave of absence on a/c ill health—

John[l] presented it to the Governor—Andrew Curtin—who approved it—saying it would be much the best—when it is possible—for parents to take sons home for treatment. Fy! I doubt it in case of chronic homesickness—or babyishness—

October 19, 1862 Sunday. Orderly S. Barnes is quite sick—Had him sleep with me. cared for him—Sergt Bohn died at 9 A.M.[34] I was called for, but when I reached Hospital he was just gone—Poor fellow I closed his eyes—Capt Tarbutton wants to allow only one

33. This is almost certainly not Lt. Valentine H. Bohn, but rather Sgt. Henry S. Bohn, another member of the company. Cormany probably confused the rank of the two Bohns when he made this entry (see Oct. 19, 1862).

34. Bohn, 22, died of typhoid fever. See *H16PC*, p. 14. He had been a farmer in Franklin County before enlisting. "Reg. Descriptive Books," 16th Pa. Cav., NA.

man to go with him home. Old Tyrant of a Man—John Karper[l] and Billy[m] left at 1 P.M. for Home—Our Boys on Guard duty.

I am doing for Barnes again for the night——We had a fine talk on religion—war—Home, &c.

Heaven bless Pet, pussy and their Samuel.

October 20, 1862 Monday. Barnes some better—Wrote to Mollie[ii]— Susie[mm] & Pa Bowman[aa]—Mrs Bohn came to see her husband not knowing that he was dead—and on his way home—Poor woman is almost distracted—

Capt came with 5 new men—Pet sent me some cakes and pies, and such a good letter with the Capt. Dear Lord bless her now, while I am enjoying these luxuries, and evermore, and keep her and our precious baby well and happy.

October 21, 1862 Tuesday. Cool—Our Company is badly demoralized on a/c delay in obtaining their Bounty money——Lieut Bohn came at noon with one Boy—Capt Sollenberger borrowed $100 (?) and distributed it amongst the most needy of the Men—

Evening Capt went to Harrisb'g Orderly S. Barnes stayed with me. Is about well—O but those articles Pet sent me are good. Thank Heaven for a good wife.

October 22, 1862 Wednesday. Our Co will soon be full—Lots of drafted men coming in to camp—wondrous and ludicrous how strangely some act—They know nothing at all about soldiering. Seems they cannot realize that they must sleep out doors——Met Col Orr and Squire Hammond—Orrstown gentlemen–Friends of my Fathers[a]—I enjoy Soldiering comparatively well—So many things I can do for fellows as well as learning things myself—and having such a precious darling wife at home, praying for me, and doing all to make me happy, create in me thoughts and feelings of joy and happiness that most men do not know nor feel. But Jesus, my all, caps the climax—

October 23, 1862 Thursday. Capt.—in last night—I do sleep so sweetly out here, breathing such good pure fresh air—Company is filling up finely—am kept quite closely at work in Captains quarters—

October 24, 1862 Friday. A very busy day—company would have been full—but 4 men were rejected on a/c poor horsemanship Mailed a letter to Pet and received one. O such a good one—

Every letter seems more valuable, more endearing, and if possible, binds me more inseparably to her.

I am all alone and still not alone for God sees me, is all around me, and meseems my Rachels guardian Angels are flitting around making us both so happy in each other, though fifty miles apart—

Slack Sheet—This is fun! Sometimes quite rough—Slack Sheet performance——A heavy canvass say 10 or 12 ft sq. One or two strong men take hold—very firmly at each corner—a soldier in almost undress is caused to stand in the center—and is told to be sure to keep on his feet—as much as possible—now by a strong and very sudden jerk at each corner the man goes up—and the men keep the canvass as nearly taut as maybe—and when the man comes down, and strikes the canvass, head, or feet, or seat first, another sudden jerk sends him up again—and this is repeated to the no small amusement of the crowd of 100—1000 or so—a Captain commands the guard, and sees that no serious injury is done, but sure a fellow gets some pretty rough handling, while it lasts—and the more good naturedly he takes it the shorter the treatment usually lasts—At the Captains "enough" the subject is excused and another victim is brought on—and amused ???? This performance is often a most side-splitting affair—lasting about an hour—

October 25, 1862 Saturday. Capt slept in Tent last night—Recruits are coming in again—Great bustle in all camp—Drilling—Uniforming—sending citizen duds home—Sent mine to Rachel in Box—

Some boys acting up badly—Hassan and Mahaffy drunk—Mahaffy our first man in Guard House—

October 26, 1862 Sunday. Had our last two men exam'd—If they pass then our Co is full—P.M. Stormy—rainy—Rumor we may leave here soon—

Read and prayed a good deal in tent—Upon the whole the day was passed pretty pleasantly—

October 27, 1862 Monday. Stormy rainy night also this morning—50 men on Guard cleared about noon—Capt in City on Company business (?)

October 28, 1862 Tuesday. Drying up fast—I made out alphabetical list of all our men—"Residence—When & Where enlisted, &c—an extensive job—Men are in better cheer—seeing brighter prospects of getting their money. Strange! how little of men, many men really are murmuring, complaining and wishing, when they certainly know that all of it avails nothing—and makes them more miserable.

October 29, 1862 Wednesday. Capt & I went to Hd Qrs to compare Lists—Find Muster Rolls &c, &c, all OK—Rec'd blanks to fill out— Got room at National Hotel[35] Commenced at 4 P.M. to make out the 5 Rolls—Wrote till 11 P.M. and remained at Hotel so I slept in a bed—and got up early—a fine Breakfast.

October 30, 1862 Thursday. Worked on our Rolls till 12½ P.M.— when we dined and then went over to Hd Qrs to have my Rolls inspected—All O.K. so far as my work was concerned.
(One Captain—Gowen—has made out 5 setts and none right yet) We returned to Camp for supper—Took Blank Pay Rolls along to fill up—I wrote till late in tent and got the four Bounty & Premium Rolls all OK. Well I am as happy as a man can well be on my success—Oh! for a glimpse now of my Precious wife, and our dear little pussy—Rachel proves to be the one perfect woman—wife and Mother—more than all else of the world to me.
No matter how hard-worked & tired I may be, to close my eyes, and think of her as all mine, and forever mine is joy complete.

October 31, 1862 Friday. Took all A.M. for men to sign the Rolls. Hd Qrs pronounced them very good—Capt got a gallon of brandy $4.50—
I took one drink—for stomachs sake. On hunt for Deserters—none found in City Guard House—Oh what a hard place for men with mind and soul to be in—

November 1, 1862 Saturday. Capt in City—Lieut Bohn with me
Musings Is it possible I am where I am, and can it be I am what I am? A soldier for my country? far away from my Darling and no assurance that I shall ever see her again. O! I dare not think of that. Still should it be so, I die in defense of my country. I have a Hope, yes assurance we will meet again—Heaven bless my dear little family this evening.

November 2, 1862 Sunday. Captain S. and some 50 of H. Co went down City to Bethel Ch. at 10½ A.M.—Heard a real good sermon.
O! It seemed so nice so glorious to sit under the droppings of the Spirit in the Sanctuary—but oh how infinitely better it would have

35. In downtown Harrisburg.

seemed had my Pet and Pussy been along—Rev Deatrich and Lady called on me—are old Chambersburgers—

Eve am well and happy—

November 3, 1862 Monday. Routine

November 4, 1862 Tuesday. Routine and made out Co Requisition for our Equipments.

Evening two Ladies (?) called on Capt., whereupon I left the tent But Cap and Lieut put their arms about them, before I got out—O where are their marriage vows?[36]—Never will I be untrue to my Dearest one. If I do let me wither on the spot——

November 5, 1862 Wednesday. Routine—

November 6, 1862 Thursday. Quite Cold. Soldiering a little unpleasant—made out and sent in a list of Chambersburg or Franklin Co Boys entitled to their Bounty—p.m. Company marched to Harrisburg for our State Bounty—No go—not enough money in Treasury today—

Boys awfully out of humor—almost mutinied[37]—

Eve. J. R. Fetterhoff & I strolled into the Camp of drafted Men— Great xcitement—object to being used to fill up old regiments—Held indignation meeting—A man "broke guard" was shot in leg— stopped sure[38]—

Letter from Pet. She does write me such splendid letters. So full of true womanliness—Thank God for a dear good devoted wife—and a precious Daughter—

---

36. Prostitution flourished during the war, especially near large army camps and in the major cities. Venereal disease became a major problem, and the army had already begun efforts to regulate and supervise prostitution. Prostitutes are still referred to as hookers after Gen. Joseph Hooker, who was in command of the Army of the Potomac when the formal supervision of camp followers was attempted. Wiley, *Billy Yank*, pp. 257–62.

37. Many of the men had been drilling at Camp Curtin for over two months, waiting for enough recruits to form a full regiment. Though home was only a short train ride away, they could not leave the camp; though they had been promised cash bonuses for enlisting, they had received nothing; though they were willing to fight, they had not been sent into action.

38. Men drafted by the state of Pennsylvania under the Militia Act of 1862 were formally liable to nine months' militia duty. They objected to placement in regular volunteer units because the latter would almost certainly see more active duty than the drafted militia and because the regular volunteer units would probably be more difficult to get out of after their nine months' obligation had expired.

November 7, 1862 Friday. Cold—Froze ½ inch in tent—Orderly Barnes carelesness made me spill ink on my coat and valise—I wiped it up quickly with his Co Roll Work—I sure was deliberate and he in high passion—some doings—Snowed and blowed all day—

November 8, 1862 Saturday. More descriptive Lists measuring of Men &c—Capts wife came to see him—Orderly Barnes has all day been careless—left things lie around—to the confusion of my papers, and his own. I became completely indignant and in presence of the Capt—1st Lieut. and some others, I stood on my rights and soldierliness, and told him that in these quarters there must be a place for everything and things must be kept in place or he must move out. In a passion he at once moved out.

November 9, 1862 Sunday. Cold—Sergt Barnes acts crusty, and silly—sends men or mere boys to Hd Qrs—or to me, to inquire—or transact business which he should see to personally—but he shows the caliber of a 12 yr old boy rather than of a U.S. Soldier—and Orderly Sergt at that—But Barnes will learn, and change, or else go down into the ranks—I vow[39]—
Some 60 of us went to Church—Sergt Armstrong came in after church, drunk. To avoid a scene his chums shaded him—
Musing—Would that I could see my Darling and little one this Eve—Oh! how precious they are to me, even tho far away—yet so very near and dear.

November 10, 1862 Monday. All is on the stir preparing to moving over to our new camp—Camp McClelland[40]—Team took tent and we marched over about 9 AM—Pitched tents at once—Camp has beautiful country surrounding it—and at once strikes one as being romantic in appearance—This done hastily—we went to City for our Bounty, and received it promptly—
Many of the Boys got a little boozy, and came back chipper, but went to work to fix up quarters in soldierly fashion—Many Men came to settle a/c's Pay in money advanced by Captain and other loans &c. &c—

---

39. This was the same Orderly Sgt. Solomon B. Barnes whom Samuel nursed through a serious illness barely two weeks earlier (see Oct. 18, 19, 20, and 21, 1862).
40. Camp McClellan, about a mile north of Harrisburg, had been established by the 17th Pennsylvania Volunteer Cavalry to reduce the congestion and overcrowding at Camp Curtin. *PV*, p. 950; *History of the Seventeenth Regiment Pennsylvania Volunteer Cavalry*, Henry P. Moyer, comp. (Lebanon, Pa., 1911), p. 27.

247

November 11, 1862 Tuesday. Frosty—John A Smith was out Bee-Stealing last night—came in badly stung—Shot in the calf of a leg. Pretty seriously hurt—not much honey—

I put in much of day taking in money towards buying a Horse to present to our Captain—

Men are so clamerous to go home with their money and to see dear ones—

The Capt has very much trouble on that account——

November 12, 1862 Wednesday. Busy time receiving Arms and accouterments for the Men—Had to move Capts tent again to be on the exact spot—Bully for military exactness[41]——

Now I strike the job! That of making out The Company Books. Smith was taken to Camp Curtain Hospital today on a/c Bee and shotgun stings—Evening. All things move off smoothly except about 6 or 8 skedadlers are still out—I am well and happy. I now have $123—towards buying the Horse for the Captain.

November 13, 1862 Thursday. Cold, Frosty, Frozen hard—Barnes—Croft and I got Pass to go out on Special business—We bought a fine little Black Stallion—$115—for Captain—Brought him in at dusk—Formed hollow square around the horse—Barnes on him—Croft and I on either side of him—Lieut Snyder brought Capt Sullenberger from his tent and into the □ Saying "Captain W. H. Sollenberger in the name of our good old Uncle Sam, and by request of Co H 16th Regt we as a Committee present you this Horse as a mark of respect, hoping he may carry you safely through this three years service." We dismounted Barnes and mounted the Captain and he made a neat little speech calling out 6 or 8 rounds of Cheers from the Company and the gathered crowd.

It was a complete surprise to Captain Sullenberger—First in order. The Capt. dismounted and after some effort, succeeded in leading his horse through our Head Quarters tent—while inside the Horse was treated to Bread—crackers and apple—and so formally "mustered in" and The Captain treated the Company—

November 14, 1862 Friday. Capt got his Horse shod—I wrote most of day in Co. Books   Recd our Sabers and Belts in P.M.   Had Dress Parade.

---

41. *Army Regulations* (1861, revised 1863), paras. 524–36 and pl. 2, stipulated the precise form a cavalry camp was supposed to take. This new unit was still trying to do everything by the book.

Eve. recd a good letter from my Darling—O how glad and joyful it makes me.

November 15, 1862 Saturday. Wrote a lot——p.m. Capt gave us a Saber Drill—

Find it hard on the wrist Eve called on some of the Boys. I do so nearly everyday or eve. Have some good times with them. Read a lot in my precious Bible—meditate and pray more recently, and so feel and am more spiritual and joyful—Ah! God is a good pay-master—I need much grace to keep me well poised—I have many perplexing cases to meet—amongst the Men.

November 16, 1862 Sunday. Froze hard—Had such a sweet dream about Pet and Pussy. My Darlings. Read in Bible awhile—Wrote some to Pet—

One of our men—Lane—is gone—Suspicion is that he is a Rebel and has returned to his own—

p.m. McGowen and I went over to Camp Curtin Hospital to see Nelling and Smith (The Honey Man) Both are doing well—Absalom S. Hartman has small pocks, and will die in a day or so.[42] No one knows whom to address—Evening Lieut Snyder and a lot of us went to Church—on returning I wrote to Pet—and read some in my Bible—O how good is God to me and how sweet to love and be loved by wife and baby. This soldier life agrees with me and I enjoy my clerking for the Captain—But I also drill & train so as to be a good soldier all around.

November 17, 1862 Monday. Spent most of day on Co. Books. Finished Co. descriptive Book.

The men are good, only too good to me, tempting me with cigars and things I am better without.

O for complete control of my appetites. Yesterday—by order of The Captain I wrote a "trap" letter, and by it found out that one of our Men is not "true blue"—Kept original and sent a copy—He'll "smoke" a little.

November 18, 1862 Tuesday. Ate 20 raw oysters last night—am O.K. on it—Mailed big letter to Pet. I am so taken up with thoughts

42. *Army Regulations* (1861), para. 1261, required that each inductee be vaccinated against smallpox. But because the *states* actually recruited and inducted most men, this Federal regulation became one of many not enforced. The result was needless tragedy. Brooks, *Civil War Medicine*, p. 120; Adams, *Doctors in Blue*; Wiley, *Billy Yank*, p. 125.

of her and Baby that at times I am about ½ unmanned, and need to brace up and be real soldierly—

Now here goes to fix up our Hd Qrs tent—Then take a Sabre Drill—and help men to fix up towards drawing their Horses very soon. Everything moves on slowly yet surely as if there was still something to be done, a little more preparation, and still a little more, to get ready to kill our fellow-men. every man of us is a challenge to fight a dual—but the challenge came from them, when they fired on our flag, and began to invade our homes and firesides. And pity the littleness of the man(?) who would not risk his little life to save his country his Home, his fireside——

November 19, 1862 Wednesday. Have caught cold—Threatened with pleurisy—cold chilly day—everything seems cold, cheerless, heartless. No one near to love and be loved by—Oh! to lay my head upon her bosom—and feel the stroke of my Darling Rachels hand upon my weary brow—Read my Bible—Rubbed me down—Retired.

November 20, 1862 Thùrsday. I had a poor nights rest on a/c pleuratic pain and "stitch" in my side, and back and under my left shoulder blade—

Took several drinks of Brandy—Fixed heating appliances—Drank hot water and exercised myself—Put in most of day being good to myself.

November 21, 1862 Friday. Capt stayed out—I slept well—stormy—rainy cleared at 10 A.M.—Will Karper^m returned from home—Not in good condition, nor is he sick physically—Not much doing save trying to keep dry & comfortable. Capt failed to get pass for me to go home. I resolved—by his consent—that I would risk it—and find my own way—I'd face Guards and find a way to pass——

November 22, 1862 Saturday. Didn't sleep well—my mind too full of throughts of getting home—Answered to Roll call. and at 6 A.M. started for Harrisburg. Took breakfast at Bomgardner House Got on Cars in good time. No patrols about—i.e. in sight—Got to Chambersburg 11 A.M. Found Pet had gone out to Uncle Gelsingers—Got me a dish of oysters—and started to Uncles—5 miles—afoot—Got ride part way on a wagon. Found Pet and Aunty just back from St. Thomas—There were some greetings just then—Darling and Baby so well and happy—My! What a delightful evening we had all around—Thank God for dear good wife and angel daughter—

November 23, 1862 Sunday. Cold and Stormy—We didn't sleep much last nite. Pet had so much to tell me of her xperiences and I so much to ask about and besides, our reunion so buoyed up our affections, that we had a great deal of loving to do.

Then too our little Pet, Cora, was a little restless, all of which detracted from sleep—All well and happy this morning—Spent the day reading, talking and loving—Took long walk in P.M.—O it does seem so pleasant, yes more so, to walk with and to be with my dear wife and precious little Daughter—Aunty and Uncle are so very kind to us—Aunty gave Pet so many things—Linen—Towels—and usables numerous—

November 24, 1862 Monday. Pretty Cool—Uncle and Aunty took us and the things Aunty gave Darling to Chamb'g—to the Plough Home—Put things in, then went to Reboks[pa] to dine—Ah! we can feel that our welcome is about run out there—Well! Pet now settles down in her rooms at John Ploughs—in Chamb'g a darky white washes them today—

P.M. Hired buggy—went out to my Ma's[b]—Left Pussy with Ma[b] and went on the Brother Johns[d]—on the old Homestead—where I was born via Harbisons—chat with "old Missy"—and Sam Sollenberger—Suppered at Bro Johns[d]—Reboks[pa] were there too—at 7 ock returned to Mothers.[b] Spent evening very pleasantly. I surely have a dear, good Mother[b] and precious sister[y] with her would God, Old Daddy[ba] were more of a manly man—

November 25, 1862 Tuesday. Pleasant—We have decided to set up now at Ploughs—Mother[b] gave Darling a Bedstead and some bedding—also a lot of dried Peaches, cherries, &c Bread, butter, apple butter, and Daddy[ba] took them to town and we 3 followed—soon had all up in her rooms—Left Baby with Ploughs girls, and Pet & I went downtown to buy Essentials for kitchen & room—Went into Hokes store for some things—was met by My Captain—I saluted him, we shook hands Startled me with the news "Our Reg't is under marching orders to strike tents at 7½ A.M. tomorrow" I should report myself in Camp by 5 ock this P.M. It was then 11 and at 1 P.M. my train leaves Chamb'g——Some hustling necessary—I told Pet and we hastened to get our things and have them up in our rooms as quickly as possible—Put up the bedstead. Stove not up yet. Plough promised to help my Darling to fix up—and to see that she had wood, chop it for her, and see her well cared for in all things and I would foot the bills—

Now Pet and I had prayers—Then gave the parting hand with tearful eyes—and I was off to my Regiment—

The intended celebration of our 3rd Wedding Anniversary was thus abruptly broken off—The Capt had not reported me absent—Don't intend to punish me except as a burlesque—

We had a great time on the way to Harrisburg—At Carlisle, met and talked with McElhaine and E Holler and other friends a few minutes—

Arrived at Camp at 5 P.M. in good shape—

Eve am well but not fully happy. As Our Anniversary was spoiled, and after all we do not strike tents til Friday—I am so sorry, so very sorry! My Darling Pet will have so much to do and see to—I must write and send her an Anniversary letter of some length—

O that she may keep well and happy—little matters for unworthy me—Now I just know how gently her hand would come over my mouth and some kisses on my forehead.

XII

Rachel Begins Her Life Alone
May 20, 1862–February 1, 1863

*R*achel *wrote only two entries in her journal during the period between the birth of her daughter and the enlistment of her husband in the Union army. When she resumes a more regular record, she and Cora are living with Samuel's mother and stepfather on the latter's farm north of Chambersburg. While Samuel's mother feels some loyalty toward her daughter-in-law, Daniel Byers clearly does not. By December, Rachel and Cora have moved into town, where they lodge in the home of Jonathan Plough and his two daughters, Annie and Emma.*

May 20, 1862   Our little babe is now two &½ weeks old. It is a wee tiny little bud of undiscribable lovliness. I am not strong enough yet to do much. I take care of the little Pet nearly altogether. I am troubled with piles these few days which is very painful. The babe is pretty good, has taken several crying spells, had cholic.

June 15, 1862   I am quite neglecting my journal, the little baby is such a little dear pet that the journal is forgotten. I am helthier than I have been for some time (years) & through the week am as busy at sewing to get things in moving & traveling order as can be. The first of August is

September 21, 1862   Chambersburg Penna At Mother Cormany Byers'[b] Well this is a long jump in my journal. My Sml has kept a daily account of the intervening time so I thought it unnecessary for me to do so too—but now we are separated he has gone to defend the rights of his country in Sulenbergers Cavalry company.   It went hard to see him go.   for he is more than life to me. When he told me that he had enlisted, I felt an undescribable heaviness in my heart.   we prayed earnestly over it.   I became calm & felt more resigned, at times still I am overcome, tears relieve me very much, my heart always seems lighter after weeping freely   In daytime I get along very well but the nights seem very long. I pray for him quite often & trust he will be spared to me—

September 25, 1862 I am not very well today. Guess I worked too hard. & have two more boils my arm is quite lame & stiff. Yesterday old dad[ba] allowed it was better to to commence with a child when quite young to break off bad habits. this he remarked after seeing the baby suck my finger often whereupon I replied that I would have a time with her when I got to myself. Last night the little thing cried for the finger I did not give it, this morn he allowed it would not hurt her it would keep her quiet The old inconsistent dog—he seems more like a sneaky dog than any thing else in his actions & I am not going to give up for him & spoil my child by it I have commenced to break her of it & it would be wrong to let her conquor Mother[b] talks up for me when he says any thing—We have been working at the peaches. Elly,[y] Mother & I have carried over (¼ mile) about three bushels this week—old dad[ba] had no time he said Today he passed there on going to mill so he brought some. Ma[b] picked them up. I know she rues she ever married him.

[Undated] While sitting here alone in my snug warm room I have been thinking O so much of the brave men who these cold nights have to suffer so severely while walking their lonely beat. I think of all, & pray for all, yet when I look at the dear little one in the cribb

December 26, 1862 Fryday.[1] At 10½ A.M. I went to Rebuks[pa] to help along with the butchering. L.[p] told me I could not help any so I sat a little while in the room thinking whether to stay or to go home. Just at this time Aunt Elenor came. So I soon decided what to do. & got on my shawl and fixed baby and came home with her. L.[p] did not wish me to go but my judgment told me I had better. Aunt brought me ½ doz. egs. & a small roll of butter. I dressed myself and went down street with her & helped her pick a dress. Called at the P.O. on my way home & got a letter from My Samuel with an order for fifty ($50.) dollars, his county bounty. I took it down to Mr. Hoke & had him draw the money & left it in his care taking a receipt for it from him.[2] Made the acquaintance of Mrs. Detwiler & sent word with her to John Karpers[l] about Billy[m] &c. Called on Mrs. Barnes, her sister is at the point of death having had an illegal child & the father to it is in the army.[3] Saw a soldiers funeral pass. a very large one.

1. Rachel and Cora are now rooming with the Ploughs in Chambersburg.
2. Jacob Hoke, whom Rachel knew through her church, was proprietor of J. Hoke and Company, one of Chambersburg's largest dry-goods stores.
3. Mrs. Barnes's husband was the orderly sergeant whom Samuel had first nursed then quarreled with. This is Rachel's second reference to an illegitimate pregnancy (see her entry for July 7, 1860). Nineteenth-century illegitimacy rates are impossible to

Evening It is raining. I cannot but think of the poor soldiers & breathe a prayer for them. O! that this war would once come to an end.

December 31, 1862 Wednesday. The last day in the old year. I have put in the day pretty severely. I washed & have a dreadful sore boil. I have suffered wonderfully with it. The baby has cried so much all day I could hardly get my clothes out, but I did get them out & got my carpet laid so things look in pretty good trim now. L^k & Naoma Rebuk were in a little while this evening. My boil opened while they were here, it ran considerably & I feel much relieved. I gave L.^{k} a teacup full of maple molasses along home. Yesterday I was much disappointed. J. Karper[l] promised to take a box of edibles along for my Samuel. (He went to Washington to get William[m] home. W. is sick at the hospital) he said he could not take them but would call for them in time. That was the last of J. Karper.[l] He did not want to be bothered & took that way to get out of it. I think he might have done that much for me or rather for Samuel after he has done so much for Billy.[4] I had my things packed in a satchel, he told me he could not go out to camp but after I proposed it—said could leave them at the depot. I went down street as soon as he was gone got a box & repacked the things, Nailed it, put the address on all ready so he would not be detained, but as above stated he never came for the box. It seems very small dirty trick of him. My things have come at last, only 5 teacups & one little plate broken. There were about a bushel of nice apples in the box which were pretty badly bruised, but are still very good.[5] Such a shooting as there is all over town tonight[6]

January 1, 1863 Evening. This seemed indeed like New Years Day, being the first day I have my room fixed and carpet down. Emma P. was up playing with the baby considerably. This morning I called to

---

assess with any precision, but references like these lend credence to the argument that its incidence was relatively higher than might be supposed, especially if cases where hasty marriages ensued are counted in. See, for example, Daniel Scott Smith and Michael S. Hindus, "Premarital Pregnancy in America, 1640–1971: An Overview and Interpretation," *Journal of Interdisciplinary History* 5 (Spring 1975), 537–70.

4. Rachel is unaware of the resentment that John Karper felt toward his brother-in-law, whom he blamed for luring his son William into the army. See Samuel's diary, Oct. 10, 1862.

5. Apples were use as padding for the chinaware.

6. The shooting marked New Year's Eve.

Mr. P. for my New Years gift. So off he ponied & cut me off a slice of liver to fry & brought me ten eggs. This p.m. Rebuks children were here, if I had those boys to train awhile I think they would act differently. They are so quarrelsome & impudent. I had to reprove them several times. After they were gone, Mr P. allowed it seemed very quite up here. Henry R.[pa] was in this a.m. & offered to get & fix me up a box to put my dishes in also a lounge if I wished it, both he & L[l] act the part of friends lately. It is getting quite cold again. I got me bonnet fixings this a.m. I expected a letter but did not get any, got the Phren. Journal. Religiously I vow to commence anew with more earnestness God helping me.

January 3, 1863 No letter this week from my Samuel. What can be the cause. I feel anxious. I looked some for him home tonight, still I hardly expected it. I feel a little sad and disappointed. Yesterday I fixed my winter bonnet over. It looks pretty well. Today Henry Rebuk[pa] fixed up a box for me with a shelf for cobboard. I have my things pretty well fixed now, which makes it seem quite homelike. J. Karper[l] & wife[k] were here today. Mrs K.[k] brought me a chicken. She took dinner with me. I took John K.[l] round the cape for not taking that box along to Samuel, he tried to hatch up some excuse but could not do much. Hannah[k] hated it.

January 9, 1863 Fryday. Rec'd a letter from Home. A slip from Mother.[bb] I was so glad that I could not but weep. I feel sad all day. The thought that next I hear from my Samuel may be that he was killed rings in my ears continually. They (His Company & Reg.) have been ordered to join Burnside. I rec'd a little box with little curiosities that he gathered in his rambles. He writes me many very good letters. Every letter seems almost like a message from the dead. A soldier was burried in the Reformed graveyard across the street. The first I ever saw burried. I could not help shedding a tear for the brave soldier, perhaps thinking that such may be the fate of my poor Samuel makes me so sad. I made knit a little hood for Cora, it's pretty. I am fixing to go to see my Samuel in case he cannot come to see me. I must now write to Hattie

January 21, 1863 Tuesday. Have had the company for nearly two weeks now of Miss M. Hanson, a schoolmate at Wes. (O. U.) Was glad to see her. It will seem lonely to sleep all alone. I deposited the county bounty of James Witherhill at J. Hokes today, also sold M. Hanson the Matrons Manuel & Maternity on credit & loaned her the

H Encyclophedia.[7] I also called on J. Wilt & brought him some maple suger. J. W. is very low with consumption Called on Mrs. Sulenberger[8] & Mrs. Barns. Got a loaf of bread at the bakery for dinner. P.M. M. H. left. I was just getting the house into order when C. Grafton came. She took tea with me. I still have much trouble with my little girl. I invented all kinds of machines to break her of that bad plan but instead of forgetting, it has grown on her to almost a mania. I pray the Good Lord to help me. Yesterday M. H. & I visited at Mr. Wilts. M. kept my & Mrs Dixons, children in the evening & we went to church. I gave in my name to be united with the church & was rec'd. I feel so much as if not fit to be a member of any church, still there I feel best at home, & my highest aim is to be a good christian. My light is giving way, so I will retire.

January 22, 1863 A.M. Wrote a letter for Mrs Barns to her husband. I am well so is Cora. It is still cloudy & rainy. It has been quite unpleasant all week. I fear my dried fruit will spoil on the balcony this damp weather. I covered the box to keep the snow out. I think it so mean that I cannot keep my box on the garret. Mr. P. said he did not like this mixing up, but how could it be mixed up when none of their things were near. & as to the mice making nests in my papers, I could easily have moved them—He just wanted to show his authority & I am going to show my independence soon. I have written a piece for the Herald of Health.[9] Must now copy & send.

January 26, 1863 Monday. It is cloudy and rained a little—is not cold. I do get so provoked with the family I am living with. Mr. P. scarcely ever has time to do any thing for me at the time I want it done. It seems to me he wants to show his authority by making me wait. Annie has been in my room but once to make a call & some

---

7. The "Matron's Manuel & Maternity" is almost certainly *The Matron's Manual of Midwifery, and the Diseases of Women during Pregnancy and in Child Bed, Being a Familiar and Practical Treatise, More Especially Intended for the Instruction of Females Themselves, But Adapted also for Popular Use,* by Frederick Hollick, a prolific author whose medical literature Samuel had sold in Canada. Hollick's publishers claimed that this book was in its hundredth printing by 1848. It was a popular and important source of information on sex and sexuality, including contraception and abortion. The other book was probably Russell T. Trall's *Hydropathic Encyclopia: A System of Hydropathy and Hygiene* (New York, 1853), another Fowlers and Wells book.

8. The wife of Samuel's captain.

9. The *Herald of Health* had begun in 1845 as the *Water-Cure Journal* and continued through the end of the century as a vehicle for medical, hygienic, and dietary reformers.

three or four times on errands. Emma comes in pretty often to play with the baby & baby likes her too. Mrs. Sulenberger was here yesterday, we had a long talk about going to the Potomac to see our husbands & take provisions for them. I am all on tiptoe at the idea of visiting them in camp. It will give us such a good idea of camp life & we can sympathize better with the poor soldiers. Mr. P. was to get me what I need but he does not do so. I asked him this morning for corn meal but he could spare me none he said. At first he seemed anxious to provide for me & overcharged me so shamefully. Of course I told him of it—Since he sees he can make nothing off me he does not have it to spare. he has been treating me more like a dog than a human being with human feelings. As soon as my wood is all I am going to some other place unless things change. Evening. Went down to Mrs B's to get her to assist in splitting the yarn that Mrs Rebuk[P] ordered & left on my hands. I thought in that way I could use it to crochet a little sack for Cora. We worked at it a little while when I said I wish I could sell it. I would teach whoever bought it to knit it into a hood. She (Mrs. Barns) was right in for it. took 5 hanks @ 12½ (62 c) Mrs. Keller came while I was there. I told her that I heard she was quite uneasy about her husbands watch & should have told some one he would not give it up. "I never said such a thing, don't believe it Mrs C. &c she said. Cora had slept but little today so she went to sleep early. Mrs. McGowan called in on her way to church—told me that Mr. Raher was to preach—so I just left baby & went—told Mr P. that I was going. We had a good Sermon, & a good meeting throughout—

January 27, 1863 Tuesday. Mrs. Barns came pretty early to learn to knit hood. She did not do much, her little girl acted so ugly. Evening went to Rebuks[Pa] & kept the children while they went to church. I rec'd a letter from my Sml—they have left again. O! War! War!!

January 28, 1863 Wednesday. This morning on waking all was white out of doors. It has snowed all day. This evening it is getting cold & stormy. O! My poor poor Samuel I cannot help weeping as I think of him. likely he is out with not even a cloth tent to shelter him. O! My God—Haste the end of this war, & bring my dear dear Samuel back to again.

February 1, 1863 Sunday. I have recieved several letters from My Sml. the orders for march were countermanded on account of the storm & the impasable roads Still he will not be allowed to come

258

home, but wishes me to come to see him. Capt. S. wants his wife to come too—so we are going together.[10] My Sml tells me not to start until he writes again. I have been very busy preparing to go to see him. I have been trying hard to get to Mothers[b] befor I go to Dixie but it seems imposible—The meeting is still protracted in our church—The interest seems to be increasing again. Cora is beginning to creep & gets up at chairs &c She is in a measure forgetting that ugly habit & plays very nicely on the floor, but whenever she gets sleepy & wet & (it seems so) when I have work to do— she is at it.

10. It was not uncommon during the Civil War for wives to visit husbands at the front, especially after the armies had settled into winter quarters.

XIII

Samuel Goes to the Front

November 26, 1862–February 17, 1863

This section follows in detail the deployment of the 16th Pennsylvania Cavalry from Harrisburg, through the Washington area, to join the Army of the Potomac, which was bogged down along the Fredericksburg-Rappahannock line of the Virginia front. It concludes with Samuel's first real leave back home after a two-and-one-half-month absence.

November 26, 1862 Wednesday. Captains wife sick—went to see her——Lieut Snyder assisted me in selecting my Horse—Mostly "red tape" today—I took my Horse through some drill—maneuvers &c &c. Lieut Bohn ill—Took him in—gave him his medicine—

Spent most of eve writing up my Diary and a letter to Pet—

Poor dear! It is just too bad I did not have another day or so with her & Baby—

November 27, 1862 Thursday. A day of bustle and confusion packing up etc.—Evening Capt returned

At 5 ock Roll Call a number men were absent. Lest they should be missing in the morning a squad was sent to City—A Doz of us. We visited some 6 or 7 whore-houses, found Brough—Bradley—Arnold—White—Earich & May—On way to camp met some coming—we took them back.

I got only little naps curled on Caps trunk—Orderly Barnes at an all night dance—we missed him—He came in time to call the Roll—and escaped

November 28, 1862 Friday. Early call—3 A.M.—Soon on job—Striking tents, rolling up—packing &c To move—–from Camp McClelland Harrisburg Pa., to Bladenburg near Washington D. C. I prepared all the Captains and my things—Our Company Books, Rolls &c by boxing &c and sent them to R.R. St'n at Harrisburg before 7 ock A.M., when we started—with Our Horses for the cars.

Capt had to take charge as Maj Fry is utterly inefficient as a horseman[1]—

1. William H. Fry owed his position to influence rather than ability.

260

Whoopee! Maj Fry and his horse fell down an embankment some 5 ft high—not hurt much—Took til noon and after to get our 1,200 horses aboard—

Left Harrisburg about 4 ock P.M.—I rode in car with The Officers—Maj Fry ordered Sergts McGowen and Zook out of Officers Car, but treated me well—I had set up Pea-nuts and Cigars—reached Baltimore 10½ ock P.M.—Men had their army grub—The officers and I went to Hotel—Good supper—Most of us slept in the cars—some officers got pretty boozy and men too.

November 29, 1862 Saturday. I am quite unwell—Sore throat and diarhea—Am using Gin and smoking for relief²—ate some breakfast out of my Haversack—The first time.

We marched through Baltimore—Fed our Horses at B&O Stock yards—at the "loading places"—

We were kept there til sundown. can see no good reason why. But then our train moved on. I again in Officers Car—Capt Sollenberger and I had two seats, and we covered them pretty well. The Men occupied all kinds of cars from 2nd Class to cattle cars. We reached Washington about 10 ock P.M. and turned in at Soldiers Retreat³ where a bowl of good Coffee, bread, and Cold Pork awaited us—

O how good it tasted!—Now we were marched to the sleeping department, where we all lay upon the floor and slept—Over 1,000 of us—The others were with the train—sleeping in Box Cars—

After all Uncle Sam is pretty good to his Boys.

November 30, 1862 Sunday. I got up early—My bowels are bad Had a long talk with Miller one of the Hospital Assistants of our Regiment—Our 1st acquaintance Seems a fine little fellow—About 8 ock we got a good soldiers breakfast after long fooling about it—Our Maj Fry is certainly a poor shoat—The fellow has too much gass and brass and not enough real get up & do! 9½ A.M. unloaded our Horses. Was quite a job—took us til 11 ock to get them limbered up and into line—we then took them to water and next fed them off the ground—not far from the White House—

---

2. Tobacco was thought to have medicinal qualities.

3. Following a period of confusion and disorder early in the war, the Soldiers' Retreat, or Soldiers' Rest, had been built to systematize the feeding and housing of the thousands of soldiers who passed through the capital. The institution functioned quite well from 1862 onward. Margaret Leech, *Reveille in Washington, 1860–1865* (New York, 1941), pp. 185–86.

The White Houe is a splendid edifice in appearance—although unfinished[4]—

One sees so many places both in Cities and Country where the war has made its mark.

So many unfinished buildings—so many barracks, drill sheds, and places laid waste as regards normal intention—We formed Column as soon as our horses were through eating—and marched out the Baltimore Pike about 7 miles to near Bladensburg[5] and got to work putting up our tents—Our Darkies[6] and I "pitched" the Captains—all worked nicely until dark—when we had it fairly ready for sleeping—(Coming through Baltimore many flags were hung out as we passed doors and windows and waved as we passed along—of course we cheered them lustily—

We stopped a little while near a home at the B&O end of the City. Women and children brought us bread buttered, apples, and water in abundance. A huge flag was hoisted at the end of the Bridge for us—How we did cheer!)[7] Eve I am quite unwell—Bowels bad. O how I wonder how my dear little family is getting along. Heaven bless them and keep me above the waters. O for more religion—

---

4. Cormany probably meant the Capitol rather than the White House. The railroad yards were close to the Capitol, but some distance from the White House; the Bladensburg Turnpike up which they were headed ran from the area of the Capitol away from the White House; and the Capitol dome was then under construction. For confirming map, see *OMACW*, pl. VI, no. 1, and pl. VII, no. 1.

5. Bladensburg, originally a landing on the Anacostia River, lay just outside the District of Columbia. The town had enjoyed a brief period of boom prior to the early 1830s, because Congress refused to let railroads enter the District itself. Passengers bound for the capital city from the north disembarked in Bladensburg and took coaches into the District. When Congress reversed itself on the railroad issue in 1835, Bladensburg resumed its quiet existence as a small market town. Maryland Writers' Program, *Maryland: A Guide to the Old Line State* (Works Projects Administration; rpt. New York, 1973), pp. 471–72.

6. The status of these blacks is not clear. Blacks were employed by the army as laborers, and some may have been assigned to the 16th Pennsylvania. Others, especially those from the war-torn border states and upper South, became private servants to officers and enlisted men, preferring such marginal employment to life in refuge camps or army work details. The army recognized the latter in several of its official regulations. See, e.g., *Army Regulations* (1861 and 1863), paras. 782, 1610; Bell Irvin Wiley, *The Life of Billy Yank: The Common Soldier of the Union* (Garden City, N.Y., 1971), p. 315; idem., *Southern Negroes, 1861–1865.* (New Haven, 1938), pp. 341–42; Harry F. Jackson and Thomas F. O'Donnell, *Back Home in Oneida: Hermon Clarke and His Letters* (Syracuse, 1965), p. 94.

7. The passage that Cormany put in parentheses does not fit chronologically, but he had no space to insert it where it belonged, in the entry for Nov. 29.

December 1, 1862 Monday. I slept pretty well, wrapped in my blanket, on the ground—Bowels still rather bad—Rained some during night—I worked busily all day fixing up Capts Quarters—I eat my meals with the Capt. Cap bo't some cabbage, potatoes, &c. Today I got up bed, writing and eating table &c &c. Feel some better. The Gin preparation seems helping—Capt made a chaff tick and filled it with leaves—so we are in a fair way for some comforts.

December 2, 1862 Tuesday. Slept well—made out our Companys Monthly Report—a nice little job—Drew my saddle—Like our new Camp. Am as happy as may be, being not quite well—My chief regret is my coldness religiously—There is so much to lead astray—and so little to draw me to God—Still God is good to me, and checks me by the Spirit when I might otherwise go astray—I need much resisting grace—

December 3, 1862 Wednesday. I like this place—

Croft & I got Pass from 9 to 12—We did up Bladensburg—The Main Battery & Fort Lincoln[8]—Both seem quite formidable as earthworks of stubborn clay—P.M. Wrote considerably—Our 1st Regimental Drill on horseback came off variously. Eve wrote to Darling—wish I could see her—Hope she is as well and happy as I could wish to see her—

December 4, 1862 Thursday. Had to cough a lot last night—Bugler and Corporal Lawrence returned. Made out requisition for wood for Captain and for the Company—

Our Hd Qrs Chimney seems to not know its functions rightly—Puffs too much smoke inside of our quarters—

The Boys are fixed up pretty comfortably now—and do a good deal of "Saber Drill" "Drill afoot" and regular Cavalry drill—some Horses, like some men are too stiff headed, or necked to move easily and together promptly—

P.M. Got a quart of oysters for our supper—Jolly time—Eve I visited Crofts & Cables qrs—nice social hour together—

Read a while in my Bible—am well and happy. Oh that I knew that my Darling and Pussy were the same—

---

8. The Corps of Engineers established a large circle of defensive forts and batteries around the greater Washington area. Fort Lincoln guarded the Bladensburg Pike where it crossed into the District of Columbia. John G. Barnard, *A Report on the Defenses of Washington to the Chief of Engineers, U.S. Army* (Washington, 1871), pp. 28, 52–53; Benjamin F. Cooling, *Symbol, Sword, and Shield: Defending Washington During the Civil War* (New York, 1975).

December 5, 1862 Friday. Ugly Cough—Grooming a distempered horse is no soft snap—so many of our horses are affected[9]—

Rainy—snowy—windy—but we sing—whistle and go in on anything vigorously that belongs to the art of Cavalry soldiering—

Did lots of reading—Read Pres Lincolns Message to Congress—A great paper indeed[10]

Long for a letter from Darling

December 6, 1862 Saturday. Very Cold! Snow and slush 3 inches deep—Read most of A.M. Billy Karper[m] dont brace up. Goes to Hospital again—I wrote letters J. B. Kimmel—Bell Kimmel—and my Pet. Evening good letter from Darling—She certainly is too good a wife for a man like me. I feel unworthy such love and affection as she xpresses—O how good God is to me—

December 7, 1862 Sunday. Very Cold Took a real good Bath—Read and wrote most of A.M. P.M. visited our boys in Hosp. Keller very low—Fink midling and Billy Karper[m]—principally home sickness—occasionally slight fever—wants a discharge from Army—

Finished a letter to Pet, and Orderly Barnes and I strolled to P.O. nice walk and pleasant talk—

Called on Croft-Coble—had a nice sing—I was called on to sing in Sergt Majors quarters.

---

9. Wartime conditions were hard on horses as well as men. Distemper, also known as "the strangles," was a troublesome, though only occasionally fatal, disease of the respiratory system and throat glands. Horses coughed, lost energy, ran high fevers, suffered throat abcesses and diarrhea, and had difficulty breathing. It is now known to be an easily transmitted infectious disease. George H. Conn, *The Practical Horse Keeper: A Manual on the Stabling, Care and Feeding, also First-Aid Treatment of the Common Diseases of the Horse* (New York, 1955), pp. 246–53. Contemporary books prescribed laxatives and liniments. John Hinds, *Farriery, Taught in a New and Easy Plan: Being a Treatise on the Diseases and Accidents of the Horse* (Philadelphia, 1849), pp. 130–34.

10. Few historians would agree with Cormany's assessment, and it is rather puzzling that Cormany himself approved the piece so heartily. Even though Lincoln had issued a preliminary emancipation proclamation Sept. 22, 1862, after the Confederate invasion was turned back at Antietam, the president used his annual message of Dec. 1, 1862, to propose a program of gradual (to 1900), compensated emancipation as the best and final solution to the slavery dilemma. The message upset many abolitionists, who considered it retrogressive, dismayed many blacks, who feared Lincoln might not go through with the Southern emancipation he had promised ten weeks earlier, and confused many Congressmen, most of whom chose to ignore it. Roy P. Basler, ed., *The Collected Works of Abraham Lincoln* (New Brunswick, N.J., 1953), V, 518–37; Richard N. Current, *The Lincoln Nobody Knows* (New York, 1958), pp. 227–29; James G. Randall and David Donald, *The Civil War and Reconstruction,* 2nd ed. (Boston, 1961), p. 384.

After Roll Call read some in my precious Bible on retiring. Day after Day, passes away, and soon will come the last one. Oh! for grace so to live that I may greet it with Joy—

December 8, 1862 Monday. Very Cold. Snow dont melt much—I furnished Franklin Co commissioners with List of F Co Boys with date of Enlistment &c P.M.—Commenced to make out our Co H Pay Roll—Requires careful work.

Eve 4 Sergts—McGowen, Zuck, Armstrong & Harrison and some privates—Goodman &c. were in my tent a long time keeping me from work—but was nice socially—

December 9, 1862 Tuesday. Still Cold—Called at Hosp. Billy K^m is as old grannyish as ever. Keller is very low—Fink pretty bad—Got a bottle of bitter cherries put up in Brandy for my Bowels—Eve had a splendid sing in our quarters—Am so glad Pet & pussy keep so well and happy. Thank the Lord

December 10, 1862 Wednesday. Very Cold. My horse died last night—

Keller and Fink some better—Finished Muster Roll of Co. H.

Took part in Dress Parade—OK Capts and lieuts were reported to Col. I reported Serg't McG. Cap gave him fits—Becker was put in irons for deserting his post—At dark—Keller was thought to be dying, but didn't—so I returned to tent and wrote some to Pet—

December 11, 1862 Thursday. Wrote for Pet til 11 ock last eve. Cold—Finished Co Dis. Book[11]—Feel some better—Am too busy to think of getting sick—Poor Keller will die I think—I gently broke it to him as a possibility—found he had been thinking on the matter—Confessed that he had been a christian but "backslid"—He desired it and I read for him, out of my testament. He seemed so glad I read verses in Rom 12–14—and Heb 12——The Name of Jesus and The promises caused his face to become illumined—During prayer and silence his lips moved and a few whispered words were understood such as "Jesus" "save" or "Saviour"—and his. he wore a satisfied expression—Returned to my tent and wrote til past 12 ock—

11. Probably short for "company description book"; description books contained the master rolls for each unit, with the required information about each individual. The one Cormany refers to here is in the National Archives.

December 12, 1862 Friday. Warmer—Keller still drowzy—I wrote in Company Books & a/c and also finished an 8 page letter for my Darling, and also a paper of 4 pages on our late anniversary—that was all broken to pieces by Marching Orders. I mailed the bunch—Evening I feel quite unwell—use some Gin—and keep knocking around—too much to do to stop—Later, Keller seems a little stronger but it may be only the rally often preceeding going out—I talked considerably with him. He seems now to be at peace, and whispered "O if I get well, I will be a different man"

December 13, 1862 Saturday. I slept well—Feel pretty good—Bathed—Took dose of Gin—preparation Then wrote til breakfast—Made Descriptive List for White and Lawrence—Called on Keller Karper^m & Fink—Fink is improving Karper^m dont want to, and Keller will soon pass over—I work on Co H Clothing Roll—Fetterhoff, Hassler & I rode over to 17th Regts Camp—Tried my new horse—well he is pretty good on the go—
Eve Ord. Barnes was in my tent awhile—I read for him some—of my Anniversary paper. Sent to Darling—Barnes said he believed we were the happiest couple in the world, and I believe it to be true—

December 14, 1862 Sunday. Barnes called for me to go along—we went over. Keller was manifestly soon to go—once he seemed to be gone—then on request we turned him over and he sat up and asked for a drink. We gave it, he said, "I aint dead yet" "I was almost gone"—a little later he said "My Jesus, O My Jesus" and in a moment he was gone. At 12-Midnight—Keller slept away without a struggle[12]
He was carried out into the open field, and 4 men stood guard—Glessner, Fetterhoff, Meister & Fletcher—With Corporal McElroy—

December 15, 1862 Monday. I had planned to take Keller home—by permission—It was declared that the body was unfit for transportation—and must be buried at once in the Govmt Burying ground not far away—Men were detailed to dig the Grave—others to escort the body—to the spot selected by The Capt. and myself—in due time—at 1 ock P.M. The Coffin arrived—The Hospital Stewards placed the body in it—Decomposition was going on fearfully—which showed that the impracticability of planing to take the Body home—Lieut Hazelton of Co I was detailed to act as Chaplain. At

12. William H. Keller, 21, a carpenter from Cumberland, Pa., died of typhoid fever H16PC, p. 14.

4:30 P.M. The Escort, followed by Co H—resorted to the Corpse— and it was borne to the place for burial —The Acting Chaplain announced the 502 hymn in the U. B. Hymn Book, which was "lined," and sung by the Boys—an appropriate prayer was offered by Act'g Chaplain—and a few remarks closed up the Career of One of Our Boys. I am to send to Mrs Keller the few little effects of the Husband—That U.B. Hymn Book being the most to be prized by the widow & Child.

Musings: My soul feels sad, and yet, I'm glad—Sad that one so young should have to leave a young wife and child. Glad that hope in Christ later banishes sorrow and awakens joyful assurance of re-union by and by—

How soon I may go, leaving my dear little family. God only knows. O for grace to live daily so as to leave them posative assurances that they may meet me in Heaven by and by—Yes, I shall live close to my Redeemer, In Him is our Assurance.

Aside from Funeral and specials slept til 7½ this morning. am well and happy as could be expected under the circumstances. Feel very serious, yet happy in my Redeemer—Oh! I do love Him, and shall serve Him while I live—

Did a good deal of writing today, between times, when funeral affairs were off—

Evening—Wrote Obituary to send Mrs Keller, and a letter to my Precious Wife, who is to read the Obituary to Mrs. Keller—I do thank God that I am the Husband of such a wife as is mine and that we have such a precious little Daughter.

December 16, 1862 Tuesday. Rained and stormed all night and still keeps it up—10 ock—

I made out Inventory of Kellers clothing—Finished up Co Hs Clothing Book for signing—

P.M. Colder still—Drew our Carbine Slings—Capt—sick—Rheumatics—

I have threats of Diptherea—Recd O such a good letter from Darling—Just the best one ever—

December 17, 1862 Wednesday. Had such a sweet dream about Darling. Am well(?) and real happy—Order—Be ready on 3 hours notice to move—Issued Carbines &c to such as had none yet. Musings: Wrote some letters—symptoms of Diptherea bother me by spells—Hope and pray it dont breakout—I am as happy as could be expected of me, being so far from home, and from my Darling and pussy. Still Jesus is my Friend—is with me. Him will I trust and serve til I am called Home, to my home in Heaven—Thank God for a hope that reaches far beyond the shores of time—where my Pet and I shall never be separated thus, as now. Oh how I long to be there. How sweet the words "A Home in Heaven"—I need grace to keep busy doing the right faithfully every day, and all the while, so preparing for that Home and sweet Rest—

December 18, 1862 Thursday. Very Cold—Clear & Beautiful—
Finish Clothing Rolls and Books—Orderly Sergt Barnes and I went in to Washington—Did up The City—Capitol Buildings &c. Passed lots of Patrol. None challenged us—Had Oysters, Ale and Cigars. P.M. More sightseeing—Great !!! Returned to Camp 4 P.M. Got all our Horses shod and we will doubtless soon be off for Dixie—I take a new Horse—call him "Jeff Davis."

December 19, 1862 Friday. Very cold I slept cold—Consigned some unfit Horses to Quarter Master Jas R. Robison—
Took a Carbine Drill—P.M. Another Carbine drill—Later—Croft and I mounted our horses—Fully equipped and took a ride to Fort Bunker Hill[13]—When thus armed and mounted and uniformed one feels more like a real Soldier—
O that by one great daring act I could end this rebellion—Eve: Got letter from Pet. O such a good, good, good one, and one from J. W. Adams[kk]—Good sing at Sergt Majors Office til "Tapps" (Lights out!)[14]

December 20, 1862 Saturday. The ride yesterday had very good effect on my cold and throat—
I wrote a Charge against the Authorities at Chambersburg for not arresting Bender & Bowser and insisted on prompt action[15]—
Eve Cap—Orderly and I long chat—O that this war might soon end, and I might be again with my Dears—

December 21, 1862 Sunday. Cold—Roll Call—Breakfast—Dress Parade—and Company Inspection and my feet nearly frozen—

13. Fort Bunker Hill occupied high ground west of the 16th Pennsylvania encampment. Barnard, *Report on Defenses,* pp. 27–28; OMACW, pl. VII.
14. Maj. Gen. Daniel Butterfield had modified an old bugle call for lights out in July 1862. His version, known as taps, caught on quickly among Civil War buglers and has remained standard ever since. See Russell H. Booth, "Butterfield and 'Taps': What Really Happened at Harrison's Landing in 1862?" *CWTI,* 16 (Dec. 1977), 34–39.
15. William Bowser, the regimental saddler, was eventually declared a deserter. Michael Bender returned for duty. *H16PC,* pp. 20, 29.

My new horse acts pretty well—Drew a lot of pistols—25—and returned the Ballance in Box—P.M. & Eve wrote to Pet—I take great pleasure in writing her all about all my trials & feelings & how I long to press her to my bosom, and tell her how dear she is to me—And best of all she appreciates and reciprocates all my love and demonstrations. Read awhile in my Bible, and prayed, thanking God for His word. I make all these records of my thoughts & feelings, socially, religiously, as a soldier and a husband—So were I to be taken, My Darling would know about my state of mind and heart almost daily.

December 22, 1862 Monday. Dress Parade and Drill in A.M. P.M. On drill again—we had a splendid time—Chief maneuvering was that of the Cavalry Charge, both Squadron and Regimental—The Boys and Horses are leaving—I wrote letter, and orders signed for Pet to draw My Co. Bounty,[16] Capt Sullenbergers, and Sergt Armstrongs Lieut Snyders wife got his—

December 23, 1862 Tuesday. Warmer—Lots of drill—Foot, Saber and Mounted and ordinary routine—After all we may lie here sometime to become proficient as Cavalrymen—

December 24, 1862 Wednesday. Captain issued an order concerning grooming Horses well, and promptness at Roll Call—I was on Drill and Parade in A.M.—
Wrote a lot of Bounty Orders for our Men—P.M. Drilled again—Those charges are made with too much carelesness—My! I wish the men would think the movements out, or through, and then act to the point—
Am wondering so why I have no letter from my Pet.
Hope all is well with both—Lieut Snyder and 4 or 5 Men went to City. Ordered by the Colonel—I had a good long sing with a squad of the Boys before "Tapps."

December 25, 1862 Thursday. Warm—Fine—
——CHRISTMAS——
Warm "Merry Christmas" from all the officers. 11 ock Orderly Barnes Sergt Peters and I went on the hunt of a Christmas Dinner—Two Mr. Shaws turned us off, but a Mr. Bell set up a fine one—with

16. Rachel was able to draw the money four days later. See her entry for Dec. 26, 1862.

a little old rum to drink—Had a fine social time—Returned to Camp at 2 P.M.—Then Capt S and I took a ride out around The Forts—

Eve—A letter from Pet—A very good one—Only, the 1st part was so blue—broke me all up—Old Plough is not true to her—dont chore for her as he promised—She has to carry her Flour, meal &c &c—and he dont care—I see her trudging, slavishly, and not well—and has the blues—and I am not there to help her out, and caress her, and demonstrate my love—and arrange for her greater comfort and wellbeing—I never was so broken up, never so pitied her. I wept like a Boy—til my pillow was wet, and the precious one has no one near in whom she can confide and be comforted by—and I am to blame—I won her heart, and took her from amongst her friends—

God bless her. Thou only canst.

December 26, 1862 Friday. Up early—My sleep was poor—and I am blue this morning—meditation and prayer cleared me up.

I wrote her of our Christmas dinner—My ride—and some about the effects of the first part of her letter on me, and how I now see how, and will see that she is better cared for.

I was on Dress Parade, and Drill—but kept constantly thinking about my precious and our pussy—

P.M. Drilled again—I was thrown, or rather I had to jump off my horse—my saddle turned while we were in the act of a Charge—a moment later and I would scarcely have escaped alive, but I did escape almost unhurt—and finished the drill——

Eve—I have a bad cold on my Lungs—Reading Pets letter over, and then my response—to it, cheered me up, and I know my letter just sent will cheer her up.

December 27, 1862 Saturday. Drilled in AM vigorously——P.M. General Policing and cleaning up quarters—I have a bad cough. I keep thinking so very much of my Darling and Pussy and their surroundings. I long so to see them, and wonder are they well and real happy—

Pets last is O such a good letter. Everytime I read it it seems better—O I do thank God that I ever became the husband of such a wife, a wife like whom there is not another on earth—never was—and never will be—Only the grace of God can ever make and keep me worthy of her love and devotion—

December 28, 1862 Sunday. Pleasant Am quite unwell—Cough—Pain on my breast—Was excused from Dress Parade—Lay on my bed resting up—thinking of me dear God given little family—and dozing the time away——

P.M. so pleasant. Barnes and I took a ride across country towards Ft. Slocum.[17] Crossed hills, hollows, brushland, everything that came to be on our route—

Spent a while at the old British Church, built 1717 & repaired 1770—Some very old grave-stones—from 1793 to 1800. one of a woman aged 120 years.[18]

How I wished Darling could share the joy of seeing these Old Relics—

December 29, 1862 Monday. I remained in Quarters most of A.M. reading, writing, &c—

Am improving physically and am happy too—even if I am not quite up to standard—Worked some on Co Pay Roll.

Wrote some for Pet—It is such a relief to sit and write her all about my feelings and condition and what I'm doing.

December 30, 1862 Tuesday. Cloudy—Spent most of day on Co Rolls. My! What an amount of Red Tape there is in Army Reports &c. Eve—6:30—Company called out—Capt called "Attention! We are to march tomorrow A.M. 6 ock." Three deafening cheers for the Order, and three for our Captain——I finished 2 Rolls—Cap & I rode to City—I got Gin Med—Finished letter to Pet in evening. Some 28 pages—I am well & happy—I love my Jesus, and seek to serve Him so He will ever love and own me as His own—Heaven bless my Pet and our pussy.

December 31, 1862 Wednesday. I didn't retire at all last night. Wrote nearly all night on our Rolls—in my Diary—and on a letter to Pet on closing of old year 1862, and about our moving—

I packed up Captains and my things—at 3 ock this morning "Tat Too" was blowed & Roll was called, and all were preparing to go. At 4 ock A.M. orders came to tear up and destroy nothing—6 ock marching order countermanded. The weather cloudy—drizzly, pretty cold—9 ock the Whole Regiment was called out—Mounted— and Mustered for pay, which took til 2 P.M.

17. Another of the forts ringing Washington, Slocum was about four miles west of the 16th Pennsylvania camp. *OMACW*, pl. VII; Barnard, *Report on Defenses*, pp. 51–52.

18. St. Paul's Church, now in Rock Creek Park. It was founded in 1712, erected in 1719, repaired in 1775, and rebuilt after a fire in 1921. Interments had begun in the cemetery in 1719. Writers' Project, *Washington: City and Capital* (Works Projects Administration, Washington, 1937), pp. 618–22.

It was very cold to sit still on our Horses minus overcoats—After Co H had mustered—They watered their Horses and returned to Camp to feed horses, and dine, but instructed to keep ready at a moments notice to march away. Thus we did—lounging about in our tents, and as evening was coming on, we settled down more and more as if to Stay. Evening, some of the Boys recd boxes from Home with good things to eat—and as we were liable to be ordered out any hour—They were the more generous, and so I with others had Pie, Cake and many good things to enjoy.

Evening did but little save fix up our bed for sleeping and write these items of the days doings—I am pretty well, and as happy as usual—This is the last of 1862—Soon the old year will have run its course, and the last favor will have been afforded—the last opportunity to accept or reject passed over—O that all would improve their golden moments as they fly, and learn and do their Makers and Saviours Will—I am one year nearer my Eternal Home! Thank God a Home in Heaven will be my lot when my work is completed here—O for grace to continue in the narrow way—and labor more arduously for my own as well as for my fellowmens advancement in Manliness, True & efficient soldierliness, and above all actual Godliness—

Twere such delight to close the old year, and begin the New with my dear precious little family—I do thank God for my darling wife and our precious Baby—

No letter from Pet today—I feel so disappointed—and yet so happy—The last one was so good—I close my eyes full of cheer on a/c of the blessings of the old year—and shall go to sleep—humming the good old doxology—Good night 62——

1863

January 1, 1863 Thursday. New Years Morning—Remarkably pleasant. Pain on my breast worse, otherwise I feel better—Slept til past 7 ock. Worked on Pay Rolls most of day—No letter from Pet. sorry.

January 2, 1863 Friday. Still in our old Camp.

But close to readiness to move out anytime now—I do a lot of writing on Rolls—I bought a pair of grained Cavalry Boots for $10— come up to my knees. Dandy. Eve letter from Pet—O such a gloriously good one—Answered Pets letter to mail in the morning. ORDERS. To march in the Morning at 8 A.M. Did a lot of final-packing-up touches of office things. Books, Rolls, &c

January 3, 1863 Saturday. Pleasant Morng—Roll Call—Breakfast—Horses in good shape—arms and accouterments in order—Tents down, and in general readiness to be off quickly—

Did not move out till 20 of 12—A Fine Column—

New Men of 3 months training—New Arms and Accouterments—Bright Flags & Guidons—marching "by Fours" about 1200 Men with some 44 Commissioned Officers and the necessary Wagons with Q.M. and commissary supplies following the Column—

Proudly and Bravely our Regiment moved along Pennsylvania Avenue—uproariously cheered by the populace and saluted by Soldiers singly and in squads enroute—

We crossed Long Bridge,[19] went through Alexandria and encamped for the night near Forts Lyons and Ellsworth[20]—Pretty tired Boys were we. I slept in the open air. The pale moon shining on my face—and frost, bordering on snow, falling all over me—

January 4, 1863 Sunday. Pitched Caps Tent. Did some writing on Co pay-rolls. We drew ammunition—Eve I wrote to Pet—am well and happy—Drawing ammunition brings up the idea of going into ACTUAL WARFARE, and makes one feel the importance of the situation—Life is at Stake.

Yet, I feel as though I would pass through this war safely. I seem assured of this in my inner self——

January 5, 1863 Monday. Very pleasant opening day. Regimental line formed and all men tried their arms, i.e., Carbines and Revolvers—Sharps & Colts—Quick dinner—Pack up—and at noon start—Passed camp of 2nd Pa. Cav—march through very ugly country—crossed the Aquiteck Creek—and lay over for the night—I mail a letter for Pet—Have severe pain in my breast and head—

Kept our Horses saddled all night—being in enemys country—ready for surprise—

19. Long Bridge spanned the Potomac River from the intersection of 14th Street S.E. and Maryland Avenue to a point of land approximately four miles upriver from the center of old Alexandria. It was then the only bridge across the Potomac from Washington itself; an aqueduct crossed upstream at Georgetown to a point six miles above Alexandria.

20. These forts guarded the Little River Turnpike and the Orange and Alexandria Railroad as those arteries approached Alexandria along Hunting Creek. What Cormany calls Fort Lyons was actually Fort Lyon, named for Nathaniel Lyon, the pro-Union commander of the St. Louis arsenal who was killed in August 1861, at the Battle of Wilson's Creek while trying to save Missouri for the Federal government. Cooling, *Symbol, Sword, and Shield*, p. 69; Ezra J. Warner, *Generals in Blue: Lives of the Union Commanders* (Baton Rouge, La., 1964), pp. 286–87.

January 6, 1863 Tuesday. Rubbed our horses down. Brekfast—
Brush up, and limber up good—Read & Meditate a little and start at
9 A.M. Soon run into where the Rebel Pickets had lain, not far from
ours, passed some burned wagons, old camp, &c. Passed old Pol-
nick Church[21]—Crossed the Ocquacon, an awful ford—went over
the late battle ground of the 17th & 2nd Pa Cav. with Genl
Steward—Saw some dead Horses—Stopped for the night where
their fight had commenced[22]—Had rained all P.M. Snowed and
stormed in the night—So we had "hardening experiences"—

January 7, 1863 Wednesday. Cold morning. Started betimes—
moved all day, rather slowly, passed old rebel camps—also passed
General Gearys Division of Infantry[23]—and reached Dumfries by
Sundown where we put up for the night. A little short of men and
horse-feed, but made the best of it all.

January 8, 1863 Thursday.[24] Lay all night in the brush—Both damp
and cool and in a fighting mood—
Were sent out scouting—Caught our first Reb—Major West left
him off on some score—scouting &c. &c. Caught sight of Genl

21. Old Pohick Church, where George Washington had been a member, was six
miles south of Mount Vernon on the main road from Alexandria to Fredericksburg.
Charles W. Stetson, *Washington and His Neighbors* (Richmond, 1956), pp. 157–62.

22. This action had been part of the so-called Dumfries Raid, an attempt by J. E. B.
Stuart to disrupt the Union supply and communication lines between Alexandria and
Fredericksburg. The clash had taken place on Dec. 28, 1862. Stuart was a clear victor;
the 17th Pennsylvania Cavalry apparently deserted the 2nd Pennsylvania Cavalry as
the skirmish began, and Stuart captured 100 prisoners before returning to the safety
of Confederate lines on New Year's Eve. H. B. McClellan, *I Rode with Jeb Stuart: The
Life and Campaigns of Major General J. E. B. Stuart* (New York, 1969), pp. 196–202.

23. John White Geary (1819–1873) was a Pennsylvania military and political figure
of national importance. He had been a prominent and successful officer during the
Mexican War, became the first elected mayor of San Francisco in 1850, served as
territorial governor in Kansas during 1856 and 1857, and was now building a distinguished Civil War record that would reach a peak at Gettysburg. After the war, Geary
was twice elected governor of Pennsylvania. *DAB*, IV, 203–04; Harry M. Tinkcom,
John White Geary: Soldier-Statesman, 1819–1873 (Philadelphia, 1940); David Montgomery, "Radical Republicanism in Pennsylvania, 1866–1873," *Pennsylvania Magazine of
History and Biography* 85 (1961), 439–57.

24. The 16th Pennsylvania Cavalry had now joined the main body of the Union
Army of the Potomac and this section begins Cormany's account of life at the front.
The Union army had been badly defeated at Fredericksburg on Dec. 13, 1862, and had
withdrawn to the northern bank of the Rappahannock River, occupying Falmouth
and Stafford Heights opposite Fredericksburg itself. Morale was at a low ebb, the
January weather was miserable, and confidence in Maj. Gen. Ambrose E. Burnside,
the commander responsible for the Fredericksburg debacle, was nearly nonexistent.

Seigels[25] Camp—but scented a chance for Meat on the Chamausie Creek—on our rounding tour—We killed 7 or 8 Beeves and 3 Hogs, and pressed a farmer to haul the meat to our Camp at Dunfries— Got back at dark almost exhausted—

January 9, 1863 Friday. A few men had remained at Camp with things. I turned in to sleep with Coble and McCleary—and though more than half sick—was on the job early with the rest of the Boys— and soon our column was on the March—I broke aside to a house for a cup of coffee—a fine looking lady gave me a cup of dandy coffee, and complimented me on my good looks besides—Oh! Thanks.

Passed a good many 5th & 6th Division soldiers near Stafford—I Bought 2 Pies for 50¢—Good—Good—We stopped for the night 1½ miles beyond Stafford—in a woods—

I about sick—and tired, and our Men and Horses seem ½ starved—Nice place to put up—Law me! how I want to see Darling & Pussy—

January 10, 1863 Saturday. Cloudy—On the move—Got to near Falmouth at noon and reported to Genl Butler—commenced to rain, about 4 P.M. Were turned into the woods to encamp—Everything wet and still raining. Yes pouring at times—Capt Sullenberger sick. I not at all well. The men and horses ½ starved. An awful time of it. Put up Caps and Lieutenants Tents, and lay in our wet clothes on the wet ground to sleep. Soon each pile of a man was warm— steaming—Sleeping sweetly—drying out—happy and I explored a lot of Dreamland.

January 11, 1863 Sunday. Rain over—Unlike Sunday, we went to work to put up Quarters—Captains Head Quarters is to be a big Shanty—We laid out the plan, and commenced on it. Did enough so we could be measurably comfortable—

Got fairly supplied with Feed and Rations, so we filled up—I am really quite unwell in throat and chest—and lean a little homesick- ward—Am so glad my dear little Family is more comfortable than I am today—

Now I get down to writing Pet a long Sunday letter—after closing my eyes a little while and looking at them and loving.

January 12, 1863 Monday. Feel better—Men busy fixing up as if to stay—I finished off Pay Rolls, and Quarterly Clothing a/c and

25. Gen. Franz Sigel commanded the Union's 11th Corps.

handed them in to Colonel—John Snyder, Bro of Lieut A. J. Snyder called to see us——Lieutenants and Men worked on Capts Qrs— same work going on for each Captain & The Lieuts—I long for a letter from Pet—re-read the old one.

January 13, 1863 Tuesday. Rather pleasant—Not feeling well— Worked on Capts Qrs most of day—and til midnight—I gathered and burned pine & other limbs to give the men light—Log walls— Ground roof—Stone Jambs, stick-clay-daubed chimney—

January 14, 1863 Wednesday. Fine—Dress Parade—on return worked on Cabin—Put up Bunk and Bed—Still no letter from Pet. O How I long for one, and still more to love, kiss and caress Darling and Baby—

Evening, Sergt Peters played violin several hours for us—Orderly Serg't Barnes danced some for us—Jolly time—

January 15, 1863 Thursday. Cloudy—I worked all A.M. putting up shelves &c &c. in cabin— P.M. Went over to Tylers Brig. Suttler.[26] Bought 40 lbs Potatoes for $2.00—Eve Mail came in from Washington for Regiment—Two such good ones from Pet—one from John & Bell Kimmel—I wrote til past 11 ock for Pet——

January 16, 1863 Friday. Rained—No Dress Parade—stormy— Mailed letter to Pet. Our Hd Qrs Cabin does well—No. 1—The men are busy on putting up quarters—I had good time reading in my Bible and in prayers till 10 ock—

January 17, 1863 Saturday. Colder—Daubbed cabin outside, and banked up ground all around 3 sides—am pretty well—Capt is worse—wrote some for Pet—I am as happy as a soldier—as a Man—as a husband & father, and as a Christian, seeking to become better—

January 18, 1863 Sunday. Bitter Cold! Sundayed up—Then had General Inspection. Wrote some for her—I do so want to see her

26. Sutlers were civilian merchants appointed under army regulations to sell goods not provided by the army itself to soldiers in the field. Each regiment was permitted to appoint one sutler who traveled with the regiments during active campaigning and built semipermanent stores during periods of winter encampment, as here. Although the troops appreciated the availability of such articles as tobacco, books, butter and liquor (the last item was sold illegally), they resented the usually astronomical prices and terrible quality of sutler goods. Donald P. Spear, "The Sutler in the Union Army," *CWH* 16 (June 1970), 121–38.

and pussy—Want her to Come. Capt wants Mrs S. too to Come. P.M. Barnes & I sought for a place in a home nearby—to keep them—
Failed.

January 19, 1863 Monday. Cold—Wrote part of day—am pretty well. Received, Oh! such a good dear letter from Pet, and a slip from Minnie Hansen[27]—am so glad Pet is so well—happy and contented—Eve. worked on quarterly report awhile.

January 20, 1863 Tuesday. Cold—Wrote some—Chopped a lot of wood in A.M.—P.M. was out on Drill—seemed fine—as we have had but little for sometime on a/c of being on the go so much—having unfavorable weather—and fixing Winter Quarters.
The Col took the Regiment to see the Grand Division move— There seems to be a general move of The Army all around—we do not.[28] Company drew 6 Gallons old Rye Whiskey for the Men— Wrote letter to Pet—Well and happy.

January 21, 1863 Wednesday. Rained all night—Awful muddy. Bought a Pipe and tobacco to smoke on a/c of my Throat—Cabin leaks some—rain soaking thru. Capts better—Eve Lieut Snyder boozy. We had a big time in Caps Tent—

January 22, 1863 Thursday. Rained all night—Awful soldiering this[29]—At 11 AM our 2nd Squadron ordered out on picket duty—all the officers—Co H—and 60 men went.
I left in charge of quarters and got the Kitchen into Hd Qrs Cabin. Eve Yank Smith pestered me til 10 ock—I wrote some to Pet— Oh! That I could see her—

January 23, 1863 Friday. Cleared—pleasant—Saw that all men curried and attended their horses well. I chopped some wood for our Hd Qrs. P.M. got a good letter from Pet—3 from Canada—all OK—

27. The friend from Otterbein who was then staying with Rachel in Chambersburg.
28. In a desperate attempt to make up for his blunder at Fredericksburg, Burnside gained Lincoln's permission to attempt a rare winter offensive. The general movement Cormany detects was the beginning of that maneuver.
29. The rain on January 21 and 22 rendered the clay roads of Virginia impassable, and Burnside's offensive quite literally bogged down. Nicknamed the "Mud March," this fiasco destroyed all remaining confidence in General Burnside, whose resignation was accepted by the president on Jan. 25, 1863.

Eve Saw that all in camp did things well—Then wrote Pet til time for sleep—

January 24, 1863 Saturday. Laid in some stock. Commissary Saddler Long and I got up a high breakfast—I wrote most of AM—Noon Capt returned from Picket—very unwell.

I am so well and hardy now—and happy withal—more devotional—

January 25, 1863 Sunday. Foggy—Capt very unwell—Wrote most of day to Pet and Canada folk—Ed Miller is off—I drew his little Bounty for him—Gave it to Captain—a little crookedness in the case I allow[30]—

January 26, 1863 Monday. Talk is another move soon—Cap S and I draw a plan for a new Hd Qrs Cabin should we move—Good letter from Pet and Mrs Sullenberger—Eve our men come in from picket all sound—

January 27, 1863 Tuesday. Drizzly day—Finished and mailed Pet large letter. Company arranged to divide up into "Messes" P.M. received Orders to march tomorrow at 8 AM—Eve well and happy—

January 28, 1863 Wednesday. Snows awfully—Regiment moved this AM—Capt Sullenberger & I remained in quarters till over Noon—Still snowing—P.M. we got into new camp—Mud 6 to 20 inches deep—Eve the snow is now 6 to 8 inches deep—perfectly awful—a few growl, but the mass sing, whistle—and "drive ahead" all for our Country—We—Capt, Lieuts, and I slept in "Wall Tent"[31]—

January 29, 1863 Thursday. Worked—as best we could for the Snow & Mud—Putting up our Officers Quarters—Capts—Lieuts— and Barnes sick and had an awful day of it—So much wet snow on ground and trees—Eve I was wet from head to foot, and all the others were about the same but we turned in and doubled up in our

---

30. Edward R. Miller was eventually listed officially as a deserter. *H16PC*, p. 20. Cormany noted on the margin of his transcript that Miller was "never heard from" again. He is obviously puzzled as to why his captain should end up with Miller's bounty bonuses.

31. Only officers were issued the desirable, semiprivate wall tents. *Army Regulations* (1861), paras. 1607, 1609; John O. Billings, *Hardtack and Coffee: The Unwritten Story of Army Life*, Richard Harwell, ed. (Chicago, 1960), pp. 38–42.

Wall Tent, a little crowded of course but soon became warm and slept gloriously—save some twisting and groaning and snoring in spots—

January 30, 1863 Friday. All up and at it. Lieut Snyder and I worked all day on our Quarters and the men also—all getting on finely Eve—somewhat in shape—Am very tired, but dried out now and wrote a while to Pet—Rumors of another move, also of some Furloughs, Oh! to see Pet—

January 31, 1863 Saturday. Pleasant day—Slept little last night. So full of thoughts of Pet and Pussy—Worked most of day on cabin— Made out Forage requisition for Co H—p.m. Got letter from Pet, O the dear Darling! Would that I could see her and our Baby Pussy— Eve Wrote Furloughs—Hope to get one and go to my Dear Ones soon—

February 1, 1863 Sunday. I worked hard all day on our Hd Qrs Cabin. Seemed little like Sunday—Men out picketing—Eve do some reading and praying—and resolving to be a more pious man, a brighter light to the Men about me.

February 2, 1863 Monday. Colder—
I am quite unwell today—Cant do much work. Capt & Lieut helped some. Sergt Peters put up a chimney. Seems quite like a house—Capt got Leave of Absence.

February 3, 1863 Tuesday. Very Cold—We slept in our new cabin Fl'd Qrs I saw Captain to station & off home—My Little Max (horse) ran or jumped over me—tramped my leg—bruised me so I can scarcely walk. Very painful. Did little work—some strolling—

February 4, 1863 Wednesday. Coldest yet—Am very stiff and bruised—Kept in quarters all day—John Morehead called to see me—Lieut and Men came in off Picket. Nearly frozen—

February 5, 1863 Thursday. Snowed all day—Am very stiff still— Sat around the fire all day—Many officers called in to see me and our quarters—all pronounce H Co's Hd Qrs the best yet.

February 6, 1863 Friday. Blustry and rainy all the Night—Slept poorly. I kept thinking of Pet & Pussy, and dreamed of Pussy—was tossing her. She laughed and crowed greatly. No day to be out doing——

P.M. Got my Furlough to go home—Rec'd a great letter from Pet— I start for Chambersburg in the Morning—nothing happening to hinder——Praise the Lord, and thanks to Uncle Sam.

February 7, 1863 Saturday. Pretty Cold—Left Camp for Station at 6 A.M. Took train at 8 for Landing.[32] Missed Boat, but got on Tug at Noon, and reached Washington D.C. at 7 P.M.—Put up at Soldiers Retreat—Good q'r's, but poor order—Several fights. Little sleep.

February 8, 1863 Sunday. Breakfasted at "Soldiers Retreat." Took 8 A.M. train for Baltimore arrived at 10—Had to lay over til 9 P.M.— Strolled about the City—Had an oyster dinner, fine—Long talk with a Dover Delaware Man—Arrived at Harrisburg at 3 AM—

February 9, 1863 Monday. Lounged around napping occasionally—Breakfast at National Hotel—Took 8 ock train for Chambersburg arrived at 11. I was surprised to John Karpers[l] at Depot— Expecting "Billy's"[m] Corpse. (Poor fellow. We left him in hospital near Washington—very homesick, and a little unwell—Now he has closed out—and I did not know of it) When they saw me step off the train they supposed I was bringing him home for burial—and I was so surprised to be thus met by a company of Kinsfolk to face the loss of "Will Karper"[m] and bear him out to the Karper home—
"Wills"[m] Uncle Bill Karper acted real meanly to me as tho I was the cause of it all.
Sure I was desirous "Will"[m] should go with me—become a soldier good and true—but he hadn't the stuff in him—and for lack of it, colapsed.
I have this comfort to carry. I did all in my power to be helpful in the effort to make a soldier of him—But all efforts failed, and when he became ill—from worry, and we could not do what was best for him in Camp, I got him into Hospital, called to see him every few days—often took other Boys with me and we tried to interest and amuse him—and get him to "brace up"—but when we left Washington for the Front I bade him goodbye—The Hospital Fellows assured me "Will"[m] will be well cared for"—and I have no question they did what they promised. But poor Will's[m] mind was made up—and he simply run down, and out, and went Home. After The Karpers[l] left without the Body.

---

32. The Fredericksburg and Potomac Railroad ran approximately fifteen miles to Aquia Creek Landing, the Union army's major supply base at this time, which was about thirty-five miles by water down the Potomac estuary from Washington.

I struck up street. Surprised some folks! Found Pet and Pussy well and looking O so well and happy—I believe Pussy knew me. She just fairly clung to me. Spent the evening O so very happily with my dear little Family. Mrs Orderly Barnes called—was full of inquiries about her S.B. and others.

February 10, 1863 Tuesday. Cloudy—Had a very sweet nights rest—How delightful to lie in the embrace of one so good, so dear, so true, and to have our little one climbing all over and about us before going to sleep—

Rained lightly all day. I was busy all the day attending to matters for Pet, Baby and myself—and for some of the Boys—Saw Captain Sullenberger—Billy Karpers[m] Corpse came today. I made arrangements for us to go to Funeral tomorrow—Eve Capt called, also Henry Rebok[pa]—Spent the Eve very pleasantly. How blessed I am! I do and how thankful that our God has blest me with such a dear good Darling Wife and Sweet Little Baby Girl.

February 11, 1863 Wednesday. Cool—threatens snow—We went to Wm Karpers[m] Funeral. A large gathering of relatives and Friends. Revs Snyder—Kuntz & Zacharias officiated—We went home with Mothers.[b] Had a delightful evening visit—Snowed and stormed all P.M. I am pretty well and O! so happy.

February 12, 1863 Thursday. Pretty cold—Started home at 9 ock. Had such a delightful P.M.—Rev J. Dickson visited us and prayed with us. We had such a glorious time altogether, especially during prayers

February 13, 1863 Friday. Spent A.M. going about arranging things, seeing friends and loving my dear ones—P.M. We went to St Thomas to visit Brother Bernards[q]—Mrs Dave and John Woodall call to see me and hear direct from their soldier husbands, and send money with me for them to come home on Furlough as soon as they can be secured, also Mrs Rohrabaugh $10. Saw Harry McClearys also—Eve Barny[q] and I called a while at The Store and Hotel and chated with Dr Van Trice, Joe and Peter Holler—Lydia Strock was at Barneys[q]—Had some pleasant talk with her—no reference to our past—

I was arrested by Patrol—Of course my Furlough let me out—

February 14, 1863 Saturday. Cold My visit with Bernards[q] Family has been delightful and Rachel my Darling enjoyed it also, only my old girl being around seemed a little wee bit embarassing.

Returned reaching Chamb'g 11 A.M. P.M. called on Mrs Lieut Snyder—and laid in some Gin and Brandy for medicinal use—Sister Sarah[u] took supper with us. Darling busy baking til bed time. Buns—cakes &c for me to take along—My! how well I am and Oh how happy to be with my little Family these few days

February 15, 1863 Sunday. Cool—Slushy—Left Baby with sister Lydia Rebok[p] and Pet and I went to U.B. Church—Brother Dickson preached a good sermon—We took dinner at Henrys (Reboks).[pa] P.M. had a number of callers, amongst them Cous B. Y. Hamsher. real pleasant talks, chiefly about the war—my soldiering &c &c Eve. Pet, Pussy and I certainly did have a romping time of it— Our little one surely does enter into the joy of it all—Pet & I certainly are the happiest two in one in the world—I want to be worthy of her love & devotion.

February 16, 1863 Monday. Snowy—unpleasant—Capt. Sullenberger and I arrange to go together— on [10] ock train—
It went hard to part, but hope of soon meeting again not to part soon, gives us joy—Surely this war will soon be over, and I will be home to stay——at 10 ock I got on the train. Capt failed, so I got off at Shippinsburg, and returned in the Evening—Pet and Baby so very glad to see me back—Rainy—had a charming evening together—and I had a long talk with John Plough, discussed some of Darlings difficulties, owing to some of his forgetfulness or neglects—am quite certain matters will now and hereafter be more satisfactory—

February 17, 1863 Tuesday. Snowy & blustry Goodbye hugs and kisses repeated, and Capt & I took 8 ock train—Dined at National. The 2:20 train left us—our time a little slow—Capt S. and Capt Fischer & chums were roving, drinking &c. &c.—Got Cap to bed at 9:30—I wrote to Pet and retired at 10 ock—awful sorry to thus miss being on time on my return—

XIV

Rachel in Chambersburg

February 14–June 13, 1863

*E*xcept *for visits with other 16th Pennsylvania wives, Rachel has little contact with the rest of the world, and she writes despairingly on March 6, 1863, that circumstances were forcing her to "live the life of a hermit in a large town."*

———————◆·◆·◆———————

February 14, 1863   Monday. Since I last wrote in my journal I have been very busy sewing & getting ready to go to visit my dear precious husband in the army on the Potomac. Last Monday was the day set to start, but to my great joy he came to visit me—arrived here on last Monday noon. His Capt. came a few days before or I suppose we would have started. I am better satisfied as it is than if I had gon to Va. to see him. The week was spent *very pleasantly*—On last Wednesday W. F. Karper[m] was burried. We were to the funeral. In the evening we went to Mothers.[b] Henry R.[pa] took Strocks horse & buggy home & we took theirs to go to Mothers[b]—had a very pleasant visit. Fryday we went to St. Thomas.   Sat, after we got home, I baked pies bread & cakes—Sister Sarah[u] took supper with us—Sunday Lydia[p] kept Cora while we went to church—Dickson preached—Took dinner at Henry Reboks[pa]—Came home soon after dinner—I took a nap, had a number of calls—All forenoon Pet & Capt. were packing & fixing to start. My heart felt sad all day—Thomsons[v] took dinner with us.   As soon as dinner was over we had to say "Goodbye." How could I prevent those tears even if the room was full of people. Henry R.[pa] came before I had the table cleared off so I got him to eat dinner too. Thompson[v] went with my Sml to the depot. As soon as he returned all left & I was again *all alone*. All afternoon in spite of me the tears would come. I feel so very very lonely——

February 17, 1863   As I had the above written, my dear Husband stepped into my room again. O! but I was glad—it seemed like a meeting after a long absence. It is so sweet to *love* and *be loved*. This morning he left.   he bade me goodbye with the expectation of coming back before leaving, but he came not & by this time I suppose he is on the way to Baltimore. It did not seem near so hard to part in the way we did for I thought he would come back. still I feel lonely. I heated my dried fruit &c to keep off loneliness. I feel so much relieved when I think that it will not be long until he will come home to stay, for he is going to get a discharge—I do not feel well this evening—have not for a few days have a bad cold & a very sore mouth.

February 18, 1863   Sultry & rainy. Mouth better. Baby good. Mended clothes all day—Annie P. went to Shipensburg for a sleigh-ride with Hazelet—wore my hood—Evening—Rec'd a letter from my Sm'l. Through the carelessness of his Capt. had to lie over in Harisburg where he wrote me from—He speaks of the wicketness of military men & asks my sincerest prayers for his preservation—O! for more religion—I feel very much on the background—My greatest desires are to become more spiritual.

February 19, 1863   It is still cloudy & rainy. Did a large washing—Ate dinner with Ploughs. I wanted to excuse myself but they would not take it. Annie kept the baby for me all day—My Smls army clothes were very hard to wash & would not get nice so I laid them out on the snow to bleach. I cleaned my room & have everything pretty well fixed up. My mouth is much better. I am very tired this evening. O! for more religion. I think much on the all-important subject—I desire to be good & do good.

February 20, 1863   Cora does not seem well—is fretful. I think she must have earache by the way she acts, poor baby—am making a sunbonnet for her. I am well—feel lonely—

February 21, 1863   Hung up my clothes & such a time as I had with them—they were all covered with coal dust—I could not get it all off. Cora is worse—I fear she will be real sick—O! that my Samuel were here—I feel very often like crying with the poor little sufferer.

February 22, 1863   Cora is still worse—looks badly—has a real bad cough. I sometimes fear we will not be able to keep her. I give her watertreatment. If my Samuel could only be at home now. I wrote letters to him & to Clem.[cc] It snowed much last night & all day as fast as posible. Snow is pretty deep. Quit snowing this evening.

February 23, 1863   Cold. Cora quite sick—has a rash on her much like the measles.   her ear has been running for two or three days, her eyes are red & watery—nose running—has considerable fever—I bathed her when she wakened this morning & put the wet bandage on her & compress on her breast. At ten oclock gave her a wet sheet pack & put on compress & bandage again.   Afternoon changed compress & bandage—evening—A tepid bath followed by cold doushe, gave her a tepid injection & put the bandage & compress on her again—She sleeps a good part of the time & seems to sleep sweetly— is very restless when awake—wants to be with me all the time. I know she feels real sick. Her feet will not stay warm. I pray the Good Lord for wisdom in treating her. I feel disappointed that I got no letter from my Sml. How can I help feeling anxious about him.

February 24, 1863   Cora has been quite sick all day—is red full of measles. Still she has fever & her feet are inclined to be cold. I bathed her this morning. Did not put the wet bandages on until the fever came again.   bathed her in the afternoon & this evening again—She takes but very little nourishment & what she takes she mostly throws up. She is now sleeping sweetly. I got some saffron and made tea for her but she would not take it—so I put the compresses on her again & a warm brick to her feet. It seems very lonely to be all alone with a sick child. O! that my Samuel were here— Motherin-law[b] took dinner with me today & brought me a crock full of milk—some smearcase[1] & a few apples. She is a good mother. She thinks so much of Samuel

March 2, 1863   Delightful spring morning—calm and beautiful. The sun is just peering over the mountain top. Clouds overspread the greater part of the heavens & at this moment are arrayed in the richest colors. The birds are singing sweetly. All nature seems to thank their maker for the sweet repose & preserving care of the night. I just returned from the P.O.   Mailed a letter with $40 of money in for my Samuel.[2] I dreamed of him last night—but the beauties of the morning have quite driven out my dream however delightful it may have been. I am well. Cora has been playing in the cradle for the last hour—I hope she will be good today—She is not right well yet—is cutting teeth but is quite over the measles. I feared for a few days that we would loose her & now constipation of the bowels seems to have taken a firm hold—I keep applying the water in different ways to remove the difficulty—Yesterday she was very

1. German for cottage (and sometimes cream) cheese.
2. Although Union soldiers were, for the most part, provisioned by the army, they had to buy some supplies from sutlers. Moreover, as Samuel's diary shows, cavalrymen frequently bought their own horses rather than ride government-issued mounts they disliked. Hence funds were at times sent from home, further depleting the family's already strained resources.

fretful. It was rainy windy & stormy—The introduction to young lady March was rather disagreeable & it is clouding up pretty thickly now. Cora has been pretty well today—Still she cries much & wants to sit on my lap all the time, or be carried out—she is weak & looks pale.

March 3, 1863 It has been cloudy & stormy all day & this evening it is raining a little. Cora is worse—her bowels are so constipated which throws her into fever—I scarcely know what more to do with her. I keep the wet bandage on her abdomen almost constantly— give her sitzbaths daily—packed her today. Gave her an injection which moved her bowels well—her gums seem very sore—being much swollen. Can see the teeth shining through. George came home this noon—quite unexpectedly—he belongs to the 126th Reg. P.V—[3] They seem all joy over there ever since. No doubt it seems like getting into another world to get out of the army & be home a few days again. Wrote to M. E. Hanson—Intend writing to Sister Susie[nn] this evening.

March 4, 1863 Wednesday. Finished & mailed the letter to Susie.[nn] Bernard Cormany[q] returned from the Potomac. He went down for a sick soldier, but the one he went for was well—insted of a sick one he brought two dead—O! the troubles of this war. Our men had a skirmish & a Mr. Hammond out of Co. H. was killed. some more are missing.[4] Cora has been very crabled today—cried nearly all A.M. P.M. played some —evening cried again. My room seems in- fested with ants—

March 5, 1863 Thursday. Cold—Yet clear & sun shining—will be warm—Cora did not sleep well—Cried much this morning—but is playing now—Can see that she does not feel well yet—her teeth are not through yet—Evening—Mrs Sulenberger called twice today once to get Capt's address & with Mrs. Barns. Mrs. B seems in good spirits. Pussy is much better—played a good deal—I mended stock- ings & made new out of old ones all day—

March 6, 1863 Fryday. It snowed last night & has been cloudy all day—is not cold. Cora cried so much today. her bowels are consti- pated. I gave her an injection which would not opperate for so long—I have a great deal of trouble with her—it almost seems as if

---

3. Pennsylvania Volunteers.
4. See Samuel's entry for Feb. 25, 1863. Charles Hammond of Company H was killed. *H16PC*, p. 15.

all ills come upon her. I some times feel as if we had done wrong to bring such a little angel on earth to suffer—To have all this upon me, & Samuel away. O! I cannot help getting blue sometimes. I try to be happy. The question sometimes comes to my mind—Does he really love me? I was brought here among strangers. After a month's visiting was left here in a town of strangers—in a back room, among a selfish family, with my babe. I cannot get out without I take her along—She is heavy to carry—so I stay in my old back room from Monday till Sat. & from Sat. till Monday—hear & see nothing. In short live the life of a hermit in a large town. Well—well! No better room could be gotten, but how could he leave me thus. I must write no more. I am too blue—Hope morning will bring better feelings.

March 10, 1863 Tuesday. Spent yesterday afternoon at Mrs. Barns' to help her finish her hood—She is wonderful slow at seeing into anything—just like a child. So I proposed to finish her cap if she would finish my baby stockings. She was glad for the chance, so today I finished it & took it home—She seemed very much pleased with it—I got no letter—feel much disappointed but heard through others that my Sml is well—My little Cora is not at all well, has taken cold & is teething—Still her bowels are constipated.

March 11, 1863 Made Naoma Rebok[pb] a pair of slippers—Also a pair for Hatie

March 12, 1863 Washed & finishe a pair of Slippers for My Samuel. am very tired. got a letter from My Sml at last. Such a good one. Cora is still not right well. I think she has the whooping cough. Weather cold—

March 13, 1863 Quite cold—put a cradle quilt in the frame—Rec'd another letter from Samuel—Also from Mo—Kimmels. Feel pretty happy. Sml writes such good letters, his religion certainly is a reality with him.

March 14, 1863 Pleasant. Not so cold. I baked & ironed & finished the quilting of the cradle quilt. Rec'd papers from My Sml. O! such good ones.

March 15, 1863 Pleasant this morning. P.M. It is thundering & snowing. I never heard of such a phenomenon before It seems very strange. It is snowing very fast just now

March 25, 1863 Wednesday evening—It has been unpleasant & rainy all week until today it cleared off & was warm & pleasant— The birds were singing merrily—the tiny grass blades are beginning to peep out from the ground. I baked today had good luck. Rec'd a letter from Bina Reeder. No war news of any account. I mailed letters on Monday to (J. W. Adams'[kk] & Fathers[aa])—Samuel—& Kimmels & 3 papers to Sml. Cora is getting better of the whooping cough.

March 28, 1863 Saturday. It is snowing all morning very fast— snowed part of the night. Sleighbells are ringing again. My little Cora was sick all night—had high fever. I got up several times when she would get very restless & bathed her in cold water after which she would sleep awhile again. It seems to me abdominal truss which I am wearing on her to cure Umbilical Hernia hurts her.[5] I wear it as loosely as posible. The part under the knob in the instrument is quite red—She cuts her teeth so hard too—her gums are very sore. One (of the three late ones) tooth is through. The gum around it looks like an old wound—very sore. I do pity her so very much— She seems quite sick this morning, is sleeping now & seems to sleep sweetly. hope she will be better when she wakens. Received a letter from Sml on Thursday evening & yesterday evening one from S.S.W's.[ee] L[dd] writes but short. I am writing a letter to brother Amos[hh] in Cal.[6] allso 1 to H. Hively & 1 to M. Hanson & 1 to Samuel before I go to Orstown if I can   if not, I will write while there—The birds are singing.   Evening   Cora is better again. Mrs. McGowan called a few minutes. Just now (8 P.M.) Annie called in to see me—I did not know her she had such a funny old fashioned dress & large collar on—her hair parted and put up the duchest   O she looked like a fright—she put a bonnet & cloak on to suit & called at

---

5. An umbilical hernia can produce a protrusion at the umbilicus, caused by a defect in the abdominal wall. The truss was designed to push the protrusion back in, where the abdominal wall might heal over it. William A. N. Dorland, *Dorland's Illustrated Medical Dictionary*, 25th ed. (Philadelphia, 1974), pp. 706, 1650.

6. Rachel's brother Amos had joined the staff of the Sacramento *Union*, one of the leading newspapers of the far west. He continued his career in journalism, earned degrees in civil and mining engineering in Europe, headed the California geologic survey for five years, helped establish the Cariboo mining district of British Columbia, was a ranking member of the Canadian geologic survey, and founded the town of Anacortes (a phonetic version of his wife's maiden name), Wash., where he finally settled down. He died in 1894. See *BHWT*, I, 28, and *The Anacortes Story*, Dan Wollam, comp. (n.p., n.d.), which reprints a portion of Amos's reminiscences that first appeared in the Anacortes *Progress*, Aug. 14, 1890.

Wamplers[7]—Such a laughing as they are having—Indeed I laughed until my face ached of being stretched so—

March 30, 1863 Monday. Got up at six oclock A.M. took two letters to the office & got some soap at Hubers, 1 lb of Harisons soap to try. like it well. I washed, took up my carpet & cleaned my room & have my carpet down again. O! but I am tired—my feet fairly ache. Cora was very fretful all day—she does not seem well at all—I very much wish for Mr. Cormany home since the baby is sick so much. I sometimes hardly know what to do with her. If she were only not ruptured. It seems só hard to have to wear that truss on her. I hope she will be cured. Those mean ants are out again this evening. I just killed three. I judge they will live high while I am gone.

May 3, 1863 I left on the 1st April as per expectation with H. W. Rebok.[pa] baby was very troublesome on the way but slept well the first night. I staid at Reboks[pa] from Wednesday 1st until Tuesday morning April 7th during which time she & I made visits in Orrstown, & Mr. Wises & Dan Keefers & called at R. Hubers & Mr Sherks. A few days after she and I went to Sam Reboks a distance of 3 or 4 miles. She drove—On Tuesday morn they took me to J. Karpers.[l] K-s would have fetched me but I told them I could as well go with the childer when they were taken to school. Staid at J. Ks[l] until Thursday 9th When Hannah K.[k] took me to J. Cormanys,[d] where I staid until Sunday 12th. Went with them to Salem to preaching & from there they took me to D. Byers'[ba] (Mother-inlaws)[b] Staid at Byers' until 27th Byers brought me to town. I enjoyed the visit well at all places—especially J. Cormanys[d] & Mothers.[b] On the 25th I rec'd a letter from My Samuel that they expected to get into a great fight. I could stay no longer, for I could not hear of the army movements & could not get my mail for so long. It seems nice to be in my own room again. I forgot to state that the baby got better every day & now is quite well & fat & lively stands alone & walks along the chairs & wall &c. Today she is a year old. She has been a little crabit. the day was beautiful— Yea lovely—All nature smiled. This P.M. we had a heavy thunder-gust—The air is so very pure now—I get letters from my Sml quite frequently—Still they had no battle yet—I fear the next news will be of one for I see in the paper that all but a reserve of the

7. The Wamplers lived across Front Street and a few houses down from the Ploughs. *AFCP*, p. 24.

Potomac army have crossed the Rapphannoc.[8] My God protect my husband. It almost seems as though I were trouble hardened. I am cheerful & at least not very unhappy, trusting in God for the result. I get a daily paper which keeps me pretty well posted.[9] My greatest trouble is that I am not a better christian. O to be better.

May 5, 1863 I am busy making a traveling dress, thinking I may need it—for should my Samuel be wounded I will go to him if possible. I feel uneasy about him all the time since the fighting has commenced in earnest. Wonder whether they are out in this drenching rain. poor fellows how can they live through all those hardships. My constant prayer is for the preservation of My Dear husband. Cora is well.

May 11, 1863 A beautiful day. I washed (& cleand house) feel tired. just at dusk the bells rang so that I thought surely there must be fire somewhere, but none could I see or hear of—when lo— Babylon (Richmond) the great is fallen is fallen. our men have taken the capital of the Conthieveracy. I can hear speaking & cheering from my room.[10] It rained nearly yes all week until Saturday. I got & made me a traveling suit & am all ready to go to my dear Samuel should anything befal him. Cora is crabit as usual on washday, is full of prickly heat. Cried nearly all evening but sleeps now.

May 23, 1863 A great day—The 126th Reg. Pa. Vol. are returning home.[11] Every body seems to be on the street in their Sunday best. I feel blue—here I am all alone—cannot get out unless I carry my big

8. The Union army had begun a major offensive, known later as the Chancellorsville campaign.

9. The press reported Union maneuvers promptly, often to the consternation of Union commanders who hoped to surprise their opponents. Like Rachel, Lee read the major nothern dailies to keep up with the movements of the Union army, and he was said to have gained as much knowledge of his enemy's activities from the press as he did from his own scouts and spies.

10. This rumor was false. As part of his plan for a grand offensive in the spring of 1863, General Hooker, then in command of the Army of the Potomac, had sent Brig. Gen. George Stoneman with two cavalry divisions on a long raid behind Lee's main force, which was concentrated around Fredericksburg. Although Stoneman missed an opportunity to destroy Lee's supply wagons, he did manage to reach the outskirts of Richmond. There he threw a temporary panic into the thinly defended city. Reports that Stoneman had reached the Confederate capital no doubt triggered the premature celebration that Rachel notes.

11. See David Rowe, *A Sketch of the 126th Regiment Pennsylvania Volunteers* (Chambersburg, 1869).

baby & even when I do go I have to stray along like some lost sheep by myself. So many things combine to make me blue. Last evening Emma P. kept the baby for me while I went on an errant down street. When I got home, they had taken the baby to my room & laid her in the cradle & left her—shut the doors so they would not hear her cry. She (the baby) got frightened & cried dreadfully & this morning her abdominal rupture is worse again. I suppose the girls thought they would make a fine haul on my dried fruit again but I got ahead of them & locked it up & took the key along, quite too much of it has been carried off for me. If Orpho Wampler & Emma Plough don't make bad women I shall be much mistaken. Another thing that makes me feel badly is that My Samuel has been duped so by his captains. It makes me too mad. Philip Karpers[j] were here last Monday & wanted me to go home with them—"right or wrong"— on a visit of two or three weeks. When it all came out they had just gotten their spring lot of sewing, so it would be quite convenient to get me to visit there & make their clothes. Nary a time do I make such visits when I can help it. I visited there two weeks last fall & helped to do their fall sewing. After this when I go visiting I want to visit & when I am to go out to sew, I want it understood that I go to sew & not to visit.

10½ A.M. The 126th just arrived. All the town bells are ringing. I wish I could have gone down street to see the arrangements. May go this P.M. The flags are all nicely trimmed with beautiful mottoes. A great dinner awaits them at the Franklin Hall. Well the ringing of the bells is dispersing the clouds somewhat.

Evening. At noon Mrs. McGowan called in & took Cora along so I went down street. the crowd was very great. everybody seemed joyful. the soldiers seemed very glad to get home once again. I got Mr. Cormanys picture also money & letters—he is not well—hope he will get home soon. he also had a talk with Capt. & Lieut. about their conduct toward him. I hope they will do him justice, he also sent me a relic of the Chancelorsville battle in the shape of a very odd book. He writes me a good letter. Cora walks. Commenced on the 19th.

Mrs. McG & I were out calling—It has been very warm.

May 25, 1863 5 A.M. The bells all over town are ringing & have been ringing more than an hour over the fall of Vicsburg.[12] Now

12. Again the rumor was premature. General Grant had just completed a brilliant circular sweep that carried him to the outskirts of Vicksburg. Unable to storm the city directly, however, he initiated siege tactics. The great fortress city, thought to be impregnable, finally fell on July 4, 1863.

Samuel Cormany. Probably the photograph Rachel received May 23, 1863.
Kiefer Family.

they are tolling, wonder what now. Now all is quiet save the music of birds. Now they are tolling again—Last evening we had a sprinkling of rain—everything is growing so nicely.

May 29, 1863 Was to P.O. got nothing but my Telescope feel "blue" As if every body shunned me—as if ashamed to let others know their acquaintance with me. O! If Samuel wre only at home so we could go west. I do not feel like dressing in my best to go to P.O. & the long & short—if people that do not wish to recognize me in my calico need not do so at all—I wish I were not quite so sensitive.

May 30, 1863 It is cloudy & looks for rain this morning. Hope it will rain, we need it very much. The earth is very dry. Just as I had put by my writing last evening I thought I heard mice in my cobboard. I raised the curtain & such a skedadling. At first I thought they were young mice but soon found that they were black roaches. such a time as I had killing them. they are an *ugly* thing.

June 1, 1863 Morning 6 oclock. It is right cool after the heavy rain of yesterday & day before. Pussy May did not sleep well at all last night. She coughs so hard. has taken cold. is still sleeping. I wrote a long letter yesterday for Samuel. will mail it today. I am working at my hair wreath. It begins to look pretty. July Wampler & Annie Plough were in to see it & nearly went off about it being so pretty I want to finish it as soon as I can, so as to get at my drawing. P.M. Was to Mrs McG's for milk. she is going to join with me in taking a daily paper. She kept Cora while I went down st.—Evening she & I went to classmeeting—took Cora along—but she would not be good so Mrs. McG. took her to the kitchen & kept her so I could get to class once—We truly had a good meeting. There was a german preacher from Baltimore present—an odd genious, but very pious. he got very happy, spoke english, but it came out rather broken. O that I could once get real happy too.

June 2, 1863 Evening Do not feel at all well. Cora still does not seem well. have been walking about a little this evening. Was to see Granny Royer & got Reubarb from her for 5 cts, to make pies.

June 5, 1863 Yesterday I was nearly sick enough to go to bed & was in bed part of the time my teeth ached so dreadfully—In the evening I took a hot footbath & put a cold compress on my face & went to bed early. I had been in bed but a short time when Mrs. Sulenberger came. she told me of her troubles—she & Sulenberger had quite a spat about the children. she felt badly—he was out so late at night still at the tavern too, but they talked it over & she says they have it plastered up again. O! it is dreadful for man & wife to fall out. She talked here until 10 oclock[13]—Cora then got awake I nursed her & then both of us went to sleep. she slept until about 4 this morning. nursed & went to sleep & is still sleeping—My face is very much swollen this morning otherwise I feel better. I received a letter from My Samuel too—he is nearly well again, they were out on a scout & expected to have a battle soon—Last evening, Mrs. McGowan sent me a basket of potatoes, nearly ½ pk I judge. she is so kind. I must now get me some breakfast—not having eaten anything since yesterday noon & then only a bite

June 11, 1863 On Monday morning early Bro. Dickson called. He was barely out of the house when Fred Karper called—he paid me 50¢ for making Maggies silk sack The doors were scarcely shut after him when Miss Flora called, & as soon as she was gone John Cormanys[d] came & staid until after 3 P.M.

Tuesday P.M. Mrs. John Huber called—In the evening Mrs Capt. Sulenberger & her Fanny who is a *very bad girl*. Wednesday morning, an old school friend Mr. Whistler called. I was glad to see him. Anthony Holler brought him up. P.M. of same day I got my photographs. got six of $1. Also saw the suprintendent about schools for the girls (sisters Mollie[ii] & Susie[nn]). he thought there was no doubt but that they could get schools. Evening Rec'd two letters from Sml.

Today (Thursday) Baked this A.M. had good success. Mrs Barns called, staid but a few minutes. I blackened my stove. Moved my large cubbard box on the balcony & had a general fixing up. Am very tired this evening. It is raining I have had the greatest bother with cockroaches. They got into my box of bedclothes. I wonder what will come next.

June 13, 1863 Having completed the dress (made out of my last years traveling skirt of which was good) for Mammy Royer. I took it

13. William H. Sullenberger had been a master mechanic and an apparently happy and successful husband and father before he helped organize the Chambersburg cavalry unit. According to Solomon B. Barnes, Sullenberger became, during the early years of the war, "quite a hard drinker at times like the rest of the other officers." He had been discharged from the army in March 1863 because of bad health (see Samuel's entry for March 11), but he had returned home a different man, probably an alcoholic. In 1878, William deserted his wife and moved to Omaha, Neb., where he lived out his life with another woman. See Sullenberger's Civil War Pension File Application 511996 and Certificate 318189, and the depositions attached, NA.

Rachel and Cora Cormany. Taken in the studio of J. Keagy, Chambersburg, this is one of the photographs Rachel refers to in her entry for June 11, 1863. Kiefer Family.

down this P.M. Found the old lady in bed resting, she having baked &c which tired her, I handed her the dress & said there was something for her "Fer mig, vas ists dan" A dress, "Ach mien guter Gott", "vas soll ich don fer dich thun"[14] I told I wanted nothing, but she wanted to give me something. I told her when she got young & could work well & I old & could not—then she should help me. The tears came to her eyes—She then took me to the garden— gave the baby all the ripe strawberries she could find. I had intended to buy some, but they had sold all ripe that morning, but I am to have the next lot. She took me to the cellar & gave me a drink of currant wine, gave the baby roses. She talked a long time about religion, related her conversion &c. &c. which was quite interesting. When I started away she would give me two large light cakes. She evidently wanted to show that she was grateful for the gift I brought her. I hope it will fit her. I had her dress pattern—unknown to her.

14. "For me? What is this?" A dress [answered Rachel]. "My Gracious, what shall I do for you?" I am indebted to Professor Beverly Smaby, an expert on the Moravians of Pennsylvania, for this translation and for her observation that Rachel's transcription follows no known dialect or standard variant of this period. It simply contains mistakes. Rachel's knowledge of written German was apparently limited, notwithstanding her familiarity with the spoken language. This is further confirmed by the fact that she gives the German in English characters; written German was still rendered in script during this period.

XV

From Chancellorsville to Gettysburg

February 18–July 6, 1863

Rejoining his unit after visiting Rachel, Samuel finds himself more and more frequently involved in actual combat. This section includes the Union offensive that was rebuffed at Chancellorsville and the Confederate counter-offensive that culminated in the Battle of Gettysburg. The observations of a common Union trooper during this period are valuable because these were the two campaigns in which momentum, confidence, initiative, and combat superiority shifted from Gen. J. E. B. Stuart's Confederate horsemen to the recently reorganized Federal cavalry under Gen. George Stoneman. When the 16th Pennsylvania pursues retreating Confederates right through Chambersburg, Samuel is able to slip away for a brief reunion with his wife and daughter.

February 18, 1863 Wednesday. Snowing—Sleeting—Very disagreeable—The 9:20 failed to come in til 11 AM—we boarded it and were off reached Balto 4 P.M. Laid over til 8 P.M.—In the mean time we had an Oyster Supper and several drinks—Capt became pretty boozy—I had quite a time with him. Reached Washington at 10 ock. Put up at Hotel—

February 19, 1863 Thursday. Took Boat for Acquia Creek landing at 8 A.M.—awfully crowded—Arr at 12 M. Took train for Potomac Creek Bridge, where Serg't P. met us with Horses—

The Boys seemed glad to see us again—Capt. Lieuts and I spent the evening merrily—a little too merrily—I surely am retrograding some. Suffering in real character—I must say no oftener—Throat or no throat.

February 20, 1863 Friday. Warm—Awfully Muddy. Am well, and would be happy but for being a little irregular yesterday and yesterday evening[1] Tho very very little, yet I chide myself, ask pardon, and am forgiven—and will be firm. Had I not been firm—the Captain would hardly have made the return without some disgrace—

---

1. A reference to his increasingly frequent use of alcohol.

297

Wrote til late for the Boys on a/c Township and County Bounty—
Wrote J. R. Orr—also letter to Pet. Retired late.

February 21, 1863 Saturday. Cold—Wrote most of day making out
Pay Rolls—Routine—Men ordered out on Picket—

February 22, 1863 Sunday. Snowed—Bad time for our Picket
Boys—Poor Cap—too much of this weather will fix him—Snowed
and Stormed all day—6 or 8 inches of snow—and awful cold—Wrote
to Pet. O that I were a better Man.

February 23, 1863 Monday. Very Cold—Sergt Peters slept with
Lieut Bohn and I—I worked all day on Pay Rolls—Serg't Peters
helped me—Eve—Read—pray—Think. For years I have not felt so
keenly so great a loss of religion, peace and joy of mind & heart—
My Lord I am thine—and will be evermore—

February 24, 1863 Tuesday. Cold—Worked on Pay Rolls til noon—
P.M. Warmer—Lieut Bohn and I had a spat—Eve all our men called
to go out on picket in the morning. Wrote letter to precious Pet—
Feel better mentally and spiritually than I have for somedays—am
resolved to live a better, more consecrated life by His grace—

February 25, 1863 Wednesday. Very cold, but clear & sunny. Finished and mailed letter to Pet—P.M. Our Pickets got into a fight—All
of Regt went to the rescue. I along—We got on the ground about
dark—had little to do—Boys greatly excited. Poor Hammond shot—
Rebs withdrew—Too dark to follow. Danger of Ambush surprise.[2]

February 26, 1863 Thursday. Rainy Day. I acted Orderly for Capt.
Sullenberger and Major White—of Genl Greggs Staff.[3] Looking over

2. This encounter, substantially larger than the cavalry's routine contact with the
enemy in the course of picket duty, is listed in the official records of the war as the
action at Hartwood Church. Frederick H. Dyer, *A Compendium of the War of the Rebellion* (New York, 1959), p. 1566. Rachel referred to Hammond's death in her entry for
Mar. 4, 1863.

3. Shortly after succeeding Burnside, General Hooker reorganized the Army of the
Potomac. The army's many cavalry units, which had generally worked with separate
infantry units, were consolidated into a cavalry corps under the overall command of
Gen. George Stoneman. The 16th Pennsylvania was assigned to the 2nd Division,
commanded by Brig. Gen. David McMurtrie Gregg. Liaisons from Gregg's staff were
attached to the various regiments under his control. Matthew Forney Steele, *American
Campaigns* (Washington, D.C., 1951), I, 161; Dyer, *Compendium*, p. 1566; *DAB*, VII,
596; *OR*, ser. I, vol. XXVII, pt. I, pp. 166–67; Ezra J. Warner, *Generals in Blue: Lives of
the Union Commanders* (Baton Rouge, La., 1964), pp. 187–88.

the teritory, and the field of yesterdays fight on the Picket line—Saw a dead Reb. burried beside the road—as they fell back—On our return to Picket Camp—I acted Commissary Sergt by order of Major——Eve rain over—I am not well but pretty happy—

February 27, 1863 Friday. But little sleep for several nights—Took naps sitting by a wee fire—huging our arms. Lay in the woods near pickets til 3 ock then our squad was ordered back to Camp—Potomac Creek way up—Had to swim our Horses across—Got very wet. My horse swam low—the rascal!

February 28, 1863 Saturday. Pleasant—I worked on Rolls most of day—Mustered for Pay in P.M.—Eve made out report of the Battle on Picket line—Brother Bernard[q] came to see me—Slept with me— Am so glad to see him, and enjoy such a good visit—

A Brother seems very dear—at such a time as this—

March 1, 1863 Sunday. "Barney"[q] enjoys army rations right well, but prefers absence of body during Picket-line-Fighting such as we just had—which I am writing up for Head Quarters today. H. Co lost "Hammond" Killed. Lyons, Nelling, Hart, Shelly, Garverick, and Bradley Prisoners (6)——Evening Brother left for Chambersburg. Sent a note to Darling by B[4]—Capt S. seems poorly—I badly used up.

March 2, 1863 Monday. Cool—Busy on Rolls and Reports all day— Capt miserable. Talks of resigning—I hope he will not—I am kept too busy to be otherwise than "pretty well thank you."

March 3, 1863 Tuesday. Spring like—Writing as usual—a little unwell—Capt & I had a long talk on religion. I feel now I shall be able to be a really better Man—nearer my ideal as Man, Soldier, Christian—

March 4, 1863 Wednesday. Same routine—only I am happier—and more hopeful of becoming able to endure the hard parts of the service—the exposure—which so often about upsets me, but I'm improving. S. B. Barnes was re-instated as Orderly Sergt—I had been acting in his place. Since his irregularity for which he was reduced or suspended—I wrote for him his xplanation and petition and Captains recommendation of it to the Colonel—and he was restored—

4. Rachel noted Bernard's return in her entry for Mar. 4, 1863.

I pitied him—tho he was to blame—I believe in him and rest assured he will act worthily now.

March 5, 1863 Thursday. Finish Co Rolls—Compare—Find O.K. I am really quite unwell—So is Captain S—I wrote his application for Discharge on a/c poor health and increacing[5]—

March 6, 1863 Friday. Fine day—Handed in Our Pay Rolls—Ord. Barnes and I went to 126th   Saw Shearers boys, Dave Kindig, John Clippinger, John Gillen, Lieut Slothe—Rev A. J. Hartsuck. Had a splendid time—also went to see Sim Whistler, grand time—Got home late and tired—Recd such a good letter from Pet. Enclosing me $40.00[6] Hammonds Bounty to turn over——

March 7, 1863 Saturday. Am quite ill with Diarhea and pain on breast—Surgeon set me off duty——Finished Inventory of Q.M. and Inspection Report.

P.M. wrote for Pet—long letter—Eve miserable and depressed—

March 8, 1863 Sunday. Capt S recd request to call on Col Jones of 3rd Pa Cav[7]—P.M. Cap and I went to Camp of 3rd called on Lieut Bauchman &c.   Jolly time—some toasts drank—Came back to camp 5 P.M. a little boozy—retired soon—Very sick in the night, all to myself—

March 9, 1863 Monday. Am sorry I took rather much. Though what I drank was good for my diarhea—and I feel the better physically—Did some writing for Co "H" and some letters—Wrote long for Darling—My! O My! how liable one is to be overcome to evil and let ones influence count on the wrong side.

March 10, 1863 Tuesday. A routine day—adding a lot of talk about examination as to my ability to stand soldiering.

March 11, 1863 Wednesday. Sent in request for examination. Filled out Co. descriptive Book and brought up all our Books to date.

Eve Captain Sullenberger recd an honorable Discharge, and will soon leave us.

---

5. I.e., worsening.

6. See Rachel's entry of Mar. 3, 1863.

7. Lt. Col. E. S. Jones commanded the 3rd Pennsylvania Cavalry, which was also in Gregg's division of the Cavalry Corps.

March 12, 1863 Thursday. Cool—Pleasant The Col has recommended 1st Lieut Snyder for Captain and no doubt he will get the rank—

I got up petition for Ord. Sgt Barnes to become 1st Lieut—The men sign it willingly—Cheerfully—got some 40 names—and the Colonel approves it. 2nd Lieut Bohn makes a hideous fuss about it, but he has no one to blame but himself, his own inactivity and inefficiency.

I am quite unwell—have such severe pain on my breast, with cough, and misery in my head—

March 13, 1863 Friday. Lieut Bohn awfully up and disagreable. Lieut Snyder and the Men off Picket—Surgeon Harrman[8] examined me thoroughly—Guess my chance for discharge is very limited and doubtful. I need to brace up and throw off my attacks & ailments—

Heard from our Prisoners in Parole Camp[9]—are O.K. I am some better. Thank the good Lord.

March 14, 1863 Saturday. Cold—Made out Descriptive List for our Prisoner Boys for Parole—

Wrote letter to Clem Bowman[cc]—Made the grand round calling on the Men—Find I am likely to be made Orderly Sergeant[10]—It would seem "tough" to jump all the Sergeants and Corporals—

March 15, 1863 Sunday. Spent A.M. leisurely—P.M. called on some 126th Boys—Division Surgeon came to discharge sick and disabled Men—No chance for me. I'm O.K. Yet—McAlvey—Smith—Pitulka and Waltmyer—4—are to go. I make out their Discharge papers for them—

8. The 16th Pennsylvania had three medical officers: a surgeon and two assistant surgeons. Augustus F. Hermann was one of the latter. "Reg. Descriptive Books," 16th Pa. Cav., NA.

9. These were the men lost during the skirmish at Hartwood Church two weeks earlier. The prisoners had evidently been paroled by the Confederates; they were released to the custody of the Union in exchange for a promise that they would not participate further in military activities. Paroled men were generally assigned to army camps where their actions could be formally monitored, rather than sent home. The parole camps thus became prisoner-of-war facilities where the army watched over its own men. This paradoxical situation was only one of many confusing aspects of the larger issue of POWs during the Civil War. See James G. Randall and David Donald, *The Civil War and Reconstruction*, 2nd ed. (Boston, 1961), pp. 333–39.

10. Cormany had campaigned to create this vacancy by petitioning for the promotion of Solomon Barnes. Since Cormany had acted for Barnes when the latter was temporarily suspended for disciplinary reasons, he must have realized that he was in line for this appointment.

Eve all quiet. Sunday evening-like—Restful after so much excitement—

March 16, 1863 Monday. Capt S. Lieuts and I had a long talk on re-officering the Co, and new non-commissioned officers to fill vacancies occasioned by promotions—It is great how they confer with me—a mere private—and company clerk, as though I were one of the Commissioned Officers—and had real authority—

The men are off on a scout. I made out the Morning Report as tho Ord. Sergt—giving a/c of Discharges &c—&c—

I am much better, and am contented—Shall do my duty, and more, and be a Man and bide my time for any promotion—Wrote Pet—O to see her!

March 17, 1863 Tuesday. Sweet Spring seems here—at midnight drums beat, and troops near us struck tents—and prepared to move out.

News—an attack is to be made on Fredericksburg—Sick hurried to Hospital—Everything on the qui vive—I sent letter to Pet and called on Rosenberry and others—Am quite well and happy—Capt Sullenberger and Lieut Bohn went to Falmouth—came back in Eve "pretty tight"—Saw an awful specimen of the degradation incident to Army Life—Horse racing under the eyes of Genls Hooker, Humphry, Siegel, Pleasenton, Sumner and any amount of other Commisioned Officers.—3 Men Killed and 4 Horses[11]—

March 18, 1863 Wednesday. All quiet again in Cavalry Camps—Wrote for Pet, J. W. As,[kk] J. Karpers[l] &c. Hear hard cannonading somewhere—Eve our men came in all O.K., but had a lively fight[12]—are all in great excitement, but no one wounded—only a

11. While gambling at cards and dice was extremely common among the troops, horse racing seems to have been indulged in only occasionally. Bell Irvin Wiley, *The Life of Billy Yank: The Common Soldier of the Union* (Garden City, N.Y., 1971), p. 250. This reference suggests that it may have been regarded as an officers' sport. Brig. Gen. Andrew A. Humphreys headed the 3rd Division of the 5th Corps; Maj. Gen. Franz Sigel had been a corps commander under McClellan; Brig. Gen. Alfred Pleasonton commanded one of Hooker's new cavalry divisions; Maj. Gen. Edwin V. Sumner had been a corps commander before retiring when Hooker was promoted.

12. This operation had been designed to drive Confederate cavalry units away from their positions west of the Army of the Potomac and to secure Kelly's Ford, a key crossing of the Rappahannock River. Hooker was planning an offensive that would involve a long westerly swing across Kelly's Ford. *H16PC*, pp. 35–36; *PV*, pp. 950–51.

Picket Fight. Lieut Snyder came near being shot—Manifested great bravery—Eve—finished letter to Pet—

March 19, 1863 Thursday. I acted Orderly Serg't at Guard Mount. P.M. was on Drill—Fine time—Now, as fine weather is here and fields are drying up we may look for lots of Drilling and maneuvering—Eve letter from my Pet—O how I do love my Darling—Wish I could see her now and Pussy too.

March 20, 1863 Friday. 4 inches snow   Good indoors—Wrote and worked all day on Captain S's transfer of U.S. property—Have more of my old symptoms of Diptheria, otherwise quite well—God bless my Darling and Pussy—

March 21, 1863 Saturday. Snow making Mud. Write most of day—

March 22, 1863 Sunday. Drying up—Lieut Bohn recd his discharge papers this morning[13]—
    Treated the Boys—

March 23, 1863 Monday. Lieut Bohn left this morning—all in a hurry—and quite dishonorably—leaving most of his matters unsettled. Sorry for his lack of Soldierly qualities—

March 24–27, 1863 Tuesday to Friday. Routine—am very busy all the time working on Captains papers, wind up &c.   Frequently feel as though I could endure this sitting and writing so steadily no longer—Symptoms of Diptheria on the increace—but the work must be done, and the Capt cannot do it, and he depends upon me—So day by day I'll stay by the Job to the finish—

March 29, 1863 Sunday. Rest from office work—Read my Bible & meditate some—am not fully happy. Find myself below my ideal as a Christian Soldier—Wrote some to Darling.

March 30, 1863 Monday. Routine—Men do some Drilling and I am on Captains work—I shall hardly obtain the Lieutency however desirous. The Officers are to have me—I see it would seem unjust to advance me "over" those 12 Serg'ts from a private—

---

13. This was the rheumatic Valentine H. Bohn. Cormany had campaigned to promote Bohn's rival.

March 31, 1863 Tuesday. Finished the Captains papers and business, and a letter to Darling—

April 1, 1863 Wednesday. Cold. At 1 ock last night we were aroused, and ordered to be ready to move out on a moments notice—At 9 this A.M. all was quiet—and normal—

April 2, 1863 Thursday. Routine day—

April 3, 1863 Friday. Wrote all A.M. in Co. Clothing Book——P.M. Capt Sullenberger and I went to Stafford Court House to see his Brother—Got some spiritus frumenti—and shame to admit—I was some the worse for it—Tho my throat seemed the better—

April 4, 1863 Saturday. "Bill" put me to bed last night—I cut up shamefully. Tore the Captains Coat—Struck orderly—and am not yet over it entirely—
  I believe they doped me—I slept most of day, or at least remained in bed doing penance—My throat and head are O.K.—

April 5, 1863 Sunday. Snowed again—Feel badly this morning. Oh! that I had maintained my integrity—Wrote Pet all about it—I wanted her to have it at first hand and not as a "rumor"—I feel so badly—But a merciful God forgives me, and I believe my Darling will—and I resolve, by Gods grace to be a better Man—

April 6, 1863 Monday. Went with Capt. S. to Acquia Landing to see him off—Got transportation for Captains and Capt Hursts, horses. Got to Camp by 2 P.M.—Eve, I feel somewhat sad and lonely to lose the Captain—Tho fact he was not much soldier nor patriot—nor Christian—Tho a jolly, easy to please fellow—But he was a snare to me in drink—Said too often I needed it, or it would be good for my throat, cough, &c, &c. and it was—or seemed to be—and the Dr. at times said the same or perhaps adding rock candy—

April 7, 1863 Tuesday. Snow gone. Fine—Worked on Co Books—Clothing a/c &c. Wrote Brother Bernard^q—Clem^cc &c—Feel quite unwell—my throat worse again—and it depresses me so—I want to be a No. 1 soldier—To be relied on anytime anywhere and all the time—But my greatest aspiration is to be withal a good Christian and a deserving husband—fully deserving of the wife I have and the Daughter we have—

April 8, 1863 Wednesday. Have a very sore tongue and throat. Diptheria seems sure. Except this morning Diarhea set in which I hope is carrying off and counteracting the disease—Hot water drinking, and enemas seem to help—

April 9, 1863 Thursday. Pleasant—warm—The birds are singing— and all things seem springing into life. Lieut Snyder—to be Captain—came in off picket with all the Boys O.K.—

He seems awfully blue on taking the responsibility of being in Command—"My God" escapes his lips every few minutes—I feel badly for him—but I'll stand by him and know how to help him in the details of caring for the Company—and he is fairly good in Drill &c—

No letter from Pet. Oh! Why?—

April 10, 1863 Friday. Everything business & bustle—McAlvey and Waltmeyer went home on Discharge—Am still very unwell. Bowels bad, but throat improving—wrote again to Pet—What can the matter be? Oh for a letter from Home—

April 11, 1863 Saturday. I. A. Smiths, Pitschkas & Finks discharges came—

My throat and all much better. Tobacco was suggested and I used some—with seeming good effect—I am now in good hopes of soon being up to normal again—

April 12, 1863 Sunday. Feel pretty well now—General inspection— Expect to march very soon—P.M. Marching orders—Move in the morning. I went with Snyder to seek to be Mustered as Captain— failed—

April 13, 1863 Monday. Break camp 7 A.M.[14] Fall in with 6th Cavalry and Tarbucks Battery—6 pieces artillery near Station—Column started about 8 ½ ock southward—Heard cannonading frequently frontward and leftward—We moved about 20 miles—Our advance had a light skirmish about 4 P.M.—Halted—alert for the night—I sat on my saddle—leaned against a tree—took little naps—holding my horses rein in my hand—Am actually very unwell—tooth and headache, sore mouth & throat &c.

---

14. This entry signals the beginning of three weeks of maneuvering that will culminate in the Battle of Chancellorsville, May 1–3, 1863.

April 14, 1863 Tuesday. We start again at daylight—I must hold out—after making 10 miles—at 11 A.M. we halted in Column— Much firing in direction of the River—and frontward—Expecting every moment to be ordered to advance and go in—now dispite my bad throat and head I felt perfectly calm and willing almost eager to go into a fight—It will go with me as will be best for trusting in God, what have I to fear?—The whole Army seems on the move—In every direction the country is swarming with Soldiery—

I lay awhile on the ground—The sun roasting my cheek—and drawing the pain out-o-me. Eve. Looks like rain—Put up our Hd Qrs Fly—men all at a wide awake ease—Slept til 3 ock A.M.

April 15, 1863 Wednesday. Rains a little—Awfully dark—Fed Horses—ate a little ourselves, and at 5 AM were in Column, on the march—about 5 Mls took us to ½ mile from River, where we halted—and 1st two squadrons were ordered to "Prepare to fight on foot"—We threw off our Overcoats and Sabers, and fell into ranks—Stood two hours in heavy rain—Kept Amunition dry— Moved a short distance˙ forward—our advance engaged the Rebs lightly. Infantry They fled—we followed a short distance—firing on them at ¼ mile range—No casualties on our side—But I do not believe they could say as much—

We were ordered back to mount, and then after establishing a Picket line—all fell back ½ mile—and put up—I was wet to the hide—so were many—But my throat was better[15]

April 16, 1863 Thursday. Rainy night—I slept on a Pole bed—But kept pretty dry—Mouth, tongue and throat still not well—but mending. In camp all day—Fly & Dog Tent Camp—I wrote a lot for Pet——Evening a merry time—our Darkey "Carter" full of funny stories—and experiences—which he let loose freely for our amusement. Wrote more for Pet——We expect to move out in the morning, and ho! for a fight—Sent in Letters—

April 17, 1863 Friday. I slept well—Got up at 6 AM—Ate very little—have been eating less than ½ ration since Sunday 12" My lips awful thick but mouth, throat & head much better Cap Bro't in

15. Cormany's regiment was part of a cavalry operation designed to disrupt Confederate detachments upriver from Fredericksburg and thereby ensure an unobstructed sweep across the upper Rappahannock for the main infantry offensive, which was to follow. The marches that Cormany describes were a series of circles and crisscrosses that extended as far upstream as the Orange and Alexandria railroad crossing.

a chicken—Cook it—and soak hard tack.[16] Big Dinner—Lie in temporary tents all day—orders to move in the morning—How I do long
for some place with my Darling to give me rational treatment—

April 18, 1863 Saturday. Slept well, but throat far from well—Yet
I go ahead with my daily duties—I dread any thought of applying
to our Doctor—and risking Army Treatment. About ½ of the Regiment went out on a foraging expedition—I got Canteen full of
good milk—and a few walnuts—Dispatch came Hasten back to
Camp—we did—and found our fellows had been shelled out of
the woods—Had broken camp—so we gathered up our things and
quickly and quietly followed them marching close to Bealton Stn,
where we put up our "shelter tents" again—and made believe
comfortable—Had a Hare for supper. Oh for a letter from Pet and
Pussy. or still better, to be able to spend Sunday with them and
give my throat a chance.

April 19, 1863 Sunday. Fine—Feel a little better after good sleep—
Mailed letter to Pet—wrote answer—I fixed up Captain Snyders
Papers, and saw him Mustered in as Captain of Co H—
    Eve marching orders again—

April 20, 1863 Monday. Broke up Camp—Stood "To Horse" from
8 to 11 AM Then started—and rain started too—but we moved on—
Eve we camped at Woodburn Church—on Pike—18 miles from
Culpepper.[17] O how damp and dreary to try to sleep on the wet
ground with only a few brush to keep one off the wetness—

April 21, 1863 Tuesday. Feel a little better—River too high to
ford—lay over all day—Cleared up, and we dry off. I wrote to
Darling, and do little aside from the necessary—Eve. I feel worse—
Oh! to have my darling wife stroke my eyes and forehead, and say
words of love and comfort to me this evening—But for my dear
family I'd pray God to take me Home. But, ah! no! I want to, and
shall, live for a purpose, and with them by and by after the war and
for them all our days, and we all 3 for God.

---

16. Hardtack, an unleavened flour and water cracker, was generally softened by
soaking in soup or coffee. Wiley, *Billy Yank*, pp. 237–39.
17. The "Pike" was the Warrenton Turnpike, which ran from Culpeper Court
House across the Rappahannock near Sulphur Springs, through the town for which it
was named, and then northeast toward Centreville and Alexandria. *OMACW*, pl.
XXII, no. 4.

April 22, 1863 Wednesday. Cool—but pleasant—Capt Snyder and six of Co H. Capt Robinson and five of Co D. and I as Orderly—went on a foraging expedition—Got 2 sacks of corn and a bunch of chickens and when we returned to Camp, found all had gone—We followed—Through Warrenton—which is a splendidly built village, but looks awfully desolate on a/c of the War. We camped on the West Branch of the Orange and Alexandria R.R. and cars brought us forage for our horses, but man-feed was very limited—Hard tack and weak chicken broth—and a few bites of chicken today—I feel better this eve.

April 23, 1863 Thursday. Rains awfully—Very temporary quarters, but fairly dry. I wrote some for Pet. A.M. cooing, and crowing—and singing and growling and laughing fills the air at times with a Babel of Sounds, and jolification has the great majority—P.M. Lieut A and I went to Warrenton—hoping to be able to buy something for our mess—We got 4 hoe cakes for $1.00 ½ doz eggs 25¢—and on returning to Camp we ate all but one hoe cake for supper—Has cleared.

April 24, 1863 Friday. "We lay Low"—Keep damp, but good natured—and I am about well now—Being short of rations is good for soldiers—we play that anyhow—Wrote more for Pet. Sent her letter. No mail for me—Fy-didle-de-dee—I say that to scare off the blues—

April 25, 1863 Saturday. Cleared finely—Got supply of Bread today and a few things more—Thank the Lord and Commissary. Not much doing save drying up. Writing letters—Chatting—and Keeping ready for anything.

April 26, 1863 Sunday. Very Pleasant day—Read most of day in 3 Telescopes Pet sent me[18]—Wrote some for her—am quite well, save ugly cough—and am decidedly more happy than a little while ago—

April 27, 1863 Monday. Fine—not much doing—I wrote a great lot for Pet. Oh! for a letter. Sent one to her—

April 28, 1863 Tuesday. Took our Horses out to graze in AM——
P.M. Drilled—Regimental Drill——
  (Thus—starting in to graze—and Drill—would say to observers we are settling down to remain awhile—) 9 ock P.M.—Marching or-

18. See Rachel's entry for Mar. 25, 1863.

308

ders——We started soon—Marched til 3 ock AM—29th—when we struck Bealton Station, where we lay til 6 ock A.M.—Feeding a little and then took up the march for Kellys Ford on the Rappahannoc River—We crossed on pontoons at noon——about 4 P.M. we had an engagement lasting til dark—We drove the Rebs back by rapid firing, and steady, but determined advancing—a few shells fell very near our advance men, but nothing fearing we moved onward towards Culpepper C. H.—driving the enemy until ordered to halt at dark.[19]

April 30, 1863 Thursday. We lay on our arms all night——Soon run into the enemy, and engaged them. i.e., their rear—at Culpepper—They stood a little—returned some fire, but soon were driven out and we went on near Rapidan and at 10 A.M. encamped near Slaighten and Cedar Mts—

The enemy showing no disposition to fight us, or to make any strong resistance, we Picketed well, and rested—Keeping in best of readiness should they become ready to attack us—

May 1, 1863 Friday. Very warm—Mail 2 letters from Darling—1 of Clem.[cc] Canonading near River.

We not in it, but look to be called into action anytime—Am well, and happy, and resigned—will stand in my place and do my work manfully whatever may threaten me, or be my fate.

P.M. Grazed our Horses—Then in Eve went on picket—Later I patrolled the line—Find the Rebs have burned the R. R. Bridge.[20]

May 2, 1863 Saturday. Clear—Warm—We marched to Culpepper and Fredericksburg Road, and then towards F'dksb'g til 9 ock—could hear the canonading near Chancellorsville——

Went into camp near bank of Rapid Ann—i.e. bivouacked—We were surprised—fired into by Rebs across the River—Elys Ford—We fell in dismounted—and fired across—Had a bustling time in the dark—a squad of our fellows mounted & charged across the Ford driving the enemy and scouring the hillside—Found the enemy had

---

19. Hooker was now launching his main offensive, and thousands of infantry were also crossing the Rappahannock at Kelly's Ford on April 28 and 29. Cormany's cavalry detachment had been ordered across the river to break the Confederates' token resistance and then to stand guard, or picket, on the extreme right (due west) of the Union infantry advance. Cormany's division was responsible for patrolling a line that approximated the route of the Orange and Alexandria Railroad from the Rappahannock, through Culpeper Court House, to the Rapidan River.

20. The Orange and Alexandria railroad bridge over the Rapidan River.

2 killed and 4 wounded left behind and we had 1 killed and 1 wounded.

We now fell back a mile and camped—leaving a good squad to Picket the Ford &c—²¹

May 3, 1863 Sunday. Hot & clear—We hear heavy canonading and musketry about Chancellorsville—We rest all AM—P.M. ordered out cross the Rapidan at Ealys Ford—and passed between the contending forces—i.e. where they had been fighting—Saw many dead, and wounded soldiers—we crossed the U.S. Ford on pontoons and went on picket near Richards Ford—Awful is result of Battle.

May 4, 1863 Monday. Hot—Slept little—wide awake morning—We were relieved at noon—Hear heavy firing on amunition train—and Johnies likely took 6 out of 8 old canon belonging to a battery protecting the moving train—We were ordered to fall back to Hartwood Church. I met John Gillen and Al Huber—Rumor has it we are defeated in this fight—Movements seem so confused—and air seems charged with uncertainty.

May 5, 1863 Tuesday. Encamped near Hartwood Church—Sent letter to Pet—Had desperate coughing spell last night—Lie over all A.M.—P.M. saw Gillen and Huber again—Seems we are falling back—whipped—But an occasional defeat makes a good soldier a better fighter, and knocks a coward out—

May 6, 1863 Wednesday. Cloudy—rainy—disagreeable——8 AM— ordered to move out 4 Miles—into a woods, and go into Camp— muddy sure—Some of our Dumfries Boys came in—How restful we all are—

May 7, 1863 Thursday. Wrote for Pet—Am well except a troublesome cough—P.M. Started for our old Camp near Acquia Creek—left Apr 13"—Rained awfully—arrived about Midnight—Old Hd Qrs Co

21. Cormany's cavalry division has now come back eastward down the Rapidan to secure the key fords directly behind the main Union advance: Ely's Ford, Richards Ford, and U.S. Ford. On the same evening that the 16th Pennsylvania helped secure Ely's Ford, Lee and Jackson launched a daring counterattack against the main body of Union infantry that pinned the confused Hooker against the river. If the Confederates had taken the fords, they would have had Hooker trapped.

H. Cabin all O.K. Save the chimney had melted. We lay on the ground—The Colonel slept with us—Had our Fly up.

Rained heavily during the night—

May 8, 1863 Friday. Cloudy—Good news of the progress of the war in general—Our move accomplished a lot in way of information, experience.

May 9, 1863 Saturday. Yesterday P.M. and today—wrote for Captain—also mailed letter to Pet—Oh! for one from her—and I do so long to see my dear ones—

News today still more encouraging—more victories than we—who were in it—knew of—of course a company—a squadron, a regiment or a brigade may seem to be whipped—and may retreat—and not even in the best of order—when in fact such movement gives way for another, resulting in decided success[22]

Evening rec'd a letter from Pet. not quite up to her usual standard—But maybe my eyes are a little blue. Had to change my quarters—take in Sergt Peters—He is so rough—I do feel so badly this Eve—so blue. Everything seems blue—wrong. Well yes! But it only seems. It is not.

May 10, 1863 Sunday. Warm—Write Pet—Am unwell with cough and pains in my limbs—

Eve Pay Master Major Potter came—I rec'd $72.35 as pay up to March 1st over five months—I am vexed that I get only Privates pay while I do more than any Sergeant in the Co. I have been made a fool of I see. I obtain nothing for all the clerical work I have done for the Captain—who resigned, nor for his successor Capt Snyder, and The Lieutenants—But I have fared some better on a/c of being associated with The Officers Mess &c.

May 11, 1863 Monday. Went over to 126th—Sent $70—by him to Darling——

Eve somehow I am blue—wish I was out of U.S. Service, or had a letter from Pet, or were a better Man, or were worthy the real good I enjoy above many.

22. William Swinton, a contemporary war correspondent, concluded in 1866 that "not the Army of the Potomac was beaten at Chancellorsville, but its commander." *Campaigns of the Army of the Potomac* (New York, 1866), p. 307. Swinton's tart comment is still impressed upon cadets at West Point in the army's own textbooks. Steele, *American Campaigns*, p. 171. Union forces had given out as much punishment as they had taken, and most historians believe that the Union army might have advanced to victory rather than retreated to embarrassment.

May 12, 1863 Tuesday. Hot day—Our General Stoneman Raid proves to have been a grand success after all[23]—Quiet day in Camp—

May 13, 1863 Wednesday. Little doing—save I went with Lieut Barnes to be mustered in as Lieut—Failed—O such a good letter from Pet! and one from the Kimmels—

May 14, 1863 Thursday. Am really in a bad way—Coughed most of night—Worked most of day on New Pay Rolls. Rec'd letter from Cousin D. Eckerman in Western Army—I am really very weak. If only I were with Darling. She would soon doctor me up rationally—no medicene—no powders—no stuff—

May 15, 1863 Friday. Awful rain storm during the night—Cooler—Worked on Rolls—I am about same physically.

May 16, 1863 Saturday. Pleasant—Had a regular raking up talk with Capt Snyder—Told him how unjustly he treated me—all considered he either lied or else possessed more ignorance than belonged to a Captain—I tried to assure him that I felt best to entertain the latter view—and would "stick to him"—

May 17, 1863 Sunday. Had a good bath—Things move off nicely as may be—Our Lieut Col—whom we have scarcely seen—is asked to resign by all the field Officers—and Major Stroup has resigned—also a mere figure head[24]—

May 18, 1863 Monday. Grazed our Horses—I mailed letter to Pet—At м—we moved to a New Camp—Fell right to fixing up—Lots-o-bother. I slept under little dog Tent[25]

23. While Cormany's division stood rear guard for Hooker's infantry attack, General Stoneman had taken most of the rest of the Union cavalry on a deep raid toward Richmond. Although the raid produced few tangible results, it had an important psychological impact on the self-confidence of the Union cavalry. Stephen Z. Starr, *The Union Cavalry in the Civil War*, vol. I, *From Fort Sumter to Gettysburg, 1861–1863* (Baton Rouge, La., 1979), p. 365. This was the raid that produced the false rumor in Chambersburg that Richmond had fallen. See Rachel's entry for May 11, 1863.

24. The lieutenant colonel forced out was Lorenzo D. Rodgers of Venango County, Pa. Stroup was Maj. John Stroup of Mifflin County. *PV*, pp. 950–51. The removal of Rodgers made possible the promotion of the popular and previously mentioned John K. Robison.

25. I.e., pup tent.

May 19, 1863 Tuesday. Warm day—All busy putting up quarters—
Capt Snyder on the right—Orderly Serg't and mine next—Orderly &
Serg't Peters awful lazy—

May 20, 1863 Wednesday. Awful hot—Orderly Sergt & I got our
q'r's finished—I took a bath—Recd from Pet the Rel. Tel. —P.M.—
My! how nice to enjoy nice new quarters—
Eve Mailed letter to Pet—

May 21, 1863 Thursday. Capt. Snyder and I have talk to a finish.
I to do all his writing—as heretofore—and he pays me $10 per
month from the time of his Muster as Capt.[26]
Not much doing—mailed letter to Pet—but receive none. Feel depressed. How much I need frequent letters from my Darling—

May 22, 1863 Friday. Fifteen men called out—
Mail another letter to Pet—and mailed it—P.M. recd none again—
O for a letter—Routine—

May 23, 1863 Saturday. Very Hot—Caught a U.S. Horse—at large—
Took a swim—No letter—Wrote and mailed another—A lounging
P.M.—Played "7 up".[27] Eve wrote for Pet til 11 P.M.—

May 24, 1863 Sunday. Very Hot——I am 25 years old today!
Had a "speck and oyer" for breakfast.[28] Takes some effort to keep
bright with no word from Pet for so long—
P.M.—Letter comes from Pet—O such a good one—All's Well!
Thank the Lord for such a Darling as is mine——Eve. Letter from
J. W. As.[kk] March at 5 A.M. tomorrow—I write til late—Fix some
towards moving out.

May 25, 1863 Monday. Misty—drizzly—Our Column starts a 6
A.M.—Am quite unwell—Didn't ride in ranks much—Just drizzle
enough to lay dust nicely—An uneventful day—Put up for the
Night at Deep Run—

---

26. Such arrangements were probably illegal, but they were so common that Congress eventually tried to curb their abuse. See *Army Regulations* (1861, revised 1863),
pp. 566–67.
27. A card game similar to pitch.
28. "Speck" was a Pennsylvania German colloquialism for fatback; "oyer" was a
colloquial or phonetic version of the German word for eggs.

May 26, 1863 Tuesday. Cloudy but fine all day—Reached Bealton Station near 4 P.M.—Pitched our shelter Tents—and fixed up cosily—all dandy——Eve. Orders to move at 4:30 A.M.

May 27, 1863 Wednesday. Pleasant—Column moved early—4th Pa Cav to Kellys Ford—16 Pa Cav to Richards Ford and 3rd to U. S. Ford.[29] Got there in P.M. Found fine place for our 16th Bivouac—Not well—I do so much need spiritual uplift.

May 28, 1863 Thursday. I put up pretty fair ¼s for myself. P.M. Capt S., myself and 7 men went on a scout—saw three Rebs— Scattered them at a distance—Had a fine talk with a lady in a partly ruined home—a Miss Patton—Eve was at the Ford—exchanged greetings with Johny pickets across River[30]—

May 29, 1863 Friday. At Midnight last night 82nd Pa Reg Inf. re- lieved us—We took up the march for Deep Run. Put up temp'y quarters—I took a swim. Things are going smoothily at Hd Qrs— Capt & I O.K. since late talk—21st. So long between letters from Pet—I am really quite unwell—Yet I keep mum and do all my duty—as Clerk and Soldier too—

May 30, 1863 Saturday. Our Sutler came up to us—I wrote and mailed letter for Darling. Oh! to see her and our precious pussy— We hear some firing towards Elys Ford—

May 31, 1863 Sunday. Moved out at 3 A.M. Struck Bealton Station at 9 ock—We Fed and breakfasted, and drew rations, and took up the march down the R.R.—near Catlett Station we maneuvered for a battle but enemy made no stand—nor advance on us—A Battery came up—Our Regt lay behind the Battery as support—and the Brigade away back of us—strong support in case of a fight—which seemed immanent. But the enemy withdrew and picketed—and en- camped on arms.

29. Like the two armies, the opposing cavalries spent the weeks after Chancellors- ville maneuvering for key positions and probing for weaknesses. The Rappahannock River remained the basic dividing line between Union and Confederate forces, but both sides made occasional forays into the other's territory.

30. Impromptu trucemaking was extremely common during the Civil War. News could be exchanged, items could be traded, and curiosity could be satisfied through tacit agreements to suspend hostilities for a brief period, especially when neither side was engaged in a major action.

June 1, 1863 Monday. Pleasant—Lay in camp—wide awake—I was sick all night. Am unwell today—Wrote most of day for Pet & Cap. Sullenberger—Wrote application for Leave of Absence for Lieut Armstrong.

June 2, 1863 Tuesday. Extremely Hot—I went to Dr LeMoyne—I am sick in almost every conceivable way. Dr. gave me a few pills—P.M. Moved our tents a few hundred yards—Great lack of water. O for plenty of good water for drinking and bathing—

June 3, 1863 Wednesday. slightly cooler—Endless am't of Orders—Doctor gave me more pills—am really sick. O that Pet were here—P.M. A dishonorable Discharge came for Lieut Armstrong He left at once. Seemed glad to get away—He never seemed to me as really patriotic—

June 4, 1863 Thursday. A general Inspection—all our saddles condemned and 18 Horses—57 Ponchos—am so sick—Vomit furiously—am so weak—Eve wrote for Cap't—goes hard—Capt told me great secret—is trying to have me Commissioned as 2nd Lieut—a lot of Sergts & Corporals ahead of me in rank—so can't well be—

June 5, 1863 Friday. Wrote all day for Cap't could hardly make it, but did—Sent off our I.C. horses—Saddles &c—Eve recd Marching Orders, all on the qui vive—
   Capt told me he guessed I'd get there—To 2nd Lieut—

June 6, 1863 Saturday. Regiment left at 3 A.M.—all afoot, except The Captains—O! I got such a good long letter from Pet—I wrote 25 pages for her—I rest in Camp—Feel much better this eve—Rumors of an impending battle. Nothing posative—

June 7, 1863 Sunday. Took a good bath, am much better—Caught the first "grey back"[31] on my clothes. Read some in my Testament—Time for meditation and prayer today—P.M. Got such a good letter from Pet—Eve. anwered it promptly—

June 8, 1863 Monday. Mailed for Pet—men back to Camp—looks like a move.
   Noon Orders to pack up, ready to move out on a moments notice—Packed Blankets and stuff—and soon ordered to mount on

31. I.e., a louse.

them and we were off in column—Awful dusty—Got to Morrisville about 9 P.M. Slept til 2 AM when we were aroused to Feed and Eat to be off soon—

June 9, 1863 Tuesday. Took up the march at 4 ock this A.M.—via Crittenden Mills and Tannery 4 miles from Kellys Ford. We heard canonading at the River. Buoyed us up—tho some got pale—yet every man looked ready for the fray—Reached Mount Holly Church—near the Ford by 7:30 AM—Could see plainly the raging of the Battle—from where we were bivouaced on hill in woods—quite a squad, whose horses were unfit to go in being "condemned" &c &c.

Lieut Barnes & I went to the Ford and saw some interesting movements.

Later we took a swim, as our fellows were forcing the enemy back—P.M. Capt and I went down again—away off, we saw four Rebs skedadling "full tare"—Also soon saw lots of prisoners and wounded brought back and taken off—Many had saber cuts and stabs—Am just too sorry that I and our squad could not perform our part in this days fighting.[32]

June 10, 1863 Wednesday. Enemy driven through Culpepper some distance—Then at dusk our men put out Pickets, and we fell back into town, and farther, and bivouaced for the night—

This morning we lay-on-arms—Rebs make some advance, as if about to attack us—but we were ready—lay in woods all A.M.— Noon odered to march in 20 min., got ready—lay waiting til about 5 P.M.

I wrote some for Pet—Poor dear will see a/c of the fight—and O how anxious she will be—but I cannot get a letter off to her yet—We went into Camp near Licking Creek about 11 P.M. Sleepy, tired, and almost choked with dust. I am well—cheerful and happy—only longing for a competent horse.

32. The Battle of Brandy Station was the largest cavalry action ever fought in North America. Hooker had ordered Pleasonton to cross the Rappahannock, discover where Lee was headed, and disrupt what looked like the earliest stages of a Southern offensive. The Union cavalry, some ten thousand strong, crashed into an equal number of Confederate cavalry in the fields around Brandy Station, Fleetwood Hill, and Beverly Ford. Though a drawn battle by objective measures, it was considered a psychological boost for the Union side. Pleasonton had accomplished his mission and the Federal cavalry had made Stuart look ill-prepared for a surprise attack. The 16th Pennsylvania was forced to do guard duty at the river fords because, as noted in Cormany's entry for June 5, they were without saddles and very short of horses. See *H16PC*, p. 37, and *PV*, p. 951.

June 11, 1863 Thursday. Warm but fine breeze. I put up our quarters and then took a nap—Later, got a splendid—O the best kind of a letter from Pet—She is such a good dear—Oh! to see her and caress her and Baby—Eve wrote for her—Had tomatoes for supper—1st of the season—Hot sultry—

June 12, 1863 Friday. Mailed letter to Pet—Not much doing—Branded our new horses—All old ones inspected again—Two condemned—General preparings for a move—a "fall back"?

June 13, 1863 Saturday. Not much going on—I read and wrote some—P.M. Orders—"Be ready to March tomorrow at 7 ock A.M.—Retired early—slept well—Health good—Thank God!

June 14, 1863 Sunday. On the line of march early—Struck Warrenton Junction. Put up in the woods—Ordered to grind all our Sabers—

Wondrous trains falling back past us, while we grind—We press into service lots of Grind Stones. With sharp and pointed sabers we propose to meet Johnies sharp swords—

I had a fine bath—First good mess of cherries—Orders to march again soon—This fall-back looks squally—

June 15, 1863 Monday. The Regiment draws new Horse Equipments—Took line of march at noon via Manassas, Great Fortifications. 9 P.M. we put up in old rebel camp near Bull Run—News comes "Rebels in Chambersburg." Men incensed—Here we are burning old Rebel Camps while they are destroying our public property at home, and distressing our wives and babies[33]—

June 16, 1863 Tuesday. Lay in camp all day   Graze our Horses—and take general good rest up—Chambersburg news confirmed—Oh! how I wonder how my Darling and Pussy are getting along—Am well, but too anxious to be real happy.

June 17, 1863 Wednesday. Took up line of march at 5 A.M. Crossed Bull Run at R.R. Bridge—Went several miles wrong—had to retrace and make up lost time. Very hot! Got a mess of good cherries—About 4 P.M. got to Aldie at Bull Run Mountains. Had a hard fight—

---

33. This report was true. Lee had begun his second major invasion of the North, a drive that was turned back two weeks later at Gettysburg. Cormany's regiment was near Manassas because Hooker, politically unable to leave the capital unguarded, was using his cavalry to cover the main approaches to Washington until he could be certain of Lee's direction. As a result, the Confederate thrust up the Cumberland Valley into Chambersburg had been almost unopposed.

Confederate prisoners captured at the Battle of Aldie. Photographic Division, LC.

Rebs fall back—we capture 2 Majors, 3 Captains—4 or 5 Lieuten-ants—75 Men. A canon ball fell very close to me, but I was not hurt—Tho bullets whizzed all about me—not one quite touched me. Thank God. Went into camp at a splendid spring near Hotel and Picketed[34]—

June 18, 1863 Thursday. Hot—Took fine Bath—At 10 AM took up the march via Dover Mills—to Middleburg—a fine little village—Reb skirmishers met us close to town, and we pressed them hard for several hours with hard firing—and little dashes—Then lined up and at it again—I fired 45 to 50 rounds of cartridges. I was struck in my hat once—The fence was struck many times very close to me—and slivers flew about me and my horse, but I stood my ground till enemy began to yield some. Then was foremost charging into town—cap-tured a few—saw some dead on the streets—The wounded escaped, either with their comrades—or were taken in and concealed—We lost none—Had a few wounded—Held the place—Scouted out after the retreaters—Came back—established a Picket line and Reserve. Then fell back 1½ miles and put up for the night—The Brigade camping near us—I was never so completely exhausted—being on the firing line about all day—either dismounted or mounted—mostly mounted—Turned cool, cloudy, rained some—not much sleep.

June 19, 1863 Friday. Early onwarded, having called in our Pickets—Our whole Brigade charged down the hill—through the town at a frightful rate of speed——Formed for battle soon outside of town—Soon the ball opened—Foot and mounted skirmishers. Then canonading   Lieut Barnes with H Co skirmished and held the extreme left, advancing all the while slowly—Hard fighting all day on center—In lull of battle—I got Hoe-Cake and butter for Dinner—and in P.M.—Our left—remaining almost in status quo—we ar-ranged matters so Lt. Barnes and 12 of us ate supper at one farm house—Chicken—Hoe cake—butter & coffee—A few at a time—a

---

34. Lee left Stuart in northern Virginia both to screen the Confederate advance and to monitor Hooker's response to it. Union cavalry, in the series of skirmishes that Cormany is describing, kept Stuart pinned up against the Blue Ridge and thereby prevented the Confederates from gaining information that might have helped Lee position his invading army more advantageously than he eventually did. These limited engagements played a significant role in determining the outcome of one of the most critical campaigns of the war. They also confirmed and reenforced the subtle increase in confidence and effectiveness that the Union cavalry had begun to demonstrate during Stoneman's Raid and again at Brandy Station. Roy P. Stonesifer, Jr., "The Union Cavalry Comes of Age," *CWH* 11 (Sept. 1965), 274–83. These battles are known by the names of the towns Cormany mentions: Aldie, Middleburg, and Upperville.

little in rear of our skirmish line——Evening encamped near the town (Middleburg)—Rained—Got very wet—bivouacking—

June 20, 1863 Saturday. We did some foraging—Killed calves and chickens—Milked cows, got hoe cake—and had a kind of early morning Feast-o-good-things——Captain Snyder got a clip yesterday—not serious however—Evening rains some—The enemy still falling back, and our men following them without much fighting—but enough so we are sure they don't slip away—General Steward certainly is failing to get to Washington, as per his recent promise to his officers and men as reported to us by prisoners taken the other day[35]—Lay on arms all night—

June 21, 1863 Sunday. Cloudy—We advanced early, and were soon engaging the enemy—Our artilery did good work—everytime they opened on us, a few shots from Tidball Battery would make them move back—Shells from them frequently fell and exploded very uncomfortably near to us, but we stood our ground, knowing that Tidball would soon make them fall out of range again by a short retreat to a new position[36]—Our boys the meantime seeking to flank them—but usually were met by force we thought not best to really charge upon hastily—or rashly——Thus we fought our way onward—Every step hotly contested—finally forcing them through Upperville—by a heavy saber charge led by 1st Maine and closely followed by our regiment——driving the enemy into The "Gap" in the mountain.[37]—beyond Upperville—We lost only a few killed, and had some wounded—while the enemy lost many killed—left on the ground—took with them many wounded—and we took a good many prisoners—

June 22, 1863 Monday. We picketed close to Upperville—and near the Gap—I stood Post—Some picket firing—Rather unhealthy on picket line—
The Boys found a barrel of whiskey—Got plenty to drink—Some

35. This report confirms Stuart's desire for a dramatic thrust that would offset his embarrassment at Brandy Station and reestablish the bravado and superiority that characterized his cavalry command during the first two years of the war. Three days later, Stuart received a vague order from Lee which, loosely interpreted, left open the possibility of repeating his famous ride around the Union army.

36. Cormany's expression of confidence supports the contention that a key factor in the success of the Union cavalry from this point forward was an increasingly effective use of artillery. Stonesifer, "Union Cavalry," pp. 281–83.

37. Ashby's Gap in the Blue Ridge.

rather too much—many filled their canteens—Strict orders caused the Command to be very cautious—and escape any drunkenness. Feeding & breakfasting was rather hurried—On orders, we fell back to Dover Mills—the enemy following us—pretty closely.

But having accomplished our end, we simply fell back in excellent order—our rear well protected—Once they came too close, and we "about faced" and made a good charge—to their surprise—and captured three pieces of artillery which would soon have been playing on our column—

We laid several bates later, but they failed to bite—

They had paid too dearly for the first. On reaching Dover Mills we laid on arms for the night. Got a quiet good nights sleep on banks of Mill Race—Pickets behaved.

June 23, 1863 Tuesday. Rested awhile—Then moved to the woods. Near Mrs Chancellors Home—Got a mess of fine cherries—By request I carried a note from Mrs Chancellor to Colonel Robison asking for a "Safe Guard"—Col sent me—Good!—I got a fine Dinner and splendid supper.

I had a fine chat and sing with Mrs C and her little girl—She is a No 1 singer, and conversationalist—Late in night I had to return to Company.

Stood "To Horse" all night—

June 24, 1863 Wednesday. Returned to Mrs Chandlers early—Set me up a luxurious breakfast—At 10 A.M. we were moved to Mill-Race. Sorry I am to leave such a perfect Lady without safeguard——

P.M. I caught a fine mess of large fish by hand—along the race— Took two good swims and feel first rate—Capt Snyder came back to Company today—flesh wound in arm nearly well—Oh! to see my Darling wife and precious Cora or even to hear from them—

June 25, 1863 Thursday. Took an early swim—Mailed letter to Pet—Eat lots of fresh fish—"Foine."

P.M. All astir—expecting to move, turn in our shelter tents & Blankets. Orders come to move in the morning.

I rode out to say good-bye to Mrs. Chandler & little girl—Had a pleasant chat. The Boys have troubled her very little—Kindly gave me some splendid smoking tobacco as I was leaving—God bless kind hearts everywhere.

June 26, 1863 Friday. Rainy—Recd 2 such good letters from Darling and one from Clem[cc]—Pet gives details of the Rebs trip to and through Chambersburg—10 A.M. we took up line of march. A very zigzag course—very hilly—fine farms—rainy day—very little show for foraging! About 9 P.M. we struck Grove Creek on Leesburg Pike—Lay on arms—but later encamped—Rumor—Rebels at Carlisle—and our destination Gettysburg Pa.

June 27, 1863 Saturday. We lay in field on Pike all A.M.—Misty—I am well and happy, but do so long to see my little family—To embrace and caress them——at Noon we move to the Fort between Edwards Ferry [and] Leesburg—sent scouts to town—saw a few Johnies disappearing—at dusk we fell back to Edwards Ferry—and at 10 P.M. we crossed [the Potomac] on pontoons—drew rations, and then marched on 15 miles via Poolesville to Barnesville by daybreak—

June 28, 1863 Sunday. Fed and rested til noon. Then took up the march via Fyatesville[38] to Frederick City—we can see a clear difference between the people here and over in Virginia—Everyone greets us with welcome looks and words—Ladies waive their h'd'k'fs &c &c and all seem to look to us for protection against invasion—Pretty fair nights rest for men and horses—

June 29, 1863 Monday. Rainy—We draw rations & a little feed— Hosts of infantry passing all the time—Also artillery[39]—We took up line of march at 10 A.M. Great Union demonstration in Frederick City. March on via Liberty, a short ways past New Windsor. Saw many splendid fields of grass and grain and met many welcomes, variously and variedly expressed and manifested Smiles—Cheers, waving flags, bows, bread & butter, pies, cakes, coffee, milk (butter & sweet) and sparkling spring water supplied to everyone who would partake—Saw some artillery boys quite drunk, and some cavalry fellows acting like vandals by riding through grass and grain fields. We kept our 16th pretty well in line—our Colonel being a good Presbyterian Farmer. Camped for the night near New Windsor—We lay "to Horse" all the night in a dampening drizzle—all in good spirits—

June 30, 1863 Tuesday. We moved out early to within a few miles of Westminster and drew up in line for battle—our advance moved on—and the Reg't supported—met little resistance in taking the City—Took 8 prisoners.

38. Actually Hyattstown, a hamlet just southeast of Frederick, Md.; not to be confused with the Washington suburb of Hyattsville.

39. The entire Army of the Potomac was moving north to meet the Confederate invasion.

The Regiment halted close to the City—We got some eatables—The people were ecstatic to see our troops driving out and following up the "Johnies." They did all in their power for us—The Rebs had acted awful meanly—Took everything like hats, boots, shoes, clothing &c—The streets and fence corners were strewn with their discarded old ones. Some of them, yes many, were almost able to join in the march, being so full of lice[40]—Soon we were called on to muster for pay—still near town—and at noon took up the march Manchester—I never saw more cherries, ripe and ripening, and better crops then are to be seen hereabouts—

Lieut Barnes & I got a fine supper at Mr. Bingamins—Fine ladies about. Exultant on our arrival, and almost worshipped us as their protectors—i.e., our soldiers—

For the night we picketed and laid ready—I stood Post two hours—

July 1, 1863 Wednesday. I had a fine chicken breakfast—and a feast of other good things. Took up march for Hanover. Very fine rich country—and such fine water—Settlers are Old Style People. Many Dunkerds. We were given any amount to eat all along the way—The Rebs who had passed this way acted very meanly—All around—demanding setters to pay money to exempt horses from being taken and barns and houses from being burned—One old man said he paid $100 to exempt 2 horses—another paid $23 to save his horse—Still another—$100 to save his barn. We found this hideous thing to be quite common[41]—

We struck Hanover at dark. Found N.C. R.R. badly torn up[42]—During the day we heard heavy canonading—and later musketry firing—in the direction of Gettysburg. Rumor was, "Theres a Battle on at Gettysburg" and was not hard to believe——Some of our Cavalry had fought desperately here today, early—Charging into the enemy's rear and flanks—

Killed some 30 rebs and hustled large forces on their way. So they had to abandon their dead and some of their wounded[43]—

40. Many sources agree that the people of Maryland and Pennsylvania were repelled by the appearance of the ragged, unkempt, and poorly supplied Confederates.

41. See Rachel's diary for numerous references to this same practice in and around Chambersburg.

42. The Northern Central Railroad, which ran north from Baltimore to York, Pa., included a spur line through Hanover to Gettysburg.

43. Stuart's main cavalry force had made a long loop below, around, and now almost back through the Union army. Just as he was about to reunite with the main Confederate army, Union cavalry under Brig. Gen. Judson Kilpatrick engaged his

We lay on arms in a field for the night—we were well fed, but awfully tired and sleepy—A shower of rain failed to awaken me—I was lying in a furrow, an old furrow. I partially awakened in the night feeling coolish on my lower side—but didn't fully awake. In the morning I discovered that water had run down the furrow—and I had "dam'd" it somewhat and so was pretty wet from below, while my poncho had kept me dry from the top—

July 2, 1863 Thursday. More or less Picket firing all night—We were aroused early, and inspection showed a lot of our horses too lame and used up for good action—So first, our good mounts were formed for moving out, and were soon off—with the Brigade and took Reb. Genl. Steward by surprise on the Deardorf Farm—on right and rear of the army line—where Steward was expected to at least annoy the rear of Genl Mead—But our boys charged him—and after severe fighting dealt him an inglorious defeat and later in the day came in and lay on arms in the rear of Meads right—While our mounted men were paying attention to Genl Steward, we fellows had our horses cared for and were marched down to the right of the main line—to occupy a gap and do Sharpshooting—at long range, with our Carbines—we soon attracted attention, and later an occasional shell fell conspicuously close—but far enough to the rear of us so we suffered no serious harm. Towards noon firing became more general and in almost all directions—and we were ordered to our horses—and joined our returned heroes, and lay in readiness for any emergency—The general battle increaced in energy—and occasional fierceness—and by 2 P.M. the canonading was most terrific and continued til 5 P.M. and was interspersed with musketry—and Charge-yells and everything that goes to making up the indescribable battle of the best men on Earth, seemingly in the Fight to the Finish——At dark, our Cav Brig—2nd Brig 2" Div—was moved to the left—many wounded came in—Taken as a whole from all one can see from one point—it seems as tho our men—The Union Army—is rather overpowered and worsted[44]—

Lay on arms to rest—Little chance to feed and eat.

---

troops and forced them to make another long circular detour, during which they were again attacked, and Stuart himself was nearly captured. This forced Lee to suffer a last critical day without the bulk of his cavalry.

44. Cormany fought most of the second day at Gettysburg beside infantry forces on the right wing of the Union position. Two Confederate brigades had temporarily reached the top of Cemetery Hill, and Southern troops were entrenched for renewed attack at the base of Culp's Hill. The Confederates very nearly turned the Union right flank, but Confederate commanders, deprived of cavalry reconnaissance, never fully

July 3, 1863 Friday. Canonading commenced early—and battle was on again in full intensity——at 10 ock we were ordered to the Front and Center, but immediately removed to the right of the Center—had some skirmishing. Pretty lively—Our squadron almost ran into a Rebel Battery with a Brigade of Cavalry maneuvering in the woods. They didn't want to see us, but moved left-ward and we held the woods all P.M.—All seemed rather quiet for several hours—From 1½ til 4 P.M. there was the heaviest canonading I ever have heard—One constant roar with rising and falling inflections[45]—

Our Boys opened 54 guns at the same time on the Rebel lines and works from a little conical hill, Cemetary Ridge. We were picketing in the rear and on the right of it—Many shells came our way—some really quite near—But it is wonderful how few really made our acquaintance.

July 4, 1863 Saturday. The great battle closed and quieted with the closing day—Some firing at various points—

Our Regt layed on arms with Pickets out—on the ground where we had put in most of the day—Rather expecting attack momentarily—

Rained furiously during the night—We had fed, eaten, and were standing "to horse" when about 6 ock NEWS CAME—"The Rebs are falling back!" and "Our Forces are following them" and our Regt went out towards Hunterstown reconnoitering. We found some confederates who had straggled, or were foraging, not knowing yet what had happened and was taking place—Of course, our Boys took them in—Making a little detour I captured two. Sergt. Major J. T. Richardson and Private Cox 9th Va Cav—disarming them and bringing them in—I guarded them—while the Regt gathered in some others—P.M. Captain Hughes came along and paroled them—and

---

realized how much they had weakened the Union line in Cormany's area. Consequently, though battered, even beaten, Union defenders remained at the end of the day basically where their commanders had placed them. Glenn Tucker, *High Tide at Gettysburg: The Campaign in Pennsylvania* (Indianapolis, 1958), pp. 282–306. Samuel's name appears on the Pennsylvania monument at Gettysburg.

45. The Battle of Gettysburg reached a climax on July 3, when a Confederate effort to break the center of the Union line failed disastrously. That effort, which featured the massive infantry offensive known as Pickett's Charge, began with what still remains the largest artillery duel ever waged in North America. The sound of that duel, reverberating through the valleys of south central Pennsylvania and northern Maryland and back and forth among layered air inversions, was said to have been audible 140 miles away. Jack McLaughlin, *Gettysburg: The Long Encampment* (New York, 1963), p. 136. Later, Union field gunners played a crucial role in repelling the infantry offensive and inflicted heavy casualties on the retreating Confederates after their attack had been turned.

we were ordered to camp near Hanover—where we first lay on arriving near Gettysburg—

Evening awfully muddy and disagreeable—I saw much of the destructiveness of the Johnies today—

July 5, 1863 Sunday. Rained awfully during the night. I got very wet—

Early we took up the march for Chambersburg[46]—Crossing the battlefield—Cemitary Hill—The Great Wheat Field Farm, Seminary ridge—and other places where dead men, horses, smashed artillery, were strewn in utter confusion, the Blue and The Grey mixed—Their bodies so bloated—distorted—discolored on account of decomposition having set in—that they were utterly unrecognizable, save by clothing, or things in their pockets—The scene simply beggars description—Reaching the west side of the Field of Carnage—we virtually charged most of the way for 10 miles—to Cashtown—Frequently in sight of the Rebel rear guard—taking in prisoners—in bunches—We captured some 1,500 wounded men, and 300 stragglers—we went as far as Goodyears Springs, where we rested (?) for the night. (I had to guard a Reb all night.)

July 6, 1863 Monday. Had a good breakfast. Turned my prisoner over to others—We took up the march—via Fayeteville for Quincy—I told Corp. Metz I intended going on—To Chambersburg—To see wife and Baby—and would report in the morning again. He understood and I slipped away—and was soon making time for home—I got a fine "10 oclock piece" at Heintzelmans—on approaching Chambersburg I was assured there were still squads of rebs about town—Near town I was met by town folk inquiring about the battle. I was the first "blue coat" they had seen—and the first to bring direct news of the Enemy's defeat—as communications had been cut. As I struck the edge of town, I was told "The Rebel rear-guard had just left the Diamond." So I ventured out 2nd Street and ventured to strike Main near where Darling and Pussy lodged—and behold They were at the door—had been watching the Reb Rear leaving town—and Oh! The surprise and delight thus to meet after the awful battle they had been listening to for passing days—My horse was very soon stabled. My Cavalry outfit covered with hay—

46. When Lee decided to retreat, he divided his forces into two main columns. The first headed west through Cashtown, Greenwood, and Fayetteville to Chambersburg, where they would turn south down the Cumberland Valley. The other proceeded directly southwest from Gettysburg toward Hagerstown. The 16th Pennsylvania pursued the first of those columns in the direction of their own home town.

and myself in my citazens clothes—So should any final "rear" come along, I would not be discovered——

To attempt to describe my joy and feelings at meeting and greeting my dear little family must prove a failure——We spent the P.M. and evening very sweetly and pleasantly, but only we had a few too many inquiring callers.

XVI

Chambersburg During the Gettysburg Campaign

June 14–July 6, 1863

Chambersburg lay squarely in the middle of the valley up which Lee launched his second and last grand offensive in June 1863. The evacuation of local militia units left the town undefended, and it was rapidly occupied by the advancing Southern army. Chambersburg was used as a central staging area by the Confederates; its importance to their operations increased when the massive confrontation began to develop in Gettysburg, approximately twenty-five miles east across the South Mountain ridge. Following their defeat at Gettysburg, the Confederates withdrew from Chambersburg toward the Potomac River. Hot in pursuit was Samuel's regiment, and Samuel himself was among the first Union soldiers to reenter the town.

June 14, 1863   Read the R. Telescope & wrote letters this A.M.— P.M. went to S. School, took Cora along—she did pretty well—was in Bro. Hokes Bible class. How much better I feel to get out to religious gathering. Intend to go more. Mrs. Dulany was there with her little one too. I got such a good book to read. Some excitement about the rebels come.   Evening the excitement pretty high.

June 15, 1863   Monday. This morning pretty early Gen Milroys wagon train (so we were told) came.[1] Contrabands[2] on ahead coming as

1. After repelling Hooker's attack at Chancellorsville, Lee had launched a new offensive, thrusting up the Shenandoah Valley, across the Potomac, through Hagerstown, Md., and then up the valley between South Mountain ridge and North Mountain ridge in Pennsylvania. His first major target was thought to be the Pennsylvania Railroad at Harrisburg. Maj. Gen. Robert H. Milroy, whose Union troops had been stationed at Winchester, Va., had lost more than a third of his command during the three previous days as his small force had been driven before the main Confederate army. Most of Milroy's remaining men had dug in near Harpers Ferry, but his supply wagons were still scurrying for safety just ahead of the invaders. See Glenn Tucker, *High Tide at Gettysburg: The Campaign in Pennsylvania* (Indianapolis, 1958).

2. Contrabands were black refugees. That usage had been initiated by Gen. Benjamin Butler who, though technically bound to return refugee slaves, had instead declared them contraband of war and put them to work. John G. Nicolay and John Hay, *Abraham Lincoln: A History* (New York, 1890), IV, 388.

fast as they could on all & any kind of horses, their eyes fairly protruding with fear—teams coming at the same rate—some with the covers half off—some lost—men without hats or coats—some lost their coats as they were flying, one darky woman astride of a horse going what she could. There really was a real panic. All reported that the rebels were just on their heels. Soon things became more quiet—& all day government wagons & horses were passing through. For awhile before dark the excitement abated a little—but it was only like the calm before a great storm. At dusk or a little before the news came that the rebels were in Greencastle & that said town was on fire. Soon after some of the our guard came in reporting that they had a skirmish with them. Soon followed 100–200 cavalry men—the guard. Such a skedadling as their was among the women & children to get into the houses. All thought the Rebels had really come. The report now is that they will be here in an hour. If I could only hear of My Samuels safety—Many have packed nearly all of their packable goods—I have packed nothing. I do not think that we will be disturbed even should they come. I will trust in God even in the midst of flying shells—but of course shall seek the safest place possible in that case—which I hope will not come to us. I have just put my baby to sleep & will now sit at the front door awhile yet— then retire, knowing all will be well.

June 16, 1863 Retired at 11 oclock. All was very quiet, so we concluded that all those reports must be untrue about the Reb's being so near, or that they had struck off in some other direction. Mr. Plough took his horse away so as to be on the safe side. So Annie and I were all alone. At 11½ I heard the clattering of horses hoofs. I hopped out of bed & ran to the front window & sure enough there the Greybacks were going by as fast as their horses could take them down to the Diamond. Next I heard the report of a gun then they came back faster if possible than they came in. But a short time after the whole body came. the front ones with their hands on the gun triggers ready to fire & calling out as they passed along that they would lay the town in ashes if fired on again. It took a long time for them all to pass, but I could not judge how many there were—not being accustomed to seeing troops in such a body—At 2 oclock A.M. all was quiet again save an occasional reb. riding past. We went to bed again & slept soundly until 5 the morning. All seemed quiet yet. We almost came to the conclusion that the reb's had left again, leaving only a small guard who took things quite leasurely. Soon however they became more active. Were hunting up the contrabands & driving them off by droves. O! How it grated on our hearts to have to sit quietly & look at such brutal deeds—I saw no men among the contrabands—all women & children. Some of the colored people who were raised here were taken along—I sat on the front step as they were driven by just like we would drive cattle. Some laughed & seemed not to care—but nearly all hung their heads. One woman was pleading wonderfully with her driver for her children— but all the sympathy she received from him was a rough "March along"—at which she would quicken her pace again. It is a query what they want with those little babies—whole families were taken. Of course when the mother was taken she would take her children. I suppose the men left thinking the women & children would not be disturbed. I cannot describe all the scenes—now—Noon—The Rebel horses with just enough men to take care of them & their teams, have just pased through town again on the retreat. Wonder what all this means. Just now the news came that the dismounted rebs are drawn up in line of battle out at McClures & expect a fight—so they sent their horses to the safe side of town in case a retreat is neces- sary. Some are walking or riding by every few minutes. The horses & wagons were taken back again. Evening—Had a good sleep this P.M. so had Pussy, & will retire trusting in God for safety.

June 17, 1863 Had quite a visiter last night. She came and aske whether I was Mrs Cormany. I told her I was. she then told me she was preacher Millers daughter, & that they had fled from the Reb's & she had no place to stay. So of course I told her I would keep her. I afterwards learned that she was a thief &c but I had promised to keep her so I put all little things out of reach, & fright- ened her by telling her I always had a loaded pistol near so I could shoot if anyone molested me. She acted quite strangely—before go- ing to bed—wanted me to blow the light & get in bed & she after having shaken off her fleas would lock the door & come too—but I let her know that I lock my own door & that she is to get into bed— she slept all night & left early this morning. All was so quiet during the night that I veryly thought the Reb's had left—but they are still here. All forenoon they were carrying away mens clothing & darkeys. shortly after dinner their horses & wagons were taken on the retreat again. Yes Generals and all went. Saw Gen Jenkins,[3] he is

3. Brig. Gen. Albert Gallatin Jenkins, a graduate of Harvard Law School, had been a member of Congress before the war. He resigned his seat to assume command of Confederate forces in western Virginia. During the Gettysburg offensive his cavalry brigade led the Southern drive up the valley along the railroad line from Hagerstown through Greencastle to Chambersburg. Official records confirm his time of arrival exactly when Rachel notes seeing him. *DAB*, V, 43–44; Vincent J. Esposito, *The West Point Atlas of American Wars*, (New York, 1967), I, map 93. The bulk of the Southern

not a bad looking man—Some of the officers tipped their hats to us. I answered it with a curl of the lip. I knew they did it to taunt us. The one after he had tipped his hat most graciously & received in answer a toss of the head & curl of the lip took a good laugh over it. There were a few real inteligent good looking men among them. What a pity that they are rebels. After the main body had passed, the news came that our soldiers were coming & just then some ½ doz reb's flew past as fast as their horses could take them. we learned since that one of them fired Oaks warehouse & that he was very near being shot by the citizens.[4] Among the last to leave were some with darkeys on their horses behind them. How glad we are they are gone—None of our Soldiers came.

June 18, 1863 Was up early & commenced washing. Got done till noon. Quite a number of the neighbors washed—Soon after dinner the town was all in excitement again—the report came that the reb's are coming back. Plough was so badly frightened that he fairly shook. Talked so snappy & ugly when I asked him anything. I do not like to be snubbed by him or anybody—but guess it's best to bear all. I have not been frightened yet.

June 19, 1863 The excitement is still high. I have slept well every night so far knowing that my Heavenly Parent watches over me at all times. Ironed this morning & baked a loaf of brown bread. feel a little blue. I feel troubled about Mr. Cormany—we are penned up so here that we can hear nothing. All kinds of reports are flying about—still the excitement has abated considerably. Mended all my clothes & put every thing away. Read about the great revivals of ,56 & ,57. felt much happier than in the forenoon, enjoyed a sweet season of prayer.

June 20, 1863 Went to bed early & slept well all night. This morning there is great excitement again. The report came last night that

---

cavalry was still far to the south and east, trying to screen Lee's invasion and monitor the Union response. See Samuel's entry for June 17, 1863.

4. David Oaks, a dry-goods merchant, also managed the Oaks and Caufman warehouse beside the railroad depot on the edge of Chambersburg. John M. Cooper, *Recollections of Chambersburg, Pa., Chiefly Between the Years 1830–1850* (Chambersburg, 1900), pp. 7, 11. Most analyses of the issue of the destruction of civilian property during the Civil War focus on Sherman's actions in the South in 1864 and 1865. It can be argued, however, that his actions differed from previous practices on both sides only in their self-conscious effectiveness. The Confederates were doing somewhat randomly in the spring of 1863 what Sherman—and many others on both sides—decided to do more systematically as the war dragged on.

40,000 or 50,000 infantry & some artillery have taken possession of Hagerstown—that the camps extend nearly to Greencastle—things surely look a little dubious.[5] If we could only have regular mails. a mail came last night—but was not opened until this morning—Got a letter from My Samuel. it is but short. He is still safe—but were under marching orders again. it has been over a week on the way—I almost feel like getting out of this to some place where the mail is uninterupted, but then I fear, My Samuel might chance to come here & I would not see him so I shall stay—Will write to him now.

June 21, 1863   All was pretty quiet until near noon The news came that the rebels are near here—which caused great excitement again. soon after a reg. of the N.Y. Greys came (militia) so all excitement died away[6]—Wrote a letter (or finished it rather) to My Samuel.   Read such a pretty S. School book

June 22, 1863   This A.M. the N. Y. 71st (militia) came & one battery.[7] we felt safe then.   the mail came again, but this evening every soldier left us again & the rebels are reported within 8 or 10 miles.[8] Guess there will be nothing to hinder them from coming

5. These reports were substantially correct, for the main body of Lee's army was now pushing up the valley behind Jenkins's advance columns. The 2nd Corps, under Lt. Gen. Richard Stoddard Ewell, with over twenty thousand men, was in the lead north of Hagerstown; the 1st Corps, under Lt. Gen. James Longstreet, with another twenty thousand men, was in Hagerstown; and the 3rd Corps, commanded by Lt. Gen. Ambrose P. Hill, with twenty thousand more, was still at the Potomac end of the valley.

6. Once it became clear that Lee was launching a full-scale invasion of the North, the authorities at Washington issued a series of desperate calls for all available militia units from the surrounding states to converge on the Harrisburg area. See, for example, "Proclamation Calling for 100,000 Militia," issued June 15, 1863, in Roy P. Basler, ed., *The Collected Works of Abraham Lincoln* (New Brunswick, N.J., 1953), VI, 277–78. Except for Pennsylvania itself, however, only New York State sent a substantial number of militia. Since these were local troops, they were not required to wear regular army uniforms; Irish-American militia from New York City, for example, arrived in Harrisburg wearing green jackets. See Wilbur Sturtevant Nye, *Here Come the Rebels!* (Baton Rouge, La., 1965), p. 217. Hence, Rachel refers not to Confederate troops but to a New York unit known by the color of its uniforms.

7. The New York militia established a defensive position overlooking the main road south toward Greencastle. Their battery consisted of two brass howitzers. Jacob Hoke, *The Great Invasion of 1863; or General Lee in Pennsylvania . . . With an Appendix Containing an Account of the Burning of Chambersburg, Pennsylvania* (rpt. Dayton, Ohio, 1913), p. 123.

8. As soon as real fighting appeared imminent, the poorly trained and inexperienced militia unit abandoned its camp to board a train for Harrisburg. The abandoned howitzers were rescued by the citizens and sent north. Ibid., pp. 128–30.

now—suppose they will be on here by tomorrow which will stop our mail again for some time. I do indeed feel like getting out of this place on that account but do not like to leave everything behind. I do really feel like leaving. Old Plough still wants to take Annie off & leave me all by myself—not a word does he say to take me along. Oh he does seem the meanest pile of dirt I have seen for some time. He seems too mean for any use. Indeed I believe I shall pack up & leave in the morning. I cant bear to think of being shut up without any news another week.

June 23, 1863 I packed my trunk last evening ready to start to Phil'dia not knowing whether I could get away or not—went to bed at midnight & slept well till after six this morning. I expected to find the town full of rebels but not a rebel could I see—none had come— So after breakfast I took Cora on my arms & started out for a walk. met Mrs Clippinger at her door, asked her to go along for a walk, so we walked on until we saw where our men threw up breastworks but did not go near enough to examine them. Met quite a number of people (men & boys) going out as we came in[9]—we sat down by the roadside & rested a little while then started on. just as we got to the edge of town or near it—two men came riding as fast as their horses could go—one said "The d——d buggers fired on us. the other looked as pale as death his mouth wide open—his hat lost—he was too badly frightened to speak. They me[t] a few of our Cavalry at the edge of town—they whirled & put off. I got a little frightened when those two men made so ugly & the cavalry-men warned us to go into the houses, looking so fierce with their hands on the gun triggers ready to shoot—all at once I got so weak I could scarcely walk, but that was over in a few minutes & I could walk faster than before. The people were wonderfully frightened again, such a running. The streets were full–It was not long until the reb's really made their appearance—I do not think that they are Cav. but mounted infantry—they most of them have nothing but a musket to fight with. They rode in as leisurely as you please each one having his hand on the trigger though, to fire any minute—so now I judge we are shut out again for awhile—I just wonder what they want this time. They are part of those that were here last week. P.M. just ate a piece & fed my baby—both of us took a good nap

---

9. The citizens of Chambersburg "helped themselves to what they pleased of clothing and other articles" abandoned by the New Yorkers until the arrival of the Confederates, who were forcibly collecting supplies themselves. Hence the "men & boys" headed out to the camp. Ibid., pp. 129–30.

after our walk. Evening—The Reb's have been cutting up high. Sawed down telegraph poles, destroyed the scotland bridge[10] again, took possession of the warehouses & were dealing out flour by the barrel & mollasses by the bucket ful—They made people take them breat—meat—&c to eat—Some dumb fools carried them jellies & the like—Not a thing went from this place.[11] Three canno[ns] went through when they came—but just now they took them back. wonder what that means again. from 7 to 15 thousand infantry are expected on tonight. they are reported to be at Greencastle by a man just from there. Well whatever betides us the good Lord is able to protect us. And He will protect us. Old Plough wanted Annie to go with him to the country but she would not go & leave me here alone. That was mean in Plough. Annie told me herself—It shows what a great heart he has.

June 24, 1863 Another eventful day has passed—All morning there was considerable riding done up & down street. At 10 A.M. the infantry commenced to come & for 3 hours they just marched on as fast as they could. it is supposed that about 15,000 have already passed through, & there are still more coming. Ewel's brigade has pas. I do not know what others. Longstreet & Hill are expected this way too. It is thought by many that a desperate battle will be fought at Harisburg. This P.M. the Rebs are plundering the stores. some of our merchants will be almost if not entirely ruined—I was sitting on Jared's poarch[12] when a young man (rebel) came & shook hands with Mr. Jared—a relative, his brother is in this army too. He was raised here—His mother is burried here—Mr. Jared told him he ought to go & kneel on his Mothers grave & ask for pardo[n] for having fought in such a bad cause. against such a good Govern-

10. The Cumberland Valley Railroad crossed Conococheaque Creek at the hamlet of Scotland, about three and one-half miles northeast of Chambersburg. Jenkins's men had destroyed the bridge a week earlier. See Nye, *Here Come the Rebels!*, p. 141.

11. Even though there was substantial political opposition in this area to the Lincoln administration, and some opposition to the war itself, the civilian population seems to have been uncooperative with the Confederates during the Gettysburg offensive. Confederate scouts had been fired upon, civilians had tried to hide anything they thought the Confederates might want, and the townspeople had to be forced to feed the Southern soldiers. Later, there is evidence of petty resistance, including the giving of wrong directions and the withholding of supplies. Civilian hostility was a disappointment to Lee, who hoped that his invasion might flame discord in the North and spark anti-Lincoln activity. On popular reaction in Chambersburg see Jack McLaughlin, *Gettysburg: The Long Encampment* (New York, 1963), p. 35.

12. The Jaretts lived four doors down the street from the Ploughs. *AFCP*, p. 24.

ment. The tears almost came, he said he could not well help getting in, but he would not fight in Pa. he told his officers so, he was put under arrest awhile but was released again. Now he said he is compelled to carry a gun & that is as far as they will get toward making him fight. He was in Jacksons Brig. Says Jackson was a christian & means it honestly & earnestly.[13] Some of the Rebs seemed quite jolly at the idea of being in Pa. All is quiet this evening so I shall retire after having committed myself to my maker.

June 25, 1863 Slept well last night. Got up at 6½ A.M. Got Emma Jarrett to go down street with me & got the dried fruit, paper, envelopes & stamps that I had left at Dr MtGomerys,[14] then went up the back st. to Ditmans[15] & got 4 bbs of brown sugar for 50 cts—when I got home Cora was sitting in the cradle playing. The streets are pretty clear this morning still there are plenty Greybacks about. 2 more divisions are expected on here today & tomorrow. Evening The other division that was to come today did not come, but those here have not been idle. They must surely expect to set up stores or fill their empty ones judging from the loads they have been hauling away & they take every thing a body can think of—I was across the street for water & at Aunt Maria's two rebs were talking. one was telling about the battle at Chancelorville. A body would think by his talk that he did about all that was done, at least the greatest part— he told how mean our me[n] acted in Dec. battle at Fredricksburg— he said they sent in a flag of truce to have time allowed them to burry their dead. well he helped to "toat" (as he said) off dead & wounded & behold when they came to where our men were. instead of digging graves they were throwing up breastworks, & instead of burrying the dead they left them lie where they were laid & sneaked off over the river in the night—Lee then sent a flag of truce for a detail of men to burry those dead—which was complied with but the way they were burried, hands & feet were sticking out— they (rebels) had to burry them over—He saw that did not take, so he said that both sides were to blame—& that they were too hasty in

---

13. Gen. Thomas "Stonewall" Jackson, a rigid Presbyterian, had died only a month before from a wound inflicted accidently by his own troops during the battle of Chancellorsville. Lee then reorganized the Army of Northern Virginia, placing most of Jackson's former command, including the famous Stonewall brigade, under General Ewell. James I. Robertson, Jr., *The Stonewall Brigade* (Baton Rouge, La., 1963), pp. 194–201.

14. A local physician. *AFCP*, pp. 19, 22.

15. George Dittman ran a grocery store on Front Street, four doors toward the center of town from Ploughs. Ibid., pp. 19, 24.

firing on Fort Sumpter—if they had waited a little longer he believed Pa. would have seceeded too. That did me for bragadocio so I left— It made my blood fairly boil to have to take that & not dare to tell him he lied. Plough was home this afternoon but left again. I made an apron for my baby today. Pretty reliable reports have reached us that McClellan has a heave force (80,000) at Harisburg ready for the Reb's. Also that Stoneman is at Harpers Ferry or near there with 15,000 Cav.[16] I wish every one of these would be taken. Hope this is the beginning of the end.

June 26, 1863 12½ oclock Cannon-waggons & men have been pass-ing since between 9 & 10 this morning—42 Cannon & as many amunition waggons have passed—so now there are 62 pieces of artillery between us & Harrisburg & between 30,000 & 40,000 men.[17] O it seems dreadful to be thus thrown into the hands of the rebbels & to be thus excluded from all the rest of the world—I feel so very anxious about Mr. Cormany—& who knows when we will hear from any of our friends again. It is no use to try to get away from here now—we must just take our chance with the rest—trusting in God as our Savior then come life come death if reconciled with God all is well—My God help me—I do wish to be a real true & living christian. Oh for more religion. Evening—called at Mrs Dickson a few minutes. Also at Mrs Clippingers. Numerous campfires could be seen on the fair ground.

June 27, 1863 Got up early & wakened Annie. And we flew round & put away our best bedclothes—before I got my things in order again Mrs. Clippinger came to go to Hokes where we got syrup & sugar. I also got me a lawn dress. Before we got started the rebels poured in already. they just marched through. Such a hard looking set I never saw. All day since 7 oclock they have been going through. Between 30 & 40 pieces of canno[n]—& an almost endless trail of waggons. While I am writing thousands are passing—such a rough dirty ragged rowdyish set one does not often see—Gen's Lee & Longstreet passed through today. A body would think the whole south had broke loose & are coming into Pa. It makes me feel too badly to see so many men & cannon going through knowing that

16. Neither of these reports was accurate.

17. Rachel's estimates were reasonably accurate. Chambersburg had become an important Confederate staging area by this date. Part of Lee's army continued north, up the Cumberland Valley toward Carlisle and Harrisburg. Other elements took the road east, over the ridges to Cashtown and Gettysburg. Lee himself arrived in Chambersburg on June 26.

they have come to kill our men—Many have chickens as they pass—
There a number are going with honey—robed some man of it no
doubt—they are even carrying it in buckets. The report has reached
us that Hooker & Sickel & Stoneman are after them. & at Harisburg the north has congregated en masse to oppose the invaders.
Many think this the best thing in the wor[l]d to bring the war to a
close—I hope our men will be strong enough to completely whip
them—Now it is on our side—While down there our army was in
the enemys country & citizens kept the rebels posted in our army
movements—now *they* are in the enemys country. Scarcely any are
willing to give them anything—in fact none give unless the have to
except perhaps the Copperheads[18]—The cavalry had an engagement
at not far from Carlisle—& the Reb's were driven back. This seems
to be headquarters. A hospital has been established in the school
house where the sick are put in & the wounded. Two of their
Generals are reported killed in that picket skirmish. They are going
rather fast—wonder whether there is not fighting going on in front.
They are poorly clad—many have no shoes on. As they pass along
they take the hats off our citizens heads and throw their old ones in
exchange. I was at the window up stairs with my baby nearly all day
looking at them—at one time one of them said something that I did
not like so I curled my lip as disdainful as I could & turned away
just look at he[r] he said to another   I saw a lot looking up, so I just
wheeled & left the window at which they set up a cheer. Once
before the same was enacted except the general cheer. I did wish I
dared spit at their old flag—I pity some of the men for I am sure
they would like to be out. At Dicksons they told me that 400 went at
one time—gagged the guards & got off to the mountains & on to
Harisburg to help our men. Or I believe J. Hoke told me this morning. He said too that about 1000 had deserted. I hope that all the
rebels have passed that intended to pass through—After they quit
coming once then I shall look for our men.

June 28, 1863 Slept well. Nowadays our cooking does not take
much time—nowadays being we do all our eating by piecing. At 8½
A.M. the rebels commenced coming again. Ga. troops. I was told this
morning of some of their mean tricks of yesterday & before. They
took the hats & boots off the men—Took that off Preacher Farney.
Took $50. off Dr. Sneck & his gold watch valued very highly—took
the coats off some, tetotally stripped one young fellow not far from

18. "Copperhead" was a derogatory term for a Northerner who was considered
sympathetic to the Southern cause.

town—Mr. Skinner. We have to be afraid to go out of our houses. A large wagon train & 500 or 600 Cavalry have just passed & it is now about 3½ oclock. hope all are through now. Many of the saddles were empty, & any amount of negroes are along. This does not seem like Sunday. No church.

June 29, 1863 Got up early & washed was done & dressed by ten oclock, had such bad luck this morning—first the washboard fell & broke—next the water boiled down in the boiler it got empty the tin melted off so it leaks & I cannot get it fixed as long as the rebels are here. I feel too badly about it—After I was dressed I put the baby to sleep then went to Ditmans & got a Gallon molasses for 50 cts— Also to Hok[e]s & got 3 qts syrup for 45 cts—Hoke told me that the Reb's had taken about 500 $ worth of sugar & molasses—they went into the private cellar & took Mrs Hokes canned fruit & bread—Mr H looks down this morning. The news reached us this A.M. that Stoneman & Stuart had a fight last week in which Stuart was whipped & ten pieces of artillery were taken from him.[19] Also that our men hold Hagerstown again. Also that the rebel mail carryer could not get through the lines. If our men hold Hagerstown it will not be long before they will be here. Evening. A large waggon train headed by 10 pieces of artillery & I judge a regiment of of infantry just passed. The wagons were all well loaded. I judge they are bound for Dixie—It looks as if they expected some opposition. It is reported too that the Reb mail carrier, mail & all have been captured. hope its true. I felt real badly to see those poor men going through as they did. likely many of them will be killed. There certainly is something on foot, for the ambulances were filled with sick, taking them away.

June 30, 1863 Nothing special transpired today. The Rebs are still about doing all the mischief they can. They have everything ready to set fire to the warehouses & machine shops—Tore up the railroad track & burned the crossties—They have cleared out nearly every store so they cannot rob much more—Evening—Quite a number of the young folks were in the parlor this evening singing all the patriotic & popular war songs. Quite a squad of rebels gathered outside to listen & seemed much pleased with the music—"When this cruel war is over" nearly brought tears from some. they sent in a petition to have it sung again which was done. they then thanked the girls very much & left—they acted real nicely.

19. This was news of the battles at Aldie, Middleburg, and Upperville already detailed in Samuel's entries for June 17–22, 1863.

July 1, 1863 It is very muddy this morning of yesterdays rain—in fact I believe it has rained every day this week. I was out hunting [y]east & got some at last   I have not a bit of bread left   my [y]east got sour, so of course the [y]east I set last evening is sour & not fit to use. It is reported that Gen. Jenkins is wounded & a prisoner. Also that the rebel pickets were driven in this side of Greencastle—& that McClellan drove them to this side of Carlisle & that Milroy & Sigel are making a junction over by Strasburg—A darkey, Colonels waiter heard him say that he thought that Lee made a bad move this time—he (darkey) also said that that large wagon train was hid in the woods &c that they could not get out, that they are watching their chance to slip out—he said too that the officers were very uneasy—Every one can see by their actions that they do not feel quite as easy as they would like.[20] They are chopping &c at a great rate over at the R.R. all morning. I judge they are breaking up the iron by the sound. Must now go & set my bread. Evening. Got good bread. Mrs. Fritz was here & told us of Emma Plough being sick from the fright & how the rebels have been carrying on out there. They robbed the country people of nearly everything they had & acted very insultingly.

July 2, 1863 At 3 A.M. I was wakened by the yells & howls of this dirty ragged lousy trash—they made as ugly as they could—all day they have been passing—part of the time on the double quick. At one time the report came that our men had come on them & that they were fighting—the excitement was high in town—but it was soon found out to be untrue—but the shock was so great that I got quite weak & immagined that I could already see My Samuel falling—I feel very uneasy about him—I cannot hear at all—They had quite a battle with Stuart—I almost fear to hear the result in who was killed & who wounded—still I want to know.

July 3, 1863 Started out with Cora & a little basket on the hunt for something to eat out of the garden. I am tired of bread & molasses—went to Mammy Royers & got some peas & new potatoes—Cora got

---

20. Many of Lee's middle echelon officers were openly uneasy with the tactical decision that Lee had made on the night of June 28–29 to concentrate his invading army just east of the ridge between Chambersburg and Gettysburg, near the village of Cashtown. This decision "uncovered" the Confederate army, as it were, for Lee had come out from behind the shield of South Mountain. Glenn Tucker, *Lee and Longstreet at Gettysburg* (Indianapolis, 1968), discusses some of the important disagreements among Confederate commanders and criticizes Lee for permitting them to become a major problem.

as many raspberries as she could eat. Came home put Cora to sleep then went to Mrs McG's for milk. got a few cherries to eat also a few for Cora   when I got back Daddy Byers[ba] was standing at the gate. he came to see how I was getting along & told me how the rebels acted—they robbed him of a good deal—they wanted the horse but he plead so hard for him that they agreed to leave him & while one wrote a paper of securety others plundered the house.   I guess Samuels silk hat & all that was in the box is gone. took Ellies[y] best shoes—took towels sheets &c &c—After they were gone others came & took the horse too yet—they did not care for his security. Other of their neighbors fared worse yet. He would not stay for dinner. After dinner Henry Rebok[pa] came—he walked part of the way   had an old horse but feared to bring him in—they were robbed of their horses and cattle up there—many had their horses sent away—one of J. Cormanys[d] horses was taken.[21] Henry[pa] wanted me to go along home with him but I could not think of leaving now—Samuel might come this way & if I were out there I would not get to see him. He said he had started for me when they first heard of the rebels coming but when he came to Orrstown two were there already. There are no rebels in town today except the sick—& two or three squads passed through, in all not much over a hundred if that many. One squad asked the way to Getysburg & were sent towards Harisburg. they did not go very far until they asked again, when they were told the truth they came back very angry & wanted the man that sent them the wrong way but he was not to be found. Canonading was heard all day.[22]

July 4, 1863   At daybreak the bells were rung—Then all was quiet until about 8 oclock when a flag was hoisted at the diamond. Soon after the band made its appearance & marched from square & played national airs—two rebels came riding along quite leisurely thinking I suppose to find their friends instead of that they were taken prissoners by the citizens—some 13 more footmen came and were taken prisoners.   those were willing prisoners they had thrown their guns away before they reached this. The report has reached us that 6000 prisoners had been taken yesterday in Adams Co. near College Hill— also that Carlisle was shelled. It is getting very dark cloudy—I judge we will have a heavy rain. That Will Wampler does yell and cry like a

---

21. After the war John submitted a claim for the loss of this horse. The document is in the possession of his eighty-six-year-old grandson, J. Roy Cormany, of Chambersburg.

22. This was the day of the great artillery duel and Pickett's Charge.

panther. Evening We have had a powerful rain. Wild rumors of a dreadful fight are numerous.

July 5, 1863 I was roused out of sleep by Mr Early coming into Wampler & telling him something about wounded & prisoners. so I got up took a bath dressed & went for a pitcher of water when I was told that 10, 4 or 6 horse waggons filled with wounded from the late battle were captured by citizens & brought to town—the wounded were put into the hospitals & the waggons & drivers were taken on toward Harisburg. Was also told that a great many more were out toward Greencastle—some went out to capture those but found that it was a train 20 miles long. P.M. A report has reached us that the whole rebel army is on the retreat—later that they are driven this way & are expected on soon—Have church S. School here today—seems like Sunday again Evening. At or after 4 P.M. I dressed myself & little girl and went to Mrs. Sulenbargers & while there we heard a fuss outside & when we got out lo our (Union of course) soldiers were coming in—she came along upstreet then to see them. They are of Milroys men[23]—Just at dusk they went out the Greencastle road enroute to capture the waggon train which is trying to get over the river again. It is frightful how those poor wounded rebels are left to suffer. they are taken in large 4 horse waggons—wounds undressed—nothing to eat. Some are only about 4 miles from town & those that are here are as dirty and lousy as they well can be. The condition of those poor rebels all along from Getysburg to as far as they have come yet is reported dreadful. I am told they just beg the people along the road to help them—many have died by the way.

July 6, 1863 I was sitting reading, Pussy playing by my side when little Willie Wampler came running as fast as he could to tell me a soldier had come to see me & sure enough when I got to the door Mr Cormany just rode up. I was so very glad to see him that I scarcely knew how to act. He was very dirty & sweaty so he took a bath & changed clothes before he got himself dressed A. Holler & Barny Hampshire called—next Rev. Dixon & Dr Croft & others. Eve we went down into the parlor to hear some of the girls play—Mr. C. was very much pleased with the music.

23. These were the same Union forces that had been driven ahead of the invaders two weeks before. Now Milroy's men were helping local citizens capture wagon trains of Confederate wounded, which were desperately straggling toward Harpers Ferry and the relative safety of Virginia.

XVII

Cavalry Operations in Virginia

July 7–November 24, 1863

This section opens as Samuel rejoins his regiment on the morning of July 7, 1863, after slipping away the previous night to spend some time with his wife and daughter. His entries chronicle the Union pursuit of the Confederate army back into Virginia and continue through the long summer of maneuver and countermaneuver that followed. Samuel's diary for this period contains excellent accounts of the Battle of Shepherdstown, where he is slightly wounded and commended for bravery, and of the so-called Bristoe Campaign, where his notes capture nicely both the boredom and the excitement of riding picket duty on an active front. This portion ends with Samuel's promotion to Quartermaster Sergeant.

———————————————◆•◆•◆————————————————

July 7, 1863 Tuesday. Oh! how sweet to love and be loved. I kissed my Darlings Good-bye, and at 7 A.M. started back to join my Regiment at Greenwood.

Now that I have again seen my dearest ones of Earth, have loved and caressed them profusely, soldiering seems almost a new thing again—and altogether desirable—since country, home, and dear ones must be defended.

Reached the Regiment about 9 A.M. Corp Metz had done the nice thing[1]—and he and I took our dinners at Fayetteville.

In the P.M. we marched on through Funkstown—En route 6 Rebs gave themselves up—Corp Metz & I took charge of them—We encamped near Quincy—

July 8, 1863 Wednesday. Torrents of rain all night—Got very wet—About 10 A.M. we went to Waynesboro—Turned over our prisoners—move on up the mountain via Mt A. Springs & then on 4 to 6 miles—Encamped for the night on top of the Mountain. Ceased raining and cleared up—

O how full my mind is of the loved ones down in the valley—I can

---

1. He had not reported Cormany absent without leave on the previous night.

see Chambersburg—10–15 miles away, and the Reformed Church steeple—near where Darling and Pussy are sleeping.[2]

July 9, 1863 Thursday. Started early—very zigzag course. rested several hours at Millersburg—and then went on the Middletown & encamped.

July 10, 1863 Friday. Hot—Lay in field roasting all day P.M. Moved camp a few 100 yrds. 13 of our Alexandria Boys joined us with new horses—and 3 absent without leave showed up—They had been visiting—

July 11, 1863 Saturday. NEWS Vicksburg has fallen.[3] A.M. I wrote for Pet—
P.M. Took up line of March. Passed where some of our advance had a little brush yesterday—Eve Camp near Boonesboro.

July 12, 1863 Sunday. Not much going on save "Camp rumors"— Rained furiously—Some of the Boys almost swam away.

July 13, 1863 Monday. Moved Camp 2 to 400 yrds. We receive plenty of orders. I made out some reports for Capt.

July 14, 1863 Tuesday. Started 9 A.M.—Crossed Potomac at Harpers Ferry on Pontoons—Eve our advance had a little skirmish— went into wide-awake-camp on Boliver Heights.[4]

July 15, 1863 Wednesday. Started out early to Halltown, rested awhile—had considerable skirmishing and charging all the way to Shepherdstown—we made a tremendous dash into town, surprising and capturing quite a number of Rebs—also—some invalids. There were some 30 fighting fellows and 80 invalids taken—also some provisions—Tents, &c.
I had a fine chat with some of the rebel Ladies—I do admire their pluck—what a pity their minds didn't run in a different Channel—a better channel. So the efforts of such animated feelings would not be

2. The German Reformed Church of Chambersburg was six doors down Front Street from Plough's house. *AFCP*, p. 24.

3. A Confederate force of over thirty thousand men, which had been trapped in Vicksburg since May, surrendered to General Grant on July 4.

4. Bolivar Heights was the high ground above Harpers Ferry, W. Va. West Virginia had been admitted as the thirty-fifth state in the Union less than a month earlier.

VIEW OF SHEPHERDSTOWN.

From S. Howell Brown, *Map of Jefferson County, Virginia* (1852). Maps Division, LC.

so hopelessly wasted on a waning cause tottering on its last legs—We followed the retreating closely some 8 miles—I was in extreme advance in charge of a section of our best men—We fired on them frequently—i.e., their rear and so kept them well closed up—— Evening we encamped near Mrs. Kroates—I got a fine supper.

July 16, 1863 Thursday. Has cleared—I got a fine breakfast at Mrs Kroates. Mr. K. is gone to Penna.—We changed camp at 10 A.M. ½ mile. Dined at Mrs. K's—I have been kind-o-guarding her home, seeing he is loyal and is away—

About noon, skirmishing commences.[5] Soon our Regt was dismounted and in front advancing across open field—firing at will— enemy was in a woods—long range—Sharp shooting ¼ to ½ mile—I with several, along our line, crept far out front behind stumps and rocks and picked the enemy sharpshooters out of trees. Soon our whole line was hotly engaged—Enemy advancing out of the woods—but we held our line, checking them. Soon we were under the hotest cross-fire we ever were in—and had to fall back on line with an old house and stone fence and stone piles—my buddy—was shot through the breast at my left and dropping said, "Oh I am shot—tell my Mother." and he was hushed. bullits passed close to my head. I dodged behind a stone pile and fired at the man who had shot Buddy—Raising his head above the stone fence protecting him. His bullet whizzed close to my right ear—I made a port hole by pushing up two stones and one to cap the space and putting my carbine through my head was shielded. After this the rocks were hit once—My gun was ready, and soon his head came up and he craned his neck to find me—Then my gun went off— and—I don't know—But he didn't show up to shoot again. Soon I found the men to my right and left were falling back and I was compelled to do so too. As I retreated toward the Boys, directly two rebs appeared, less than 100 yds to my right—having just emerged from some bushes and weeds—and had the drop on me. Instead of throwing up my arms to surrender—I banged away. One of them dropped his gun. The other fired wild—I fired again on the run—a small volley followed me—but I reached the fence where

5. What follows is the detailed description of a typical cavalry action. The Confederates had been continuously in retreat since Gettysburg; the Union cavalry steadily in pursuit. As their bold charge into Shepherdstown the day before demonstrated, the Union troopers had grown quite confident. Now safely across the Potomac, however, elements of the retreating Southern army wheeled around to face their pursuers in a rearguard counterattack resulting in the Battle of Shepherdstown.

our line was, and so was safe(?) again—The rebel line was coming across the same ground—a daring Flag bearer was away front. Came within 100 yds of us—I said "Boys drop that Rebel Flag" We fired—The flag fell. Another reb picked it up—another little volley and it dropped again—another picked it up, and stepped behind a lone tree—held it out, i.e., The flagpole resting on the ground—The arm extending from the tree—held the pole erect. Again our little group fired "for that arm" and the flag fell—all this while to the right and left of me and my Bunch—the regiment was firing from this fence—and the enemy was moving rather cautiously and slowly but was now very close—a little lull—BOOM! a shell drops within 20 or 30 feet of us. Explodes throwing ground over us—making an excavation large enough to roll a horse in out of sight—a piece of that shell hit my right arm between the shoulder and elbow. My first thought was "There goes my right arm"—But it was not gone—though badly bruised—

Here came the hotest time yet. Shells—Grape in front—and infantry crossfire—and a charge—Infantry against dismounted Cavalry—

Nine pieces of artillery were in play—Our Boys stood to the stone fence—A while I carried ammunition—as my arm was too sore to allow my using my carbine—In this I became a fine (?) target for sharpshooters—

We held our part of the line though they several times charged as close to our fence as 50 to 100 yards or nearer—at such times our men used their Revolvers and forced them to fall back and reform—

Kindly darkness came on so we could only fire at their fire—But we held our line against every effort they made—Their firing becoming less and less frequent. About 10 P.M. they ceased firing. Later we fired a few shots. There was no response, so we sent out a few scouts and found they had withdrawn and about 11 ock orders came for us to return to our horses—and fall back to Boliver Heights and encamp—Picket line had been established—So we gave ourselves to seeking rest and comfort—amidst rain and rain and rain. Of course, we all were very much exhausted.

The tension was fearful, for we well knew we were fighting against fearful odds———

July 17, 1863 Friday. After Battle of Shephardstown. Boliver Heights   I feel quite unwell—used up—We lay 'round resting most of day—My arm & shoulder very bruised, and lame, from a hit by a piece of rebel shell, yesterday, and the jar from so much carbine shooting—

Evening we drew some clothing for our comfort &c.

Read and meditated some   The Lord is SO GOOD to have spared me through another such terrific battle.

July 18, 1863   Saturday. Cleared up   I am very stiff in my right arm and shoulder—But have no difficulty in performing full duty.

I took a good bath in the Shenandoah River—made me feel lots better—P.M. Captain Snyder and I rode Harpers Ferry Hospital—Sergt Harrison wounded in right knee—rests easy—Poor Will Goodman and Corp'l S.A. Rorabough mortally wounded—both died soon after being taken off the field[6]—

July 19, 1863   Sunday. Fine day—Rested—My arm quite sore to the touch—and somewhat stiff—Eve we left camp, crossed the Shenandoah on Bridge—went down along the River—some grand-romantic scenery—at 10 P.M. we put up at Lovettsville—

July 20, 1863   Monday. This morning Capt Snyder announced that "for conspicuous bravery during the battle at Shepherdstown—four days ago—Sam'l E. Cormany has been promoted to Sergeant and Jerome Coble to Corporal and the Company is hereby ordered to recognize them as such at all times"—

We took up line of March early, via Leesburg—Folks look awfully surly at us as we pass—we can see our unwelcomeness—and no wonder! We defeated Lee at Gettysburg and drove his Army back to Virginnia, and only last Thursday we thoroughly defeated a large force of them at Shephardstown, and induced them to fall back here in Virginnia, and here we are! A column of Triumphant Fellows, moving along their streets, and their "Boasters" still on the retreat.——Evening we put up at a Mill on Goose Creek—I am well but suffer some from my bruised arm—

July 21, 1863   Tuesday. Marched all day—Went via Centerville. Great fortifications here. Went on across Bull Run and bivouaced—Put out two squadrons on picket duty towards Evening—Endless patches of Blackberries, and we did up quantities of the choicest berries—both Evening and morning—

6. Both Goodman and Rorabough (Rowbaugh in the official records) were from Company H. The 16th Pennsylvania lost six known dead, fifteen wounded, and eleven missing in action. Two of the missing were also from Company H. Cormany's injury was not severe enough to warrant listing his name among the wounded. See *H16PC*, pp. 15, 17, 19; *PV*, p. 952.

The Orange and Alexandria Railroad line near Bristoe, Va., as it appeared when the 16th Pennsylvania advanced along it in the summer of 1863. The tracks had been destroyed by the Confederates. Photographic Division, LC.

July 22, 1863 Wednesday. I am feeling fine—Is very hot. We took up line of march by 8 OCK. Passed Bull Run Forts and breast works, and went on to Bristow Station on Orange & Alexandria R.R.

Fine grazing and plenty of water—Nice camping ground—on the open plain—

July 23, 1863 Thursday. Very hot! Laid off all day—I worked on Co Pay Rolls—Took two good swims—wrote long letter to Pet—am well physically, mentally and spiritually. Thank the Good Lord, and my arm is about O.K. again—

July 24, 1863 Friday. Warm—sultry——We drew rations & forage and at 10 A.M. Marched via Catletts Station and Warrenton Junction to one of our old camping places, four miles from Warrenton—Put up cosily—Threw out pickets. O! The luscious berries all around—

we put up—or down—plenty. Orderly Peters and I cease to Mess together—He is not a Christian—is profane—and a little lazy—Tho we got on fairly smoothly—

July 25, 1863 Saturday. Returned to Warrenton Junc. I worked on Co. Rolls—We drew Forage and rations, and filled up with Blackberries Evening Strike Tents and march. Heavy rain & storm—Reach Bealton Station 10 P.M. Bivouac—

July 26, 1863 Sunday. Very hot—Lounge (?) around all day—A day of rest sure—I am pretty well and happy—Willing to do all my duty, and do it well. But, one may be expected to do lots belonging to some other one to do and sour on it—

And as regards my spiritual duties, or dues, would to God I could perform them better—

I find it so easy to promise my ever Faithful Lord & Saviour—but so often I fail to perform. But God knows all my hinderances.

July 27, 1863 Monday. Warm if not more so. I finish Pay Rolls—Monthly Report Wrote to Pet, also to the Provost Marshall in Chambersburg to have Sergt McGowen arrested and sent to the Regiment, as he has been long absent without leave.

July 28, 1863 Tuesday. I slept last night with Ash Rosenberry in Wagon. We lay around all day reading—talking—writing and wishing to get a move on soon—

July 29, 1863 Wednesday. Marched early via White Sulphur Springs and near Warrenton—any amount of Troops seem on the qui vive—Passed Gen'l Meads Hd Qrs and in eve went into camp 3 miles from Warrenton on the Pike—Rained furiously in the night.

July 30, 1863 Thursday. Up and off early—Crossed river at Waterloo, very deep fording went via Amesville[7]—Brigade lay there while we went on Picket near Gains X Roads[8]—I am Sergt of the guard—Rebs are near our posts—

---

7. Amissville, Va., about ten miles west of Warrenton.

8. The main road west from Warrenton forked at the small town of Gaines' Cross Roads. One branch veered northwest through the Blue Ridge at Front Royal; the other turned south toward Thornton's Gap and Luray.

July 31, 1863 Friday. Last eve I drew in our posts some and this morning placed them out again—Did some Foraging—Pork, Flour, and horse-feed plenty—and Berries without number, measure or expressable quality. Some Picket firing—not serious. P.M. Relieved from picket—so we fell back to main Reserve. Drew Rations

August 1, 1863 Saturday. We fell back to Amesville and camped in Pine Woods—
I cooked Applesauce—First of the season—Fine! with "slapjacks."
My arm and shoulder all O.K. now, and I am so well and real happy, but I do so long for a letter from Pet and pussy—This has been the hotest day out—

August 2, 1863 Sunday. Heavy canonading in the direction of Culpepper—Lay in Camp—Wrote to Pet—Heat tremendous. Read and meditate—Am well and happy, but long to be a more Manly Man, especially morally and religiously—

August 3, 1863 Monday. Made out Final Statement of Wm Goodman and S. A. Rorabaugh—deceased—Finished a long letter of 16 pgs to Pet—To be sent also to Canadian Friends——Eve I am on as Serg't of the Guard—Lieut Caughey Officer of the Guard—and Capt Snyder Officer of the Day—A dandy good crew for sure, and Alls! Well!!

August 4, 1863 Tuesday. I was out with my Guards all day—Good news from fight near Culpepper yesterday. Enemy defeated & driven.[9] Genl. Lee now at Stephensburg—Our Guards taken off—Adjutant showed some spleen—

August 5, 1863 Wednesday. HOT! Lieut Barnes, Corporal Decker—Earick Witherall, Georgie and I went out foraging—Fooled some Rebel folk badly—They took us for Mosby Men—"Confeds"[10]— We got

---

9. The skirmishing around Culpeper, the noise of which Cormany had heard two days earlier, proved inconsequential. The two sides were facing each other along the now familiar Rappahannock line and the action at Culpeper barely affected either army. E. B. Long, *The Civil War Day By Day: An Almanac, 1861–1865* (Garden City, N.Y., 1971), pp. 393–94.

10. John S. Mosby led a force of Confederate irregulars who waged a remarkably effective form of guerrilla warfare in northern Virginia. Considered a brigand by Union commanders, Mosby was lionized by the Southern people and was eventually recognized formally by reluctant Confederate officials. See *The Memoirs of Colonel John S. Mosby*, ed. Charles W. Russell (Boston, 1917). Georgie was a black servant.

15 Chickens, 1 bu Potatoes, lots of eggs—Butter and Canteens of milk &c, &c, &c. Maybe we and others didn't have a high in Camp on our return? But I say we surely did—

August 6, 1863 Thursday. New Camp—Short ⅛ mile move—I commenced to mess with John Woodall—Cooked some for Captain Snyder today. As Serg't I am trying to fill my office worthy the name—
  I am requiring men to come up to orders—and to be actual soldiers—Eve Corporal Coble—Dave Woodall—and I went out strolling—Took baths—Little swims, got lots of berries & apples—

August 7, 1863 Friday. Moved Camp to near White Sulphur Springs—A delightful location   O how it did rain, and how wet we did get, but being so awfully hot, we enjoyed it—Cooled us off for sleep—

August 8, 1863 Saturday. General Inspection day. Corp Woodall and Wm McGowen were publicly complimented by The Inspector General for having remarkably clean arms, and accouterments
  Still no letter from Darling, passingly strange!—O how I do long for one—I hope one will come soon—Eve wrote some for her—

August 9, 1863 Sunday. Routine. Finished letter for Pet—O for more letters from Home—and O for more holiness of Heart and life—We brought grain from River on Horses—Water high—

August 10, 1863 Monday. Went out on Picket between Jefferson and Amosville—Patrolled to Amosville—At night we fell back to near Jefferson—
  I made the acquaintance of Bedy Kempers family—It is such a luxury to meet congenial spirits in their home life.

August 11, 1863 Tuesday. Went out again to yesterdays line—Had Corp Metz and six men on my relief—Had a fine time. I got a nice dinner—at Mr. Kempers—I had a fine chat with him, Mrs Kemper and the Daughter—
  Exchanged with them Coffee for sugar—Coffee short in Dixie.

August 12, 1863 Wednesday. We were relieved and fell back to Jefferson—where again I had charge of a Relief—I got supper in town—awful rainy night——

August 13, 1863 Thursday.——and morning—Letter from Pet— The first since July 14. How glad I am I cannot tell. Thank the good Lord! Wife and pussy are well and happy—just as I hoped all the days—I got a fine breakfast at a house—10 OCK A.M. we were relieved and fell back to near White Sulpher Springs, went into Camp on a new tract—After putting up our shelters—Dining, and resting, and brightening up, we indulged in a Regimental Dress Parade for a change—

The evening was spent restfully—and the night ditto.

August 14, 1863 Friday. HOT! Little going on in Camp—I did some writing for Captain. Wrote 10 page letter to Pet—Letter paper size— and rec. one from her. O such a good one. I do have such a good precious wife—would God I could see her!

August 15, 1863 Saturday. Marched via Woodburn Church & Warrenton to Catletts Station—Loaded down with Roasting Ears on the way. Camped at dark, made a little supper and "lay by" Tired! Oh! how good is Sleep—

August 16, 1863 Sunday. Excessively hot and Poor water—Early we moved to a better place and put up good summer Quarters in a clean camp—Got mail—Good letter from Pet—Though very small— A restful Sabbath—am well and Happy—

August 17, 1863 Monday. Restful—Routine—Wrote letters, one for Pet—P.M. Ordered to Box up things—i.e., all excess and at 3 OCK were ordered out in "light marching order" 1 days Forage 1 days rations—We went via Greenwich and Hay Market, and encamped for the night at Greenwich—A "British Settlement" Everything looks kind of Ancient, rather poorly cared for—but little injured by the War—Don't seem to belong!

August 18, 1863 Tuesday. Very cool night—Struck early—marched through Bull run Gap—Found no Rebs—Grazed our Horses long at New Hay Market. Returned to Camp Same way—with lots of corn, Elderberries, Dust and Tiredness—Wonderfully glad to get back into Camp again—

August 19, 1863 Wednesday. Cool night—Drew rations—Lounged about Wrote up Co affairs and Letters—P.M. Dress Parade for a change—I am well, but I do so long to see my Darling and Pussy— Boys all in good spirits.

August 20, 1863 Thursday. Cool—Routine—P.M. Wrote Pet—am pretty well, and quite as happy as could be expected so far from my loved ones and so hungry for kisses and caresses.

August 21, 1863 Friday. Cool in morning. Hot through the day. I have The Boys signing Pay Rolls, and Preparing to go out on Picket. We were paid off at noon——P.M. We went on picket between Greenwich & HayMarket. Splendid place for our reserve—Lots of Roasting Ears & Apples

August 22, 1863 Saturday. Heavy rain in night a small fight in front by Pickets chiefly—close to New Hay Market—Outer Reserve dashes out—do a little shooting. The Rebs retreat—
Lieut Barnes and I with 10 Men make a scout—to Bucktown—and surrounding country—Johnies all gone—Even their pickets—
We have some great chats with Secesh Girls en route. Awful shy about telling how many Johnies were around this Morning. Some of our Boys in Camp gambling all day   Eve I with a squad patrolled outside our picket line &c. &c—

August 23, 1863 Sunday. Very pleasant—Had a fine morning swim—Routine—Mail came in—O Such good letter from Darling, and one from Brother Bernard^q—We got lost of corn and apples today. P.M. First Maine Cav relieved us from Picket duty—
We got back to Camp at dusk. Capt. S, Lieut B and I settled up a/c's. I wrote letter to Pet—am well and happy—Orders. We march in the morning.

August 24, 1863 Monday. Capt. Snyder and I went Warrenton Junction and Expressed our money home—Capts, Lieuts, Mine, & The Woodalls—9 A.M. took up the March via Warrenton, White Sulphur Springs, across the River. Encamped on old ground—I mailed letter to Pet early this Morning, John Woodall quite unwell—

August 25, 1863 Tuesday. Cool—Routine—Rest—Settling up amongst the Boys—Sending money home &c. So many of The Boys come to me to see them through little matters. I wrote letter for Gerhart—Made out Len Davis' Descriptive List—Wrote Cap Sullenberger and a letter to Pet. I am not real well—have a bad cold, cough, and pain on my breast, but what of it—I've had the like often.

August 26, 1863 Wednesday. Quite Cool—We started early on Scout via Amosville and Gaines X Road towards Little ——— and

Flint Rock.[11] Had a little skirmish and made a dash—had one man wounded and one captured—We took 7 or 8 Horses. The men getting away in brush, marsh, &c—

August 27, 1863 Thursday. Cool—Lay in Camp—General Inspection—I wrote most of day for Captain. My Evening and Morning Cough very annoying.

August 28, 1863 Friday. Almost a frost—Regiment on picket at Corbins X roads—I had charge of Patrol—all Quiet—Recd such a good letter from Pet O how much good her letters do me—How can I ever repay her goodness—devotedness, Faithfulness.

August 29, 1863 Saturday. I was placed in charge of 3 Corporals & 21 men 3 reliefs—on Picket—I was complimented by Colonel for doing my duty well. Sure I realize a weighty responsibility when in Charge of outposts, and act accordingly——wrote some for Pet by moonlight—

August 30, 1863 Sunday. a bit warmer—I slept only an hour or so—and that close to a standing Picket at Camp—I tested my outer pickets—found them extremely wide awake—wrote more for Pet by moon—We were relieved at noon—Returned to Camp—Took apples along in—Take things easy—

August 31, 1863 Monday. Work on Muster and Pay Roll we were Mustered—Wrote busily all day—a big job, but I like it. Cough still annoying—and besides—suffer pain in my left leg, side and arm—seems rheumatic Oh! to see my Darling—

September 1, 1863 Tuesday. All day on Rolls—finished job—Then made out Descriptive Roll of detachment at Hancocks H'd Qrs—I am so tired of Caps ignorance and inconsistence—am tempted to join the Regulars so as to get away from these irregularities.

September 2, 1863 Wednesday. Orders—March early—1 days rations, 1 days forage—Went via Amosvile, Keysville to Sandyhook—I with 6 men, tried and true charged on a House. Captured one Rebel—3 Horses & Equipments—the men eluded us someway—

---

11. Little Washington and Flint Hill, two small villages located between Gaines' Cross Roads and the Blue Ridge. *H16PC*, p. 39, confirms these place names and the capture of eight horses.

Had a Skirmish at a School House—Rebs withdrew—and we fell back to Regiment and Reg moved back via Flint Hill, G.S.X Road, and Amosville and 2 mls this side, and lay on arms til morning—

September 3, 1863 Thursday. Early took up the march for camp—via Jacksonville—I am really quite unwell—pain in left leg & arm &c. Recd Oh! Such a good letter from Pet—She is about to go to Philadelphia in the interest of Susie's[nn] bad leg—and an artificial one.

September 4, 1863 Friday. Went on Picket early between Jackson-ville & Hazel River I had 3 Corporals and 21 Men—Seven on a relief and 14 on the Reserve—some picket firing—The Boys find lots of Peaches and Corn to cook—But need to keep very wide awake—

September 5, 1863 Saturday. Various rumors of an attack to be made on our line by Steward Cavalry—Well they'll find us here, and our good support wide awake, and The Reg't ready for the Fray—

September 6, 1863 Sunday. We lay "to horse" all night—Pickets xchange shots frequently out front, but show no signs of advanc-ing—Will McGowen relieved me in part—I am really too unwell to do full duty on such a time as this, but I can't afford to run risks by substituting—another precious letter from Pet—

September 7, 1863 Monday. All quiet again, Find lots of Grapes—Tomatoes—&c—Noon relieved—Returned to Camp—Our Suttler has come up—

September 8, 1863 Tuesday. I feel some better warmer again—I wrote some for Pet and some for Religious Telescope—Worked some on Horse and Company Reports—and do some real good car-ing for myself—

September 9, 1863 Wednesday. Handed in Reports—sent letters to Pet—Rel. Tel. & Bro Bernard.[q]

September 10, 1863 Thursday. Went on Picket again on Hazel River near Oak Shade Church—
I had new duties assigned me—Cautious scouting, or strolling, chatted with citizens—catching news—was near the Ford—Saw 15 to 18 Rebels on other side, likely on the same errand I was—Only they caught no glimpse of my supporters—

355

September 11, 1863 Friday. At a House—got big breakfast and two Chickens to take with me for the Boys who are on hard duty— Captain Snyder is becoming awfully commanding—gives orders very gruffly to nearly every one—He needs to tone down a wee—I had some interesting talks with several Reb. Girls today, obtained some information of value—Eve there was quite an alarm started by a fool fire on the front.

September 12, 1863 Saturday. I was up ½ the night making sure no surprise should occur. I got only about 2½ hours sleep—This A.M. I met a Rebel of Co. B. 7th Va Cav midway in River—and exchanged news papers with him—We were relieved from Picket at noon—and in Eve received marching orders—

September 13, 1863 Sunday. Rained—Took up the march at 4 A.M. Crossed Hazel River near Oak Shade Church—Saw 2 Rebs near crossing—We were ordered to support Battery, near Culpepper Court House—Had a hot time—Lieut Barnes wounded—Capt Snyders Horse Killed—A Co A man killed—but we fought to win—and did. We took 3 pieces of Artilery—and 75 to 150 prisoners in a running fight—over night we lay on arms 3 Mls S.E. of C.C.H.[12]

September 14, 1863 Monday. Rainy night—Awful muddy—we marched via Cedar Mountain to Rapid Ann R.R. Bridge early—Hear Canonading not far off all day—Infantry coming up and go on—We Picket near Cedar Mountain battle field—Cloudy—Showers—unpleasant—But our men in fine spirits—

September 15, 1863 Tuesday. cleared up—On Picket—Hear Canonading—and Infantry—by spells—all day—Infantry wagons transporting to the front—or towards it—Mailed large letter to Pet—am quite well again Thank the good Lord. Oh! how good He is to me—

September 16, 1863 Wednesday. On outer Picket line all day— outposts rather quiet. Eve we were relieved and returned to Brigade near Slaughter Mountains—and camped for the night—

---

12. The operations that Cormany has been describing were part of a series of feints and raids executed by the Federal army during the late summer of 1863, while both sides concentrated their attention on theaters of action elsewhere around the country. The net result of these small clashes was not great. Lee's defensive perimeter on the eastern front remained intact along the Rappahannock–Rapidan–Blue Ridge line.

September 17, 1863 Thursday. Clear—Hot—Lay in easy camp resting all day—

Eve returned to back of Slaughter Mountain and took a good nights rest. Short of rations, but have plenty Corn—Tomatoes, Beans &c and so fill up and feel nicely satisfied and nourished— Thank the Johnies for feeding us even if we do risk our lives to "draw it"

September 18, 1863 Friday. Took up the March for the Front, towards Rapidan Station—Saw the Reb. Forts & Rifle pits—recently evacuated—we hear picket firing not far away. P.M. rained awfully all night—we remain "to horse"

September 19, 1863 Saturday. Still pouring rain—At noon we were relieved by Infantry, and reported to Brig. H'd Qrs—were ordered to Cross Mill Creek—was at flood stage—Had to swim our horses some distance—say 25 to 30 yds—in mid stream—Fortunately the landing on opposite side was down stream about 45 degrees—The men "tore up Jack in general"[13] putting Amunition, rations, blankets &c about their necks and chest, and holding carbines high—and with a yel, started in obeying orders to keep horses heads faced well up stream, at the same time giving the animal as free use of head and neck as possible. Using spurs of course to urge action—A squad of Rebels on a hillock on the opposite shore seemed startled so at our daring move as to forget their guns, until a volley from a Company of our fellows stirred them up effectually, when they fired a nervous volley over our heads and struck to the rear—We made the landing without loss of a man or Horse—Though a few were carried down stream, where the bank was high, and came near perishing, though finally landing safely and coming into Camp as victors over the flood.

September 20, 1863 Sunday. On landing last eve. we sent out scouts and found no enemy in force—and assurance that their pickets beat a hasty retreat on seeing us Crossing—and were likely going yet.

Found a good camping place. Plenty of wood and rails. So soon there were numerous fires, and Men and clothes & Things generally steaming, drying—

Picket line was put out and so the night was one of "drying up" and getting ready for Sabbath.

Remained on Picket—Did some foraging—Found plenty Corn—

---

13. I.e., behaved boisterously.

potatoes tomatoes melons—pumpkins &c. &c. &c. Today moved the reserve—and lay in main reserve this A.M. I bought 3 hams & 1 bushel sweet potatoes for $2.00 Confed scrip[14]—Boys pretty well dried by evening, and we went front on picket.

September 21, 1863 Monday. I had charge of a relief of Pickets— The Boys feasting on Ham Sweet Potatoes &c. Have a high day— But actually the Boys are almost worn out from extra duty, and lack of rest. God is so good to give me such good health, and power of endurance—O for ability to love Him more and serve Him better.

September 22, 1863 Tuesday. Quite a Frost—Hot day—Had a day of rest. Oh! so good, Wrote to Pet & Clem[cc]—I am well and happy, but do so long to see Darling and Baby—But thank the Lord we 3 are well—

September 23, 1863 Wednesday. Quite a frost—A.M. A general cleaning up of arms. P.M. Inspection—14 Ponchos—6 Horse Blankets—12 prs spurs, I C'd [condemned] am well. O to be a better Christian—I am so unworthy such health and pleasure I enjoy—

September 24, 1863 Thursday. Cold frosty—Pay Master here today. Got $31.33¢ Captain paid me $20.00—Clerking service—At 4 P.M. Orders to March—Start at once. Via Culpeper C.H. Fed at 10 P.M.—Camped on the Rapidan at 1 A.M.—Very tired—

September 25, 1863 Friday. Start again at 7 A.M. for Bealton Station and go into Camp on old Infantry Camp—A day of resting— reading—meditating and aspiring to higher Christian Soldier Manhood.

September 26, 1863 Saturday. Our squadron went out on a scout one mile beyond Deep Run—I made the acquaintance of Mr Benj. H. Dalton 916 Coates St Philadelphia whom we escorted to certain families outside of our lines—Got some tomatoes—

September 27, 1863 Sunday. Cool—I slept some twenty times during the night—I had pain in my head, jaws, back knees &c &c &c Am all out of fix—slept a dozen times today—ate nothing. I

14. Confederate scrip plummeted in value after Gettysburg; a payment of this amount, while technically a purchase, was tantamount to confiscation. Only the presence of the owner distinguished this transaction from foraging.

moved into Captains quarters—awfully miserable—our Squadron ordered on picket—

Long with me for company—

September 28, 1863 Monday. night cold—Frosty all day, am most miserably comfortable lying around in Cap's quarters—Precious Letter from Pet—O to see her—God bless her and Baby.

September 29, 1863 Tuesday. Still cold—Slept some but still feel badly. Tongue stiff. Burns sore, pain in small of my back—wrote letter to Pet and sent 100 pages Journal—

Evening took physic—seem worse—Lounged about til 2 A.M. Eased somewhat

September 30, 1863 Wednesday. Warm morning—I feel slightly better—a little appetite—Head better—can now rest and eat some and realize crisis is passed—Oh to see my dearest ones

October 1, 1863 Thursday. Fine—Better, but mouth sore still. "Billy" won a $40—race today—P.M. we marched to Rappahannock Station and encamped—Made out Blumbaughs Final Statement.[15] Am still quite unwell—Think so much of my jewels far away. Oh! to see them—Tapps! It rains but I am dry.

October 2, 1863 Friday. Rainy all A.M.—wrote some—Eve moved to Bealton. Arrived at dusk—An awful dark-rain-storm came up turned cold—no wood—nor rails—hard time getting up shelter—or quarters to rest—

October 3, 1863 Saturday. Cleared up. Fixed up pretty comfortably—Not much going on—Wrote some—mailed letter to Pet—am fairly well again. and happy—

October 4, 1863 Sunday. Fine—Routine—Inspection—O.K. all quiet in Front—Sent in Lieut Burns Final Statement[16] Also Blubaughs.

15. John Blumbaugh, or Blubaugh in the official records, died of typhoid fever. He had been a teamster in Company H. *H16PC*, pp. 14, 29.

16. Probably 2nd Lt. William J. Burns, who had been promoted from orderly sergeant earlier in the year. *H16PC*, p. 9.

October 5, 1863 Monday. Saber Drill. Special Business Expected—Our Sutler came up—O how dull camp life is compared with being in Front—doing things to make a fellow tingle all through—

October 6, 1863 Tuesday. Pleasant—Early—Ours and Capt Swans squadrons escorted a train of 25 to 30 Wagons to Hartwood Church—got back at 9 P.M. I traded 2 boxes Coffee for Butter Some Johnies tickled sure, and Yanks too—

October 7, 1863 Wednesday. Heavy Frost—I wrote considerably today—mailed letter to Pet——P.M. I was detailed Sergeant of the Guard—had 5 Corporals—and 30 Men—I had as much whiskey as I wanted—but didn't want much——Eve rainy—Stormy—dark—Gloomy letter from Pet, Poor Darling!

October 8, 1863 Thursday. On guard all day—Nothing special occurred—Eve relieved. "Billy" won another race—Capt S. very drunk—Distresses me greatly—

October 9, 1863 Friday. Heavy Frost—Hot day—Wrote to Pet—and in Diary—Had to "Tie up" Jeff D. Bad Fellow—Our Sutler robbed last night—Capt S. again drunk—I made out an official Report of his being Officer of the Day and so helped him out again—Rec'd orders to March at 4 in the morning.[17]

October 10, 1863 Saturday. Started at daybreak Went via Rap-St'n. Brandy and Culpepper to Old Camp near Thoroughfare Mountain. A fight going on in front of us—We expected to get into it too but were not needed—We Picketed near Cedar Mountain—

I had charge of a scouting party Col Robison in Command—Gave some "Johnies" a scare and stiring up I am not at all well today—

October 11, 1863 Sunday. Took up line of march at day break—Via Culpepper—Drew Forage there. Rebs follow us too closely and near C—our artillery shelled them back—and our Regiment went for

---

17. These orders inaugurated approximately two weeks of skirmishing on the right flank of Meade's line. Lee was attempting to maneuver around that end of the Union position and thus place himself between the Northern army and its own capital. Federal cavalry was sent out to scout, harass, and possible stall the Confederates while Union infantry repositioned itself further north. These actions are known as the Bristoe Campaign, after the Virginia town where the largest sustained engagement took place. See Long, *Day By Day*, pp. 419–26.

them—Then covered the retreat via Oak-Shade-Church, Jefferson to old Camp—Lay to arms, by little fires—strong Picket line out—Slept pretty well—

October 12, 1863 Monday. Early took up the March 13th Pa., 1st Maine, & 4th, and we bring up the rear. Closely pressed—General maneuvering and some fighting amongst the hills, till 3 P.M. near the Springs—Hard Skirmishing comes on, and our Battery shelled the rebel line, while we—16th—support the Battery—We got awfully shelled—5 Pieces opened on us at once. Having now ascertained their strength—Our Brigade was ordered to retreat in good order—Our Reg't was placed in rear to cover the retreat—Enemy charged us repeatedly—We greet them with volleys, and then—as they break some, we charge them with solid line driving them back, and gaining the field—Taking some prisoners—but finding hoardes of the enemy farther back—awful suspense! General Gregg[18] comes on the scene. Saying we must hold this place—and we do that thing—The other Regts supporting us and attacking the Enemy on our right and left—Fighting kept up into the night. The enemys vigor diminishing gradually—Leaving only a strong picket line in our immediate front—So at 10 P.M. we fell back to near Fayetteville—leaving a strong picket line facing theirs with a strong reserve—

October 13, 1863 Tuesday. After 10 last night we draw rations. I act Quartermaster Sergeant—We lay by and keep quiet some time. Sleep some on arms during the night—Find we have lost considerably in prisoners yesterday—also some killed and wounded—At noon we took up the March over all imaginable kinds of roads— Sometimes galloping, then walking or trotting—then halting a little while—in Column—and then advancing again We finally struck Burnt Church Xroads. We find 2nd Corps is accompanying us—We lie on arms & "to Horse"—all night—any amount of fires in all directions, and trains of wagons, moving by all night—and withal we slept pretty well—I had a long season of meditation and prayer—and am in good state of mind, heart & body or temporally and spiritually thank the good Lord—

---

18. Brig. Gen. David McMurtrie Gregg was in command of the entire division to which the 16th Pennsylvania was assigned (his cousin, Col. John Irvin Gregg, commanded the 16th Pennsylvania itself). The place being contested in this entry was a ford across the Rappahannock; Union commanders did not want Lee to be able to use it as a short cut to get behind Meade's forces before the latter could reposition themselves.

Samuel Cormany wearing a cavalry jacket and standing beside Mary, the horse he lost in the Battle of Bristoe Station. Kiefer Family.

October 14, 1863 Wednesday. Very misty & smoky—

At daybreak, we found our Division about surrounded by being fired into from all sides—We opened up with heavy skirmish lines—strengthening them where needed—keeping it up til 10 OCK, and holding the enemy well in check—The Col—R[19]—wounded—all day our Brigade and Regt had the rear to protect whenever a move was made—the enemy followed as closely as was healthy—at one time we put up a Fool battery on the road. Mounted a hollow log on some stuff, piling up green brush to partly conceal the ruse—A few men defended it some—The enemy planted a piece ½ mile back, or more—A few of our men were behind—but to the right & left of it—i.e. of the ruse—and the main body was making a nice retreat in the woods and brush—We got a good shelling however—But gained time for the body of our men to gain the desired point—

I was a very busy Serg't all day—This has been a good time to measure men, and know who were brave & deliberate, and who cowardly—who were the best fighters—The evening finds us near Bristow Station—our rear was charged and my "Mary" shot So I

19. Lt. Co. John K. Robison. This heavy skirmish took place near Auburn, Va. *PV,* p. 952.

had to leave Regiment, and abandon her at Bruntsville, and foot it. Walked all night over the hills, through the creek and mud, keeping the course the Regiment was taking—was somewhat unwell and a little discouraged—and awfully tired—but got to the Regiment again and we had a little brekfast——and

October 15, 1863 Thursday. Walked on til noon, and then succeeded in getting into our George Snyders Ammunition wagon[20]— Though it was rough riding, it was a relief—Roads are awful, and the Rebels are ever trying to flank our Regt—Snyders wagon keeps just ahead—and moves lively—and reaches the wagon train we were escorting—

General Sickles comes to his old 3rd Corpse—Wondrous Cheering—Had been away awhile—and here he meets them. Just as we find them close by for our support, and relief[21]—The Trains put up near Fairfax Station—I am in bad shape physically—but O.K. mentally and patriotically—Oh the rain and mud we have encountered this day—and the pressing of the enemy. But thank God our boys kept cool and bravely held the rebs back til we struck safety—and all without much loss—Cant tell yet how much—But I must have a Horse—I am out of my best element—

October 16, 1863 Friday. A wearisome night—Rainy and stormy—I left this wagon train, and went to the Mule train—Am real unwell, and the weather so disagreeable—Capt Snyder sent for me—sent Dandy Billy for me to ride to the Company 3 miles out from Fairfax Station—Tho rainy, I feel some better—I long to be thoroughly robust so as to be better able to do my duty as a Soldier—and to be a more thorough going Christian, so my influence would always be helpful to my comrades—and so as to be better prepared for what may await me—

20. George W. Snyder was one of the original members of Company H. He had probably taken over part of the company's teamster duties after the death of John Blubaugh. *H16PC*, p. 29.

21. Maj. Gen. Daniel E. Sickles, a political figure from New York, had commanded the Union 3rd Corps at Gettysburg. On the second day of that battle Sickles placed his men in what turned out to be a vulnerable position, and the corps suffered heavy casualties. Sickles remained with his men, however, and was eventually hit himself. To save the general's life surgeons amputated a badly wounded leg. The incident endeared Sickles to his men, but not to General Meade, who blamed Sickles for positioning his men disastrously in the first place. While the 3rd corps gave him a hero's welcome upon his return, Meade refused to restore him to command. See William A. Swanberg, *Sickles the Incredible* (New York, 1956), pp. 213–35. Swanberg gives October 18 as the date of Sickles's reunion with his men.

My trust in Him who alone knows what is for my and my Darlings good, in time and Eternity—

October 17, 1863 Saturday. The sun rises in all his native splendor and I feel pretty good in every way. Wrote up diary for some days past. Then wrote letter to Pet. O how much I do love her and long to see her and our blessed Baby—Some canonading greets our ears today P.M. we went out on picket near Bull Run—Have a pleasant Reserve I am Serg't of 2nd Relief—Feel fresh and stout and aspiring.

October 18, 1863 Sunday. Frosty—Called on Mr. Dyer—a good old Methodist—A very pleasant visit. On picket all day—Eve fell back to near Fairfax Station—drew rations and encamped for the night— Am well—

October 19, 1863 Monday. Lay near Fx Station after noon—Rec'd letter from Pet—Kimmels—Sergt Harrison—O so glad to hear from Pet again—also from the others—Took up the March in P.M.   kept it up til 11 P.M. when we encamped near Centerville on Manassas turnpike Captains Arm so slow about getting well—goes to Hospital. I am acting Q.M. Sergeant—

October 20, 1863 Tuesday. Very frosty night—Took up the march early. Moved slowly in rear of a train to where the center of our army rested at the great Bull Run battle—we hear some fighting in front of our Column—

October 21, 1863 Wednesday. Early off to Gainesville Station on Manassas G&R.R. lay close by Gen'l Meads Head Quarters[22]—Drew Forage and Rations—and in evening took up the march via Bucksville, New B. to Warrenton[23] where we encamped at midnight— rather restfully until 10 A.M.

---

22. The Manassas Gap Railroad ran west from Manassas Station, through Gainesville and Thoroughfare Gap, toward the Blue Ridge. Meade had fallen back to this area in order to concentrate his troops, avoid being flanked, and protect Washington.

23. The first two towns were Buckland Mills and New Baltimore, both on the Warrenton Turnpike. This foray was designed to discover where Lee's main forces lay. Meade was too uncertain of his enemy's whereabouts to risk more than cavalry reconnaissance. See George R. Agassiz, ed., *Meade's Headquarters, 1863–1865: Letters of Colonel Theodore Lyman from the Wilderness to Appomattox* (Freeport, N.Y., 1922; rpt. 1970), pp. 33–36.

October 22, 1863 Thursday. Took up the march at 10 A.M. for Fayetteville 4 to 5 miles from Bealton—I commence to mess with J.R. Fetterhoff—Some Rebs in sight during A.M.—Put up tents for a bivouac—soon tore them down again, and drew up in line of battle and at 10 A.M. fell back to Brigade Head Quarters—Stopped at 3 places before we pitched tents—

October 23, 1863 Friday. Fixed up quarters some canonading hearable—Later we set to snoozing liberally—I did some writing— P.M. Cloudy. Eve put up for rain—

October 24, 1863 Saturday. Rained all night—Rumors of a Rebel advance—We were in line most of day—Rainy—ate lots of luscious persimmons. Eve we went on Picket towards Beverly Ford—Very disagreeable—cold—damp—

October 25, 1863 Sunday. Changed position about noon—Picketing on Rap. St'n. reaching towards Bealton Station—Pretty good times—Bought cabbage, pumpkins, &c.&c. Eve we connected with 1st Div—4th N.Y. Cav pickets—we have only 90 men near—all told here for duty—I stood post—

October 26, 1863 Monday. Drew rations—Our line attacked some— Considerable skirmishing—Heavy Rebel force came in sight towards Bealton Station—a slight engagement—In a charge, our Regiment almost cut off by rebel force, but we out maneuvered and outshot them and came off O.K. Fell back to Fayeteville—Capt Alexander returned from Hosp.

October 27, 1863 Tuesday. Cold and icy—Relieved from Picket— went back into camp 3 mls from Warrenton Smith—Glesner— Stump—Staunton came from Dismounted Camp—
   Letter from Pet—O so good—

October 28, 1863 Wednesday. Very cold. icy. I have much pain during night—and some in daytime Rheumaticy—Wrote to Pet Made out descriptive Lists for Sergts Harrison, Flannagan and the man Witherall. wrote some for Clem.[cc]

October 29, 1863 Thursday. Looks like moving. Any amount of orders—am kept very busy—Wrote to Clem[cc] concerning a Commission as 2nd Lieut. Suggests $100 or so might enable the Senator he is doing for on health lines to secure it for me. I reply—no buying for Me—I'll secure it on Merit or Never.[24]

October 30, 1863 Friday. Cloudy—Am quite rheumaticky—wonder how my Darling is getting along. O to see her and my precious Cora—Am writing letter to Pet and Bell Kimmel. Did some Company writing—Read some—and quarrel with misery—

October 31, 1863 Saturday. Cold—Went to Doctor—Gave me some pills. Threw them away—Receive orders to make out Muster Rolls—my arm is too numb—am too unwell—Set S.B. Peters on the Job—Garverich—Brough & Nelling return from prison xperience—They fared pretty well[25]—
Good letter from Pet—

November 1, 1863 Sunday. Mustered for Pay this morning. My miseries not letting up much—would that I could go to Hospital and take a rest and so recruit my health, but alas! Those are most successful who can play off best—hardy tho they be   I am taking medicine now, not for the good it will do me, but to try to get needed rest—and possibly I may succeed in getting Pet and Cora to come to me awhile—

November 2, 1863 Monday. Cool—Packed at 8 A.M. for Picket—H. Co. was put into Major Swans Squadron—Lay in Reserve—This means good rest—so long as Pickets and outer Reserve are quiet. Cabbage and pumpkins plenty—a good restful quiet day for me. Eve feel lots better—

November 3, 1863 Tuesday. We were sent out on front to picket—in sight of Rebel Flag, and in hearing of Rebel Band—I am Sergt of 3rd Relief—We have Beef and Pumpkin for dinner and other staples. Visited my posts—saw lots of rebel Pickets, But they are peacable, and so are we. Eve—moved our Reserve—

24. Unsystematic methods of commissioning officers in the volunteer army led to influence peddling, political (as distinguished from military) decision making, and outright corruption. Samuel's brother-in-law, Clem, the water-cure physician, was now practicing in Philadelphia. He was trying to persuade Samuel to purchase the patronage of one of his patients, and thereby gain a commission. On the problems associated with volunteer officers, see Fred A. Shannon, *The Organization and Administration of the Union Army, 1861–1865*, vol. I (Gloucester, Mass., 1965), pp. 151–79.

25. A prisoner exchange freed Christian Nelling and David Gaverich, both of whom had spent eight months in Confederate prisons following their capture during the raid on Hartwood Church in February. *H16PC*, p. 19. Daniel N. Brough was apparently captured prior to Nov. 9, 1862. All three men were from Company H.

November 4, 1863 Wednesday. A very unpleasant night for me. Lots of rheumatic pains, but on the whole some better—Today things moved off smoothly. Took breakfast a house—50¢ bought pumpkin 25¢ Fist-sized cabbage 10¢—Confed scrip—
Eve returned to Main Reserve Letter from Capt Snyder from Hospital. I wish the Capt were here—

November 5, 1863 Thursday. Drew in our Safe Guards—were relieved by 1st Maine Cav. We put up in old Camp Rumors of a move—but no orders yet—Oh! to see my little Family.

November 6, 1863 Friday. Stormy—Made out Pay Rolls—Wrote all day. Am none too well, but Thank the Lord I am improving—I wonder how would Poor Sergt. Peters do were he left to himself to run this Company Machine & I am glad I can do for him or post him—

November 7, 1863 Saturday. Stormy—cold—Lots of Infantry passing towards Bealton and Rappahannock—At 3:40 we struck our tents and took up the march via Bealton to Morrisville—Canonading commenced at Rap-Stn about 2 OCK and increaced in strength til after dark[26]—

November 8, 1863 Sunday. News—1500 Rebs captured yesterday, and some artillery—Troops moving today, but no fighting within hearing—P.M. some canon hearable—Eve we went on Picket—Reserve close to Drs House at Morrisville—I am Serg't of a Relief—which to me means great responsibility—any failure in alertness may prove very disastrous—Wide Awake is the Watchword—

November 9, 1863 Monday. In off Pickett and on the march early for Kellys Ford—Camped close to Mount Holly Church—Drew Rations and Forage—Got mail—Letter from Clem^cc—is too fast for me. I am in a strait—No! will let my last of 29th ult. stand as final—Mailed letter to Pet & Lieut Barnes—We have good fires and plenty of water—

November 10, 1863 Tuesday. Snowed last night—Took up march early for Hartwood Church—Picket on River, our Squadron lay in

---

26. Meade recrossed the Rappahannock to reestablish the line that existed prior to Lee's Bristoe campaign. By withdrawing, Lee conceded the Federal commander his original position.

Reserve all day—Splendid place—Wrote some—I am pretty well and rather happy.

November 11, 1863 Wednesday. Up and off to Morrisville Thence to Elk River—Encamped—Zuck & D. Woodall came from Washington D.C.—Lots of orders but little doing—Fetterhoff & I mess again—

November 12, 1863 Thursday. Early we returned to Morrisville and encamped—all quiet—P.M. we had Inspection—Mounted—Bushwhackers very daring again. Best Treatment? Ventillation for their "inerds" made for one or two, with a Spencer-Carbine-bullet on the "Still hunt." Our Boys know how! Strenuous religion helps a Soldier do that to the Johnie seeking it—and we somehow—naturally take it that whenever a Grey back goes into the bushwhacking business he's a candidate. and we are commanded to Elect him[27]—
 Such a good letter from Pet. Oh they do me so much good—Am quite well again and happy, daily aspiring to be nobler Christian and a braver more resourseful soldier.

November 13, 1863 Friday. Cool, clear, pleasant—I worked on company clothing a/cs Zook and I got into a squall—I gave him to understand how dumb and insignificant he really is, and how he has to depend on the kindness and knowledge of others to enable him to occupy his place—Eve. Had a fine sing—a little lot of us—

November 14, 1863 Saturday. Fine—Finish clothing a/c's—P.M. wrote Pet. Eve rained powerfully—Put up better shelter—Davy W and I vowed to lead better lives. O for grace from Heaven we prayed. We "hunger & thirst" for rightness in all our Soldiering—

November 15, 1863 Sunday. Rainy night—Cleared 10 A.M.—Canonading opened in direction of Rapidan—Bushwhackers somewhat active, but very shy, we'll call em presently—Finished letter to pet— Rather restful Sabbath—

November 16, 1863 Monday. Rebels driven out of works on Rapidan—Letter from Clem[cc] concerning Commission—Throws up some hopes out a ways—I dont bank much on anything save real merit— Even went on picket with Lieut Swank and 10 Men—Fine time—

---

27. Federal troops were under orders to execute bushwhackers—pro-Confederate guerrillas and irregulars—as spies and had no qualms about killing them from ambush.

November 17, 1863 Tuesday. Drizzly—Little sleep—Am quite well—Lieut & I good time all day—Eve were relieved by Lieut Brown—McGowen, Jim Woodall, Gerhart & J. Long were in Camp when I returned from picket—

November 18, 1863 Wednesday. Maj Kennedy and Capt Rush returned to Regt from—Exchange of prisoners. Got a letter from Capt Snyder—still in Hospital—Doing well will soon come.

November 19, 1863 Thursday. Fix up Clothing Book—wrote Pet— Capt Snyder returns. bro't me a p'k'ge from Pet—O so good— Thank the Lord for a true good wife—I do know I have the best wife in the world—I sent Company history to Brig. Gen'l James Ripley by order—

November 20, 1863 Friday. Clear. fine—I dreamed most of night of my Darling—Mailed letter to her—I wrote out document for the reduction to ranks of Sergts Zook & McGowen on a/c inefficiency— drink &c—and promotion of John Woodall to Commissary Sergt. John Metz to Sergt—and was made Quarter Master Sergeant myself! Zook took it hard[28]—Such a good letter from Pet & Sister Susie[nn]— Thank the Lord for Darling & Cora—

November 21, 1863 Saturday. Rainy—Capt Snyder is "Brig. off of the day." Wrote Pet a Letter Studied Tactics. I am looking up and must be efficient—Must master Caseys Cavalry Tactics.[29]

November 22, 1863 Sunday. Fine clear—Wrote Pet, Sue[nn]—P.M. Had dress Parade. Zook & McGowen reduced to ranks—destriped John Woodall & Metz made Sergts—J.R. Fetterhoff made

28. It is not difficult to imagine the hard feelings engendered by this shuffle among the noncommissioned officers of Company H. As Samuel notes, Joseph Zook, who had been the company's quartermaster sergeant since its organization, was bitter about his demotion and replacement. It becomes clear in the next section of Rachel's diary that this shuffle had repercussions on the home front as well, for it poisoned the relationship between Rachel and Mrs. McGowen. Moreover, hanging in the background was the shadow of Clem's effort at influence peddling.

29. Silas Casey (1807–1882), a career officer and West Point graduate, headed a board of officers that revised the army's manual on tactics in 1861. *Infantry Tactics, for the Instruction, Exercise, and Manoeuvres of the Soldier, a Company, Line of Skirmishers, Battalion, Brigade, or Corps d' Armée*, published under Casey's name in 1862, became the standard manual for Civil War officers, especially in the volunteer units where few men had any formal training in military science. *DAB*, II, 560; *NCAB*, IV, 279; Mark M. Boatner III, *The Civil War Dictionary* (New York, 1959), p. 131; *NUC*, XCVII, 681.

Corporal—Woodall Com Sgt—Cormany Q.M. S'g't—Announced on Dress Parade—

November 23, 1863 Monday. Started on march at 10 A.M.—Got fairly under way—a winding way—and encamped again ½ mile from old Camp—Laurence—Hill—Hassan—May and McCleary returned to the Regiment—Drew F&R[30]—

November 24, 1863 Tuesday. Broke camp at dawn-o-day Rainy day—Cross Rappahannoc at Ellis Ford—and the Rapidan at Ealys Ford thence to Richardsville and encamped. Awfully wet & disagreeable.

30. Probably forage and rations.

XVIII

Life in Chambersburg Drags on
July 7–November 25, 1863

After the drama of the Gettysburg campaign and the surprise of Samuel's passing visit in Chambersburg, Rachel returns to the frustrating routine of trying to take care of herself and her daughter. Visits to some of Samuel's relatives in the countryside and a trip to Bucks County help break the monotony, but the psychological and financial pressures on Rachel remain unabated. In an effort to improve her situation she brings her younger sister Susie back from Philadelphia and moves into the home of Mrs. Merklein, only to have Susie fall critically ill.

July 7, 1863 Mr C. is gone again I can hardly stay in I feel so lonely. My room seems so empty—my eatable do not taste good, everything seems to have lost of its charms—soon after he left I took my girl & started out I was gone nearly all forenoon—got a man to fetch the boiler that I got spoiled by my careless thoughtfulness—to mend it. Two ladies & a gentleman called while I was away. Can not think who they could have been. Ate a piece then went to Mrs McGowans—so now 3 P.M. I am home again & Cora is sleeping. The bell just rung for some good news again—day before yesterday the news came that Vicsburg had fallen & today that our men are fighting the rebs again by Hagerstown & this side & are driving them this way—also that those of Milroys men who passed through here on Sunday captured a number of waggons and men.

July 8, 1863 Went for a pitcher of water about 11 A.M. & on my way learned that the mail had come so I set my pitcher in a window & went right down & got one from the girls (Mollie[ii] & Sue[nn]) one from brother A.C.B.,[cc] one from J.W.A's[kk] & one from my Sm'l written sometime ago. I immediately set to work answering them. Went to Mrs McG's a few minutes & partly made arrangements to go day after tomorrow for cherries—various rumers of fighting up toward the river are afloat—My God protect my Samuel. rained last night & is very wet—creek high.

July 9, 1863 It is still a little cloudy. I have look for Mr C. every evening since he left, but he came not & we cannot hear from him. The bells all over town rang a long time this morning in honor of the fall of Vicsburg—Got my paper once again. The Union arms seem successful everywhere at present. On the 4th July Vicsburg unconditionally surrendered. Another victory was gained at Helena (I think its in Arkansas) on the same day.[1] Rumors reach us again of fighting near Hagerstown. Also that Col Gregg had quite a fight on the 7th   Hope my Samuel is safe.[2]

July 13, 1863 I have beet out of town since the morning of the 10th 7 oclock at which time I started on foot to go to motherinlaws[b]—borrowed a little waggon & hauled the baby & 4 fruit jars along. Rested ½ hour at Mr. Groves where they gave me cherry pie the first I ate for this year. Arrived at Byers'[ba] at 11 A.M. was pretty tired—P.M. Ellie[y] & I went to J. Hubers to gather cherries—did not get many—the wet weather caused them to rot—got about 4 quarts after being seeded, which I canned. Cora was very tired of her ride.   She got so dreadfully frightened at a toad that she would not leave me all evening even after she fell asleep she would spring up & scream. Slept well—Sat. Morning I washed out Coras clothes—I had intended to start home again this P.M. but Motherinlaw[b] would not hear to it & said Daddy[ba] would take me home Sunday—So I staid—In P.M. of Sat Ellie[y] & I walked to J. Cormanys[d]—had quite a pleasant visit. After tea we walked back again & gathered a few raspberries along the wayside—Sunday I Thompsons[v] came—had quite a pleasant little chat—Had several pretty spirited arguments with Mother[b]—according to my way of thinking she takes quite a wrong view of the war—its cause & all about it—& feels to bitter toward the administration but I do not wonder she hears nothing but daddy Byers[ba] & Barna Hampshire the year round.   P.M. daddy[ba] took me home. I bought 2 lbs of butter & 1 doz. of eggs from him. Mother[b] gave me some beans a few potatoes & a few apples & a head of cabbage & qt of milk. It had rained pretty smart here, but out at Byers we heart the thundering & thought it canonading. I have been fussing round all morning clearing up my room & had just got done when Aunt Elenor came & brought me a sixpeny crock full of fresh butter—quite a treat surely—It is very cloudy & rainy all

---

1. Union forces occupying Helena repulsed a Confederate attack on July 4, 1863.
2. General Meade pursued the Confederate army after Gettysburg with extreme, if not excessive, caution. Only the Federal cavalry maintained steady pressure and engaged their Southern counterparts in serious battle; Rachel was hearing reports of those clashes.

morning. The town is swarming with soldiers. 3000 or 4000 have passed through within the last few days—A great battle is expected if it is not going on already. The paper states that Gregg has had a hard fight quite lately—i.e. since my Sml was home. hope he is safe. P.M. was down in the Hall with Cora. Emma was playing with her, so I did not look after her. so next I knew Emma made a fuss as if the house were on fire saying the baby had spoiled her paints. She set them on the steps & baby got them. I told Emma not to make such a fuss that I would make all right I would rather pay six boxes than have her make such a fuss. Her paints are not spoiled at all, only wetted a little.

July 14, 1863 Baked & washed today—had a very large wash—had of Samuels clothes to wash—his large overcoat & shawl—Got very good bread—Paid Emma 3 cts (postage stamp) for the pretended damage the baby did & took the occasion to ask her whether she knew who took my apples last winter—also whether she knew who took my dried peaches. Of course she knew nothing. I told her then that I knew that I had watched. she got very pale. I told her too that I came nearly seeing a little girls hand in the peach poke once— to which she enquired so quickly, "D you think it was me." I did not say that, I replied. Told her the Good Man never could take children to heaven that did such things. Told her too if any more things were taken that I would make a fuss. She is very distant since. She little thought that I knew it all. A thunder gust this evening—Still no word from my Samuel. Mrs McGowan called— Gave her a pr of Smls old pants to make her boy a pair—her man is still here yet. Baby is so full of prickly heat & consequently is troublesome. Religiously I get along as usual. O! to be more holy—

July 18, 1863 Pleasant day—Maggie[ja] & Fred.[g] Karper came to see me. took dinner with me. Mr & Mrs Peffly also came a little before dinner & dined with us. After dinner a Mr Armstrong from C. W. formerly but now one of the Blue reserves of Philad'a called to see me, thinking we might rake up old acquaintance but none could be discovered so I excused myself & went down street with Maggie[ja]— she had her Photograph taken—so had Fred.[g] his taken—It was 4 P.M. when we got back—now they set in to have me go home with them. At first I thought I could not but after being told I could get Raspberries up there & that they would bring me home whenever I wanted to go—I went—in less than an hour we were on the way to Strasburg—The folks gave me a hearty welcome.

July 19, 1863 Sunday. Early the folks began to come on their way to church & nearly 1 doz. came in to Karpers[j]—After church all who were there before churche came & took dinner, it seemed little like Sunday—Wil.[i] did not like it but could not help it all just chanced to come together so.

July 20, 1863 Went early for raspberries—got a good many—sewed for Wil.[i] the rest of the time—We had quite a time berry-ing—went in the butcher wagon   were gone about 3 to 4 hours—dried them. I staid a week at this place—Went twice for berries—the rest of the time I sewed for Mrs K.[i] This is truly a very unhappy family—Mr K.[j] is away nearly all the time droving which is a business Mrs K.[i] utterly detests.[3] Mrs K.[i] and her children are con-tinually quarreling—I do not know that I heard them speak a pleas-ant word together that whole week. They do not sit down & have pleasant family chats—all their conversation is how this or that is to be done or scolding & snapping about work not being done right—or the children that they do not want to do what their Mother asks of them. When Mrs K[i] would tell me any thing that did not just please her daughter, the daughter would contradict her. I got fairly sick of it.   & then it is nothing but work—work, work, some 1001 little jobs were to be done. I turned one of Mrs Ks[i] dresses into one for Mag.[ja]   cut & made the waist of a new—cut sleeves & made part—pleated the skirt—& did various other jobs & left as many undone that were to be done—sewed to nearly the last minute of starting. Mrs K.[i] makes a perfect slave of herself. She has good traits too & her society would be agreeable were it not for the above faults. I really pity her.

July 25, 1863 Mrs Karper[i] took me to Mr Thompsons[v] (Brother-in-laws)   she took he three smallest children along & on the way put my baby's hat on her rowdy Jim. Of course he broke it. She is so careless with other peoples things. While at her house she used my black shawl a[s] a window blind in her parlor &c &c.   We found Sarah[u] in the midst of her Saturdays work. Mrs K[i] staid until 3 P.M.—then started home—The next day Sunday 20th Mrs Mr Thompson[u] & I went to Wilson Owens for dinner. The roads were very bad. I was tired when I got there it being over a mile from Mr Ts & I carried my baby all the way.   the day was extremely warm.

---

3. Droving was a notoriously dirty occupation. Inns and roadside taverns often insisted that drovers sleep in separate quarters, or with their herds, because they stank too offensively to be allowed into the regular rooms.

July 27, 1863 Martha Hudson & I went for blackberries. each got a pk. nearly all low one—the high ones were just beginning to ripen—The next day I went all alone to a new place all of a mile from T's the next day I went again so on every day during the week—Many days Sarah[u] & I together gathered ½ bus. She heated her oven every day to dry them. O! but I did do some fancy sweating during those trips. On Monday Aug. 2nd I went out again with two vesels. this morning for the first time there were quite a number in the patch I did not get my vessels quite full—P.M. Sarah[u] gathered a few from her patch. Tuesday she gathered some again. When I went she kept the babies & visa versa—Wendesday 4th we went to Mother Thompsons for tea.

August 5, 1863 Thursday. we started at 6 A.M. & went to Mother Byers[b]—After the salutation she asked about Sammy & told me she heard he was killed—it shocked me very much & although I could not believe it yet I felt badly all day—Cora was quite fretful & took a notion to cry at the table until Mother[b] took her. She is quite crazy for her Grand Mother[b] who makes a great deal of her—the child knows it of course—after tea we started home again Cora cried on the way & set Sarahs[u] baby to crying so I could not manage the both (I had both & Sarah[u] drove) Sarah[u] had to stop & take hers. S.[u] got rather out of humor about it—we got home safely at sundown. Cora cries so much & T's[v] do not like it. O! but I wished myself home.

August 7, 1863 Fryday. I went to S's[u] patch & gathered nearly two baskets of berries. P.M. we divided our dried berries 20 qts—& got my things ready to go home next day. S.[u] gave me 1 doz. eggs—Martha H. took tea with us—After tea I went home with her & got a pk of apples.

August 8, 1863 Saturday. I was up early dressed myself & baby—got my berries ready ie the undried which I took along for pies & to can—At 7 A.M. we started Reached Chambersburg a little after 9 oclock A.M. 3 letters from my Sml were here waiting for me. Thank God he is safe yet. After reading my letters & telling Mr Thompson[v] their contents he started home. I changed clothes then set to work canning my berries. I took the large dish in which I had them & set them down to Plough & his girls & let them eat to their hearts content. Annie was baking. On leaving I left as much (if not more) as a sixpenny loaf of bread with the understanding that she give me some when I return. She soon told me she thought she could not spare me any being she did not bake much—before this she told me she thought I would come that day—Thinks I just keep it then, & sent Emma & got some sour milk & bake soda raised bread. she gave me a little more that Cora & I needed for dinner & that is all she returned. & of the beans she used of mine she returned about ⅓—My room looked as if they had been using it—their sittingroom carpet was lying on a pile in here—she used my tin boilers—used ½ doz of my eggs. (I hope she will return those) I baked me 4 small blackbery pies—cleaned my room—worked hard all day—Sunday wrote letters all day—The weather was very warm.

August 10, 1863 Monday. Cora has been quite sick all day. Poor dear just laid wherever I put her & moaned so piteously—did not cry much—Uncle Gelvixes called a little—would have taken supper had Cora been well—Mrs Mc.G sent me beans &c

August 11, 1863 Cora rested midling well—last night—she is fretful today. John Karpers[l] & the 3 smallest children visited me—I had a time getting meat—& bread—I asked Annie to lend me bread but she did not like to so I went from bakery to bakery until I got some. Annie is just getting as selfish as she was when I first come. Old Plough told me I could have as many apples as I needed for present use—& said he has no hog to feed them to & the people dont fetch them like they use to & he could not use them up fast enough &c &c &c so now I fall air to the badly bruised rotten & small ones.

August 12, 1863 Wrote letters all day. to Sml—to C.W. (fathers,[aa] Adams[kk] Weavers[ee] & Uncle Noahs) to Sisters. 13th I washed in A.M.—P.M.Mended my hoops—evening had those 2 teeth that have been bothering me so extracted. & 14th today ironed some & baked—Cora had colera morbes last night & is quite fretful today. She is sleeping now so I must go & Iron more. The stove is all taken up so I cannot iron so I will write more. This morning when washing up thing I threw water down. when I got down old Plough said you will have pretty tubs with the water splashing against them. I replied clear water does not dirty or hurt them & I throw no other kind down. I am getting tired of his reprof—the other day when Annie was ironing she had clothes on a chair to the end of the house. I was sweeping & on seeing those clothes I was right careful when first I knew old Plough came out—"Mrs Cormany—you should not sweep down here when there are clothes here"—I just said I did not sweep dow at the end—I do not relish that kind of talk—last evening he gave me a basket of apples—all were badly bruised—split—rotten or very small—still I am glad for them but it

376

looks rather badly in him to give me only what he would feed to the hogs—My teeth are still bleeding a little. O! but the pulling did hurt—after the first one was pulled I shook like a leaf—I could scarcely hold the glass straight enough to keep the water in. Its cloudy & thundering   hope we will have rain—Cora is awake—

August 16, 1863 Sunday. Early this A.M. Mrs McG sent her little girl for my baby—so I could go to church. I was glad to go to preaching once again. It was communion day—I communed but felt badly   I feel that something is wanting.   M. went for my baby but she was so good that by Mrs McG's request I left her there—Came home wrote to My Sml—at 4 P.M. went to experience meeting. Spoke told as well as I could my dark state of mind—felt after I had spoken as if wanted to creep through some hole so no one could see me & leave. I felt so ashamed of myself. After meeting was dismissed quite a number came & spoke to me. I resolved to struggle & pray until I found relief—I did not go home before I got my baby, it really seemed a long time that I had been without her. Ate a little & put baby to sleep then betook myself to prayer. Soon I felt relieved—Read in my Bible—went to bed light & happy

August 17, 1863 Fell happy—every thing goes on so smothly babys crying does not iritate me—& she does not get cross like when I am iritated. O! that I could always act & speak kindly to her I know she would be better. Went down street on an errant—& while gone Mrs McG sent me some roastingears & tomatoes. On Sat. Evening she brought me some potatoes   She is so kind to me—This morning I got word that the case for my hairflowers was completed—P.M. I went for it. Its real nice. I asked him (John Hazelett) what the charges were—"Well Mrs Cormany—I admired your hairflower so much & I thought if the case would be acceptable I would make it for you if you would make me a boquet of hairflowers of my friends hair—O! Mr H. I shall certainly [d]o that if that satisfies you &c &c & thanked him for the case—Some ½ doz. or more ladies came running to see my flowers when I brought the case home—for I carried it myself—no darkey being there at the time & thinks I whose business is it if I do carry it home   those ladies of course were disappointed when they saw the empty case—All seem anxious to see the flowers—

August 18, 1863 Worked at my hair flowers & completed the wreath & boquet for the centre—Emma took Cora out so while she was gone I went down street & got white pasteboard to line my case also ribbon to make a Union badge to tie to the stems of the boquet, & intended completing it—but my sheet of pasteboard did not reach—so I will have to leave it—Also got No 1 of Harpers War Magazines—

August 19, 1863 Got up early made applesauce & got cracked wheat for breakfast Gave Cora a morning walk to Mrs Mc Gs for milk—took my little pitcher full of applesauce along for her—have been reading & writing all day. Wrote to My Samuel—Eve. Put my hair flowers in the case looks pretty.

August 20, 1863 A.M. Went to Granny Royers for corn. she had none so she gave me a head of cabbage & a few potatoes—2 cucumbers & 2 large pears took them home & started again for corn called at 7 places before I got some. I got 1 doz ears for 6 cts—Had I not been a soldiers wife I would not have gotten any there & at least not that cheap P.M. Mrs McGowan—Mrs Sulenberger & Miss Rudy took tea with me—Had a nice little visit—Had no meat for supper, which is odd for a Pa. supper. All admired my hairflowers very much—Cora is not well. Poor baby—Did not get my dishes washed until 8½. A man (Mrs Wordabaugh's father—called to to see whether I had heard from Mr Cormany lately—they heard that our men had a heavy fight on last Monday & many of that Co were killed & among the killed were Mr Cormany & Mr Wordabaugh—I told them it could not be—that I saw nothing of any fight in the papers. Mrs W. walked from Salem church to town (4mls) & carried her babe—to see whether I had heard from Mr C. What will woman not do or endure for the man she loves.[4] The weather is very warm. Some of the six month Cav. Regiments left for Loudon Va. today. Many think this war will soon be over. The rebel cause looks hopeless. My Sml in his of last Sat—speaks very hopefully of the speedy ending of the war & his safe return home God grant it—Religiously I am getting colder again. O! to be very good—

August 24, 1863 Not very well—Neither is Cora—finished the letter to Mr C. I had not quite completed it when Miss Whistler called—she was here about 1 hour After she left I put Cora to sleep—dressed myself—had bonnet & all on went to the drawer where I always keep my portmonio to get a stamp out of it when lo—it was not there I searched immediately for it but could not

4. The rumor of Wordebaugh's death was false; Samuel mentions his application for a leave of absence in his entry for Feb. 13, 1865.

find it, so I took a few loose cents thinking after I'd get back I would search again—Called at Sulenbergers & Barn's—mailed my letter & home—Ate a little dinner—Cora still slept—& then hunted through every thing & everywhere but no portomonio did I find—I was so certain that I had put it in my drawer but it may be that I lost it last Thursday when I last had it—Or some one took it—P.M. I told Plough & also told him of Emmas "hooking" propensities—but told him I did not suspect them—Neither do I, but still deep down in my heart something still says may be Emma & Orpha W. took it the evening they were up here—but I do not wish to suspect—God knows—Evening—Old P. talked to his girls—Annie seems very distant—I have not seen Emma—Old P. just gave me a lecture about lownecked dresses—he said "It is enough to make any mans courage rise to see girls with their shoulders bare & you ought to know that Mrs C." Rather a plane hint—for I went barenecked this few days—The old scamp to think of such things & to speak of them—

August 26, 1863 Receaved a letter from my Sml. he is in good cheer. Finished cutting my carpet rags—3 P.M. went to McGowans & canned ½ bus. & ½ pk tomatoes which filled 10 qt & 1 2 qt jar (12 qts) Am not well—am sick at the stomach—Oh so sick paid my rent up to the time I start for Philadelphia—Wish I were there already

August 30, 1863 Sunday—Evening—Was to S.School in J. Hokes Bible class—he certainly is a good teacher—Pussy did not do well— she would talk—O! to be a better christian. After Christ has done & suffered so much for us we should be very good—Nothing do I desire more—I expect to be very busy this week to get ready for my tour—O! for the presence of my Savior always with me so I may always do right & undertake nothing that He cannot smile on How much shorter the days have gotten already—dark at 7—Just finished a long letter to my Sml.[5]

October 7, 1863 607 Pine St Philadelphia I left Chambersburg 3 weeks ago last Saturday in the noon train—came as far as Shiremans-town where I staid over Sunday—Monday Morning I started for White Hall but made a mistake about the county so I came very near going to Lehigh Co. instead of Bucks. I found it out just in time so I lost only 50cts by it. & got to Quakertown first instead of White

---

5. Samuel received this letter on Sept. 3, 1863.

Hall where I had to spend 40 cts that I would not have spent had I gone to White Hall first. Well so much for bought wit—The week at Quakertown was very pleasantly spent as also the 3 weeks in Hilltown among the friends & now we are in the city of "Brotherly love"—where we expect to stay until next Monday—We stay mainly on account of Susies[nn] Art. Limb—Dr Palmer is changing it considerably but feels confident that he will succeed in giving perfect satisfaction. Yesterday evening I went with Mrs Leitenberger (my hostess) to german evangelical prayer meeting. had a good meeting. Today Clem[cc] was here for dinner. P.M. Susie[nn] he[cc] & I were out looking at sewing machines I was also to the North Pa depot &c &c indeed I think I walked no less than 6 to 8 mls consequently I am quite tired. Cora is well the little dear—she is sleeping. Yesterday & today I left her. she had to cry today so I shall take her along hereafter unless Susie[nn] stays & keeps her.

October 21, 1863 In Chambersburg again Susie[nn] is with me & is quite sick with typhoid fever. She complained for some time before we left Hilltown but we thought nothing of it—during our stay in Phil'a she got worse every day—A week ago today (13th) we left Phil'a for this place. Susie was very sick so we got only to Shiremanstown that day—Next day (14th) we came on home, by which time she was so completely exhausted that we could hardly get her in. She took her bed & has kept it ever since—She has been verry sick. I really felt alarmed about her & wrote to Clem[cc] to come which he did not do—only wrote. she is much better now—All fever has left her & she is convalescent—Still is not able to help herself of any account—Last night & today Cora cried so much that my patience quite gave way—Indeed I wished I had never been born. the more I tried to quiet her the more she cried. I felt as if I were the most forsaken creature on earth. Indeed I cannot tell how miserable I felt. My crossness made the baby still more so too. I see how verry wrong I was. My God O! for thy help to do right. This evening I tried to be real gentle & mild, yet firm, she gave up soon. I often feel my unfitness to be a mother. Ploughs are as selfish as ever During all Susies[nn] illness this far Annie has never come in unless I asked her to stay with Susie[nn] while I would do errands. Well I have other rooms now & I am glad of it—I hope we will get to more agreeable people—Susie[nn] does not rest well.

October 22, 1863 This morning Susies[nn] limbs began to jerk—only big spells & every paroxism left her weaker & every paroxism seemed more severe than the one before—by evening it had extended over the whole body. I got alarmed & sent for Dr Reynolds, who uses no strong medicines   I was in a tight place surely I did not know what to do for her & I saw that she must have relief.   he gave her some stuff to act on her liver & bowels—also something to quiet her nerves so she might sleep—she had some fever again. I am very tired was on my feet all day. Wrote letters to Mollie,[ii] Clem,[cc] & home to C. W.

October 23, 1863   Susie[nn] slept pretty well. About 11 P.M. (I had just retired) I heard her making heard her saying something. I went to hear   just as I got to the bed she said—Glory—peace. I then pulled the quilt over her when she said "O! Rachel such dreams do not hurt me. I was just thinking of the 4th of July the last 4th I mean the last day when all the children will be gathered home, what a happy time it will be when all receive their happy crowns"—You feel happy do you, "Yes"—I think she was scarcely awake—I asked her this morning whether she remembered it—she said she did & said "It will be a happy time too, wont it? I asked her again whether she felt happy she said she did! That jerking is less frequent & less severe this morning—she seems inclin to sleep most of the time just like yesterday.   her tongue is some coated again.

October 24, 1863   Susie[nn] lay stupid or rather sleeping the greater part of the day—Seems to have no pain—that jerking is still not gone yet—She has considerable fever, no doubt caused by the medicine. I told the dr this morning that I thought we could get along now. If she should get worse we would call him.   he left some fever drops which she was to take every half hour—but not a bit of it did she take. I believe that his stuff is what made her more fever again. She is verry restless this evening—

October 25–November 3, 1863   Was disturbed on the 25 so I got nothing but the date down   The next day (26th) Susie[nn] took hemoragh of the bowels & her life for awhile was dispaired of—I telegraphed to brother Clemn,[cc] to come—but 2 weary days of anxious watching passed ere he came & then Susie[nn] was better   he stayed over but one night—The day he left she was worse again—Since then she has been improving slowly—On Sat. 31st Sister Mary[ii] came & Yesterday, Nov. 2nd we moved to this place (Mrs Merkliens.[6] we have our things in pretty good order now—Tomorrow My Sewing

---

6. Mrs. Merklein, or Merkline, lived half a block south and across the street from the Ploughs. *AFCP*, p. 24.

Machine will come which is an Aniversary Gift from My Samuel—I got 2 letters from him today   these last marches have nearly killed him. O I do wish this cruel war were once over & he at home to stay

November 14, 1863   Susie[nn] is able to walk about a little now—Mary[ii] is still here   Capt. Snyder & Lieut. Barns are home on furlough—both called this week. Snyder is taking a few little things along for me to him.[7] I also rec'd 2 letters from him this week his health is only midling. O I hope he will soon get home to stay   Mother[b] & Elly[y] were here to dinner today. Ellie[y] is getting married in a few weeks. If Samuel were home they would ask us to the wedding   as it is they do not want me there.[8]

November 17, 1863   Have been remodeling my silk dress. Cora was so very troublesome that I got but little done. Yesterday I was to Whites for work   he had none cut said he would have it ready today, but today it was not ready—or he was not in.[9] I feel quite gloomy, do not know why   O! My Father help me to be a good christian.   then come what will He is my stay—& comfort. I have feared something might have befallen Mr C

November 19, 1863   Mary[ii] & I were to Lieut. Barns' for supper, were a little late   On our way home we called at Annie Plough. intended to call on Julie Wampler but she was over at Annies—so we made 2 calls at once. Rec'd 3 letters—one from My Samuel, Another from H.W. Reboks,[pa] & another from Minne Hanson in which she states that S. Jennie Miller is dead. She died a "maniac." Tawny again revived his courtship & deceived her again after that her mind gave way & she died saying "Tawney is my murderer." It seems it cannot be that Jennie is no more & that D.A. Tawney is her destroyer.   both respected schoolmates.[10] Rebok[pa] writes a cheery letter. So does my Samuel. 2 strange ladies called & staid quite a while. A new england lady & a town girl—

7. See Samuel's entry for Nov. 19, 1863.

8. Samuel's youngest sister was marrying Benjamin Slichter on Dec. 10, 1863.

9. Two blocks up Front Street, near the center of Chambersburg, lived A. J. and H. M. White, "merchant tailors and clothiers." *AFCP*, p. 24. Rachel is again taking in sewing to supplement the family's meager income.

10. Sarah Jane Miller had been one of the two graduates at Otterbein's first commencement in 1857. Garst, *Otterbein*, p. 76. She died on Nov. 1, 1863. Daniel A. Tawney, who had been an undergraduate with Jennie and Rachel, earned an A.M. at Otterbein (1863) and became a Presbyterian minister. *TQRGO*, pp. 25, 29.

November 20, 1863   Went to Mrs. Sulenbergers to inquire how to proceed to get tailor work. She offered to get some for us & sure enough soon after noon she came with a bundle & helped us to get into the way of putting them together. Mrs McG- sent for me   I went. She was in trouble—had received an anonymous letter which contained no very pleasing matter. The weather is fine.

November 21, 1863   It has rained all day & is still at it. Trimmed my bonnet for the winter—Rec'd a letter from my old schoolmate H. C. Pennel.   how glad I am to hear from them again. Also rec'd the R. Telescope again. The first since the subscription

November 25, 1863   Our third Marriage Aniversary. A bright clear cold day—just one like the wedding day was—Then I was happy—I wedded the man of my choice—A bright future was looming up before me—A neat little cottage just built was awaiting for me, & having just emerged from College walls—All seemed so novel—A trip to Niagra was the first—then followed incessant parties & sleighrides in C.W. among my relatives. Now clouds arose to overshaddow our bright skys—The Rebellion broke out, & our prarie home cannot be reached, So Mr C. (my worser half) engaged himself as clerk & book keeper to the firm of Wenger & Weaver & I went in partnership with sister Lydia[dd] (Mrs Weaver) in the milliner business. We did well—Mr C. was compelled to sell liquor out by the small which grated on his conscience—He tried to quiet it for a while but its lashings became so severe that he told the firm that he could not sell any more—They remonstrated with him, told him he was overscrupulous—but he was firm—They told him they could not employ him longer if he refused to sell any part of their merchandse. So of course he was out there. We left Elmira soon after & moved to Blair into My fathers tenant house. Mr C. taught singing classes at night & in day time assisted father. Here we spent our first aniversary, & had quite a jubilant time—All the cousins near were invited & we had a big supper for them. In May of our second year a daughter was born to us—a little angel daughter. I shall never forget how proud & happy Mr C. was with "his baby" as he called—.   In August of the same year we left C. W. on a visit to Pa. his native state & friends. After our visit here we expected to go to Mo. to occupy & enjoy our Pararie home—but alas this cruel war soon separated us—he enlisted in the 16th P. Cav.   I visited among the friends awhile until near the second aniversary day—Yes until the day—for we (Mr C came home on a "french")[11] went to Mothers[b] a

11. I.e., on leave.

few days before & got things to commence housekeeping & on the 25th 1862 I moved to Ploughs Chambersburg—in another part of my journal I have an account of the vents of that day—as also of proceedings since then, but this day brings all these things to mind again. It seems as if it could not be that I have to spend this day her & Mr C in the army—& the good man only knows where he is. My God protect him & bring him safely back. In honor of the day we had as good a dinner as circumstances would permit. Sisters Sue[nn] & Mollie[ii] being here, we talked all the dinner hour of Mr C. & wishing him home—Cora, being his immage, of course was his representative too so all must wait on her as if she were a king. O! It seems so dreadful to be thus sepparated. If he only be spared to come home again that we may yet long live together I will not murmur at this cruel separation. The great sin of slavery has brought all this calamity on us—God grant us grace & strength for our day & trial— Evening—Was to prayermeeting, was called on to pray—when I thought of My poor Samuel I broke down right in the midst. I hope he is safe yet—I wrote for him but could not complete a letter & so ends the third Aniversary day—

XIX

On the Eastern Front
November 25, 1863–March 14, 1864

In this section Samuel recounts the activities of the 16th Pennsylvania Cavalry from the little-known Mine Run Campaign of November 1863 through the camp life and picket forays of January and February 1864. This was a period during which the Army of the Potomac, like other Union armies in Tennessee and the Mississippi Valley, maintained a steady but restrained pressure upon the crippled military forces of the Confederacy and waited for spring weather to launch what they hoped would be their final offensive thrusts.

November 25, 1863 Wednesday. Lay in Camp—This is our 3rd Wedding Anniversary-day—Oh! to be at home to celebrate it with Darling and Daughter. Happy the day. Thrice hallowed the hour that united us and made us one. O Lord spare me to live many years my Darlings Husband and Coras Father——

November 26, 1863 Thursday. Drew rations and Forage and Start at 6 A.M. crossed Rapidan at Ealies Ford—5th Corpse in sight.[1] Marched through "Wilderness" in direction of Spotsylvania Court House, leaving Chancellorville to the left. Crossed two plank Roads at G and encamped[2]——

November 27, 1863 Friday. awfully cold—On move early. Passed 5th Corpse near Mount Hope Church on plank road. Our 1st Bri-

1. This movement signals the beginning of Meade's last attempt to trap Lee before the advent of winter weather. These maneuvers, known as the Mine Run Campaign, were named for the stream along which Lee repositioned his defensive line to meet the advancing Federals. Lee's move proved effective, for Meade withdrew rather than risk a major thrust against such a strong position. Both armies then settled into winter quarters. See Jay Luvaas and Wilbur S. Nye, "The Campaign That History Forgot," *CWTI* 8 (Nov. 1969), 11–42.

2. This is substantially the same route Grant would later take in the spring offensive of 1864. "Wilderness" referred both to a specific place—a crossroads tavern—and to the surrounding area, which was characterized by dense second-growth forest crisscrossed by roads and boggy streams. G probably stood for Germanna, the name of a key ford across the Rapidan and also of the plank road that led south from that ford.

Cavalry crossing the Rapidan River at Ely's Ford. *Harper's Pictorial History of the Civil War.*

gade being in advance encountered the Enemy first—drove them some distance and a warm engagement took place—we were drawn up in support—were shelled some with missing effect. Soon Infantry came to our relief—Our command lost heavily charging Rebel Infantry—Some 80 wounded—35 mortally—sad affair—Lay on arms over night at Mount Hope Church.

November 28, 1863 Saturday. Cloudy—7 OCK—all quiet yet—7:30 occasional shots of Canon & Muskets—Prospects of a great fight—but the enemy fell back some. Rain set in at 11 AM—awfully unpleasant—Enemy failed to advance and attack so we lay out on arms—rain ceased—No blankets, uncomfortable—Chilly—

November 29, 1863 Sunday. Cleared up cold—Rested mainly during AM—some fighting in hearing—P.M. Some rebel Cavalry attacked, us—The 2nd Pa Cav drove them out Plank Road to Parkers Store. When we charged, and fought them severely Fetterhoff and 1 wounded, our Capt Alexander killed—an awful time, charging and being charged. Falling back as tho whipped, and having squadrons prepared to charge in on their flanks—and crossfire them with awful destruction—our retreaters then about facing and re-charging—Thus we were enabled to do fearful work on them. While our loss was not so great—and we were holding back, and at times driving back greatly superior numbers with our daring and quick acting tactics & movements. It seems they were 3 to 5 to our 1.
Lay on arms over night—

November 30, 1863 Monday. Enemy withdrew in night—So we took up march early—Awfully cold—Frozen hard—
We reported to 2nd Corpse Infantry. Lay in their rear all day near Rebel Fortifications—Saw some of their Canon, and heard some off along the Front. Eve. we fell back to our old Camp were up all night to keep warm, and be ready for any emergency

December 1, 1863 Tuesday. The coldest of the winter—thus far, such exposure, and shortness of rations, &c. tries ones patriotism—
We went out Foraging, found lots of Corn and Turnips—Our troops are falling back, gradually—Still awfully cold—We were up and ready all night expecting command to March—

December 2, 1863 Wednesday. Took up line of march at 3 OCK A.M. chilled to the bone and very heart—Crossed Rapidan at Ealies Ford at 9 A.M. Rebels follow us closely and fire on our rear guard occasionally. We throw out Pickets—or a thin skirmish line to the rear and go into Camp near The Ford—A little forage comes to us—Men seem ½ starved being on about ½ rations now 8 or 10 ds. Save what we forage from settlers occasionally—and their supplies are extremely meager—as both armies draw on them alternately.

December 3, 1863 Thursday. A little more mild—Picket firing at intervals all night   Some rations reach us. Sounds pleasing to our ears—and feels fine to have our horses filled up once more, good, and ourselves too—We have now been out eight days without unsaddling any one whole night, and have had not one good nights rest—and even now start in again on ½ rations—Eve went on Picket at Ealies Ford—

This ½ ration business is on a/c of the risks of getting wagons to us—as we are fighting and scouting in the Enemies Country—

December 4, 1863 Friday. Cool—pleasant—Rebel pickets right opposite ours on the little river, fordable at many places, nothing interesting all day,

Evening our Regt relieved and fell back to Richardsville—Mail reaches us, Letter from Pet—Clem,^{cc} H.C. Pennel, & Wm McGowen, also Copy of one from Col J. I. Gregg to Mr Conley³—

December 5, 1863 Satuday. Sent a pencil letter to Pet   Oh! for a talk with her or time to write all my feelings—and the glimmerings of hopes of promotion.

Had a long talk with Capt Snyder   says I am all O.K. for promotion. Am putting all the time I can snatch studying to Master Caseys Cav., Tactics—

December 6, 1863 Sunday. Cold—clear—We went on Picket to Germanna Ford on Rapidan.

Plenty of wood—rations and forage, so men and Horses are warm & full—

---

3. Clem Bowman has apparently remained active on behalf of his brother-in-law. Although the identity of Mr. Conley remains in doubt, making the following reconstruction a conjecture only, it is possible that Mr. Conley and "Senator Connel," who is mentioned by Samuel on April 13, 1864, are the same man: Pennsylvania State Senator George Connell from the fourth district of Philadelphia, where Clem was practicing hydropathy. Clem apparently pushed "Mr. Conley" to bring Samuel to the attention of the regimental commander, Colonel Gregg, who acknowledged the senator's interest. Connell then gave the colonel's reply to Clem as proof that he was indeed applying pressure. Clem sent a copy of Gregg's letter back to Samuel.

December 7, 1863 Monday. cold—
Have great log fires—The Infantry got 14,000,00 ft of Lumber near here for use for Winter quarters—I rode to the River to see the sight—Saw some Rebs and their works, on opposite side of River—Quiet

December 8, 1863 Tuesday. Xtremely cold—Routine day—Wrote to Pet—am well and gay, but long to see my little All. Pet & Cora—

December 9, 1863 Wednesday. Still very cold—Routine til M—were relieved and fell back to Ealies X Roads—put up good quarters. Hope we may stay awhile.

December 10, 1863 Thursday. still cold—Slept well—Mailed letter to Pet—made out Reports for Captain & Co.—Drew Forage and rations—Routine—

December 11, 1863 Friday. slightly milder—Routine day—

December 12, 1863 Saturday. cloudy—Break camp at 7 A.M. move via Kellys Ford to Bealton Station—Picketed towards Morrisville—
—awful rainy night—

December 13, 1863 Sunday. Completely water soaked—cleared up finely—try to dry up—Relieved from Picket—Lay on poles all night—Sergt Harrison—Privates Shelly—Bradley & Hassler came back to the Command—

December 14, 1863 Monday. clear—cold—Moved and camped near Bealton in a Field—Good ground, but scarce of wood—Put up shelter—Tents, Low Style—Fairly comfortable—

December 15, 1863 Tuesday. very cold—Still in Camp—Little doing—Plenty of rations now & Forage—but awfully cold—

December 16, 1863 Wednesday. Double Cold—Routine—Write Letters—

December 17, 1863 Thursday. very rainy night—Rained most of day—More than disagreeable—is horrible—Letter from Pet—

389

December 18, 1863 Friday. nearly clear—But Oh how wet, and muddy—Such exposure and conditions almost unendurable. Yet we do endure them, keep well—and actually thrive withall—P.M. we drew clothing, and evening took up the march again for Warrenton—a fearfully cold freezy windy night—reaching a camping place at 11 P.M.—

December 19, 1863 Saturday. cold, clear, windy Moved Camp early. Put up good quarters—Drew Forage and Rations—Seems like staying awhile—Awfully cold—Busy keeping warm—Evening orders "March in the morning.

December 20, 1863 Sunday. awfully cold— Struck Tents—and took up march—Didn't go far. Hit one of our old camping places—Put up in the woods—Better fires and more comfortable—Lay around Kind of Sundayified—Am so full of thoughts of Darling and Cora—and long so to see them—I am keeping midling well—Evening Marching for 6 A.M.—

December 21, 1863 Monday. still very cold—Struck out for Bealton Station—Drew Forage and rations—and lay round at Noon took up the move via—White Sulphur Springs—Jefferson to near Amesville—went into camp around huge rail fires—cooked a bean soup supper—quite a warming fill up—wrote to Pet—am O.K.

December 22, 1863 Tuesday. still very cold—Took up march at early dawn via Amosville—Gaines X Roads. Little W—Sperryville, through Thornton Gap into Luray Valley 4 miles from town of Luray where we put up—on way our Boys "Foraged" lots—Caught a Reb at Amesville—took him along—Saw a few Gaines X Roads & Sperryville—but met little resistance—Rumor says 300 to 500 Rebs at Luray—We are well picketed.[4]

December 23, 1863 Wednesday. We spent the cold night cooking and eating—Geese, Turkeys, Chickens and home made Bread. somewhat reluctantly given to the Boys at times by Johnie Farmers, and at other times, cheerfully given by ladies with the map of loyalty all over their faces—Of course we were very gentle with such—and not un-

4. The Shenandoah Valley remained an important source of supplies for the Confederate army. This raid by the Union cavalry was designed to disrupt operations at one of the key crossing points into and out of the valley and to destroy anything the Confederates had stockpiled for shipment to the Southern army during the coming winter.

gentlemanly to those who were not of "like precious faith" and handed out the Loaves with a little seeming reticense.

We marched early into Luray this morning—after our cold night of Feasting—

Took any amount of Tobacco—Leather finished and unfinished— Some partly tanned—some in preparation—and some raw hides— Of course these must be burned. The hundred of cords of dry bark serving as fuel to keep up fires during the burning, and the Tannery buildings while burning served as Consumeries into which to toss Leather. Hides &c—also The Saddlery or Establishment—a place where Saddles, Bridles and Harness were being made to supply Cavalry—Artillery and Teams with equipment added to the Furnace fires in which to Complete the destruction of the entire plant— Having done up the job pretty well we took up the counter march, and burned five more tanneries in the valley within 15 miles—Shot one and captured one Reb at Little Washington—where we laid up for a nights rest—Both men and Horses were greatly exhausted with the dashing about in the valley, keeping up the Fires. Keeping roads of access well picketed—and a general cautious lookout to avoid being surprised from any point—

December 24, 1863 Thursday. Had lots of good things to cook and eat last night and this morning—Took up line of march early— Wending our way homeward—or Warrentonward—Our Horses were well nigh done out—and we all were very badly used up— from the days and nights doings—with little rest or sleep—

Reached old camp at sundown, heavily laden with Poultry— Beef—Pork, Sausage, Meal, Flour &c for our Christmas Dinner, and some for later use—Spent hours writing Pet a Christmas letter—Tho it will be late for her—

December 25, 1863 Christmas Day Paymaster on hand. Prepared "H" Co Rolls—Some companies being paid——I am quite unwell— sore throat—stiff neck—But thank God I have neither frozen nor been shot, and am able to do justice to a dandy Soldiers Christmas Dinner Several times today—Evening do a lot of writing—

December 26, 1863 Saturday. milder—We—"H" Co was paid off this A.M.—Also had Inspection of Ordnance—Recd Blanks to make new Reports and Rolls &c. I am quite unwell—

December 27, 1863 Sunday. Had to work on Muster Rolls cloudy, looks rainy—I am really too unwell to do my pressing work—But wake up. Here goes—

December 28, 1863 Monday. Rainy—muddy—slushy—Capt Snyder, Orderly Barnes—Peters and I took our documents to the Home of Mrs Cochrans—and in a fine warm room wrote all day—Plenty of whiskey in sight, and some gone out of sight, helped to keep up spirits, and we sure did a big days work—and got the chilliness dried out of us—Oh! to see my Darling, and our Baby—and to be with them to stay—But this cannot be—until we are Victors and have saved our Homes—our Country.

December 29, 1863 Tuesday. Rain ceases—I finish Rolls—and wrote some besides—Capt S is most terribly drunk today—Too much whiskey in camp for the good of our Men, and especially the Officers—My cold is making me more than half sick—But I must keep well at my work for the Captain and the Company—

December 30, 1863 Wednesday. Clear overhead, but almost bottomless mud—We today into a new Infantry Winter Quarters which they had to leave and go on the March—Seems too bad for them, but awfully good—while it lasts for us—
    We fixed them up to suit us, and they do splendidly—
    Received a letter from Pet and Baby—Little Heart and Bird Cake in it—and Oh! it is such a good Christmasy Letter—Just lik[e] unto her own dear self—

December 31, 1863 Thursday. awful rainy—Our squadron gone to Hartwood Church. I was excused to work on Co. Clothing a/c also wrote up diary, and letter to Pet— and meditated—alone with God—I am not as well as a No.1 Soldier needs to be physically— Nor am I up to my ideal spiritually—But I press on daily to reach my ideals—So closes 1863—

New Year 1864

January 1, 1864 Friday. New Years Morn! Cleared up—My cough very annoying—and I am really quite unwell—
    The Regt gone on a Raid—I lay in quarters most of day—Our 2nd Cav. Div. gone on raid to Front Royal—Wrote and mailed letter to My Rachel—Rec'd one from her today—Eve awfully cold.

January 2, 1864 Saturday. Extremely cold day. I am long ways from being well—I wrote most of day in my Quartermaster Memorandum—Drew Forage—Our Sutler came up. Cough quite troublesome—My breast sore.

January 3, 1864 Sunday. Routine—Rest—Read. meditated—Now to strive to attain my ideal life religiously, and as a Soldier & Patriot—

January 4, 1864 Monday. Cloudy—snowing &c Wrote most of day on Captains a/c's or affairs—also a letter to Pet—These Ordnance reports are very troublesome to make out—Eve sleeted some—I wrote til 9 P.M.—Had a fine Oyster supper I feel very badly on breast and lungs.

January 5, 1864 Tuesday. Clear & very cold—Started in on my writing for Captain 10 OCK—We rec'd marching orders We packed up the things belonging to the Boys out on the Raid and placed them into Wagons then about 11 ½ A.M. took up the march via Warrenton Junction to Turkey Run on W.J.R.R.—Most intensely cold—we put up for the night in pines—good shelter—I am still quite unwell.

January 6, 1864 Wednesday. awful cold—Regiment came in off raid of five days—Cold & well wornout—
We drew up on hill-side near Turkey Run & R.R. and many commenced to put up winter quarters—We—can't see it yet. been fooled too often—so we simply shelter-tent-it for the eve and night—

January 7, 1864 Thursday. coldest yet—My shelter-Tent—pretty cosy—Sent in Ordnance Co. Report—Wrote for Pet—Cut lot of pine wood for fire—Eve mail came O such a good letter from Pet—Heaven bless her for writing me such good cheery letters and being so true and faithful to me—Surely no man I know is so happy in or a wife and Baby girl as I.

January 8, 1864 Friday. Snowed all night 3 or 4 inches deep—pretty cold! Wrote answer to Pets letter—Many of the Boys busy getting ready & putting up quarters as tho to stay—We have done nothing more than talk of it yet—as we are pretty well sheltered in our Dog tent—We ate Three Rabbits for dinner—John, Dave and I—and I am pretty well and happy, so say we all—

January 9, 1864 Saturday. Exceedingly cold—Dave went Rabit-hunting—I got a team to haul us a shanty—from a vacated camp—John helped load it—We soon had it up—And had two Rabbits for dinner—P.M. Worked on our Shanty—Finishing touches—Eve had

393

most excrutiating pain in my ankle from a slight hatchet bruise inflicted in the morning.

January 10, 1864 Sunday. Cold, clear, pleasant I put up the stonework of our chimney—Then John & I built up the "stick" part—daubing it with clay &c. and put on the roof—tent covers—and got things in fair shape to sleep in by dark—and our chimney draws very well—physically I am pretty well again but in my head and spiritually I am dull and dilapidated—Cap't and I had some words + + +

January 11, 1864 Monday. still very cold—All hands putting finishing touches on cabins—sent off 5 condemned horses—But they came back again—Don't know why. Nothing out of the ordinary—My health much better—Cough seems gone, and I am delighted—

January 12, 1864 Tuesday. ' a little more moderate Sent the Cond'd horses off again. Worked some more on Shanty. P.M. Company drew clothing—Eve I entered clothing issue into Quartermasters a/c Book   Wrote letter to Pet—

January 13, 1864 Wednesday. milder—We got out timber and laid floor into Our Shanty—Worked hard all day—Eve wrote letter to Pet—am pretty well, but out of humor, not happy—O that all men were Men indeed. So many are merely the running-gears-of men

January 14, 1864 Thursday. Snowing all A.M.—Work some improvements on my new Cavalry Jacket—Eve stewed a mess pan full of dried apples—I am quite well again and decidedly happier—

January 15, 1864 Friday. Cloudy—Muddy—Moderate Wrote all day for Capt on Ordnance accounts—Eve read O such a good letter from Pet—Dear precious one, wish I could half repay her goodness—Eve wrote a letter to Pet about 10 OCK. Well and happy—

January 16, 1864 Saturday. Fine day—I made out 6 sets of Ord and Q.M. Invoices & Receipts—Eve wrote letter to Brother John[d]—Capt got some whiskey—I got enough for my good medicinally.

January 17, 1864 Sunday. Finished letter to Pet   General Inspection of Men, Arms, quarters &c &c   Read in Testament—and Telescope—and meditated prayerfully several hours—Eve Sam McGowen got a box by xpress from Home—Pet sent me 7-½ quires of

Winter quarters of an unidentified Union cavalry regiment, January 1864. The photograph was taken in the same general area where the 16th Pennsylvania established its winter camp. Photographic Division, LC.

paper—a lot of envelopes—4 prs socks—a canteen of molasses, 2 shirts, a few dried peaches &c &c—The dear good creature—of God—is so good to me—Heaven bless her—

January 18, 1864 Monday. Raining—Drew clothing—Drawers & Boots—Wrote for Captain—Some whiskey about again—Seems Captain can't let it alone—Nor use it as not abusing himself & others—

January 19, 1864 Tuesday. Wrote most of day for Capt. Eve sung awhile at Adts quarters. Wrote to Pet til 11 P.M.—

January 20, 1864 Wednesday. Write all day for Captain—am rather unwell—This sitting so much is hard on my breast—Eve feel all unstrung & downhearted—Oh! to see my pet and pussy or even to get more letters—

January 21, 1864 Thursday. Got wood hauled for Company use. Two new recruits came today—Wrote all day—Eve got a letter. Oh! such a good one from Pet—I wrote til very late to Pet—

January 22, 1864 Friday. General inspection again today—Capt Russel Inspector—I wrote most of day for Capt. Eve such a good letter from Pet and Sister Sue[nn]—Answered Pets late—Am not in real good condition physically nor mentally—

January 23, 1864 Saturday. Spring Like—Busy day at Captains Hd-Qrs—Had the Men sign Clothing Roll—
Practiced some at Boxing with Gloves—with Blair—He had been doing some of the Boys roughly—after watching him and noting his special moves and punches, and dodges, and parrys—I chafed him a little, at once he challenged me to try him—I accepted—we had a lively time—I saved my face, and landed a right swing on his left ear—stunning him some, and he dropped back from the line—or rope—but soon came again. I parried his blow and made as though for a right on his face. He dodged, but a left under cut with all the force I had met his face and fairly lifted his head—and the blood spirted from his nose, and we quit—I felt sorry for Blair—but he had been rather abusive to some of the innocent Boys.
Evening feel a little sore and depressed on my Chest—but a well and happy Soldier—

January 24, 1864 Sunday. Spring-Like-Day Finished letters to Pet and Sue[nn]—

Inspection—Routine—Read a good deal and meditate—Sunday-like—I have a longing to be a better a more exemplary Christian and in every way a better Man and my ideal Soldier—

January 25, 1864 Monday. Spring like—Not much going on—Routine—Did some writing for Capt. Eve a splendid letter from Pet. our winter quarters are good—Rations & Forage ample—Our Camp life is quiet—Very little Drill—This is playing soldier sure enough as compared with last month—

January 26, 1864 Tuesday. Regular Spring weather—Finished a letter to Pet—Adjt-Lieut Swank, Applegarth, and I practiced Vocal Music—P.M. I practiced alone awhile Drew forage—Eve. I went with those singers to Warrenton—We had a kind of jollification—Singing on the streets. In front of several fine residences—&c—were cheered some—Got back to Camp late—

January 27, 1864 Wednesday. warm—Wrote for Capt part of day—Rec'd letter from Cous Eckerman—Bro Bernard[q] and Pet——Drew 6 Horse Covers—Eve orders. Saddle up and be ready for an emergency—To arms til 10 P.M. All quieted—and we went to rest for the remainder of the night.

January 28, 1864 Thursday. Fine—Wrote for Capt most of day—Finished and mailed letter to Pet—Eve Phrenologized a whole lot of fellows—Lots of fun—Oh! that I were real well. I'd be so much more happy and could make it so much more enjoyable for the Boys—

How I do yearn to see my Darling and Cora—

January 29, 1864 Friday. still warm—Doc Herrmans and Capt. Rushes wives came—Hermans little girl reminds me so much of Cora—Our dear little Cora!

Wrote for Capt—and some letters P.M.—I was quite feverish, lay on my lounge several hours in a kind of delirium—Eve had to make Map of Picket lines of Regiments of our Brigade—Quite a job—

January 30, 1864 Saturday. Cloudy—In quarters most of day—Finished letter to Pet—Eve rec'd one from Her—Oh! such a good one—I cannot understand why I am so nervous—Sleepless—unstrung—Too much indoor quiet, too little doing—Long to be on the drive—

January 31, 1864 Sunday. misty—Quiet—officers wives still coming in—O that my Rachel and Cora were here too—I believe I'd soon be more vigorous again. Read and meditated several hours.

Eve wrote some for Captain—Such a good letter from Pet—

February 1, 1864 Monday. Little else than routine—with some reading—Tactics—and writing to Pet Things generally going contrariwise today xcepting drawing 23 Horse Cover and distributing them amongst the Men—

February 2, 1864 Tuesday. I am feeling decidedly better—Wrote letter to Brother Bernard.⁹ I stirred up a breeze about shortage in forage ration. Led to decided increace—

February 3, 1864 Wednesday. Cool & Stormy—Wrote for Capt in A.M.—P.M. Routine—Eve good letter from Pet—

February 4, 1864 Thursday. Routine—Wrote and mailed letter to Pet—Did some company writing—No new thing came up today—

February 5, 1864 Friday. Cap. got some old Rye—Let me have some for my cough—We became quite communicative—I left, to see about a room nearby for Pet, Cora & I to stay—provided I succeed in getting permission to have her come—On my return Capt—John W. &c cut up Jack til 11 OCK in our quarters—Nonsense let loose.

February 6, 1864 Saturday. Routine—I wrote a letter for Dave Woodall to his wife—Canonading hearable towards Raccoon Ford—Enlivens the Boys a little—Eve—More and more terrific—

We had a fine supper of Pudding—Tripe—Pickles, &c

February 7, 1864 Sunday. Routine—Regular Inspection—Took a sweet nap—Wrote some for Pet—Read a good deal—Eve—Letter from Pet—Such a good one—How could I do else than love her with all my powers—John and Dave Woodall each recd box from Home—

February 8, 1864 Monday. Cool but fine—Being Quarter-master of Company H makes me a whole lot more work—Drew some more clothing for Co., Issued it to the Men—P.M. Entered it into Co. Clothing Book—Capt Snyder is still in command of the Regiment—Wants me to try to make out His ordnance Returns—Recd letter from Prof. H. Garst of O. U.⁵—

5. He was not yet a professor (see ch. 1, n. 15). Samuel must have added the title when he transcribed the diary.

February 9, 1864 Tuesday. Letter to Pet—Wrote most of day on Ordnance Reports etc—Evening—Had a fine sing with Lieuts Swank, McDowell and Applegarth—so companionable. The Boys are off on Picket at Bealton—We've had a long rest from picket duty or in fact any other duty save Camp routine and occasional drill—

February 10, 1864 Wednesday. Colder—Wrote all day on Ordnance Report and Returns—Sufficiency on hand now. Wrote letter to Pet—almost censuring her for not writing oftener. Not quite—Eve blustry and colder—

February 11, 1864 Thursday. Warmer again—Wrote all day. Am getting on slowly, but surely. Eve—a real good letter from Pet Late! Finished one for her of 16 p'gs large note paper—

February 12, 1864 Friday. Wrote all day for Captain—I am in decidedly better health and spirits—but feel need of more religion—"O for a closer Walk with God, a calm and heavenly frame A light to shine upon the road That leads me to the Lamb"—
How many times I heard my good Mother[b] sing that stanza. When I was but a little Boy and I love it too—

February 13, 1864 Saturday. Fine—Wrote most of the day for Captain. Finished all but the signing the Ord. Re'ts. to June 30"—

February 14, 1864 Sunday. Remarkably fine—Routine—Mounted Inspection—at 10½ OCK—Company Quarters Inspection 1 P.M.— Rev M. M. Rice of Brownsville Oneida Co. N.Y. was with us a while—left some good books &c—Lots of reading going on in Camp—We had preaching at 2 P.M.—and the most of the day seems quite Sundayish[6]—
More and more I aim at my ideal Christian Solder and Man.

February 15, 1864 Monday. Wrote most of Day—Capt got off 2 Boxes—2 Prs of ordnance Returns. 1st & 2nd Qrs 1863—Eve. Well, happy—My Rachel is so good, so true. O to be worthy such a wife—

6. M. M. Rice was almost certainly a field agent of the United States Christian Commission. Organized under the auspices of the YMCA, the commission provided both spiritual and material comfort to troops in the field. It distributed books and fresh food and won high marks for its efforts in Union hospitals. James O. Henry, "The United States Christian Commission in the Civil War," CWH 6 (Dec. 1960), 374–89.

February 16, 1864 Tuesday. Snowed an inch—Is windy but not very cold—I sent Dismounted Camp Receipts &c back—mailed letter to Pet—P.M. Routine—Drew 1 days Forage—Pretty cool—I am well and much happier than sometime agone.

February 17, 1864 Wednesday. Quite cold. John, Dave and I got up some wood—Made a Door for our house(?)——P.M. Drew 3 days Forage and issued it to the men—All's quiet—

February 18, 1864 Thursday. Monstrous Cold—Routine—Fixed up Companys' Descriptive Book—Wrote letter to Carrie[PP] and Lizzie[oo] Bowman——Eve Oh! such a good letter from Pet—Wrote a response—Eve Capt bro't in 2 U.S. Horses—Strays—somebody's out sure!

February 19, 1864 Friday. Extremely Cold—Laying low and keeping warm—am well and enjoying myself. Very much long to see my Rachel and Cora—Time flies swiftly, and yet how long seems the time since last I saw and caressed them.

February 20, 1864 Saturday. slightly moderated—Little doing—Routine—

February 21, 1864 Sunday. clear and cold—Inspection—Read most of A.M. P.M. Paymaster came and in Eve we were paid for Nov & Dec 1863. A few of the Boys greatly disappointed and displeased for not receiving any pay. Poor deserters—pay—now, for the pleasure they had—while "at home without leave" and we were fighting—

February 22, 1864 Monday. Men on Provost duty Paid a dull day—Mailed letter to Pet. Good news from Army in west and Southwest[7]—Not much doing here—

February 23, 1864 Tuesday. Spring-like—I rode John Woodalls Horse to Div. Review at Warrenton—we brought a lot of new Horses down—Drew 7 for "H" Company—
Evening Letter from Pet stating Mother[b] is ill—My poor Mother. Oh! that I could see her—

---

7. Union troops under Gen. William T. Sherman had captured Meridian, Miss. on Feb. 14 and were systematically disrupting the Southern railroad network in the surrounding countryside. But the campaign faltered on the day of this entry, for Confederate cavalry under Nathan B. Forrest successfully attacked a Union column near Okolona, Miss., and forced it to withdraw.

February 24, 1864 Wednesday. Warm—Routine—Letter to Pet—and Clem^cc—Sent in Lawrences Dis. List—P.M. Commenced making out Pay Rolls—Wrote my application for Furlough & Capt. S. Signed and sent it in—Am pretty well and happy—Eve drew 2 ds forage and six new horses—I have now a good mount again—May he be bullet-proof—Wrote til 10 P.M.—

February 25, 1864 Thursday. Fine day—Regimental drill from 9:30 A.M. til Noon—My horse is a noble animal—a number of new horses and no drills for a good while occasioned some irregular movements. P.M. Had Inspection—six Horses condemmed—Looks like getting reading for doing things—

Eve. A letter from Pet—Mother^b is still no better, and wishes to see me—Oh! that I could get home—Worked on Pay Rolls 'til Tapps—

February 26, 1864 Friday. Spring-like—Jim Witherill & I finished Pay Rolls—all except Recapitulation and a very few remarks—P.M. Nothing of much interest going on. Am quite well—My! but I wish my Furlough would come approved. So I might go and see my dear sick Mother^b—and Darling and Cora.

February 27, 1864 Saturday. Fine—A.M. wrote on "A peep at H Company"

Wrote most of day—Eve. our Tent came very near being burned up—Saved it Later! Capt Snyder—24 Men of H.Co. and some 75 out of other Co's went to join Genl Kilpatrick on a raid[8]—

February 28, 1864 Sunday. Fine—Seems very lonely so many of our Boys gone—but it means liveliness for them, and maybe a good deal more both to them and The Johnies—Eve I attended to Sam McGowens back—It is awfully blistered—Doc H and I and some others are tired of sore or lame backs—when it looks like business or a fight looming out in the near future &c &c[9]——Dusk—Everything

---

8. Gen. Judson Kilpatrick and Col. Ulric Dahlgren persuaded the Union high command to let them risk a winter raid on lightly defended Richmond. They selected 3,584 troopers from among the various commands then quartered in northern Virginia and headed south Feb. 28, 1864. Six days laters, they were back behind Union lines. They destroyed substantial amounts of matériel in the countryside around the Confederate capital, but they lost almost 10 percent of their men, including Dahlgren himself. See Virgil C. Jones, *Eight Hours Before Richmond* (New York, 1957).

9. McGowan, now malingering, had already been docked for a protracted absence without leave and demoted on account of his inefficiency, which Samuel attributed to a drinking problem.

looks like a move—9 P.M. Orders for every available man to turn out at midnight—John Woodall—Dick Warren—Fetterhoff—and I fell in—with the Column—Marched all night Via Rappahannoc Station—to Stephensburg—arriving at 8:30 or 9 OCK A.M.[10]—

February 29, 1864 Monday. I had charge of 2nd Platoon—Fed our horses and at Noon—bivouaced in Cedar Flats—Pretty Cold—Pretty bright prospects that Richmond my be victimised and our Boys in prison be released—what a Hallelujah time that would be![11]

March 1, 1864 Tuesday. Rained during night some—but slept pretty well—Cold Chilly morning in this Cedar Swamp—awful suspense too. No news, various rumors of some strategic movement on foot. During the day Forage came—Eve snowed a perfect streak til ten O clock at night and then cleared, bitter cold—

March 2, 1864 Wednesday. very cold—Orders to "saddle up" at 4 A.M. Everything frozen stiff, such a time to saddle up and prepare for a move is seldom experienced. Nothing of interest during day—Some quiet manouvering &c—

Eve am very "Rheumaticky"—Couldn't sleep til near mid-night. Kept thinking of my dear ones at Home. Heaven bless them and keep them more comfortable than I be—

March 3, 1864 Tuesday. Quite cold—Up at 4 A.M. Drew Forage and at 7 A.M. took up the march for Old Camp arriving at 2½ P.M.— O Joy! My Furlough has come—Also letter from Pet—Bro John[d] and Earich—Spent the evening setting business in order—and getting ready to start for Home.

March 4, 1864 Friday. Pleasant—Leave for Washington 10 A.M. Leave for Baltimore at 3 P.M. Supper at Baltimore Soldiers Rest— Left for Harrisburg 9:30 P.M. Arrived at 3 A.M.—

March 5, 1864 Saturday. Took Breakfast at National—Took 8:05 train for Chambersburg Arrived at 10 A.M.

Found my Darling and Cora well and happy, and so surprised to

10. This movement was part of an action designed to confuse the Confederates and screen the Kilpatrick-Dahlgren raid.

11. One of the objects of the Kilpatrick-Dahlgren raid was Richmond's Libby Prison, where a large number of Union officers were, in fact, able to stage a dramatic escape.

see me. and O so full of such tender greetings—The thought of loved ones. Oh! how sweet. But oh! how much more so to greet.

The P.M. seemed crowded with face to face rehearsal of experiences, and caressings—O the world of meaning in wife and little Daughter—

Eve had some callers, but callers however dear are tame things contrasted with re-uniting of Soldier-Husband and Little Family

March 6, 1864 Sunday. What a contrast between being awakened by sounding of Bugle, and by cooing. ta! ta! of Baby and caress of wife—I spent several hours trying to hire conveyance to go to Salem and then to see Mother[b]—Failed—We went to hear Dickson, a splendid practical Sermon. P.M. Got Mr. Mohler to take us out to Mothers[b]—Such a pleasant meeting—Once again Mother has her 3 children with her for a visit—a short time—

Old Daddy[ba] is very disagreeable—So down on the Northern Army—which of course includes me too.

March 7, 1864 Monday. Very pleasant Mother,[b] Ellie[y] and we went down to Brother Johns[d]—Rev J. M. Bishop was there—altogether we had a very pleasant visit—called to see Steagers—Evening John[d] and I went over to Johny Sullenbergers—We talked a dutch streak til after 9 P.M.—Hot room, and cool outside. The sudden change gave me severe cold—

March 8, 1864 Tuesday. Bro John[d] gave us their conveyance and Pet, Baby & I visited John Karpers[l] A.M. and over dinner—P.M. went over to Henry Reboks[pa] several hours. Nice visits. Then returned to Bro Johns[d] and enjoyed a good supper, and fine visit. Then Bro John[d] took us up to Mothers[b]—Katy[e] gave us along some pickles and a stuffed & smoked Bladder—

March 9, 1864 Wednesday. Pleasant—Nice morning visit—Then Pa B[ba]—took us to Chambersburg—Found all things O.K.—Read—Talked—and were at Home. The blessed Trio—

Eve took tea at Mrs McGowens—Mrs Capt Snyder called—we had a pleasant social chat—

I suffer some from misery on my lungs

March 10, 1864 Thursday. Cloudy—Pet fixed my shirts—Mammy Royer called—Rainy—P.M. We make some calls—

My cold & throat annoying—I enjoy my visit to my old Home & Kin very much, But decidedly best at our little Family Home, with Pet and Cora—

March 11, 1864 Friday. Rainy—A.M. with my dearest ones—Bro Bernard[q] called awhile—I gave him John and Dave Woodalls money for their wives—I am quite a bit out of fix—

Eve Rev J. Dickson and Winter with us for a while—a very agreeable time—

March 12, 1864 Saturday. Springlike—Pet not quite well—But loving & happy. A great many folks called on me today—Eve throat quite sore—I wrote in Mrs.. Glassers Album—Miss Wampler sang and played for us—and throughout we had an enjoyable time—

March 13, 1864 Sunday. Springlike—I reported to Surgeon. Gave me some medicine—I couldn't go to Salem Church—Plough is very little of a Man—Capt Sullenberger and wife and children called, Also Mrs Dickson—Mrs Clippinger—The Misses Hasson, and a great many others—I dedicated Miss Betty Merkleins Album—

March 14, 1864 Monday. I reported to surgeon. Felt some better but ordered Front—So I packed up to go—Took 1 P.M. train—Parting went harder this time than ever—O how sweet to love and be loved and to spend a few days and nights with my dear Pet and Cora—How I do thank God for them. For a good true loving Wife & Daughter.

XX

Irritation

December 3, 1863–March 14, 1864

*R*achel *becomes nearly as frustrated with her situation at the Merkleins' as she had been at the Ploughs'. A visit from Samuel finally offers a brief respite in March.*

<hr />

December 3, 1863 No letter from Mr C. & the paper states that the Potomac army was fighting & that communication with it & Washington was cut off. Just now Betty came in & told me that a despatch was received stating that the Potomac army was fighting & that the rebs were in force. O! My God—in pity remember My Samuel—protect him & be with him & O! grant our army a great victory.

December 30, 1863 I am all alone this evening. I have been quite neglecting my journal having company nearly all the time. Mrs Penness is spending her holy day week with us, her accounts of her sojourn in Rebeldon are quite interesting—we never get tired talking I have not heard from Mr C. for so long. I just saw in this evenings paper that they were out on an extensive raid. & got back to camp on Christmas eve. It seems very long since I last heard from him, nearly two weeks. I am quite busy in making a dress for Cora to wear to a donation party to Rev Dicksons on New Years eve. A

protracted meeting is in progress in our church now—Susie[nn] & Mrs P. went there

January 31, 1864 Just one month since I wrote I am alone at home Susie[nn] is at church. The meeting is still in progress but I think it will close this evening. I feel very much out of health—think it is cold. I would have plenty to write but am too unwell.

February 1, 1864 Suffered considerably from toothache last night so early this morning I went to the Dr's & had it extracted. I will soon be a toothless grandmother if my teeth keep on at the rate they have been going for some time.   this one was just back of the eye-tooth & will show some, but rather that than toothach. I mailed a letter to Mr C. this morning. last week I received 7 letters 5 of which were from Mr C. The week after New Year Susie[nn] Cora & I went with John Cormany[d] to the country. we spent nearly 2 weeks among Mrs Cs friends. had a pleasant visit. had sleighing most of the time. Since then I have not been very well. Charlie Merklein has been sick too. I sat up with him one night & Susie[nn] two. I do not know what is sticking in me. Just now a hog was taken past here that beat all the hogs that I ever saw for size & fatness. it could hardly waddle for fatness. The protracted meeting commenced on Christmas is still going on There have not been as many conversions as I have seen in a similar length of time

February 15, 1864 We had preaching all week. Bishops Glassbrenner & Markwood preached I was disappointed in Markwood's preaching. I expected more—Bro. Freed also from Va. preached one evening. he is quite ordinary—Bro. Stearn from Chicago frormerly from Va also—preached on Sabbath. does pretty well. Meeting, I mean protracted meeting, is closed now. I washed today had a large wash—am tired & not verry well—Cora is quite fretful, do not think she is well. Saturday Wilhelmina Karper[i] & the two little ones & Fred[g] were her for dinner. W.[i] gave me quite a downsetting about her old cloak that I turned into a coat. She talked real ugly I had taken some off—she was cross & I thought she might have acted more considerate. She said "Indeed Aunt Rachel I hate to hurt to feelings but I cant help it." I thought I wonder whether you could not help it. If she had only told me— but she harped on it so long & said a good deal that she might have left unsaid. Susie[nn] says—"That is what you get for doing all their old dirty jobs which they cant do—do it gratis & receive a scolding in the bargain if you do not make their old worn out garments look like new. It is quite handy to have a younger sister-inlaw to do all such dirty jobs. I told you this long time you were foolish to spend your time on them as you do—when they do not appreciate it in the least—They would be verry clear doing the like for you." Susie[nn] is more than half right—henceforth I will devote my time in enriching my mind & making such ornaments that my husband will be pleased with. paintings &c—He will appreciate— while weeks of labor are not by such as W.[i] as my experience heretofore as with the cloak has proved. I feel daily that I am so far below my ideal of what I should be or what I desire to be—both religiously & mentally. I do not accomplish what I wish to. My mind & soul are not in as elevated a state as I wish them to be.

Above all I am not as good a christian as I should be—O for a deeper work of grace in the heart. My anxiety for my husband has in a measure deminished—I feel so confident that he will return. O! that the time may soon come. I do long so much for him at home—for it does not seem home without him. All I do is done for the time when he is at home once again—scarcely any thing but what partains to daily wants is done for the present—I tire not in working for him—Thank the Lord for having granted me the man he has.

February 26, 1864 Fell considerably disappointed that Mr Cormany did not come home this evening. I had no particular reason to expect him home I only thought he would come. Well now I will keep expecting until he comes or I get a letter telling me that he cannot come. I baked a good many things to send to him & we have concluded to send by Tuesday if he is not here by that time. Mrs Merklein has boarders. Two soldiers and a cousin, one soldier left left this week, but the other Charlie Brown is here yet. All the young stripps of girls in the neighborhood are cracked for him—he is a wild boy—but not bad—This evening some of her friends from Hagerstown came—Betty was to much cracked for the boys to stay in. We had callers too, and of course they (Betty and those other little imps) had to stick themselves in here as they always do when we have company. Called at Mr Dulaneys Mrs D. was sitting up—she is recovering fast. Received a letter from home with Mother[bb] & Fathers[aa] photograph in.

March 1, 1864 This morning when we got up all was white with snow without—It has snowed all day & is still snowing this evening I sent Susie[nn] over to Mrs Merkleins so as to keep these boys out of my room, they cut up so ugly—Betty and Charlie Merklein are forever quarreling. Oh! how I do dislike that. Charlie Merklein is the biggest baby I have seen for a long time. We are really tormented too much with them. & they are so rough too. brake and spoil things for me It is frightful the way they tare round over this carpet. Charlie Brown is mschievous but has some honor and manliness about him while Charlie Merklein has neither and nothing else to redeem his bad qualities. Why this morning he was in here & heard Betty going up stairs, as soon as she was up he posted after for no reason that we could see than to pick a quarrel. He talks so ugly to his Mother, indeed on Sunday she & he with some others came in here and they got up the dirtiest quarrel about a pair of boots that I have heard for a long time I do not know that I ever witnessed one that seemed so degrading as that. I feel blue this evening I expected Mr C home to a certainty.   still he has not come. I feel disappointed & this constant carousing about me makes me feel badly. Maggy Glasser just came & took Susie[nn] along to Class, so Charlie B. came in here   soon Bettie came so I got both at reading a good book. I hope I will have some peace this evening now.

March 14, 1864   On Sat. March 5th my dear Husband came home. I was rejoiced beyond expression. O! I was so glad to see him, to be kissed & caressed & to love kiss & caress him. On Sunday A.M. we went to hear Mr. D. preach, got a little late—Mr. C was trying all over town to get a conveyance to take us to Salem but failed so we got too late.   in the after noon he succeeded to get old Mr Mohler to take us to his Mothers[b] by paying him $2. Mr Plough acted anything but the gentleman to him. I think I will square up pretty short with him soon & then cut his acquaintance. We had a pleasant visit at his Mothers[b]—John Cormanys,[d] J. Karpers[l] & H. Rebok[pa]   Mr C. took a desperate cold—his throat & lungs were all inflamed. Daddy Byers[ba] brought us in on Wednesday A.M.   The rest of the week we were at home. Mr C. not being well went out only to attend to necessary business. Yesterday, 13th he reported to the hospital Dr got some medicine—this morning he went again & the surgeon told him that he could not excuse him that he thought Mr C. able to go front.[1] At 10 A.M. Mr C. returned & told me   it took me so suddenly that I did not know what to say, the big tears filled my eyes. I wept freely— the tears came to Mr C's eyes. I feel O so lonely & desolate   This P.M. I wrote him a letter—also one to Sister Sue[nn]—who left this Morning—My little angel & I are all by ourselves now. I know the good Lord will be with us. He will be with My Dear husband & comfort & protect him—& comfort & protect me—Before my Samuel left we had a season of prayer together. I could not pray loud my emotions were too strong, but I know the Lord hears the silent prayer as well. Friends that come in ask me whether I am sick. I look so pale—but I wonder who would not look pale after parting with the dearest friend on earth. I am sure I do not look any worse than I feel—

1. The Union army, hard pressed for physicians, employed civilian doctors to help staff military hospitals in the North. They were empowered to grant and extend sick leaves. George W. Adams, *Doctors in Blue: The Medical History of the Union Army in the Civil War* (New York, 1952); *Revised United States Army Regulations of 1861, with an Appendix Containing the Changes and Laws Affecting Army Regulations and Articles of War to June 25, 1863* (Washington, D.C., 1863), pp. 32–33.

XXI
The Union Spring Offensive
March 14–June 30, 1864

*I*n May the Federal army launched the most massive offensive of the Civil War. Grant's advance precipitated in rapid succession a series of major infantry battles that included the Wilderness, Spottsylvania Court House, the North Anna River, and Cold Harbor.

In preparation for the offensive, the Union cavalry was reorganized, and overall command of the Cavalry Corps was given to Maj. Gen. Philip H. Sheridan, Grant's protégé. The corps' most dramatic actions during the spring offensive consisted of two large-scale raids directed by General Sheridan himself. The first penetrated the outer defenses of Richmond in May, and the second resulted in the Battle of Trevilian Station in June. Samuel rode in both raids, and his diary for this period is the only known first-hand account of his regiment's actions. This section concludes as Sheridan's raiders reunite with Grant's main army, which was then entrenching itself on the outskirts of Petersburg.

March 14, 1864 Monday. Reached Harrisburg 4 P.M.—Put up at National Hotel—

March 15, 1864 Tuesday. Took 2:40 A.M. train for Baltimore—Met Nash at Balto—our Sutlers Clerk—Good travelling companion— reached Washington 11 A.M.—Got my Pass O.K. Promenaded the City most of P.M. sight-seeing—Eve Put up in Gleasons Room with Nash[1]—Took meals at Soldiers Rest—Wrote letter to Pet—Tired—

March 16, 1864 Wednesday. Mailed letter—Took train at 9:45 A.M. for Camp—and arrived at 2 P.M. all O.K. Had some fun on route and nearly had a row—On reaching Camp Reported to Adjutant on sight. Was kindly received by H'd Qrs. and the Boys generally—

Everything looks about old style—Evening. Well for a fact I do feel very lonely—My cold cabin and no Darling to go into a good bed

1. W. H. Gleason, the regimental sutler for whom Nash worked, was later investigated and dismissed by a board of enquiry. See "Regimental Order Book," 16th Pa., Aug. 12, 16, 1864, NA.

to—no little Cora to Coo-ta-ta, Good night to me. Oh! that this cruel war was over. But a brave, loyal, soldier says, with mouth firmly set—here am I to brave it to the finish.

March 17, 1864 Thursday. Springlike—After some routine—as Q.M.Sg't. I issue clothing to the Boys—Wrote & mailed letter to Pet—Do some meditating and resolving—By His grace—who knows how to strengthen—I will be a more exemplary man, and Christian—and attain to my ideal of soldierdom—Rumors of a move in the air. Hope it comes not to pass right away. But let come when it will—Here am I—Got such a good letter from Pet this eve.

March 18, 1864 Friday. Spring-like—Read & wrote some General routine goes on Tattoo—Roll Call—Stable Call—Breakfast Then some kind of Drill—or exercise to instruct us, to make us efficient—these latter only when the weather is favorable—and we are not out on Picket—Scout—or Raid. or Manouvering for Battle——Eve Dress Parade—Col Gregg with us

March 19, 1864 Saturday. Rec'd orders at 3 OCK to be ready to march at daybreak—Some doings sure—Fine morning—8 OCK A.M.—Order countermanded So we re-encamped—We hear Canonading on the River all P.M. We had a fine Mounted Drill—made some good charges——Evening another such a good letter from Pet. I am quite unwell—Mailed letter to Pet

March 20, 1864 Sunday. Very fine—Routine—Read—meditated. Wrote to Pet—At 10 A.M. we had mounted inspection—and usual quarters inspection at 1 P.M. Eve not at all well, pain just below my right shoulder blade—Failed to get my letter to Pet finished—

March 21, 1864 Monday. Early routine—Then a fine mounted drill—Made a transcript of "A peep at H Co" to send with Capt to Chambersburg—Eve made out list of clothing needed.

March 22, 1864 Tuesday. Quite Cold Had a splendid dismounted skirmish drill—Regimental—Handed in Requisition for Clothing required for April——
Eve I had a talk with Capt on promotion. I am studying Casey's Tactics in preparation——
Snows to close the day—

March 23, 1864 Wednesday. Snow 6 to 8 inches deep—Capt started to Washington & Home. Snow fine for "balling" We had a regimental snow-balling—Big Time. Eve letter from Pet—

March 24, 1864 Thursday. Some of the Boys last night undertook to raid the Sutlers Tent—not successful. All who were in it are under arrest—I took Inventory of ordinance and Quarter Masters Property as Quarter-Master of H. Co—responsible Lieut Brown "F" Co. Commands H Co on a/c Capt Snyders absence. P.M. General Inspection by Capt Hughes—Eve Dave Croft was in with us—I'm real unwell.

March 25, 1864 Friday. Routine—Noon blustry—Wrote Sisters, Mother,[b] Mollie[ii] and Sue[nn] and Darling Eve rainy—horrible—My cough is so bad again—Oh to have my Rachel to care for me and help me out—

March 26, 1864 Saturday. Rained all night powerfully—our Cline returned from Dism't'd Camp. I wrote a letter for Dave Woodall to his Father—P.M. Orders to prepare for Grand Review Tomorrow—

March 27, 1864 Sunday. Fine but muddy—Had a pleasant Review Near M—Got Oh! such a good letter from Pet—O what a delight!—Read and meditated a good deal today—

March 28, 1864 Monday. Beautiful! Mailed letter to Pet. Issue some Pistols to men & Holsters on a/c some condemned 25th inst—P.M. We had mounted regimental Drill. I command 3rd Platoon "H" Co. attached to Maj Swans Squadron—Had a fine drill. The movements are simply delightful—My cough better. Good letter from J. B. Kimmel and a splendid one from Pet—A letter from Wife and Cora. What an uplift!

March 29, 1864 Tuesday. Routine: Then 8 men go on Picket at Bealton—Mailed letter to Pet—Had some wood hauled—P.M. set in raining—Eve drew 3 ds Forage—O so Cold! Sergt Harrison in with us, Had a good sing, and fine time til Tapps—

March 30, 1864 Wednesday. Rained all night—Routine—Brightened up at 10 A.M. P.M. Made out Invoice of property condemned last inspection, so as to "turn it in"—

411

March 31, 1864 Thursday. Fine—Mailed letter to Pet—and company drilled in manual of arms by orderly Sergeant S. B. Peters. P.M. Busy writing for Capt. and Pet—Oh how good is God to have brought us together and adapted us so well for each other enabling us to contribute so wonderfully each to the others sum of happiness—O to be a better nobler man, and soldier—

April 1, 1864 Friday. Spring-like—Routine—Drill in Manual of Arms P.M. Copied our Serenade "Stars of the summer night" to send to Darling—Clouded and commenced raining—I did writing and meditating—I have such insatiate longing to be with my Dearest ones when there is so little doing that seems to any purpose—and when practicing Drills—Movements—and exercises tending to the making of the best possible soldiers out of us, I am just so absorbed in the doing of things in fine soldierly fashion, That I think of only that one thing—God make of me a model Husband and Father—an ideal Soldier and withal an humble exemplary Christian—

April 2, 1864 Saturday. Snowed—Sleeted—Rained all night and is a wet A.M. Do only necessary routine—and write for my Pet—P.M. continues—Read letter from Pet—O so good—But must forego getting my box from Home, for the very best reason in the world. Viz. It has not arrived—I had heard it said that "this is a world of disappointments." and now I know it sure! and I don't feel as sweet about it as a good ideal man should—

April 3, 1864 Sunday. Muddy—Some routine—Send out mail—Pay Master came and paid us about noon—We are raising money to present our Capt. with Sabre, Belt &c—Eve stormy—Did some writing. I had sent Rachel $5.00 this morning not knowing of Pay Masters coming so soon.

April 4, 1864 Monday. A mere routine day—

April 5, 1864 Tuesday. Still rainy—and we lie low, and seek to be dry, and good natured—

April 6, 1864 Wednesday. Rained another night—Commenced letter to Pet—Wrote most of A.M. P.M. cooked meat and dried apples and read some in Tactics and Testament——Evening—Sung—Bathed & dressed up——Today moved our Horses on the Hill to allow quarters to dry up—

April 7, 1864 Thursday. Fine clear—Mailed letter to Pet enclosing $10.00 Also a letter to J. R. Orr—Turned in condemned ordnance— Eve drew 3 ds forage—Rec'd a splendid letter from Pet. Came while I was at a "speaking meeting" a bunch of 8–10–12 of "H" Co Boys being Christians meet in some secluded spot—for prayer and testimony occasionally. Had a good time this Eve away out under a huge Pine tree—Later, wrote for Pet some—

April 8, 1864 Friday. Springlike—Routine and Drill. Finished letter to Pet—Enclosed $5.00—Receipt came for condem'd Q.M. & Ord property—Studied Tactics—Read—Meditated—

April 9, 1864 Saturday. Rainy all day—Little doing save reading— talking—discussing Tactics &c

April 10, 1864 Cleared but Oh! the mud. Read considerably—My protracted cough seems to be subsiding some—A Rev from Maine preached for us this A.M.—A pretty good sermon. P.M. strolled to "Moriahs"—Gave me a good drink of fresh milk and nice bread, and a pie. God bless her! But I pay her all the same—Evening I was at a class meeting—Had a pretty good time, out under the old Pine Tree—Harrison, The Woodalls—Fetterhoff—Rohrabaugh—Croft— Nelling &c

April 11, 1864 Monday. Cleared up We draw Clothing &c—No trains running—2 Bridges washed out so no mail—Am decidedly better in health, and in good spirits—Read & study some and commence a letter to Pet—

April 12, 1864 Tuesday. Clear—Mud drying up fast—Drew and issued ammunition—Have a Company Carbine Drill. Then P.M. Mounted Regimental Drill. Eve a good letter from Pet—How glad I am no one knows—

April 13, 1864 Wednesday. Clear—Letter finished and mailed for Pet—Also one for Mrs Dave Woodall—Wrote letter to Senator Connel on matter of Commission—I prefer to go up regularly or on Special Merit Eve Rec'd another letter from Pet as good as can be—

April 14, 1864 Thursday. Fine—All quiet—Mailed letter to Darling—Drill! The general order of the day. Eve letter from H.C. Pennel and Capt. Snyder—Surely God was with us—I proposed that our little band recieve a name—we were unanomous—Cormany,

Fouck, Kramer a committee to suggest Name & Constitution to next called meeting—All meetings are on Call.

April 15, 1864 Friday. Routine day—a good letter from Pet—Committee met—Decided on what to recommend—Next Sab Eve—

April 16, 1864 Saturday. Rained last night, and rains today—Nothing doing in the line of soldiering save Routine—I wrote letter to Pet—Pennel—and for D. Woodall and B. May—I am so happy on a/c of being so busy for the Boys.

April 17, 1864 Sunday. Has partially cleared—Col Robison talked with me on, or concerning, Captain Snyder—his strong and weak points—we agree! also relative to a Furlough for Sam McGowen (Strange the Col should confer with me—only Q.M.Sergt—on cases away above me in rank) Finish letter to Darling—P.M. Had preaching at Head Quarters, and in Eve our band met for Pr. meeting—Committee reported, and the constitution was adopted—with name "The Christian Association of the 16th Pa Cavalry"—Object—Christian fellowship and development, by prayer, Testimony, and experiences being related—any soldier may attend, and take part, and so be a member—

There shall be a Leader, elected, by a majority present for an indefinite time—In case of the absence of the regular Leader, those assembled shall choose one of their number to lead for the time—

The Leader shall call meetings as often as he may deem favorable—

Also, any three members may call a meeting when desired—

By unanimous vote I was chosen Leader—and we had a half hour of devout fellowship in which every one present took some active part—and in which all were interested[2]—

April 18, 1864 Monday. Fine—Went to Warrenton on Grand Review—General Sheridan reviewing Officer—Whole Cavalry Corps out[3]—After review our 2nd Brigade went on a scout via Woodburn

2. Formal religion played a limited and fairly ineffectual role in the lives of most Civil War soldiers. "Christian Associations"—ad hoc organizations of men who took their spiritual lives seriously—are, however, also reported for the 13th Pennsylvania Volunteers and the 16th Connecticut Volunteers. Bell Irvin Wiley, *The Life of Billy Yank: The Common Soldier of the Union* (Garden City, N.Y., 1971), p. 272, and *CWH* 6 (Dec. 1960), entire issue.

3. The 16th Pennsylvania was placed in the 2nd Brigade of the 2nd Division of Sheridan's reorganized Cavalry Corps. *OR*, ser. I, vol. XXXVI, pt. 1, pp. 207–08. The purpose of the review was to make certain the corps was fully prepared for the advance that Lincoln, Grant, Meade, and Sheridan were planning.

Church, nearly to Waterloo, thence down the River near Sulphur Springs and then back to Warrenton and returned to Camp by 8 P.M. No dinner. No supper. No letter from Pet: a hard days ride and 3 days forage to draw first thing—Sure! our Horses first—Who wouldn't feel disappointed, and vexed—10½ OCK and a short late supper—and no letter—Tho late I wrote awhile, for Pet rather a little hard maybe—No! This has been a great day—I'll write Darling about it on the morrow when less weary—

April 19, 1864 Tuesday. Fine—Springlike—Routine. Then wrote additional and more tenderly to Pet—Such days harden a fellow up for solid soldiering—P.M. Capt Snyder returned—News that "after tomorrow all mail communications with the army to be cut off for 60 days"

No letter from Pet. Oh! the sadness of it! My heart knows no expression, and what I sent this morning was a little sharp in its beginning—wish I had it back—

April 20, 1864 Wednesday. Cloudy, Cool, Blustry—Mailed another letter to Pet—My last for 60 days—if rumor be true——General policing this morning and later a Drill. P.M. Mounted Inspection by Cavalry Corps Inspector——Eve I got a letter from Pet enclosing a Canada letter to her from Sister Sue[nn]—Dear Precious! seems just a little careless in her correspondence at times—But I am not worthy— and why should she in any way discommode herself to write to me—

April 21, 1864 Thursday. Mailed letter to Pet—We had Mounted Drill—We rec'd notice of 16 new recruits for our "H" Co—Now there will be need of a new 2nd Lieutenant—I intend to run Orderly Sergt S. B. Peters a race for the office though he and a lot of Sergts are ahead of me in rank or regular order for promotion—Some months ago A General Order was issued by the President setting forth that hereafter Commissions need not necessarily be issued to the ranking Sergts, but that any aspiring soldier might seek promotion over those ranking him—by applying to Hd Qrs. asking for a competative examination—That if such applicant proved to possess superior qualifications—then such competitor should be promoted and commissioned

Immediately I put forth Special Efforts in the study of Tactics and gave increased attention to Drill, Movements &c with a view to seeking the first opening for such promotion—This a/c's for my putting in so much time reading Caseys Cav. Tactics—To be honorable I

415

went to Sergt Peters and told him of my intentions. The Serg't used some language not nice to quote, but I simply repeated that I certainly would proceed as I had stated, and his only chance for the desired 2nd Lieutency was for him to convince the examiners that he was the superior cavalryman[4]—

April 22, 1864 Friday. Spring day—fine—Routine—Studied Tactics all A.M. P.M. Our Regt made a reconisance—via Fayeteville to Warrenton. Charged into the town, saw a few Rebs but captured none—returned to camp at dusk—

I handed the Colonel a written request for an examination as to my qualifications for 2nd Lieut of Co H instead of Sergt S. B. Peters who is the ranking Sergeant—

The Col assured me that the case would have his attention promptly—Studied til late—

April 23, 1864 Saturday. Fine—Routine—Studied Tactics most of day——P.M. Corp Coble, Privates Earich, Mahaffy, Wordebaugh & Long returned to Co. Evening—Sergt Peters and I were examined by "Board" as to which was best qualified for being commissioned to 2nd Lieutency of Co H—I feel fine over it! and can easily await the Verdict—

April 24, 1864 Sunday. Mailed letter to Pet also one to H. W. Rebok[pa]—We had preaching at 10 A.M.—P.M. The enemy does some scouting outside our picket line—Everything alert—Do some company writing—Eve very good letter from Pet—

April 25, 1864 Monday. Mailed letter to Pet. Commenced on Pay Rolls—Wrote all day. Plenty Reb scouts near picket line—Some firing—all wide awake

April 26, 1864 Tuesday. I am all day on Pay Rolls. Have much extra work on a/c of those Deserters and absent without leave fellows who have returned. The Reg off on a scout today—but brought in no Johnies—Eve wrote Mother[b] and Pet—

---

4. While advancement by seniority, not to mention by political pressure or personal favoritism, remained common throughout the army, the sanctioning of competitive examinations was one of the important reforms introduced during the war. Colonel Gregg had circulated a general order to the 16th Pennsylvania in June 1863 spelling out the procedures for calling an examination and specifying that the material in Casey's *Tactics* would be the chief subject upon which candidates would be examined. See General Order 98, June 6, 1863, in "Regimental Order Book," 16th Pa., NA.

April 27, 1864 Wednesday. Mailed letters—worked on Rolls—Drill some and talk more again.

April 28, 1864 Thursday. Finished Rolls. Save a few touches—I am well and happy, expecially in hopes of a future final happy Home in Heaven, and would be more so now if Darling could write more regularly—

April 29, 1864 Friday. Early Orders—Hustle—March out at 9 A.M. via Bealton Station—Kellys Ford—Encamped near Peoli Mills— Mailed note to pet this morning—Eve mail came up but no letter for me, why of course not!

April 30, 1864 Saturday. We are lying in a fine sod field all day— Finished Rolls and Mustered—Still no letter—

May 1, 1864 Sunday. Brigade Review and Inspection—P.M. mailed another letter to Pet. Evening rec'd a good letter from Pet—The Christian Association met in a woods—Had a good meeting, seemed helpful to all—Later wrote some to Pet—

May 2, 1864 Monday. Drew and issued clothing.

May 3, 1864 Tuesday. This is Coras birth-day anniversary. Sorry to miss it—But here come marching orders—Off at 8 A.M. Strike Richardsville whole 2nd Division encamps—I can't help Pet celebrate today—but I can think of when the dear little Angel of the household came—No doubt Darling is doing the day justice faithfully—
We drew forage at 11 OCK P.M.—

May 4, 1864 Wednesday. Aroused at 2 A.M. Marched at 4—Got to Ealies Ford at daybreak—Our whole 2nd Division and 3 Divisions (30,000) of 2nd Army Corps advanced—Captured some half dozen Johnie Pickets, and moved on to Chancellorville, rested awhile then moved on to about 7 miles from Fredericksburg on Plank Road. Our 2nd Brig was in advance and we drove the enemy about a mile and then halted and Fed our horses and ate some[5]—
I am quite well and in fine spirits—We expect warm work this eve or tomorrow, esspecially if the taking of Fredericksburg is on the

---

5. This massive advance signaled the beginning of the largest and most successful Union offensive of the war.

program, which some assert. But let come what will as I know that my Redeemer liveth, and if He has nothing more for me to do on earth, I fain would die my countrys cause defending. Yet I believe that He has something more before me to do, a life of usefulness to live, and to that end a kind providence will spare me——Oh! that this cruel war were over so I could return to the loved ones at home, and enjoy the amenities of a peaceful social, and religious life with my little family. At 4:30 P.M. The enemy attacks us—gently— carefully I am now on the skirmish line or rather a holding line— dismounted—Our advance mounted line is lightly engaged We have a fine position, with light breast works—

Just at this moment our Col. J. K. Robison[6] passed along the line and said to me "You have a good position Sergeant—Do you think you could fetch one of those Johnies from yon bars?" (a point nearly ½ mile away) I replied 'Yes! Col' and on he rode, inspiring good will, courage, energy and invincibility in the men.

Soon the mounted line advanced a little, exchanging occasional shots. Next along came General D. Mc. M. Gregg and Genl J. I. Gregg noting our lines and positions and adding to our courage— We held the line til dark, occasionally doing some sharp shooting—

In the dark we quietly slipped back some distance and "sup- pered"—a few men remaining on the line—Then we returned and they enjoyed(?) theirs as we had—Next, all lie on the line, on their arms—save a few out posts as watchers—There was very little firing on the picket line, or anywhere near.

Things being so quiet all night I took several good naps, and in my last one—Just before day, I was carried away to dreamland and was basking in the sunlight of my darlings love, kisses, and caresses when I was called by quiet orders to fall back to our Horses, Feed them, Eat breakfast and be ready.

May 5, 1864 Thursday. Early called in from line—Took up march at 8 A.M. to Chancellorville 4 mls to R.R. train for Forage—Great col- umns of infantry and heavy artilleryists from Washington D.C. act- ing as infantry—are moving front and in various directions. Their faces express business—Their step is elastic—firm—and one is in- spired with courage to be a part of such a body of Men.

---

6. Lt. Col. John K. Robison had risen to command of the 16th Pennsylvania in a reorganization that preceded the offensive of May 1864. Colonel Gregg, the former commander, now commanded the entire 2nd Brigade (six regiments) of the 2nd Division of Sheridan's Cavalry Corps. Brig. Gen. David McMurtrie Gregg remained in command of the 2nd Division (two brigades) as a whole. *OR*, ser. I, vol. XXXVI, pt. 1, pp. 207–08.

P.M. Skirmishing and canonaiding hearable in almost every direction—save in the rear—3 P.M. we were ordered out front. 1st Cav Div came up with us. We advanced to Todds Tavern[7] Met 3rd Cav Div there—we skirmished in front and on left. 5 OCK. We are lying in rear of our Battery—1st Brigade becomes engaged. 3 Div formed in the rear—all doing nice work 5½ OCK our Brigade in front (I have charge of 2nd Platoon) formed line—for business—not much engaged—enemy recedes some—So we are ordered back to Todds Tavern—Infantry fighting was on terribly—and some canonading—til after dark—We went on Picket—and at 1 OCK we were relieved and slept on arms a few hours at Todds Tavern.

May 6, 1864 Friday. We were in column by dawn. My platoon is in good shape—At sunrise heavy musketry and canonading set in—The heaviest musketry I ever heard—and continued 4 to 5 hours—about 10 A.M. Custers Cavalry[8] became engaged and soon our 2nd Division took some part—Our brigade supporting and lightly engaged came in for some shelling—tho not severe——Now our squadron supports a section of artillery—I am now sitting in front of my platoon—and in rear of artillery—making these notes—ready with my men—to dash into the fray any moment and yet may not become really engaged—as the battle tide turns——So time flies—and now 2½ P.M. it is rather quiet about us—

Awful hot—sultry—smoky—we lay on our line til 9 OCK P.M.— were then ordered back several miles—where we bivouaced, and about 11 P.M. we drew 3 days rations and forage, and "lay by til morning"—The tension was so high all day—and all energies so aroused and wound up that all our sleep was more than half awake.

May 7, 1864 Saturday. Early the famous "Clean them out" order was read to the men. The order congratulated the men on their fine work yesterday and before—and proposed that we "clean them out

7. Todd's Tavern was located at a tactically important road junction between the Wilderness, where Lee first fell upon the advancing Union army, and Spottsylvania Court House, where Grant and Meade were hoping to head next. The Federal cavalry was given the job of clearing the major roads of enemy forces, then screening the infantry advance. This assignment proved formidable, and the Union offensive nearly bogged down at the end of its first week, just as Hooker's advance had done one year earlier. Meade and Sheridan blamed each other for the confusions and failures. See Edward G. Longacre, "Cavalry Clash at Todd's Tavern," *CWTI* 16 (Oct. 1977), 12–21.

8. Brig. Gen. George Armstrong Custer, who died in 1876 at the Little Big Horn, was a rising young cavalry officer. In charge of the 1st Brigade of the 1st Division of the Union Cavalry Corps, he was directing four regiments of Michigan volunteers with great success.

today"——The cheers and roars all along the lines and every where were simply indiscribable[9]—I am well, and happy—our command grazed the horses—and rested, and at 12 OCK were ordered to Todds Tavern—we met the enemy soon—and had some skirmishing—mounted—not very severe—At 3 P.M. a dismounted line was formed by 2nd 16th & 8th Pa and 1st Maine. We put up some temporary breast works—logs—rails &c and did some fine deliberate shooting. The enemy charged our line three times, but our firing sent them back—Our artillery did some fine work shooting over us and into them. I had some pine logs before me and was sharp shooting—picking, now and then during the lull, some Johny who showed himself busy as I was—we were not supposed to advance at all, simply hold the line and await orders—A Johny got my range—I saw where his shot—ball—struck the ground in front of me—some distance—"buddy" called my attention, saying "some Johny is getting range of you" I replied "you find and peck him" a little later a ball struck a smoothe cut pine knot close in front of me—glanced, flatened some and struck me flatly above my right eye—Knocked me senseless. As I dropped on my face, I heard "Cormany's Shot" uttered by some one—Later, Capt Brooks rolled me over on my back, dashed some water from a canteen into my face, and the shock brought me to consciousness—I was in bad shape. My head became kind of benumbed, but I would not be taken from the line—but lounged around close to my post on the line—

Our part of the line kept rather quiet—but we lay on our arms til 3 OCK A.M. and then ½—every alternate man—fell back to Breakfast. Then came front and the others sent back—Thus we were fed—

Enemy faced us at 3 OCK P.M.—We formed a dismounted line put up logs, rails & as breast works in the edge of a wood and threw out Mounted Skirmishers who were soon engaged by Enemy, who were dismounted—Then our mounted men fell in our rear and we became hotly engaged. The 16th was on right of road and 1st Maine on

9. This order confirmed the fact that the Union army would continue its offensive. While the short-term effect of this decision was a serious falling out among the Union commanders about how best to proceed, the long-term effect was significant. For three years, Union commanders had ventured south, been met and bloodied by Lee, and then retreated to regroup for another thrust. Grant broke that pattern by advancing rather than retreating. He reasoned that Lee's army was probably as badly bloodied as his own; that the relative strengths of the two armies had not changed significantly. The tremendous enthusiasm that greeted this order contrasts with the dismayed frustration that had resulted from Hooker's decision to retreat from virtually the same situation one year earlier. James G. Randall and David Donald, *The Civil War and Reconstruction*, 2nd ed. (Boston, 1961), p. 419.

left of the road—The 8th Pa was on our right and 2nd Pa on left flank—The line was 3 or 4 miles long—The left flank was charged and dislodged—but 10 N.Y. came to their support and they regained their position.

The right flank was charged but held its own—Next they charged our Center and we gave them such a warm reception as to repulse them handsomely Next they bring up a piece of Artillery by hand—when a double fire from our two pieces which had just come up knocked their pice all to pieces, killing four men and one officer. Seen by our Field glasses—we see 7 of their men killed by our carbine balls also——about this time I got a Spat above my right eye—

May 8, 1864 Sunday. Thus far only 4 or 5 of H. Co. wounded, none killed yet—I have a fearful bump over my eye, but with a bandage over it—which I keep wet, I greatly prefer remaining on the line with the Boys——At 8 A.M. we mounted, and were soon again engaged in a severe fight—we were under heavy artillery fire—We charge the Battery and almost take it, but the 8th is too slow—We dismount and charge through a thicket and drive the enemy wildly and hold our point—Dan Unger shot in the leg——We held our line rather quietly, and were relieved by Infantry at 3 P.M. and Fall back to The Plank Road—Here we meet Genl. Burnsides forces—we then draw 1 days Forage & Rations—and wait——10 P.M. we lie on arms and sleep some. The roar of battle having quieted down—up at 3 A.M. Orders! Be very quiet—Strike no light—To move out at once—Keep sabers from dangling, so as to make no noise—avoid all possible noise—First ½ hour we move rather slowly, but gradually increace to rapid movement—We realiz that we are striking for the rear of Lees Army. That we are on a hazardous trip—and that it demands haste—and quiet, for a time[10]—

We find no resistance—So we know we've succeeded in slipping away unobserved. Sometime Monday night 9th we neared the North Ann River and bivouaced.

---

10. This night march signaled the beginning of a major cavalry action: Sheridan's Richmond Raid, May 9–24. Grant had responded to the lack of coordination between Meade's infantry and Sheridan's cavalry by separating the two. While the main Union army continued its relentless march south, Sheridan was given ten thousand troopers, including the 16th Pennsylvania, and an open-ended assignment to harass the Confederates on his own. He had decided upon a deep raid in force that would destroy Confederate supplies, compel Lee to divert forces away from the main front, and perhaps provoke a confrontation with Stuart's cavalry on favorable terms. He was remarkably successful in realizing these goals.

May 10, 1864 Tuesday. Wide awake! Just at daybreak the enemy opened on us with shell, and but for the dense fog hiding our maneuver we would have been awfully endangered—

At sunrise we cross the North Ann River and pass on to Beaver Dam Station where where our 1st Brigade—last evening—with wonderful tact—captured 3 engines with 3 trains of cars in which were 400,000. Rations for Lees Army—and 300 prisoners recently taken about Chancellorsville and Todds Tavern &c, and kept on the cars for safety—

Our (2nd) Brigade was supporting the 1st—which cautiously came in on the Telegraph Operator—and by persuasion of several revolvers, compelled the Operator to be mum, but order the trains—which were lying near Richmond awaiting orders—to come to the front with all speed—and the trains came—and the 1st helped themselves and started the destruction of the surplus, and this morning our Brigade came on the scene—and replenished their light haversacks well and then Joined in the hasty destruction of about everything excepting the train crews, and the 300 prisoners and the Confeds who were guarding them—

Well! We had the Confeds to turn over their arms—and the late prisoners had the pleasure of guarding them as our prisoners now—

The poor Johnies we had been fighting—Friday, Sat. Sunday—out Front—were short of rations while doing hard fighting, and were expecting these Trains to come Monday, and issue rations to them—And here we had "drawn them." Monday night and Tuesday—(Prisoners taken Sunday 8th had admited shortage in their rations—and told of being promised issue of rations very soon) and the Johnies never got them—

And now our Cavalry Corpse moves rapidly towards Richmond—while the Infantry and artillery keep up the fight—Chancellorsville—Wilderness &c some days[11]—Our column started in the direction of Richmond—and we soon find the enemy on our right and in rear—and occasionally firing on us, but our Column moves on rather rapidly regardless of their pecking—

We marched via Mt. Olivet Church—across the South Anna (I think to Squirrel Church)[12] and on to Hanover Court House and

11. In the action at Beaver Dam Station, a depot on the Virginia Central Railroad, the Confederates lost three locomotives, approximately one hundred railroad cars, ten miles of track, half a million bread rations, nearly a million meat rations, and 378 recently captured Union prisoners. Mark M. Boatner III, *The Civil War Dictionary* (New York, 1959), p. 55.

12. Ground Squirrel Bridge.

encamp for the night—The weather is most awfully hot, and the roads tremendously dusty—

May 11, 1864 Wednesday. Last night—for the first time since we crossed the River at Ealies Ford on the 4th—we got nearly a full nights sleep——At daybreak our squadron went out on Picket 1 mile west of Squirrel Court House——At 10 OCK firing commenced and we were ordered back to the Regiment. In the meantime our Division had moved and the enemy had driven our men out of the position they were holding on the Cross roads, and 2nd Brigade artilery were in position and ready to open on them when they would make a charge. They charged and the 10th N.Y. broke and fled, and somehow got into the range so the artilery could not be used to good advantage. Just at this juncture our squadron—coming off Picket with orders to join the Regiment (which had left) came marching out of the roads, and in full view of the Rebel Charge— and the 10th N.Y. skedaddle—We, although ordered off duty, and to report to our regiment—at once formed for a charge—and as the Rebs made for a second charge—and were almost sure to capture the 2 Pieces and a lot of prisoners We charged them to fine effect, saving all—and empting a number of their saddles, and causing the Johnies to skedaddle in great confusion—

This was certainly a clear case of quick initiative—and snatching victory out of defeat. A fight without orders from higher up—

Capt Snyder, who was in command of our Squadron—and the Men were very highly complimented by the Capt Commanding the Battery. Also Colonel J. K. Robison and by Genl J. I. Gregg—for our disinterested manifestation of true bravery in thus, when one would have been fully justifiable in evading the whole fracas, and breaking for the Regiment—to rush at once into a daring charge upon the enemy to the saving of 2 fine cannon & many soldiers, and a great stamped of the Boys in blue—

Soon all became quiet and we joined our Regiment in the Column, which was moving onward—soon the advance met the enemy again, offering little resistance.

They also followed up our rear closely, so that all day long we fought in front, and rear and rear-right flank by spells—

Toward evening the enemy would check our advance, using some artillery, but our men know well how. So they moved on handsomely and by a charge unexpectedly coming in on their flanks captured 3 pieces of Art'l'y and a bunch of prisoners—

The rear of our column occasionally charged the enemy rearward to prevent their coming too near and getting cross fire on the column at any point—Thus this was an eventful day, and yet with very little loss, and a steady advance towards Richmond——Evening! We did not stop, but kept up the little fight til dark and then lay on arms til 2 OCK A.M.[13]

May 12, 1864 Thursday. when we again advanced and at break of day found ourselves inside of the outer works—earth works—of Richmond. A severe fight followed—The enemy in front—on our right and in our rear—and no way of falling to the left—a rather precarious position 1½ miles from the Rebel Capital and thus attacked. There would seem to be considerable of a chance of being closed in on, overpowered and awfully whipped. We however fight them, mounted dis-mounted and with artillery for 5 or 6 hours—charging them frequently—

It was discovered that our only way out was laid with "mines"—another charge was ordered toward the right and front, our boys were in it—we took one small piece of artillery, and a bunch of cav., supporters—By close questioning at Hd Qrs—it was brought out that this bunch, with their Lieut, were the very fellows who had put down the "Mines." Immediately—with open mouthed revolvers and carbines giving them a knowing wink, they were compelled to hastily take up the "mines" and so clear the way for our action and movement with safety (?)—

By 2 or 3 OCK we had so repulsed the enemy as to be again at liberty to move forward with safety—

During this engagement, at times, we could see immense crowds upon the Forts and embank to our right—near the City—we got it that the Rebel General was so certain of being able to take us in that he encouraged the Rebel Congress to adjourn and see him doing it, and of course the People wanted to see it also—

We were not taking Richmond either, anymore than Genl Steward was taking us. But we had made Genl Lees Army go hungry—and also solicitous for their rear—We had destroyed 3 trains they needed very much—We had attracted the Steward Cavalry to leave Lees army and look out for the safety of their capital—and we were not taking Richmond now. But we were not blown up yet, and so headed our column for the Chicohominy—and the only way for us

13. Stuart had made a long sweeping run with the bulk of his own cavalry in order to reach the outskirts of Richmond ahead of Sheridan's column. On May 11, he made a defensive stand at Yellow Tavern, a crossroad hamlet just six miles north of the capital. While Gregg's brigade protected the Federal rear and flanks in the fashion Cormany describes, the head of the Federal column crashed into Stuart's roadblock. The roadblock was smashed and Stuart mortally wounded.

to cross was on a R.R. embankment—and R.R. bridge—which by the way was planked—But the enemy had a canon planted facing us—so while a good line protected our rear, and they were keeping the Rebs busy, some of our bravest were wading the swamp—and in due time dashed up—all so unlooked for—and in a wee time spiked the Canon—

There was very little support with the Canon—all attention was about Richmond—and the yanks being hemmed in over there— Now crossing on the embankment—by fours—went on rapidly— and our rear line was showing energy about fighting Stewarts cavalry back—as though we needed to get out that way—all the while the evening was approaching—and our fellows were crossing over finely, and soon we had our artillery planted just across the swamp and our line, protecting the rear so faithfully, withdrew gently, yet kept up firing, and as the last were withdrawing the enemy advanced—firing—but received no response—until our last section of 4s was safe, when our artilery greeted the enemys approach to the R.R. embankment, which they dared not attempt to cross.

Weary and exhausted, we cooked some coffee to regale ourselves. Our rations being all, we were therewith content—so we moved on to Mechanicsville and then on to Hancock Court House where we bivouaced at 9 OCK P.M.[14]—

May 13, 1864   Friday. After foraging some for our Horses, with nothing for ourselves to eat we take up the line of march—our Co "H" on the left as flankers—we strike an amount of corn, and moving on crossed a Rail Road and at mid-P.M. we bivouaced near Bottom Bridge—no fighting of any a/c during the day—and no rations—and there seems almost nothing to eat in the land we traverse.

May 14, 1864   Saturday. Rained powerfully all night. Clear and pleasant this morning   Took up the march towards Melvern Hill. Thence down to Hacketts Landing,[15] and went into camp a mile from there—Maybe we were'nt hungry—Men have turned their haversacks inside out and licked up the crumbs in the lower corners—

---

14. All of what Cormany describes is well documented elsewhere. Sheridan's maneuver through the mined defenses of Richmond and his subsequent escape across the Chickahominy River to avoid entrapment have been labeled daring and brilliant by most analysts, unnecessarily foolhardy by a few.

15. Actually Malvern Hill and Haxall's Landing. The latter was on the James River below Richmond. From that point, Sheridan was able to establish contact and communication with the Army of the James under Gen. Benjamin Butler, which was threatening Richmond from the southeast.

Yet one hears no complaining, save now and then the taunts "Have a hard tack"? "Well no!" "Almost forgot how one looks, or tastes"—

May 15, 1864 Sunday. Ours and Capt Swans Squadrons went out on a foraging expedition. We got great loads of smoked pork— Meal—some Flour—& Butter etc. scouted and covered the country for some twelve miles and got back to Camp at sunset—We also brought in some 6 or 8 mules and as many horses——Fried Pork— SlapJacks—Corn pone—Hoe Cake—Bread and gravy—a little but- ter—and a little molasses, with coffee plenty, etc. etc. was indulged in moderately (?) by all the Boys   A rain came up, dampening our ardor some—and detracting some from our joys—

May 16, 1864 Monday. Pleasant Morning—News Papers came in— Also Rations and Forage—Glorious news from Armies all around— and now surely mail will soon come in—Yes!   about sick—vomiting and purging—Ate too freely, and too rich, after so long a time of almost utter fasting—

Lots-o-the boys similarly affected. Fortunately we could just lie around all day and feed up gently and rest—

May 17, 1864 Tuesday. Early received marching orders—Carried all surplus Forage down to The Landing (Hacketts)—Just when com- pleted, orders countermanded, and we carry it back again and make ourselves as comfortable as may be—I am well but very sleepy—I went to sleep at 10 A.M. and slept til 5 P.M.—when we drew some more Forage and Rations—and issued them to the men. At dusk we rec'd orders to be ready to march by 9 P.M. with 3 days Forage and 3 days rations—

Most of our officers have been drinking freely—some are pretty drunk. Captain Snyder is awfully drunk—scarcely able to ride—But we took up the march at 9 OCK P.M. promptly—marched all night   Got to Chicahominy at 9:30 A.M.[16]

May 18, 1864 Wednesday. Crossed at Jones'–Old Bridge   clear— cloudy—rainy alternately—My bowels still quite bad—Capt Snyder still quite drunk   we bivouac from 9:30 A.M. til 4 P.M. and then took

16. Cormany's first orders indicate that Sheridan planned to reunite with Grant and Meade by taking ships back around Union lines, as McClellan had done when he extricated his army from virtually the same spot in 1862. Sheridan reversed himself, however, and what follows is a brief sketch of the cavalry's rather risky, but ulti- mately successful, attempt to reunite with the Army of the Potomac by an overland march.

up the march again, a very Zigzag route and bivouac at the Baltimore X Roads for the night—

May 19, 1864 Thursday. a good rest—At 9 A.M. our Regiment started on reconoisance—Crossed the Little Pamunky—Were at "Smiths Store"—"Old House" &c &c were within 12 miles of Richmond again—and captured 6 or 8 prisoners and 8 or 10 horses & mules and got loads of smoked pork. We returned to Camp at Baltimore Cross-roads at dusk—and encamped and camped—

May 20, 1864 Friday. We took up our line of march again at 5 OCK A.M. scoured the country and bivouaced at Coles Harbor[17] at 2 P.M.—In the evening our Regiment advanced to within ten miles of Richmond—drew up our Regiment in line, with sabers drawn for a charge The skirmishers fire some and the enemy falls back—night being about upon us, we return to Coles Harbor and bivouac—We are living pretty well these days on Ham and Eggs, Chicken, Corn Cakes—pone & hoe cake—Confiscated corn for our Horses our rations had about run out yesterday evening—

May 21, 1864 Saturday. A little foggy—nothing doing. but lying around—no mail no news—swallowed up in Johny Land—Altho I daily—almost hourly think of my dear Darling Rachel, and precious pussy Cora, yet this day more than ever I long to hear from them once again.

Oh! to be with them one short hour. Heaven protect and bless them, and me, soon to meet again—

Spent most of day in suspense—Foraged some little but both armies going over the same teritory, leave little Slept some—No forage. No rations. No visible prospects of any of either—and yet we know we shall be fed—

Canonading hearable most of day—but we know not where and in a sense we don't care.

May 22, 1864 Sunday. Cloudy—Roused at 3:30 A.M. took up the march at 4:30—Extremely hot—Very many of our Cavalry horses are playing out and being shot or abandoned on these raids—Cause? Hard marches—irregular rations—fearful strain on muscles & nerves—& lack of rest—

We arrived at White House Landing at 2 P.M.—Drew 3 ds Forage,

17. Actually Cold Harbor, where Grant's attempt to storm into Richmond would be repulsed two weeks later.

and 5 days rations—Our squadron went on picket at Tunsall Station—Gnats! Jerusalem! Will they kill us? Their bites or stings, and the after touches, seem to create misery in the marrow of ones bones—and every where a fellow lives & is at home—

May 23, 1864 Monday. Quite Hot At 9 A.M. we reported to White House Landing—and at 11 OCK crossed the Pamunky River on R.R. Bridge[18]—and loafed awhile—I took a fine swim in the river—I am quite well and happy, but I do so long to hear from my dearest Rachel and precious Cora—Our Division having gone we moved along all alone at our leisure via Lanesville, King Henry Court House and to Elliottsville, where we found the 1st and 2nd Div bivouaced. Is a very hot day—200 Rebel Cavalry who had been cut off unwittingly by our column charged across the road near Lanesville between our squadron, and the rear of the main column, which was about two miles ahead. Lucky fellows they that we didn't know of their being so near us—

May 24, 1864 Tuesday. Took up the march at 7 A.M. in the direction of Hanover Junction til within four miles, then turned in the direction of Fredericksburg and Bivouaced in the river swamp at 5 OCK P.M. 25 miles from Fredericsburg—

I enjoyed a fine bath & swim—Had a heavy shower in evening—

This is my 26th Birthday Anniversary—Thank the good Lord that I am who—where, and what I am, and who's I am—How good is God to me, unworthy tho' I be—

May 25, 1864 Wednesday. We took up the march at 8 A.M. passed Chesterfield St'n No 5 at 2 P.M. and saw the first infantry we have seen of ours since May 9th—about Todds Tavern.

We encamped at Polecat River at 4 P.M.

☞ Mail comes to us I had mailed my last to Pet May 1st and had received my last from her same day—all these 25 days we were in the enemys country—several times quite near Richmond—as noted heretofore—and entirely out of reach of Mail facilities. But today—thank the good Lord—Our mail comes up and I recieve five letters from Pet—one from H. W. Rebok[Pa]—one from Rose Karper,[n] and one from Clem[cc] and one from Jas W.[kk] and Lea Adams[jj] So we had a quiet day of reading letters from Home. Writing some—and reading "war news." We know almost nothing of what was being accomplished, save what we—cavalrymen—were doing—and we

18. The Richmond and York River Railroad crossed the Pamunkey River at White House Landing.

knew but little of that save what our own Regiment was closely engaged in—

May 26, 1864 Thursday. Rainy—I recieved my commission as 2nd Lieutenant today. Made some effort to be mustered out as Serg't and in as 2nd Lieut At 1:30 P.M. we took up the march again via Chesterfield Station & Edensville halted at 9 OCK to eat and feed—Fed our horses and I with many lay down & slept rather than to cook—We lay an hour and then moved off again via Concord Church—Edensville, Enfield marched all night and on into the new day.[19]

May 27, 1864 Friday. Halted for breakfast at 9 OCK A.M. then Cross Pamunky River at the Enfield Ferry at 10 OCK A.M. Three or four Regiments of Rebel cavalry resist us, but in vain. We drive them and cross, and bivouac and sleep—protected by a strong picket line & guard—which has little disturbance—The day is a restful one. We graze our horses some in eve. and make exchange of Pickets—Do up a pretty good supper and have a rather quiet night.

May 28, 1864 Saturday. and a cheery restful morning— At noon we took up the march in the direction of Hanover C. H. and at 1:30 P.M. the ball opens briskly near Hanover or Old Church.

On the Field Canon roar and Shells burst, Carbine balls keep buzzing wildly—At 2:30 very hotly engaged. Our Regiment in for all thats going—but I was ordered to remain with the led horses, whose riders were doing special work on the line—Already Capts Robinson and Swan are wounded—Two men in "K" Company wounded— The battle kept up til dark—Seven killed and twenty-six wounded in our 16th—Altogether it was a very severe fight[20]—After dark were

---

19. After fighting his way across the North Anna River, Grant continued his offensive by swinging slightly east and crossing the Pamunkey. The 1st and 2nd Divisions of the Union cavalry, supported by the 6th Corps of infantry, were sent to secure the best crossing sites. This placed Cormany's regiment in the vanguard of the Union army.

20. The fight pitted the 1st and 2nd Divisions of the Union cavalry, sweeping ahead of the main army, against slightly less than two divisions of Confederate cavalry under Wade Hampton, who had risen to command following the death of Stuart. Lee had sent Hampton to determine just where Grant's army intended to cross the Pamunkey and whether they had actually begun to do so. When Hampton encountered Gregg, the result was the Battle of Haw's Shop, named for a nearby hamlet. The Union side lost 340 men, including 30 officers, in this intense clash, but held control of the roads they were sent to secure. See Robert A. Williams, "Haw's Shop: A 'Storm of Shot and Shell,' " *CWTI* 9 (Jan. 1971), 12–19.

relieved by The Sixth Corps—infantry—and we fell back to Hano-vertown ferry and bivouaced at midnight. Had rather a quiet rest.

May 29, 1864 Sunday. The Infantry have the job now and we lie 'round and rest. Towards evening we move down down the River some four miles to Edmonds or New Castle Ferry—This is most beautiful farming Country—

I got a shell from the cabinet of Edmund Ruff who—it was said—fired the first shot on Ft. Sumpter[21]

Near his place we bivouaced for the night—

May 30, 1864 Monday. Very fine morning—Splendid nights rest 17 miles from Richmond

I took a swim in the Pamunky River—In P.M. we moved out and had a little fight near Old Church—were on the line til 9 P.M.—Bivouaced at Old Church—Our mail came to us. Glad Boys—I have one from Pet. Oh! such a good one—We drew 2 days Forage and at 11:30 were ready to sleep.

May 31, 1864 Tuesday. Awfully hot—orders—Our Brigade (2nd) detached to General Smiths Command—(Butlers Old Command) we report to White House Landing, and lie 'round—After dark we draw 2 days Forage and 3 days Rations, and bivouac near Tunsalls Station at 11:30 P.M.—Any amount of Infantry passing in the direction of Cole Harbor[22]

June 1, 1864 Wednesday. Capt Snyder let me have the little Grey—as mine—She was a capture—all used up—I had done much to fit her for service again——Pleasant day We marched at 10 A.M. in direction of Cole Harbor. halted within 3 miles—1st Cav Division

21. Edmund Ruffin, an extreme advocate of Southern secession, had been given the symbolic honor of firing the first shot toward Fort Sumter in April 1861. Marl-bourne, one of his estates, was less than four miles from the Haw's Shop battlefield and located on the road down which the Union cavalry withdrew. Ruffin was one of North America's leading advocates of scientific agriculture, and his interest in geology and paleontology had stimulated him to acquire an excellent collection of shells and fossils from which Samuel probably seized his souvenir. See Avery Craven, *Edmund Ruffin, Southerner: A Study in Secession* (Hamden, Ct., 1964), pp. 239–40; and Ruffin's own *Diary*, 2 vols. (Baton Rouge, La., 1972, 1976). Ruffin committed suicide in the days following the Confederate defeat.

22. These movements presaged the Battle of Cold Harbor, which featured a poorly conceived frontal assault by the Union army on the outer defenses of Richmond. This assault was the one decision of the entire war Grant most regretted. *Personal Memoirs of U. S. Grant* (New York, 1886), II, 269–77.

Pontoon bridges over the Pamunkey River at Hanovertown, Va. This is where the 16th Pennsylvania rested after the Battle of Haw's Shop. The photograph was taken by Timothy H. O'Sullivan in May 1864, the same month that Samuel was there. Photographic Division, LC.

and our 1st Brigade are fighting hard—Enemy makes strong showing near Coal Harbor—at dusk the fight still goes on fiercely, and the infantry comes to our relief—

We lay over for the night in rear of the Infantry—

June 2, 1864 Thursday. We took up the line of march at 8 A.M. made a reconnaisance in force—and run into the enemy on extreme left of our line on the Chicohominy, and had a severe—a savage—fight—quite a number killed and wounded—Tho as it happened the 16th did not get into the hottest this time.[23]

The Chaplain of the 1st Maine Cav was shot through the breast by a solid shot and killed instantly while waving his hat—and encouraging the men who were making a good charge—

In the evening our Cavalry was relieved by infantry as much of the days fighting was against Rebel Infantry—and on their first dash they took in 512 of the Rebel Infantry—We now took up the line of march for Bottom Bridge—Rained heavily, went into camp, greatly alert however—

June 3, 1864 Friday. Rainy night—Cloudy morning—I put up my Shelter Tent for the first time since we broke camp, about a month ago—

I spent most of A.M. writing   P.M. Johnies tried to shell us some from across the river—So Captain orders me to the R.R. Train to do some writing for him, a cozy place in the car—

June 4, 1864 Saturday. I commenced to correct the disputed Ordnance Report—The train moved at 2 P.M.   I went along to near Coal Harbor four miles to the rear and continue my clerical work—Eve rains—

June 5, 1864 Sunday. Rainy—A.M.   I write in a large tent   Finish the Ord. writing and then commence writing for my Rachel—Wrote her a long letter, and one for J. B. Kimmel—Rose Karper[n]—H. W. Rebok[Pa]—I write til night—Seemed more like Sunday than for sometime. Save the heavy cannonading hearable all day—

June 6, 1864 Monday. I started for the Regiment   Got outside of our lines being mis-directed, but no harm comes from it—about

23. Grant later acknowledged the significance of this foray because it confirmed the fact that his army could cross the Chickahominy River without major resistance should he decide to do so. Ibid., II, 269.

noon I joined my Regiment and obtained my discharge as Sergt, and a very good letter from my Darling, and one from A. C. Bowman.[cc] and—for a change—the Boys were awaiting orders to strike tents &c.

Towards Evening—orders came[24] and we march via Summit St'n to New Castle Ferry and stop on the River Bank and rest on Arms—I had a fine time today—got as much milk as I wanted to drink—and was kind of free-and-easy—

At 11 P.M. we quartered for the night—

June 7, 1864 Tuesday. Cloudy—Routine—Drew Forage and took up line of march at 9:30 via Sharon Church and Brandywine to Herring Creek   bivouaced at 4:30. Made application to be mustered in as 2nd Lieutenant. Made out Rolls &c &c—

June 8, 1864 Wednesday. Up betimes—Routine—I was mustered as 2nd Lieutenant at 5 OCK A.M.—Donned my shoulder-straps and took off my Sergt's stripes—

Sergt Flannagan and Corpl Coble assisted me gleefully!

I took the squadron to Water—i.e., to water the Horses—At 10 OCK we took up the line of march via Beulah Church 24 miles and encamped near Polecat Station—

Grazed our Horses in a 100 acre clover field—Got lots of Corn, Meat, Meal, Milk, &c &c

June 9, 1864 Thursday. Moved out at 8 A.M.—I am placed in Command of the rear guard of the 2nd Brigade, 2nd Division of Cavalry Corps—and acted as assistant Ins. of March—Passed Wrights Store near Milford Station, Trynesville and Nathan Hancocks Store and turned in to Camp near Youngs Mill—

Captain Snyder and I mess together—

24. These orders assigned the 16th Pennsylvania to another major cavalry raid. Grant wanted Sheridan to move up the Virginia Central Railroad, thus destroying one of Richmond's arteries, and rendezvous with a Federal force under Gen. David Hunter, who was supposed to be clearing the Shenandoah Valley of Confederate forces. When he learned of these movements, Lee countered by dispatching Hampton to intercept Sheridan, which he did near Trevilian Station, a depot on the Virginia Central Railroad a few miles above the town of Louisa Court House. Though Hampton lost heavily and eventually abandoned his roadblock, Sheridan's losses were sufficient to make him turn around and rejoin the main army rather than push forward. This aborted venture is known as the Trevilian Raid. See Jay Monaghan, "Custer's 'Last Stand'—Trevilian Station, 1864," *CWH* 8 (Sept. 1962), 245–58.

June 10, 1864 Friday. Rained some in the night—I slept well. Is a pleasant morning. I took the squadron to Water—and we marched out at 9 ock. via Levys Stores, Strynersville, Baldys Tavern, Good Hope Church. Crossed South Ann River and in several miles went into Camp—and the 16th was the Picket Regiment—and our Squadron the main reserve, while I had charge of the outer reserve and outposts—Our foraging parties are being fired into very much—

June 11, 1864 Saturday. I am suffering from a severely enflamed eye—Took up march at 7 A.M. in a few miles we struck Stoods Tavern near Lobillia Station, and at 8 ock we were fronted by the enemy and were in line of battle with Genl. Custer on the right, and our 2nd Brigade on and in left of R.R. by 9:30 the fight rages furiously two of the Platoons of our Squadron hold a manouver on the extreme left—rather specially their own—for some time—but with flanking effect. P.M. The whole line charges with splendid results—Capturing 750 prisoners—Our regiment lost 4 killed and 10 wounded—The Brigade's loss was very small comparatively—We had a very responsible position, and on our wild and dashing, mounted charge upon the enemy's right, getting almost in rear of their artillery—we caused them to concentrate on the center—and put up a hot resistance—which gave our dismounted line a rather confused and demoralized mass to charge into. We mounted fellows were exposed very much to the fire of sharp shooters—My "Gayety Grey" (my mare) seemed a particularly attractive object—or rather her rider—which was somewhat annoying to my sensative ears—
But we gained the day and held the Field—Darkness coming on, the enemy fell back—and soon we too withdrew to the main position, and bivouaced, throwing out a picket line—The night was quiet—no p'kt firing—A fine shower of rain.

June 12, 1864 Sunday. A beautiful day—Got some commissary whiskey—We had a generaly restful A.M. In camp, I watered and grazed the squadron—The 1st Division is fighting all day more or less P.M. all hands tearing up R.R. track, or turning it up-side-down—The process is rather simple—A joint is first broken on one side. Men stand shoulder to shoulder—say one thousand abreast along the rail—a few with fence rails, and chunks, pry the rail and ties up for 100 or more feet, underpinning the one side, for a short distance—the the height of several feet—Now, at the word of command, every man lifts harder and harder, and soon the men at the broken joint, have the ties in perpendicular position while those next are nearly so. Continuing the lift and tearing up, while now the ties and rail at the break are beyond the perpendicular and so bear down and at the same time remaining spiked to the ties—help in the overturning process—so when once fairly started the R.R. track is turned upsidedown with considerable speed and the extreme strain and twist, of the turning over mass, twists and otherwise damages nearly every rail

At 11 OCK P.M. we took up the march. Crossed the south Anna, and encamped—or rather bivouaced for the night—a pretty tired lot of Boys

June 13, 1864 Monday. Seems as tho my eyes were poisoned wonderfully sore—Otherwise I am very well and happy   We lay around resting   Did some foraging   Capt Snyders squad of Foragers were fired into—no one hurt. The shooter too far off—

June 14, 1864 Tuesday. We had Turkey for supper last eve and again this morning   Took up the march at 5 A.M.   Stopped for dinner at 10 OCK P.M.   Grazed—rested—til 4 P.M.   Then moved a short distance and encamped 3 miles from Todds Tavern—Found many of ours and some of the Rebel dead lying unburried—some results of May 5th–6th–7th work

June 15, 1864 Wednesday. Very hot and dusty—Took up the march at 8 OCK A.M.   Went through Spotsylvania and amongst the earthworks and fortifications—It is wonderful that men should build such works for defense, but still more so that they should abandon them with so small punishment to the assailing party—

We encamped near the Mattapony River at 9 OCK P.M.

June 16, 1864 Thursday. Lay 'round til 9 A.M.—Got fine mess of Cherries   So did lots of the Boys—Marched at 9 to Bowling Green— once a fine town, but now all in ruins—Took our time to see—and moved on some ten miles towards Newtown where we encamp'd at dusk—My eyes decidedly better—

June 17, 1864 Friday. Ready to move out—at 7 A.M.   Soon on the way—

I was ordered to take charge of all dis-mounted men of the 16th and march them on flanks of the artillery   Is a Bore! Indescribably hot and dusty—

We passed Newtown & on in the direction of Dunkirk—to within 2 miles then to the left, along Mattapony river some ten miles, where we encamped at 8 P.M. 3 miles from Walkerton Mills—

435

June 18, 1864 Saturday. Keeps awfully hot—I took out a foraging party—Got lots of corn—some sugar—saw some Johnies They skedaddled—

At 8 A.M. We march down the river—Passed King and Queen C. H. and Col Dahlgreens empty grave and the place he was assassinated.[25] Bivouaced 2 miles down the river at 2½ P.M. At 5 P.M. moved ¼ mile—

I was ordered in Command of "I" Company—"C" and "I" Cos constitute a squadron. Lieut Caughy com'ds squadron—I took them to water—

June 19, 1864 Sunday. Sultry—awfully dusty—after routine I see the squadron well watered   Start out at 7:30 A.M.   march 21 or 22 miles to near Dunkirk. Encamped at dusk   I had command of Rear Guard on todays march. Eve my eyes are rather worse—but well and happy otherwise—Sent letter to Pet—

June 20, 1864 Monday. Hot—sultry—dusty—We crossed the River at 7 A.M.   mail came—Recd letter from Pet—Drew 1 days forage and rations—(Now that I am no more Quarter Master Sergeant—The handling of Feed and Food has fallen to another. But having Command and the care of Co "I" places me under heavier responsibility—)   After taking supplies we moved on the White-house-Landing   Encamped before sunset—I never saw worse dust—Our Cav Corps Train all driven across the River by a Rebel Raid and dash made upon it. But they failed to get the booty[26]—

June 21, 1864 Tuesday. Foggy—Regiment aroused at 2:30 A.M. to march—dismounted at 3 OCK—We crossed the bridge at break-o-day—Found a few of the enemy   drove them 1½ miles, and put up temporary breast works—after a short engagement—we charged—

25. During the raid on Richmond, Col. Ulric Dahlgren had been shot by Virginia militiamen, who may have been acting in reprisal against Dahlgren's hanging of a local guide suspected of giving false directions. After papers allegedly found among Dahlgren's effects indicated his intention to kill leading Confederate governmental officials, Dahlgren's remains were disinterred and secretly reburied as an act of disrespect. *Harper's Pictorial History of the Civil War* (New York, 1866, facs. rpt.), p. 523, and Meriwether Stuart, "Colonel Ulric Dahlgren and Richmond's Union Underground," *Virginia Magazine of History and Biography* 72 (1964), 152–204.

26. As is clear from Cormany's description, the Federal cavalry took a long looping route back toward Grant's army. The party was repeatedly struck, though never with seriously damaging results. The return took longer than the advance because Grant's army had swung down around Richmond, across the Chickahominy and James rivers, and into a strong position opposite Petersburg.

and drove them near Tunsall Station and held our position or line till 6:30 P.M.—Enemy withdrew. We left out a picket line and support and re-crossed the River—took our supper—Then took our horses and all over to near our line and bivouaced—or rather encamped lightly—

June 22, 1864 Wednesday. Still immensely hot and dusty—We drew in our dismounted pickets and support, and our squadron threw out a mounted picket line near the Tunsall Station—

The enemy had fallen back towards Richmond and Bottom Bridge—Our pickets brought in one Reb—they caught napping—The 4th Pa relieved our Regiment at sun set, and we made ourselves confortable.

June 23, 1864 Thursday. A cool night—Good sleep—some canonading going on in direction of Richmond—All "to Horse," and march at 5 OCK AM. We go to Landing We tore up Bridge & Wharf, awfully hot job, and dusty—Took up line of march again at 9 OCK A.M. via New Kent C.H to "Long" or "Jones' Bridge, and encamped at 6:30 P.M.——At 10:30 when all were soundly asleep we were ordered to pack—to march immediately. We marched 1½ to 2½ miles and bivouaced—

June 24, 1864 Friday. Marched at 6 OCK A.M. via Charles City Court House—a few miles beyond we drove in the Enemy pickets—and kept up light skirmishing till 2:30 P.M. when it became more firm. Our lines were charged many times, but we repulsed them and held our ground, or line handsomely—

All rather quiet for a little while—our line intact—I had dismounted, and was sitting on a Stump—close in front of my Company "I"—and was writing—making notes of our doings—Whereupon a Reb Sharp Shooter was getting range of me—one of my men seeing an occasional puffing up of the ground rather close in front of me caused by the enemy's bullet—remarked "Lieut! That Johny has pretty close range of you" I replied I observe, just then a bullet struck the stump, between my feet, taking with it a bit of my boot and barely grazed my left ankle—inside—slightly removing a little cuticle—but doing me no harm save what a boot-mender can repair.

A little later both Infantry and Cavalry charged us—We are being flanked and greatly outnumbered—and a general falling back takes place—with some regiments amounting to almost a stampede and panic—through some woodland—Our old 16th in good order—

holds the extreme rear, firing as they fall back, thus keeping the enemy from coming too close—Lieut Caughy receives a wound— and I take command of the squadron—We are under awful firing— As we came out of a wood, The Col J.K.R with the 1st squadron faces the charging enemy and they pour volleys into them—thus retarding them—and the while I rallied my squadron some distance in the rear or rearward on the opposite side of the road—on an elevation. And we lustily sang the song "We'll rally round the flag Boys" Others, who had fallen back without orders, rallied to us, and soon order was restored, and we presented a solid front—I warned the squadron that the Colonel would very soon be coming back to our right on the opposite side of the road—Every man to be at aready but not to fire a shot until I gve command Fire!—Then to pour it in with precission—and continuously, until the Reg't had time to form further back on our right and rear.

Soon our Boys came. The Col calling Steady! Steady Men! as they passed us—and for a wee, the dense dust and firing of the enemy revealed to us their approach while we were invisible to them— When they came to about 100 yds of us, upon order "FIRE!" Such a volley greeted them as checked them all and dismounted many— and the same was repeated several times, when an effort to flank us made it necessary for us to "By fours, right about face" and move to the rear steadily, firing occasionally to the rear or "rear-right-oblique"—Soon we were opposite to the Regiment again— and then was their turn to greet any who rallied and drove (?) us. Thus by "eschelon" we held the enemy back—until night relieved us from further pressure and we bivouaced at Charles City Court House—

June 25, 1864 Saturday. No enemy annoying us we start out early—The dust and heat of yesterday and today beggars description—We move on to Wilcox Landing—I am in command of the rear guard—Arrive at noon—I take a swim—We feed and eat and in P.M. our squadron on Reserve Picket—mail arrives—No letter from Pet—Long for one—Oh! to become a better and more noble Christian man and soldier—To reach my ideals—

June 26, 1864 Sunday. Hotest of the year—Lay in reserve all day. Did some fine sleeping—P.M. Recd a good letter from Pet—Quiet along the picket line all day—Eve. 8th Pa Cav relieved us Another letter from Pet—A shower! To lay the choking dust I went to the landing for eatables—Officers rations scarce—My eyes still somewhat sore. Hope the dust may be kept down now—

June 27, 1864 Monday. Cooler—Wrote all A.M. for Pet—Dined on Tack & water—At 2 P.M. went to Landing got some Oysters, Tomatoes & Brandy, a special put up—An awful rain storm, I got thoroughly wet—nothing of interest transpiring—Thank the Lord I am kept so well and happy

June 28, 1864 Tuesday. Very pleasant day—No dust—We moved to the Landing at 5 A.M. and lay around awaiting Transportation til 3 P.M. then were taken across by Boat,[27] and we encamped 1½ miles from Fort Powhattan—I and Tom went to the Fort Commissary for rations for our Mess—Eve a letter from Pet—

June 29, 1864 Wednesday. Routine—Pleasant day—all quiet—I write lots—sent letter to Pet—at 4 P.M. we took up the march—were on the move all night zig zaging around and at dawn found ourselves at Prince George Court House—we halted til 9 A.M. and breakfasted—I was in Command of Rear Guard again.

June 30, 1864 Thursday. We marched on to the Assamossack—or Black water swamp and mills—arriving at 3½ P.M. Lay around til dark and then camped for the night—During P.M. were mustered for Pay—

27. I.e., across the James River estuary to reunite with the rear guard of the main army. The front itself was about fifteen miles west of the ferry.

XXII

"I am so tired of this way of living"
March 21–November 25, 1864

The war is now in its fourth year, and its psychological impact upon the lives of Elizabeth Jane Snyder, Mrs. McGowan, and Jonathan Plough becomes apparent. Its material impact is dramatized in one of the most flagrant and controversial acts of the entire conflict: the deliberate burning of downtown Chambersburg by Confederate soldiers on July 30, 1864.

———————◆•●•◆———————

March 21, 1864 Feel better than I have for some time. Last week I really though I was————. but it was something else. I am sure I am well satisfied as it is. I tried to be cheerful under it but could not. I could do nothing but week. as soon as a change came I felt like another person. my appetite returned. I could sleep again & feel cheerful. Indeed—I did not think that I would be affected as I was about such a thing. It is well I was mistaken both for————& myself.[1] I am sewing carpet rags & telling the girls stories to get them to help me—I can work again with a will. last week I could not do so. It has been quite cold for some time, especially so today. This morning my stovepipe caught fire. Mrs Merklein nearly went off the handle about it. she flew & flurried about like an old cluck when the hawk is after her yound ones. It almost made me fidgety to see her performing—She had the chimney all in ablaze when only the sparks were flying. O! deliver me from such people. Mrs McG. was at a sale & by my orders bought me a rocking chair for 75 cts with cushion on back & seat—

April 4, 1864 Moved from Mrs Merkleins to Mrs McGowans—Had quite a time getting my things hauled—Bettie M. & Mattie Jarret carried a number of things. they helped me like good girls—so did Mrs M. & Charlie—Mrs Mc was sick still she got the dinner for us— Mr Harmon hauled two small loads for me—Could not fix much— am tired—Yes real tired[2]

1. Rachel thought she might be pregnant after Samuel had been home on leave.
2. The McGowans also lived on Front Street, four blocks south of the Merkleins, near the outskirts of residential housing about ten blocks from the Diamond. *AFCP*, p. 24.

April 6, 1864 Got Armstrong boy with the little waggon to fetch the rest of my things—Am not well—was right sick all night. went up to help get my wood out—when I got back here three country women whose husbands are in the co Mr C is in were here for dinner—Just at noon John Grafton came so I had quite a houseful for dinner & I sick—

April 11, 1864 Mother[b] Ellie[y] daddie[ba] & John Cormany's[d] visited me—I was so glad to see them all but daddie[ba] & he is a nuisance anywhere & everywhere—he is too stingy & selfish to live in a world with other people—he has 70 lbs lard to sell but would not sell me any—I pity Mother[b] that she has to be tormented with such a dog—Ellie[y] is going to houskeeping her husband[z] says old dadd[ba] has knocked her round long enough—I really this days visit. After they were gone C. Fuller called I enjoyed her call too. Mrs Mc has been sick in bed since Fryday I wait on her & take care of her things in general—Got 3 letters, such good ones

April 12, 1864 My 28th Birthday—Wrote a letter to Mr C. also one to Mr McG—for Mrs Mc. Prepared supper for my sisters but they did not come. rec'd 2 letters from My Samuel verry good ones too—Am so tired that I can scarcely get along—I went to the depot & took Cora along—which was too much after having been on my feet all day—

April 13, 1864 This Morning Maggie Karper[ja] came to stay a week she brought me several qts of wheat—4 inches bologne (home made) & maybe ¾ lb butter & a little tallow so now I am to help her make her summer outfit & board her for that. such friends—after her Mother[j] acting as she did about the cloak I altered for her for nothing.[3] I think I shall not hurt myself cooking or sewing for her. she wanted me to run with quick to get her things & then sit like a slave & sew for her all week but she is not going to get it over me this time—I have been looking for my sisters for some time now still they are not here—Evening Sisters Mollie[ii] & Susie[nn] came to stay with me awhil. I am so glad they are once here—I have been looking for them so long. Maggie Hamilton & Miss Mahler came to Mrs McGowans. I do not know where to store all to sleep—

April 20, 1864 Wednesday Eve. M. K.[ja] is at last gone after "pestering" us a week with her sewing—It is a shame the way they impose

3. See Rachel's entry for Feb. 15, 1864.

on me   bring only a mouthful so to speak & a bundle of sewing—She asked me to cut—fit & help make her dress—& wanted me to ask my sisters to help—she said she would pay me—Well I did help her—I stuck so closely to it that I did not as much as get my necessary Mending done—I have been short of money for sometime & I got quite out—& out of butter so I asked her to loan me some.   at first she thought she could not—still she gave me a quarter—which I never intended to give back if she did not pay me some—well when she left she said—You—can just keep that quarter I had intended to give you something anyhow." Now if I were not a soldiers wife & had plenty—I would not mind it—but they are rich & know my circumstances as well as I do   By the help of sisters & Mrs Mc I gave her some hints that I think she could not help taking. I do not want them to come very soon again I am sure—If there is any snapp about the family I think they will not come soon again—

April 22, 1864   Evening. Recieved a letter from My husband.   he seemed verry low spirited, on account of not receiving letters from me regularly, as also the fact that communication between the army & the friends at home is stopped for 60 days—In all probability fighting will commence in earnest now verry soon—I cannot help weeping every time I read his letter—I scarcely know what to do with myself—

April 25, 1864   Have not been well for several days.   took cold—& I feel so worried about my husband—I feel like sitting & weeping all the time. I cannot work.   & that last letter—whenever I think of it such a sense of depression & heaviness comes upon me that I can scarcely help asking the good Lord When—O! when will my troubles cease. Another reason that I feel depressed for is that I am just out of money—flour—wood—potatoes—& in fact out of nearly everthing—Just now I am tired of living—God speed our release from this dreadful suspense of 60 days & from war & the troubles of war—If I only know that my husbands life would be spared I could rest easy—but if should he be taken—all would be gone—.   A few days after the above was written I received a letter from my husband stating that the 60 days suspension of mail was only a rumor   I also received letters with money. Truly the Lord provides for me. Sister Mollie[ii] remarked that it seemed as if an unseen hand was providing for me—

May 22, 1864   Last Thursday Sisters Mollie[ii] & Sue[nn] left for home in C W.   I felt so lonely & had not been well for a week or more & since the 2nd inst had received no tidings from my husband.   when

442

I returned from the depot—I was almost ready to declare myself sick enough to go to bed—My charge—J. Grafton had the measles so he needed a good share of my strength to attend to him. Mr McGowan (the lady of whom I rented) is sick too & has been since I live here. The lady living with her M. Hamilton was sick too & went home next morning. Well Thursday P.M. was spent rather uncomfortably all round—Evening came & with it a letter from my Precious—O! the light that letter brought with it. I was so glad I scarcely knew what to do with myself. I kissed the little missive, run all through the house proclaiming my fortune, hurried my few duties over then struck for Mrs Snyder to tell her but she having had the same good fortune was on her way to tell me & I met her a few doors from so we returned together.[4] Our brave husbands have seen hard marching & hard fighting. My Precious bears the mark of a minnie ball[5] on his forehead he writes me—Thank the Lord that they are still spared. This AM. I attended class & preaching—I was happy in class—O! this glorious religion of Jesus Christ I am not well today—feel much out of fix   My little girl has been very unwell—but she is quite over her spell & is as mischievous as she well can be—here she comes so goodbye My old Journal—Rec'd a letter from Minnie Hanson last evening—

May 29, 1864   Sabbath P.M.   This is a clear beautiful day. Yet quite cool. I have been quite sick during the week was confined to bed two days—the rest was spent between the bed & chair. John Grafton boarding with me I had to cook when I was scarcely able to be out of bed

May 30, 1864   A beautiful Morning—Am still far from being well John G. leaves me this morning.   he did not tell me of his intention to leave until Sat. evening, so now of course I have more bread than I can eat in two weeks—I fear my meat will spoil. I got potatoes just the other week to do until I get new ones—so there is $1[.]50—or

---

4. Elizabeth Jane Snyder married Adam J. Snyder, a tanner, in 1856. Snyder had difficulty with alcohol, which was exacerbated, as Samuel's diary makes clear, by the pressures of the war. After he abandoned his wife in 1866, she lived alone in Chambersburg taking in washing and ironing. Since she and Adam never formally divorced, she was able to draw a widow's pension after Adam died in 1890. She died in 1910. See his pension file, NA.

5. Cf. Samuel's entry for May 7, 1864. The term was derived from the name of the inventor of this type of bullet, Capt. Claude-Etienne Minié. M. Pierre Larousse, *Grand dictionnaire universel du XXIe siècle* (Paris, 1874), p. 38; *Nouvelle biographie générale* (Paris, 1861), p. 598.

more out of my pocket His bed I have to wash & room to clean which is altogether too much trouble to be put to not to receive any remuneration for—Well these are the thanks I get for putting myself to a good deal of inconvenience to accomodate him. If his sister & guardian had not set in so hard for me to take him I never would have had this bother. I pittied John when I was told how he was knocked about through this world. John worked for me in my lot[6]— & really he did not do the work half—I dropped the potatoes & he covered them, when I went over the piece some were sticking out— He made a horrid job of digging. & worse of planting corn, just before he left he hoed my potatoes, well—a child of 8 or 10 years would have done it as well. I have to hoe all over. & in sawing the wood he fooled round that we are at double expense & trouble. Indeed it is too bad

June 2, 1864 I arose at 5 AM. & got myself ready to hoe my potatoes but when I got out it was raining so of course I donned another habbit & now am conversing with my most trusty friend My Journal. Cora is still sleeping. There Mr Mahler of Martinsburg Va. has just come—Now Cora is awake—Breakfast over It is still raining I received a letter from Mr Cormany—he is still safe & well—he writes that he received a Lieutenants commission shortly before. I told Mrs Mc— she did not seem to like it she said a good many things that were meant to cut—& were hard to take. I made no replys for I knew it would only make it worse. So I just work along in my old even stile & she seems to have gotten pretty well over it—It made me feel very badly She watches closely but I will show her that I am the same as before. She remarked so short—Yes—Some are favered & others are not—What her man got he got honestly & if they got what was due them they could live better too. Well I do not know how things are—it seems unjust that he is kept out of his pay so long[7]—

June 7, 1864 I am still getting better—I cough very much by spell I weeded my garden this A.M. also Mrs Mc's little onions I

6. The use of part of McGowan's large vacant lot was doubtless one of the advantages of moving to the outskirts of the town.

7. The army considered McGowan AWOL during part of the summer of 1863 and docked his pay accordingly. Samuel, in fact, had drawn up the order for his arrest (see Samuel's entry for July 27, 1863). Mrs. McGowan's bitterness is compounded by Samuel's promotion, tainted as it was by Clem's influence peddling, for officers received much higher pay than enlisted men.

want to show her that being a Lieut's wife does not change me. I also helped her to make soap so I got only a few stitches sewed. My cough bothers me much. Cora put very strong lie in her mouth this morning which took the cuticle right off—her lips were only touched with it they are much swollen & sore. A despatch came this P.M. that Capt Harmony was killed. They have had desperate fighting before Richmond last week O! How I long for if but a few words from my husband—to know he still lives[8]

June 18, 1864 I am well, but had a very sore mouth this last week It is well again—but very tender. Cora is well—is sleeping just now The weather is quite warm. My garden looks nice I will soon have beans to cook. Fruit will be plenty if nothing gets over it. I have not heard from my husband for some time. I do wish I could hear. O if he were only once safely at home again to stay—On last Monday the Liberty pole was again raised in the diamond it is materially larger than the one the rebels sawed down I feel blue. I wish I had more religion.

July 19, 1864 Just a month has passed since I last wrote in my journal. I have had frequent communication with my husband during this month. his health is good, he has been in some desperate battles of late, he sent me his commission last week, he seems in good spirits. I long so to see him I wish he were home to stay. Since I last wrote I was a week at Orrstown drying cherries & left Cora with Mrs McG. We have had wonderful excitement about the rebels coming again. they were at the state line & state any amount in M'd Now report says they have gone back again Making for Richmond as fast as they can. We fear here that being they were so successful this time they will try it over & come in Pa. also N. Rebok[pb] is spending a week in town she sems to have changed much for the better since they moved down there. Cora is well & talks nearly every thing quite plainly.

July 26, 1864 Cool this morning. Rained Sunday night & nearly all day yesterday. a nice soaking rain. All has been quiet for a few weeks about the rebels coming—last evening the excitement broke out again & all night farmers were going North with horses &c. A thousand rumers are afloat. If the rebels intend coming I wish they would hurry so the fuss would be over once—

8. Union casualties had been very heavy during the spring offensive of 1864.

August 6, 1864 Just a week this morning the rebels turned up in our devoted town again. before they entered they roused us out of our slumbers by throwing to shells in. this was between 3 & 4 A.M. by 5—the grey back hordes came pouring in. They demanded 500,000 dollers in default of which the town would be burned—They were told that it was imposible to raise that amount—The reb's then came down to 100,000 in gold which was just as imposible. when they were informed of the imposibility they deliberately went from house to house & fired it. The whole heart of the town is burned. they gave no time for people to get any thing out. each had to escape for life & took only what they could first grab. some saved considerable. others only the clothes on their backs—& even some of those were taken off as they escaped from their burning dwellings. O! the 30th July 1864 was a sad day to the people of Chambersburg. In most of cases where the bulidings were left money was paid. They were here too but we talked them out of it. We told them we were widdows & that saved us here. About 3000 were made homeless in less than three hours. This whole week has been one of great excitement. We live in constant dread. I never spent such days as these few last I never spent—I feel as if I could not stay in this country longer. I feel quite sick of the dread & excitement.[9]

August 16, 1864 Just received a letter from My sister & the home folks in general—All write in urging me to come to C.W. to preside

---

9. In an effort to relieve the pressure on besieged Petersburg, Lee sent a force under Gen. Jubal Early to threaten Washington. Early was able to drive quite easily to the outer defenses of the capital, where President Lincoln himself came under fire at Fort Stevens on July 12, 1864. Realizing that his limited forces could not successfully storm Washington itself, however, Early turned instead to lesser targets. The action against Chambersburg was conducted by one of Early's subordinates, Brig. Gen. John McCausland. The damage included the destruction of 537 buildings (266 of which were residences or businesses) along with roughly a million dollars worth of private property. Extensive looting and robbery by Confederate enlisted men accompanied the systematic burning of the buildings themselves. Early, who took ultimate responsibility for this action, claimed he was operating in full accord with the laws of war and was exacting legitimate retaliation for the destruction of civilian property by Union troops under orders from General Hunter in the Shenandoah Valley a month before. Benjamin S. Schneck, *The Burning of Chambersburg, Pennsylvania* (Philadelphia, 1864); Jacob Hoke, *The Great Invasion of 1863; or General Lee in Pennsylvania . . . With an Appendix Containing an Account of the Burning of Chambersburg, Pennsylvania* (rpt. Dayton, Ohio, 1913); and Jacob Hoke, *Historical Reminiscences of the War; or Incidents Which Transpired In and About Chambersburg During the War of the Rebellion* (Chambersburg, 1884). McCausland published his own version of the incident in *Annals of the War Written by Leading Participants North and South* (Philadelphia, 1879), pp. 770–74.

Burned out buildings along Chambersburg's Main Street. This photograph was taken a few days after the Confederate raid of July 30, 1864. Photographic Division, LC.

at brother Clems[cc] watercure. I scarcely know what to do. I will write to Mr C. immediately. I can hardly refuse when urged like they do. I have been under the weather i.e. lowspirited for some time. I feel so troubled about almost every thing. I have felt since the last rebel visit to our place as if I could not stay here. I have not received any anss on that subject from Mr C. I had almost made up my mind to spend the winter in Camp with him. Now I do not know what to do—I know I will sleep but little this night for thinking. I rather think the call too urgent to let it go. My health is good, as is also Coras. Cora is getting spoiled—the children here tease her so much that I hardly know what to do. I cannot be whipping all the time. God direct us how to do so the most good will come—

August 20, 1864 Cloudy & air pleasant. Slept pretty well. Cora coughs so much that I was awake often. I feel somewhat alarmed about her. She has had this cough for so long. Such a set of fighting dogs & cats John & Annie are.   they just fight all the time. Annie is an illgrained child & John is rough like boys are. We have had a few days quiet now but the rebel fuss is commencing again. I am so tired of this excitement   John Plough—My stingy landlord, is insane & in the assylum in Harisburg. After the burning he went to McCanicsburg where, I am told he ran the streets hallooing the rebels were after him to take his money.

August 29, 1864 Since I last wrote I spent a week in the country. Bro. John C.[d] was in with his carriage & took Sewing Machine Cora & I along out—His horse got frightened at the cars & very nearly run off with Cora & me—John[d] had him by the bridle & it was all he could do to hold him. I was much frightened but did not know it until all was over—I spent a pleasant week. Sat—I was at the Salem S.S. celebration   from there John[d] brought me home. Mrs Mc seems so queer   not at all like at first. I hardly know what to make of her actions. She is so short & dry. I intend to do as near right as I know how & trust to providence for the rest. It makes me feel badly

September 2, 1864 This has been a pleasant day.   it seems like fall.   I was sewing all day. The Mrs Minichs are still here but intend leaving soon. Mrs McG. is still so crusty, she cuts me off so short before others.   she gains nothing by it I am sure. I felt very badly about it & cried over it & prayed over it & still she acts so ugly—I try all I can not to seem to mind it. She talks as if my husband at fault that hers does not get his pay when away from his reg. last summer. She seems to delight to find fault with him.   that gets my duch up. as long as she picks at me I can grin & bear, but she had better not pick much at my Samuel or she may get some back. In fact I am afraid to do anything for fear of being snapped. She seems to take every chance to give me a snapping & makes chances. Mrs Snyder noticed it when she was here. Mrs Minich spoke of today. She said I need not tell her anything—she has lived here too & had to go through the same ordeal that I am going through now. Said We know Mrs Mc. She is a good neighber but a bad landlady—Mrs M. thinks it is jealousy that makes her act this way—I will try to bear it The good Lord will make it all right If I trust Him.

September 3, 1864 Cloudy, but no rain. Received $30. by express from Father[aa] the ballance due me on Susies[nn] old account. had to pay express on it which I think not quite right & I think they might have thought that far too. I think I would have thought of it. It loolks rough to loan money without interest, discommode my self to oblige others & then have to pay all expense in getting it. I think it a little hard that they did not send the yarn for a hood as I had requested & never say a word about it either. I must not let hard or bad feelings arise. The Lord will be true when all others fail. Mrs. Mc. is quite changed today. she can talk to me again which makes it seem like another place. I feel so sad—so very sad this evening, like weeping. O! for more religion to keep above the troubles of earth. I took my onions to the grocery—got a cantelope, 4 cakes & 18 cts for them, which is better for me than the onions. I know what I think right & good but here I have to keep my opinions to myself to keep peace. I find though I will get along better by being a little independant. & I will take my part henceforth.

September 6, 1864 Still rainy, & gloomy—I went to P.O. every night for some time I am getting tired of it. Mrs Mc & I had a talk she thought I was displeased. we talked the matter over & all is right now again. I am sure I am glad. She knows what was talked only between Mrs. M. & I, so I think she must have been eaves-dropping. both Mrs M's say she is in the habit of doing that. She has many good qualities & she has her faults with the rest of us. & she acknowledges it. I have found her very kind & her ill health has a tendency to make her moody—

September 7, 1864 Recd. a letter from my husband. replies to former letters. little else. Only he says he is appointed Act. Adjutant. Mrs Mc—also got a letter from her husband. he tells her that $136.16. were kept off him—she seems down about it. I do not wonder she needs it badly. Today Mrs Mc— Grandmom & I baked in the oven. I helped Mrs Mc—prepared her apples & P.M. we ironed. I had little for myself so I helped her. It is the same in washing. I think I shall quit washing every week, why should I help a half day for my few pieces. There is no use in it. I am getting so fleshy. I would rather get poore[r] in flesh. both Cora & I are so well. Spiritually I glide along pretty evenly. May be more so than is best. I desire to be good—

September 12, 1864 Sat. Evening. This A.M. Mrs Mc & I went out to the country to get butter. we got none. We brought a load of chipps home. I was very tired. P.M. I went down street to get a few necessary things. got my $20 broke. went to see Scofield about those picture frames but he was not at home. Called to see M. Barnitz—she was not in—Came home. paid Mrs Mc this quarters rent—which would be due Oct. 1st I dislike wonderfully to owe any one.

September 13, 1864 Sunday Morning. It rained very heavy last night & this morning it is very wet. Many apples were blown down so Mrs Mc went & picked them up. It was not her morning. she got about ½ bushel, wonder whether she will divide I am sure I did when the storm blew them down. I did not pick up on her morning once & when she did not pick up on her morning I gave her half. Bro. Dickson is away & some quack is going to preach so I shall stay at home

September 20, 1864 Returned today from the country. I started last Thursday to walk out—took Cora along. Rode with D. Richardds about a mile walked the rest of the way Cora walked fully half way. I had to wonder that she walked like she did. Daddy[ba] was quite friendly, unusually so. Fryday Mother[b] & I peeled an oven full of peaches & Sat. A.M. peeled more peaches. She & I went to John Cormanys.[d] we had quite a pleasant visit. Had sweetpotatoes & fried veal for supper. Had to start in a hurry when the horse was hitched for he would not stand. Sunday we staid at home. I read old letters & wrote a letter to My Dear. Monday peeled peaches in A.M. P.M. went to see sister Elly[y]—took her a few apples grapes & peaches that daddy[ba] knew nothing of. This A.M. daddy[ba] brought me home. Mother[b] gave me about 1 lb. butter, 9 eggs, 4½ qts peaches dried, 1 pk of apples & 16 bunches of grapes & part of a loaf of bread. Mother[b] is a dear good soul. I often feel as if she were almost robbing herself—but then I think it is not out of her pocket &

such little things who will miss it there & how good it comes to me. Mrs McG. seems a little dry to me again. She says she feels blue. I do not understand the woman Mrs Peffly gave me two crocks full of such nice peaches which I pickled, & I got some small tomatoes & put along I think they will be so nice

September 25, 1864 Beautiful day—cut apples all A.M. & put them in the sun to dry. Mrs J. Eckerman called at noon. was in too great a hurry to eat dinner so I gave her a piece. Mrs C. Minnich & Mrs Wiester visited Mrs McG. Grandpap Mohlers boiled applebutter today—I stirred a little. Was to P.O. this evening, intended to mail a shirt to Mr C. but postage would have been 87 cts. which was too high. something detained the upper train so I went into Mr Fullers until the mail was changed, they were picking off grapes for wine, had two very large tubs full, They gave me ½ doz. bunches along home, I gave the children all some. Rec'd a head of cotton with stems & seed by Mail. Mr C sent it. Its so nice.

September 27, 1864 It is cloudy and rains by spells—We are glad for the rain. Tuesday I got Grandpa Mohler to plow my potatoes, he charged nothing for plowing them. I got only about 1½ bushel, last year the same patch yealded from 12 to 14 bus. We washed in the A.M. Wednesday A.M. we ironed. P.M. I mended & now I have my things all in good trim. Daddy Byers[ba] was here to ask me to come & keep house for them while they go to visit an aunt up the country. I told him I would come. I am only to be company to their girl. he is to come for me today or tomorrow. I have everything in trim to leave now but some cut apples which are not quite dry. Mrs Mc would attend to those for me—I received no letter this week from my husband. but got the little box with the head of cotton. he is so good—so mindful of me to send me such mementoes as he thinks will please & interest me. If only this war were once over that he could come home & stay with us. Cora talks so much of him. she looks down st. then says Pappa want da't at all to come. Of late she talks so much about him & I know should he come home she would not know him.

September 28, 1864 Still cloudy & rains by spells. A.M. went down st. called on Mrs Snyder. fook her a doz. nice apples for dumplings & a mess of tomatoes, she had a letter from her husband—he is not well & writes that my husband has sore eyes, poor sould I wish he were home so I could by care & kindness cure them for him, bought me a shawl border—P.M. cut out underclothes. Bro. Dickson called. I do like his calls   Indeed I think if our ministers all were like he our church would be more spiritual— He took Mr C's address & said he would write to him.   had prayer before he left. Evening I took a mess of tomatoes & a doz of apples to Mrs John Christ. I felt sorry I had taken them I think she is not in need of any thing—she was out at camp selling pies & cakes. If I had to give I would love to hunt out the poor & bring them things.

November 3, 1864   Returned from Orstown on the 1st   Cora fell the day before & got quite sick of it, had high fever the two follow-ing day.[10] I went to J. Karpers[1] to dry apples, according to a pressing invitation from them.   when I came there there was not an apple to dry. "the wind blew the apples down so they had to make ci-der."   Well I sewed & in that way paid for cider & apples I got there. I sewed some for Reboks[pa] too. I made my circular. Have headache hence I will retire.

November 5, 1864   Weather changeable, raw & cold—I baked this AM   bread would not raise. I suppose my [y]east was bad, cleaned up my room & did other little chores.   P.M. dressed to go down st.   asked Mrs Mc if Cora could run with her children or stay with her. I never saw such eyes as she made. I forgot to state that just at dinner time she got strangers & was pretty well crowded with work   I offered to assist her but she said she had nothing for me to do   well—I thought then I will hurry my work & then go down st—& get me a bonnet shape & make my bonnet yet today, & when ready I went out as above stated. She said, I have to much to do to keep her & I think you might have helped me clean up this kitchen having strangers & every thing left for me. If it had not been for your baking I would have it cleaned, & you made dirt as well as I did. This she siad just as short & cross as it well could be said. Tears started in my eyes before she got through   I went & took out the carpet & shook it—then swept the yard & wanted to scrub the kitchen but she would not let me   Of course I took a real cry after I got to my room—Now I ate in my room all week & part of the time cooked in here. I do not see how I made much dirt only in baking today. I want to do my part & rather suffer wrong than do wrong—

10. Samuel's sister Lydia wrote Samuel almost three weeks later to tell him that Cora was still not fully recovered from the effects of this concussion. See note to Samuel's entry for Nov. 24, 1864.

November 17, 1864 Weather cloudy & rained some—baked bread
& pies, had good luck. I feel sad—Yesterday Maggie Hasson was
here to see Mrs McG to tell her what news she had in the letter from
her brother. I overheard some thing about the officers & the privates
just have to take it, & I heard Mrs McG say "she is right out here" I
was pealing potatoes at the table outside—they then whispered
something. I was at the P.O. Tuesday evening. I got a letter for
myself but none for Mrs Mc—she spoke rather insinuating—Said
"Well this evening (Wednesday) I am going down myself & if I dont
get a letter I am going to see about it" She is cross at Mr C & told
me what he did to her man—I told her I did not beleive it. Well all
week she acts very strange—in fact since Mr C's promotion there
has been something off & on. she is not like the same person she
was before The good Lord knows I try to do right toward her I do
not know whether I am mistaken, but I just feel as if she were
talking about me There must be something on foot or I would not
feel like I do—Last evening she got letters—she came in the door
rather quiet & fired up stairs & today never said a word that she had
gotten a letter she seems offish—quite so—If I have done ought to
make her act thus I do not know—Lord have mercy & help us live
like christians should. O! how I sigh for my own home—My Lord
Grant that we may soon get there. I am so tired of this way of living.
In this world we need expect nothing but vixations but we strive for
a better one—

November 19, 1864 It is still cloudy—I am well Cora is well all
but her face is still sore—I expect Mrs Rebok[P] this evening, she will
stay a few days. I must confess I am almost homesick. I do want to
see my parents. Strange that a married woman should talk so—still
it is all so—were my husband at home it would not be so—but really
I can hardly stay any longer—My God give me grace to overcome—
Still how can I help weeping over it & sighing for the loved ones at
home—I am the only one away now—soon thanksgiving will be
here & still I will be here alone in a strange land Three are in
heaven, the rest will all be at home on that day—Flow on tears, you
are my relief

November 25, 1864 This is the fourth Marriage Aniversary. The
day was bright & sunny—Lydia (Sisterinlaw)[P] spent nearly a week
with me she came last Saturday. The week was spent right pleasantly. Wednesday she & I with our babies took dinner with Mrs W.
McClintok—She was sick with a beeting in her head—still we had a
fine time of it—We supped & spent the evening with Mrs B.

Hampshire   The day was spent very pleasantly (Thursday)—Yesterday was thanksgiving. L^p & I concluded not to go to church—So I stitched some collars on the machine & tucked a skirt for her babe.   then got dinner—P.M. we went to Mr Dicksons intending to take supper with her—but Mr Rebok^{pa} came soon after we were there & persuaded us to go along to Levi Oilers—so home we came—fixed thing up a little then started. I dreamed so sweetly of my husband that he had come home & we were talking when I awoke & here it was on my 4th aniversary—Soon after breakfast we started home & at 11 oclock they started for home. The rest of the day I spent at home except going to P.O.   I received such a good cheery letter from my husband. I had left Cora with Mrs Mc   I went up stairs sat down a little—told her there was nothing there for her—but that I got a letter—she replied—"I did not expect any thing so I was not disappointed Mrs Cormany—not in the least. I am satisfied when I get one a week—I dont look for more—I was just saying to Pauline this evening—I wish I had as good times as some people"—Why take the times good   "I am not like some people—when I have work to do I do it & not leave it come all at once"—O I think just so I get it done   By this time I was half way down stairs & I just think what is it to her when or how I do my work. If she would mind her own business & let me alone it would be better for her—Well I suppose it seems hard to her that My husband gets along so much better than hers—well—I feel sorry for her & him—I wish them both well—It sometimes seems a little hard that the spleen should be vented on me when I have nothing to do with it.

XXIII

The Siege of Petersburg

July 1–December 8, 1864

Following the Richmond and Trevilian Raids, Samuel's regiment rejoined the main portion of the Army of the Potomac at the end of June in order to help Grant's forces surround the key railhead city of Petersburg, Virginia. The siege that resulted was destined to last some nine months. Samuel's regiment is used to probe for weaknesses in the Confederate defensive perimeter and to make forays against suspected sources of Confederate supply or reenforcement. Samuel figures personally in the death of the Confederate general John R. Chambliss on the Charles City Road, August 16, 1864.

July 1, 1864 Friday. Cloudy misty—Marched at 9 A.M. 3 or 4 miles to Jerusalem Plank Road[1]—Bummed around in the hot sun til 3 PM Then made a scout to the Nottaway River—in the direction of Stony Creek Station—Saw only one Johny and him we brought in with us at 1:30—and camped til morning—awfully hot—

July 2, 1864 Saturday. Took things easy til P.M. then marched via Prince George Court House to about 3 miles from City Point[2] and encamped—making ourselves as comfortable as the extreme heat and choking blinding dust would admit of—

July 3, 1864 Sunday. A Quiet sabbath for once—Time for reading— meditation and conversation—and prayer—only Routine—

July 4, 1864 Monday. Took up march at 7 A.M. to near Light-house Point—and encamped   Had Inspection of Horses 3 condemned for "I" Company—Took a ride to Cav Corps Hd Qrs at Point—

---

1. The Jerusalem Plank Road ran nearly due south from Petersburg. The 16th Pennsylvania was operating behind and occasionally beyond the left end of the Union army's main siege lines. Its object was to help extend the siege line ever farther around the southern perimeter of the city and simultaneously to prevent any Confederate counterattack against the Union's potentially vulnerable left flank.

2. City Point had become the Union army's chief depot for supplies arriving by ship in the James estuary.

The Union supply depot at City Point as it appeared when Samuel was sent there to fetch fifty horses, July 1864. Photographic Division, LC.

July 5, 1864 Tuesday. I was ordered to take the dismounted men to City Point—Drew 50 new Horses—Had a rough time introducing them to the idea of marching by fours, and in any kind of order— Got to Camp 9 P.M. I had supper at 10—mailed a letter to Pet— Took a little xx and retired—

July 6, 1864 Wednesday. Hot but a fine breeze stiring all day— Turned in the Q.M. Dept 3 Horses and recipted for new ones— wrote letter to Pet—and put up my commission as 2nd Lieutant to send home—News comes Rebels are striking Chambersburg.[3]

July 7, 1864 Thursday. The finest breeziest night in a long time Mailed Comm & Letter to Pet—Wrote to Mrs D. Woodall & Bro Bernard.[q] Lay around most of day—did some reading & writing— Evening I was at the meeting of the Christian Association of the 16th Pa Cav—It was a good meeting really uplifting to all present. I am well and happy—but longing to hear oftener from Darling & Pussy.

July 8, 1864 Friday. Made application to have "Lilly"—My Iron Grey Mare which we took in from Johnies—doctored up—and put into good shape—appraised as I wish to purchace the animal—Not much doing, in fact chances are poor here today for much doing or thinking outside of routine. My health is fine and my eyes are near normal—and my prayer daily is for that steadfastness of heart that will make and keep me invincible to the gross evils constantly lurk- ing around to entrap one and injure his ideals—

July 9, 1864 Saturday. 6 OCK A.M. we go out on Picket to Prince George Court House   Had a fine place for Reserve—I spent the day rather pleasantly—Lieut Caughy and I called on the Loyal Mr. Sher- man made the acquaintance of old Lady—Mrs David Sherman— They seem to be noble people[4]——Evening relieved by 6th Penna. and returned to Camp at dark.

July 10, 1864 Sunday. Very hot night—Letter from Pet   Good but so short—Inspection. Had my mare "Lilly" appraised—Price Ninety Dollars[5]   Too hot for anything but sweating and panting—

3. See Rachel's entry for Aug. 6, 1864.

4. The Sherman property, located about a mile north of Prince George Court House, is shown on the army's own maps of the Petersburg area. See *OMACW*, pl. LXXVII, no. 2.

5. Cavalrymen were allowed to buy their mounts from the government at a price set by a professional appraiser, if they wished to retain them for future campaigns or postwar service.

July 11, 1864 Monday. Pleasant breezy morning. Took the squadron to water—Inspected Co "I"—am proud of my boys and they delight in pleasing me. Wrote letter to Pet—I feel a little unwell—10 OCK very hot again. considerable fighting and canonading hearable this A.M.—P.M. a General Corps Inspection Eve our men drew 2 days forage and 3 days rations and marched at dusk—Sergt Fritz sent to Hospital Company has his horse, equipments, and arms to care for—

Marched all night—Tuesday break-o-day 12th found us at Prince George Court House—we moved on to the left of the works of the Army of the Potomac on Jerusalem Plank Road

July 12, 1864 Tuesday. Breakfast at 10 OCK A.M. P.M. we had a little fight on the plank road—2nd Pa Cav had the hotest of it and lost 1 Major—1 Lieut and 21 men captured and 4 killed—We had no casualties——Evening 16th and 8th made a reconisance to Lees Mill—2nd Swamp and on almost to Plank road—were fired into—bullets buzzed some but went a little high or wild—so we suffered no casualties—Returned to Camp at 11:30 P.M. Sleepy—tired—without dinner, or supper coated with dust and simply rolled in to sleep My! what a glorious sleep I had—and most of the men likewise.

July 13, 1864 Wednesday. Aroused at dawn—Fed—Breakfasted and were ready to march at 5 OCK A.M. I took our squadron to water—we killed time til 11 A.M. when we marched for Lees Mill Warwick swamp where we encamped at 4 P.M.—a good place to lay up—Capt Snyder—Capt Day—and I had Hd Qrs in a cool shady shed—Outside was extremely hot & dusty—All quiet—no canonading—No infantry firing hearable—Am well & happy—I do so long for a letter from Pet, a strange lull—All in wonder Whats brewing? Whats up? What is up? That all is so quiet?

July 14, 1864 Thursday. Cool breezy night where we lay. Hot but airy morning—I sent letter to Pet written 11th At 7 A.M. went out on picket near 2nd swamp on Petersburg and Norfolk R.R.—Our mess had first new potatoes for Dinner—P.M. Lieut Brown shot by a Bushwhacker—9 buckshot through his leg—bone not injured—I had my company in Wilsons Reserve—Our lines very much annoyed by lurkers of the lowest order or grade—But, we'll soon peck-m-out. and get rid of them as we have previously, elsewhere—

458

July 15, 1864 Friday. I slept most of the night, a man of "F" Co wounded last night on post in breast, slightly, by a whacker, was sent out with me with my "I" Co. to scout & scour the country where the shooting occurred. We scoured 1½ miles of country, but found no enemy—So we returned to Caughys Reserve—and had some of my men posted—I spent the day rather agreeably—Ripe Apples—New Potatoes plentifull Huckleberries ripening—Hot and dusty! Very little firing on Picket line—

July 16, 1864 Saturday. I slept, leaning up against a hugh pine—some alarms along line—Everybody on high tension of alertness—I was sent out with 26 men to do scouting—which is a thing I enjoy—always feel alive at. Captured a Rebel mail, the Post Masters Blanket and commission.[6] drove in Capt Malabones pickets 1 mile from Disputanta Station[7] and P.O.—Return safely and had Fowl, Potatoes and fine ripe apples for Dinner——Eve. were relieved from Picket duty by 1st Cav Div and returned to old camp two miles from Light House Point at 9 P.M.—

July 17, 1864 Sunday. Hot—dry—dusty very much—Recd O! such a good letter from my Darling—Thank the good Lord for such a good precious wife—Changed Camp into woods. Fine place.
I am well and happy and doubly so knowing that my Rachel and Cora are well and O so devoted to me—

July 18, 1864 Monday. Cloudy—Mailed letter and Relics to Pet—Took a little morning ride—Then had a sleep of two hours—Feel finely—Had my Company "I" rebuild their tents and the squadron fix up in style—P.M. feel quite dull and tired Got a little stimulent—Read a/c of Rebs in M'd etc. Eve our Darkies had a jubilee for our amusement and their Joy!

July 19, 1864 Tuesday. It rains, O Joy! It rains—Recd splendid letter from Pet! Rained all day long so there was nothing doing but

6. Samuel wrote a short letter on the back of this commission and sent it home to Rachel. Issued in February, 1863, by Confederate Postmaster General John H. Reagan, the document appointed John F. Brochwell postmaster at Disputanta. Samuel's letter, dated July 16, 1864, at "Picket Reserve, 2nd Swamp, Norfolk & Petersburg R.R.," repeats almost verbatim what Samuel recorded about the incident in his diary. His letter ended with the line, "Preserve this commission," which Rachel evidently did, for the memento was among the family papers.

7. A depot on the Norfolk and Petersburg Railroad, southeast of where the Union army was concentrated.

routine and being glad—Health—good spirits—fine, everything Eve Capt Cole of 4th & Lieut Hal called—Darkies had
another Jubilee. Dancing, "patting Juba" &c[8] Hear heavy cannonading & musketry, out on Infantry line—

July 20, 1864 Wednesday. Fine!—I left Dr LeMoyne have Funkeys
Horse for a time—Not much of interest going on—I assisted Sergt
Brewer D Polly[9] to get his discharge properly on foot preparatory to
being mustered as 2nd Lieutenant—
    Hear canonading most of day P.M. Had General Inspection—1
Horse—4 S. Blankets, 1 Saber—5 S. Tents Condemned—

July 21, 1864 Thursday. Routine—Mailed letter to Pet, went to Brigade Commissary bought $5.00 worth of rations—Living is expen-
sive—Lieut Billings returned to Regt   Eve Cap & I took baths—The
Christian Association Met off in the woods, had a real good meeting—O this is fine to steal a little while away and enjoy fellowship
and communion with God—Oh! to be with Pet and Pussy a while to
love & be loved.

July 22, 1864 Friday. Cool—Routine—Mailed letter to Pet—Brother
Bernard,[q] Mrs. D. Woodall. Lots of orders and poppycockism—
nothing serious xcept discipline

July 23, 1864 Saturday. Cool quiet night—Routine—By permission
of Lieut Col Robison I made a trip—with Sergt Woodall—taking my
Orderly along—to know better the line in Front of us—i.e., to know
the lay of the land. Called on Lieut Kindig of Infantry—not in—
Dined in Fort Warren[10] with Lieut Gracy—Saw some Johnies, and
many interesting sights, met many old acquaintances of other
days—and early home life—Returned via City point, met Wm
Weston—who accompanied me. We Called on Saml Wise—and

    8. Patting Juba was a system of handclapping and bodyclapping to maintain com-
plex rhythmic patterns as background for certain types of chants and folk songs.
Dena J. Epstein, *Sinful Tunes and Spirituals: Black Folk Music to the Civil War* (Urbana
and Chicago, 1977), pp. 141–44; Kenneth M. Stampp, *The Peculiar Institution: Slavery
in the Ante-Bellum South* (New York, 1956), p. 369.
    9. Bruer D. Polley had been a sergeant in Company "A" since the organization of
the 16th Pennsylvania. *H16PC*, p. 22. Like Cormany, he was now moving up to a
commissioned rank.
    10. To solidify its siege lines, the Union army built an extensive network of fortifi-
cations designed to prevent Lee from breaking out of the slowly tightening noose
around Petersburg. Cormany was touring this impressive string of trenches, impedi-
ments, and earthwork fortresses.

Sam Mohler[11]—Orrstown boys—Returned to Camp at dark. Friend Weston along. Days observation big with valuable information as to the lay of the land & lines—

July 24, 1864 Sunday. Took my "Lilly" (mare) to Q.M. Robison to have her branded as mine—I made out Bronson D Pollys Rolls to muster in as 2nd Lieutenant—Accompanied him to muster-in and along then to Corps Suttler—Weston now returned to his Battery— We had Co inspection towards eve all quiet—Nothing of interest—

July 25, 1864 Monday. Rained all night—I am detailed Officer of Camp Guard—with 48 men—Capt McDowell Regimental and Capt Snyder Brigade Officer of the day—"Orders" a plenty—I made out requisition for 12 rations for our mess (caps & mine). Eve Capts' Snyder & Robinson had an interesting game at Sucker, and we had plenty of Lemon Punch—that punched.
At mid-night I made the rounds of all Guards—
All O.K.

July 30, 1864 Saturday. We had some doings—scouting—etc about Warwick Swamp—Lees Mills &c

July 31, 1864 Sunday. We had a little brush with the Johnies yesterday P.M. at Lees Mill—we drove the enemy across Warwick Swamp. Our rations and forage run out yesterday—so we are having a hard time—P.M. we were relieved and moved to Price George Court House and encamped in the woods close by—awfully hot & sultry. I am well—and seem happy—but its a tight job when I know my men are hungry.

August 1, 1864 Monday. Still awfully hot—We are ordered to put up camp—I am on duty as Regimental Officer of the Day—
I had the camp thoroughly cleaned up, and all things placed in tasty shape, both for the Men and the Horses—And to the Joy of all Rations and Forage arrive—I drew 5 days for our mess—Cap & I.   I took a fine swim in Monster deep hole—mail letter to Pet—There are exciting rumors of Rebels raiding in Md & Pa. and the evacuation of Petersburg—
Wonderful rumors circulate amongst the Men, especially when not very actively employed, or engaged—

11. During his most recent leave Samuel had hired one of Mohler's relatives to convey his family to his mother's farm. See Samuel's entry for Mar. 6, 1864, and Rachel's entry for Mar. 14, 1864.

August 2, 1864 Tuesday. Hot—Routine—Capt Day relieved me as Regimental Officer of the day—Recd very good letter from Pet and wrote and mailed one—Nothing new—The Boys are pretty well fixed up now—P.M. Reg't went on Picket—Our main reserve is at Mt. Sinai Church and Lieut Caughys' reserve at Mocks and Cap Snyders at Bishops.

August 3, 1864 Wednesday. So we have a good line—well protected by two small bodies near and a large one some farther back— On all day—I rode along the line some, inspecting, at intervals—all quiet—P.M. Lieut Polly relieved my company and we went into Caughys' Reserve—

I took a good sleep in Lieut Caughys Tent. Plenty of apples and mellons to feast on

August 4, 1864 Thursday. Still on picket—I called at some of the neighbors (?) on the line—looking for information—Johnies—and last, but not least, for chickens, potatoes, apples and mellons, &c P.M. Moved my company to main reserve—Took picket men, and scouted some—Made the acquaintance of Miss Russel, a Governess in a Rebel Home, and a Miss Bryant—wide awake ladies—Good talkers—Jolly—Posted on war affairs—Know well how to be agreeable and yet nicely reserved—We gratefully took along some extra melons—apples S&I Potatoes[12]—

August 5, 1864 Friday. Relieved from Picket in P.M. by Kotzes command—Moved to a new camp. Light House Point fixed up nicely— Rations came up, I am well and get along finely physically—and in military lines, but rather retrograding spiritually—God bless poor me and help me keep closer to my ideals—

August 6, 1864 Saturday. Lying in Camp—Fixing up as tho to stay right here—nothing new—about same amount of noise out on the front as usual—I did some letter writing—Bought a Cavalry Vest of Van Wagner for $4.00—A monotinous day—

August 7, 1864 Sunday. Fine shower last night   Lieut Polly and I took a round to the Front—Had a view of Petersburg The blown up Forts—&c. &c[13]   The lines are very close together at some places—

12. Sweet and Irish.
13. Only a week earlier, Federal forces had tried to penetrate Lee's defenses by tunneling under the Confederate line and blasting it. While Federal miners succeeded

So the men can call to each other and talk, when it is understood there shall be no firing—Saw Rev J. L. Kephart, Lieuts Gracy and Kindig. A nice time—Returned to Company at 8 P.M.

August 8, 1864 Monday. Still very hot—I carried a dispatch for General Gregg to Col Kimes to command the Brigade Pickets—I had two orderlies—rode some 18 miles. Considerable exposure at several points, but no incidents——

Eve I took a fine swim—and later **Capt Snyder**, Lieut Caughy and I put away some fine Sherry—Some little **cheery**—Plenty of rumors, but not much of interest doing today—

August 9, 1864 Tuesday. Early orders to march at 8 A.M.—**started** at 11—reached Prince George Court House at 2½ P.M.—**Commenced** fixing up a fine camp—Companies in good cheer. Eve I with **Companies** "I" and "L" escorted Genl J.I. Gregg to the Front, along a part of the line—and back—in good shape—a dandy dash—

August 10, 1864 Wednesday. Routine—Capt Ressler with details from "C" & "I" Companies dug a well—at 12 ft. found supply of water—War news interesting—

August 11, 1864 Thursday. Orders. Change directions of camp—Co's "C" & "I" put into 1st squadron, Capt Snyder com'd'g—General cleaning up all over camp—Finished our well—regimental well—Plenty of fine water—Got some medicine from Dr. Harman for darhea which has been annoying me several days—Eve Dr H. & I take a ride out and have a good swim—

August 12, 1864 Friday. Our camp very comfortable—Rumor says we will lay here a month—A very large percent of the Regiment would prefer to be on the drive and fight to the finish rather than enjoy (?) a nice comfortable camp, and its monotony—

Eve Oh Joy! A good letter from Pet, poor dear! She is at times so frightened by "Cheesetown Rebels" or Copperheads residing about there, and too by Chivalrous Rebels who have been raiding about frightening women & children—But the raid is over and I am so happy to know there will not soon be another, and that my precious

---

in exploding 8,000 pounds of powder beneath their target point on the morning of July 30, 1864, the infantry assault that followed was hopelessly bungled. The eroded and partially refilled remains of the crater—originally thirty feet deep—are still visible at Petersburg Battlefield National Park.

ones are safe and sound and too that I am so sure Our God will take care of all three of us til the war is over.

August 13, 1864 Saturday. Routine—Then commenced diging wells for Horses to water—about noon received orders to prepare to March at 4 P.M.—Command seemed delighted to know, or think a move, and a doing of something, was about on. Wrote letter to my Darlings—Off on time—A thoroughly zig zag route traversed to Point of Rocks, where we crossed the Appomattox at 11 OCK P.M. We lay over an hour or more—Feeding—Then on again and crossed the James River at dawn-o-day—at Jones' neck—Here we Fed and breakfasted and fed and rested quietly.[14]

August 14, 1864 Sunday. Awfully hot—my diarhoea is worse—but feel well—At 11 A.M. we advance on the Gravel hill road to within 10 miles of Richmond—We see some very hard fighting by our in-fantry. Our 1st Maine—2nd Pa and 13th Cavalry had some taste of it too—while our "16th" were picketing—scouting, and taking care of the flanks, and rear, but not much into it——Evening and night were rainy—I got fearfully wet—

August 15, 1864 Monday. Were moved back and placed to support a Battery—later relieved—lay by not far away—I with "I" Co act as Provost—Soon some very hard fighting comes off. We as a Regt not in it at all—Tho we hear it—near us—most of the day—and I wish "I" Company—keep moving about to make sure no surprise is sprung—I realize I am weakening some from my diarhea. But I must stick to my company, brace up and keep out of Hospital—
    Encamped at night where we lay most of day—

August 16, 1864 Tuesday. Broke camp and started out at 5 OCK A.M.—Struck the Charles City Court House road—and the 16th advances out that road   we soon became engaged, and charged the Rebs out of their works beyond the swamp, and they retreat. The country is considerably wooded, sometimes heavily again lightly, with underbrush and clearings, and small farms—The road gener-

---

14. This movement was part of another attempt to penetrate the Confederates' defensive line. Grant had reason to believe that the Southerners were overextended in their efforts to protect both Richmond and Petersburg. He hoped a skillful assault upon the long thin line between the two cities might succeed in breaking through. The plan called for a major infantry attack near Deep Bottom, coupled with a cavalry rush up the Charles City Road toward Richmond itself. Gregg's division, including the 16th Pennsylvania, was given the latter assignment.

ally is crooked and winding, with occasional stretches of straight road, so one could see ¼ or ½ mile or more ahead—and all the while there were little hills or undulations to obstruct the view—Our Regiment—followed the retiring enemy—principally on the road—Tho we had skirmishers out, at times, on the right, or left, or both sides of the road. The Column or body moved generally in the road—— Captain Rush had command of the extreme advance and Captain Ressler supported him with his own company and a portion of Capt Rushes.

The enemy fired occasional shots, but kept well out of our way— General J. Irwin Gregg—our 2nd Brigade Commander, and some of his staff came up on our right, and advanced to the front—for observation——Soon the General sent his Adj't General Maitland to Col Robison instructing him to send a better (adapted) man to take the place of Captain Rush—as The Advance——Col Robison turned to me—I was riding beside him—and said a few words, as to who was out there &c, whereupon I proposed to take 20 men of "I" Company and go out and relieve Capt Rush—This was agreed upon, and I took my men and moved along the side of the column, past Rush's support, and there, beside the road stood Genl Gregg—holding up his bleeding right hand—which a sharp shooter had tapped—As I and my 20 passed—The General said "Cormany avenge that" I replied "all right General. We'll do our duty. (I was not aware of the Genls wound—had only partially understood his words, but gave a response that I knew would convey my determination. The Generals aid, Maitland, told me about it afterwards) and very soon, with my 20 choice men I was at the head of the column and now Ressler and Rush were my supports, and I and my trusty fellows were moving forward—Captains R and R were usually 200 to 300 yards back and The Colonel with the Regiment were ¼ to ½ a mile farther back still—

Occasionally we were fired on from the front, or obliquely from the brush, to which my men quickly responded, but all the while kept moving steadily on.

Now we came to a bend in the road. We could not see 100 yds ahead. My men were in five sections of 4s, About 8 or 10 ft apart. I rode beside my 1st section. bullets buzzed above and about us occasionally—as we came into a piece of straight road, I saw before us in the road—not 200 yds away, a fine looking man in grey, well mounted—"Halt"! he disregarded, but wheeled to get away. My Command "1st section Fire" Sent four spencer carbine bullets after him. He reeled to the left of the road—fell from his horse, and we— 21—were with him—His right hand was over his bosom as he lay on his back—Close to his finger tips—near the middle of his breast, were two bullet holes showing where two of the four shots had come through him from the rear as he vainly tried to get away. Dead! Of Course he was. I ordered one of my men to give me his sword, and belt and pipe—I noticed he was an Officer—but my support and The Colonel now coming up. They took charge of Brigadier General J. R. Chambless body[15] And so I moved out again with my men, and we soon found some forces before us—We exchanged some shots, then, "Front into line" we gave them several volleys—Now my support came up, and formed on our right and left and fired a volley—Then "at will." I realized the enemy were weakening so with my 20 men I charged them—and was followed by my support, and they took to the woods, and to the rear—we followed cautiously—firing occasionally—whenever a Johny came into sight—which became less and less frequent—for some reason— In ½ a mile or more we halted at the edge of the woods, where we had a fair outlook of ½ mile or more—Here we waited til my support and the Regiment came up close—Now I moved on again. The Supports taking care of my flanks—we met nothing formidable, but were fired into rather frequently—by sharpshooters.

As I was riding along in front of my first section, a shot was fired on my right—The bullet passed clean through my "Fancy" dun mare— close in front of my knees and saddle flaps—The animal dropped on her knees too dead to turn over—I remained "a straddle" til my feet struck the ground—One of my Braves dashed to my side with "Lieutenant you can have my horse" I thankfully accepted—Transferred some of my accouterments—Told him to take my saddle—bridle, &c and break for the rear as fast as he well could—And we moved on again in good fashion—The whole affair not occupying 5 minutes. Soon firing commenced again—and became more lively, and we returned fire carefully—seeking to make every shot count—and to show that a few shots could not send us back—By and by we came to a slight curve in the road—with timber and underbrush on both sides—and a little hillock. I saw something looking suspicious— "Halt Men"—"Quiet"—"Divide right and left off the road" "Steady—so—O.K. Boys" "Keep your nerves"—"Do you see that bunch of brush and twigs—at the bend—on the little hillocks"—

15. Brig. Gen. John R. Chambliss, a West Point graduate whose father had served in the Virginia Secession Convention and in the Confederate Congress, was the highest ranking officer on either side to fall in the Deep Bottom campaign. Ezra J. Warner, *Generals in Gray: Lives of the Confederate Commanders* (Baton Rouge, La., 1959), pp. 46–47. Lee himself was deeply troubled to learn of Chambliss's death and wrote that "his fall will be felt throughout the Army."

"Those high brush hide our movements"—"Now men! There's a canon planted right there at that bend. Not ½ a mile away" The Johnies have a trap for us—and are watching—but they have not had any good glimpse of us yet"

"They plan to "rake the road" Should we come along on it—— Now "Ed! you go back—keep out of the road—Tell Capt Ressler ++++ and go on tell the Colonel too—he'll come right up &c" Soon the Col is with me and we plan a trap for them—Back ½ mile or more—So if my advance becomes engaged with any force worth while—and I fall back—and they follow—which we will aim to have them do, there will be som excitement yet this evening—So the Colonel—went back giving orders to Capts Ressler & Rush, and then to the Regiment—The plan is complete, on me and my men rests the opening—and developing—and ascertaining what forces we have been in touch with nearly all day—

It soon comes now—I tell my men—Keep off the road unless ordered on. Be much alive to hearing commands—Keep Cool, and now we are expected by our Colonel to be heard from—So Men! in a moment do good aiming—put 20 bullets into that "Brushpile"— Battery—close to where you know the artillerymen are usually located before opening fire. Now, Ready—Aim FIRE——There is some stir about that masked battery, and next it speaks fiercely, and the shot tears up the road some distance and explodes near where we had been just a little before. Now we send another volley from the brush and another shell greets us. Then a rather heavy volley from infantry cutting the brush about us—and we know we have more force before us than we care to attack, as the shadows of night are falling closely, and so we quietly fall back to our support— keeping our rear well guarded—and the while receiving occasional shots from our friends—The enemy, and sending back sufficient lead to make their following somewhat hazardous—Darkness gathers—and we—our whole command falls back, and goes into camp near where the ball opened in the morning. At once putting out a good picket line and support—and our tired horses were fed and cared for—and our weary hungry men feasted on Hardtack— pork & coffee—and retired wakefully   Recapitulations &c.   5 OCK this A.M. started out Charles City Road—Charge Rebs out of works—Heavy Skirmishing—Genl. Gregg Comes to the front—I— with 20 "I" Co am placed to take the advance—Genl. Gregg slight wound in right hand—Brig. Genl. J. R. Chambliss killed by my men. I obtain his sword and belt—much weak resistance—some sharp shooting—my "Fancy" "Dunn" mare shot by lurking Reb on our right in the brush—I obtained this fine animal—dunn in color with

Confederate Brig. Gen. John R. Chambliss. From Ezra J. Warner, *Generals in Gray: Lives of the Confederate Commanders* (Baton Rouge, La. 1959).

darker spots on thighs—white main and tail—and of delightful movement—rather peculiarly.

John Dullinger (Father of Laundryman Dullinger of Mount Pleasant, Pa.—) had "drawn" the animal—and rode it a long time—I had frequently tried to exchange with him—offering him at one time $10 "to boot" if he would favor me, but "Johny" as I always called him said no I want to keep "Dunny"—

By and by an order came from Brigade Hd Qrs for a good reliable man to be sent up for help in the ambulance corps and hospital— The Colonel sent Johny—Soon Johny returned saying he had no need of a horse—and had to "turn him in"—so I lost no time in persuading the Col allow me to have "Dunny"—After a few month—I had to abandon her Dead!

August 17, 1864 Wednesday. Have diarhea again—I am really weak—but I cannot think of leaving my companys interests in anothers hands—They—Heaven bless the "Boys"—fight so nobly with and for me that nothing but the actual necessity can separate us—

Exchanged our pickets and "lay round" rather restfully—

Had Inspection and turned in a few wounded and played out horses—and some equipments—

P.M. Capt Snyder—returned to the Regt. Is some better—Eve we moved into the woods—Rains a little—There is some Picket firing

August 18, 1864 Thursday. Chiefly resting up—not at par—P.M. we go on Picket on "Gravel or Middle Road" and "Charles City Road"—Rebs made attack on our whole picket line—not very severe, but they found us ready everywhere, and they withdrew and quieted down—or rather we repulsed them—Eve Rained some— Later some firing on our pickets by concealed Johnies.

August 19, 1864 Friday. Cloudy—rainy—With "I" Co—we lie in main reserve—Large mail came to us—Very good letter from Pet— Good news from Mobile[16]—Still quite unwell and weakened— Eve—Rainy—Things look quite squally—We expect an attack—But are not to bring on an attack—needlesly—

August 20, 1864 Saturday. Rainy—Wrote and mailed letter to Pet— —We are expecting to be driven (?) off this line, everything in our rear has withdrawn—Cap Rush and I sent to picket Chas City road—Johnies reserve at one point in full view—I signaled for a Johnie to meet me between the lines—on friendly terms. Each of us waving a paper "Com on"—We met—and talked over the days fighting 16th—He knew Genl. Chambless personally. I had on the

---

16. Two weeks earlier a fleet under Adm. David G. Farragut had achieved one of the most significant naval victories of the war at Mobile Bay.

Genls sword—which he recognized.[17] I pulled out the Genls pipe—he said he saw The Genl smoking that pipe on that morning—I asked him did he know the Genls family. Said they were neighbors in Lynchburg, Va—I asked could he deliver the Pipe to Mrs. Chambless. Assured me he could—so I handed it to him with these instructions. "Tell Mrs C. you saw the officer who gave the order to fire—and had the General not been more brave than judicious he might have escaped, by surrendering—as my men were too near for him to expect to escape"

I gave the fellow some sugar and coffee—and he gave me some fine "Kilikanick smoking tobacco"[18]—each appreciating the others gift kindness and bidding adieu. All the while the men at the post of each side stood at a ready for any emergency—

We also exchanged Richmond and Philadelphia papers——at 10 P.M. we quietly brought in our pickets, and through mud & rain & darkness wended our way to the Pontoons and crossed the river about mid-night and rested on our arms—

August 21, 1864 Sunday. At dawn we crossed the Appomattox and moved on to 1½ miles from Pr. Geo. C. H where we fed and breakfasted at 10 A.M.—and dried our Blankets—

In the P.M. we moved on to the Jerusalem plank road and put up for the night—

Desperate fighting within hearing during the day, on the Weldon **R.R.—by** infantry[19]—At 10 P.M. we were aroused and ordered to **move near the** R.R. got into an awful swamp—and lowlands—later **found meadow lands** to rest on—

August 22, 1864 **Monday.** Spent A.M. drying our duds—

P.M. again **move up to the** R.R. and go into Camp—Eve I call on some 21st Cav Boys—**Chaplain** J.L. Kephart and others—and we are

17. The Chambliss sword has been passed down through the Kiester-Kieffer line of Samuel's family and is now in the possession of Donald E. Kieffer, a great-great-grandson.

18. Killickinick was the most popular brand of smoking (as distinguished from chewing) tobacco in America at the outbreak of the Civil War. It was manufactured in this soldier's home town of Lynchburg, Va. Robert R. Heimann, *Tobacco and Americans* (New York, 1960), p. 154.

19. The Weldon Railroad ran south from Petersburg toward Weldon and Rocky Mount, N.C. On Aug. 21, the infantry succeeded in extending the Federal siege lines across those tracks. This left the Southside Railroad, which ran west from Petersburg toward Lynchburg, as the only major artery of supply still open to the besieged Confederates.

The Federal pontoon bridge over the James River, 1864. Photographic Division, LC.

showered with rain—Oh! such awful rainy times and bad water and poor health. Diarhea, to weaken a fellow—

Then too I come so short of my ideal of a Christian—I seem nearer my ideal of a soldier, in my official capacity as the commander of Company "I."

August 23, 1864 Tuesday. A pretty good nights rest—A.M. we moved out the R.R. scouting. Found lots of corn—apples and some fine potatoes, and some Hard Cider, and so had rather a jolly Dinner time. P.M.—we advanced to Reams Station—and scouting found the enemy in force, and disposed to fight and so we were soon into it briskly.[20] The whole Regiment becoming engaged in rather irregular fashion, charging and counter charging—

By an unexpected dash from some brush in my rear, my "I" company was cut in two, and for a moment seemed to be at the point of hard usage, but—some squad of the enemy had been cut off from their own command—in the confusion—and so charged through to get to their line, doing my men little damage just then, and receiving little themselves, so I immediately reformed my men and dashed after them some distance—at the same time our Regiment—to my right and left—taking in the situation did some good work—carefully firing "at will" and soon our line was well formed and slowly advancing and forcing the enemys line back——Darkness came on—we had a good line, but ceased advancing and firing as there came no response from the enemy.

We remained on the line til 10 P.M. when, leaving a line of pickets we fell back some distance to suitable ground, and bivouaced for the night——Our loss today—so far as known now—is 2 killed and 7 wounded, all of them taken care of by ourselves—

August 24, 1864 Wednesday. We rest—Is very hot—I am exceedingly weak today on a/c of diarhea—Lie around til noon—P.M. go on picket on yesterdays battlefield, The enemys line in sight, but they are real quiet and peacable—Eve write letters—

August 25, 1864 Thursday. We had a quiet A.M. on the picket line—I took a good bath and put on "clean duds"——At 9:30 A.M. skirmishing commenced on the railroad—and 11:30 canonading, and

20. Ream's Station was a depot on the Weldon Railroad about five miles south of where the Union infantry had established its position astride the tracks. Gregg's cavalry division had been assigned to help several units of infantry destroy the Weldon Railroad as far south as they were able to penetrate Confederate defenses.

soon the enemy charged our reserve—being ready we checked them handsomely—Then charged them and drove them some distance but they came dismounted and supported with Infantry and too numerous for our picket force so we fell back to our works—old temporary works—Our Reg't moves to left of works and makes a fine stand—firing carefully and doing good work in the way of checking the enemy line and thining it out some. The 11th Pa some way became demoralized and retreated—leaving our bully old 16th to hold the line—repel the enemy by a desperate charge—and causing them to leave the field. We now after dark placed a line of pickets—and support it—lying on arms—in Reserve til 12 ock mid-night[21]—

We had three men killed—Cline, Hill—and _____. and six wounded of our Reg't——About 1 ock we move back and encamp on Plank Road some 3 miles north of Reams Station.

August 26, 1864 Friday. A day of quiet and restfulness—No enemy annoying our outposts Our Boys are pretty weary and short on sleep—I am using "commissary whiskey" today to straighten up my "inerds"—Rains some today in eve nothing startling—

August 27, 1864 Saturday. Commenced work on Pay Rolls Corp Washabaugh on old "H" Cos Harry Shively on "I" Co—I wrote letters to parents of the 3 Boys killed the other day—Wrote a letter to Pet and sent it.

August 28, 1864 Sunday. Restful day—Letter writing all the go today—Lieut Barnes returns today—P.M. we move camp a mile north of Plank Road—

Stretch Picket line for the Horses—Everything moves along finely today—I am much better—and yearn to attain to my own ideal as a Christian—Soldier—Adjutant—Man—

August 29, 1864 Monday. Fitting up Camp—making out Pay Rolls—I reduce Corporal Thomas—and————and Sergeant Clive to ranks for conduct unbecoming their stripes. And Promote to Corporalship privates Wagoner and Shively on a/c merit—

Things are moving off briskly—and methodically—and my health is better.   Thank a kind Providence.

---

21. When the Confederates counterattacked the railroad demolition operation on Aug. 25, many recently recruited Union infantry regiments buckled in panic while the seasoned cavalry forces fought effectively enough to save a rout.

August 30, 1864 Tuesday. Early routine—General Inspection by Capt Phipps—Saddled up as tho to move—

P.M. Go out on Picket 3 mls south. Capt Barnes commanding "G" Co on out post duty.

I do a little scouting with several orderlies—Call at some homes, see some fine looking southern girls, and enjoy some joviality and sociability—

August 31, 1864 Wednesday. Regiment musters for pay—I receive letter from Pet and O so rejoiced to hear again from my dearest ones on Earth—

P.M.—Our squadron—Cos "I" & "C" relieve Barnes on Picket—Nice quiet time—call and chat with those same Ladies again—Make round of inspection with Col Robison—Is pleased with our line, and Reserve—"Everything lovely" is The Colonels pronouncement—

September 1, 1864 Thursday. Cool by night and Hot by day. Captain Rush relieves us and we return to Camp—

My horse falls with me, and hurts me some—but I simply Thank God it was no worse and keep on duty—

Evening   The enemy makes a charge on the pickets of the 4th Pa joining our line—We are called out to their support. Enemy is thoroughly routed—and quiet is established with no loss to us, but surely some to them—as some of their horses are seen running without a soldier in the saddle—

We keep alert and at dusk Capt Ressler and I made a little scout to the bridge on the enemys line, but found no Johnys—

September 2, 1864 Friday. Very warm—all quiet—Capt Carey relieves Capt Rush on picket—

Nothing of special interest "on the board"   Except Our Co "I" made a scary dash into the Rebel lines in retaliation for theirs of yesterday with no one of our saddles emptied—We keep well on the alert—as we see signs of "a coming"—But they came not all keep quiet—Mail came—Letter from Pet—

September 3, 1864 Saturday. Hot—We are relieved by 1st Maine Cavalry—Return to Camp—Finish up Rolls for pay and have our Horses Inspected by Capt Phipps—"I" Co. two condemned—All quiet—I am feeling some better physically—Very busy times Lieutenant Polly is acting Adjutant—

September 4, 1864 Sunday. Routine—Received Order No 53, assigning me to "Acting Adjutant 16th Penna Cavalry" I took up the duties at once—Wrote and worked in the office all day[22]—

I dined with Col Robison and Surgeon—Dr. LeMoyne—Recd delightful letter from Pet—Eve: Alarm on Picket line—The 13th Pa ordered out—

September 5, 1864 Monday. Very warm—Am writing all day in office, regimental business, and letter to Pet—I am better physically and seek to become better spiritually, mentally, and as a military man and officer—Everything moves along lively. Some indications of a pending battle. Evening—on invitation—attended an "Ale Party" over at the 4th Pa Cav—Lots of good cheer socially, some military discussions, and experiences on tap—and some tapped more Ale than was really conducive to finest decorum—

September 6, 1864 Tuesday. I finished and sent in to Brigade Hd Qrs my Monthly Return—also monthly return of Deserters. Hitherto our Command has used Sharps Carbine—a breach loding—single-shooting gun——Today I make Requisition for the famous Spencer Carbine—a seven-shooter—carrying a thousand yards—I hope we get them soon—as our efficiency would be increaced approximately seven fold in a dismounted fight[23]—

News comes "Atlanta has fallen"—great jollification[24]——The 2nd

22. The regimental adjutant functioned as an all-purpose staff officer and assistant to the regimental commander, in this case, Col. John K. Robison. Adjutants typically supervised regimental paperwork, prepared written orders, and organized the flow of business at regimental headquarters. From this point forward, the official papers of the 16th Pennsylvania (most of which are preserved at the National Archives) contain a large number of documents drafted or written by Cormany, or executed through his orders.

23. The breech-loading Sharp rifle had already provided Union cavalry with a better weapon than the standard muzzle-loaders carried by infantry on both sides throughout the war. With the advent of Spencer rifles, however, this slender edge became a dramatic advantage. Union troopers could fire the seven-shot Spencers fourteen times per minute while mounted, even faster when dismounted. Cavalry units equipped with these repeaters came to be openly feared by the Confederates, which added significantly to the surging confidence and field effectiveness of Northern horsemen. Fred A. Shannon, *The Organization and Administration of the Union Army, 1861–1865*, vol. I (Gloucester, Mass., 1965), pp. 129–42, discusses the decision to begin issuing Spencer rifles on a major scale.

24. Sherman had forced the Confederates out of Atlanta on Sept. 1 and occupied the city the following day. Both in terms of military significance and in terms of Federal morale, this was without question a major victory. It also helped push many wavering supporters back into Lincoln's camp on the eve of the presidential elections.

Corps is fortifying near us and our Cav are preparing for an attack that may be made any time—

September 7, 1864 Wednesday. Am called on for report of deserters in Jan, Feb, Mch & Apr 1864—

I join in the Head Qrs Mess with The Col. and Dr. LeMoyne—I sent in application for leave of absence for Major Swan. Mail letter to my Rachel—I am kept very busy in my official work in office as also on all Parades—Drills—& Reviews.

I have much to learn but delight in acquiring ability to be of service to my regiment, and to do my work well, and enjoy commendation from my superior officers day by day—

September 8, 1864 Thursday. Fine day to enjoy—am well—Capt Snyder went on hunt of his horse—I feel very sensibly the responsibilities of my position.

So many officers and men looking to me to help them in their Reports—i.e., show them how, and to deal justly with them in the matter of detailing them for Picket duty—Guard duty—and any other duty. Eve I called on the "Boys"—in general—an hour—all over camp—They appreciate all little attentions from Head Quarters—

September 9, 1864 Friday. Maj Swan starts on leave—The Reg't went on Picket—I remain in office—Capt Snyder returns—Corp Witherill got his horse—I made out Field Return & Loss & Gain Report. Worked some on "H" Co clothing a/cs—Evening seems stilly, lonely, quiet, so few in Camp—

Lieut McDowell, Dr Harrman and I took a ride to Fort Warren—Pleasant time—

I put on a Camp Guard—

September 10, 1864 Saturday. My yesterdays Reports returned for correction—Oh! that I were once fully initiated into this Adjutancy and perfect in my work—which is so varied   I finished "H" Co's Clothing Book to 1st yearly settlement—Sent in application for Sick Leave 20 days for Capt Olliphant—I put on a Camp and H'd Qrs Guard—

September 11, 1864 Sunday. Cool night—Lots of Orders from Brig. Hd Qrs—Had camp policed or cleaned, and things generally prepared for Inspection. Wrote letter to Pet and Ellie^y—am pretty well—
—P.M. Inspector failed to come—Cold in eve—am chilly.   Throat ailing some—

September 12, 1864 Monday. A good many men have Ague—Sent in Loss and Gain Report, and Lots of others—
Noon Regiment came in off Picket—all O.K.—
I called on the Boys, all around, welcoming them back to Camp—and recd my reward—Eve Capt Cary, Lieuts Barnes, Polly, and I took a ride out to Works. Some rebel sharpshooters tried us, but were poor shots—we took in sights and returned O.K.

September 13, 1864 Tuesday. Nothing of special interest up, but plenty to do in the Office—Had a w melon feast at noon, Made out report of casualties in engagements of 16th ult—Leave came for Capt Oliphant—any amount of orders came in and of Reports called for—

September 14, 1864 Wednesday. I sent in charges, preferred by Col Robison against an "A" Co. man. Make report of officers and men doing service at Sheridans Hd Qrs. Still no letter from my Darling—

September 15, 1864 Thursday. Slept on my new Bunk in Office Was aroused at 10 P.M.—Orders to march at 3 A.M. with 1 days forage and 2 days rations——We started on time and reported to General Warrens Head Quarters at dawn-o-day[25]——Went on a scout or reconoisance in force—Our Reg't—The 4th Pa Cav and General Baxters Brigade of Fifth Corpse of Infantry[26]—
We drove in the enemys pickets via Poplar Springs Church over the Hawks Farm to Clemens Farm—Had some rough little skirmishes but suffered no casualties of note—but got back to Genl Warrens Head Quarters and lay in woods til 8 P.M. I had the honor to become acquainted and have some talk with both Generals Warren and Baxter. Both were very affable, especially the latter—I spent some time in their tents—We got back to Camp about 10½ ock P.M.——Mail had come in—Recd such a good letter from Pet.

25. Maj. Gen. Gouverneur K. Warren was in command of the 5th Corps infantry from March 1864 through the Battle of Five Forks in April 1865. A well-educated officer interested in cartography, mathematics, and science, Warren's feud with Sheridan resulted in his court-martial after the war. *NCAB*, IV, 68–69.

26. Brig. Gen. Henry Baxter, who had risen from captain of a local company of Michigan volunteers, was a 43-year-old veteran of the California gold rush. He had been severely wounded in the Peninsular campaign of 1862, again at the Battle of Fredericksburg in 1863 (where he led the famous boat assault across the Rappahannock), and again during the Battle of the Wilderness (where two horses were shot out from under him). Ezra J. Warner, *Generals in Blue: Lives of the Union Commanders* (Baton Rouge, La., 1964), pp. 25–26.

September 16, 1864 Friday. Slept late—Routine—Sent in Reports &c due at Brigade Hd Qrs at 8 ock—Received marching orders. Started instanter, out the plank road to the Col Procter farm—Then P-M—on to the swamp and Bridge—Had a little fight there, but no loss—Got back to Proctors about 11 P.M. Very tired and sleepy. Fed our Horses—Suppered and then rested on arms til 2 ock A.M. when a supply of ammunition came up for all the men. After drawing, and stowing away a good supply—We started towards the Weldon R.R.

September 17, 1864 Saturday. at dawn The 16th and 8th Pa Cav left ballance of The 2nd Brigade at Poplar Church and advanced 2½ miles to the Weldon R.R.—We met little opposition. So, after gathering all possible items of news from citizens, White & and black, and a few captured Johnies—We returned to the Church--and thence the whole expedition returned to Camp. Weary Sleepy, &c. All prepared to appreciate rest and sleep—

September 18, 1864 Sunday. All is quiet out front—Slept late—I am almost tuckered out—and have considerable writing to do—
P.M. Regiment went on Picket. I went along—Inspected the line. Then returned to Camp and wrote I do so long for a letter from Pet. Dr. Herrman and I take a ride—

September 19, 1864 Monday. I sent in my Tri-monthly-Field &c Returns—Loss & Gain report, Casualties a/c &c &c——Recd Commision for Luther Day—P.M. I visited picket reserve & line. O.K. Wrote letter to Pet. The U.S. Christian Commission brot us some peaches—
I induce Harry Shively to be sent to Hospital—Is a decidedly worthy young man, needs care—Has outcome.
I have James Hart taking care of my Horse &c—

September 20, 1864 Tuesday. Dr. Herrman and I rode out to the Pickets & Reserve—All's quiet—P.M. News of big victory by Genl. Sheridan[27] Eve Marching orders! To be ready to break Camp on short notice—Reg't relieved from Picket by Infantry Late draw For-

27. While the main Union army kept Lee pinned along the Petersburg line, Grant sent Sheridan to clear the Shenandoah Valley of Confederate forces. If Sheridan succeeded, the Southern army would be deprived of one of its most important remaining sources of basic foodstuffs and light manufactured goods. On Sept. 19 Sheridan had taken a long step toward his goal by defeating General Jubal Early near Winchester in the Battle of Opequon Creek.

age and Rations. Call for report of "Fighting Strength—sent it to Brig. Hd Qrs—After all the stir we lie down and sleep.

September 21, 1864 Wednesday. Quiet night—I slept finely—I have James Hart caring for my Horses   Regimental Inspection at 10 A.M. by Capt R.J. Phipps—P.M. Sent all condemned and surplus arms, stoves, horses &c to Hd. Qr. Cavalry Department by Lieut Polly in charge—Eve. Mail letter to Pet—and make out Monthly Inspection Report and sent to Brig. Hd. Qrs—Lieut Swank returned from leave—Sergt Major Applebaugh called and by request I reduced him to the ranks, and promoted Sergeant Russel R. Peeler to Sergeant Major—Applebaugh was to be promoted by some Order higher up—maybe at Brigade Hd. Qrs[28]

September 22, 1864 Thursday. Finished Inspection Report and sent it in by noon—P.M. wrote out some special orders to cover yesterdays doings—Oh! for more letters from Darling and our precious Cora.

Eve had a general social officers meeting at 2nd Brig. Head Quarters. The Generals Gregg and General Davies present[29]—It was a truly pleasant hour to be thus associated with the men away above us in rank and yet in many ways simply our equals! Our Comrades! and to find we had so many things in common, while all the while we were ever ready to lift our hats and recieve orders from them and obey[30]—

September 23, 1864 Friday. News confirmed of Genl Sheridans great victory[31]——Very busy in office—Feel much indisposed to work—Our Officers Mess opened at M. [i.e. noon] today   my Inspection Report returned for correction—Corrected & returned

September 24, 1864 Saturday. Sent in all my weekly Reports by M—war movements seem to be progressing favorably every-

28. Applebaugh was willing to relinquish his office to a friend because he had already arranged a promotion for himself.

29. David McMurtrie Gregg, commander of the 2nd Division; John Irvin Gregg of that division's 2nd Brigade; and Henry E. Davies, Jr., who led the division's 1st Brigade. Davies, 28, a New York City lawyer who had risen to brigade command from a captaincy, was described by contemporaries as "unpolished, genial, gallant." *DAB*, III, 101–02; Warner, *Generals in Blue*, p. 113; Mark M. Boatner III, *The Civil War Dictionary* (New York, 1959), p. 223.

30. On the democratic nature of the Union army and its sense of camaraderie, see Shannon, *Organization and Administration*, I, 167–72.

31. Sheridan followed his success at Opequon Creek with an even more decisive victory at Fisher's Hill on Sept. 22.

where. Troops all in glowing spirits—Eve S'g't Herbert returned to office for duty—Got the best letter from Darling. What a delight to have a precious wife and sweet little daughter at home—safe and happy and all the while loving abody and so often sending expressions of tenderest love and constant devotion.

September 25, 1864 Sunday. Beautiful day—Starts in restfully Read, meditate, and write to Pet—Usual Inspection——P.M. Lieut Barnes and I took a ride to Appomattox[32]—Had a fine view of Petersburg—Genl Butlers works &c &c returning to camp—via along The Line to the Jerusalem plank road &c Eve. I am hungering and thirsting for the righteousness that will bring me to the attainment of my ideal of a man, a soldier, a Christian Officer—

September 26, 1864 Monday. Very busy A.M.—Letter from Pet— P.M. Took a ride after dress parade Evening Had some musical entertainment—God bless those musical soldiers who bring so much heavenliness around Head Quarters at intervals—

September 27, 1864 Tuesday. Busy A.M. straightening out official business—
Noon took a ride to Brigade Commissary for some supplies—a dull day in Camp—Receive Orders to go on Picket tomorrow.

September 28, 1864 Wednesday. Cool—Reg't went on P'k't—
I remained in my office shaping up things nicely—I am not feeling real well—This diarhea attacking me so often and so severely keeps me too weak for the satisfactory performance of my many duties.
Had just retired when orders came to be ready to march at 4 A.M. with 3 days rations and 2 days Forage—

September 29, 1864 Tuesday. Started at 4 A.M. But order countermanded and we resume our Picket line—The enemy hovers along in sight of our picket line quite frequently during the day—Sometimes quite a squad in sight. They are peacable however, and so are our Boys—
Heavy canonading along the main line—at intervals——Eve! All quiet on our p'k't line now.

September 30, 1864 Friday. Pretty restful night for us. Considerable fighting hearable however, and there is lots of excitement, and

32. The river, not the town. Samuel's regiment was stationed just east of Petersburg.

ominous movement of troops of all kinds—and in various directions[33]—We have a fine time, and yet are liable to have a surprise
sprung upon us at any time—and yet not a surprise for our men
understand that the thoroughly wide awake watchful soldier is not
surprised—

October 1, 1864 Saturday. Rained some in the night—All quiet
along our line—Many rumors afloat but no fully reliable accounts of
anything really doing—An all days waiting—Eve prospects brilliant
for a general engagement and our Regiment is fairly itching for it to
open up—

October 2, 1864 Sunday. Still on picket, and in readiness—all
day—

October 3, 1864 Monday. On same line   nothing special for our
Re'g't—
   The Division have had a severe fight—which for once—our old
16th escaped—But we have been on the strain, or tension—or
wound up to the fighting pitch now 3 or 4 days and nights

October 4, 1864 Tuesday. Still on picket on the same line and wide
awake—The enemy annoy our outposts some but make no deffinite
offensive move—
   Lieut Russel of the 1st Maine Cav reported to Col Robison with
150 dismounted men to support our line if needed—I put some on
as Camp Guards—and hold the principal part in Reserve—

October 5, 1864 Wednesday. Still on line   some troops are returning to their camps—on our right and left, lines have advanced
some—we remain—and rest rather quietly—

October 6, 1864 Thursday. All's quiet—weather fine—much cavalry is leaving for camp—
   P.M. we were relieved by the 13th Pa Cav.   Lieut Russel and his
150 men sent to rejoin their Regiments 1st Me Cav   We return to
Camp—we left Tuesday 29th Sept—and proceed to put up good fall
quarters near Fort Stevens[34]   At dark Major Dyer came. His clerk
slept with me—I wrote a letter to Pet—

33. Grant had ordered forceful probes both north of the James near the Richmond
end of the line and west of the siege trenches, in an effort to extend them.
34. Almost certainly Fort Stevenson, part of an outer ring of fortifications south of
Petersburg.

October 7, 1864 Friday. Busy Pay Day throughout the Regiment—I received my pay as Sergeant—til Lieut Muster $32.00 Then Pay as Lieut from May 27 to Aug 31st $347.97 Total $380.10¢——Everything is quiet out along the line—Eve wrote to Pet—Sent her $100—Paid up all bills due the Boys—Suttler—&c Drying blankets &c one of the jobs of the day—Eve cool—windy.

October 8, 1864 Saturday. A call for Tri-monthly return, Tri monthly Field returns, Loss and Gain items—Report of Deserters—Their Descriptive Lists— &c. &c.

P.M. sent in recommendation for Promotion of Sergt M. Cannon by order of Col J. K. Robison—

Eve called to see Harry Shively in Hospital—Is better—and I am delighted—Orders come for Regiment to go on Picket in the morning.

I am a little overworked these days—Need some better help—Late! Write to Pet

October 9, 1864 Sunday. Frosty morning. Regiment went out on picket early—I did office work—Then rode out and reviewed the Picket line, and called a while in the Reserve with Col Robison and other officers, returning to Camp and office early—

October 10, 1864 Monday. Regiment still out on Picket—Am busy in my Office on reports & corrections—All sent in by noon—

P.M. Dr. Herrman and I took a ride to Picket line and Reserve—Took out some Election Literature—mailed a letter to my Rachel and Cora—The Darlings!

October 11, 1864 Tuesday. Cool—not much doing in office

P.M. We held our Election—Regiment returns a strong Democratic majority—Hard to a/c for.[35]

October 12, 1864 Wednesday. Everything lovely in Camp and Office—P.M. Regiment came in off Picket—Eve. all settled down to irregular routine—

35. Pennsylvania, like many other states during this era, held separate elections for state offices prior to the national election day in November. Until 1864, however, a man could vote only in his home district. Republicans led a successful effort to amend the state constitution to allow soldiers to vote in the field. See Josiah H. Benton, *Voting in the Field: A Forgotten Chapter of the Civil War* (Boston, 1915), pp. 189–203. Cormany had some right to be puzzled by the result; Pennsylvania's soldiers as a whole voted 17,888 Republican to 5,232 Democratic in this election.

October 13, 1864 Thursday. Cool—Stormy—Quiet out on line.

P.M. Some stir on foot, an attack seems to be anticipated—After dark our Spencer Carbines arrive—with ammunition—We have a great time issuing them by night—Our men pleased we realize greatly increaced power and efficiency—

October 14, 1864 Friday. Very Frosty—I slept cold—

We issued many special regimental Orders & Circulars &c

Relieved Lt. A. W. Guernsey by Lieut E. Dunn as Acting Regimental quartermaster—Extra-daily-duty-men reduced materially—Col and I decided that too many men were "serving" officers who should be in line—Some of the officers feel it—but their duty is to hire—and ours is to see that our enlisted men are on the line—I may be derided a little, but God knows I shall pursue a straightforward course and let consequences be what they may—The 16th must be ideal, not only reckoned such—Col Robison and I are fully of one mind on that and on all other points—

October 15, 1864 Saturday. Regiment went on Picket again—I am very unwell.

Bloody passages—Have a hard time getting out Reports due—but my help stands by me—and in they go to Brigade Hd Qrs by noon—all quiet about Camp and on line.

October 16, 1864 Sunday. Fine autumn day. Am feeling very weak, but inspected the Camp and sent up my Inspection Report to Brig. Hd. Qrs—

P.M. Lieut Dunn accompanied me on my round of inspection of Picket line and reserve.

Eve feel some better—Letter came from my Rachel and one from Dr. A. C. Bowman.cc

October 17, 1864 Monday. Cool and clear—Busy A.M. in office—Went to see "Harry" my colored man—Paid him $15 and dismissed him—Got another, a good one, right away—and put Our black Colby in charge of the other two[36]—

P.M. The 21st Pa Cav Reported to our (2nd) Brigade—I called on some of their officers—I recd a letter from Adjt Fretz—Poor fellow is not doing well—

---

36. Officers associated with regimental headquarters apparently had sufficient servants to require the establishment of a formal hierarchy among them.

October 18, 1864 Tuesday. Cloudy, warm, Regiment came in off Picket—Leave came for Lieut Burns—Capt Snyder applies for Leave—Lieut Chamberlin tenders his resignation—Our men busy learning to handle & load their new Carbines—

October 19, 1864 Wednesday. Busy A.M. in office—Am pretty well again P.M. We had Regimental mounted drill—a fine time—The men perform most of the maneuvers finely—But we find that it is important to have drills—dress parades—Saber practice—Exercise in the handling of Carbines and Revolvers quite frequently to keep all men in practice, and capable to perform the needed thing at any time and at all times—

October 20, 1864 Thursday. Am very busy in office in A.M. On self xamination find myself now well able to perform my duties as Adjutant of the Regiment both in the Office—on Drill—Dress Parade and on the Field in action. Wish I could say as much of myself religiously.

October 21, 1864 Friday. Our Regiment goes out on Picket relieving the 1st Maine—

I called on Rev J. L. Kephart the Chaplain of 21st Pa Cav—we had quite a profitable talk—for me—Genl Sheridan is having glorious victories and we are "not in it" with him and our Cavalry Boys. But here is our post of duty, and we are obeying orders[37]—I am pretty well, and keep thinking so much of my Rachel and our Cora. Oh! to see them, love and caress them. The good Lord bless and keep them happy—

October 22, 1864 Saturday. I have quite an experience clearing the camp of bummers[38] and sending them out to the Reg't on Picket—&c &c am also busy in office—Capt Snyders Leave came—Goes to see sick wife—Dr. LeMoyne, Lieut Dunn and I enjoy a fine sociable evening in my office.

---

37. Two days earlier, at Cedar Creek in the Shenandoah Valley, Sheridan had won perhaps his most famous battle. His success was dependent in part upon the role that units like Cormany's were playing. By maintaining maximum pressure against the Petersburg siege lines, Grant prevented Lee from transferring troops to the valley.

38. I.e., malingerers. As the siege wore on, soldiers on both sides began to realize that they would probably spend the winter at Petersburg. Under such circumstances chores like picket duty seemed less and less pressing.

October 23, 1864 Sunday. Quiet sabbath morning—I inspect the Camp—All's fine. Rev J. L. Kephart visited me we had a fine chat—Mail came. Fine letter from Rev J. Dickson—P.M. Lieut Dunn & I took a ride to the Regiment on Picket—I inspected the line some for the Colonel—

October 24, 1864 Monday. Regiment came in off Picket—O.K.— Capt Maitland a.a.g.[39] 2nd Brig called to see me, also Brigade Quartermaster Robison Maitland & I selected a site for New Camp to move in P.M.—Moved to new camp in Battery No 37—PM.

Put up fine quarters for Col. R., but only temporary for me, as I have the tip—move again soon—This move, and "fix-up", seems to observers—Enemy spies, and almost any one outside the inner circle—like settling down for the winter—and to our Boys is fine discipline—Preparing them to obey orders, asking no questions— and to proficiency in case of an alarm, or surprise attack—to be able to strike tent and be ready to mount, and for action, in a few minutes—

October 25, 1864 Tuesday. Fine—cool night—Very busy morning— well and happy—but realize my need of greater firmness in resisting evil, and persistance in efforts to attain my ideals as a soldier, an officer—and above all an exemplary Christian manhood—

October 26, 1864 Wednesday. Cool—numerous orders—circulars, &c General indications of a move soon—10 A.M. Received Orders "Be ready to move at 3 P.M."—At once sent in all surplus and unusable ordnance, equipments, &c Took up line of march via near old picket line to Yellow House, bivouaced at dusk, wide awake—Orders to be ready to move out at 1:30 A.M.——Col Robison and I slept together by a fine fire—kept up by our Darkies.

October 27, 1864 Thursday. 1:30 A.M. Cloudy—Threatens rain— Lay by awhile, Took up the March at 4 A.M. towards Dinwiddie Court House Soon ran into Enemys pickets They fall back several miles slowly, and we don't hurry them—next they resist rather stubbornly—3rd Brigade charges them, and they fall back and make another stand—but soon are on retreat again. About noon we become engaged in front—on the left and in rear—Some

---

39. Acting adjutant general.

hard fighting sets in—Our Regiment is ordered to the Front—and we charge them out on Boynton Plank Road to within six miles of Petersburg[40]—

Here—several hundred yards to our right, I observe "Genl Grants Head Qrs Flag" There is a lull in our fighting—awaiting orders—

The Col allows me to dash over to see the General and his staff—I ride up to within 150 to 200 feet of the flag. Genl Grant sits upon a rock at the foot of a hugh old oak—His orderly and Horse near him—and about him stood Generals Meade, Hancock, Gregg & Mott,[41] and others, holding a consultation—There was high tension easily to be seen—Genl. Grant was smoking—deliberately raising his cigar to his lips, taking a puff or several, then lowering it while he said something I could not understand—While thus engaged, once, as the hand & cigar were rising and were ½ way to his face—A Rebel shell exploded in the tree top, but the Generals hand never faltered, but reached his face and he took his puff leisurely—Then— with a word to his Generals—Grant mounted his horse, and the group moved to the right and rear, and in a minute another shell landed where the group had just been—and exploding played havoc with the big tree[42]—

I dash back to the Col. and soon—about 3 P.M.—hard fighting opens up—Our regiment becomes very hotly engaged and keeps at it—holding the enemy in check, and later charging them back a short distance on the plank road—and on the left of the road—through a woods—and across an open field or meadow, here we ran into rebel infantry—So tarried in the woods—dismounted—sent our Horses rearward into a protected dent in the woodland, and as darkness was

40. Cormany was involved in a major attempt to extend the Union position west- ward, across the Boydton Plank Road that ran southwest from Petersburg. If that artery could be cut and Lee's lines flanked, the Confederates would have no choice but to abandon the entire Richmond-Petersburg area. With winter setting in, Lee realized the seriousness of this threat and countered with a major action of his own that eventually blocked the Federal thrust at Hatcher's Run. The campaign takes its name from that small, swampy creek.

41. Gershom Mott, who had risen through the ranks of New Jersey's volunteer structure, was in command of the fourth infantry division at this time. Warner, *Generals in Blue*, pp. 337–38; *DAB*, VII, 287–88.

42. This incident is also reported by Horace Porter, one of the officers in Grant's party, in *Campaigning with Grant*, ed. Wayne C. Temple (Bloomington, Ind., 1961), pp. 309–12, and by Theodore Lyman, an officer assigned to Meade's staff, in *Meade's Headquarters, 1863–1865: Letters of Colonel Theodore Lyman From the Wilderness to Appomattox*, ed. George R. Agassiz (Boston, 1922), pp. 250–51. The exact details of the incident vary from observer to observer, indicating the possibility that Grant and his party may have come under fire more than once as he reconnoitered the enemy's position along Hatcher's Run.

creeping over us—we formed a line along a "worm fence"[43] at the edge of the wood—where we could see dimly across the open meadow 100 to 200 yards—to the edge of the wood where we could hear the enemy—orders to us were "Hold that line at all hazards old 16th"—Our dismounted men lay on the ground, mostly—5 or 6 feet apart—Each man could fire 13 shots—7 carbine, and 6 revolver—without stopping to load—and to re-load took 2 to 4 minutes——Darkness prevails—The line is complete—I bear the order along the line—to the officers not to open fire until the command comes from the Colonel—Then fire carefully—very carefully—carbines first, then if the line comes on, use Revolvers—always aim to kill—as I walked along the line, in the dark—giving the Colonels orders, and returning again, a good many Johny bullets passed me with a buzz—and as I neared the Col. on the right, in looking over my left shoulder I could see a few of the enemy coming out of the woods—I greeted the Col with "All orders given to the whole line" and the Col's reply was "Bully Adjutant, and they are coming"——and so they were, and at the Command, FIRE! There was something deadly going on—and it was kept up til some of the enemy were within 40–50 yards of our fence, when the boys did such awful execution that the enemy broke & ran back—our boys yelling like Hyenas and kept "shooting at will," and cries of the enemy wounded, fairly vent the air.

But they were desperate   They re-formed in their wood and our men re-loaded and a new line came, but could not move our men, and the old fence was some protection to us, while they must come across open space. So! tho some came very nearly across, they were so few, as to stand no show at all——They no more rallied, nor came out to attack us—we tarried 'til 9 ock P.M.—when in the rain—orders came for us to "Mount and move up to the plank road" where we lay til 11 P.M.   Kind of bivouaced. I used 2 rails, laid on end on a 4 rail high fence, and the other on the ground—just far enough apart so I could not fall through—and so found an hours sleep, and the Col did about as well, sitting on a flat rail, in a fence corner close by, and the Regiment, largely lying on the ground—sleeping too—but every man near his horse—and ready to mount and go in if occasion required——But occasion didn't require—we had done our work so thoroughly that no enemy wanted to attack us[44]—At 11 P.M. we take up line of march, on return trip—awful rainy and disagreeable—and slow moving—

43. Split rails laid at angles to create a zigzag line of fence.

44. The Union failed to achieve its goal in the Hatcher's Run operation and retired to its old siege lines for the winter, but the Confederates suffered severely when they tried to turn their successful defensive action into a counterattack of their own.

October 28, 1864 Friday. At dawn of day we bivouac at Yellow House—we find our loss has been pretty heavy—But God pity the Johnies. Scores & scores of their brave boys must have fallen in that old field or meadow.

We had Five killed, Twenty-two wounded and there are seven missing yet—We picket from Col Wyants to Vaugn Road—P.M. we are moved down to picket on left of Weldon R.R. to near plank Road—Towards evening clears up finely.

Everything seems to be resuming its old position &c I am well, but awfully wearied and sleepy, and inexpresibly thankful that I have been able to do my duty well these eventful days—Col and I sleep by a fine fire—Do pretty well at it—we have a restful night—

October 29, 1864 Saturday. Regiment remains on Picket. I return to old camp and have men put up Colonels Quarters, and I get busy on Office work. Returns, &c.

I hand in my Monthly Report—Field Report, and Report of Enlisted men employed as Servants to Officers—This class is being reduced some.

October 30, 1864 Sunday. Our Pioneers[45] busy completing Head Quarters in good fashion—I wrote long letter to Pet giving a/c of late fight &c—I have slight neuralgia in left side of head and upper jaw—So am keeping quiet and restful—

October 31, 1864 Monday. More reports called for—So am busy in office—Have Pioneers at work on Hd Qrs—at 9 A.M. had my desk moved out of Colonels tent into my double-wall-tent-sized-new-office—and set them to work finishing the Colonels Personal quarters——Noon: Regiment came in off Picket duty, in good trim but weary. made out and sent to Brig. Hd. Qrs. Complete "Picket Report"——Eve: In my qrs—Drs LeMoyne & Herrman Lieuts Swank, Dunn and I played "Muggins for the Apples"—I enjoy the social game, but saw that it was gambling, and resolved never again to gamble at Cards or in any other way—Though as a social game, in camp, I will not condemn the pleasant passtime and amusement—

---

45. Engineering and construction teams were frequently comprised of black soldiers at this point in the war. Colonel H. L. Scott, *Military Dictionary: Comprising Technical Definitions: Information on Raising and Keeping Troops; Actual Service, Including Makeshifts and Improved Material; and Law, Government, Regulations, and Administration Relating to Land Forces* (New York and London, 1864), p. 463.

November 1, 1864 Tuesday. Indian Summer Day—Now that I have large office room, I put in Extra Desk for the Serg't Major and Clerk—So I shall have them do much of the writing I have been doing—and I shall examine their Work Reports, and sign them when correct—and send them out—Have Serg't Maj making out our monthly return of deserters &c

I am directing and assisting him when necessary—

P.M. Everywhere we are making preparations as tho we were to remain here some time—Building chimneys &c &c

November 2, 1864 Wednesday. Fine weather, some storms, but for-a-that is pleasant—We are all very busy in the office today on various Reports called for.

I am only beginning to get into the run of matters—as acting Adjutant—so as to make things move off easily—I feel the responsibilities resting upon me as the Colonel's special man—to look after the whole Regiment for the Colonel, and see that the Colonel knows the condition existing in each company—and everywhere, as regards doing duty of every kind, and being an honor to the Command—Oh! that I were a better man, more worthy the position I occupy in this Regiment, and more capable of seeing and doing whatever I should and directing others in all things pertaining to a faithful adjutant.

God make me what I should be in all things, or guide me to make myself such—

November 3, 1864 Thursday. Camp all quiet—Lots to do in my Office, but with such good quarters, and dependable help, I am getting along finely.

I am happy I can so easily get along without whiskey too.

My throat and stomach being so much better—and now I must overcome a tendency to being harsh in matters of discipline, and in the use of language that is unbecoming. O for special grace, so as to overcome all evil, and be a thoroughly good man in every sense of the word—

O to be as good an example, Spiritually, as I seem to myself to be in the military sence—

Capt Snyder returned this eve from Chambersburg, and brought me Oh! so good a letter from my Pet—

November 4, 1864 Friday. We remain in Camp—nothing special doing—Men resting and polishing up generally—Some office work— a fine Dress Parade—Mounted—

Eve at Doc LeMoynes—Brig H'd Qrs—Muggins! Yes—jollily—

489

November 5, 1864 Saturday. All reports made out and sent in before noon, and office ready for Sat-½-holi-day——P.M. Recd order for Reg't to go on picket in the morning—Snyder tells me my Rachel is not as well as usual, and Cora too seemed ailing—Oh! That I could slip in to see, love, and caress them this evening, and occularly demonstrate the love my heart so strongly feels—

November 6, 1864 Sunday. Early routine. Then Regiment went to Plank Road on Picket—I read & Wrote some—spend the day rather pleasantly and restfully—I sent in an application for a pass by U.S.M.R.R.[46] to City Point and return—Business at Dismounted Camp—Eve Pass Approved—

November 7, 1864 Monday. Cloudy—rainy—Took train at Hancock Station at 7:30 A.M.—direct to Dismounted Camp   Attended to business promptly—amidst awful torrents of rain and sheets of mud—

I had the honor to share a seat with General Hunt—Chief of Artillery[47]—on down trip—Got back to station at 5 P.M.—Genl. Gregg was going on train, so I had the pleasure of riding his horse back to Camp—and the Generals Orderly took him.

This has been a wearisome day—I suppered lightly and retired early.

November 8, 1864 Tuesday. Election Day. Regiment voted on Picket—398 votes cast——

216 for Lincoln and
182 for McClelland

A Lincolns Majority 34——I never saw an Election come off so quietly—Not even cheering. Let alone drunkenness, or quarreling[48]—

November 9, 1864 Wednesday. Regiment came off Picket—Finished up Election Returns and sent in—Men resting—

---

46. United States Military Railroad. The Union army had run a spur line from the supply wharves, storage depots, and staging areas at City Point to the siege line itself. For details, see Thomas Weber, *The Northern Railroads in the Civil War, 1861–1865* (New York, 1952), ch. 11; and Robert B. Sylvester, "The U.S. Military Railroad and the Siege of Petersburg," *CWH* 10 (Sept. 1964), 309–16.

47. Maj. Gen. Henry J. Hunt made his reputation as chief of artillery in the Union army, but Grant had promoted him a few weeks earlier to chief of siege operations. Warner, *Generals in Blue*, p. 242.

48. Lincoln's Democratic opponent was George B. McClellan, former commander of the Union army.

Terminus of the Unites States Military Railroad at City Point. Photographic Division, LC.

November 10, 1864 Thursday. Cool—Business in Office brisk—I have it by the Forelock so it cant push me, but I pull it through on a good pace——P.M. Mounted regiment at Drill
Men did finely!

November 11, 1864 Friday. Routine—Rest—10 ock Dress Parade—Fine !!! Evening rec'd Notice of decease of Adjutant Fretz—Died Nov 7"—Poor fellow—soldier gone—we hope "To Rest"—We sent up recommendation for promotion of Capt J. C. Robinson to Major—
Order Recd "Go on picket tomorrow morning.

November 12, 1864 Saturday. Cold and frosty—Regiment went on picket—Sent in Weekly Report by noon——P.M. cold and blustry—I sit beside or before my nice fire in my roomy cozy quarters, thinking reading, writing, and directing office work—Happy, yet aspiring to a nobler, an ideal, manhood and perfection as an Officer—

November 13, 1864 Sunday. Very cold night and morning Read and meditated all A.M. and re-resolve to strive to attain my ideals of completeness in everything I have to do with—

P.M. I rode out to call on the Colonel—the reserves, and ride along the picket line with soldierly greetings for the Boys exposed on the outposts—

Eve read some—wrote to Darling—very cold.

November 14, 1864 Monday. Reg still out on Pkt—Office routine—

P.M. very cold and blustry——Eve Genl Gregg came—Had a good reception for him—a general fine time—at Brig. Hd. Qrs—2 Brass Bands Brig—Flag Presentation—Fine little speeches from many—and general good feeling prevailed—

November 15, 1864 Tuesday. Busy day in office—Finished copying muster & Pay Rolls—

Eve wrote long letter to A. G. Russel,[49] Harrisburg Pa. concerning commision of Serg'ts Heslop and Hilburn—Regt comes off Picket—

Col Robison told me he would now recommend me for promotion to 1st Lieut and Adjutant to fill the place of Former—Lt. Fretz deceased Nov 7″ 1864——Mailed a long letter to Pet and received one—

November 16, 1864 Wednesday. Very cool nights and morning. I wrote a long letter for Col Robison to Genl A. L. Russel concerning commissions—sent his recommendation for me to be made 1st Lt. & Adjt   Copied Letters—Orders &c into our Reg. Order Book—Oh! how I do long to see my Darling and our Cora.

November 17, 1864 Thursday. Regimental Inspection by Capt R. J. Phipps—I accompany him all through—The Capt is a fine sociable—sensible man—

---

49. Adj. Gen. Alexander L. Russell (1813–1885) supervised the official records of Pennsylvania's volunteer units, so promotions had to be registered with his office. Cormany evidently abbreviated Russell's rank in this day's entry ("A. G." for Adjutant General) and Russell's given name in the entry that follows ("A. L." for Alexander L.). Pennsylvania Historical and Museum Commission, archival reference section, Harrisburg.

P.M. set teams to hauling away all camp refuse—and it makes things look fine—

I turn over to Sergt Major the making out of all Inspection Reports—examining and signing them myself before sending them up—

November 18, 1864 Friday. Busy in Office. Sergt Maj and Clerk wrestling with Inspection Report—P.M. Regiment had a fine mounted Squadron Drill—Afterwards I called on Capt Phipps—and A. A. Genl Maitland—nice chat—

General Gregg calls me in to his tent, wants me to give some special attention to writing up 2nd years History of Reg't.   I do not see how to get at many facts, as my predecessors have made so few notes of events—

Evening sets in to storming and raining—Oh! for a letter from Pet.

November 19, 1864 Saturday. Storm keeps up—very busy A.M. in office. Send in the following reports &c Inspection Report—Report of Services Rendered—Tri-monthly Morning Report—Tri-Monthly Field Return—Loss & Gain Casualties—all in by noon——P.M. Still more office work to see done—and I have James McCurdy—Tailoring for me—making some changes in clothing as to fitting &c——Eve. This seems like "Saturday P.M." My weeks work done—George has my quarters cleaned up finely and now 8 P.M I commence to write a letter to Pet. To have my Saturday evening visit—

November 20, 1864 Sunday. Cold, Blustry, Rainy all day—How glad! We have good quarters—Read—meditated—wrote a lot for Darling—I am well and happy but would be decidedly more happy could I once get to see, and talk with, love and caress my Darling Rachel, and our Dear little Cora.   Oh! that could be Heaven!

November 21, 1864 Monday. Still disagreeable—Poured down rain all night—and is faithfully at it now and yet the Regt goes out on Picket—Study of U.S.A. regulations and Caseys Cav tactics—drill—etc. Am quite well and happy—Recd good letter from Pet and wrote and mailed one to her.

November 22, 1864 Tuesday. Cleared last night—Is quite cool Office routine—and some preparation for public presentation of new Flag at Hd Qrs 2nd Brig 2 Div—at 6:30 this P.M.—we had a grand time—some patriotic speeches, and some congratulatory—many officers of other commands with us, and also, there was too much whiskey in evidence to suit some of us—

Later I visited Rev J. L. Kephart.

November 23, 1864 Wednesday. ¼ inch ice—Directed Office affairs—and Studied Tactics &c—P.M. I went out to the Regiment—on Picket an hour or so—Boys are jolly—Major Swan and Lt. Day returned from Leave—Eve fine letter from Pet—So full of sunshine—makes me long to go home a while to my blessed ones.

November 24, 1864 Thursday. ¼ inch ice—Office routine. Regt came in off Picket. Nothing special up—I am well, and anxious to see my Darling Rachel and precious Cora—So I sent in application for "leave of absence" for 12 days[50]—Eve. The men are now settled down cosily and quietly in their good quarters for the night—

November 25, 1864 Friday. Still cold—but O.K. am straightening up all office affairs in anticipation of my "Leave"

P.M. my Leave came approved good for 12 days—will start Sunday—Eve wrote letter to Bro Bernard.[q]

November 26, 1864 Saturday. Busy day—Pushing office work and directing Serg't Major and Clerk as to doing things during my absence. We got Saturday Reports in by noon. P.M. initiated Lieut J. P. Crawford to act Adjt during my absence[51]—Evening Packed my valise so as to start in the morning—

---

50. This application has survived in Samuel's service file in NA. Cormany justified his request for a leave by appending a letter from his sister Lydia, written at Chambersburg Nov. 18, 1864: "Brother Samuel, I am glad to write you that I am well. I came to see your little family on the 17th and am sorry to write you that your little daughter is still suffering, from the severe fall she had a week ago. the shock seems to have affected her brain—she is kind of dull and drowsy and falling away. Your wife is very much distressed. at times it almost seems she would lose her mind. I am often at a loss know what to do for her and Cora. Cora in her spells so often calls for you. 'Oh write to Pappa to come home to poor baby &c. And I thought perhaps by writing you of the state of affairs you might perchance be able to home and see them. I intend to remain here until they get better or worse. I hope for the former, while the latter is to be feared. Mother was in to see us a few days ago—The friends generally are well—write soon. and do come if you possibly can. As ever Your sister Lydia A. Rebok." See Rachel's entry for Nov. 3, 1864.

51. The original order stating that Crawford was to act for Cormany during the latter's leave is in "Regimental Order Book," 16th Pa., NA.

November 27, 1864 Sunday. Left Hancock Statn 7:30 A.M. Boarded the Boat Daniel Webster[52] at 10—Mr. Jacobs, Q.M. Clerk and I take a state room $1.50—Took dinner and supper on Boat—Witnessed the burning of the "Grey Hound", Genl Butlers dispatch boat, an awful sight[53]—The voyage was rather agreeable, would have been more so but for fog, mist, smoke—

November 28, 1864 Monday. Struck 7th St. Wharf at Washington, D.C. at 6:30 A.M.—a very pleasant clear day—obtained breakfast at National Hotel—Later called on Major Clark—drew 3 months pay—Took train 2:50 P.M. for Baltimore—Took tea there and at 7:30 P.M. left for Harrisburg. Arrived at 12:30. Put up at U.S. Hotel. Well, happy and too full of thoughts of home to sleep well—

November 29, 1864 clear, coldish, started for Chambersburg 8:15 A.M. arrived 11 ock. Met my Darling by surprise. O how sweet to meet and greet a wife, so good so true. Precious little Cora knew me. O the joy of it all—P.M. made a very few calls, but spent most of my time—as nature would suggest—to devoted man and wife, and precious little girl—talking and loving. Oh! what a happy man I am being blest with so good and devoted, and child so precious.

November 30, 1864 Wednesday. A little cloudy—Went to Whites, bargained for a Cavalry suit of clothes—
Engaged Horse & Carriage to go visiting—Called on and acquaintance of Miss Rebecca Shively—Found her a very agreeable and intilligent Lady[54]—Spent the evening at Home, with my Darling wife and Cora—Oh! how delightful to be once again at home—sweet Home—

December 1, 1864 Thursday. Pretty cold—made several calls up street—at 10 ock went out to Mothers[b]—dined there. Then took Mother along to Sister Ellas'[y]—Not at home—so we went to Brother

---

52. The *Daniel Webster* was an Aspinwald steamer, which had seen duty as a hospital ship earlier in the war. Anne L. Austin, *The Woolsey Sisters of New York: A Family's Involvement in the Civil War and a New Profession, 1860–1900* (Philadelphia, 1971), p. 54.

53. Some of Butler's correspondents alleged that the spectacular burning of the Greyhound resulted from a plot against the general. Nonetheless, Butler himself escaped injury. See *Private and Official Correspondence of Gen. Benjamin F. Butler During the Period of the Civil War*, vol. V (Norwood, Mass., 1917), pp. 370–71.

54. This is the sister of Corp. Henry "Harry" Shively, Cormany's friend and protege from Company I.

Johns[d] at 4 P.M. Had a fine visit, but I feel sad to think how little of the true patriot my Brother possesses—He seems a little "coppery" but I try to hope it is only in appearance and conduct, and not in deep reality—Evening we had a sweet season of Family Worship— as of old, when as children we used to kneel daily, morning and evening, with Father[a] and Mother[b] in prayer and worship—

December 2, 1864 Friday. Cloudy—we visited at Henrys,[pa] (H.W. Reboks), John Karpers[l]—Had a little chat with Wilson Owens—Eve went to Sister Wilhelminas[i] (Phillip Karpers[j]). Received a very warm reception—Eve called at Uncle Dan Gelwixes—Oh! how sweet it is to visit thus once more my sisters and have my dear good Mother[b] along as of yore, and at the same time bask in the sunshine of my Rachels love and goodness—

December 3, 1864 Saturday. Rainy—we visited Sister Sarahs[u] a few hours very pleasantly—and dined together. Then in P.M. we went to Sister Ellies[y] It seems so odd and comical(?) to see Ella[y] dandle a baby. All her own baby too, and only so few years ago she was "Little Ella"[y] an innocent flaxen haired little girlie——Eve. Clear and cool. 8 P.M. we returned to Mothers[b] what a gala day this has been—

December 4, 1864 Sunday. Cool—We went to Salem Church—Oh! how sweet to occupy the old pew as of long ago, but how changed. To my right sat my Rachel and our little daughter, and all around old familiar faces—Some Ladies I used to think I loved. But ah! how many seats are vacant—or others occupy them—Mothers & Fathers gone to rest. Dined at Mothers.[b] Sarah's[u] & Ellas'[y] were there—nice re-union indeed Eve we and Ellas[y] went to Aunty Gelsingers. Spent such a pleasant evening together with the dear good Uncle & Aunty and all together

December 5, 1864 Monday. Returned to Chambersburg by 9 A.M. Ella[y] dined with us—P.M. did some shopping and called on Mrs Lieut Barnes—Evening Pet and I called on Miss R. H. Schively. Had a fine little visit—I am well, and Oh! so happy to be at home with my "little all"—O! that I were worthy such a loving devoted wife. God truly is good to me to bless me thus—

December 6, 1864 Tuesday. Cloudy—I heard that Brother Bernard[q] is at home so in P.M. I hired a horse & buggy and we went to visit him and his family—Found them Butchering and so very busy—We spent the evening rather pleasantly all around. But, however much I enjoy my visits to dear kin and friends my Rachel and Cora are the main stream of my pleasure and enjoyments—I am sorry to see in my brothers such a degree of hatred towards the Administration and conduct of the war—Oh! That their eyes were opened to see properly the real situation—But Thank God! None of these things move me.　And I am glad I was prompted to come away from quiet peaceful Canada, voluntarily, and to enlist as a defender of our glorious Union and that my Darling too has the same spirit.

December 7, 1864　Wednesday. Returned to Chamb'g by 9 A.M.— went to Artist to sit for vigniette for self in Adjt Suit—and for Pet too—Got my new suit, a little in advance of my Commission, but I have long been acting Adjt, and my recommendation has gone in, and is sure of approval——Made a few calls in P.M.　Evening received many calls. A very pleasant one from Miss Schively and Miss Wampler. Am busy preparing to return to my Soldier Home, and Adjutant work. I am sorry to leave—and happy to know—My Rachel is with me, and seeks to be, at all times, contented with her lot, and even prides in her Soldier Husband—

December 8, 1864　Thursday. Cold. Ground frozen hard—Attended to business preparatory to going back to the Front　Bade adieu to my Darling Wife and precious Cora, and exchanged tenderest kisses and caresses, and at 1 OCK P.M. boarded train for Harrisburg　Put up at City Hotel—Retired at 9 P.M.　Filled with sweet thoughts of my Darlings—and breathing a prayer for them and myself I soon fell asleep—

Samuel in his new uniform. Taken at H. Bishop's New Sky Light Gallery, Chambersburg, this is the photograph referred to in Samuel's entry for Dec. 7, 1864. Kiefer Family.

XXIV
Rachel Moves to the Country
December 7, 1864–February 10, 1865

Three weeks after Samuel returned to the Petersburg front, Rachel and Cora moved out to the farm of Samuel's aunt and uncle, Eleanora and Isaac Gelsinger. Eleanora and Samuel's mother were sisters, and Eleanora had shown kindness to Rachel on several previous occasions. This older couple lived approximately three miles northwest of Chambersburg on a secondary road. Though Rachel likes the Gelsingers, she begins to chafe under the boredom and isolation imposed by life in the countryside.

December 7, 1864 My little Cora & I are all alone—I feel so lonely. Mr Dear Husband was home on leave of Absence—he spent 10 days very pleasantly with me. We hired a horse & carriage & visited all his friends   We had a real pleasant time his Mother[b] was with us 3 days—I think it cannot be that I have to live alone now again. I went with him to the depot. I kept pretty good control of my feelings until I came home. I cannot keep from weeping. I feel quite lost, I know Cora does too, for she keeps talking constantly about her Pappa—She often comes to me & says—"Dont cry Mamma— Pappa will soon come"

December 31, 1864 Another busy month has passed   I was too busy to write in my journal—After my husband left I set to work & knitt or crocheted him a pair of pulseheaters & a pair for the Col. braided & souled him a pair of slippers, crocheted him a lounging cap—made him a shirt, & prepared some little fixing for christmas. Made & braided Cora a cloak. Made a bonnet over for sisterinlaw beside doing my own work & preparing to move. Well now I have moved.   Last Wednesday Dec. 28th Mr. Allison brought my things & Mr H Deal brought me out in the carriage. Everything came safe, but my sewing machine had the treadle stick split off. Motherinlaw[b] came to see me & ate dinner yet for the last time with me. We did not get here (My Husbands Aunt Elenors) until 4 P.M.   Auntie had supper ready for us—I left Mrs McG. in good feeling, she was very kind ever since Mr C was home. Well now I am safely fixed here. I felt homesick the first evening. I wept—I wanted to go to my

fathers[aa] house. I could hardly work at my things. I put little away—
On Thursday I went at it with a will & got things straightened up &
now I am better fixed than since in this country. I have a place to
put my things where they will keep nice & where I can get them
without hunting an hour for them. I have been fixing up my &
Coras clothing a little & begin to feel at home   Antie is kind to me &
seems to sympathize with me.   she & Uncle make so much of Cora
& Cora likes them she is perfectly contented here—only once did
she mention Mrs McGs name & says not a word about John & Annie
McG—I am glad she is so well contented. She has not been well
since out here   The first night we were here she broke out full with
chicken pox   she is very full & I know she must feel badly—she
does not rest well at night. She is better today—but at best is frett-
ful—Today Mr Allison went to town   I got him to get my mill
wheat—& enquire for letters, he brought me no letters but a small
teabox containing two beautiful china teacups & one china saucer &
one common saucer & 2 common cups. All rebel relics I suppose all
were taken when on the last raid. I have such a dear kind husband—He does any & everything he can to make me happy He is
so tender & so kind & loving to me.[1]

January 2, 1865   New Years day passed off very quietly   a few of the
neighbors called. & I wrote letters & read all day—Sat. evening Mr
Allison brought me a small package which John Hassen brought from
Mr Cormany to me   I opened in their pressence—it contained an
oldfashioned tea box in which were packed two beautiful china teacups & two odd shaped stone ware cups one stone ware saucer & a
china saucer—rebel relics—Nice keep sakes. He is ever thoughtful &
kind—I washed today—quite a large wash—got done in good time.
Put Clems[cc] books out to air & read the remainder of P.M. Cora is about
well again. She is sleeping. My health is splendid.

January 6, 1865   Time passes slowly here. It sems as if I had been
here a month & it is but a week.   every thing is so quiet. My mail so
irregular & uncertain. If only my paper would only come once. It is
raining all day & is freezing ice on the trees, the rain is keeping a
continued patter on the spout outside, which makes every thing
within more gloomy—O! What a world we have—full of sin &
trouble   Auntie & I have been taking turn about in reading Parson
Brownlows adventures among the rebels.[2] Auntie likes to read & so

---

1. See Samuel's entry for Dec. 25, 1864.
2. William G. Brownlow, *Sketches of the Rise, Progress, and Decline of Secession; With a
Narrative of Personal Adventure Among the Rebels* (1862). "Parson" Brownlow, a former

do I—& we have plenty of books—still I get lonely—If only this cruel war were once over so my Dear Husband could be with us & we together at our own home—I am nearly homesick to see my parents, I have it very good here—Auntie is so kind.

January 16, 1865 It is now near three weeks since I came here—I like it very well—I feel better contented than when living in town— My expenses are much less. The people more agreeable—I have more room to put my things & where they will stay nice. & the place in every way is much pleasanter On the 13th I rode to Chamb-g horseback—enjoyed it—got another letter from my Samuel—He wants me to go to Camp—He seems almost homesick to see me—I think I will go unless he gets home. Saturday P.M. Rev. J.C. Smith came here—preached in the schoolhouse—I went with him down—Sunday Aunt E, Cora & I went to the red³ schoolhous to hear him preach. He is quite an agreeable man. Aunt & I just finished a letter to J. B. Eckerman⁴—I write about 2 a week to Samuel since I am here.

January 23, 1865 It is raining this morning but not very cold— Yesterday we did not go to preaching the roads were too bad—It had snowed & sleeted on Saturday P.M. Rec'd but one letter from My Samuel last week—So I wrote but one—I am about ready to go to camp—Am just waiting for a pass—Nothing new happens out here. My Harpers Weekly keeps me posted on the general war news & the "Telescope" adds some too—spiritually I get along pretty well—I need more religion

January 25, 1865 Extremely cold. Had sleighers. Yesterday I commenced my drawing again. Read in Fowlers works.⁵ Am much inter-

---

Methodist minister, edited the *Knoxville Whig* in Knoxville, Tenn. at the outbreak of the war. Because he remained loyal to the Union, Brownlow was first imprisoned, then deported to the North. His book, coupled with a lecture tour, made him one of the best-known symbols of Southern loyalism. He later became governor of Tennessee and had a sometimes brilliant, sometimes violent career as a Republican politician during Reconstruction.

3. Probably short for Red Bridge, a tiny hamlet less than a mile from the Gelsinger farm.

4. Joseph Eckerman, one of Aunt Eleanora's and Samuel's mothers's brothers.

5. Orson S. Fowler, a leader of the phrenological movement and an advocate of hydropathy, wrote also on health, hygiene, diet, and related subjects. He and his brother Lorenzo were principals in the publishing firm that produced and marketed most of the literature Samuel sold in Canada. See John D. Davies, *Phrenology, Fad and Science: A Nineteenth-Century American Crusade* (New Haven, 1955); and Madeleine B. Stern, *Heads & Headlines: The Phrenological Fowlers* (Norman, Okla., 1971).

ested. Sent letter to Samuel. Recd. 3 on the 23rd. Practice jimnastics some for my health[6]—I feel better by it. Sunset clear & beautiful

January 29, 1865 Every thing goes on so quiet here that one cannot but wish for an end of winter—The cold too has been so intense that I could not keep warm. Still my time is not wasted. I read many things which instruct. I do not hear preaching or get to prayer or class as I would wish—but the Lord is here too—

February 2, 1865 Started to Chambersburg at 8.45 A.M. I went in to Dr Platts[7] to get teeth plugged & extracted. While Aunt E. drove up to Mrs McGs left Cora there & horse also—came back but nothing being done to my teeth she went shopping. My turn came at last & Dr Platt went in on them with a will. The filling was a little painful—especially pressing the gums back so as to get a wedge in between the teeth—That done the worst job came—extracting—he took the best one first   Well I got a little noisy & considerably nervous—Now for the achy tooth.   it broke off—next the gum had to be cut so as to get at the root.   then pressing his nippers down & taking hold & pulling with all strength & twisting to make it come— O! Ye Gods—I thought part of the head was coming along. Well I did ouch considerably.   the tears came & I shook like a leaf—O Horors, on teeth pulling—If any one wants to wish me any great good—I hope that great good will be that I may never more need to have any more teeth pull—I was at Mrs McGowans she was very kind, but not well—well all I saw seemed particularly glad to see me   Capt. Snyder was at home—I did not get to see him but left a letter & vignette of myself for him to take to Mr C-y. Am sick.   feel wretched—Will retire early—

February 3, 1865 Feel like another person today so much better How glad I am my teeth are out—My gums are sore but not near as bad as I thought they would get—I mended all day Yesterday Aunty

6. The hygienic movement associated with the Fowlers strongly advocated exercise and gymnastics. See Russell T. Trall, *The Illustrated Family Gymnasium; Containing the Most Improved Methods of Applying Gymnastics, Calisthenic, Kinesipathic, and Vocal Exercises to the Development of the Bodily Organs, the Irrigation of Their Functions, the Preservation of Health, and the Cure of Disease and Deformities* (New York, 1864).

7. George Fisk Platt (b. 1835) studied medicine at Yale and dentistry at the Pennsylvania College of Dental Surgery in Philadelphia. After graduating in 1860, he practiced in Chambersburg. From August 1862 to May 1863 he served in the Union infantry, then returned home. George O. Seilhamer, *Biographical Annals of Franklin County, Pennsylvania* (1905; rpt. Evansville, Ind., 1978), pp. 198–99.

got me a dark gingham apron & today she made it—I had eated very little for a few days on account of toothache but today my appetite came—Had a letter from My Dear—I wish he were home—

February 8, 1865 Yesterday & today is very cold & unpleasant—A very deep snow fell yesterday & it drifted in every corner—This morning we had a time shoveling snow—This AM I rec'd a letter from Minnie H. of Vicsburg—How much letters cheer me. I wrote one to L. K. Miller Westerville. Worked at my drawing—& am progressing finely   Cora is very stirring is is so full of pranks that I fear Uncle & aunt will tire of her. O! for grace & wisdom to bring her up as I should—As the Lord would have her. I enjoy religion more than formerly.

February 10, 1865 Beautiful day—Am not very well—Nothing new has transpired except that I finished my picture yesterday. It is a perfect success. Wrote letters to L. K. Miller & R. Winter. I feel lonely. So lonely—Cora seems even more so than I.   she is so bothersome. & wants to be climbing on everything.

XXV
Winter Along the Petersburg Line and Home on Leave
December 9, 1864–March 31, 1865

Despite a general slowing of military activity during the winter, the 16th Pennsylvania Cavalry remains active in the siege of Petersburg, and Samuel relates several incidents of interest. Included among them are an overt example of officer cowardice and an encounter with Confederate guerillas. On February 17, Samuel is granted another leave and returns to Pennsylvania. While with his family he becomes severely ill. A local doctor authorizes him to remain at home through the end of March 1865. This section concludes as Samuel heads back toward Petersburg after the expiration of that extended leave.

December 9, 1864   Friday. Got up at 2 A.M.—Took train for Baltimore at 3 ock—and arrived at 7.   took an oyster breakfast—and at 9 started—Took train for Washington D. C. arriving at 11 AM—all my business attended to by 12—I met Lieut S—and Capt Taylor well soaked—Dined at 2 P.M. aboard the "Dictator"—at 3 P.M. was nearly left behind by some nonsense—

Evening turned out cold and blustry—Got a State Room with Capt Church, a congenial officer—Retired at 9 OCK.

December 10, 1864   Saturday. Very stormy night, awful boating—Many Seasick—about 6 A.M. things looked squally & scary to greeny. 8 A.M. cleared up—reached City Point at 4 P.M. Soon struck camp—Cav. Div. gone—Army on move—Everything looks like a general get up on foot—Mud Mud Mud   I turn in with Lieuts McDowell & Dunn—O! how different from at home with Darling & Cora

December 11, 1864   Sunday. Just returned from leave. Cold, muddy, icy &c

I meet many and conflicting rumors of the commands, and army movements—The office has been quite well kept up during my 12 ds absence—First I wrote and sent a big letter to Pet—Find the Regt is off—likely on p'k't.[1]

Spent rather a dull day in office and surroundings—Oh! that this cruel war were over so all could go home—

Evening a few of our men came in and report that the Regiment is coming—will be in soon—I am well and happy, much more so for having been to see my Darlings—Found some accumulated mail & official business awaiting me—There are seven commissions—and one of them is My Comm as 1st LIEUTENANT and ADJUTANT.

December 12, 1864 Monday. Awfully cold and stormy—Set the Pioneers to fixing up our Head Qrs—

Regiment came in about noon—Awfully glad to see the dear old Boys——Made preparation to Muster out as 2nd Lieutenant and Mustered in as 1st Lieut and Adjutant—Worked in office til late— Major Swan and I slept together—very cold—

December 13, 1864 Tuesday. Extremely cold this morning. I was Mustered out as 2nd Lt.—and in as 1st Lieut and Adjutant 16th Pa Cav today. Thus my Regt honors me again—

I have always done my duty or my level best for My Captain, My Company "H", for the Regiment, and for The Service. Especially for the Cavalry Service. And in return the Regiment has ever done grandly for me.

1st. as a simple Private and clerk for the Capt. I became a sharp-shooter and "for conspicuous bravery" at Shephardstown July 16" 1863 The—Col J. K. Robison—promoted me over the whole list of non-commissioned officers to the rank of Sergeant—and as such I served at times as Orderly, and also as Quarter Master Sergeant.

2nd. Later—After a competative examination—with the ranking Sergt, S. B. Peters, the Colonel recommended me for the 2nd Leuten-ancy of "H" Company—and May 27" 1864 I was commissioned, and June 8" 1864, I was mustered in and June 18" Col Robison assigned me to the Command of Co "I" (all I Co officers being sick—or wounded).

3rd. Next Sept 4th 1864—Our Adjutant being sick—in Hospital— The Col promoted me to the Office of Acting Adjutant (Adjt Fretz died Nov 7th 1864)[2] and Dec 13" 1864 I was mustered as First Lieut. and Adjutant

---

1. Most of the 16th Pennsylvania Cavalry was on what became known as the Hicksford Raid, another foray southward along the Weldon Railroad.
2. Official records confirm the death of Major Isaiah Fritz. *PV*, p. 957.

Thus I have been well treated—but not without determined faithfulness in everything to which I was appointed or assigned—and so, now, I have honor conferred again, and resolve to magnify the Office—

Turned in to be helpful to some others preparing to Muster—Rendered Tri Monthly to Hd. Qrs. Eve recd such a precious letter from Pet—What a Darling she is.

December 14, 1864 Wednesday. Cold—very busy day in office—My Serg't Major and Clerk do finely. Rumors of a move coming on—Eve Dress Parade. Major Swan commanding—Col. Robison returned from "Leave"—The 8th Pa. Cav. Band gave us a fine serenade—Head Quarters in Glee—Some of Brigade staff and officers of 8th & 21st Cav spent the evening later with our Major J. C. Robinson—and I worked in office til late—Wrote to Pet and meditate.

December 15, 1864 Thursday. My office clerk went on "leave." I have Kephart of "I" Co. instead. Full of work all day—The Reg't busy preparing to move camp—I have the "Pioneers" at work all day on new Hd Qrs—

Capt. Snyder kindly lets me have "Billy"—Billy is a neat little bay horse, accustomed to the race track, and to hurdle racing—but too light for a 225 lb man to ride day by day in Army life, but O.K. for me at 135 lbs—Eve send a big letter and my Commission to Darling—and Lieut Swank and I have a fine sing—Then I spend a while in meditation, prayer and new resolves—

December 16, 1864 Friday. Regiment preparing to move.
New Winter Quarters going up. I am very busy in office. Have Corporal Schively acting Sergeant Major—does finely—

December 17, 1864 Saturday. Sent up my Reports betimes—
Moving day for the Regiment. Eve have a detail to move office over into new place and I put up in Colonels Qrs temporarily—

December 18, 1864 Sunday. Am busy all day with a lot of men building quarters, altho it is Sunday. The weather and business demand that we work industriously—while the whole Regiment is busy on the job—we got my office under roof—

December 19, 1864 Monday. Threatens rain—I finish and send in my Tri-Monthly Report on time—an order issued by Col making Corporal Lewis Sergeant Major—I send it to him—Eve we move my

Office Desks into the new house—and it seems the making of a very cozy place—am well and happy—Late: Col & I have a fine talk on religious subjects & morals.

December 20, 1864 Tuesday. Rainy night and today—am busy finishing up my office. For reasons I do not know Corporal Lewis declines the promotion to Sergeant Major and I at once suggest, and intercede, that the Colonel allow me to have Corporal Schively instead and I think I can make the point—

December 21, 1864 Wednesday. Still rainy—much office business on hand, and yet am pushing finishing touches on my office and quarters. P.M. about done—Eve Lieut Barnes' Leave arrives OK— By consent of Col Robison, I issue the order promoting Corporal Harry Schively to Sergeant Major—for this I am greatly pleased on a/c of seeing, for long, real merit in this young man & soldier—

December 22, 1864 Thursday. Awfully stormy all night and today—Busy writing—and directing the Boys finishing up Office & Quarters—

Have Regimental and quarters inspection at 10 AM—Lieut Barnes starts home this A.M. Eve Both my horses gone and they seem unfindable—

December 23, 1864 Friday. Still cold & stormy—Set Harry Schively, my new Serg-Major to work on Inspection Report.

Am very busy myself also—Eve. Still no news of whereabouts of my horses—

A very good letter from Pet—Order: To go on an expedition tomorrow—I am well and happy. Office and everything runs smoothly.

December 24, 1864 Saturday. Coldest yet—Started at 7 A.M. Our 16th & Fourth regiments and some twenty teams via Lees Mill to William Gees', got all the lumber we could haul—While the men were loading I was in the house awhile. Made the acquaintance of Miss Rosa Roder, an inveterate little Rebel—and bewitchingly beautiful—but withall exceedingly interesting socially. As relics I got a fine brass candlestick—a steel & tumbler at Gees—Also found some fine "Apple Jack—We got back to camp at 8 P.M.—I certainly became a wee bit boozy on Applejack—The deceiving thing! Went to bed at once—or soon—and had a fine nights sleep on the exciting day— Exceedingly cold Christmas Eve.

December 25, 1864 Sunday. CHRISTMAS DAY!——I sent Pet, by Hasson—a box with "Relics"[3]—Inspection at 11 ock. Wrote a long letter to Pet—Towards Eve we had Dress Parade, and recd orders for Regiment to go out on Picket in the morning—

I received a Commision for 2nd Lieutenant in "H" Co. for Sergt. S. B. Peters—whom I had defeated in competative examination last May, and though he cursed me hugely, I did what I could to help him improve—and finally to obtain this promotion—I wrote him a letter of congratulation—Made good Resolutions to keep before God and my men—as true soldier.

December 26, 1864 Monday. Rainy—300 men of the regiment went out on Picket—

I was busy in office all day—Am well and happy—Dreamed so delightfully of my Darling, and Cora last night—

Sent in application for Pass permitting Rev H. W. Rebok[pa] to come and visit the Army and me——Good news from Savannah Ga[4]—O! That this war were over—Why should men need to kill each other for the sake of peace? And yet, no peace ever came to man without blood letting—So we'll have to go ahead bleeding the Johnies I suppose til they call out Enough! May it come soon! So Johny and we can go marching home again—

December 27, 1864 Tuesday. Very busy day in office. Straightened up Journal book, Index book, &c   Harry gets on admirably—I can depend on him—I have a bad cold—very hoarse—can hardly talk— Mailed a long letter to Pet—

Pass came for H. W. Rebok.[pa] Approved. Mailed it to him—

December 28, 1864 Wednesday. Cloudy, stormy, etc. Went out to see the Picket Boys—Am really very unwell—Such a bad cough— Set Schively to work on Report for tomorrow.

December 29, 1864 Thursday. Got my chimney re-built—and eaves fixed—Got all reports in betimes—On orders sent detail of 3 officers and 73 men on Picket—and the Regiment—or the 300 men came at 2:30 P.M.——Sergt Major and I made a general "red-up" of all our office blanks, a/cs etc.——Eve Stormy. Commenced a letter to Pet— Oh! to see her & Cora to be with them, never more to part.

3. John Hasson was an original member of Company H. See Rachel's entries for Dec. 31, 1864, and Jan. 2, 1865.
4. Sherman forced the Confederates to abandon Savannah on Dec. 20, 1864. Federal forces occupied the city the following day.

December 30, 1864 Friday. Awfully cold and snow stormy—Nothing of special interest up—My cold is awfully severe—Oh this cough!—Oh! for even a little letter from Pet—

December 31, 1864 Saturday. Very cold day. Had all my Reports up by 3 P.M. My cough & hoarseness some better—Eve. finished & mailed letter to Pet. No letter from her. Must I close a little sadly for want of a letter? The year is closing, closing, closing, and with it closes many an eye bathed in tears for loved ones far away.

1865

January 1, 1865 Sunday. Extremely cold—My cold letting up. Am otherwise well and happy—I kept Holiday—Called on Capt Backer—O.S. Kindig—Capt Merideth, John Crider of the 20th.

Now the New Year has begun. I have fully determined to spend each successive day with a reference to my anticipated home beyond the river—

I spent part of the evening very agreeably with Capt McDowell. Then with Capt. Snyder.

January 2, 1865 Monday. Most beautifully clear and bracingly cold—Busy day in office—I wrote a little missive to Miss R. H. Schively—Harry's sister—Regiment busy putting up "mangers" for the Horses—am quite well again save a little cough—And why is it I get no letter from Pet? Oh! Why this seeming neglect?

January 3, 1865 Tuesday. Still very cold—I wrote recommendation for Lieutenant Swank to be commissioned as Captain of "D" Company and Pealer and Andrews for 1st & 2nd Lieuts. Same Co.

P.M. Started up Quarter Master accounts—Eve snows—Lieut Barnes returns from Leave. Brought me a pair of slippers, 2 prs wristletts & a fine lounging cap. Rachels own "hooking" and making and a lot of Christmas presents from Pet and Cora—and a big fat letter. What a dear good wife I have[5]—

January 4, 1865 Wednesday. Snowed 1½ or 2 inches last night. Clear cold day—Busy day in office—Quiet in camp—routine—Finished letter to Pet. Am well and happy in prospect of ere long having my Darling & Cora being here with me awhile—God bless them.

5. See Rachel's entry for Dec. 31, 1864.

January 5, 1865 Thursday. Snow all gone—sent team for brick & lumber for Serg't Major and me—P.M. I called on A.A.G. Maitland and we had a fine social visit—Eve commenced papering my part the office—making it look fine—

January 6, 1865 Friday. Cold cloudy—Letter from Pet—Finished papering my room.

PM. Rainy—Tent leaks in front part—Wrote Pet in eve—Also to Rev Slichter. Am well and happy, and seeking to show myself and actually be a more noble man and officer of my Country—

January 7, 1865 Saturday. Stormy day. Sent up my reports in A.M. My office is now in fine running condition—With Serg't Major Schively now fairly well posted as regards Reports demanded and most of the routine office work my actual work is greatly reduced—Eve very cold, am well and happy—Wrote some more in reply to Pets letter—

January 8, 1865 Sunday. Very cold—We had Sunday morning Inspection—Being ordered, I sent in my Tri-monthly this P.M. Major West was to see us. Recd another letter from Pet. Answered all and sent in evening mail—I feel kind of sad to know the truthfulness of a few statements in Pets last letter—I have not quite kept up to my own ideals of a noble man. The husband of such an ideal wife. But some one has colored tales and so stirred up my Darling—and she cannot fully realize how hungry one becomes for good things during long campaigns, and how one is liable to spend more than is meet when banqueting evening chance to occur—after victories—

January 9, 1865 Monday. Cloudy—Cold—Regiment went out on a Foraging expedition and scout via Disputanta Station on Norfolk and Petersburg R.R.—1½ miles south. We got lots of corn—Guerillas prowl around and fire into our rear as we come away. Have quite a fight here. a rear-end engagement—At one stand we have 2 men killed, 3 men wounded, and several horses killed or disabled—and are getting away—and emptying a good many of enemy saddles— At this juncture I call out my old Company I—and we charge them furiously, driving them back and recovering our dead and wounded, and leave theirs for them to gather up later——The enemy now withdraws. "I" company falls in with the regiment, and the "return-to-camp" movement is set in motion. After going some distance, the Colonel halts the command and sends the disabled— The Corn—&c towards camp—well guarded——Scouts are sent out to anticipate any enemy that might seek to flank us, and also sends Captain Rush rear-ward with a squad of 8, 10, or more men to find out if any force was following us.

And I took a platoon—16 or 20 "I" company men to support Captain Rush in case of attack. And Regiment proper rested by the roadside awaiting results——The Captain moved along ½ mile or more, and I kept in sight—when underbrush and evening shades allowed sight. Some distance to the front of the Capt I could see an opening of the road into a clearing or farmland—but betwixt me and the Capt was underbrush, so as to measurably obstruct view— Several shots were fired. Then all was quiet—and I charged steadily with my men—to sustain Capt R. and his men if needs be. There was no more firing. We could hear rushing through the woods to our right but could not see distinctly at all—and no shots being fired I simply rushed forward to the support of Rush—On reaching the opening I found no man in sight——I at once sent out 3 or 4 men 100 or more yards as feelers, and formed the rest of my platoon in line at a ready, and set to investigating immediately the road and ground—No horse tracks were plain save such as had moved on the road to this opening, and they had chiefly turned to the right and into the woods rearward. So I or we were of the opinion that the Captain and his men had struck for the regiment. No enemy appeared anyhow—

Now I examined the road through the open and the "barrens" on either side carefully, and found no signs of an enemy, or anyone having been on the ground—save about ¼ mile out the road, across the open, were some indications that a horse had been there at some time.

But all effort to stir up an enemy utterly failed—So I gathered my men, and discussed the situation a little. When I decided thus, my orders were to follow, and support Capt. Rush and his men, if needs be—I did so til he eluded me and I was left in a strange predicament. I waited—with my men, where the shots had been fired——Some of my men seemed quite certain the Captain and his men had gone back hastily to the Regiment—i.e., They had "ske-daddled," and I was without anybody to support, and without any call from the men I was to support, and so without orders, and darkness was gathering rapidly now.

So with my men well in hand, I started on the retreat and before long I was halted by a picket on the road and we were "passed" into the Reserve and to the Regiment—There sat Col Robison by a fine fire, with some officers and men about him, who had been for a short time discussing what had become of Cormany and his men?——First

511

a big cheer rent the air. Then my response "We are all here" and we formed a semi-circle to demonstrate my report—and we were more than heartily cheered—

The camp rumer had been just put afloat that "Adjutant Cormany and all his men were likely killed or captured. Captain Rush had run into a large force of the enemy and had only escaped by a quick "right about face" and a rush into the woods, and a dash to the rear—

The last he had seen of me, he said, and my men, was as he retreated in the woods—he saw us charging right into the face of the force he had so dexterously escaped from without the loss of a man. (except Cormany and his men who were supporting me) But rumor was very rapidly dispelled—and—Captain Rush—The poor fellow was put to shame by the report we rendered—and our actual presence, without a scar—and without even having seen a Johnny—To which every man assented. Now all pickets or outposts were called in—no one of them had seen an enemy nor heard one in the gathering darkness—and we rather hastily returned to Camp—and I at once—about 8 P.M. sent up my Report of our days doings to Brigade Head Quarters.

Col Robison told me to "go to his quarters and place Capt. Rush under arrest til further orders." So I resumed my side arms, and went up. on meeting him I said Captain Rush—The Col orders me to demand your arms and place you under arrest. To be confined to the limits of this camp, until further orders from our Commander Col. John K. Robison—

The Captain handed me his sabre, belt, and revolver, and I very quietly withdrew and returned with them to the Colonels Quarters[6]—
—I retired late, and Oh! so weary—and sad! over the days happenings——Yet summing up was—1st a thorough scouting of the country designated. 2nd a little fight in which we thoroughly routed the enemy with heavy loss to them, and some loss to us—3rd we secured a lot of corn &c and 4" Capt Rush disgraces himself—

January 10, 1865 Tuesday. Rainy Stormy A.M.—I am well this morning, but have such an intense desire to see and converse with my Rachel. Oh! what a dreary world this would be without one to love even though so cruelly separated—

I am proud of old "I" Company. How grandly she stood by me yesterday, even as ever of old—

Rained all day—This evening I feel more sensibly than ever the

6. Augustus H. Rush had served as captain of Company E since Nov. 1862. *H16PC*, p. 8; *PV*, p. 974.

weightiness of the responsibilities resting upon me as being so closely associated with Our Colonel Robison.

January 11, 1865 Wednesday. Clear and beautiful overhead, but awfully watery beneath. Keep well and happy—Nothing of special interest on foot today—but plenty of work in the office—Evening Sergt Maj. Schively alnd I talked til 11 ock—military affairs—Phrenology, Psycology &c.

January 12, 1865 Thursday. Cold—Busy day on Pay Rolls—Reports &c. Beautiful moonlight night! Mailed a nice letter to Pet. Oh for a stroll in some gravel-walked-park with my Darling at my side and Cora chirping along—

January 13, 1865 Friday. We completed a Roster of Field and Staff Officers in Regt. since organization to Dec 31" 1863. Eve delightful letter from Pet.

January 14, 1865 Saturday. Clear—beautiful—fine for the season! I help Harry on Roster touches—to finish—I made a tour of The Regiment on the Picket line & Reserves——MUDY——New orders recd regulating the Furlough business—O.K. Eve recd letter of Dr Herrman and wrote one to John B. Kimmel—Am well, but do so hunger and thirst after my ideal rightness, as a man, a Christian and a Soldier, and especially as a noble Adjutant.

January 15, 1865 Sunday. Rather poor rest—Beautiful day—Corp Merideth called to see me—Eve had a fine social and musical time at Brigade Head Quarters—Made acquaintance of Genl Irvin Curtain[7]— The General and General J. Irvin Gregg spent an hour with us—we delighted them with some of our songs——Returned to Reg Hd Qrs at 9 ock wrote for Pet til 11 ock—I am so inclined to feeling blue— Pshaw! Foolish man! After so much pleasure crowded into the day.

January 16, 1865 Monday. Clear Cold—Regiment came in off Picket—and detail of 81 Men 4 Officers under Command of Maj J. C. Robinson went out on Special point. Busy all day on Regimental History——Eve had a fine long talk with Col Robison on the

7. John Irwin Curtin, Governor Andrew Gregg Curtin's half-brother, was a brevet brigadier general in the Pennsylvania Volunteers, then serving with the 9th Corps infantry. Mark M. Boatner III, *The Civil War Dictionary* (New York, 1959); New York *Times*, Jan. 2, 1911, p. 9.

Religious Moral & Military duties of The Man The Soldier. Our views do most charmingly coincide or harmonize.

I am so glad of this—And we are of one mind to do our level best to make our Regiment The model Cavalry Regiment. With this idea uppermost, I close the day and retire in earnest Prayer to God that I may be favored with wisdom and power to do well my part.

January 17, 1865 Tuesday. General Inspection at 9 A.M. by Maj Swan—Busy day in Office—Called on A.A.G. Maitland on official business—on "Leaves." Eve. letter from Pet—a little agrivating—and I responded a little harshly—Now what a shame I should allow any small thing to mar my happiness and induce the least unkind reflection on my Darling or even anybody else—The dear Lord help me to reach and keep up to my ideals as a devoted husband to the best woman and wife in the world—

January 18, 1865 Wednesday. We had regulation Guard Mount for the first time since I am Adjutant—It had been done any-old-way for some time—We—Col & I—decide its performance will add to good and better discipline—Busy day in office——Eve—Write to Pet—rather appologetically—Heaven bless me and mine, and prepare us to fulfill Thy great design.

January 19, 1865 Thursday. A new Orderly Sergeant out of "C" Company. We had "Mounted Guard Mount." I bought trimmings, Feather, Eagle, Cross sabres in gold, Cord & Tassel for my best hat, costing $9.00 All this in compliance with orders from Head Quarters 2nd Brigade Eve mailed a nice letter to Pet—Wrote til 11 P.M. Capt Snyder is on a grand spree—

January 20, 1865 Friday. Very Cold—First we had a mounted Dress Parade—Came off finely—At 10 A.M. had Mounted Review and then Guard Mounting—The men full of inspiration and vim throughout the whole. We kept a kind of holiday—Eve we had an Inspection of Horse-Covers—The Inspectors were Maj. J. C. Robinson, 1st Battallion, Capt. Ressler, 2nd and myself, 3rd—Snyder still on bust. Harry and I wrote in office til 11½ P.M.——

January 21, 1865 Saturday. Rained all night—rainy morning. Had Mounted Guard Mount——Office full of work. Rains and sleets all day—Am dry and comfortable—well and happy, but Oh! how I would enjoy this evening at home with my pretty Pet and precious Cora. Heaven bless me and them, and prepare us for usefulness in time and happiness in Eternity——Eve Capt Snyders Leave came approved.

January 22, 1865 Sunday. Cold—misty—disagreeable—Had Inspection—after reading and meditation I wrote letters to Dr. Herrman—Uncle Jerry—and a long one to Pet. I tell her how precious She is to me, how I appreciate her continual devotedness to me, how I long to be worthy of all her love and devotion and strive to be better, and a more noble Christian Soldier every successive day—

January 23, 1865 Monday. Rainy—Misty—Routine Study Tactics—Eve we have a Recitation—1st time—

January 24, 1865 Tuesday. Cold—Blustry—Had Dress Parade in A.M. and mounted Squadron Drill—Then in P.M. We had regimental Mounted Drill—and some work in office—Capt McDowell returned from leave. Eve Tactics recitation. Major Swan leaves tomorrow on recruiting service.

January 25, 1865 Wednesday. Very Cold——Guard Mount—Dress Parade and Mounted Squadron Drill in A.M. and in P.M. Mounted Regimental drill—Dreadfully cold—After drill, very busy in office—up till midnight—am suffering some from cold on my lungs—

January 26, 1865 Thursday. Very Cold—Dress Parade—Guard Mount—and Sq. Drill in A.M. and Regimental Mounted drill in P.M. My leisure is quite limited in these days of so much parade drill &c, but we realize it to be fine for the discipline and vigor of the men—I left office work for "Harry" to do, and I occupied my leisure writing a long letter for Pet—Wrote til 10:30 P.M.

January 27, 1865 Friday. Awfully cold—We had no drill—Put the men to work fencing up Camp P.M. mailed a long letter to Pet. Had recitation in Tactics—Recd a good letter from Pet—answered it in part—Sergt Major & I had a nice evenings chat—and he extended to me the compliments of his sister, who greatly appreciates the interest I take in her "Brother Harry"

January 28, 1865 Saturday. Still very cold—Sent in my Saturday and Tri-monthly Reports on time. Corpl Merideth called to see me. I wrote to Dr. Herrman—and Capt Snyder—and some to Pet. Am quite unwell, awful gripings in stomach and bowels—But after drinking lots of hot water and enjoying(?) a good vomit—I am O.K.

January 29, 1865 Sunday. Clear and Cold—We turned out on Brigade. Review at 10 A.M. P.M. I called on Mr Davis's, Then visited Lieut Powders of 207 and saw some of the Boys. "Billy" broke my new bride-bit. Eve wrote letter to Cousin Martha Hampshire. I am pretty well now again—Recd letter from Capt. Snyder—

January 30, 1865 Monday. More moderate—Dress Parade and drill in A.M. Recd very unjust & insulting circular No. 17 from Head Qrs. 2nd Brigade concerning the appearances of our Regiment on Review—at least so it seems to me—But—Sure! it will never be said again of us. Mailed letter to Pet, and one to Capt Snyder—

January 31, 1865 Tuesday. Fine   Companies A,B,C,D,E,F,G,H, & I went out to Picket—Sergt Major busy on returns and I on Historical Sketch—Am feeling unwell—depressed on my lungs—retired early—Colonel came in to sleep. Capt McDowell in command of Pickets—

February 1, 1865 Wednesday. Standing Order—Be ready to march on short notice if called on. Are ready. Routine of Office Work.

February 2, 1865 Thursday. Routine—It seems as tho a move was in the wind—Keeping Office affairs squared up—

February 3, 1865 Friday. Mild—Confidential Order "Be ready to move out on short notice"   Sure will be. Evening I was at Brig. H'd qrs to a social and musical Party—and we did have a fine time sure.

February 4, 1865 Saturday. Moderate—Routine—I recd such a very good letter from Pet this A.M.——Oh! how happy I am to learn that Darling has so materially changed her mind on that one great subject—of having a Boy—some sweet day, not too far away—Thank the Lord—Finished a letter of 12 pages to my Darling——Late recd orders to move out at 2:30 A.M.—I didn't go to bed—Dozed a little before the Fire up to 1 ock A.M.—When I slipped along all company Head Quarters and stirred up all Officers—Attention! Quietly. Feed—Breakfast, and be ready to mount at 3 A.M.—

February 5, 1865 Sunday. 3 AM took up line of march via Tuckers—Reams Station across the creek—The 13″ Cav. charged the Malone Bridge & captured a few rebs and wagons, and all went on to Dinwiddie Court House—The 16th was sent on Boydton Plank Road towards Petersburg and captured Ten Mule Teams, one ambulance and some

25 rebs.[8] I made a little dash on the enemys scouters—some were dressed in our uniforms[9] and my 20 were roughly dressed, and at first only myself and an orderly were in sight—the others were in a cut in the road a short distance back—I saw ½ doz or more about a barn about ¼ mile away. I beckoned them to come up—after a little tarrying, one advanced slowly. I told my men—softly—keep low but ready—as the Johny came nearer—he hesitated—I called "You alls Mosby Men aint ye" Ans came "no were North Carolina scouts"— Well we're trying to find our man Mosby. Come along to the fence so I can hear you better. Maybe you can help us—&c &c. So he advanced a little—and I quietly said over my Orderly—"up cover him." and quickly drew my revolver—now he was less than 75 yards away, covered by a Carbine and Revolver and I called out—"Come on!" "Hurry up"—"You are my man" "Hands up"—now my men came up—and the fellow was limp—as he faced a lot of carbines—He ventured "Who are you all." I threw my overcoat cape back, exposing my shoulder straps—saying, off with that Belt and those arms. My orderly assisted him, and brought them to me—I am Adjutant of the 16th Pa. Cav. and you are my prisoner—Who are you? "I am Adjutant Cook. 24th North Carolina Infantry" How come you here? My regiment lies in on the line—I came with a little cavalry scouting party of Mosbys men (?). How many were there down at that Barn you came from? Not many! I asked you how many about—Pointing to my squad he said about that many—All right—Corp Metz, you and Reasoner take this Adjutant back to the Colonel—Treat him kindly— and tell the Col. I'm after a squad of Mosby men—

Now with my men we dashed across the field towards the Barn— Found no one but a Darkey who told us "Dem's all dun gone long ago—towards de lines—Petersburg——So we hastily returned to our regiment, and in evening we returned to near Rowanty Creek. Roads awfully bad—never saw them worse and its very cold. We bivouac Feed—Eat—and dose some.

February 6, 1865 Monday. At 2 ock A.M. we took up the march and struck the Vaugn Road at day-dawn—I had a bottle of coffee as a

8. Federal commanders had hoped to capture a large Confederate wagon train that was believed to be trying to slip supplies into Petersburg along the Boydton Plank Road. Instead of wagon trains, the Union cavalry met a determined counterattack that precipitated a sharp clash near Gravelly Run, which Cormany will describe shortly. Boatner, *Civil War Dictionary*, p. 217.

9. The besieged Confederate army was desperate for decent clothing, and many Southern soldiers were wearing parts of captured Union uniforms by the early months of 1865.

bracer. We crossed Gravel Run 1½ miles from Hatchers Run and "lay-over" about 11 A.M. The enemy attacked our rear—Our 3rd Brig. and 1st Brig fought some Infantry—Opened pretty lively—and became heavy—real intense. At 3 P.M. our regiment was ordered in and we had an awfully hot time—we made a desperate charge and captured 36 prisoners—and lost 2 killed and had 3 officers and 19 men wounded, but we made a second charge, and drove the enemy across Gravelly Run—Emptying a great many saddles and firing furiously into the fleeing enemy——After dark, firing ceased—all became quiet, and we fell back a short distance allowing the enemy to take up the wounded i.e., their wounded, while we placed a picket line where the charge began, and the Regiment bivouaced farther back, at a wide-awake and ready. Awfully cold. Stormy, snowy—no wood to build fires with but pine—green pine. Oh! such indiscribable weather and circumstances. 2nd Brigade and Regimental Head Quarters all together, and all being smoked alike. But my! how patient all are.

February 7, 1865 Tuesday. Morning—sleeting, raining, blowing and freizing—at 8 AM we form line of battle, and remain in position all day—anticipating attack—as we had taken a lot of ground—I never saw or was out in more awfully disagreeable weather for so long. Sure! These conditions do try mens souls. The Infantry are fighting kind of easily all day—Each knows well the other is there and ready.

Near night fighting becomes terrific for a few hours—on infantry lines close by—

After dark—we draw 1½ days forage, most of our men are out of rations—We bivouac on same ground as last night. Slushy—icy—watery, awful place to sleep—The Col. Dr Le M. Capt McDowel & I sleep under one Fly—

February 8, 1865 Wednesday. A chilly slim breakfast——8 ock A.M. we took up the march for Yellow House. Bleak and cold the wind—We are ordered on picket on Weldon R.R. at the Forks of Reams station and Dinwiddie Court House road—Very muddy, yet cold the wind doth blow——In eve, we are relieved by Infantry at dark we bivouac near by—Awful cold, never endured so much—So much suspense—attack liable any moment on our outposts—and chilly cold—so little wood for fire to warm at—and pretty short of rations—Ah! but such a good letter from Pet. Got a cup of tea at Brig. Hd Qrs. Col Robison, Cap Caughy, Lieut Polly & I slept—Just before going to sleep, our rations arrive—are issued, but men are too tired, and scarce of wood to cook. Lastly, orders received to march at 9 ock A.M. tomorrow—Three cheers for The Red, White and Blue, and Good night.

February 9, 1865 Thursday. Extremely cold—We took up march at 7:30 A.M. via Yellow House, and reached our camp quarters by 9:30 nearly frozen—Found Capt Snyder—Lieut Crawford and Capt Kesslop back from "leave"—Found a good letter from Pet—We make out our Reports—and thaw out—but in early evening retire. Thanking the good Lord for comfortable quarters—

February 10, 1865 Friday. Still very cold—I sent up morning reports early. We had Guard Mounting in A.M. P.M. Sent in 7 applications for furlough—Wrote Pet in response to her last two letters which were exceedingly good.

February 11, 1865 Saturday. Still cold—Reports go up promptly— Rev D. S. Truckenmiller, who is candidate for Chaplaincy preached for us this P.M. very fine sermon—Eve Received a very good letter from Pet and one from Miss Schively—

February 12, 1865 Sunday. Cold and Stormy—We had usual Sunday Morning inspection—Regiment in splendid condition—Read in my Testament, and enjoyed usual meditation—I feel some better spiritually, and am restful in my Heavenly Fathers will—He doeth all Things well my daily—constant—longing is to be enabled to do His will in every detail of my military life and in my Spiritual and Social as well—I wrote and mailed long letter to Pet—Heaven bless her and our precious Cora.

February 13, 1865 Monday. Very Cold Still—Had a fine Guard Mounting—Then a general straightening up of the Office Books and files—

Sent in application for Leave of Absence for myself, and Furlough for Truman C. Wordebaugh—I am happy in my endeavor to do my whole duty towards my God—Myself—My Family and last but not least to those under, around, and above me in the service of my Country.

February 14, 1865 Tuesday. Moderate—Summond to attend Court Martial of Capt Rush Capt Barnes Acting Adjt—for me—Case failed to come up—So I returned to my Office—

February 15, 1865 Wednesday. Case came up. I gave testimony and my men coroborated all[10] P.M. worked in office—I wrote Dr. A. F. Herrmans application for Discharge—and some private matters for Colonel.

February 16, 1865 Thursday. Cloudy—Misty—A fine dress parade and mounted drill—All reports are made out and gone up—
Eve My Leave of Absence came.[11] Busy preparing to be off duty—We had a great thunder storm—Cleared at 10 P.M.—Lieut. Barnes is to act Adjutant during my absence.

February 17, 1865 Friday. GO ON LEAVE Left camp at 6:30—Sergt Major took me to Station—Took train for City point—and boarded The Thomas Brady at 9:30—Started at 10:30—Our stateroom $1.50. Suppers $1.75—River very rough in evening—worse & worse 10:30 retired—Just a little seasick, but lying and musing of home, and my Darlings, who doubtless are now lying side by side—sweetly sleeping—and perchance innocently dreaming of me—How sweet to have old morpheus carry ones loved ones around—cosily—and safely all the night—while a fellow is being tossed around on a none too comfortable bunk—and deliver them safely to the new day when it opens for business—Good night!

February 18, 1865 Saturday. After all I had a good sleep—Got up at 5 A.M. and after a fine wash went on deck—Clear morning—Bay calm—but considerable ice afloat bumping our boat fearfully at times. Reached Annapolis at 8:30 A.M.—Train gone—Store baggage. Get mess Oysters—Stroll some—Put up at National Hotel—Had the honor of forming the acquaintance of Major General Charl Schurz[12] and Capt Szbad—Aid-de-Camp on Genl Warrens Staff (a hungarian).
Lively talk on the situation. They were greatly interested in our late Cavalry exploits and successes, as I related some of them in response to their questions or inquiries.
Left Annapolis at 2:30 P.M. Fare $1.60—Arrived at Washington D.C. at 5:30. Put up at Clarendon Hotel—Found our Old Ex Major West there. Gay and happy as usual. Took supper at 7 ock. Then

---

10. Rush was dismissed from the service Mar. 21, 1865. *PV*, p. 974.

11. On Feb. 13 Samuel had applied for a leave on the grounds that his uncle appeared to be near death and that his two younger sisters and their families were about to emigrate to Iowa. See his service file in NA.

12. Schurz was a nationally recognized German-American political leader. See his account of the Civil War years in *The Reminiscences of Carl Schurz*, ed. Frederick Bancroft and William A. Dunning, vol. III, 1863–1869 (Garden City, N.J., 1917).

went to Canterbury. Tkt. 75¢—amusement sure![13] returning to Hotel 12 ock—Sleep failed me an hour. Am so disappointed on a/c of delay—no train out for Harrisburg til Monday, so good night! Heaven bless and protect me and mine, and check the rending of Our Own dear Fatherland—

February 19, 1865 Sunday. Beautiful day—I called on Major Clark for Pay due—After several hours fooling he put me off til Monday so I returned to Hotel and read—meditated, talked, &c Good news from Genl. Sherman.[14] Day passes of quietly—Stroll the City some. Find much to interest. Returned at 10 P.M. Tired, sleepy, and a bad cold.

February 20, 1865 Monday. Old Rye and loaf sugar eases up my cold early——Breakfast at 8 ock—called on Major Clark—refused to pay me the extra $10 per month for responsibility as Commander of Co "I" but referred me to Chief Clark—he referred me to 2nd Auditor—and he back to Chief Clerk, and then he sent me back to Major Clark who next referred me to Major Dyer, and I finally obtained the full amount due—Ah Yes! Importunity is a big thing in such cases. Weary and worn I returned to Clarendon at Noon—having spent three hours getting my dues—Dined and settled bill and at 4:30 took train for Baltimore—Wait til 10:40 for Train for Harrisburg and arrive at 2:30 A.M. Tuesday—Rest up at National Hotel—

February 21, 1865 Tuesday. Reached Chambersburg 11:30 Dined at Cousin Anthony Hollars—Called on Miss Shively—very pleasant—Christ Brant took me out to Uncles—not at home, but Pet & Cora were there—well and happy and our meeting and greeting was never so sweet—Uncles returned at dusk—Cheerful greetings—Sleighing is fine—

February 22, 1865 Wednesday. Quite Cold—Wrote a letter to Sg't. Maj. Shively—My cough is very troublesome and my head painful. P.M. We hooked up in "Uncle Isaacs" old sled and went to Mothers[b]—Spent the evening very pleasantly—Stephen Huber called to see me.

13. Canterbury Hall, once the home of the Washington Theater Company, was being used to present variety shows. Writers' Project, *Washington: City and Capital* (Works Projects Administration, Washington, D.C., 1937), pp. 143–44.

14. Sherman's army had captured Columbia, S.C., on the night of Feb. 17, 1865, and the Confederates had almost simultaneously evacuated Charleston. It was becoming clear that the South could not hold on much longer.

February 23, 1865 Thursday. Wintry—Visited Bro Johns[d] in A.M. Had a fine visit. But cannot but feel sorry that Brother takes such a dark view of this war——P.M. went to John Karpers.[l] The actual treatment is good enough but I can't but feel that there is a coldness on a/c of Williams[m] being called away by death, and I induced him to enlist—Noah Zook called to see me—Spent eve rather pleasantly.

February 24, 1865 Friday. Snow is going—We went to Henry Reboks[pa] at 9 A.M. Had a warm wholesouled reception and treatment altogether—Western emigration is the chief topic now-a-days[15]— Henry & I shot mark—Eve John Karper[l] called—My cough & headache bad—

February 25, 1865 Saturday. Went via Orrstown—calls—and on to Bro Johns[d] for dinner—Bro—gone to Chambersburg. P.M. called at Ellas[y] a wee and at Pap and Steve Hubers for Tea. A very pleasant time all around and returned to Mothers[b] in Eve.

February 26, 1865 Sunday. Omited Salem—Bro Johns,[d] Ellas[y] & we dined at Mothers[b]—P.M. visit pleasant xcepting too much fault finding with the war and administration—a little too coppery—

February 27, 1865 Monday. Put in A.M. at Mothers,[b] Dave Byers came over dinner—P.M. Pet and I went to John Hubers spent the evening very agreeably. Some true demonstrations of loyalty here and in addition, plenty of good apples & cider and sociability til 9 ock—returned to Mothers[b]—

February 28, 1865 Tuesday. Went to Ellas[y] at 8 AM. A very pleasant time—meeting and greeting old acquaintances whom I had not seen for a long time. Eve returned to Mothers.[b] My cough and misery increaces.

March 1, 1865 Wednesday. Early, we went to Chambersburg— Conferred with Dr Reynolds—Says I have attack of Pneumonia and will not be able to travel to army this week. gave me some medicine and will call to see me on the morrow——Went Home to Aunty's severe pain on breast & between shoulders—

March 2, 1865 Thursday. It rains—my cough very severe, and— and my misery great—So I can't walk without a cane—Dr. R. came

15. The families of both of Samuel's younger sisters, Sarah Cormany Thompson and Eleanora Cormany Slichter, were preparing to move to Iowa.

to see me—certified to my inability to travel and report for duty for at least 15 days[16]—

Sent same to S.B. Barnes, and—He (the Dr.)—reports to A.A.G. U.S.A. and Hd Qrs, Cav Corpse—

March 3, 1865 Friday. Am in pretty bad way—In bed most of day. Towards eve feel a little easier—

March 4, 1865 Saturday. Rainy—feel a little better. Cough loosens some—PM pains scatter some—Eve took a rousing bath and am hopeful the worst is now over and by next week I can return and report for duty.

March 5, 1865 Sunday. Clear and cold. Feel a little better. Walk out to the pump—look over the snow-clad hills but soon wanted to be indoors and sitting, or lying down—Read a good deal—Wrote to Capt Snyder & Sergt Major Shively am really very little better this evening—

March 6, 1865 Monday. Clear cold—Uncles went to Church. I walked out a little—I feel anxious to get to the Regiment. Oh to be a better man, a nobler Christian—I am so happy in my Darling, and Cora, and Friends, and I want to be a nobler exemplar of Jesus my Saviour—Eve am a little more feverish—

March 7, 1865 Tuesday. Pet & I walked over to Allisons. He is drafted and must go—The family moves. The walk exhausts me. Makes me feel a little blue—cant get to see Bro Bernards[q] and Sister Sarahs[u]—

March 8, 1865 Wednesday. A very fine spring like day. The blue birds are chirping & the wrens flit about—Pain has almost subsided entirely, and I hope soon to be able to travel and re-join my Regiment—I know Sgt. Maj. Shively and the clerk will keep Office matters straight—But the Colonel will be wanting companionship &c.

March 9, 1865 Thursday. Springlike—Muddy—Am in good cheer hoping by 14th to be able to go to the Front—Still have some symptoms of fever—Extreme pain in my head & back of neck and weak-

---

16. This certificate is in Cormany's service file, NA. Dr. Samuel F. Reynolds attested that Cormany was "laboring under the effects of a violent cold which has brought on a violent cough with much pain and inflammation of the lungs."

ness & pressure on my breast, and severe coughing spells—But all may soon subside—

March 10, 1865 Friday. Fine springlike—I feel today that while in some respects I am stronger, but in general I am weaker, especially so on my lungs—I walk out some, but it excites my cough—

March 11, 1865 Saturday. Recd letter from my Sergt Major Shively— a good one, makes me wish I could—weak as I am—in an instant transfer myself to the Adjts Office of the 16th Pa Cav—Eve Rev J. C. Smith was to preach a S.H.—½ mile away—Wife & I walked up—but I was completely exhausted on our return—

March 12, 1865 Sunday. Fine day—walk out some—Birds are singing cheerily—My present xtension of Leave of A—is good for only 4 days more, and how I fear I shall not be able to safely travel to the Front. I love to be with my little Family—but since duty calls, I'd much rather be in my office, dispatching business for my Regiment, My Country and so My God.

March 13, 1865 Monday. However nice the weather, and however well I am taking care of myself—I seem to improve so slowly—

March 14, 1865 Tuesday. Pet rode to Chambersburg to confer with Dr. Reynolds, a bad day—eat nothing—Eve took emetic—after 3 or 4 doses operated powerfully—I became quite dilirious—Sweat profusely—7 ock took 4 pills—high fever—Poor sleep.

March 15, 1865 Wednesday. 4 A.M. Pills operate freely—Rains all day—Dr. Reynolds failes to come on a/c of rain & mud—am exceedingly weak—abed all day—

March 16, 1865 Thursday. Too weak to get up—11 A.M. Dr. Reynolds comes—seems pleased with effect of medicine—gave me new supply—Expressed his opinion that I would be unable to travel to duty for 15 or 20 days more, will forward Affidavit to that effect, or rather "Affirmed Certificate" to Army Head Quarters[17]—

17. This certificate is also in NA. Reynolds wrote that Cormany had developed "bilious fever, with cough and inflammation of the lungs," and extended the leave through April 1, 1865.

March 17, 1865   Friday. Am awfully tired of lying in bed. Eat a little dinner sitting on the big rocking chair——p.m. walk out on porch a little by the aid of a cane—

Eve I feel really I'm getting better now, after the severe operation of the late medecine—O! that I were even now strong enough to start for City Point—and to occupy my office again—

March 18, 1865   Saturday. Fine spring day—Rested medium—Feel a little more like myself today—Dr failed to come—I was up and out a little—but found myself too weak for much exercise—

March 19, 1865   Sunday. Fine spring day—Bro Bernard[q] made me a nice visit—Doctor Reynolds came at noon—Calls me doing well— left me some more medecine—My appetite improves some and with it my Strength—Mr Lehman called to see me—I am pretty happy, but not as I have been—Ah! how fickle is health, how feeble is life—

> Heaven guide me homeward—
> Earth forgotten lie
> Hopes cherished often fade
> Ere they bloom, they die——

March 20, 1865   Monday. Folks gardening—I looked on and lent a little help and advice. Oh! how I enjoy being able to be out in the sunshine to breathe the pure air, hear the birds singing, and see busy Farmers passing by to and fro—moving shopping, getting ready for the spring and summer work.

March 21, 1865   Tuesday. Clear & warm—Pet washed and Aunty went over to Mr. Wagoners. The old Gentleman died yesterday about 10 A.M.   Sisters Ella[y] came, and P.M. Ben[z] & I walked across the Fields to The Foust flitting[18]—They set up a big dinner——P.M. Ben[z] and I had a long talk on the war—He seems to have about the correct idea—Eve I feel very much tired out after such a busy day—

March 22, 1865   Wednesday. Fearful stormy night   Clear morning—Ellas'[y] started home in A.M.   PM wrote letters to My Harry and Capt Snyder—Eve feel much better, but still quite week—Anxious for news from The Front—Oh! that this cruel war were over, and all mankind feared God, and kept His Commandments or even sought to know and keep them—

---

18. The Fousts lived a little less than two miles from the Gelsinger farm. *AFCP*, p. 13.

March 23, 1865 Thursday. Stormy-Sunny-Snowy-Calm and almost anything else alternately. Indoors most of day—reading and enjoying my Darlings—

I feel my need of being a nobler better man—O for grace divine, and strength abundant to enable me to come up to my own ideal of a man mentally, morally, spiritually, & physically—

March 24, 1865 Friday. Very Stormy—Nothing special transpiring—My mind rambles and considers the extreme varieties of the human mind and kind. All aiming for happiness, and Oh! how differently—Those certainly succeed best—who labor much for the good and welfare of others, in securing Joy for themselves. Rev J. C. Smith preached at S.H. I couldn't go—

March 25, 1865 Saturday. Snow stormy—Rev J. C. Smith called to see me—nice visit—Uncle and Aunty went to Chamb'g—I wrote to J.B.K.s P.M. read war news. Inquirer[19]—Genls Sherman—Scoffield and Sheridan are doing much as they please—and it seems as tho they would soon drive The Rebs to the wind up—

March 26, 1865 Sunday. In Uncles Buggy we 3 started at 8½ ock for Mothers[b]—Got pretty cold—Ella[y] was there too—Sarah[u] failed us—A delightful visit and luscious "Chicken Dinner"

P.M. We walked down to "Rocky Spring"—to Uncle Sam Hubers—Had a fine short visit—Eve feel somewhat fatigued but am gaining nicely—

March 27, 1865 Monday. Beautiful Spring day—Went to Chambersburg—Called on Mrs Capt Snyder—Left Cora there. Put Horse & Buggy to the Horse Stable—Attended to various items of business— Called on Lieut Barnes' Family. Whites, Hokes, Miss Paulines, Mrs Mc Gowens and Sollenbergers—Got Cora and returned to Uncles about 5 P.M.—I was very tired—but Dr Reynold tho't I might venture to travel in a few days—News of a great fight at Hatchers Run—and victory. My how I wonder what part our old 16th played—one thing I know, whatever was given them to do they did well[20]—

19. *The Philadelphia Inquirer* was featuring letters from a correspondent attached to the headquarters of Maj. Gen. John M. Schofield. On Feb. 22, forces under Schofield's command had captured Wilmington, N.C., thereby closing the Confederacy's last major port.

20. Sheridan had rejoined Grant on the Petersburg front, and the Union army was maneuvering to trap Lee in Petersburg by severing his remaining supply and escape routes. There would soon be a Union victory at Hatcher's Run, but this news report was premature.

March 28, 1865 Tuesday. Spring birds are singing cheerily—I am gaining in strength—and feel pretty well—Chore some for Uncle Isaac—Eve visit Fousts—

March 29, 1865 Wednesday. Misty morning—Cleared at 9—I am planing to start for The Front tomorrow—Spent the P.M. very pleasantly, with Darling & Cora—Uncles being away—

March 30, 1865 Thursday. Rained so uncle didn't want his horse & buggy taken out so I made the best of it by chatting with precious Pet & Cora and Aunty. O how sweet to have congenial spirits hovering around—

March 31, 1865 Friday. Rainy—Pet took me to Chambersburg and we had our lovely parting, and I took the 1 ock train for Harrisburg—I met Capt Bricker at Carlisle and Charly & Tom Harris in H'b'g we did up the City some—and then retired—Oh how different from last night—Furlough—on a/c sickness was xtended so as to cover from Feb 17″ to March 31st and then some—

XXVI
Rachel's Notes on Samuel's Leave
February 21–March 31, 1865

Though her entries are lean, it is evident that Rachel enjoys the round of visiting and activity that characterizes Samuel's extended leave.

———————————◆•■•◆———————————

February 21, 1865 We have had beautiful weather for three or four days. Sat. I looked for my Precious home but he did not come. I felt disappointed. I could have wept—but buoyed up. now I think he will surely come tomorrow. Yesterday Aunty Cora & I went to Abram Ebersoles to Classmeeting. had a pretty good meeting—all were strangers & yet I felt that they were really brethren & sisters. Had I been placed there with my eyes sealed—I might have thought my self seated in a similar meeting in my native Canada—so similar are the workings of the Holy Spirit. O! that my heart were more filled with that spirit. I am longing—longing for my husbands return. Speed thee old time. & yet how swiftly time flies. Eternity will be at hand before we are aware of it—even if we do live out our three score years—So far the winter has been cold—we have had a great deal of snow the sleighing is still quite good. This has seemed something like a Canadian winter. My gums have not quite healed up yet—still so near that they do not hinder my eating. My health is good—Cora is well too—

March 5, 1865 My Precious Husband came as per expectation on 22nd—He was quite out of health. 23rd we started to Motherinlaws[b] in sleigh. when about 3 miles on the way the sleigh broke. tied it— then it commenced raining & kept on the remainder of the trip. Motherinlaw[b] was quite surprised to see Samuel—Next day we dined at J. Cormanys[d]—P.M. went to J. Karpers[l] staid till A.M. of 25th From there went to H. Reboks[pa]—staid there until Next Morning. then started back to J.C.'s[d] called on M. Hamilton— dined at J.C's[d] spent P.M. at Stephen Hoovers—a pleasant visit— Rained nearly all P.M. went to Mothers[b] in evening. Sunday 27th intended to go to Salem church—but Samuel felt to much indisposed—so we staid at home. Ben[z] & Ellie[y] & J.C's[d] came there after church & spent P.M.—28th A.M. were boored by Dave Byers &

kept from making the visits we had intended. P.M. went to John Hoovers   Had quite a pleasant visit Tuesday   Went to Ellies^y sale^1— Things went only midling well—still they went well on an average. Wednes. came home—Samuel sick. Sleighing very bad—Thursday Dr Reynolds called—Samuel got him to write a certificate of his inability to return to the fron at present—which extends his "leave" 15 days. He is some better today—still is not able to ride, is scarcely able to walk. This is a beautiful day—

March 28, 1865   Beautiful day—Pleasant—Calm—My Pet is still at home—had his "Leave" extended 15 days again—which will expire next Sunday. His health has been improving slowly for a week or more now—still he is weak. Last Sunday we went to his mothers^b in the carriage—It was very cold.   he was nealy played out by the time we got there. Yesterday, 27th we were in Chamb-g—small pox were so bad that we called at but a few places—Got some virus to vaccinate our little daughter—This A.M. Pet put the posys on Coras & my arm^2—Mended my circular & dress that I got cut at the buggy yesterday, its too bad—

March 31, 1865   Rained most of day—washed buggy after I got home   Took My Dear to town today.   he started for the front again. I had a lonely ride coming home. Really it does not seem right that husbands should go & leave their wives. Such are the cruel fates of war. I just feel as if I did not care much where I would be knocked to I feel so forsaken.

1. The Slichters were selling some of their possessions before moving to Iowa.
2. Home vaccinations against smallpox were common during the nineteenth century. In using a bit of the virus fluid itself, Samuel was probably following Russell Trall, for the common practice was to use smallpox scabs. *Hand-Book of Hygienic Practice: Intended as a Practical Guide for the Sick-Room* (New York, 1864), p. 274.

XXVII
The Appomattox Campaign
April 1–10, 1865

Lee is finally forced to abandon Petersburg, and he makes a desperate run for the safety of the Appalachian Mountains. Grant immediately orders his cavalry to try to overtake the fleeing Confederates and to pin them down until his main infantry forces could move in for the kill. The 16th Pennsylvania Cavalry is among those in the forefront of the chase, and as a result, Samuel is involved in the capture of the Confederate general Richard S. Ewell. At Appomattox Court House Samuel's regiment helps establish the advantageous Union position that convinces Lee to surrender rather than fight on.

April 1, 1865 Saturday. Left Harrisburg at 2:50 A.M. Met Col Young of 4th Pa Cav on the train—Left Baltimore for Washington D.C. 9:50 A.M. Arrive 11:30. Col and I put up at Clarendon Hotel for dinner. 2:30 Took Boat "Dictator" There were Col Young, Capt Lebo—Capt Robbins & I of our 2nd Cav. Division—Col & I took state room together—The River Calm, Breezes cool & refreshing—The journey fatigues me very much indeed—Slept til 8 ock then up and breakfasted—

April 2, 1865 Sunday. At Fortress Monroe Maj Taylor, and our Chaplain came aboard—and our company enjoyed a beautiful ride, and very pleasant companionship—
On nearing The Point the Shipping was all bedecked with Stars and Stripes—and all around was bustle—We were entering the atmosphere of action. News were cheering—yes buoyantly hopeful—Had an Oyster Stew at Our Sutler Van Wagners—Then rode in Ambulance to near Cavalry Department—I put up with Lieut Dunn——Am very weak and exhausted from the Journey—Wrote letter to Pet—Found my Horse an Servant both gone—no one knows the exact whereabouts of the Chief part of the Command—Some very gloomy news concerning our regiment—Heavy fighting hearable—But Lt Dunn shows me much kindness and I get a good nights sleep.

April 3, 1865 Monday. Morning News——Petersburg fell into our hands at 5 A.M.—at 8 ock Captain Robins—Lieut Dunn and I start for Petersburg—Pass over some of the recently hotly contested works and lines. We enter the City—and from 10 to 11 we rode around to see the sights—See very many places throughout the City where shot and shells left their marks. In some places they played havoc and must have caused great alarm at the time of landing—

We met Captain Harper of Genl Greggs Staff—who showed no little kindness in this that he accompanied us to "Southerland Station—near which—we would find our Regiment—and so we did—

My! What a warm greeting from Officers and Men on a/c of their Adjutants return—

It was surely delightful—But I was so fatigued by this time I could hardly dismount or mount—But to be again well enough to take my place—with the Colonel at the head of The Column—and hear from his lips an account of the wonderful doings, and achievements of the regiment during my absence was decidedly refreshing.

P.M. we started out on the march—were on the move til 10–11 OCK, and encamped on the Vamoose road—near V-creek—a great day—Everything everywhere on the move—and everybody wild with excitement over the recent victories, and the brilliant prospects before us, now that the old lines of battle are broken up—Petersburg is taken, and we have the Rebels on the run, And we are in good trim to keep it up.[1]

April 4, 1865 Tuesday. Marched via Manburg, Amelia Court House to Dannville R.R. near Geedersville[2] where we found General Phil Sheridan and lots of Cavelry at about 3 A.M.—in the night—The march has been very wearing. O how sleepy and tired I am. Ah! Yes! Just to lie on a couch now a while, and have my Darling stroke my throbbing forehead, and eyes—Oh! That would be heavenly. We bivouaced a while and slept—a nap—til 4 A.M.

April 5, 1865 Wednesday. Then we fed our horses and breakfasted—and rested—I am still weak, but strange to say, there is such exileration in these events, and my connection with and rela-

---

1. The Confederate plan of retreat was to flee west up the Appomattox River Valley toward the shelter of the Appalachians, then to try to unite with the remaining Confederate forces still fighting under Lt. Gen. Joseph E. Johnston in North Carolina. Since both sides realized this was Lee's only chance, the final campaign took on the character of a giant race toward the foothills near Lynchburg.

2. Jetersville, on the Richmond and Danville Railroad, was about forty miles due west of Petersburg.

The first Federal wagon train to enter Petersburg following the Confederate evacuation, April 1865. Photographic Division, LC.

tion to them—that I am strengthening up manifestly, daily——At 8
A.M. we took up the march via Amelia Springs, to the Support of
Genl Davies who was bringing in a host of prisoners, mules, and a
Battery, having destroyed 110 wagons laden with supplies.

We soon became engaged, and pressed by infantry and cavalry—
in greatly superior numbers, and retired rather precipitately—commenced to scatter some—but The Colonel and I rallied small bodies,
and charged. Others braced up and rallied to us and so we made 5
or 6 charges against vastly superior numbers, constantly becoming
more solid and formidable, and victorious—The Regiment lost or
suffered 10 wounded, and 8 missing—But gained our point and the
enemy retired, and we went into bivouac Camp at Gedersville[3]—

April 6, 1865 Thursday. Up and in line by 8 A.M.—See Reb Trains,
moving paralell with our road for several hours—Our Reg't was
ordered to move towards it. Soon we found ourselves engaged, and
supported, but met with too much force, so we withdrew some,
and, moved on paralell. Then dismounted and charged again—
pouring in Carbine fire. Then coming close up used our revolvers
fiercely, and drove them so we scooped in 20 to 30 wagons—Setting
fire to them and sending back the mules, to our rear—

Next we flanked some Rebel works—But here mounted men came
up, gained the line on us, and Captured Genl Ewell—and his staff
&c—&c—and we divided the glory amongst us any old way[4]——At
dusk we went into Camp, much fatigued, but in better spirits than
last night—But hungry, sleepy, and about played out—

No time to cook—eat—sleep or anything but "go in on them."
Oh! to be fully well, & stronger, so as to be able to fully enjoy this
wild adventurous work of crushing the Southern Cause. Sending
the ragged half fed Johnies home—and straightening things up so
we could go home too to stay—I to my Darling and precious Cora
and other dear ones.

April 7, 1865 Friday. Cloudy—Rained Some—We moved on at 6
ock A.M. across the Appomattox—

3. The job of the Union cavalry in this campaign was to slow the enemy by
hit-and-run tactics, to support the infantry whenever it was able to overtake an
enemy unit, and to maintain constant contact with the main body of Confederates lest
they shake off their pursuers.

4. Lt. Gen. Richard S. Ewell, one of Lee's corps commanders, surrendered himself, his staff, and what was left of his two divisions near Sailor's (sometimes Saylor's
or Sayler's) Creek. His own account of the incident is in *OR*, ser. I, vol. XLVI, pt. I,
pp. 1292–95.

Sketch of the surrender of Ewell's Corps. From *Battles and Leaders of the Civil War* (New York, 1956).

Rebels burned the long R.R. Bridge and set fire to the Road Bridge[5]—We move on to Farmville—Awfully hilly—we ford the river in town——We find wonderous amounts of Tobacco stored in warehouses. Navy Plug—fine brand—and the Famous Kilikenick— smoking—by the ton—Sure! The boys laid in as good supply—as the exigencies of the case would admit, in passing through—once fairly out of town we were apprised of a large wagon train which was moving across our road at right angles going south or S.W. This train we were instructed to charge, and seek to capture, or destroy— Our Captains were ordered to keep their commands well in hand— and "by Column of fours" we advanced—on almost a charge—and soon were fired upon by the train escort, which we ignored, moving right on—to make a charge, which The Colonel and I were discuss- ing—when a bullet hit the Col in the leg, and another hit our Chief Bugler,[6] when the Col said "Go on in Adjutant—I'm hit," and he rode off to the right, and I led on.   nearing the train and just ready to order the Charge—I discovered that a force of rebs was advancing on our left, and in front—Infantry—mostly—I at once conferred with Captain Snyder—Com'd'g Co "H" right behind me and de- cided best to fall back, and re-form. Thus avoiding the cross-fire from our left, and ascertaining something more as to the strength of the enemy, and the support—if any—we had to depend on—This was a trying time, but our men did brave work—They repelled the enemy, and at the same time, about-faced—So the column now had its front in the rear—and we were falling back carefully—and it was for the Capt—who was really Senior Officer now, and myself—as Adjutant—to get to what was (a little while before) the rear—and command further movements—

The road was narrow—so it was difficult for the Captain and myself to pass the men in column and instruct, or order the officers in passing what to listen for, and keep doing as they were falling

---

5. The "long bridge" carried the Southside Railroad across the Appomattox River between Sailor's Creek and Farmville. Retreating Confederates damaged it severely, but Union troops arrived in time to save the smaller wagon bridge (Cormany's "Road Bridge") beneath it. Since neither infantry nor artillery could ford the Appomattox at this point, saving the wagon bridge prevented the possibility of a major snarl in the Federal pursuit. George R. Agassiz, ed., *Meade's Headquarters, 1863–1865: Letters of Colonel Theodore Lyman from the Wilderness to Appomattox* (Freeport, N.Y., 1922; rpt. 1970), pp. 351–52; Mark M. Boatner III, *The Civil War Dictionary* (New York, 1959), pp. 274–75.

6. Official accounts confirm the wounding of Lt. Col. John K. Robison, the regi- mental commander, at Farmville, Va. The official report, however, had Robison hit while leading a saber charge. The regiment's chief bugler was Ferdinand F. Rohm. *PV*, pp. 956–57.

Railroad bridge over the Appomattox River near Farmville, Va. The road bridge at grade can also be seen, lower right. Photographic Division, L.C.

back—I "jumped the fence" and rode in the field and so was making good time towards reaching my point, when suddenly a huge ditch—or washout—8 or 10 feet wide, and 6 or 8 feet deep confronted me—it was bridged on the road—but there was a high fence to my left, and a squad of rebel infantry coming out of the brush 100 yds to my right—demanding my surrender—I gave my horse the rein, and my two spurs and he cleared the gully—only his hind feet did not go quite far enough, but by throwing myself forward after a little moments awful struggle—he recovered himself and we went on—

I can't see why those 30 or 40 rebs didn't shoot me—Guess they were too cock sure I'd land in the gully—and be their game—or else too startled looking at the awful venture to remember they had guns. A minute later, they fired a volley after me, and the bullets buzzed like bees over head—but not one touched me or my horse— Soon Cap. Snyder and I had our Regiment reformed in open field and ready to resist any ordinary force likely to turn out on such an

536

occasion or to move against them either. But all this while the train had kept moving out of danger at rapid rate. We lost during these 15 or 20 minutes—2 officers and 15 men wounded—one officer—The Col—wounded and a prisoner—Also 15 men captured—and one killed—The whole affair was very exciting and but for our long experience we would have been badly used up——We remained on the line til dusk—Then moved back through town—Cross the Appomattox and move on to Pamplin[7] Station—we had no time to cook or eat all day—save eating raw pork and hard tack—"On horse" and "to horse" til 2:30 A.M.—O my! I am awfully weak and weary & sleepy—Col Robison being wounded Captain Snyder assumes command, which means greatly increaced responsibility for me—For the Captain always depended a whole lot on me even when I was Company Clerk, and does doubly so now that I have been so long Adjutant and right hand man to the Col.

April 8, 1865 Saturday. Clear—fine—Busy rendering Reports &c &c til 10 ock   Then moved out, met no resistance—Massed at Poplin Station where we captured 3 Engines and some rolling stock. did some reconnoitering and in P.M. marched around via Evergreen Station to Appomattox Station and went into camp about 10 P.M. weary—sleepy—and hungry—The day has been beautiful——General Sheridan—by a yankee trick—captured three trains of cars from the Johnies—The Trains had come up from the Southern department, not well posted as to latest doings &c.

April 9, 1865 Sunday. We had a late supper about midnight—good fresh mutton, and potatoes—biscuit—milk & Coffee——Slept til about 6 AM and had a dandy breakfast akin to supper—and at 8 A.M. mounted and moved out, and soon met the Enemy in force—A general engagement seemed pending—The rebel Cavalry fell back before us, and on our right, our Infantry and Artillery seemed to be forming into line—facing to the right—or Appomattox ward, The enemy cavalry disappeared from our front, and our regiment was ordered to dismount No 1—in each section of 4—taking care of the horses of Nos. 2, 3, & 4 so our dismounted men—with our 7 shooting Carbines, and 6 shooting revolvers, and abundance of ammunition—on direction moved to the right, and front, and formed in line of battle our right connecting with the Infantry line—our men lying on the open ground about 4 or 5 feet apart—each one capable to

---

7. Poplin.

shoot 13 times without re-loading—and instructed to hold his place at all hazzards—we were to hold our line by all means.[8]

The ground was elevated somewhat directly in our front, and receded again at about 100 yards—so we we were hidden from the enemys line, but could hear them in forming to advance.

I passed along in rear of our boys, instructing each officer—to allow no firing by any means until the Command came from Captain Snyder or me from the right—completing these instructions—I returned to The Captain on the right—who at once ordered me towards the Center of the line—

Very soon I had reached the center, I heard the enemys coming—one could see their double line—with steady tread, but they saw us not—lying on the ground—but a quick Attention! Fire at will! rang out, and our line opened—with deadly aim—and volley after volley was poured into the approaching lines with terrible effect—

In vain their Officers tried to hold their men—and keep advancing—Too many fell, and too many others wounded fell back—and then too, the lay of the ground would occasion all but well taught & drilled shooters to shoot too high—overshoot. This was their failure——But they came on—in some fashion—til some were quite close—The cloud of smoke was blinding—our men knew no faltering—but with a yell, as if to Charge—many arose—using their revolvers, and now the scattering enemy broke to the rear, across the little rise of ground—leaving many dead wounded and dying   I ran along our line ordering "Men! Load up quickly—Carbines first—Bully! Boys! you never flinched a bit. You may have to do it again, but you Cant do it better—I returned to the Captain—reported what I had done and he fairly flooded us all with praise "Bully!" was his word—
—We could now hear the enemy on the job of rallying—and could easily understand how difficult was their task. Again, I ran along the line with "They'll come again—Do as before. Dont fire til you have the command, but remember the lay of the land—and just exactly where the chests of the bodies are and aim there &c"   and soon, on they came—steadily—over the rise—and into view—next again the Command—and the boys poured in as before, and the enemy overshot as before—and their retreat again was as much or more of a skedaddle and our boys fairly followed them but were commanded to

8. Sheridan's cavalry, including the 16th Pennsylvania, had ridden ahead of Lee's main force and was well positioned astride the Confederates' sole route of escape. Union infantry was closing in behind, and if the cavalry could hold the Confederates until the infantry arrived, Lee's position would be hopeless. W. Birkbeck Wood and James E. Edmonds, *Military History of the Civil War with Special Reference to the Campaigns of 1864 and 1865* (New York, 1960), pp. 302–03.

re-load to the limit—as they may obtain reinforcements—and try us harder——"But Boys we must hold at all hazzards"——Re-loading proceeds quietly—and the response "ready" ripples along the line— I report to the Captain our line in fine trim—We hear words of Command coming across from the enemy—"Get into line there" "Right Dress" "All at a ready" &c. &c. We can hear—while our boys are lying low, resting—waiting for orders——From the Enemys side we can hear—dimly—Forward! and we know they are coming Behind us—comes a solid line of Colored Troops—to take our place—Fine fellows⁹—The transfer is made quickly—We fall back in fine order—and They receive the rebs with a volley—followed by some "grape-and-canister,"¹⁰ and we are sure we did our part well—and the darkies would be able to finish up the oncoming Rebs in good shape—

Returning to where we left our Horses—we found that in the mean time a body of rebel Cavalry had come dashing in and captured some 45 of our horses, and the men caring for them and were getting away with them, but part of our Brigade came on the scene—in the niche of time—and succeeded in re-capturing the Horses, and the men caring for them, and also a bunch of the daring-dashing Johnies. A good many of our mens "haversacks" were gone, otherwise little damage was suffered by the capture and re-capture.

The marvel of it all is we didn't lose a man, only had a few wounded slightly—and now our Regiment is soon mounted again, and in Column of fours, moving towards the left with our 2nd Brigade, or as part of it. The First Maine Cav was in the lead—our 16th was next, and The 4th Pa and 8th followed. A great open field was before us and to our left—

The order came to prepare for a Brigade Charge—in regimental formation—The body was promptly alligned—1st Maine—16th Pa—

9. These black soldiers were infantrymen, and with them came most of the Union 5th Corps under Gen. Edward O. C. Ord. The noose around Lee had now closed, and the cavalry could fall back. Burke Davis, *To Appomattox: Nine April Days, 1865* (New York, 1959), p. 375. Black regiments participated fully in the operations of the Army of the Potomac during 1864 and 1865; some twenty-two black regiments had seen action in the siege lines before Petersburg. Dudley Taylor Cornish, *The Sable Arm: Negro Troops in the Union Army, 1861–1865* (New York, 1966), p. 266.

10. Grape was a form of artillery shot consisting of groups of solid iron balls. Canister, which produced a spray of small projectiles and slugs, allowed field pieces to function like giant shotguns at short range. Some authorities dispute the use of grape during the Civil War. Unless Cormany was confused in his terms, this reference certainly suggests that it was used at Appomattox. Boatner, *Civil War Dictionary*, pp. 119, 354.

4th Pa—8th Pa—and (8th Michigan ? possibly)——one regiment be-hind the other 30–40 paces apart——At the far side of the open space—in the edge of a woods rebel cavalry was visible—about half a mile away—

Everything had quieted down—The irregular firing in places—along the infantry lines—going on during the morning hours—had all ceased—

The Command now given to our Brigade was "Prepare to Charge!" "Draw Saber." Every Sabre was bare. Just then! away! far! off! to our right our ears caught the sound of Cheering—But the command came "Forward—Guide Right—March!" and the brigade—en-masse moves steadily—slowly—men clasp the hilt of the sword tensly—awaiting the final "CHARGE!" to be given   But a moment and it was given a great line of the enemy cavalry now appeared out from the woods—a few shots were being fired by 1st Maine—The cheering on our right became plainer The Brigade Charge started—Now a Staff officer, on a black Horse—came dashing up towards the Brigade Head Qrs Flag exclaiming "For Gods sake Stop that Charge!"——an occasional shot still goes off—The Rebels show the white flag, and Their Bugle blows "Cease firing" and Ours blows the HALT! and all is quiet an instant—

O what a lull! What a wondering Why?——Flags of Truce meet—Whats' up? The News! "Generals Grant and Lee are coun-selling"—Next Comes the Cry,

"LEE SURRENDERS!

"Ye Gods!" What cheering comes along in waves from far off to the right, becoming more intense as taken up by those commands nearer to us. Now our Brigade lets loose more fully as the news is confirmed. Hats and caps uplifted on the points of Sabers are whirled and waved overhead—and with tearful voices—Scores of overjoyed men exclaim "Now I can go home to Wife Babies Mother Sister Sweetheart, and our Country is forever safe——

The tension, and nerve of Our Regiment has been on tremendous strain all day, and for five days now—In fact day and night. Before night—Genl Gregg—who had been captured about the time Col Robison was wounded—returned to Brigade H'd Qrs—paroled—Other prisoners returned to their Commands.

At night fall—we simply bivouac—on nearly the same ground—and rest for the night—Captain Snyder & I have our Fly up as shelter—

April 10, 1865 Monday. Slept finely, All in Joy that Lee has sur-rendered—

Some villain stole my Hat and Boots during the night—The Command saddled up at daylight as though all might not be Safe afterall. Evidently the fellow could not "put on" my boots—as the ground showed—not a hundred yards from where I had lain—and so he tried to cover them with loose ground—and left them. Fortunately a bit of one leg protruded—and a soldier who had walked out a short distance—for a purpose—saw the ground peculiarly tramped up, and a bit of nice leather in sight—took hold of it and pulled, and up came a pair of fine Cavalry Officers boots, of small size, some one not far away—who had heard of my loss—at once brought or directed the fellow with them to me—and sure they were mine. They slipped on nicely—With my thanks and some reward, the finder passed on to his Company—and I rejoiced, But my Hat never came. We ate early breakfast and at 7:30 we took up the march via Appomattox Court House—

Saw the Site where Genl Lee Surrendered to our General Grant, and hosts and hordes of surrendered Rebs all about the place and surrounding country—and many of our troops too, seemingly in charge of affairs, and affairs generally in a kind of promiscuous condition—In tarrying a bit I met my old time Friend "Bill Peacock" and we enjoyed a little chat—

We moved on to Prospect Station and encamped at 3 P.M. rained at times all day—making matters a little disagreeably joyful—But with it all, we closed the day "After the surrender" with a sumptuous Ham—eggs—and Slap-Jack supper, and other good things Our Mess Wagon and our Head Quarters darkies brought up——

This seemed delightful after nearly a week of getting on along almost any way—and at times no way—except as we ate things largely raw and cold—and an occasional cup of coffee—

XXVIII
Waiting for Samuel's Return
April 2–August 13, 1865

On April 2 Lee abandoned Petersburg and on April 9 he surrendered to Grant. But the period that follows is not one of triumph for Rachel. Instead, it is full of tension, tedium, frustration, and depression. Samuel's life was no longer in danger, but he could not obtain a discharge from the army and his letters showed that boredom and temptation were taking their toll. Rachel herself remains isolated on the Gelsinger farm with her infirm in-laws, and she has trouble with her daughter, who is going through a stage of misbehaving. The result is misery for Rachel, and it nearly overcomes her. By the second week of May, she writes of wishing to die; a month later she repeats the same sentiment.

April 2, 1865 Beautiful day—Roads muddy—Aunty Cora & I went to Red Schoolhouse in buggy—Quarterly meeting there. J. P. Bishop preached good sermon. Had sacrament. My eyes pained me very much when I got home, could not read as that increased the pain. Evening went again—walked down with Mahaffys girls—Young people behaved shamefully—was very tired when I got home.

April 3, 1865 Beautiful day—Not very well—washed a tremendous wash—Am nearly played out. P.M. read a little—eyes quite painful, retired early—

April 4, 1865 Rainy day. daughter had Croup last night for first time, seemed almost strangled, sat up a long time to watch her. A.M. Ironed—& fixed up the beds. P.M. mended & finished putting on a border on Auntys shawl. Cora seems quite lively—playes nicely with her dolls—feel tired. News has reached us that Richmond & Petersburg have falled—Salutes were fired

April 5, 1865 Cloudy most of day—Rained last night. Aunty & I fixed up the flowerbeds. News of Richmond being taked confirmed—heard no particulars yet. Aunty was called on to help prepare for a funeral at Mr Wolfs—a son was killed in battle & brought home. Had a time milking—Cora was afraid of cows.

April 6, 1865 Raining—Mr P. brought no paper for me—next time I will tell the one I send myself—The old maxim if you want a thing done do it yourself—if not send, has been verified too often of late. I am quite out of patience waiting for mail—& I have to wait just to suit useless whims in others—Aunty has gone to Wolf again. A bad day for a funeral—

April 12, 1865 This is my 29th Birthday. Not a very gay day for me. Uncle & Aunt are both sick. Still they are not bedfast. I do the milking & in fact all the work. O! how I dislike those cows—there are two that the butcher ought to have, they kick & switch & carry on high—I know if they were mine that I would not be bothered long with them. Wrote a letter to my Dear.   What would I not give to know just where & how he is. God will protect him—

April 14, 1865 Uncle & Aunt are quite sick—especially Uncle—Dr Maxel was her again, was here yesterday, thinks they are doing very well. I churned butter—Made yeast—& prepare for baking—feel very tired. Anna Mary Wagonar stays with me—she came last night. It takes quite a few steps until all the work is done up—I fear Uncle wont get well—he has such a hollow cough—

April 15, 1865 Baked bread pies & cake—every thing got very nice, did the cleaning &c—Well I nearly gave out before I got done. Quite a number of the neighbors have called to see the sick. This P.M. a neighbour came in & told us a dispatch had come that Perident Lincoln was assassinated. The report is that the President was going to a theatre & was shot just as he stepped on the plattform to go in, & that he died this morning. Also that Sec. Seward had been indisposed and an attempt was made to assassinate him—O! how dreadful it seems. The one that shot the Pres. was caught—I feel like weeping over the nations loss. My God what does it all mean—Is anarchy & destruction coming upon us? When will the end be—My God hasten the time when peace shall reign again. O! for a word from my dear husband. Hope he is safe & well—Uncle & Aunt are much better, sat at table to eat supper. again.   It seemed quite lonely without them. I am very tired head aches considerable. It is raining was cloudy & rainy all day—Tobias Crider stopped & talked

Rachel Bowman Cormany. Undated photograph by the Soule Studio, Chambersburg. Kiefer Family.

a little bit—He is a good old man. O! that I were a better christian. Report was incorrect as to the place.[1]

April 21, 1865 It is very cloudy & foggy—I baked today, had very good luck. Went to Mr Pickens for eggs for Aunty to set some hens—I do nearly every thing in house & barn. Mr Lehman attends to the horse—Yesterday I worked some in the garden. I nearly gave out. I do not think I was intended for such work. At any rate I cannot stand it. I have considerable to do, get very tired sometimes. Yesterday Aunty gave me a new linnen sheet for helping them & doing their work for them. I Rec'd a letter from Samuel. O! how the few lines relieved me, for it was only a few lines—Also Rec'd a letter from H. H. Frazier. such a good one. Our Photograps sent to her were lost. She speaks of coming to see me & spend a month here. Aunty hoped she would bring some one to take care of her horse—I told her she would bring no horse. I know as stingy as the people in this country are a months visit would be considered a dreadful thing. The way Aunty spoke I think she would rather not have her come I will propose to pay her boarding when she once writes she is coming—I would gladly do it in order to have her here. I hope she will come. I do not know what kind of people these are in this country. Now Uncle & Aunt have been right sick. Many thought Uncle would not get well again & indeed is not of of danger yet. I wrote the fact to Motherinlaw[b] She sends word she is not able to ride & Byers[ba] won't bring her—Word was sent to Uncles brother & sisters. None have come near yet. We are told his brotherinlaw was at a neighbers. had to pass in sight & did not come to see them. I could not help but pray inwardly that I might not die in Pa—I either want to be among strangers or with friends that think it worth coming to see us at least when it is thought death might soon separate us. O! I do not like this country. The people all or nearly so seem so closefisted It seems to me they (many) think as much of a cent as western people of a dollar

April 24, 1865 Monday. Weather beautiful. Dug some garden. that is almost killing work to me. P.M. fixed up some of my clothes. Mrs Beard came & brought me a letter from my Sisters & brother. Yesterday Motherinlaw[b] & Byers[ba] were here. Came Saturday P.M. & left yesterday P.M. John Gelsinger came too on Sat & left when they did. Everything moves off smothly. If only the war were over & our loved ones at home.

1. I.e., the place of the assassination. This line was added in the same ink as the next entry. By then Rachel knew Lincoln was shot in his own box rather than upon the platform of Ford's Theater. The reports were otherwise accurate.

April 27, 1865 Beautiful clear warm day. Planted flowers this A.M. then cut & sewed at a dress for Cora. Uncle & Aunty are getting pretty well again. Had a letter from Home on Monday & one from My Dear on Tuesday. How those letters cheer me. I feel a little lonely—Cora is so full of her play. I find that she often annoys the old people. I try to make her be good so my stay here will not be greivous to them. God grant grace to do right.

April 30, 1865 Beautiful day. Wrote to My Precious. Was so verry lonely

May 10, 1865 It has been cloudy all week & rained every day—Brother Amos[hh] spent last week with me. I had not seen him since Nov—/59. He had many very interesting naratives of his travels to relate to me. He has changed much. has become so much more manly—but in religion the most important of all—he has retrograded. Since he is gone I feel so lonely—Cora is so full of her fun & pranks—that she annoys the. old people. I whip & punish her often but it is no sooner over than forgotten & the same thing done again I feel this evening as if it would be a blessing to the world in general & myself in particular if Cora & I could just shut my (our) eyes never to open in this world—It is not right to feel thus. Hence I pray for Grace to live right & to overcome evil. In seven weeks I have received but three letters from my husband which is so unusual that I do not know what to make of it. He has always been so punctual in writing. O! how wretched I am.

May 23, 1865 Has cleared off again after four days of rain & five of cloudy weather It seems nice to have sunshine again. Brother Amos[hh] returned last night. He seems quite done out with the journey—he had to walk from Gettysburg. the freshet took the bridges so the stage could not run. Do know when my Dear will get home. hope soon.

June 5, 1865 It is clear & very warm. This morning I picked a large dish full of strawberries. A week ago today brother Amos[hh] left—I went along to the depot I did not like to see him go. still I knew it must be. I got no letter from Mr C. O I wish he were home so I would not have this trouble with my mail.

June 10, 1865 Well as usual I feel as if I were a burden to every body & myself in particular. The greatest cause of feel thus is that I have such a trouble with my little girl—she is so restless & mischievous. tares round & is in every thing she should not be torments Aunty & Uncle so that I know they must be anxiously waiting for Mr C. to come home to take us off. Really I feel tired of life. It seems to me I am just in other peoples way—I think if I could only be in my own house, so that Cora would not torment other people & make life unpleasant to them. My mind is fully made up that longer than this summer I will not live around this way—I feel as if I wanted to run off—I do not want to see any body or talk to any body—more like creeping into a dark corner & weep that my tears might swell to a torrent.

June 18, 1865 Weather very warm inclined to be gusty—Aunty Cora & I were at the Red schoolhouse to preaching. Mr. Quigly quite a young man preached—did right well. Reminded me of Jake Burgner—I had almost made up my mind at first sight that I would not like him on that account his manner of speaking is pleasing. Think he will make a good preacher. Had letters from my Dear this last week. he has got over his "Blue" spell. I feel so much relieved. when he gets low spirited, he gets down so dreadfully. Had a letter from Amos[hh]—he sent the money I gave him. He is still for Va. land[2]—brotherinlaw J. W. A.[kk] is ready to join in—My Dear has not rec'd the letters in which Amos[hh] states what he intends doing or would like to do—I was in town yesterday. Rec'd letters from Western from sistersinlaw.[3] They do not like it there. & intend leaving as soon as they can sell—They are all homesick.

June 20, 1865 Cloudy—rained a little—Aunty & I were over at Betts to finish the tree we bought. We pay 3 cts per qt. for what we pick. it was very wet & unpleasant from yesterdays rain. I seeded all we got. If it does not rain we will go to Mr A. Beards for some more this P.M. I stand this kind of work very well—feel well—but get very tired sometimes. O! how I delight to work with fruit when I know it is for my loved ones. I keep thinking all the while that I am working so hard that my Dear Husband will be home to help enjoy them in the winter.

July 1, 1865 Very warm & sultry. Am not very well. We have been fetching cherries from A. Beards by the ½ bushel. they had so

---

2. Many Northerners considered investing in Southern land immediately after the war. With its economy destroyed and the status of its black agricultural labor force still uncertain, land there could be purchased quite reasonably.

3. Sarah Thompson and Elly Slichter, who had emigrated with their husbands to Iowa.

many that the invited us so strongly to fetch—said they could not work them near all away. It was dreadful work to carry them home a mile. & I am nearly worn out with it. Aunty is worse than I—still it paid, for each has 3 pks unseeded & 1 pk seeded dried—Had a letter from My Samuel—he is killing himself in that office I wish he would come home I am getting along here as well as could be expected with my mischief of a girl. I often fear the old people will tire of her. I try to make her good, but it seems I cannot talk or knock any thing into her.   but I must keep trying

July 5, 1865   Very warm day. Had a little sprinkle of rain—finish a dress for Aunty which I commenced on Monday P.M.   Everything goes smoothly. Just got done drying fruit & put it all away today. now I am ready to pitch into something else. Religiously I get along pretty well.

July 14, 1865   Weather cloudy. Aunty Cora & I started before 7 oclock to go to my motherinlaws.[b] Went through Chambersburg.   fixed all the business we could—I went to Mrs Sulenbergers to get patterns for aprons for Cora. Staid perhaps ten minutes. When I got back, I found that Aunty was rather displeased that I staid so long & having failed to get the patterns in the morning was to call for them in the evening. I told Aunty so—she told me so short, that she would not drive back there again. She was quite short in the grain for a little while, We had quite a pleasant visit at Motherinlaws,[b] who had a letter ready to mail for me so anxious she was to hear from us & Samuel, I was sick part of time there. Got my pattern on the way home after all the fuss, Got home by dark. I milked & put it away then all was done. Really people look at & make as much fuss of a visit of ten miles off—as many would to go 100 miles.

July 16, 1865   Sunday. Cloudy Aunty & I were at meeting last evening & brought the preacher Mr Quigly along home with us. This morning we fully intended to go to the Red Schoolhouse & had Cora dressed & myself partly—to go when a thunderstorm came up so we did not go. At noon Adam Plums came so the day was spent in talking rather pleasantly & now evening is here. I prayed this morning that I might spend the day in such a way that this evening I might be a days journey nearer heaven. I did one thing wrong. I ate too hearty a dinner so that I felt stupid. I want to live for heaven or lay up treasures in heaven so my end may be peace. I long so for my Dear home, especially since I rec'd his last letter.

548

July 28, 1865 Weather extremely warm. Yesterday Aunty Cora & I were at Louden to see Mrs J. Eckerman. It began to rain soon after we started & rained till we got to St Thomas. Had fair weather after that. Our visit at Louden was not so very pleasant   Mrs E. was very busy baking & had little time to spend with us. Aunty got on a bumblebees nest & got badly stung. Could hardly get a man to hitch up for us when we wanted to go home. We took supper at B.A. Cormanys[q] at St Thomas. Had quite a pleasant visit there. Cora played so nicely with the children & wanted to stay—got home in good time. I was out for huckleberries this A.M.   got very few. Left Cora at Mr Lehmans. Ate some splendid rhubarb pie there after we came in with our berries. Cora wanted to stay & they all plead for her so I left her   It seems so quiet without her. I would soon get lonely without her. I try daily to live a christian.   God helping me I hope to reach heaven.

August 6, 1865 P.M. It is warm but cloudy—looks much for rain. Was to meeting at Brick schoolhouse (Bigley & Leymaster).   Had class after preaching. A good time. Good old Brother Leymaster got so happy that he fairly leaped for joy. There were but few there— but such a good feeling prevailed. Little Cora did pretty well.   she went home with Wagoners girls   she thinks so much of them. The letters I receive from my Samuel cause me much anxiety. He receives so few letters from me which makes him so low spirited. I wish he were home. God can comfort & protect him from evil. I have given him into His care & felt that all will be well.

August 11, 1865 Received such good letters from Mrs Danforth & Mrs M.A. Fisher—Mrs Danforths contains so much news. Poor Lydia D. went to Africa as a missionary   Married a missionary there & after two years died. Lydia was a dear girl—a very devoted christian. I wish I were as good as she. She has gone to her long sought home. O! I feel like living nearer my Saviour. I want to get to heaven too. Mrs Fishers is a good letter too. She sighs to be released from this prison house to go to join her dear husband in the realms of eternal day—Aunty has taken Cora to spend the day at Mr Lehmans. I was disappointed in not getting a letter from My Dear husband. My God be with him. Keep him safe from all harm & evil & bring him safely home is my constant prayer   The Cars have just whistled which tells me I must get supper.[4]

---

4. The Cumberland Valley Railroad passed within about a mile of the Gelsinger farm as it approached the northwestern edge of Chambersburg. *AFCP*, p. 13.

549

August 13, 1865 Sabbath Morning. A beautiful cloudless morn. Last evening Aunty & I went to the Brick Schoolhouse to here Mr Quigly preach. I think him a promising young man. The young men talked so much that Mr Beard went out to silence them. It had a good effect. After preaching Mr Beard handed me several letters he had lifted for me. We hurried home. One was from my Dear. How eagerly I read. He has been tempted so severely & seems so much depressed in spirits. I fell on my knees & tried to pray to the Lord in his behalf as he requests. O! I felt as if my heart would break. I feel so for him. I told the Lord all but all seemed dark. but before I went to bed I could feel that all is well. I could by faith give my Dear in the hands of the Lord & Feel that He who protected my Dear from the dangers of the battle field could also protect him from the missiles of Satan. O! He will keep him. I take the promises of His word for my trust I feel assured all will be well. I feel that I am so sinful & shortcoming daily. Thad daily I can do no good I have no merits of my own. all my hope is in the mercy & goodness of God. I love my little daughter & my greatest desire is to train her up for the Lord. I find it takes a firm hand to deal with her—she seems so pervese & selfwilled little as she is. I often feel the task of bringing her up too great that I am not competent to bend the little immortal mind in the right direction. I often pray for grace, wisdom & help from above. O! I want to be a holy christian. Do good while here & gain heaven at last.

XXIX
From Occupation Duty in Virginia to Reunion in Pennsylvania
April 11–August 27, 1865

Samuel is not immediately discharged after Lee's surrender but is ordered instead to Lynchburg, Virginia, as part of a peacekeeping force. During the anticlimactic months of demobilization, Union soldiers, including Samuel, sought the comfort of whiskey and the company of Southern women.

April 11, 1865 Tuesday. Cloudy—a time of resting—11 A.M. we march as rear-guard of our Cavalry Corpse wagon train via Hampton Sidney College—Prince Edwards Court House to Sandy Creek where we go into camp for the night—

We cannot fully realize the great change in the general aspect of affairs—No hostile enemy seen or heard of—we go into camp as tho at home or near our homes—

April 12, 1865 Wednesday. Took up line of march at 6 A.M.—crossed Sandy Creek—passed Sandy Creek Church and moved on to Berksville Station,[1] where we encamped at 2 P.M.—Lieut S. B. Barnes reported to the Regiment—Also our Chaplain—who amounts to very little to the Regiment or rather has not as yet—— Oh! That officers and men would give vent to their Joys in a nobler way than by excesses and drunkenness—

April 13, 1865 Thursday. Rainy—We took up the line of march at 6:30—we passed Max's Mill and Nottaway Court House, and station, crossing the Creek and in a nice upland woods went into Camp.—

---

1. Actually Burkesville, a village near the point where the Richmond and Danville Railroad crossed the Southside Railroad. Cormany's regiment was proceeding back toward Petersburg along the Southside roadbed.

Many rumors, and much news as to General Sherman and Genl Johnson—and affairs away down South—but little that is truly reliable²—

I am quite well again and happy—hoping no more guns need be fired to secure permanent peace—and that SOON I can return to my Darlings to Stay!

I mailed a letter to her today—

April 14, 1865 Friday. Clear—Cool—pleasant. Joyous!

A monstrous Mail reached us today—I recd a blessed fat one from Darling, one from Martha Hampsher, and some on Office business—I am real hardy—well and happy—but long to be still a better, nobler man—

April 15, 1865 Saturday. Rainy day—Capt Snyder & Lieut Barnes took out a foraging party—captured a wagon—also apple Jack—got some trophies—Is a general time of drunkenness amongst the Officers—Capt Snyder goes on awfully—were our dear Col Robison here there would be some putting under arrest—Have severe diarhea, but yet would be happy, but for the drinking of the Officers.

April 16, 1865 Sunday. Major Fry came from dismounted Camp— where he had long been strutting—and commanding the dear old boys—who had lost their Horses in this great campaign—The Maj seems like a recruit amongst the old Veterans of the 16th—of course, when the Col was wounded, Capt. Snyder took Command, and when Fry came up he was Senior, and took Command, now that danger is over—and puts on a sight of airs. My health is better today—

No one knows how glad I am that I got back from my Furlough and Sick extension, in time to enter fully into this campaign and was permitted to share in the glorious doings ending in Genl Lees surrender and above all that I am so well, and have been preserved so exceptionally and wonderfully—

April 17, 1865 Monday. Clear—fine—took up line of march at 7 A.M. down The R.R. to 4 mls from Ford Station and Camped.

As we passed Dismt'd Camp—Brave Maj Robinson³—who has been enjoying himself there—dismounted me in the Column and

2. Sherman's army was operating in North Carolina, where an outmanned Gen. Joseph E. Johnston was still trying to resist as best he could. Sherman and Johnston would formally suspend hostilities on April 18, 1865.

3. James C. Robinson had not participated in the chase to Appomattox.

demanded his (U.S.) horse—or rather the horse he had been riding when with us—My horse had been disabled, and The Maj was away, his(?) horse was available, so I appropriated him, and here bravely dismounts me on my line of duty, simply because The Maj could do so—and he could do it because his cowardly soul was too little to do any more noble thing—Evening I reported his conduct to Brig. Hd. Qrs. and I agreed to pass it over, or under, as too small to spend any time on.

April 18, 1865 Tuesday. Beautiful day—Marched about 6 A.M.— reached Petersburg 2 P.M. and encamp—Maj Robinson showed some more of his xtreme littleness—I refused to give him more notice than rank demanded & promptly started off on a ride. I called on Uncle J. B. Eckerman—viewed some of the Rebel works and part of the City of Petersburg—Our Head Quarters Desk came up and we establish regimental Hd. Qrs—preparatory to business tomorrow. I am pretty well, but not nearly as happy as if Col Robison were with the Command instead of these Figureheads of majors— Fry & R.

April 19, 1865 Wednesday. Boys busy in office on Reports. I help Chaplain to get mustered in   Uncle J. B. Eckerman called——Spring is here—Trees are leafing and blooming—Hills and valleys are green and glorious, air is balmy—and every thing seems gay and happy, and yet We all mourn, aye! more. For The Great Man—Great above all others in U.S. is Dead! by an Assassin——and Who can Fill the vacancy?

April 20, 1865 Thursday. Good letter from Col Robison. Beautiful day. Office work abundant, but Sergt Major and Clerk are mastering it finely and I need only look it over, verify it, and sign the Reports, St'm'ts, &c.

Chaplain and I take a ride to Forts Mahone and Sedgwick[4]—

It is astonishing how close the two contending armies lay—Well may they say "Our enemies were worthy our steel"——I am real well now—Recd letter from Pet—

---

4. The forts, Confederate and Union respectively, faced each other across the Petersburg line. Only fifteen hundred feet apart, their forces had shelled each other so constantly that they came to be known as Forts Hell and Damnation to the men. *The Photographic History of the Civil War*, V, 217; Thomas Chamberlin, *History of the One Hundred and Fiftieth Regiment Pennsylvania Volunteers, Second Regiment, Bucktail Brigade* (Philadelphia, 1905), p. 267.

April 21, 1865   Friday. Fine. Routine. Eve. went to Cav. Corps Hospital—Splendid time with our wounded Officers, Col Robison—Capt's Heslop & Oliphant, Lieuts Barnes & E.[5]—went to Cav Depot—Lodged with Lieut Billings about 12:30 P.M.—

April 22, 1865   Saturday. I returned to Camp at Noon—Had Inspection Then changed Camp, put up pretty nicely—Our dismounted men came back—"George" came to be my Boy again[6]——Eve—Our Quartette, Chaplain—Swank, Brooks & I sang—Foine!

April 23, 1865   Sunday. Fine—Busy—Very good letter from Pet—— P.M. Marching Orders—To move 5:30 in the morning   Chaplain preached—I wrote 4 page letter to Pet—am well—I thirst to be a nobler better Man.

April 24, 1865   Monday. Ready at 5:30. Sent off 95 horseless men to dism't'd Camp—Later unsaddle—await orders—all day—at 7:30 P.M.—went 12 mls and bivouac at Dinwiddie Court House—

April 25, 1865   Tuesday. Took up march at 6 A.M.   made good time, struck main Calvary Column at noon at "Buckskin Church"— we made some 37 miles, and encamped at dusk—

We passed through some very fine country—Found plenty of meat, meal, Poultry, Mules, Horses and Forage, and of course appropriated all we needed—Major Chaplain—Doctors & I mess together—and it was pretty good "pickin" we had—My George knows to "lay in" care for, and do up for use—

April 26, 1865   Wednesday. Start 5:30 on Boynton Plank Road leaving it often, halting often—Fair farming country—Too much spirits arounds for the good of troops—we made about 20 miles—put up near Boynton—

April 27, 1865   Thursday. Start up again 6:30 A.M. and passed through Boynton, crossed staunton river at Skipryan farm and en-

---

5. Lt. Col. John K. Robison had been wounded at Farmville on April 7, 1865 (see Samuel's entry for that date); Capt. Frederick W. Heslop at Dinwiddie Court House on Mar. 31, 1865; and Capt. Henry W. Oliphant at Sailor's Creek on April 6, 1865. There is no record of Lt. Solomon Barnes being wounded since Sept. 13, 1863, but he may have been hurt in some minor way in the drive to Appomattox. "E" was almost certainly Lt. William H. Everhart, who had been wounded with Oliphant at Sailor's Creek. *PV*, pp. 956, 984.

6. Cormany's black servant. See entries for Aug. 5, 1863, and Nov. 19, 1864.

camped at 8 P.M. having scoured the country all day from place to place—Strange it seems to travel thus all about this country so recently occupied by The Enemy and find no one to molest us in any way. Surely this people was ready to lay down arms and quit—

My health is splendid—now, and spirits good. Excepting the annoyances created by the wounding and absence of Col Robison, resulting in the return of Major Fry and Maj J. C. Robinson both itching for the honor of Commanding Our War-worn—battle scarred—regiment, now that all danger is a thing of the past. But it don't set well on the Boys who won our record—or made it to be commandeered by fellows who scarcely ever saw rebels, or smelled powder—

We all of us long for the the speedy restoration of our Col. and for his return.

The dear old Colonel Can't return too soon for the Joy of Head Qrs—especially of The Adjutants office—

My! how little three years of posing as a Major has done for Fry—Maj Robinson did see a little service as a Captain, but has almost none of the real worth as a Commander of Col John K. Robison—(I know this effusion is a little breach of true military discipline—but my Diary won't be read for some years—and so dont hurt The Boys)

April 28, 1865 Friday. Delightful day—Took up march at 7 ock—Crossed the Danville R.R. at Scottsburg Stn went via Hailifax Court House to S. Boston crossed the Dan river and encamped for the night—Recd dispatch that Genl Johnson had surrendered about same time as Genl Lee.[7]

April 29, 1865 Saturday. Move at 7 ock—Recrossed the Dan, and marched via Suttville Station to Staunton River, crossed at Mosley's Ferry and encamped within a mile[8]—A heavy shower at dusk, and cleared right after—Our rations come up—This mess is not nearly as nice as to be alone with my "George"—

April 30, 1865 Sunday. Quiet—restful—til 11½ A.M.—when we again took up the march—a fine country—down the Lunenburg Court House road and encamped near Maherring river at 8 P.M. O Yes! The Regt mustered for pay at 10 this A.M.—and our Chaplain

7. General Johnston had first asked for terms on April 14, but did not formally surrender until April 26, 1865. E. B. Long, *The Civil War Day by Day: An Almanac, 1861–1865* (Garden City, N.Y., 1971), pp. 676–83.

8. Sheridan had his cartographers chart the route of this cavalry reconnaissance to South Boston on the Dan River. That official map is reproduced in *OMACW*, pl. LXXIV, no. 1.

took to messing alone again today—He suits better to mess alone, and I am sure we are more of a Mess without the Gentleman—

We had no Chaplain through the war, and the dear fellow cant create an atmosphere suitable to even us good Boys. Fact!

May 1, 1865 Monday. Up and off at 6 A.M. crossed the Mahoning, passed through Lunenburg—and lots-o-fine-lands, and encamped at 3 miles from Black and White Station towards evening. This is dandy playing—soldier—sightseeing—keeping well and happy—of course, our circulating all around in this Jerusalem of secessiondom gives the Elect Rebels a chance to see the make up of the Cavalry fellows that harrassed them and their braves, and finally brought them to their knees, and bro't out the spirit of obedience in them, with some of the spirit of loyalty sprouting up here and there, now and then, but the crop is not very startling yet.

May 2, 1865 Tuesday. Weather fine—marched at 6 A.M.—Drew rations at B and W Station—and "around and abouted" to see and be seen and towards evening turned in and encamped about 18 miles from Petersburg—

We found vegitation very much advanced on this trip. Wheat heading out, Cherries Coloring, Clover blossoming, and the little Chickens hopping and peeping about Houses—Cabins—barns &c. and the little and bigger darkies—some black, some yellow, some more or less so, in evidence, a great deal

Eve! I am thinking very much today—by spells of events—reaching a crices at "Carlisle Hill" Canada three years ago—rather approaching it.

May 3, 1865 Wednesday. Hip-hooray! Coras birth Day——

Took up march at 6 OCK A.M. we struck The Boydton plank Road 7 miles from Petersburg

Saw some of the effects of the hard fighting of the opening of the Spring Campaign, where Picketts Div of Hills Corpse was captured—Got into Petersburg about noon—Crossed the Appomattox—& R.R. and encamped on N. Side at 4 P.M.—

Well and happy as usual—but Oh! to be at home this evening to help Darling Celebrate This The 3rd Anniversary of Coras birth day, No. 3.

May 4, 1865 Thursday. A Large mail came to us, but none from Darling—Business in office great and pressing—Commissions came for Lieut Swank as Captain Sergt Andrews as 1st Lieut 2 Lieut Puler as 1st Lieut—Sergt Beecher 2nd Lieut Sgt Maj Schively 2nd Lieut and J. Coble as 2nd Lieut—P.M. Two letters from Pet—Oh such dear ones—wrote and mailed one for her and Bro. Amos.[hh]

May 5, 1865 Friday. Booming office work making out back Returns &c &c Sergt Maj (now Lieut) and Clerk doing finely and will soon catch up—

I am pretty well, but am so tired of my office under the present incumbent Com'd'g Officers—Mere "up starts" as compared with Col Robison and assuming more authority over me and my office, and things generaly in one day, than Our old veteran Col attempted in a week, and the Col knew more at a glance than they together do in a week—I just do need special grace, and wisdom to treat them with due(?) respect—To be a real Man—and carry myself and my office above "pettyness"—and noticing commandeering and strutting—

Tendered my resignation and Request for Discharge to be forwarded tomorrow[9]—

May 6, 1865 Saturday. Major Fry also resigned—The Majors and my requests forwarded same time this A.M.

I do want out of Service now, as I doubt whether our dear Col J. K. Robison will be able to take Command of the Regiment again, and I cannot do much for The Boys—under present conditions.

Very busy in Office all day—Capt Chas H. Miller once adjt—but defective—called on Maj Fry—Capt Snyder and others—were very gay indeed not very military—and by evening were much under the influence of "Spiritus Frumenti"

Dr Cox and I had a fine walk and Chat by moonlight this Eve—we had an atmosphere of Our Own—far above the line of whiskey soaks—

I do want to go home, to my dear ones, and away from all this vice, and unballanced Officialdom—and yet it seems selfish to wish to be relieved from the place where I can still be of some help to the "old Boys—and, Lord I want to be helpful to these fellows—

It surely can't be long til "we'll all go marching home again! Hurrah! Hurrah!——

May 7, 1865 Sunday. A sweet balmy air, and misty sunshine—Major Fry sober and OK this morning—The Major, Dr Cox and I

9. Cormany's letter of resignation, dated May 6, 1865, survives in "Pennsylvania Regimental Letter, Endorsement, Journal, and Miscellaneous Book, 16th Cavalry," NA.

took a fine ride. Lay over at a fine Farm House. Dinner for three, and it was fine—Paid $2.00

P.M. In office—wrote long letter to Pet—and one for D. Woodall for his wife—Am pretty well and cheerful this Eve—Has been a pretty sunny sabbath throughout—But I am O so anxious that Col Robison returns, so I may have something of a liveable life on military lines. Chaplain preached at 6 P.M. So the Sabbath closed with a little period of uplifting exercises, and some fellowship with a hom-ish flavor

May 8, 1865 Monday. Fine—Rather warm—New Order—"March for Linchburg in the Morning"—Busy clearing up Office work—and all preparations—for a move into a new part of the State to us—
I spent part of the evening at Brigade Head Quarters—

May 9, 1865 Tuesday. Form line for marching 7 ock. Pass through Petersburg via Southerland Station to Fords Depot, and encamped at 6 OCK about 20 miles from Petersburg

Am well, and as gay and happy as an Adjutant can be who has so many things to aggravate and perplex him—Oh! That all who would be, really were, men or at least acted The Man, and the true Soldier—

May 10, 1865 Wednesday. Fine for marching—we passed Black and White Station, thence to Nottaway Court House and Station and went into Camp at 6 P.M.

Major Fry bought himself some "Mess kitt" and proposes to mess alone—or by himself, to our utter satisfaction—The command drew abundance of Hay—so we have happy horses as well as Men—We made 25 miles today——Jolly night of it—warm—

May 11, 1865 Thursday. Move out at 7 A.M. Struck Berksville at 10 OCK—Drew rations & Forage, wonderful crowd of citazens, and parolled prisoners mingle with the men, asking for Rations—The "Boys" are generous to them—O how changed to see the Negro, The soldier, and the Chivalry in one mass, press to the Commissary Department for rations, on equal terms and footing, and how nobly our men acted. It was a real Joy! We moved on to Bush River and encamped—a great Hail-storm swept over us, with rain, and not only drenched us, but so demoralised our horses, that mens nerves were put to severe test—but after ½ hours tension the sun came out, and the drying process went on quietly—But the night was rather an uncomfortable one, and The boys were glad to hail a warm rising sun—

May 12, 1865 Friday. Clear—Dried off til 8 A.M. and started via Prince Edwards Court House to Pamplin Station etc making about 25 miles—encamping near the Station at 9 P.M.—We suppered George dressed a pair of chickens for breakfast—and I retired 11½ OCK—I am quite well, and much more happy since Cap Snyder and I mess alone again with My George for Cook, and no up-starts to awaken discord—

May 13, 1865 Saturday. Very pleasant. Took up the march at 8 OCK, Having filled up with chicken Stew Potatoes & Bread Went via Evergreen Station and Appomattox Station—over the ground where our Cavalry had the last fighting. Then on to Concord Station 11 miles from Lynchburg, and encamped at a beautiful place about 4 PM

Everything is lovely, and many things move off more smoothly than previously, since Capt Snyder and I mess, and yoke up together and are free from pestifferousness.

May 14, 1865 Sunday. Fine—clear—and a general day of rest—

Our Chaplain preached at Church at Concord at 11 A.M.—Capt Phillips and I got a fine dinner at Mr. G. W. Staples in Concord—

P.M. I wrote, and mailed letters to Pet and Col Robison—

How I do long for a letter from my Pet, and still more to be with her and Cora—safe at Home—

May 15, 1865 Monday. I went to Brig Hd. Qrs attended to some B. B.[10]

Major Robinson and I dined at Mr Staples—P.M. Adj't of 8th Pa. Cav. Drs E and Cox and I went calling at widow Davis, widow Evans, thence to Camp, thence to Mrs Burfords, where we had a fine supper, and made acquaintance of The Misses Gussie, Nannie and married Sister Mrs. Davison—spent til 11 P.M. very pleasantly—in a general social way.[11]

---

10. Brigade business.

11. The last Confederate forces in the west did not formally capitulate until early June, and the Federal government remained divided over the future status of the Confederate states. Consequently, it seemed appropriate to leave a military presence at key points such as Lynchburg, an important railroad junction (see Robert C. Black III, *The Railroads of the Confederacy* [Chapel Hill, N.C., 1952], p. 283 et passim). The sociability Cormany describes probably reflects some combination of resignation, peacemaking, ingratiation, and business sense (Union soldiers paid for their meals).

May 16, 1865 Tuesday. Recd news of Capture of "Old Jeff Davis"—Some Jollifying on a/c[12]—

Receive orders to move tomorrow—Did not put up office here as we seemed unsettled—no mail came—

Dr. Cox and I took Tea at Mrs Davis Thence went to Mrs Burford again where we spent the evening very pleasantly indeed—Returned to Camp about 11½ OCK.

May 17, 1865 Wednesday. Up betimes, and on line of march by 7 OCK—to a point some 6 miles from Lynchburg—where we went into Camp—We had a mess of Mulletts for supper—Eve Capt Snyder and I went to Lynchburg called at 2nd Brig. Hd Qrs. Thence went down street—Saw the sights—Met fun half way—Took in an open southern dance—simply as onlookers, was rather naughty—being out til 3 OCK—

May 18, 1865 Thursday. Office shaped up—any amt of business for Serg't Major and clerk—Sent in Tri Monthly Return, Ditto field Return, and list of men whose term expires prior to Oct 1" 1865—Indications are that we will soon be mustered out of Service—Am a little unwell physically and more so spiritually—O what a feeble thing is man! When shall I ever attain to my ideal of a Man, a real noble image of the handiwork of God, an example for other men to follow, to imitate, a man who can always easily say no to the appearance of Evil—and yes to every duty, or opportunity to do the noble, manly Soldierly thing—I am so thankful for the confidence my men repose in me—even more so the honors my Superiors Confer upon me so many times—I must maintain the inner worthiness of all honors conferred—

May 19, 1865 Friday. Took up the line of march at 6:30 A.M. up main street in Lynchburg—then up fifth to College Hill. Encamped about noon in a fine open wood, near The Fair Ground.[13]

Put up Hd Qr's and got down to business—I am very much depressed in Spirits. Evil thoughts perplex me ever and anon, and my

---

12. When Lee notified the Confederate government that Richmond could not be held, President Jefferson Davis fled south. He was captured May 10 near Irwinsville, Ga. See Hudson Strode, *Jefferson Davis: Tragic Hero, The Last Twenty-five Years, 1864–1889* (New York, 1964), pp. 216–26.

13. The fairgrounds abutted the Orange and Alexandria (later Southern) Railroad tracks on what was then the western edge of Lynchburg. Richard B. Lloyd and Bernard K. Mundy, *Lynchburg: A Pictorial History* (Virginia Beach, Va., 1975), Harry W. Cumby map of "The original seven hills of the city of Lynchburg."

passions, how they long to rule me. Thou God art my refuge and strength and my Keeper.

May 20, 1865 Saturday. Very fine weather—Quite warm, but a fine breeze stirring all the while—Busy all day in Office—Capt's McDowell and Day detailed as Provost Marshalls—Capt Snyder sent to arrest some parties—

Evening Dr Cox and I visited The Pratts Hospital—Find many deformed & crippled Rebs there—

Set up fine supper for us—Later Mr Burford was up to see us, at Our Hd Qrs. we had a fine chat on the new Situation—

May 21, 1865 Sunday. Hot but breezy—Had Inspection—Boys made good showing—Called at Mrs Creasys' a while—

Had preaching at 10 A.M.—P.M. rained a shower —at 4:30 Dr Cox and I started out for a ride—called at Mr Burfords, were received warmly. Had a fine mess of lucious cherries—and a fine supper—and lots of sociability—an awful thunder shower came up—waters came up high—Awfully dark—Had to remain til morning—were up til 12:30,

May 22, 1865 Monday. Left for Camp at grizzly dawn—Found Beaver creek still high—but fordable. Struck Camp at 6:30 A.M.

All hands busy in office all day—Evening do some retrospecting—I am so well, but by no means as happy as I should be—I have retrograded some spiritually, am too much given to fun and foolishness for spiritual growth. I almost despair of ever becoming a real model man, much less my ideal of a perfect man, and a model Soldier.

May 23, 1865 Tuesday. Very fine day—Our camp is so delightfully shady—and such fine breezes stir the air most all the time. I got Corp Lem Rivers of I Co. to help square up office accounts, and work generally. Greatly pressed with business in the office—keep every helper strictly on the Job all the day——Close the day reviewing my Year with prayerful heart—So often I have said Oh to be a man after my own heart—With this as the key note of all my prayer,

> "I lay me down to sleep,
> and Pray the Lord my soul to keep
> If I should die before I wake
> I pray the Lord my Soul to take,
> and This I ask for Jesus sake. Amen!"

May 24, 1865 Wednesday. Beautiful is the weather. I am 27 years old today. How swiftly glide the years, and make such slow progress—In some respects I am less a Man than I was a year ago, in others I've advanced—Great God! how shall I control myself all around and in all cases—always correct and erect and immovable—Lord be Thou my keeper——Major Fry called to Genl Greggs Staff—So J. C. Robinson is in Command of our Regiment. Orders from War Dept for many back returns which other Adj'ts failed to send in when due—Glad mine went in on time—

Eve took a ride to town

May 25, 1865 Thursday. Very warm—Men made some Changes in Camp—Office force busy all day, nothing special for my fellows, but to keep up to the dot, ready for any kind of inquiry or report—Am well physically, but it seems my mind and soul are caving in—I do so need my Rachel to fill me out, and stand beside me, and bring me to my best, and keep me there as she alone can by His Grace.

May 26, 1865 Friday. Rains and blows—Mostly laying off in office—and "let her drive"

P.M. Ride out with Maj Bell—Get some old apple brandy or Jack—Eve Capt Snyder & I go to town—Lynchburg—and 2nd Brig. Hd. Qrs—

Had a long confidential talk with Capt Maitland, A.A.AG of J. I. Greggs Staff on military lines—Indulged some in "Apple Jack"—Got pretty lively—In fact a little unmanned—

That stuff is so deceptive—I've vowed and vowed, and sinned again. Twere better not to vow. But here I am—ashamed—to know, we both have been foolish—not viscious but too giddy for the rank and place we occupy—The Boys don't see our foolishness—Tis well! Their respect would suffer a little shock! We separate! and soon find our bunks, and sleep, and so things go once in a long while. But God forgives—and soon I'll be at Home, and be myself.

May 27, 1865 Saturday. Clear! Busy day in Office—wrote to Dr. Herman, socially, and on Reg. affairs—Evening take myself to account severely for irregularity of last evening—I must control my inclinations to go astray thru the social glass or canteen—

May 28, 1865 Sunday. Beautiful morning—Fine Inspection at 8:30—Preaching at 10—at 11—I with Lieut Peder and ten men made a scout to New London—The place where Patrick Henry made his great war speech—which still rings in the ears of great men[14]—This is a very wild, romantic country—I had a fine chat with Wm C. Burton Esq. and a delightful southern Lady at the home—Returned to Camp at dusk. Mr. Creasy spent the eve with Dr. Cox and me at our Hd Qrs.

May 29, 1865 Monday. Blustry-warm-cold-rainy &c. Very busy all day in Office—i.e. My Sergt Major and Clerk are, and I am in and out periodically directing things—Am just fighting Blues constantly. P.M. spent a few hours with my special Friend, Assistant Adjutant General—Capt Maitland—in town—a grand man and soldier, and True Friend

Eve recd such a good letter from my Rachel—would that I were worthy her perfection. and devotion, and trueness—

May 30, 1865 Tuesday. Fine—Dr Cox and I started P.M. for Mrs Burfords, Concord—on way met Col Robison on his way to the regiment—Had a little Joytime on the road—Then we went on, got to Burfords at 4 ock—a Fine supper—lots of cherries—and a very agreeable evening socially—We started for Camp about 9:30—Reached Camp at mid-night—in good trim—Seems like a new Era dawns upon us now that Our blessed Colonel Robison is with us again—It starts up my old fount of happiness again.

May The Col never leave us.

May 31, 1865 Wednesday. Office crowded with work

O how glad I am that Col Robison has returned. His Fatherly presence is a blessing, but makes me feel my littleness, and see wherein I have been retrograding—but Oh what a help—what strength he will be to me—Wrote such a candid letter to Pet—deplored my lack of attaining my own ideals—and my little lapses— What a wonderful ideal she seems to me, Yes really is.

June 1, 1865 Thursday. Very warm—Busy all day in Office—I am getting to see a little daylight, and end of reports, for a time—

14. Cormany refers to a speech more famous in his day than now. Henry was defending a former army commissary agent who had been sued by a former loyalist, John Hook, for compensation and damages for two steers that Henry's client had seized to feed revolutionary troops. Henry rehearsed the suffering of the patriots, the glorious victory at Yorktown, and the nobility of the American cause; then ended with withering ridicule of the tightfisted loyalist and his mean-spirited claim. Hook barely escaped tar and feathers by fleeing the courtroom. See Henry Howe, *Historical Collections of Virginia; Containing a Collection of the Most Interesting Facts, Traditions, Biographical Sketches, Anecdotes, etc., Relating to Its History* . . . (Charleston, S.C., 1845), pp. 213–14.

I need rest. Oh how I want a letter from Pet, how I want to talk with her, or even time to write her a long letter—I fear my last makes her feel sad

I was so candid—My God bless my Rachel and Our Cora—

Evening The Colonel and I took a ride—7 ock in the 4th Pa Cav—Brig. Hd. Qrs—Lynchburg &c &c

O how much more happy I am now that The Colonel is here, and here to stay—and that he has lost none of his Fatherliness—nor Commanding dignity and personality.

June 2, 1865 Friday. Very busy on Reports—I feel some happier than for some time. I trust I shall yet attain that degree of Manhood perfect, which I so much admire, and so sincerely desire, and hold myself on line to attain.

June 3, 1865 Saturday. Office routine—Am quite well, and real happy. Everything moves methodically and smoothely—P.M. Dr Cox and I call on the Misses Edwards. we had an agreeably sociable time—They are literary & musical—and sunshiny withal—

June 4, 1865 Sunday. Very warm. The Col and I went to Methodist Church—Dr Cox—D Ellenshaw and Lieut Burns followed—Heard a pretty good sermon—and fine music—Audience chiefly Ladies and children—only a few men—Eve Chaplain held services in Camp

June 5, 1865 Monday. Mail—Good letter from Pet and Brother Amos[15]—Put in day close to business—I stand it finely—Nothing new or of special interest save the presence of our Colonel is more than a ballance wheel to all movements—P.M. Dr Cox and I call at the Edwards Home—enjoy cheery chat—one feels the uplift of respectable ladies in a cozy home, causes me to think so much of My Pets, and makes my Darling seem more precious to me, and arouses deep longing to be at home with her, and our little One—Eve wrote and mailed a good letter to Pet—

June 6, 1865 Tuesday. Busy day—plenty of agravations by careless officers and their reports making extra work for my helpers. P.M. The dismounted men from City point commenced coming this evening at dusk——Major J. C. Robinson and Lieutenants Brown, Peters

---

15. Amos had been visiting Rachel. See her entries for May 10, 23, and June 5, 1865. Amos wanted to know whether Samuel would join him and their brother-in-law, James W. Adams, in Southern land investments.

& Polly came——Makes quite a stir to have all these officers and men—many of them dubbed Bummers—Come in and crow, now that all danger is past, and "playing Soldier" is on—

June 7, 1865 Wednesday. Pleasant day—Did some re-organizing of Regiment, and made some Camp changes—Set on Foot some general Policing, and fixing up Camp and Quarters—Very busy in Office—The force is quite efficient—I am suffering from dull toothache—use chloroform, is a speedy remedy—acts instantly[16]——Dr and I call a bit at Miss Mollies—I am done there now—Indications touch the point of being questionable, or liable to become such—

June 8, 1865 Thursday. Fine day—Col orders better discipline—Had a Guard Mount of 45 Men, 3 Corporals, 1 Serg't and one Com'd Officer acting as Regimental Officer of the day and Officer of the Guard—

Returned Lindley to his Company, and detailed George Brown for Clerk—P.M. Finished up 4 lb Package of Returns called for, and mailed them to Hd. Qrs.——Eve good letter from Pet & Bro A. B[hh]—

Doctor of 8th Pa Cav called—Dr Cox & I took a moonlight stroll am well and happy—Too busy for anything else.

June 9, 1865 Friday. Special! Our Col Robison is placed in Command of 2nd Brigade—Lieut Crawford returns to duty with Reg't & Co—Otherwise routine—

June 10, 1865 Saturday. Routine—O! to bask in The sunshine of my Darlings Love—To look into her bright eyes and press her to me, heart to heart—

June 11, 1865 Sunday. Routine, and office work til 4 P.M. Eve Dr Cox & I took a walk to town, promenaded with The Misses Edwards to the Cemetery—We had not a really pleasant time. My Rachels spirit was with me all the time, and so filled my eyes and soul that I could not see Miss Sallie Edwards, however companionable she is socially, and religiously—and however much our group had in common—There arose continually the longing Oh! That my Pet were

---

16. Chloroform, opium, and various essential oils were commonly packed into tooth cavities to relieve pain. T. Lindley Kemp, *The Medical Guide to the Preservation of Health and the Knowledge of Disease; Being an Outline of the Principles of Physiology, Pathology, and Therapeutics, Designed for Popular Use* (London, 1853), "Dictionary of Surgery for Popular Use," pp. 26–27.

here! My Pet my all——at dusk we returned—and soon I was asleep in my tent, dreaming of Darling and Cora—

June 12, 1865 Monday. Cloudy—Sultry—rained some. Some companies are working on muster-out Rolls.—I feel the pressure of my close confinement to Office work—From dawn til 11–12 ock—I must soon get out of this, and home to my dear ones—my all—

June 13, 1865 Tuesday. Extremely warm—Twenty men of A Co. mustered out today—I completed the muster-out-papers of the Non-Commissioned Staff who go out. Busy day as usual in Office—Col Robison returns to Command of Regiment—Recd details for Majors Robinson—Snyder—Capt Cary—Lieuts Reeder and Puler

June 14, 1865 Wednesday. Very busy—Four of Non-Comd Staff, Thirty Three, of C Company—Thirty 8 men of G mustered out—
Great bluster and xcitement up in regiment on a/c of some being mustered out, and others kept in service[17]—
I wrote an Address for Col Robison—to Officers and men—Subject—Past association how pleasant the recollection—and a parting advice—Read it on Dress Parade—wondrous cheers!!!

June 14, 1865 Thursday. 36 men of Co "B"—35 of "H" Co—23 of "I" Co mustered out—
I read an Address from Major Snyder to "H" Co—which I had written—and then I made an xtempore speech to the outgoing Boys—with a warm goodbye to it——"H" Co and I called on the Colonel and gave the parting hand and 3 rousing cheers for Him and the Whole 16th——"I" Company waited on me (I commanded them some time when I was 2nd Lieut) in the evening—I made a little speech to them Shook hands with each and all—and received of them Three rousing Cheers and a Tiger[18]——There is a sadness in the parting from those with whom we have fought The Enemy so often, and with whom we have been so closely connected for so long and in so many ways—

---

17. The Army of the Potomac had begun mustering out volunteer forces under a series of orders issued in May. *OR*, ser. III, vol. V, pp. 1–3, 20–23. Enlisted men were being released in a prescribed sequence that was roughly related to their length of service.
18. A howl-like cheer or yell; sometimes a growling pronunciation of the word "tiger" building to a crescendo.

June 16, 1865 Friday. Rainy day—We settle down to the work of re-organization, and correcting the Records—

June 17, 1865 Saturday. Rainy—Routine office work—Recd a fine letter from Pet. Wrote some in response—and am so refreshed by reading Darlings good letter, and meditating on the preciousness of My Darlings

June 18, 1865 Sunday. Hot—Usual Inspection—Wrote most of day for Pet. Rather gloomy I fear—Eve Dr Cox and I called a bit at Edwardses—A cheery set they are—Returned to Camp at dusk—
This Evening finds me somewhat depressed in spirit—I lack in the Joyous assurances which usually are mine to enjoy—

June 19, 1865 Monday. Sultry day. Office full of work—Sergt Major and Clerk doing finely—They need little of me today—Finished letter, and mailed to Pet & Bro Amos[hh]—
I am ashamed of myself—Why should I feel so blue? True I am greatly tempted to sin, but I am not yielding, and am resting in My Saviours grace to keep me from falling—and enable me to even be a helper to keep others from going astray and from falling into habits not in keeping with a high type of manhood.

June 20, 1865 Tuesday. Not quite so busy in Office work   all a/cs pretty well straightened up—
Eve—a social time, a lot of Officers in my Quarters—Game of "smut"[19] and other amusements. Drink ruled out—Later. Am pretty well, and more happy, but Oh! I do so much long to be once again with my Darling—To see—love—caress her, and share with her the Joys of caressing our precious Cora—
With no Fighting, no long marches, no rough-and-tumbling-it, no sacrifice to an End, Soldiering is a dead service (?)
An occasional Dress Parade or Scout—to show off—Inspection—Guard Mount & Police duty as a matter of form & discipline seem so nearly a farce. They tire an old Fellow or a lot of them, after having seen so much smoke of battle—and shared so many desperate encounters where life squared up to life, and one or The other must enjoy(?) The worst of it all—Yes! There was enjoyment in it all, as compared with these days and events of "playing the Soldier"—

19. A card game.

June 21, 1865 Wednesday. Nothing exciting—nothing new! Doc Cox and I took rousing baths. So feel better mentally and physically Eve another Jolly time for an hour on "Smut"—I got in once for the first time.

Time moves along monotimously O for something exciting—Tragical, Big, to look back over at bed-time as an achievement—

June 22, 1865 Thursday. Most beautiful morning—such a cool balmy breeze floats through my Head Quarters—

The Sgt Maj & clerk busy but not crowded—Day of routine—Eve Doc Cox and I called on The Misses Edwards—an hour, quite a diversion and Jolity, both for the family and for us as well—wrote awhile for Pet.

June 23, 1865 Friday. Busy in office in A.M. all well and happy—

P.M. Dr. Cox and ride out to Mrs. Burfords—Cordial reception agreeably pleasant time all the while, and a magnificent supper Then jollity in general til 10 ock—

We started homeward via a roundabout way—striking Lynchburg and arriving at Camp at 2 ock. A great night ride sure—so bracing!

June 24, 1865 Saturday. Routine generally

I finished 8 page letter to Pet—and then some to others—I am well, and happier than for some time—a fine letter came from Pet—oh how her letters do buoy me up—

June 25, 1865 Sunday. Routine—Lieut Peters called on me in A.M. I called on Mr Shoemakers—It rained so we had no services—Eve nothing new nor stirring.

June 26, 1865 Monday. Beautiful day—Office busy. I made out the "Character Roster" of the officers of the Regiment—Designating those who desire to remain in service to full enlistment—of 3 years—

Great rain storm in P.M. wrote some for Pet—

Col. Robison and I get on so nicely—never a jar —Leaves so much to me, relies fully upon me—and I never disappoint him.

June 27, 1865 Tuesday. Beautiful day a little lull in office—Dr Cox and I went to city at 10 A.M. Called on Maj. Snyder—saw some of the workings of the employment Agency System—looks hard—I accosted a Rebel Major who had been drinking some—I took in a fine dinner—Called on Dear Maitland, White, Capt Moss &c &c and

568

others—Some 16 of us officers had some "mint julips"—some too much, got quite boozy, and made themselves ridiculous—Doc and I put up at a Boarding House for a fine dinner—and quiet. Some got too high for others of us—But we must not abandon any of our Fellows about midnight got all hands pretty well regulated, and Doc Cox and returned to Camp, about 2 ock A.M. rather ashamed of ourselves for having been drawn into such a crowd of officers and such hilarity—

June 28, 1865 Wednesday. Fine day—Routine in office and camp I am ashamed over last nights escapade—am resolved to shun any possible repetition.

New move—companies B, G, D, I, K, L, M,—200 men went to Lynchburg City—on Provost duty

June 29, 1865 Thursday. Maj W.H. Fry reported to Regt. again, under a special order—very busy in office—moved out all the clerks and now have all the room to myself—It is fine—I enjoy it so much better—and the Sergt Major and clerks have more freedom—I am well, and pretty happy. Long so much for a letter from Pet. Oh! to see her and Cora—

June 30, 1865 Friday. Beautiful—Mustered in A.M.—we have wonderful bother getting out company monthlies—These new Sergeants (since re-organization) try ones patience horribly[20]—P.M. Thundered, Stormed & rained awfully. Took a dash to city in eve. just a wee.

July 1, 1865 Saturday. Office rushed—nothing new—4th Pa. Cav. started home this morning—Eve oh! for a letter from Pet, but alas none has come, and I keep wishing on. Oh to see her—to put my arms about her and lovingly to caress her my own dearest Darling One—

July 2, 1865 Sunday. Fine balmy morning—went to Baptist Church in A.M. P.M. Dr. Cox and I went to Mrs. Burfords. Dr Davison returned from prison—we had a splendid visit and a luscious supper—returned to Camp at 10 ock. Rode much of the way sleeping—

---

20. Commanding officers were ordered to consolidate the remaining troops into coherent units of appropriate strength. Whenever possible, volunteers from the same state were to be combined, thus expediting their eventual dispersal at government expense back to their original points of enlistment. Ibid., pp. 20–23.

July 3, 1865 Monday. Fine—I have much easier time now that Sgt Maj and clks are alone, and so most of the work of my office—I simply look over their work, approve, sign it and forward to Hd. Qrs—

Nothing new!—the 4th is coming! How I would love to be home, and awaken on the 4th with the smiles of my devoted Rachel first to meet my eyes, and her Kisses and caresses first to cheer my soul, and then to toss and fuss with our Cora, and hear her coo and cheer

July 4, 1865 Tuesday. Hot—A Parade at 9 A.M. Declaration of Independence read—Passed in Review—Music by the Brig Band— Had a little business in office Seemed little like Independence Day rather a kind of Sunday soldiering this—

Eve we had sports—sack Races—open foot races—&c &c &c Dr Cox and I called on Mrs Burfords, at the R. R. Station in the city, just a passing while.

July 5, 1865 Wednesday. Hot, sultry, took noon nap—office work goes on O.K. Eve. Dr Cox and I called on the 8th Pa Cav—some pleasantries—awfully hot—still no letter from Pet. seems all too bad. Seems so long. But one is coming!

July 6, 1865 Thursday. Routine—not rushed. Took fine sleep— Time for reading and thinking—Took supper at McBryants—

July 7, 1865 Friday. Breakfast also—Rations delayed—attend a Public Horse Sale—

Evening retired early—at 11 ock Lieuts Kindig and Patten came to call on me—were pretty boozy—High time

July 8, 1865 Saturday. very hot. 21st Pa Cav started home—Got my quarters fixed up finely—Sent off Our Pay Rolls today—wrote and mailed letter to Pet, and am longing for one from her

What a wonderful affair Our Mail System is—we write and ad-dress & stamp and Uncle Sam does the rest—Letters get there—

July 9, 1865 Sunday. Cloudy—sultry—had inspection and quiet— P.M. Dr Cox & I Took a ride—to Mrs Beufords were cordially re-ceived and entertained—had a delicious Supper Turkey, Chicken &c &c &c

Evening we took a delightful walk—Miss Jenny Davis and Sergt Dedecker were there also—we left about 11 Ock. Got to Camp 1 ock

July 10, 1865 Monday. Routine—Consolidation seems all the theme—

July 11, 1865 Tuesday. Received notice that the order re-instating Major Fry is revoked. So he goes—all on the qui-vive awaiting orders for the Consolidation of 16th & 8th Pa. Cav am longing for letter from Pet—

July 12, 1865 Wednesday. Rec'd orders for consolidation—at once we get on the job—and aided by my Sergt Major I consolidate the Twelve companies into Six, and Col Robison approves and signs it. Thus everything moves off smoothly—

July 13, 1865 Thursday. Details of consolidation going on smoothly—I am well and in fine spirits—save the longing for a letter from Pet—none in 3 weeks—how long the time seems—

July 14, 1865 Friday. Completing the officers part of Records—nothing new—I wrote letters home for Abr Rosenberry and J. Long—My how they appreciate my doing it for them—

July 15, 1865 Saturday. Office busy on Records Genl Custer arrived this P.M. Eve rec'd Oh! such a good long letter from Pet—How rejoiced I am over it—To know that Darling and ours are well and happy is my greatest solicitude

July 16, 1865 Sunday. Powerful shower no inspection—wrote a long letter to Pet—10 pgs. offl. size & some
  Eve. severe head ache—oh! to lay it on the bosom of my jewel and have her stroke it well in a minute—

July 17, 1865 Monday. Consolidation up. Capt Kendall tries to overthrow my—Col Robisons plan of consolodating—There is quite a stir. But we stand o.k. only I am bothered greatly by Company Com'd'rs not being prompt and paying poor attention to orders—Eve Dr. Cox & I go to city for a change—

July 18, 1865 Tuesday. Capt Kendall has knocked our plans on the head—we now sit down and give all over into his and General Greggs hands and say "Let them rip"—It will be all over with soon anyway—

July 19, 1865 Wednesday. My feelings are almost insupportable—Oh that I could undo—O whiskey! thou demon! May I never put thee to my lips again—God being my helper I shall be a better—a nobler man—can my Rachel forgive me! I know she will—

I write and confess to her at once, and as God forgives me so does she also I am quite sure. Office work is easily handled these days—and I am well and equal to all of it—

July 20, 1865 Thursday. Fairly busy in office all day. Spend a good deal of time in my private office, reading my bible, meditating and praying—Oh! for strength to make and keep good, my vows to be the ideal man. I have so often promised myself, and vowed to God I would be—

July 21, 1865 Friday. Very hot & sultry.
As usual busy! nothing new—

July 22, 1865 Saturday. Telegram to make up muster out Rolls at once. That all the Cavalry is to be discharged with the Deptmt of Va at once—I read the order to the regiment in solid body company formation—I never saw such a Jubilant outburst prevail amongst Men & officers. Not even at the surrender—Commenced briskly on The Rolls——

July 23, 1865 Sunday. I made out an original muster out Roll for Non-Commissioned Staff. All busy—all A.M. on Rolls Field and Staff and Companies—

Noon. Received orders to drop making out muster-out Rolls and go on with Consolidation—Soon There was quite a Murmuring in Camp. Evening came very near a mutiny—There was a beginning but we got it stopped. My how cool the Col is, and how he seemed to look to me as a reliable stand by—

I never saw such a feeling of rebellion manifest in the Regiment before—It seemed more a determined remonstrance against being trifled with—But the Col's "We'll be Men to the end" was enough—All quieted down like Men![21]

21. The process of demobilization provoked a great deal of trouble throughout the Union army. Many men resented temporary assisgnment to strange units, especially if some of their friends got to go home instead. Officers squabbled over who commanded whom as the contraction and consolidation continued (see Cormany's entries for July 17 and 18, 1865). Beleaguered paymasters frequently ran behind schedule, and irregular paperwork often delayed the departure of soldiers who were otherwise free to go home. Several outright mutinies occurred, and not all of them could be hidden from the public. See, for example, New York *Times*, June 16, 1865, and Baltimore *Sun*, July 1, 1865.

July 24, 1865 Monday. Consolidation goes on again—Maj Robinson—Capts Caughy, Robbins & Ressler, and Lieuts Brooks, Jones, Crawford and Barnes who had been m. o. 21st & had muster out revoked were m.o. today and started for home this P.M.—I was in city this P.M.—Trying to see my Horse——Col Robison ordered to command 8th Penna Cav—

July 25, 1865 Tuesday. very busy. am well and pretty happy—wrote letter to Pet—brief, mails are irregular these days—
   I am so inclined to be short, quick tempered—impatient and the many "criss-cross" orders incite me. I am so tempted to curse lack of discipline—and prompt obedience to orders—O for the Control of myself I used to have, when we were actually doing things.

July 26, 1865 Wednesday. Very busy squaring up a/cs Books, &c preparatory to a move and a grand turn in of all Government Books &c in our offices—

July 27, 1865 Thursday. orders to Turn in all U.S. Horses, pack up Ordnance & Q.M Stores preparatory to shipping—Consolidation announced as being complete—But it is not really so on official Papers.

July 28, 1865 Friday. Went to Brig Hd Qrs. Saw Genl. Gregg—Got the consolidation papers into better shape—Very busy preparing for a speedy move—still no letter from Home. Oh! why this long silence?

July 29, 1865 Saturday. Very hot—Had a mounted Dress parade, and afterwards marched through Lynchburg Va and returned to camp—Rec'd orders that six companies should turn over their horses, and move in the morning at 4 A.M.—Had a very busy time straightening up things preparatory to their move—
   Today the 2nd Brig made its last mounted showing.

July 30, 1865 Sunday. The six companies did not "get off" til 10 ock—Shame to note. Most of our officers and some of the men are drunk. i.e. are far from being the fine looking, and noble acting soldiers they should be——about 10" we rec'd orders to March at 4 P.M. (The other 6 companys) We marched to Grace Church, near Robison B'd'ge—Halt at 8 P.M. Slept in Church—a rainy night—I am thinking so longingly of my Darling—

July 31, 1865 Monday. I rode in to Lynchburg. Took breakfast with Quartermaster Robison and Commissary McDowell[22]—Rainy Rainy and more so. I secured Transportation by R.R. to Richmond—called on General Curtis[23]—Receive orders that we go by Boat, on a/c The Appomattox river being too high to ford—Rained all day—we simply "lie round awaiting Boats—3 came down about 9 P.M.—We slept in Grace Church—

August 1, 1865 Tuesday. Up at 4 Ock. Breakfast &c at 6 Ock A.M. our Head Quarters and Oliphants Squadron get aboard The John Randolph—and two squadrons boarded the Gov Guenant and started. At 11 Ock Major Snyder & Captain Barnes boarded the W. Smith, with horses &c &c aboard the Va— Tho somewhat of confusion prevailed at times, we moved out, and got along finely until we struck the mouth of the Tye river where some literally "stuck in the mud"—and a great time was enjoyed(?). We made slow progress, but kept on the move—many of us slept on deck—

August 2, 1865 Wednesday. Breakfasted at 7 A.M. as best we could, and then got a little more of a move on and glided along nicily—In the P.M. we had a boat race on a wild scale—The Randolph was beaten—

Evening Halted for supper at "Allen Farm" near Columbia—a great time—we saw much of the effects of Sheridans last raid. "All aboard"! and on we go again for all night

August 3, 1865 Thursday. very hot. Lieut Cannon and I swam a race—behind our Boat, for 2½ miles—Great xcitement—I excell Canon was the verdict—

Arrive at Richmond at 4:15 P.M. I reported to Genl. Gregg at Genl Terrys.[24] I had the honor of being introduced to the Genl. and

22. Bvt. Capt. James K. Robison had been quartermaster of the old 16th cavalry; William A. McDowell had been the regiment's commissary sergeant. *PV*, p. 957.

23. Newton M. Curtis (1835–1910) had won a Congressional Medal of Honor and a brevet major general's rank for his heroism at Fort Fisher six months earlier. After the war Curtis enjoyed a successful political career in New York, culminating in his election to Congress during the 1890s. Ezra J. Warner, *Generals in Blue: Lives of the Union Commanders* (Baton Rouge, La., 1964), pp. 106–07. Curtis left his own impressions of the war in a volume entitled *From Bull Run to Chancellorsville; The Story of the Sixteenth New York Infantry, Together with Personal Reminiscences* (New York, 1906).

24. Maj. Gen. Alfred Howe Terry (1827–1890) rose through the ranks of Connecticut's volunteer forces to command of the expedition that captured Fort Fisher, N.C. That success helped earn him a commission in the regular army, which, unlike most volunteer officers after the Civil War, he accepted. Terry remained in the army until he retired as a regular major general in 1888. Warner, *Generals in Blue*, pp. 497–98.

press his excellencys hand in a cordial greeting——we drew rations—Rained—Slept on the Boat—Col—Doc Cox and I took a little promenade and bust in the City—

August 4, 1865 Friday. awfully hot—we brekfasted at "Enrick," Restaurant—Our last boat came in at 10 A.M.—having been detained—
Our command marched across the River to Manchester and Encamped. The 8th Boys joined us, and put up quarters for Shade—Hotest weather I ever saw. Many of the men fell to the ground—fairly wilted by the oppression of heat—Getting out of U.S. service seems a hard road to travel—Oh! for mail—for a letter from "pet and pussy"—

August 5, 1865 Saturday. Office pushing Muster-out-rolls—Spent a while in the City on business.

August 6, 1865 Sunday. very hot—Genl. Gregg out—we have general Inspection—Under the new regime of consolidation—It's Col J. Irwin Gregg now is senior in command of the regiment. Lieut Col J. K. Robison next, or practically in command—and in fact—as Adjutant so long—I almost run the regiment now in the preparations for mustering out of service.
P.M. we had a Dress Parade. a Band played to enliven up the affair—
Mail came, but naught from Darling—How hungry I am for a letter from her—

August 7, 1865 Monday. Genl Gregg in Camp 9 Ock til 3—My office very busy all day—we turned in saddles and equipments—Evening fine Dress Parade—also rec'd such a good letter from Pet—Oh! how glad I am—

August 8, 1865 Tuesday. Cool—stormy—Office very busy on Rolls all day—
We xpect to muster out in a few days—P.M. wrote to Pet. I feel so feeble religiously, and so unworthy the preciousness I possess in Darling and Pussy——Eve—Dress Parade—

August 9, 1865 Wednesday. ordered to be ready to muster out by 11th—I run fine pens in my office today—Fine fellows—completed five Muster out Rolls—and Field and staff this evening—Received another very good letter from Pet—She's a Darling even if I am not as good as I am striving to be—my ideal is difficult of attaining, and more so is the maintaining—

Up til 12 Ock on finishing touches. Signing the clerks work, and meditating and praying—

August 10, 1865 Thursday. cool, blustry—I administered Oath of Office to Brevet Major General J. Irwin Gregg, U.S. Vols. as Brevet Lieut colonel of U.S. Army—regulars[25]—

Office rushed all day Eve. rec'd another O such a good letter from Pet—wrote on rolls, & reports 'til late in the night—I read and re-read the dear precious letter—Oh that I were worthy such a good wife. and such utter devotedness—

August 11, 1865 Friday. Up early—went to city—Richmond—in A.M. on office business—

U.S. Inspector went through my Office Books—Declared in Good condition—

P.M. Dress Parade—Then mail came in—another letter from Pet— —Later Captain Kendall Commenced to muster out our command— at 7 Ock P.M. Finished at 11 P.M. So the 16th Pa Cavalry is no more—we are all private citizens. Now again, as we were three years ago.

Many of us will be better citazens, for having gone through the experiences of three years vigorous cavalry war fare—

How proud we are to have been in the last struggle—The Surrender

August 12, 1865 Saturday. I was placed in charge of all Regimental Books and company Records &c and all muster out Papers[26] and the

---

25. Officers who intended to remain in the service had to be formally mustered out of the volunteers, then sworn into the regular army.

26. The army made a concerted effort to see that accurate records were prepared and safely deposited with the appropriate authorities. General Orders No. 94, the master plan for demobilization, contained the following separate and explicit command: "The commissary of musters of the division to which the regiment belonged in the field will take possession of the copies of muster-out rolls intended for the field and staff, companies, and paymaster; also the company and regimental records, with all surplus blank rolls, returns, discharges, &c., in possession of regimental and company commanders, or other officers, and after boxing them up place them, whilst en route, under the special charge of a discreet and responsible officer of the regiment. The sole duty of said officer will be to care for and preserve said rolls and records whilst en route, and on arrival at the State rendezvous where payment is to be made to turn them over to the chief mustering officer or his assistant at that place." *OR*, ser. III, vol. V, p. 22. Cormany was the "discreet and responsible officer" for his regiment.

Wharves at Rocketts, Va., showing captured Confederate guns and Union transport ships, 1865. Photographic Division, LC.

command broke camp at 10 Ock A.M. marched to Rocketts[27]—boarded a Boat and at 2 P.M. Head Quarters on "The Edward Everett" with five companies and a Band—Five companies on "The Eagle"—and the remainder and private Horses on "Lancer"—

We Suppered on the Boat—and "laid over" all night—

August 13, 1865 Sunday. Beautiful—we struck Fortress Monroe at 10 Ock—I went ashore. Bought some papers &c we move on finely—Dinner and supper aboard—Everything moves along smoothly—I do some writing in P.M. My sergt Major made out Monthly Return as a matter of form.

I am well, and abundantly able for all duties notwithstanding the strain and extra duties of recent weeks—Am not at all satisfied however with some irregularities in Conduct which I would fain

27. Rocketts, Va., a landing on the James River, was immediately adjacent to Richmond. *OMACW*, pl. XVII, no. 1.

undo One can simply repent and re-resolve—by His grace—to become more noble and avoid lapses and so attain ideals long striven for—

We made fine time during the night arriving at Baltimore

August 14, 1865 Monday. at 2 Ock this A.M.—and had our Breakfast aboard—

Disembarked at 10 A.M. and did some marching to limber up—and at 2 P.M. Ballance of our boys came up—and we all boarded a train for Harrisburg—Pa. A jolly ride sure—arriving at 11 P.M. The men bivouaced, and officers put up at Hotel near the Bridge—very warm.

August 15, 1865 Tuesday. we marched through the city and out to old Camp Curtin. Bands playing, and tattered colors flying——"A tents" put up for the men and "Wall tents" for the officers—and soon all were rather comfortable—Many wives of the boys came to meet and greet their returned husbands—A motley crowd looked us over—agents and bad women played their arts on unwary men in the camp—

P.M. I took the "Rolls"—"Discharge papers" etc etc to the Chief Mustering Officer of the State—I had to make some corrections—

August 16, 1865 Wednesday. Blustry—I completed the Rolls and took them to the Chief M.O. at 1½ ock—

I find much to do in office to straighten up matters, & records in general, preparation to turn all in and be released from all further responsibility Has been a very busy, trying day to me—It seems as though The whole Regiment was on my hands to be finally and properly disposed of and set loose—

August 17, 1865 Thursday. Cool and windy—This A.M. I turned in finally, the Regimental and Company Records and was free!!

The men seem very impatient to be paid off now and finally Discharged! I spent the evening in the city promenading with fellow officers—Going from one Hotel to the other—where groups of officers were stopping—Chatting over xperiences—saying good bye— and shame to say some were "pretty full"—Too much so for the satisfaction of others—about 10 Ock I struck for my Hd Qrs and was thankful!

August 18, 1865 Friday. Camp seems dull—this waiting is monotinous——P.M. Cos "A" "B" & "C" were paid off, and finally discharged—Eve Dr. Cox & I spent a while in city—Bedtime O! to be at Home.

August 19, 1865 Saturday. Ballance of Regiment being paid off—Non commissioned Staff paid at 4 P.M. "F" Co last, at 5 P.M.—Moved my things to City Hotel—Dr Cox—Ellershaw and Everhart also.[28] Evening we pass around some. Meet many groups of officers—and men—and their friends who have come to meet and greet them on their homecoming—

All too many are drinking and being disorderly—But they are now Citazens, and our official control is nil—Tho our influence still counts somewhat as mild restraint—But whiskey blunts respect in a measure and one is measurably helpless—

August 20, 1865 Sunday. a rest and quiet day——Read some—meditated and prayed, alone at my Hotel—

One can scarcely escape excesses amongst so many who think so little on that line.

August 21, 1865 Monday. Up early—and find still some business that demands my attention in order to have our regiments closing out to be satisfactory and close to perfect—and this is my ambition—Finding things in The Department in such condition that I could not close out for a few days likely. I decided and aranged to go home and see my Darlings—and then return again and finish up affairs in leisurely fashion and Satisfactorily to myself and to the State Department

At 1:30 P.M. I took the train for Chambersburg—with my "George"—colored man Servant—and my effects—arrived in Chamb'g about 4:30—and employed conveyance to take us and baggage out to Darlings—at Uncle Gelsingers—

Black "George" was a Refugee and had been my faithful man, a year or more—seeing to my Horse or Horses—to my effects—and caring for my commissary and cooking—and being without a home, or friends other than I had afforded him—naturally enough he desired to accompany me—to be with me—to do for me—and have me care for him—So I consented to take him with me and agreed to do my best to help him and treat him as a dependent which he surely was in the broadest sense—

Our arrival was a surprise sure—and the greetings I received were next to heavenly.

O what a joy to press my Darlings to my bosom and know that now we can plan to be together. Yes! day by day to be at home, together, and live with and for each other.

---

28. All three men, Thomas C. Coxe, William Ellershaw, and Isaac F. Everhart, had been surgeons in the 16th Pennsylvania. *PV*, p. 957.

August 22, 1865 Tuesday. Oh the Joy of it all! To have seen the end of the war—and be safe at home——George goes to work for "Uncle Isaac" Pet and I unpack and straighten up matters and things—a rainy day—mostly indoors—Aunty and Uncle seem so glad now that I am safe—and well, and strong—and "out of the war" though they are a little proud of it, that "Sammy was a soldier" and "Got pretty well up"—

Evening we retired to our room early—Darling and I had a long talk over a few lapses—and a long fervent prayer, with confession—and sense of pardon—and Oh such peace and joy was ours. That "After all" we have each other—and love each other with an ever increacing love and devotion—

August 23, 1865 Wednesday. We visited Brother Johns[d]—Found them well and happy as usual.—Dined together——p.m. went to Mothers[b] met with very warm reception—spent the evening very pleasantly—

Thank the Lord for a good kind Mother[b] and a true, good and devoted wife, and precious little Daughter—Oh! to be worthy of them.

August 24, 1865 Thursday. Pet took me to Chambg early—Took the 8:35 train for Harrisburg—Capt Barnes along—I pitched into business at once, and put in good time—but there was so much that I came to get my final pay at 2½ ock—Item, Aug 24" Pay from June 1" 1865 To Aug 15" 1865 including 3 mos pay proper Rec'd $1258.77¢ in full I met Van Wagner our old Sutler—Paid him a bill—

Met Col Robison—we had a delightful talk over old times—Col presented me with a hat—we put up at Jones House—and put in a jolly evening—

August 25, 1865 Friday. Cool. I was ready to start home but Major Snyder detained me so I missed the train. Then I turned in and helped Major Snyder through with his settlement. Dined at City Hotel—after dinner Col Robison and I promenaded some—What true Yoke fellows we are—as true as steel to each other——I took the 1:35 p.m. train to Chamb'g—Pet met me in town, and took me out—what a joy permeates such meetings, trips and arrivals home—

August 26, 1865 Saturday. Cool and breezy—I read most of a.m.— p.m. Straightened up my money a/cs—and then Pet, Cora and I went to Adam Plums—A fine visit—Lots of Grapes, pears, and fruits—returned after tea.

Eve Rev J. C. Smith preached at the School House—

August 27, 1865 Sunday. at home all day—Read a good deal—and talked more—an entire Sabbath of rest—

On retiring, I opened to Pet the very worst features of my short-comings and lapses—during my army life—and how God had graciously forgiven me every one and how I found it always the hardest to forgive myself—and keep from censuring myself, and to cease from casting my eyes backward and harboring "blues" because I saw my ideals marred—

We so earnestly prayed together, and sought divine help to let the dead past hide its gloomy spots—and looking unto Jesus, rely on Him to work in us and help us to help each other to overcome all evil and to acquire or attain to our ideals as Husband and Wife—as Heads of our Family—as Christians, in the Church and world—Oh! the peace, the joy, the rest that came to and possessed us, and how sweetly we fell asleep in each others arms——

XXX

Rachel and Samuel Reunited

August 27 and September 1, 1865

The Cormanys' reunion is bittersweet, both a triumph and a poignant reminder of how much they had endured.

———————————◆•◆•◆———————————

August 27, 1865 Joy to the world—My little world at least. I am no more a war widow—My Precious is home safe from the war. I am so thankful that he is once more home & that to stay. I am happy all the time now. I do not feel now as if I were alone in the world—as I had so often to feel during his three years absence & now that the war is over I hope we can once get to our own home & live as God intends we should. We are certainly a happy little family—God grant that we may be a good family too.

September 1, 1865 Evening. Just home from camp meeting. spent the greater part of the week there. This has been indeed the saddest week of my life My heart is almost broken. It is with the greatest effort that I keep up—I have prayed God for grace to overcome. He has answered my prayer in a measure & has comforted my soul. I have felt really happy in Him. It takes all the powers of my mind & soul to bear up under this my greatest of sorrows so as to hide the anguish of my heart. I have forgiven with all my heart & have resolved to try to forget it. & put forth my greatest efforts to make him happy. He seems almost heartbroken over his missteps & I feel that it needs an effort to save him from despair. He has vowed to me that henceforth no such misteps shall befall him. God will help him & we shall be happy again. May be I should not have put this on paper—but my mind seemed so overburdened & the smothered feelings must escape or—— O! for more of God & heaven in my soul—"I long to be there & his Glory to share & to lean on Jesus breast"—God help us to be useful here so as to answer the end of our creation fully—

Epilogue

The Cormanys continued to attend the camp meeting near the Byers farm until September 1 and then began a round of visiting relatives in the Cumberland Valley. They stayed for several days with John H. Cormany on the farm where Samuel had grown up. On the fourteenth they visited overnight with Samuel's sister Wilamina Karper, whose husband John had gone to Virginia to look at possible land purchases. On the fifteenth and sixteenth the Cormanys stayed with Samuel's sister Sarah and her husband, Isaac Thompson. Isaac took them to Bernard Cormany's farm, where Samuel, Rachel, and Cora remained a few more days. But by September 14, Samuel's diary had begun to reflect his impatience with the long round of visits and his desire to take his bride to the house he had built for her in Missouri five summers before.

After a week of packing and saying goodbye, the Cormanys left Chambersburg on September 27, 1865. They sent 972 pounds of household equipment on ahead of them by rail to Macon City, Missouri, where their friends the Kimmels had agreed to look after it. The firm of Oaks and Lynn handled this freight shipment for them; David Oaks was the same man whose warehouse had been destroyed by the Confederates during the Gettysburg campaign. George, Samuel's black servant from the war, went with them, wearing a new suit that the Cormanys had bought for him. Samuel reasoned that he would be able to use a hired man on his new farm, and he felt a sense of responsibility toward George. As things worked out, George served a sort of agricultural apprenticeship with the Cormanys and was able within a year to go off on his own and "command good wages."

The Cormanys stopped their first night out with Col. John K. Robison and his family in Juniata County where Robison established in later years a highly successful career in law and politics. From there the Cormanys took a train through Pittsburgh to Cleveland and then made a sidetrip to Oberlin to visit the Danforth family. Rachel had roomed with Mrs. Danforth when she attended Oberlin's preparatory school a decade earlier, and they had kept in touch since (see Rachel's entry for Aug. 11, 1865). While there, Samuel and Rachel were both impressed with the preaching of Oberlin's president, Charles Grandison Finney.

On October 2, the Cormanys traveled by rail from Oberlin to Grand Rapids, Michigan. Both Samuel and Rachel noted separately that the trip was unpleasant; the coaches were extremely crowded and the expressions of a young Irishman celebrating his return home from the war were not exactly what Rachel was accustomed to hearing. This time their stopover was lengthy, for Rachel's father had bought a farm fourteen miles south of the town and her two youngest sisters were attending school in Grand Rapids.

The Cormanys remained with the Bowmans, "rejoicing at the lost soldiers' return" as Rachel phrased it in her one entry about the visit, through October and into November. Samuel's more numerous entries describe helping with the potato harvest and hunting for small game and wild birds. Rachel was plagued by boils and poor health, and on October 27 Samuel noted that "one of our cherished hopes is dashed to atoms which casts a cloud over us for the time." He was referring to their hope of having another child, the child Rachel had finally agreed to try for as the war was drawing to a close. Two days later they "talked over the matters," however, and they both felt much better. On the night of November 2, they had "a long consultation, and Lovers talk & Vows"; it is reasonable to assume that they decided to keep trying to increase their family.

On November 13, Rachel's mother and father took the Cormanys to Kalamazoo to catch the train for Michigan City and points west. Passing through Quincy and Danville, Illinois, the Cormanys reached Missouri on November 16, 1865. Life was difficult for the Cormanys. They were able to spend their fourth anniversary together on their own farm, but the octagon house Samuel built in 1860 had suffered severely from five years of vacancy and vandalism. Rachel was seriously ill through most of December 1865 and January 1866. It was not until the end of February that she could even go out for a visit and begin to meet her neighbors. She found the closest ones "kindhearted" but "almost illiterate & consequently ignorant." Moreover, she and Samuel were "again disappointed in our hopes & desires" for another child.

In the spring of 1866 Samuel planted crops and organized a United Brethren church. He also reorganized the community Sunday school he had launched with the Kimmels in May 1860. But Rachel remained depressed. "Why did I not die when a child," she wrote after a tiff with her husband on April 16, 1866. "O, God thou alone knowest why my life is prolonged. O! help me to do right at all times. I am all alone. O! how lonely to be alone away out in the country at night. I feel distressed beyond expression."

Notwithstanding the loss of both Cormany diaries after 1866, it is possible to reconstruct the broad outlines of what happened to Samuel and Rachel in later years. The most important sources in putting that outline together included family Bibles, newspaper obituaries, formal death certificates, army pension records in the National Archives, and a long narrative letter that Rachel wrote in 1889 to one of her old professors, J. E. Guitner. The letter was Rachel's response to an Otterbein alumni survey.

The Cormany's situation in Missouri never improved. They found themselves entangled in the bitter local politics of the Reconstruction era and, according to Rachel, "Kulux bullets came near accomplishing that in which the war failed. viz—making one more widow." They found " 'Borderruffian' life decidedly uncongenial." In October 1868 they sold their farm and joined a small party that was emigrating by prairie schooner to the plains of southern Kansas. There Samuel began to preach at frontier missions and Rachel opened a school.

The Cormanys finally seemed content. Rachel became pregnant shortly after their move and gave birth to Jacob Benjamin Cormany on October 17, 1869. But the son Samuel had wanted so badly lived only six weeks. The Cormanys turned "with renewed vigor" to their mission services. Samuel took up the Cherokee circuit of the United Brethren church; Rachel and Cora helped with the farming while he was away. Rachel became pregnant again in 1870, and a second daughter, Harriet May Fraxier Cormany, was born May 18, 1871. Fortunately, Hattie survived.

In 1873 Samuel contracted "brainfever" and malaria. Doctors urged him to move farther north, so the Cormanys requested a different circuit. To their delight they were assigned to the Waterloo area of Canada. Samuel served there from April 1873 to May 1876. Rachel bore her fourth and final child at Waterloo in the summer of 1875. But the baby, a girl, lived only ten days. From May 1876 to February 1878, Samuel served the United Brethren district of Fonthill, Ontario, just west of Niagara Falls.

Because Samuel's health failed to improve, he resigned from circuit riding in 1878 to try to recuperate in northern Michigan. There the Reverend Cormany served a small community church and began some modest business ventures "to secure the means to educate our daughter." Cora, now sixteen, became the district school mistress. Two years later, in 1880, an admittedly proud Rachel sent her off to Otterbein.

During the 1880s Rachel became very active in the Women's Christian Temperance Union and in the national kindergarten movement. She also tutored private students in German. Cora graduated from Otterbein and in 1885 married the Reverend Lawrence Keister, who would later become president of another United Brethren school, Lebanon Valley College in Pennsylvania. Business took the Cormanys to Pittsburgh in 1886, and the following year Samuel and Rachel were appointed Superintendent and Assistant Superintendent of that city's Protestant Home for Boys.

In the 1890s Samuel resumed his ministerial career by accepting a pastorate in Bradenville, Pennsylvania. From there he went to the Second United Brethren Church of Johnstown, Pennsylvania. Hattie established herself as a music teacher in Johnstown, but her parents began to fail. Samuel's poor health forced his retirement from preaching early in 1898, and Rachel fell ill in the autumn of that same year. Rachel was confined to her bed as winter approached and by January 1899 it was evident that she had cancer and would not recover. On Saturday evening, February 18, 1899, Rachel Bowman Cormany died. She was sixty-two years old. She is buried in Johnstown's Grand View Cemetery.

Samuel, now disabled, lived alone for several years in various small communities around Johnstown. In one of those towns he met Almeda Truxel, whom he married April 6, 1904. They lived in Mt. Pleasant, Pennsylvania, and apparently subsisted on the Federal pension that had been granted to Samuel under the Invalid Veterans' Act of 1890. Samuel's old commander, John K. Robison, supported Samuel's pension application with a letter of testimony that cited Cormany's exploits during the war. But Almeda was dead by 1915 and Samuel went to live near his older daughter, Cora Cormany Keister, at Scottdale, Pennsylvania.

By 1920 Samuel could no longer take care of himself. He had endured nearly thirty years of heart trouble, rheumatism, and lung disorders, but now began to suffer from prostate cancer and bladder infections. Cora, herself no longer young, had to hire a nurse to care for her father during his last lingering months. Samuel Cormany finally died April 20, 1921. He was not quite eighty-three years old. He is buried beside Rachel in Johnstown.

Index